Fodor's 2016

NORTHERN CALIFORNIA

Excerpted from *Fodor's California 2016*.

WELCOME TO NORTHERN CALIFORNIA

It's easy to tap into the good life in Northern California. Between rounds of golf at Pebble Beach, winding drives along the iconic Big Sur coast, or scenic treks through Yosemite National Park, you can indulge in a wealth of top-notch outdoor activities. In Napa and Sonoma, eating and drinking are cultivated as high arts. You can sip wine at picturesque vineyards and then dine at stellar locavore restaurants. Urban pleasures await in San Francisco, too, where cable cars zip through vibrant neighborhoods lined with chic boutiques and cutting-edge museums.

TOP REASONS TO GO

★ **San Francisco:** This diverse city beguiles with natural beauty and contagious energy.

★ **Wine Country:** Top-notch whites and reds in Napa, Sonoma, and beyond.

★ **Feasts:** Cutting-edge cuisine, food trucks, fusion flavors, farmers' markets.

★ **Stunning Scenery:** Picture-perfect backdrops from the Golden Gate Bridge to redwoods.

★ **Outdoor Adventures:** National park excursions, hiking, and golfing are all excellent.

★ **Road Trips:** The Pacific Coast Highway offers spectacular views and thrills aplenty.

Fodor's NORTHERN CALIFORNIA 2016

Publisher: Amanda D'Acierno, *Senior Vice President*

Editorial: Arabella Bowen, *Editor in Chief*; Linda Cabasin, *Editorial Director*

Design: Tina Malaney, *Associate Art Director*; Chie Ushio, *Senior Designer*; Ann McBride, *Production Designer*

Photography: Jennifer Arnow, *Senior Photo Editor*; Jennifer Romains, *Photo Researcher*

Production: Linda Schmidt, *Managing Editor*; Evangelos Vasilakis, *Associate Managing Editor*; Angela L. McLean, *Senior Production Manager*

Maps: Rebecca Baer, *Senior Map Editor*; David Lindroth and Mark Stroud, *Cartographers*

Sales: Jacqueline Lebow, *Sales Director*

Marketing & Publicity: Heather Dalton, *Marketing Director*; Katherine Punia, *Publicity Director*

Business & Operations: Susan Livingston, *Vice President, Strategic Business Planning*; Sue Daulton, *Vice President, Operations*

Fodors.com: Megan Bell, *Executive Director, Revenue & Business Development*; Yasmin Marinaro, *Senior Director, Marketing & Partnerships*

Copyright © 2016 by Fodor's Travel, a division of Random House LLC

Writers: Michele Bigley, Christine Ciarmello, Cheryl Crabtree, Denise M. Leto, Daniel Mangin, Steve Pastorino, Fiona Parrott, Jerry James Stone, Claire Deeks van der Lee, Christine Vovakes

Editors: Luke Epplin, Salwa Jabado, Teddy Minford

Editorial Contributors: Linda Cabasin, Daniel Mangin, Amanda Sadlowski, Amanda Theunissen

Production Editor: Evangelos Vasilakis

ISBN 978-1-1018-7849-1

ISSN 1543–1045

All details in this book are based on information supplied to us at press time. Always confirm information when it matters, especially if you're making a detour to visit a specific place. Fodor's expressly disclaims any liability, loss, or risk, personal or otherwise, that is incurred as a consequence of the use of any of the contents of this book.

SPECIAL SALES

This book is available at special discounts for bulk purchases for sales promotions or premiums. For more information, e-mail specialmarkets@penguinrandomhouse.com

PRINTED IN THE UNITED STATES OF AMERICA

10 9 8 7 6 5 4 3 2 1

22

CONTENTS

Fodor's Features

The Ultimate Road Trip: California's Legendary Highway 1 22
California's Missions 58
Chinatown 169
Cable Cars 181
Wine Tasting in Napa and Sonoma . . . 320
Eureka! California's Gold Rush 493
Tahoe: A Lake for All Seasons 523

ABOUT THIS GUIDE

Fodor's Recommendations

Everything in this guide is worth doing—we don't cover what isn't—but exceptional sights, hotels, and restaurants are recognized with additional accolades. **Fodor's Choice** ★ indicates our top recommendations; and **Best Bets** call attention to notable hotels and restaurants in various categories. Care to nominate a new place? Visit Fodors.com/contact-us.

Trip Costs

We list prices wherever possible to help you budget well. Hotel and restaurant price categories from **$** to **$$$$** are noted alongside each recommendation. For hotels, we include the lowest cost of a standard double room in high season. For restaurants, we cite the average price of a main course at dinner or, if dinner isn't served, at lunch. For attractions, we always list adult admission fees; discounts are usually available for children, students, and senior citizens.

Hotels

Our local writers vet every hotel to recommend the best overnights in each price category, from budget to expensive. Unless otherwise specified, you can expect private bath, phone, and TV in your room. For expanded hotel reviews, facilities, and deals visit Fodors.com.

Top Picks	**Hotels & Restaurants**
★ **Fodor's Choice**	🏨 Hotel
Listings	⤺ Number of rooms
✉ Address	🍴 Meal plans
✉ Branch address	✗ Restaurant
☎ Telephone	🍸 Reservations
🖷 Fax	👔 Dress code
⊕ Website	🖃 No credit cards
✎ E-mail	Ⓢ Price
🎟 Admission fee	**Other**
⊙ Open/closed times	⇨ See also
Ⓜ Subway	☞ Take note
✛ Directions or Map coordinates	🏌 Golf facilities

Restaurants

Unless we state otherwise, restaurants are open for lunch and dinner daily. We mention dress code only when there's a specific requirement and reservations only when they're essential or not accepted. To make restaurant reservations, visit Fodors.com.

Credit Cards

The hotels and restaurants in this guide typically accept credit cards. If not, we'll say so.

EUGENE FODOR

Hungarian-born Eugene Fodor (1905–91) began his travel career as an interpreter on a French cruise ship. The experience inspired him to write *On the Continent* (1936), the first guidebook to receive annual updates and discuss a country's way of life as well as its sights. Fodor later joined the U.S. Army and worked for the OSS in World War II. After the war, he kept up his intelligence work while expanding his guidebook series. During the Cold War, many guides were written by fellow agents who understood the value of insider information. Today's guides continue Fodor's legacy by providing travelers with timely coverage, insider tips, and cultural context.

EXPERIENCE NORTHERN CALIFORNIA

WHAT'S NEW IN NORTHERN CALIFORNIA

Foodie's Paradise

Great dining is a staple of the California lifestyle, and a new young generation of chefs is challenging old ideas about preparing and presenting great food. The food-truck frenzy continues to fuel movable feasts up and down the state. You can find food-laden trucks at sports and entertainment venues, near parks and attractions, and on busy roads and boulevards—and the ensuing lines of hungry patrons.

Diners are also embracing the pop-up concept, where guest chefs offer innovative menus in unconventional settings for a limited time. These pop-up engagements are hosted anywhere from inside a warehouse to outside in a field. Visitors can look for local pop-ups listed on foodie websites such as Eater (⊕ www.eater.com).

California chefs continue to shop locally for produce and farmer-sourced meat, and many restaurants proudly display their vendors on the menu. Chefs and foodies alike engage in discourse on the ethics and politics of food and farming.

Wine Discoveries

California offers oenophiles ample opportunities for new discoveries beyond the traditional California Wine Country. Areas such as the Petaluma Gap and the Sierra Foothills offer plenty of vineyards to explore. Visitors to Lake Tahoe can even take in some wine tasting at the Truckee River Winery, claiming to be the highest and coldest winery in the nation.

Family Fun

Both kids and adults will be fascinated by the creatures on display in "Tentacles: The Astounding Lives of Octopuses, Squid and Cuttlefishes," the newest exhibit at the Monterey Bay Aquarium.

San Francisco's Exploratorium continues to challenge and fascinate visitors of all ages. With trees as tall as they come, the Children's Redwood Forest in Humboldt Redwoods State Park is a great place for kids to romp through some awe-inspiring landscapes.

All Aboard

Riding the rails can be a satisfying experience, particularly in California where the distances between destinations sometimes run into the hundreds of miles. The best trip is on the luxuriously appointed Coast Starlight, a long-distance train with sleeping cars that runs between Seattle and Los Angeles, passing some of California's most beautiful coastline as it hugs the beach. For the best surfside viewing, get a seat or a room on the left side of the train and ride south to north.

Homegrown Hospitality

Agritourism in California isn't new, but it is on the rise, with farm tours and agricultural festivals sprouting up everywhere. Wine country is a particularly fertile area—spurred by the success of vineyards, the area's lavender growers and olive-oil producers have started welcoming visitors. Sonoma Farm Trail Tours include walking the land and a farm-driven dinner with paired wines.

State of the Arts

California's beauty-obsessed citizens aren't the only ones opting for a fresh look these days: its esteemed art museums are also having a bit of work done. The San Francisco Museum of Modern Art is expected to reopen in 2016 after a major expansion project that will vastly increase the museum's exhibition and support space.

NORTHERN CALIFORNIA PLANNER

WHEN TO GO

Because they offer activities indoors and out, the top California cities rate as all-seasons destinations.

Early spring—when the gray-whale migration overlaps with the end of the elephant-seal breeding season and the start of the bird migration—is the optimal time to visit Point Reyes National Seashore. Yosemite is ideal in late spring because roads closed in winter are reopened, and the park's waterfalls—swollen with melting snow—run fast. Autumn is "crush time" in all the wine destinations, both in the north and south. Ski resorts typically open around Thanksgiving (they sometimes remain in operation into June).

It's difficult to generalize about the state's weather. As a rule, inland regions are hotter in summer and colder in winter, compared with coastal areas, which are relatively cool year-round. Fog is a potential hazard any day of the year in coastal regions. In the mountains, winter brings snow at elevations above 3,000 feet and summer is sunny and warm, with an occasional thundershower.

Microclimates

Mountains separate the California coastline from the state's interior, and the weather can sometimes vary dramatically within a 15-minute drive. On a foggy summer day in San Francisco, you'll be grateful for a sweater—but head 50 miles north inland to Napa Valley, and you'll likely be content in short sleeves. Day and nighttime temperatures can also vary greatly. In Sacramento, the mercury hits the 90s and occasionally exceeds 100°F on August afternoons. Yet as darkness falls, it sometimes plummets to 40°F.

CAR TRAVEL

Driving may be a way of life in California, but it isn't cheap (gas prices here are usually among the highest in the nation). It's also not for the fainthearted; even the state's scenic highways and byways have their own hassles. On the dramatic coastal road between San Simeon and Carmel, twists, turns, and distracting vistas frequently slow traffic; in rainy season, mudslides can close the road altogether.

On California's notorious freeways, other rules apply. Nervous Nellies must resist the urge to stay in the two slow-moving lanes on the far right, used primarily by trucks. To drive at least the speed limit, get yourself in a middle lane. If you're ready to bend the rules a bit, the second lane (lanes are numbered from 1 starting at the center) moves about 5 mph faster. But avoid the far-left lane (the one next to the carpool lane), where speeds range from 75 mph to 90 mph.

AIR TRAVEL

Air travelers beginning or ending their vacation in San Francisco have two main airports to choose from: San Francisco International (SFO) or Oakland International (OAK) across the bay. The former lands you closer to the city core (ground transportation will take about 20 minutes versus 35), but the latter is less heavily trafficked and less prone to pesky fog delays. BART, the Bay Area's affordable rapid-transit system, serves both airports.

If your final destination is Monterey or Carmel, San Jose International Airport (SJC), about 40 miles south of San Francisco, is another alternative.

WHAT'S WHERE

The following numbers refer to chapters.

3 The Central Coast. Three of the state's top stops—swanky Santa Barbara, Hearst Castle, and Big Sur—sit along the scenic 200-mile route. A quick boat trip away lies scenic Channel Islands National Park.

4 Monterey Bay Area. Postcard-perfect Monterey, Victorian-flavored Pacific Grove, and exclusive Carmel all share this stretch of California coast. To the north, Santa Cruz boasts a boardwalk, a UC campus, ethnic clothing shops, and plenty of surfers.

5 San Francisco. To see why so many have left their hearts here, you need to visit the city's iconic neighborhoods—posh Pacific Heights, the Hispanic Mission, and gay-friendly Castro.

6 The Bay Area. The area that rings San Francisco is nothing like the city—but it is home to some of the nation's great universities, fabulous bay views, Silicon Valley, and Alice Waters' Chez Panisse.

7 Napa and Sonoma. By virtue of award-winning vintages, luxe lodgings, and epicurean eats, Napa and Sonoma counties retain their title as *the* California Wine Country.

8 The North Coast. The star attractions here are natural ones, from the secluded beaches and wave-battered bluffs of Point Reyes National Seashore to the towering redwood forests.

9 Redwood National Park. More than 200 miles of trails, ranging from easy to strenuous, allow visitors to see these spectacular trees in their primitive environments.

10 The Southern Sierra. In the Mammoth Lakes region, sawtooth mountains and deep powdery snowdrifts create the state's premier conditions for skiing and snowboarding.

11 Yosemite National Park. The views immortalized by photographer Ansel Adams—towering granite monoliths, verdant glacial valleys, and lofty waterfalls—are still camera-ready.

12 Sequoia and Kings Canyon National Parks. The sight of ancient redwoods towering above jagged mountains is breathtaking.

13 Sacramento and the Gold Country. The 1849 gold rush that built San Francisco and Sacramento began here, and the former mining camps strung along 185 miles of Highway 49 replay their past to the hilt.

14 Lake Tahoe. With miles of crystalline water reflecting the peaks of the High Sierra, Lake Tahoe is the perfect setting for activities like hiking and golfing in summer and skiing and snowmobiling in winter.

15 The Far North. California's far northeast corner is home to snowcapped Mount Shasta, the pristine Trinity Wilderness, and abundant backwoods character.

1

Crescent City
Yreka
Goose Lake
0   75 mi
0   75 km

Klamath
Redwood National Park
Alturas

9
Mt. Shasta
Burney
CASCADE RANGE

Arcata
Weaverville
Shasta Lake
Eureka
Redding
15
Lassen Volcanic National Park
Susanville

Ferndale
Red Bluff
Pyramid Lake

Garberville
Chico
Paradise
Reno
NEVADA

Leggett
Willows
Oroville
Grass Valley
Truckee

Fort Bragg
Willits
Sacramento Valley
Yuba City
49
Lake Tahoe
★ **CARSON CITY**

Mendocino
Ukiah
Clear Lake
Auburn
South Lake Tahoe

Boonville
Placerville

Point Arena
Woodland
7
★ **SACRAMENTO**

Gualala
8
Healdsburg
Elk Grove
13
Yosemite National Park

Jenner
Santa Rosa
Napa
Fairfield
Jackson
Bridgeport

Sonoma
Lodi
Sonora
Mono Lake
10

Novato
5
Berkeley
Stockton
11
SIERRA NEVADA

SAN FRANCISCO
6
Oakland
Modesto
Yosemite Village
Mammoth Lakes

Fremont
Turlock
Bishop

Palo Alto
San Jose
Merced

Santa Cruz
Gilroy
Chowchilla
Kings Canyon National Park
Big Pine

San Luis Res.
Los Banos
Madera

Castroville
San Joaquin Valley

PACIFIC OCEAN
Monterey
Salinas
Fresno

Pacific Grove
4
Soledad
Visalia
12

Carmel
Tulare Lake Bed
Porterville
Sequoia National Park

Big Sur
5
Coalinga
Kernville
China Lake

San Simeon
Paso Robles
Bakersfield
Ridgecrest

San Luis Obispo
McKittrick

Santa Maria
Tejon Pass
TEHACHAPI MTS.
Lancaster

Lompoc
3
Santa Barbara
Ojai

Santa Barbara Channel
Ventura
Oxnard
Pasadena

NORTHERN CALIFORNIA
TOP ATTRACTIONS

San Francisco's Cable Cars

(A) Pricey and touristy for sure, but a chance to ride on one of San Francisco's classic cable cars should not be passed up. Clutching a handrail while riding downhill on one of the exterior running boards can be exhilarating or downright frightening, depending on whom you ask. Sitting inside offers a tamer ride, yet you can watch the gripman at work, listen to the clanging of the bell, and take in the sights as you roll by. It is easy to incorporate a ride into your itinerary, as the cable cars pass by some of the most popular sights in the city.

The Golden Gate Bridge

(B) Catching that first glimpse of the iconic Golden Gate Bridge is bound to take your breath away. Completed in 1937, the art-deco suspension bridge has become the internationally recognized symbol of San Francisco. While often swathed in an otherworldly fog, on a clear day the city and bay views from the bridge are spectacular.

Monterey Bay Aquarium

This aquarium is one of the nation's most spectacular and most respected. A multistory kelp forest, the million-plus-gallon tank in the Open Seas exhibit, and a dramatically lit jellyfish experience are just some of the highlights. The aquarium also impresses behind the scenes with its extensive marine research programs and conservation efforts.

Napa Valley

(C) Despite impressive wines being produced throughout the state, the Napa Valley remains California's original and most famous destination for wine. Although the vineyard-blanketed hills are undeniably scenic, the wine itself (preferably accompanied by the area's famed cuisine) remains the big draw here. From household names to producers with a cult following, budding oenophiles can educate their palettes on scores of tours and tasting sessions.

Point Reyes National Seashore

(D) Aside from the namesake seashore, this Marin County preserve encompasses ecosystems that range from woodlands and marshlands to heathlike grasslands. The range of wildlife here is equally diverse—depending on when you visit, expect to see gray whales, rare Tule elk, and almost 500 species of birds.

Yosemite National Park

(E) Nature looms large here, both literally and figuratively. In addition to hulking Half Dome, the park is home to El Capitan (the world's largest exposed granite monolith, rising 3,593 feet above the glacier-carved valley floor) and Yosemite Falls (North America's tallest cascade). In Yosemite's signature stand of giant sequoias—the Mariposa Grove—even the trees are Bunyanesque. Needless to say, crowds can be supersize, too.

Redwood National and State Park

A United Nations World Heritage Site, this park along California's north coast is one of the most serene spots on earth. It holds groves of towering ancient redwood trees, including the world's tallest tree at nearly 380 feet. Drive along the Redwood Highway to experience the majesty of the trees.

Lake Tahoe

(F) Deep, clear, and intensely blue, this forest-rimmed body of water straddling the California–Nevada border is one of the continent's prettiest alpine lakes. That environmental controls can keep it that way is something of a miracle, given Tahoe's popularity. Throngs of outdoor adventurers flock to the California side to ski, hike, bike, and boat. On the Nevada side, where casinos are king, gambling often wins out over fresh-air activities—but natural wonders are never far away.

QUINTESSENTIAL NORTHERN CALIFORNIA

The Beach

California's beach culture is, in a word, legendary. Of course, it only makes sense that folks living in a state with a 1,264-mile coastline (a hefty portion of which sees the sun upward of 300 days a year) would perfect the art of beachgoing. True aficionados begin with a reasonably fit physique, plus a stylish wardrobe consisting of flip-flops, bikinis, wet suits, and such. Mastery of at least one beach skill—surfing, boogie boarding, kayaking, Frisbee tossing, or looking fab while catching rays—is also essential. As a visitor, though, you need only a swimsuit and some rented equipment for most sports. You can then hit the beach almost anywhere, thanks to the California belief in coastal access as a birthright. The farther south you go, the wider, sandier, and sunnier the beaches become; moving north they are rockier and foggier, with colder and rougher surf.

The Automobile

Americans may have a love affair with the automobile, but Californians have an out-and-out obsession. Even when gas prices rev up and freeway traffic slows down, their passion burns as hot as ever. You can witness this ardor any summer weekend at huge classic- and custom-car shows held statewide. Even better, you can feel it yourself by taking the wheel. Trace an old stagecoach route through the mountains above Santa Barbara on Highway 154; track migrating whales up the coast to Big Sur; or take 17-Mile Drive along the precipitous edge of the Monterey Peninsula. Glorious for the most part, but authentically congested in some areas, Highway 1 runs almost the entire length of the state, hugging the coast most of the way.

Californians live in such a large and splashy state that they sometimes seem to forget about the rest of the country. They've developed a distinctive culture all their own, which you can delve into by doing as the locals do.

The Wine

If California were a country, it would rank as the world's fourth-largest wine producer, after Italy, France, and Spain. In those countries, where *vino* is barely considered an alcoholic beverage, wine drinking has evolved into a relaxing ritual best shared with friends and family. A modern, Americanized version of that mentality integrates wine into daily life in California, and there are many places to sample it. The Napa and Sonoma valleys come to mind first. But there are other destinations for oenophiles. You can find great wineries around Santa Barbara County, San Luis Obispo, Monterey Bay, and Gold Country's Amador County, too. All are respected appellations, and their winery tours and tastings will show you what all the buzz is about.

The Outdoors

One of California's greatest assets—the mild year-round weather enjoyed by most of the state—inspires residents to spend as much time outside as they possibly can. They have a tremendous enthusiasm for every imaginable outdoor sport, and, up north especially, fresh-air adventures are extremely popular (which may explain why everyone there seems to own at least one pair of hiking boots). But the California-alfresco creed is more broadly interpreted, and the general rule when planning any activity is "if it can happen outside, it will!" Plein air vacation opportunities include dining on patios, decks, and wharves; shopping in street markets or elaborate open-air malls; hearing almost any kind of music at moonlight concerts; touring the sculpture gardens that grace major art museums; and celebrating everything from gay pride to garlic at outdoor fairs.

NORTHERN CALIFORNIA TODAY

The People

California is as much a state of mind as a state in the union—a kind of perpetual promised land that has represented many things to many people. In the 18th-century, Spanish missionaries came seeking converts and gold. In the 19th, miners rushed here to search for gold. And, in the years since, a long line of Dust Bowl farmers, land speculators, Haight-Ashbury hippies, migrant workers, dot-commers, real estate speculators, and would-be actors have come chasing their own dreams.

The result is a population that leans toward idealism—without necessarily being as liberal as you might think. (Remember, this is Ronald Reagan's old stomping ground.) And despite the stereotype of the blue-eyed, blond surfer, California's population is not homogeneous either. Ten million people who live here (more than 27% of Californians) are foreign born. Almost half hail from Latin American countries; another third emigrated from Asia, following the waves of Chinese workers who arrived in the 1860s to build the railroads and subsequent waves of Indochinese refugees from the Vietnam War.

The Politics

What's blue and red and green all over? California: a predominantly Democratic state with an aggressive "go green" agenda. Democratic Governor Jerry Brown, who was elected to the office for the second time in 30 years, is moving the progressive agenda ahead with policies that make California the greenest state in the nation, supporting green construction, wind farms, and solar panels.

The Economy

Leading all other states in terms of the income generated by agriculture, tourism, entertainment, and industrial activity, California has the country's most diverse state economy. Moreover, with a gross state product of more than $2 trillion, California would be one of the top 10 economies *in the world* if it were an independent nation.

Due to its wealth ($61,094 median household income) and productivity, California took a large hit in the 2007 recession, but the Golden State's economic history is filled with boom and bust cycles—beginning with the mid-19th-century gold rush that started it all. Optimists already have their eyes on the next potential boom: high-tech and bioresearch, "green companies" focused on alternative energy, renewables, electric cars, and the like.

The Culture

Cultural organizations flourish in California. San Francisco—a city with only about 825,000 residents—has well-regarded ballet, opera, and theater companies, and is home to one of the continent's most noteworthy orchestras. Museums like San Francisco Museum of Modern Art (SFMOMA) and the de Young also represent the city's ongoing commitment to the arts.

The Parks and Preserves

Cloud-spearing redwood groves, snow-tipped mountains, canyon-slashed deserts, primordial lava beds, and a seemingly endless coast: California's natural diversity is staggering—and efforts to protect it started early. Yosemite, the first national park, was established here in 1890, and the National Park Service now oversees 32 sites in Cali-   fornia (more than any

other state). When you factor in 280 state parks—which encompass underwater preserves, historic sites, wildlife reserves, dune systems, and other sensitive habitats—the number of acres involved is almost as impressive as the topography itself.

Due to encroaching development and pollution, keeping these natural treasures in pristine condition is an ongoing challenge. For instance, Sequoia and Kings Canyon (which is plagued by pesticides and other agricultural pollutants blown in from the San Joaquin Valley) has been named America's "smoggiest park" by the National Parks Conservation Association, and the Environmental Protection Agency has designated it as an "ozone nonattainment area with levels of ozone pollution that threaten human health."

There is no question that Californians love their 280 state parks. Nearly every park has its grass-roots supporters, who volunteer to raise money, volunteer as rangers, and work other jobs to keep the parks open.

The Cuisine

California gave us McDonald's, Denny's, Carl's Jr., Taco Bell, and, of course, In-N-Out Burger. Fortunately for those of us with fast-clogging arteries, the state also kick-started the organic food movement. Back in the 1970s, California-based chefs put American cuisine on the culinary map by focusing on freshly prepared seasonal ingredients.

Today, this focus has spawned the "locavore" or sustainable food movement—followers try to only consume food produced within a 100-mile radius of where they live, since processing and refining food and transporting goods over long distances is bad for both the body and the environment. This isn't much of a restriction in California, where a huge variety of crops grow year-round. Some 350 cities and towns have certified farmers' markets—and their stalls are bursting with a variety of goods. California has been America's top agricultural producer for the last 50 years, growing more fruits and vegetables than any other state. Dairies and ranches also thrive here, and fishing fleets harvest fish and shellfish from the rich waters offshore.

NORTHERN CALIFORNIA TOP EXPERIENCES

Hit the Road

Kings Canyon Highway, Redwood Highway, Tioga Pass, 17-Mile Drive, the Lake Tahoe loop: California has some splendid and challenging roads. You'll drive through a tunnel formed by towering redwood trees on the Redwood Highway. If you venture over the Sierras by way of Tioga Pass (through Yosemite in summer only), you'll see emerald green meadows, gray granite monoliths, and pristine blue lakes—and very few people.

Pan for Gold

Though California's gold rush ended more than a hundred years ago, you can still feel the forty-nine fever on the western face of the Sierra Nevada in Columbia, a well-preserved town populated by costumed interpreters, where you can pan for gold or tour a mine. Or visit Bodie, an eerie ghost town in the eastern Sierra that remains in a state of "arrested decay."

Think Globally, Eat Locally

Over the years California cuisine has evolved from a mere trend into a respected gastronomic tradition: one that pairs local, often organic or sustainable, ingredients with techniques inspired by European, Asian, and, increasingly, Indian and Middle Eastern cookery.

See Eccentric Architecture

California has always drawn creative and, well, eccentric people. And all that quirkiness has left its mark in the form of oddball architecture that makes for some fun sightseeing. Begin by touring Hearst Castle—the beautifully bizarre estate William Randolph Hearst built above San Simeon. And Lake Tahoe's Vikingsholm (a re-created Viking castle) is equally odd.

People-Watch

Opportunities for world-class people-watching abound in California. Just saunter the rainbow-flagged streets of San Francisco's Castro neighborhood or the century-old boardwalk in time-warped, resiliently boho Santa Cruz.

Be Transported

San Franciscans take cable cars seriously—and riding on one is a must-do. You may even want to visit the (free!) Cable Car Museum to get a handle on the inner workings or just ring a gripman's bell. But, the city's options for vintage public transport doesn't end there: the lesser known F line streetcars are every bit as photogenic, and they have shorter lines.

Go Wild

California communities host hundreds of annual events, but some of the best are organized by Mother Nature. The most famous is the "miracle migration" that sees swallows flock back to Mission San Juan Capistrano in Orange County each March. In the Pacific Grove, masses of monarch butterflies reliably arrive for their winter vacation every year in October. If you can't make it there, visit the butterfly sanctuary in the California Academy of Sciences in San Francisco.

NORTHERN CALIFORNIA'S BEST ROAD TRIPS

Visit Fodors.com for advice, updates, and bookings

THE ULTIMATE ROAD TRIP

CALIFORNIA'S LEGENDARY HIGHWAY 1

by Cheryl Crabtree

One of the world's most scenic drives, California's State Route 1 (also known as Highway 1, the Pacific Coast Highway, the PCH) stretches along the edge of the state for nearly 660 miles, from Southern California's Dana Point to its northern terminus near Leggett, about 40 miles north of Fort Bragg. As you travel south to north, the water's edge transitions from long, sandy beaches and low-lying bluffs to towering dunes, craggy cliffs, and ancient redwood groves. The ocean changes as well; the relatively tame and surfable swells lapping the Southern California shore give way to the frigid, powerful waves crashing against weatherbeaten rocks in the north.

HIGHWAY 1 TOP 10

- Santa Monica
- Santa Barbara
- Hearst San Simeon State Historical Monument
- Big Sur
- Carmel
- 17–Mile Drive
- Monterey
- San Francisco
- Marin Headlands
- Point Reyes National Seashore

Give yourself lots of extra time to pull off the road and enjoy the scenery

STARTING YOUR JOURNEY

You may decide to drive the road's entire 660-mile route, or bite off a smaller piece. In either case, a Highway 1 road trip allows you to experience California at your own pace, stopping when and where you wish. Hike a beachside trail, dig your toes in the sand, and search for creatures in the tidepools. Buy some artichokes and strawberries from a roadside farmstand. Talk to people along the way (you'll run into everyone from soul-searching meditators, farmers, and beatniks to city-slackers and working-class folks), and take lots of pictures. Don't rush—you could easily spend a lifetime discovering secret spots along this route.

To help you plan your trip, we've broken the road into three regions (Santa Monica to Carmel, Carmel to San Francisco, and San Francisco to Fort Bragg); each region is then broken up into smaller segments—many of which are suitable for a day's drive. If you're pressed for time, you can always tackle a section of Highway 1, and then head inland to U.S. 101 or I-5 to reach your next destination more quickly.

WHAT'S IN A NAME?

Though it's often referred to as the Pacific Coast Highway (or PCH), sections of Highway 1 actually have different names. The southernmost section (Dana Point to Oxnard) is the Pacific Coast Highway. After that, the road becomes the Cabrillo Highway (Las Cruces to Lompoc), the Big Sur Coast Highway (San Luis Obispo County line to Monterey), the North Coast Scenic Byway (San Luis Obispo city limit to the Monterey County line), the Cabrillo Highway again (Santa Cruz County line to Half Moon Bay), and finally the Shoreline Highway (Marin City to Leggett). To make matters more confusing, smaller chunks of the road have additional honorary monikers.

Just follow the green triangular signs that say "California 1."

HIGHWAY 1 DRIVING

- Rent a convertible. (You will not regret it.)
- Begin the drive north from Santa Monica, where congestion and traffic delays pose less of a problem.
- Take advantage of turnouts. Let cars pass you as you take in the ocean view and snap a picture.
- Mind your manners: Don't tailgate or glare at other drivers.
- If you're prone to motion sickness, take the wheel yourself. Focusing on the landscape outside should help you feel less queasy.
- If you're afraid of heights, drive from south to north so you'll be on the mountain rather than the cliff side of the road.
- Driving PCH is glorious during winter, but check weather conditions before you go as landslides are frequent after storms.

HIGHWAY 1: SANTA MONICA TO BIG SUR

Hearst Castle

THE PLAN

Distance: approx. 335 miles

Time: 3-5 days

Good Overnight Options: Malibu, Santa Barbara, Pismo Beach, San Luis Obispo, Cambria, Carmel

SANTA MONICA TO MALIBU (approx. 26 miles)

Highway 1 begins in Dana point, but it seems more appropriate to begin a PCH adventure in **Santa Monica.** Be sure to experience the beach culture, then balance the tacky pleasures of Santa Monica's amusement pier with a stylish dinner in a neighborhood restaurant.

MALIBU TO SANTA BARBARA (approx. 70 miles)

The PCH follows the curve of Santa Monica Bay all the way to **Malibu** and **Point Mugu,** near **Oxnard.** Chances are you'll experience *déjà vu* driving this 27-mile stretch:

mountains on one side, ocean on the other, opulent homes perched on hillsides; you've seen this piece of coast countless times on TV and film. Be sure to walk out on the **Malibu Pier** for a great photo opp, then check out **Surfrider Beach,** with three famous points where perfect waves ignited a worldwide surfing rage in the 1960s.

After Malibu you'll drive through miles of protected, largely unpopulated coastline. Ride a wave at **Zuma Beach,** scout for offshore whales at **Point Dume State Beach,** or hike the trails at **Point Mugu State Park.** After skirting Point Mugu, Highway 1 merges with U.S. 101 for about 70 miles before reaching **Santa Barbara.** A mini-tour of the city includes a visit to the magnificent Spanish **Mission Santa Barbara** and a walk down hopping **State Street to Stearns Wharf.**

SANTA BARBARA TO SAN SIMEON (approx. 147 miles)

North of Santa Barbara, Highway 1 morphs into the Cabrillo Highway, separating from and then rejoining U.S. 101. The route winds through rolling vineyards and rangeland to **San Luis**

Santa Barbara

Obispo, where any legit road trip includes a photo stop at the quirky **Madonna Inn.** Be sure to also climb the humungous dunes at **Guadalupe-Nipomo Dunes Preserve.**

In downtown San Luis Obispo, the **Mission San Luis Obispo de Tolosa** stands by a tree-shaded creek edged with shops and cafés. Highway 1 continues to **Morro Bay** and up the coast. About 4 miles north of Morro Bay, you'll reach **Cayucos,** a classic old California beach town with an 1875 pier, restaurants, taverns, and shops in historic buildings.

The road continues through **Cambria** to solitary Hearst San Simeon State Historical Monument, better known as **Hearst Castle**—the art-filled pleasure palace at **San Simeon.** Just four miles north of the castle, elephant seals grunt and cavort at the **Piedras Blancas Elephant**

Big Sur

TOP 5 PLACES TO LINGER

- Point Dume State Beach
- Santa Barbara
- Hearst Castle
- Big Sur/Julia Pfeiffer Burns State Park
- Carmel

Seal Rookery, just off the side of the road.

SAN SIMEON TO CARMEL (approx. 92 miles)

Heading north, you'll drive through **Big Sur,** a place of ancient forests and rugged shoreline stretching 90 miles from San Simeon to **Carmel.** Much of Big Sur lies within several state parks and the 165,000-acre **Ventana Wilderness,** itself part of the **Los Padres National Forest.** This famously scenic stretch of the coastal drive, which twists up and down bluffs above the ocean, can last hours. Take your time.

At **Julia Pfeiffer Burns State Park** one easy but rewarding hike leads to an iconic waterfall off a beachfront cliff. When you reach lovely **Carmel,** stroll around the picture-perfect town's mission, galleries, and shops.

HIGHWAY 1: CARMEL TO SAN FRANCISCO

San Francisco

THE PLAN

Distance: approx. 123 miles

Time: 2-4 days

Good Overnight Options: Carmel, Monterey, Santa Cruz, Half Moon Bay, San Francisco

CARMEL TO MONTEREY
(approx. 4 miles)

Between **Carmel** and **Monterey,** Highway 1 cuts across the base of the Monterey Peninsula. Pony up the toll and take a brief detour to follow famous **17-Mile Drive,** which traverses a surf-pounded landscape of cypress trees, sea lions, gargantuan estates, and the world famous **Pebble Beach Golf Links.** Take your time here as well, and be sure to allow lots of time for pulling off to enjoy the gorgeous views.

If you have the time, spend a day checking out the sights in **Monterey,** especially the kelp forests and bat rays of

Monterey

the **Monterey Bay Aquarium** and the adobes and artifacts of **Monterey State Historic Park.**

MONTEREY TO SANTA CRUZ (approx. 42 miles)

From Monterey the highway rounds the gentle curve of Monterey Bay, passing through sand dunes and artichoke fields on its way to **Moss Landing** and the **Elkhorn Slough National Estuarine Marine Preserve.** Kayak near or walk through the protected wetlands here, or board a pontoon safari boat—don't forget your binoculars. The historic seaside villages of **Aptos, Capitola,** and **Soquel,** just off the highway near the bay's midpoint, are ideal stopovers for beachcombing, antiquing, and hiking through redwoods. In boho **Santa Cruz,** just 7 miles north, walk along the **wharf,** ride the historic roller coaster on the **boardwalk,** and perch on the cliffs to watch surfers peel through tubes at **Steamer Lane.**

SANTA CRUZ TO SAN FRANCISCO (approx. 77 miles)

Highway 1 hugs the ocean's edge once again as it departs Santa Cruz and runs northward past a string of secluded beaches and small towns. Stop and stretch your legs in the tiny, artsy town

Davenport cliffs, Devenport

of **Davenport,** where you can wander through several galleries and enjoy sumptuous views from the bluffs. At **Año Nuevo State Park,** walk down to the dunes to view gargantuan elephant seals lounging on shore, then break for a meal or snack in **Pescadero** or **Half Moon Bay.**

FRIGID WATERS

If you're planning to jump in the ocean in Northern California, wear a wetsuit or prepare to shiver. Even in summer, the water temperatures warm up to just barely tolerable. The fog tends to burn off earlier in the day at relatively sheltered beaches near Monterey Bay's midpoint, near Aptos, Capitola and Santa Cruz. These beaches also tend to attract softer waves than those on the bay's outer edges.

Half Moon Bay

TOP 5 PLACES TO LINGER

- 17-Mile Drive
- Monterey
- Santa Cruz
- Año Nuevo State Reserve
- Half Moon Bay

From Half Moon Bay to **Daly City**, the road includes a number of shoulderless twists and turns that demand slower speeds and nerves of steel. Signs of urban development soon appear: mansions holding fast to Pacific cliffs and then, as the road veers slightly inland to merge with Skyline Boulevard, boxlike houses sprawling across **Daly City** and **South San Francisco**.

Golden Gate Nat'l. Recreation Area

San Francisco

Daly City

Pacifica

South San Francisco

Moss Beach

Pillar Point
Half Moon Bay

El Granada

San Mateo

Hayward

Half Moon Bay

Belmont

San Francisco Bay

Palo Alto

San Gregorio

Pescadero Point

Pescadero

Mountain View

Bolsa Point

Pigeon Point

Santa Clara

Año Nuevo State Park

Point Año Nuevo

Boulder Creek

Los Gatos

San Jose

Saratoga

The Forest of Nisene Marks State Park

Davenport

Pacific Coast Highway

Santa Cruz

Soquel

Capitola

Aptos

Watsonville

Monterey Bay

Elkhorn Slough National Estuarine Marine Preserve

Moss Landing

Castroville

17-Mile Drive

Cypress Point

Pacific Grove

Pebble Beach

Carmel Bay

Monterey

Salinas

Carmel

Carmel Valley

0   10 mi

0   10 km

Point Sur

Big Sur

HIGHWAY 1: SAN FRANCISCO TO FORT BRAGG

Mendocino Coast Botanical Garden

THE PLAN

Distance: 177 miles

Time: 2-4 days

Good Overnight Options: San Francisco, Olema, Bodega Bay, Gualala, Mendocino, Fort Bragg

SAN FRANCISCO

The official Highway 1 heads straight through **San Francisco** along 19th Avenue through **Golden Gate Park** and the **Presidio** toward the **Golden Gate Bridge.** For a more scenic tour, watch for signs announcing exits for 35 North/Skyline Boulevard, then Ocean Beach/The Great Highway (past Lake Merced). The Great Highway follows the coast along the western border of San Francisco; you'll cruise past entrances to the **San Francisco Zoo, Golden Gate Park,** and the **Cliff House.** Hike out to **Point Lobos** or **Land's End** for awesome vistas, then drive through **Lincoln Park** and the **Palace of the Legion of**

Golden Gate Bridge

Honor and follow El Camino del Mar/Lincoln Boulevard all the way to the Golden Gate Bridge.

The best way to see San Francisco is on foot and public transportation. A **Union Square** stroll—complete with people-watching, window-shopping, and architecture-viewing—is a good first stop. In **Chinatown,** department stores give way to storefront temples, open-air markets, and delightful dim-sum shops. After lunch in one, catch a **Powell Street cable car** to the end of the line and get off to see the bay views and the antique arcade games at **Musée Mécanique** (the gem of otherwise mindless **Fisherman's Wharf**). For dinner and live music, try cosmopolitan **North Beach.**

SAN FRANCISCO TO POINT REYES

(approx. 37 miles)

Leaving the city the next day, your drive across the Golden Gate Bridge and a stop at a **Marin Headlands** overlook will yield memorable views (if fog hasn't socked in the bay). So will a hike in **Point Reyes National Seashore,** farther up Highway 1 (now called Shoreline Highway). On this wild swath of coast you'll likely be able to claim an unspoiled beach for yourself. You should expect company,

Point Reyes National Seashore

however, around the lighthouse at the tip of Point Reyes because year-round views—and seasonal elephant seal- and whale-watching—draw crowds. If you have time, poke around tiny Olema, which has some excellent restaurants.

POINT REYES TO MENDOCINO

(approx. 131 miles)

Passing only a few minuscule towns, this next stretch of Highway 1 showcases the northern coast in all its rugged glory. The reconstructed compound of eerily foreign buildings at **Fort Ross State Historic Park** recalls the era of Russian fur trading in California. Pull into **Gualala** for an espresso, a sandwich, and a little human contact before rolling onward. After another 50 miles of tranquil state beaches and parks you'll return to civilization in **Mendocino.**

Point Reyes National Seashore

TOP 5 PLACES TO LINGER

- San Francisco
- Marin Headlands
- Point Reyes National Seashore
- Fort Ross State Historic Park
- Mendocino

MENDOCINO TO FORT BRAGG

(approx. 9 miles)

Exploring Mendocino you may feel like you've fallen through a rabbit hole: the weather screams Northern California, but the 19th-century buildings—erected by homesick Yankee loggers—definitely say New England. Once you've browsed around the artsy shops, continue on to the **Mendocino Coast Botanical Gardens;** then travel back in time on the **Skunk Train,** which follows an old logging route from **Fort Bragg** deep into the redwood forest.

Leggett
Rockpoint
Westport
Laytonville
① 1
Fort Bragg
Mendocino Coast Botanical Gardens
101
Caspar
Mendocino
20
Little River
Willits
Albion
Elk
128
Navarro
Calpella
20
Point Arena
Philo
Ukiah
Manchester
ANDERSON VALLEY
Point Arena
Boonville
Anchor Bay
Hopland
Gualala
Yorkville
Kelseyville
Pacific Coast Highway
Stewarts Point
Cloverdale
Horseshoe Cove
Salt Point State Park
Fort Ross State Hist. Park
Geyserville
Fort Ross
Healdsburg
Jenner
101
Duncan Point
116
Santa
Calistoga
Carmet
Rosa
Bodega Bay
Sebastopol
Bodega Head
Bodega Bay
Tomales
Tomales Point
Sonoma
Tomales Bay
Marshall
Petaluma
Inverness
Point Reyes Station
Point Reyes
BOLINAS RIDGE
Drakes Bay
Olema
101
Point Reyes National Seashore
San Rafael
FARALLON ISLANDS
Bolinas
80
Bolinas Bay
Stinson Beach
▲ Mt. Tamalpais
Muir Beach
Richmond
Marin Headlands
Golden Gate Nat'l. Rec. Area
Sausalito
Golden Gate Park
0   15 mi
San Francisco
0   15 km
Oakland
280
101

PACIFIC OCEAN

GREAT ITINERARIES

SANTA BARBARA WINE COUNTRY, 3 DAYS

It has been over a decade since the popular movie *Sideways* brought the Santa Barbara wine country to the world's attention, and interest in this wine growing area continues to grow. On this trip you will explore one of the most beautiful cities in the West, enjoy time along the gorgeous coast, and then head inland for a delightful wine-tasting adventure. This itinerary makes a perfect add-on to a trip to Los Angeles, or for those driving the coastal route between Los Angeles and San Francisco.

Day 1: Santa Barbara

(2 hours by car from LAX to Santa Barbara without traffic.)

Santa Barbara is a gem, combining elegance with a laid-back coastal vibe. It provides a tranquil escape from the congestion of Los Angeles, and a dose of sophistication to the largely rural central coast.

Start your day at the beautiful **Old Mission Santa Barbara**, known as the "Queen" of the 21 missions that comprise the California Mission Trail. From here, head to the waterfront and spend some time enjoying the wide stretch of sand at **East Beach** and a seafood lunch at one of the restaurants on **Stearns Wharf.**

Next stop is a tour of the **Santa Barbara County Courthouse** and the beautiful red-tile roofed buildings of the surrounding downtown. Don't miss the incredible views from the top of the courthouse tower.

Back on the ground, enjoy superb shopping along **State Street** and consider kicking off your wine tour early with some tastings along the **Urban Wine Trail**, a collection of tasting rooms spread over a few blocks between downtown and the beach. Enjoy the lively dining and nightlife scene downtown, or head towards tony **Montecito** for an elegant dinner or overnight stay at the ultra-exclusive (and expensive) **San Ysidro Ranch.**

Day 2: Santa Rita Hills, Lompoc, and Los Olivos

(Without stops, this route takes about 2 hours by car. Plan to linger, and to detour down side roads to reach the wineries.)

Take the scenic drive along the coast on Highway 101 before heading inland towards Buellton. Exit onto Santa Rosa Road to begin your loop through the Santa Rita Hills. This area's cooler climate produces top-notch Chardonnay and Pinot Noir. Vineyards line the loop as you head out on Santa Rosa Road and return on Highway 246 towards Buellton. **Lafond Winery and Vineyards, Alma Rosa Winery,** and **Ken Brown Wines** are just a few of the wineries found along this route. Don't miss a stop at the so-called **Lompoc Wine Ghetto,** located midway around the route. Several tasting rooms are clustered together in an industrial park downtown including well-regarded producers such as **Stolpman** and **Longoria.**

Back on Highway 101, head north about 6 miles before exiting towards **Los Olivos.** Here you can park the car and spend the rest of the day exploring on foot. Tasting rooms, galleries, boutiques and restaurants have made this former stagecoach town quite wine-country chic. **Carhartt Vineyard** and **Daniel Gehrs** are just two of the producers with tasting rooms in town. Los Olivos is a good base to overnight in, or stay just outside of town at the lovely **Ballard Inn.** Or, dine at the chic locavore **Root 246** restaurant and stay at the **Hotel Corque** in nearby **Solvang.**

PACIFIC
OCEAN

Days 3: Solvang, Foxen Canyon, and the Santa Ynez Valley

(The drive from Santa Ynez to Santa Barbara is about 45 minutes by car via Hwy. 154.)

Start the next morning with pastries at the Danish town of **Solvang**, 10 minutes south of Los Olivos. The collection of windmills and distinct half-timber architecture of this village is charming, even if it is touristy. Spend some time exploring the town before hitting the road.

The towns of Los Olivos, Santa Ynez, and Solvang are located just a few minutes apart, with wineries spread between them in an area known as the Santa Ynez Valley. Heading north from Los Olivos, the Foxen Canyon wine trail extends all the way to Santa Maria. Expect some backtracking along your route today as you wind between the towns and venture into Foxen Canyon. The tour at **Firestone Vineyard** is worthwhile, but very popular. The tasting rooms throughout the Santa Ynez region can get crowded, but there are plenty to choose from—if you see a tour bus parked outside one winery, just keep driving to the next one. Don't blink or you might miss the tiny town of **Santa Ynez** itself, but it is worth a wander or a stop for lunch.

When you've had your fill of the wine region, take scenic Highway 154 over the San Marcos Pass and back to Santa Barbara. Wind down the day with a stroll along the beach, and perhaps one last glass of wine at sunset.

MONTEREY BAY, CARMEL, AND BIG SUR, 4 DAYS

In a nutshell, this drive is all about the jaw-dropping scenery of the Pacific Coast. Visitors pressed for time often make the drive from Monterey through Big Sur in one day. However, those who linger will be rewarded with more time to venture off the road and to enjoy the solitude of Big Sur once the day-trippers have gone.

Day 1: Monterey

Monterey, with its federally protected national marine sanctuary and its world-renowned aquarium, is the perfect spot to kick off your tour of the coast. Start the day with a visit to the enthralling **Monterey Bay Aquarium.** Exhibits such as the dramatic three-story kelp forest near the entrance give you a true sense of the local marine environment. For an even closer encounter, take yourself to the water on a kayak or whale watching tour. While undoubtedly touristy, the shops and galleries of **Cannery Row** still make for an interesting diversion and it's fun to watch the colony of sea lions at **Fisherman's Wharf**. There are plenty of excellent dining and lodging choices within walking distance of downtown, so enjoy a seafood dinner and an evening stroll before hitting the road the next morning.

Day 2: 17-Mile Drive and Carmel-By-The-Sea
(The 17-Mile Drive's Pacific Grove entrance gate is 15 minutes by car from Monterey.)

If your visit falls between October and March, begin your drive with a quick detour to visit the migrating monarch butterflies at the **Monarch Grove Sanctuary** in the charming Victorian town of **Pacific Grove**.

Enter the scenic **17-Mile Drive** through the tollgate off Sunset Drive in Pacific Grove. This scenic road winds its way along the coast through a hushed and refined landscape of stunning homes and the renowned golf links at **Pebble Beach**. Perhaps the most famous (and photographed) resident is the **Lone Cypress**, which has come to symbolize the solitude and natural beauty of the coast. Even though the drive is only 17 miles, plan on taking your time. If you stop for lunch or souvenir shopping, enquire about a refund on the entry toll.

Upon exiting the drive, continue south to the charming town of **Carmel-by-the-Sea**. Spend the afternoon browsing the town's boutiques and galleries before walking to **Carmel Beach** for sunset and dinner at one of the many fine restaurants here. Similarly, there is no shortage of stylish, but pricey, lodging. Venture outside of the village for less expensive accommodation.

Day 3: Big Sur
(30 minutes by car.)

The coastal drive through **Big Sur** is justifiably one of the most famous stretches of road in the world. The winding curves, endless views, and scenic waypoints are the stuff of road trip legend. Keep your camera handy, fill up the tank, and prepare to be wowed. Traffic can easily back up along the route and drivers should take caution navigating the road's twists and turns. While you will only drive about 30 miles today, allow several hours for hikes and stops.

Heading into Big Sur you will first come upon the extremely photogenic **Bixby Creek Bridge**. Pull over in the turnout on the north side of the bridge to get that perfect shot. About 10 miles down the road look for a small cluster of services known as Big Sur Village just before the entrance to **Pfeiffer Big Sur State Park**, the perfect place to stop for a hike.

One mile south of the park, watch carefully for the sharp turnout and unmarked road leading to **Pfeiffer Beach**. Following the unpaved road 2 miles toward the sea you may question whether you are lost, but your perseverance will be rewarded when you reach the secluded beach with its signature rocky arch just offshore. Don't miss it!

There are several lodging options around this portion of Big Sur, ranging from rustic to luxurious. If room rates at the legendary **Post Ranch Inn** are not in your budget, consider splurging on the nine-course tasting menu at its spectacular cliff-side **Sierra Mar** restaurant instead. Alternatively, the terrace at **Nepenthe** offers decent food and gorgeous views at a lower price point. Be sure to check the time for sunset when making your dinner reservation.

Day 4: Big Sur to Cambria
(About 2 hours by car. Allow ample time for hiking and 2 hours to tour Hearst Castle.)

Start the morning off with a hike in **Julia Pfeiffer Burns State Park**, popular for its waterfall tumbling dramatically into the sea. Back on the road, several scenic overlooks will beckon as you head through the southern stretch of Big Sur. Treasure hunters should consider a stop at **Jade Cove.**

As you enter **San Simeon**, don't miss the **Piedras Blancas Elephant Seal Rookery.** Depending on your timing, you might catch a late afternoon tour at **Hearst Castle.** If not, you can make a reservation for a tour early the following morning. End the day with a walk at **Moonstone Beach** in the town of **Cambria**, 10 miles south of the castle and overnight in one of the reasonably priced lodgings here.

From here, you can continue your travels south through the central coast to **Santa Barbara.** Or head inland to visit the **Paso Robles** wine region before returning to Monterey via Highway 101.

SIERRA RICHES: YOSEMITE, GOLD COUNTRY, AND TAHOE, 10 DAYS

This tour will show you why Tony Bennett left his heart in San Francisco. It also includes some of the most beautiful places in a very scenic state, plus gold-rush-era history, and a chance to hike a trail or two.

Day 1: San Francisco

Straight from the airport, drop your bags at the lighthearted **Hotel Monaco** near **Union Square** and request a goldfish for your room. A Union Square stroll packs a wallop of people-watching, window-shopping, and architecture viewing. **Chinatown**, chock-full of dim sum shops, storefront temples, and open-air markets, promises authentic bites for lunch. Catch a Powell Street **cable car** to the end of the line and get off to see the bay views and the antique arcade games at **Musée Mécanique**, the hidden gem of otherwise mindless **Fisherman's Wharf.** No need to go any farther than cosmopolitan North Beach for cocktail hour, dinner, and live music.

Day 2: Golden Gate Park

(15 minutes by car or taxi, 45 minutes by public transport from Union Square.)

In **Golden Gate Park,** linger amid the flora of the **Conservatory of Flowers** and the **San Francisco Botanical Garden at Strybing Arboretum,** soak up some art at the **de Young Museum,** and find serene refreshment at the **San Francisco Japanese Tea Garden.** The Pacific surf pounds the cliffs below the **Legion of Honor** art museum, which has an exquisite view of the **Golden Gate Bridge—** when the fog stays away. Sunset cocktails at the circa-1909 **Cliff House** include a prospect over Seal Rock (actually occupied by sea lions). Eat dinner elsewhere: Pacific Heights, the Mission, and SoMa teem with excellent restaurants.

Day 3: Into the High Sierra

(4–5 hours by car from San Francisco.)

First thing in the morning, pick up your rental car and head for the hills. Arriving in **Yosemite National Park, Bridalveil Fall,** and **El Capitan,** the 350-story granite monolith, greet you on your way to **Yosemite Village.** Ditch the car and pick up information and refreshment before hopping on the year-round shuttle to explore. Justly famous sights cram Yosemite Valley: massive **Half Dome** and **Sentinel Dome,** thundering **Yosemite Falls,** and wispy **Ribbon Fall** and **Nevada Fall.** Invigorating short hikes off the shuttle route lead to numerous vantage points. Celebrate your arrival in one of the world's most sublime spots with dinner in the dramatic **Ahwahnee Hotel Dining Room** and stay the night there (reserve well in advance).

Day 4: Yosemite National Park

(Yosemite shuttles run every 10–30 minutes.)

Ardent hikers consider **John Muir Trail to Half Dome** a must-do, tackling the rigorous 12-hour round-trip to the top of Half Dome in search of life-changing vistas. The merely mortal hike downhill from Glacier Point on **Four-Mile Trail** or **Panorama Trail,** the latter an all-day trek past waterfalls. Less demanding still is a drive to Wawona for a stroll in the **Mariposa Grove of Big Trees** and lunch at the 19th-century **Wawona Hotel Dining Room.** In bad weather, take shelter in the **Ansel Adams Gallery** and **Yosemite Museum;** in fair conditions, drive up to **Glacier Point** for a breathtaking sunset view.

Day 5: Gold Country South

(2½–3 hours by car from Yosemite.)

Highway 49 traces the mother lode that yielded many fortunes in gold in the 1850s and 1860s. Step into a living gold-rush town at **Columbia State Historic Park,** where you can ride a stagecoach and pan for riches. **Sutter Creek's** well-preserved downtown bursts with shopping opportunities, but the vintage goods displayed at **Monteverde Store Museum** are not for sale. A different sort of vintage powers the present-day bonanza of **Shenandoah Valley,** heart of the Sierra Foothills Wine Country. Taste your way through Rhône-style blended Zinfandels and Syrahs at boutique wineries such as **Shenandoah Vineyards** and **Sobon Estate.** Amador City's 1879 **Imperial Hotel** places you firmly in the past for the night.

Day 6: Gold Country North

(2 hours by car from Amador City to Nevada City.)

In **Placerville,** a mineshaft invites investigation at **Hangtown's Gold Bug Mine,** while **Marshall Gold Discovery State Historic Park** encompasses most of **Coloma** and preserves the spot where James Marshall's 1849 find set off the California Gold Rush. Old Town **Auburn,** with its

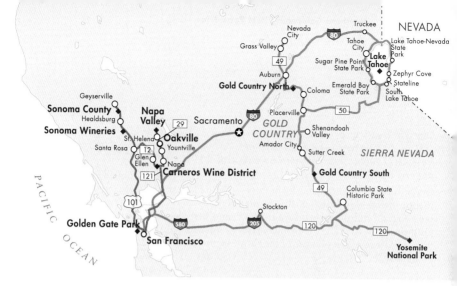

museums and courthouse, makes a good lunch stop, but if you hold out until you reach Grass Valley you can try authentic miners' pasties. A tour of **Empire Mine State Historic Park** takes you into a mine, and a few miles away horse-drawn carriages ply the narrow, shop-lined streets of downtown **Nevada City**. Both Nevada City and **Grass Valley** hold a collection of bed-and-breakfast inns that date back to gold-rush days. For more contemporary accommodations backtrack to Auburn or Placerville.

Day 7: Lake Tahoe
(1 hour by car from Nevada City, 2 hours from Placerville.)

Jewel-like **Lake Tahoe** is a straight shot east of Placerville on Highway 50; stop for picnic provisions in commercial **South Lake Tahoe**. A stroll past the three magnificent estates in **Pope-Baldwin Recreation Area** hints at the sumptuous lakefront summers once enjoyed by the elite. High above a glittering cove, **Emerald Bay State Park** offers one of the best lake views as well as a steep hike down to (and back up from) **Vikingsholm**, a replica 9th-century Scandinavian castle. Another fine, old mansion—plus a nature preserve and many hiking trails—lies in **Sugar Pine Point**

State Park. Tahoe City offers more history and ample dining and lodging choices.

Day 8: Exploring Lake Tahoe
(Sightseeing cruise lasts 2 hours.)

The picture-perfect beaches and bays of **Lake Tahoe–Nevada State Park** line the Nevada shoreline, a great place to bask in the sun or go mountain biking. For a different perspective of the lake, get out on the azure water aboard the stern-wheeler MS *Dixie II* from **Zephyr Cove**. In South Lake Tahoe, another view unfurls as the **Heavenly Gondola** travels 2½ miles up a mountain. Keep your adrenaline pumping into the evening with some action at the massive casinos clustered in Stateline, Nevada.

Day 9: Return to San Francisco
(About 4 hours by car from Tahoe City.)

After a long morning of driving, return your rental car in San Francisco and soak up some more urban excitement. Good options include a late lunch at the **Ferry Building,** followed by a visit to the **San Francisco Museum of Modern Art,** or lunch in **Japantown** followed by shopping in **Pacific Heights.** There is excellent people-watching in the **Castro** and the **Haight.** Say good-bye to Northern California at one of the plush lounges or trendy bars in the downtown hotels.

Day 10: Departure

(SFO is 30 minutes from downtown both by BART public transport and by car, without traffic.)

Check the weather and your flight information before you start out for the airport: fog sometimes causes delays at SFO. On a clear day, your flight path might give you one last fabulous glimpse of the City by the Bay.

THE ULTIMATE WINE TRIP: NAPA AND SONOMA, 4 DAYS

On this four-day extravaganza, you'll taste well-known and under-the-radar wines, bed down in plush hotels, and dine at restaurants operated by celebrity chefs. Appointments are required for some of the tastings.

Day 1: Sonoma County

(1½–2 hours by car from San Francisco, depending on traffic.)

Begin your tour in Geyserville, about 78 miles north of San Francisco on U.S. Highway 101. Visit **Locals Tasting Room,** which pours the wines of special small wineries. Have lunch at nearby **Diavola** or **Catelli's,** then head south on U.S. Highway 101 and Old Redwood Highway to **Healdsburg's J Vineyards and Winery,** known for sparkling wines, Pinot Grigio, and Pinot Noir. After a tasting, backtrack on Old Redwood to Healdsburg. **Hôtel Les Mars** and **h2hotel** are two well-located spots to spend the night. Have dinner at **Chalkboard, Bravas Bar de Tapas,** or **Campo Fina,** all close by.

Day 2: Sonoma Wineries

(1 hour by car from Healdsburg to Glen Ellen.)

Interesting wineries dot the countryside surrounding Healdsburg, among them **Dry Creek Vineyard, Jordan Vineyard & Winery,** and **Unti Vineyards.** Dry Creek produces Zinfandel, Jordan makes Cabernet Sauvignon and Chardonnay, and Unti specializes in Zinfandel, Sangiovese, and obscure Italian and Rhône varietals. In the afternoon, head south on U.S. Highway 101 and east on scenic Highway 12 to **Glen Ellen.** Visit **Jack London State Historic Park,** the memorabilia-filled home of the famous writer. Dine at **Aventine Glen Ellen** or **Glen Ellen Star** and stay at the **Olea Hotel.**

Day 3: Napa Valley

(Glen Ellen to St. Helena is about 30 minutes by car without traffic. St. Helena to Yountville is about 15 minutes by car, without stops.)

On day three, head east from Glen Ellen on Trinity Road, which twists and turns over the Mayacamas Mountains, eventually becoming the Oakville Grade. Unless you're driving, bask in the stupendous **Napa Valley** views. At Highway 29, drive north to **St. Helena.** Focus on history and architecture at **Charles Krug Winery** or let the art and wines at **Hall St. Helena** transport you. Take lunch downtown at **Cindy's Backstreet Kitchen.** Check out St. Helena's shopping, then head south on Highway 29 to Yountville for more shopping. Start at celebrity chef Michael Chiarello's **NapaStyle,** inside **V Marketplace.**

Stay overnight at **Bardessono** or the **North Block Hotel,** both within walking distance of Yountville's famous restaurants. A meal at **The French Laundry** is many visitors' holy grail, but dining at **Bouchon, Bistro Jeanty,**

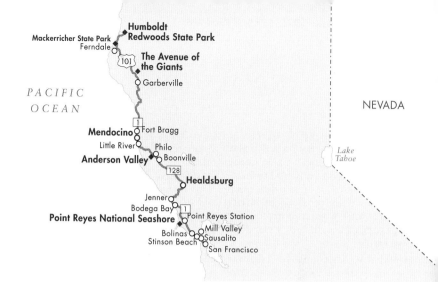

Redd, or Chiarello's Bottega will also leave you feeling well served.

Day 4: Oakville to Carneros

(Just over 1 hour by car from Napa to San Francisco, without traffic.)

After breakfast, head north on Highway 29 to **Oakville**, where sipping wine at **Silver Oak Cellars, Nickel & Nickel**, or **B Cellars** will make clear why collectors covet Oakville Cabernet Sauvignons. Nickel & Nickel is on Highway 29; Silver Oak and B Cellars are east of it on Oakville Cross Road. Have a picnic at **Oakville Grocery**, in business on Highway 29 since 1881. Afterward, head south to Highway 121 and turn west to reach the Carneros District. Tour the **di Rosa** arts center (appointment required), then repair across the street to **Domaine Carneros**, which makes French-style sparkling wines. There's hardly a more elegant way to bid a Wine Country adieu than on the Domaine château's vineyard-view terrace before heading back to San Francisco. Give yourself plenty of time to get to your departure airport; traffic is generally heavy as you close in on the Bay Area.

THE BEST OF THE NORTHERN COAST, 5 DAYS

Hit the highlights of Northern California in one itinerary: scenic coastal drives, quaint windswept towns, wine tasting, culinary delights, and majestic redwood forests. This route can be done as part of a longer trip north towards the Oregon border, or as part of a loop back down to San Francisco.

Day 1: Marin County and Point Reyes National Seashore

(Without stops, Pt. Reyes National Seashore is about 1½ hours by car from San Francisco on Hwy. 1. Pt. Reyes Lighthouse is 45 minutes by car from the visitor center.)

As you head out of San Francisco on the Golden Gate Bridge, be sure to pull over at the **scenic lookout** on the north side and take in the sweeping views looking back at the city skyline. If you haven't yet checked out the picturesque harbor community of **Sausalito** just north of the bridge, now is your chance. It will be hard not to linger, but there is much to see today. Bidding San Francisco farewell, you will quickly find yourself in the natural beauty of Marin County.

Exit the 101 onto Highway 1 at the chic suburb **Mill Valley,** and head towards **Muir Woods National Monument.** Walking among the coastal redwoods, it is hard to imagine San Francisco lies just a few miles away. However, the proximity to the city means that Muir Woods is often crowded and parking can be difficult if you don't arrive early.

From Muir Woods, continue on Highway 1 past the laid-back beach towns of **Stinson Beach** and **Bolinas** before continuing on to **Point Reyes National Seashore.** Spend the remainder of the day at the park tidepooling, kayaking, hiking one of the many trails, or exploring the **Point Reyes Lighthouse.** In the winter, be on the lookout for migrating gray whales.

The tiny town of **Point Reyes Station** offers a selection of shops and dining options, including **Tomales Bay Foods,** a provisions stop favored by foodies. Spend a quiet evening in town and overnight at one of the small inns nearby.

Day 2: Healdsburg
(Pt. Reyes Station to Healdsburg, via Jenner, is 2 hours by car.)

Continue north on Highway 1 past **Bodega Bay,** made famous by the Alfred Hitchcock movie *The Birds.* At Jenner, known for its resident harbor seals, turn on Route 116 and follow the Russian River inland taking time to stop at a winery or two along the way.

Ditch the car in **Healdsburg** and enjoy strolling through the appealing town square with its excellent selection of tasting rooms and boutiques. The town is home to many acclaimed restaurants and luxurious hotels and is an excellent place to stop for the night.

Days 3 and 4: Anderson Valley and Mendocino
(Mendocino is 2 hours by car from Healdsburg. Budget plenty of time for stops in Anderson Valley to ensure the end of this scenic drive is done in the daylight.)

Driving north on the 101 from Healdsburg, pick up Highway 128 at Cloverdale and head into the **Anderson Valley.** This wine region is famous for its excellent Pinot Noir and Gewürztraminer, and the laid-back atmosphere of its tasting rooms can be a refreshing alternative to those in Napa Valley. **Navarro Vineyards, Roederer Estate** and **Husch Vineyards** are all recommended. The small towns of **Boonville** and **Philo** have several high-quality dining options, and the latter is home to the **Philo Apple Farm**'s beloved farm stand.

Continuing on to the coast, Highway 128 follows the Navarro River through several miles of dense and breathtaking redwood forest ending at the ocean. From here you meet up again with Highway 1 as it winds its way along a spectacularly scenic portion of the coast.

With their excellent dining and lodging options, the towns of **Mendocino** and **Little River,** just to the south, are great choices for your overnight stay. Spend the next day and a half exploring the area. Opportunities for stunning coastal walks abound, including **MacKerricher** and **Van Damme State Parks.** Hike through the unique **Pygmy Forest**in Van Damme and visit the **Glass Beach** in Fort Bragg. Be sure to save some time to explore the town of Mendocino itself with its quaint New England–style architecture and selection of art galleries and boutiques.

2

Day 5: Humboldt Redwoods State Park and the Avenue of the Giants
(Mendocino to Eureka via the Avenue of the Giants is 3 hours by car.)

Driving north on Highway 1, the road eventually curves inland and meets up with U.S. Highway 101 near Leggett. Head north on the 101 to Garberville, a good place to take a break before heading on to the Redwoods.

For all the hype, a drive through **The Avenue of the Giants** will still take your breath away. Pick up a copy of the self-guided tour as you enter the 32-mile stretch of road running alongside some of the tallest trees on the planet. The drive weaves through portions of the larger **Humboldt Redwoods State Park.** Take time to get out of the car and take a short hike through Founders Grove or Rockefeller Forest.

Continue on to **Ferndale,** a picturesque town of colorful Victorian buildings that is now largely a tourist destination. You can overnight here, or carry on to the regional city of **Eureka** for a wider variety of dining and accommodation.

From here, you can continue your way up the coast through the **Redwood National Forest** and on to the Oregon border. Alternatively, you can head south on the 101 and either return to **San Francisco,** or easily combine this itinerary with a trip to **Napa Valley** and the rest of **Sonoma.**

THE CENTRAL COAST

From Ventura to Big Sur with
Channel Islands National Park

WELCOME TO THE CENTRAL COAST

TOP REASONS TO GO

★ **Incredible nature:** The wild and wonderful Central Coast is home to Channel Islands National Park, two national marine sanctuaries, state parks and beaches, and the rugged Los Padres National Forest.

★ **Edible bounty:** Land and sea provide enough fresh regional foods to satisfy the most sophisticated foodies—grapes, strawberries, seafood, olive oil, and much more. Get your fill at countless farmers' markets, wineries, and restaurants.

★ **Outdoor activities:** Kick back and revel in the California lifestyle. Surf, golf, kayak, hike, play tennis—or just hang out and enjoy the gorgeous scenery.

★ **Small-town charm, big-city culture:** With all the amazing cultural opportunities— museums, theater, music, and festivals—you might start thinking you're in L.A. or San Francisco.

★ **Wine tasting:** Central Coast wines earn high critical praise. Sample them in urban tasting rooms, dusty crossroads towns, and at high- and low-tech rural wineries.

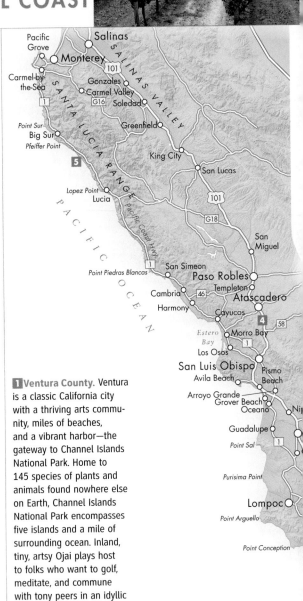

1 Ventura County. Ventura is a classic California city with a thriving arts community, miles of beaches, and a vibrant harbor—the gateway to Channel Islands National Park. Home to 145 species of plants and animals found nowhere else on Earth, Channel Islands National Park encompasses five islands and a mile of surrounding ocean. Inland, tiny, artsy Ojai plays host to folks who want to golf, meditate, and commune with tony peers in an idyllic mountain setting.

2 **Santa Barbara.** Down-home surfers rub elbows with Hollywood celebrities in sunny, well-scrubbed Santa Barbara, 95 miles north of Los Angeles. Its Spanish-Mexican heritage is reflected in the architectural style of its mission, court-house, and many homes and public buildings.

3 **Northern Santa Barbara County.** Wineries, ranches, and small villages dominate the quintessen-tially Californian landscape here. The quaint Danish town of Solvang is worth a stop for its half-timber buildings, galleries, and bakeries.

4 **San Luis Obispo County.** Friendly college town San Luis Obispo serves as the hub of a burgeoning wine region that stretches nearly 100 miles from Pismo Beach north to Paso Robles; the 230-plus wineries here have earned reputations for high-quality vintages that rival those of Northern California.

5 **Big Sur Coastline.** Rugged cliffs meet the Pacific for more than 60 miles—one of the most scenic and dramatic drives in the world.

GETTING ORIENTED

3

The Central Coast region begins about 60 miles north of Los Angeles, near the seaside city of Ventura. North along the sinuous coastline from here lie the cities of Santa Barbara and San Luis Obispo, and beyond them the smaller towns of Morro Bay, Cambria, and Big Sur. The nearly 300-mile drive through this region, especially the section of Highway 1 from San Simeon to Big Sur, is one of the most scenic in the state.

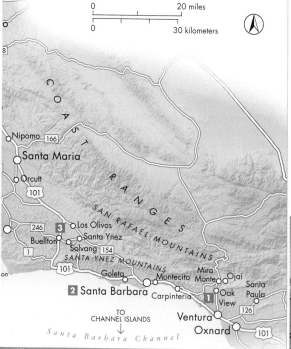

Updated
by Cheryl
Crabtree

Balmy weather, glorious beaches, crystal clear air, and serene landscapes have lured people to the Central Coast since prehistoric times. Today it's also known for its farm-fresh bounty, from grapes vintners craft into world-class wines to strawberries and other produce chefs incorporate into distinctive cuisine. The scenic variety along the Pacific coast is equally impressive—you'll see everything from dramatic cliffs and grass-tufted bluffs to wildlife estuaries and miles of dunes. It's an ideal place to relax, slow down, and appreciate the abundant natural beauty.

Offshore, a pristine national park and a vast marine sanctuary protect the wild, wonderful underwater resources of this incredible corner of the planet. But not all of the Central Coast's top attractions are natural: Ventura, Santa Barbara, and San Luis Obispo are filled with sparkling examples of Spanish-Mediterranean architecture, bustling shopping districts, and first-rate restaurants showcasing regional foods and wines.

PLANNING

WHEN TO GO

The Central Coast climate is mild year-round. If you like to swim in warmer (if still nippy) ocean waters, July and August are the best months to visit. Be aware that this is also high season. Fog often rolls in along the coastal areas in early summer; you'll need a jacket, especially after sunset, close to the shore. It usually rains from December through March. From April to early June and in early fall the weather is almost as fine as in high season, and the pace is less hectic.

GETTING HERE AND AROUND
AIR TRAVEL

Alaska Air, American/US Airways, and United fly to Santa Barbara Airport (SBA), 9 miles from downtown. United and US Airways provide service to San Luis Obispo County Regional Airport (SBP), 3 miles from downtown San Luis Obispo.

Santa Barbara Airbus shuttles travelers between Santa Barbara and Los Angeles for $50 one-way and $95 round-trip. The Santa Barbara Metropolitan Transit District Bus 11 ($1.75) runs every 30 minutes from the airport to the downtown transit center. A taxi between the airport and the hotel districts costs between $22 and $40.

Airport Contacts San Luis Obispo County Regional Airport ✉ *903 Airport Dr., off Hwy. 227, San Luis Obispo* ☎ *805/781–5205* ⊕ *sloairport.com.* **Santa Barbara Airport** ✉ *500 Fowler Rd., off U.S. 101 Exit 104B, Santa Barbara* ☎ *805/683–4011* ⊕ *flysba.com.* **Santa Barbara Airbus** ☎ *805/964–7759, 800/423–1618* ⊕ *www.sbairbus.com.* **Santa Barbara Metropolitan Transit District** ☎ *805/963–3366* ⊕ *sbmtd.gov.*

BUS TRAVEL

Greyhound provides service from Los Angeles and San Francisco to San Luis Obispo, Ventura, and Santa Barbara. Local transit companies serve these three cities and several smaller towns. Buses can be useful for visiting some urban sights, particularly in Santa Barbara; they're less so for rural ones.

Bus Contacts Greyhound ☎ *800/231–2222* ⊕ *www.greyhound.com.*

CAR TRAVEL

Driving is the easiest way to experience the Central Coast. U.S. 101 and Highway 1, which run north–south, are the main routes to and through the Central Coast from Los Angeles and San Francisco. Highly scenic Highway 1 hugs the coast, and U.S. 101 runs inland. Between Ventura County and northern Santa Barbara County, the two highways are the same road. Highway 1 again separates from U.S. 101 north of Gaviota, then rejoins the highway at Pismo Beach. Along any stretch where these two highways are separate, U.S. 101 is the quicker route.

The most dramatic section of the Central Coast is the 70 miles between San Simeon and Big Sur. The road is narrow and twisting, with a single lane in each direction. In fog or rain the drive can be downright nerve-racking; in wet seasons mudslides can close portions of the road.

Other routes into the Central Coast include Highway 46 and Highway 33, which head, respectively, west and south from Interstate 5 near Bakersfield.

Road Conditions Caltrans ☎ *800/427–7623, 888/836–0866 Hwy. 1 visitor hotline (Cambria north to Carmel)* ⊕ *www.dot.ca.gov.*

TRAIN TRAVEL

The Amtrak *Coast Starlight,* which runs between Los Angeles and Seattle via Oakland, stops in Paso Robles, San Luis Obispo, Santa Barbara, and Oxnard. Amtrak runs several *Pacific Surfliner* trains and buses daily between San Luis Obispo, Santa Barbara, Los Angeles, and San Diego.

Metrolink Regional Rail Service trains connect Ventura and Oxnard with Los Angeles and points between.

Train Contacts Amtrak ☎ *800/872–7245* ⊕ *www.amtrak.com or www.amtrak california.com.* **Metrolink** ☎ *800/371–5465* ⊕ *metrolinktrains.com.*

RESTAURANTS

The cuisine in Ventura and Santa Barbara is every bit as eclectic as it is in California's bigger cities; fresh seafood is a standout. A foodie renaissance has overtaken the entire region from Ventura to Paso Robles, spawning dozens of restaurants touting locavore cuisine made with fresh organic produce and meats. Dining attire on the Central Coast is generally casual, though slightly dressy casual wear is the custom at pricier restaurants.

HOTELS

Expect to pay top dollar for rooms along the shore, especially in summer. Moderately priced hotels and motels do exist—most just a short drive inland from their higher-price counterparts. Make your reservations as early as possible, and take advantage of midweek specials to get the best rates. It's common for lodgings to require two-day minimum stays on holidays and some weekends, especially in summer, and to double rates during festivals and other events. *Hotel reviews have been shortened. For full information, visit Fodors.com.*

WHAT IT COSTS			
$	**$$**	**$$$**	**$$$$**
Restaurants	under $16	$16–$22	$23–$30	over $30
Hotels	under $120	$120–$175	$176–$250	over $250

Restaurant prices are the average cost of a main course at dinner or, if dinner is not served, at lunch, excluding sales tax of 8%–8.25% (depending on location). Hotel prices are the lowest cost of a standard double room in high season, excluding service charges and 9%–12% occupancy tax.

TOURS

Many tour companies will pick you up at your hotel or central locations; ask about this when booking.

Cloud Climbers Jeep and Wine Tours. This outfit conducts trips in open-air, six-passenger jeeps to the Santa Barbara/Santa Ynez mountains and Wine Country. Tour options include wine tasting, mountain, sunset, and a discovery adventure for families. The company also offers a four-hour All Around Ojai Tour and arranges horseback riding and trap-shooting tours. ☎ *805/646–3200* ⊕ *ccjeeps.com* ⌦ *From $89.*

Grapeline Wine Tours. Wine and vineyard picnic tours in Paso Robles and the Santa Ynez Valley are Grapeline's specialty. ☎ *888/894–6379* ⊕ *gogrape.com* ⌦ *From $109.*

Santa Barbara Wine Country Cycling Tours. The company leads half- and full-day tours of the Santa Ynez wine region, conducts hiking and cycling tours, and rents bicycles. ☎ *888/557–8687, 805/686–9490* ⊕ *winecountrycycling.com* ⌦ *From $80.*

Stagecoach Wine Tours. Locally owned and operated, Stagecoach runs daily wine-tasting excursions through the Santa Ynez Valley in vans, minicoaches, and SUVs. ⊠ *Solvang* ☏ *805/686–8347* ⊕ *winetours santaynez.com* ✉ *From $155.*

Sustainable Vine Wine Tours. This green-minded company specializes in eco-friendly Santa Ynez Valley wine tours in nine-passenger Mercedes Sprinter vans. Trips include tastings at limited-production wineries committed to sustainable practices. An organic picnic lunch is served. ☏ *805/698–3911* ⊕ *sustainablevine.com* ✉ *$150.*

VISITOR INFORMATION

Contacts **Central Coast Tourism Council** ⊕ *centralcoast-tourism.com.*

VENTURA COUNTY

Ventura County was first settled by the Chumash Indians. Spanish missionaries were the first Europeans to arrive, followed by Americans and other Europeans, who established towns, transportation networks, and highly productive farms. Since the 1920s, agriculture has been steadily replaced as the area's main industry—first by the oil business and more recently by tourism.

Accessible via boat or plane from Ventura and Santa Barbara, Channel Islands National Park is a series of five protected islands just 11 miles offshore where hiking, kayaking, and wildlife viewing abound.

VENTURA

60 miles north of Los Angeles.

Like Los Angeles, the city of Ventura enjoys gorgeous weather and sun-kissed beaches—but without the smog and congestion. The miles of beautiful beaches attract athletes—bodysurfers and boogie boarders, runners and bikers—and those who'd rather doze beneath an umbrella all day. Ventura Harbor is home to myriad fishing boats, restaurants, and water-activity centers where you can rent boats and take harbor cruises. Foodies can get their fix all over Ventura—dozens of upscale cafés and wine and tapas bars have opened in recent years. Arts and antiques buffs have long trekked downtown to browse the galleries and shops there.

GETTING HERE AND AROUND

Amtrak and Metrolink trains serve the area from Los Angeles. Greyhound buses stop in Ventura; Gold Coast Transit serves the city and the rest of Ventura County.

U.S. 101 is the north–south main route into town, but for a scenic drive, take Highway 1 north from Santa Monica. The highway merges with U.S. 101 just south of Ventura. ■ TIP➔ Traveling north to Ventura from Los Angeles on weekdays, it's best to depart before 6 am, between 10 and 2, or after 7, or you'll get caught in the extended rush-hour traffic. Coming south from Santa Barbara, depart before 1 or after 6. On weekends, traffic is generally fine except southbound on U.S. 101 between Santa Barbara and Ventura on Sunday late afternoon and early evening.

ESSENTIALS

Bus Contact Gold Coast Transit ☎ *805/643–3158* 🌐 *www.goldcoasttransit.org.*

Visitor Information Ventura Visitors and Convention Bureau ✉ *Downtown Visitor Center, 101 S. California St.* ☎ *805/648–2075, 800/483–6214* 🌐 *visit venturaca.com.*

EXPLORING

Mission San Buenaventura. The ninth of the 21 California missions, Mission San Buenaventura was established in 1782 but burned to the ground in the 1790s. It was rebuilt and rededicated in 1809. A self-guided tour takes you through a small museum, a quiet courtyard, and a chapel with 250-year-old paintings. ✉ *211 E. Main St., at Figueroa St.* ☎ *805/643–4318* 🌐 *www.sanbuenaventuramission.org* 🎟 *$4* 🕒 *Sun.–Fri. 10–5, Sat. 9–5.*

Museum of Ventura County. Exhibits in a contemporary complex of galleries and a sunny courtyard plaza tell the story of Ventura County from prehistoric times to the present. A highlight is the gallery that contains Ojai artist George Stuart's historical figures, dressed in exceptionally detailed, custom-made clothing reflecting their particular eras. In the courtyard, eight panels made with 45,000 pieces of cut glass form a history timeline. ✉ *100 E. Main St., at S. Ventura Ave.* ☎ *805/653–0323* 🌐 *venturamuseum.org* 🎟 *$5, free 1st Sun. of month* 🕒 *Tues.–Sun. 11–5.*

Fodor's Choice ★
Ventura Oceanfront. Four miles of gorgeous coastline stretch from the county fairgrounds at the northern border of the city of San Buenaventura, through San Buenaventura State Beach, down to Ventura Harbor in the south. The main attraction here is the San Buenaventura City Pier, a landmark built in 1872 and restored in 1993. Surfers rip the waves just north of the pier, and sunbathers relax on white-sand beaches on either side. The mile-long promenade and the Omer Rains Bike Trail north of the pier attract scores of joggers, surrey cyclers, and bikers throughout the year. ✉ *California St., at ocean's edge.*

WHERE TO EAT

$$ SEAFOOD
🍴 **Brophy Bros.** The Ventura outpost of the wildly popular Santa Barbara restaurant provides the same fresh seafood-oriented meals in a spacious second-story setting overlooking the harbor. Feast on everything from fish-and-chips and crab cakes to chowder and delectable fish—often straight from the boats moored below. [$] *Average main: $22* ✉ *1559 Spinnaker Dr., in Ventura Harbor Village* ☎ *805/639–0865* 🌐 *brophybros.com* ✍ *Reservations not accepted.*

$$$ AMERICAN Fodor's Choice ★
🍴 **Café Zack.** A local favorite for anniversary and other celebratory occasions, Zack's serves classic European dishes in an intimate, two-room 1930s cottage adorned with local art. One standout appetizer is the lobster and sweet corn in a curry cream sauce. Entrées of note include seafood curry and filet mignon, the latter typically crusted in peppercorns or topped with porcini mushrooms. The crowd-pleaser for dessert is Zack's pie, with chocolate ganache poured into a pecan-cinnamon crust and topped with whipped cream and caramel sauce. [$] *Average main: $25* ✉ *1095 E. Thompson Blvd., at S. Ann St.* ☎ *805/643–9445* 🌐 *cafezack.com* 🕒 *Closed Sun. No lunch Sat.*

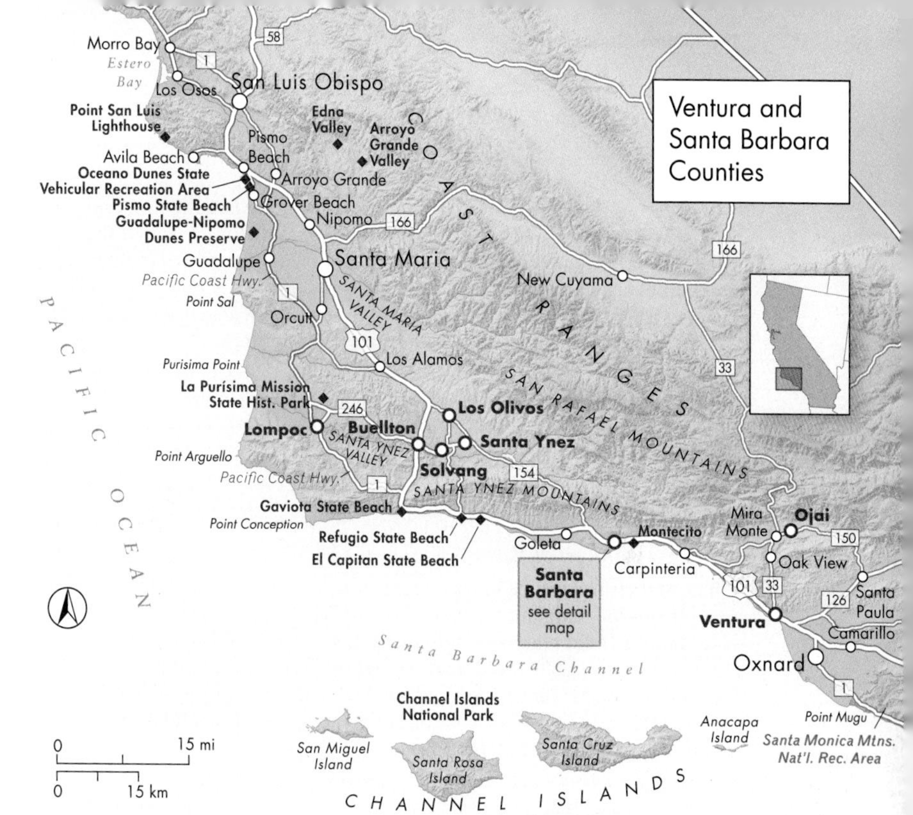
Ventura and
Santa Barbara
Counties
Morro Bay
Estero
Bay
Los Osos
San Luis Obispo
Point San Luis
Lighthouse
Edna
Valley
Arroyo
Grande
Valley
Pismo
Beach
Avila Beach
Oceano Dunes State
Vehicular Recreation Area
Pismo State Beach
Arroyo Grande
Grover Beach
Nipomo
Guadalupe-Nipomo
Dunes Preserve
Guadalupe
Santa Maria
Pacific Coast Hwy.
Point Sal
Orcutt
SANTA MARIA
VALLEY
COAST RANGES
New Cuyama
PACIFIC OCEAN
Purisima Point
Los Alamos
SAN RAFAEL MOUNTAINS
La Purísima Mission
State Hist. Park
Lompoc
Buellton
Los Olivos
Santa Ynez
SANTA YNEZ
VALLEY
Solvang
Point Arguello
Pacific Coast Hwy.
SANTA YNEZ MOUNTAINS
Gaviota State Beach
Point Conception
Refugio State Beach
El Capitan State Beach
Goleta
Montecito
Carpinteria
Mira
Monte
Ojai
Oak View
Santa
Barbara
see detail
map
Santa
Paula
Ventura
Camarillo
Oxnard
Santa Barbara Channel
Channel Islands
National Park
San Miguel
Island
Santa Rosa
Island
Santa Cruz
Island
Anacapa
Island
Point Mugu
Santa Monica Mtns.
Nat'l. Rec. Area
CHANNEL ISLANDS
0
15 mi
0
15 km
58
1
166
166
101
33
246
154
150
101
33
126
1

$$ 🍴 **Lure Fish House.** Fresh, sustainably caught seafood charbroiled over
SEAFOOD a mesquite grill, a well-stocked oyster bar, specialty cocktails, and a wine list heavy on local vintages lure diners into this slick, nautical-theme space downtown. The menu centers on the mostly local catch and organic vegetables, and includes tacos, sandwiches, and salads. Regulars rave about the shrimp-and-chips, cioppino, and citrus crab-cake salad. [$] *Average main: $19* ✉ *60 S. California St.* ☎ *805/567–4400* 🌐 *www.lurefishhouse.com.*

WHERE TO STAY

$$ 🏨 **Crowne Plaza Ventura Beach.** A 12-story hotel with an enviable loca-
HOTEL tion on the beach and next to a historic pier, the Crowne Plaza is within walking distance of downtown restaurants and nightlife. **Pros:** on the beach; near downtown; steps from waterfront. **Cons:** early-morning train noise; waterfront crowded in summer; most rooms on the small side. [$] *Rooms from: $169* ✉ *450 E. Harbor Blvd.* ☎ *800/842–0800, 805/648–2100* 🌐 *cpventura.com* 🛏 *254 rooms, 4 suites* 🍽 *No meals.*

$$ 🏨 **Four Points by Sheraton Ventura Harbor Resort.** An on-site restaurant,
RESORT spacious rooms, and a slew of amenities make this 17-acre property—which includes sister hotel Holiday Inn Express—a popular and practical choice for Channel Islands visitors. **Pros:** close to island transportation; mostly quiet; short drive to historic downtown. **Cons:** not in

the heart of downtown; noisy seagulls sometimes congregate nearby. $ *Rooms from: $160* ✉ *1050 Schooner Dr.* ☎ *805/658–1212, 800/368–7764* ⊕ *fourpoints.com/ventura* ⤴ *102 rooms, 4 suites* ⦶ *No meals.*

SPORTS AND THE OUTDOORS

The most popular outdoor activities in Ventura are beachgoing and whale-watching. California gray whales migrate offshore through the Santa Barbara Channel from late December through March; giant blue and humpback whales feed here from mid-June through September. The channel teems with marine life year-round, so tours, which depart from Ventura Harbor, include more than just whale sightings.

Island Packers Cruises. A cruise through the Santa Barbara Channel with Island Packers will give you the chance to spot dolphins, seals, and sometimes even whales. ✉ *Ventura Harbor, 1691 Spinnaker Dr.* ☎ *805/642–1393* ⊕ *islandpackers.com.*

CHANNEL ISLANDS NATIONAL PARK

11 miles southwest of Ventura Harbor via boat.

On crystal clear days the craggy peaks of the Channel Islands are easy to see from the mainland, jutting from the Pacific in such sharp detail it seems you could reach out and touch them. The islands really aren't that far away—a high-speed boat will whisk you to the closest ones in less than an hour—yet very few people ever visit them. Those adventurous types who do will experience one of the most splendid land-and-sea wilderness areas on the planet.

Channel Islands National Park includes five of the eight Channel Islands and the one nautical mile of ocean that surrounds them. Six nautical miles of surrounding channel waters are designated a National Marine Sanctuary, and are teeming with life, including giant kelp forests, 345 fish species, dolphins, whales, seals, sea lions, and seabirds. To maintain the integrity of their habitats, pets are not allowed in the park.

GETTING HERE AND AROUND

Most visitors access the Channel Islands via an Island Packers boat from Ventura Harbor. To reach the harbor by car, exit U.S. 101 in Ventura at Seaward Boulevard or Victoria Avenue and follow the signs to Ventura Harbor/Spinnaker Drive. An Island Packers boat heads to Anacapa Island from Oxnard's Channel Islands Harbor, which you can reach from Ventura Harbor by following Harbor Boulevard south about 6 miles and continuing south on Victoria Avenue. Private vehicles are not permitted on the islands.

BOAT TOURS

Island Packers. Sailing on high-speed catamarans from Ventura or a mono-hull vessel from Oxnard, Island Packers goes to Santa Cruz Island daily most of the year, weather permitting. The boats also go to Anacapa several days a week, and to the outer islands from April through November. They also cruise along Anacapa's north shore on three-hour wildlife tours (no disembarking) several times a week. ✉ *3550 Harbor Blvd., Oxnard* ☎ *805/642–1393* ⊕ *www.islandpackers.com* 🎫 *$36–$147.*

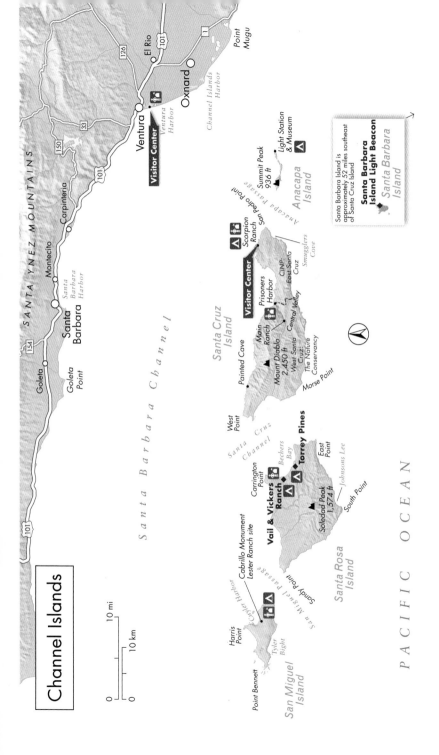

Channel Islands

Santa Barbara Island Light Beacon

Santa Barbara Island is approximately 52 miles southeast of Santa Cruz Island

Santa Barbara Island

Anacapa Island

Summit Peak 936 ft

Light Station & Museum

San Pedro Point

Anacapa Passage

Santa Cruz Island

Scorpion Ranch

CINP East Santa Cruz

Smugglers Cove

Prisoners Harbor

Central Valley

Visitor Center

Main Ranch

Mount Diablo 2,450 ft

West Santa Cruz: The Nature Conservancy

Painted Cave

Morse Point

West Point

Santa Cruz Channel

Santa Rosa Island

Bechers Bay

Torrey Pines

East Point

Johnsons Lee

Vail & Vickers Ranch

Carrington Point

Soledad Peak 1,574 ft

South Point

Cabrillo Monument
Lester Ranch site

San Miguel Passage

Sandy Point

San Miguel Island

Cuyler Harbor

Harris Point

Tyler Bight

Point Bennett

Mainland

Point Mugu

El Rio

Oxnard

Channel Islands Harbor

Ventura

Ventura Harbor

Visitor Center

Carpinteria

Montecito

Santa Barbara

Santa Barbara Harbor

Goleta

Goleta Point

SANTA YNEZ MOUNTAINS

Santa Barbara Channel

P A C I F I C   O C E A N

0   10 mi
0   10 km

EXPLORING

TOP ATTRACTIONS

Channel Islands National Park Visitor Center. The park's Robert J. Lagomarsino Visitor Center has a museum, a bookstore, and a three-story observation tower with telescopes. The museum's exhibits and a 24-minute film, *Treasure in the Sea,* provide an engaging overview of the islands. In the marine life exhibit, sea stars cling to rocks, anemones wave their colorful, spiny tentacles, and a brilliant orange Garibaldi darts around. Also on display are full-size reproductions of a male northern elephant seal and the pygmy mammoth skeleton unearthed on Santa Rosa Island in 1994.

On weekends and holidays at 11 and 3, rangers lead various free public programs describing park resources, and from Wednesday through Saturday in summer the center screens live ranger broadcasts of hikes (at 11) and dives (at 2) on Anacapa Island. Webcam images of bald eagles and other land and sea creatures are shown at the center and on the park's website. ⊠ *1901 Spinnaker Dr., Ventura* ☎ *805/658–5730* ⊕ *www.nps.gov/chis* ⊘ *Daily 8:30–5.*

Santa Cruz Island. Five miles west of Anacapa, 96-square-mile Santa Cruz Island is the largest of the Channel Islands. The National Park Service manages the easternmost 24% of the island; the rest is owned by the Nature Conservancy, which requires a permit to land. When your boat drops you off on a portion of the 70 miles of craggy coastline, you see two rugged mountain ranges with peaks soaring to 2,500 feet and deep canyons traversed by streams. This landscape is the habitat of a remarkable variety of flora and fauna—more than 600 types of plants, 140 kinds of land birds, 11 mammal species, five varieties of reptiles, and three amphibian species live here. Bird-watchers may want to look for the endemic island scrub jay, which is found nowhere else in the world.

One of the largest and deepest sea caves in the world, **Painted Cave,** lies along the northwest coast of Santa Cruz. Named for the colorful lichen and algae that cover its walls, Painted Cave is nearly ¼ mile long and 100 feet wide. In spring a waterfall cascades over the entrance. Kayakers may encounter seals or sea lions cruising alongside their boats inside the cave. The Channel Islands hold some of the richest archaeological resources in North America; all artifacts are protected within the park. Remnants of a dozen Chumash villages can be seen on the island. The largest of these villages, at the eastern end, occupied the area now called **Scorpion Ranch.** The Chumash mined extensive chert deposits on the island for tools to produce shell-bead money, which they traded with people on the mainland. You can learn about Chumash history and view artifacts, tools, and exhibits on native plant and wildlife at the interpretive visitor center near the landing dock. Visitors can also explore remnants of the early-1900s ranching era in the restored historic adobe and outbuildings. ⊠ *Channel Islands National Park.*

WORTH NOTING

Anacapa Island. Most people think of Anacapa as an island, but it's actually comprised of three narrow islets. The tips of these volcanic formations nearly touch, the islets are inaccessible from one another except by boat. All three have towering cliffs, isolated sea caves, and natural bridges; Arch Rock, on East Anacapa, is one of the best-known symbols of Channel Islands National Park.

Wildlife viewing is the main activity on East Anacapa, particularly in summer when seagull chicks are newly hatched and sea lions and seals lounge on the beaches. Exhibits at East Anacapa's compact **museum** include the original lead-crystal Fresnel lens from the 1932 lighthouse.

Over on West Anacapa, depending on the season and the number of desirable species lurking about there, boats travel to **Frenchy's Cove.** On a voyage here you might see anemones, limpets, barnacles, mussel beds, and colorful marine algae in the pristine tide pools. The rest of West Anacapa is closed to protect nesting brown pelicans. ⊠ *Channel Islands National Park.*

San Miguel Island. The westernmost of the Channel Islands, San Miguel Island is frequently battered by storms sweeping across the North Pacific. The 15-square-mile island's wild, windswept landscape is lush with vegetation. Point Bennett, at the western tip, offers one of the world's most spectacular wildlife displays when more than 100,000 pinnipeds hit its beach. Explorer Juan Rodríguez Cabrillo was the first European to visit this island; he claimed it for Spain in 1542. Legend holds that Cabrillo died on one of the Channel Islands—no one knows where he's buried, but there's a memorial to him on a bluff above Cuyler Harbor. ⊠ *Channel Islands National Park.*

Santa Barbara Island. At about 1 square mile, Santa Barbara Island is the smallest of the Channel Islands and nearly 35 miles south of the others. Triangular in shape, Santa Barbara's steep cliffs—which offer a perfect nesting spot for the Scripps's murrelet, a rare seabird—are topped by twin peaks. In spring you can enjoy a brilliant display of yellow coreopsis. Learn about the wildlife on and around the islands at the island's small museum. ⊠ *Channel Islands National Park.*

Santa Rosa Island. Between Santa Cruz and San Miguel, Santa Rosa is the second largest of the Channel Islands. The terrain along the coast varies from broad, sandy beaches to sheer cliffs—a central mountain range, rising to 1,589 feet, breaks the island's relatively low profile. Santa Rosa is home to about 500 species of plants, including the rare Torrey pine, and three unusual mammals, the island fox, the spotted skunk, and the deer mouse. They hardly compare, though, to their predecessors: a nearly complete skeleton of a 6-foot-tall pygmy mammoth was unearthed in 1994.

From 1901 to 1998, cattle were raised at the island's **Vail & Vickers Ranch.** The route from Santa Rosa's landing dock to the campground passes by the historic ranch buildings, barns, equipment, and the wooden pier where cattle were brought onto the island. ⊠ *Channel Islands National Park.*

SPORTS AND THE OUTDOORS

Channel Islands Outfitters *(⇨ see Santa Barbara Sports and the Outdoors)* arranges paddling, kayaking, and other Channel Islands excursions out of Ventura and Santa Barbara, and various concessionaires at

Ventura Harbor Village (☎ 805/477–0470 ⊕ *www.venturaharborvillage.com*) arrange diving, kayaking, and other rentals and tours. Island Packers conducts whale-watching cruises.

DIVING

Some of the best snorkeling and diving in the world can be found in the cool waters surrounding the Channel Islands. In the relatively warm water around Anacapa and eastern Santa Cruz, photographers can get great shots of rarely seen giant black bass swimming among the kelp forests. Here you also find a reef covered with red brittle starfish. If you're an experienced diver, you might swim among five species of seals and sea lions, or try your hand at spearing rockfish or halibut near San Miguel and Santa Rosa. The best time to scuba dive is in summer and fall, when the water is often clear up to a 100-foot depth.

KAYAKING

The most remote parts of the Channel Islands are accessible only by a sea kayak. Some of the best kayaking in the park can be found on Anacapa, Santa Barbara, and the eastern tip of Santa Cruz. It's too far to kayak from the mainland out to the islands, but outfitters have tours that take you to the islands. Tours are offered year-round, but high seas may cause trip cancellations between December and March. ⚠ **Channel waters can be unpredictable and challenging. Guided trips are highly recommended.**

WHALE-WATCHING

About a third of the world's cetacean species (27 to be exact) can be seen in the Santa Barbara Channel. In July and August, humpback and blue whales feed off the north shore of Santa Rosa. From late December through March, up to 10,000 gray whales pass through the Santa Barbara Channel on their way from Alaska to Mexico and back again, and on a whale-watching trip during this time frame you should see one or more of them. Other types of whales, but fewer in number, swim the channel from June through August.

OJAI

15 miles north of Ventura.

The Ojai Valley, which director Frank Capra used as a backdrop for his 1936 film *Lost Horizon*, sizzles in the summer when temperatures routinely reach 90°F. The acres of orange and avocado groves here evoke postcard images of long-ago agricultural Southern California. Many artists and celebrities have sought refuge from life in the fast lane in lush Ojai.

GETTING HERE AND AROUND

From northern Ventura, Highway 33 veers east from U.S. 101 and climbs inland to Ojai. From Santa Barbara, exit U.S. 101 at Highway 150 in Carpinteria, then travel east 20 miles on a twisting, two-lane road that is not recommended at night or during poor weather. You can also access Ojai by heading west from Interstate 5 on Highway 126. Exit at Santa Paula and follow Highway 150 north for 16 miles to Ojai. Gold Coast Transit provides service to Ojai from Ventura.

Ojai can be easily explored on foot; you can also hop on the Ojai Trolley ($1, or $2 day pass), which until about 5 pm follows two routes around Ojai and neighboring Miramonte on weekdays and one route on weekends. Tell the driver you're visiting and you'll get an informal guided tour.

ESSENTIALS

Bus Contacts Gold Coast Transit ☎ *805/643-3158* ⊕ *www.goldcoasttransit. org.* **Ojai Trolley** ☎ *805/646-5581* ⊕ *www.ojaitrolley.com.*

Visitor Information Ojai Visitors Bureau ✉ *206 N. Signal St., Ste. P, at E. Ojai Ave.* ☎ *888/652-4669* ⊕ *ojaivisitors.com* ⊙ *Weekdays 8-5.*

EXPLORING

Ojai Avenue. The work of local artists is displayed in the Spanish-style shopping arcade along the avenue downtown. On Sunday between 9 and 1, organic and specialty growers sell their produce at the outdoor market behind the arcade.

Ojai Valley Museum. The museum collects, preserves, and presents exhibits about the art, history, and culture of Ojai and Ojai Valley. Walking tours of Ojai depart from here. ✉ *130 W. Ojai Ave.* ☎ *805/640-1390* ⊕ *ojaivalleymuseum.org* 🖻 *Museum $5, walking tour $7 ($15 family)* ⊙ *Tues.-Sat. 10-4, Sun. noon-4; tours Oct.-July, Sat. 10:30.*

Ojai Valley Trail. The 18-mile trail is open to pedestrians, joggers, equestrians, bikers, and others on nonmotorized vehicles. You can access it anywhere along its route. ✉ *Parallel to Hwy. 33 from Soule Park in Ojai to ocean in Ventura* ☎ *888/652-4669* ⊕ *ojaivisitors.com.*

WHERE TO EAT

$$$
MEDITERRANEAN
✕ **Azu.** Slick furnishings, piped-in jazz, craft cocktails, and local beers and wines draw diners to this artsy Mediterranean bistro known for tapas made from organic ingredients. You can also order soups, salads, and bistro fare such as steak frites and paella. Save room for the homemade gelato. 🖻 *Average main: $25* ✉ *457 E. Ojai Ave.* ☎ *805/640-7987* ⊕ *azuojai.com.*

$
ITALIAN
✕ **Boccali's.** Edging a ranch, citrus groves, and a seasonal garden that provides produce for menu items, the modest but cheery Boccali's attracts many loyal fans. When it's warm, you can dine alfresco in the oak-shaded patio and lawn area and sometimes listen to live music. The family-run operation, best known for hand-rolled pizzas and home-style pastas (don't miss the eggplant lasagna), also serves a popular seasonal strawberry shortcake. 🖻 *Average main: $15* ✉ *3277 Ojai Ave., about 2 miles east of downtown* ☎ *805/646-6116* ⊕ *boccalis.com* 🖃 *No credit cards* ⊙ *No lunch Mon. and Tues.*

$$$
EUROPEAN
✕ **Suzanne's Cuisine.** Peppered filet mignon, linguine with steamed clams, and pan-roasted salmon with a roasted mango sauce are among the offerings at this European-style restaurant. Seafood, roasted meats and poultry, and vegetarian dishes dominate the dinner menu, and salads and soups star at lunchtime. All the desserts are made on the premises. 🖻 *Average main: $28* ✉ *502 W. Ojai Ave.* ☎ *805/640-1961* ⊕ *suzannescuisine.com* ⊙ *Closed Tues.*

WHERE TO STAY

$$ ▦ **The Blue Iguana Inn & Suites.** Artists run this Southwestern-style hotel,
B&B/INN and their works and those of other local artists decorate the rooms.
Pros: colorful art everywhere; secluded. **Cons:** 2 miles from downtown;
on a highway; small. Ⓢ *Rooms from: $129* ✉ *11794 N. Ventura Ave.*
☎ *805/646–5277* ⊕ *iguanainnsofojai.com* ⇥ *4 rooms, 8 suites, 8 cottages* ⼗〇⼁ *Breakfast.*

$$$ ▦ **Oaks at Ojai.** Rejuvenation is the name of the game at this destina-
RESORT tion spa where you can work out all day or just lounge by the pool.
Pros: great place to get fit; peaceful retreat; healthful meals. **Cons:** some
rooms are basic; on main road through town. Ⓢ *Rooms from: $250*
✉ *122 E. Ojai Ave.* ☎ *805/646–5573, 800/753–6257* ⊕ *oaksspa.com*
⇥ *44 rooms, 2 suites* ⼗〇⼁ *All meals* ⼕ *2-night minimum stay.*

$$$$ ▦ **Ojai Valley Inn & Spa.** This outdoorsy, golf-oriented resort and spa
RESORT is set on beautifully landscaped grounds, with hillside views in nearly
Fodor's Choice all directions. **Pros:** gorgeous grounds; exceptional outdoor activities;
★ romantic yet kid-friendly. **Cons:** expensive; areas near restaurants can
be noisy. Ⓢ *Rooms from: $400* ✉ *905 Country Club Rd.* ☎ *805/646–
1111, 855/697–8780* ⊕ *ojairesort.com* ⇥ *231 rooms, 77 suites* ⼗〇⼁ *No
meals.*

SANTA BARBARA

27 miles northwest of Ventura and 29 miles west of Ojai.

Santa Barbara has long been an oasis for Los Angelenos seeking respite
from big-city life. The attractions begin at the ocean and end in the foothills of the Santa Ynez Mountains. A few miles up the coast east and
west—but still very much a part of Santa Barbara—are the exclusive
residential districts of Montecito and Hope Ranch. Santa Barbara is on
a jog in the coastline, so the ocean is actually to the south, instead of
the west; for this reason, directions can be confusing. "Up" the coast
toward San Francisco is west, "down" toward Los Angeles is east, and
the mountains are north.

GETTING HERE AND AROUND

U.S. 101 is the main route into Santa Barbara. If you're staying in
town, a car is handy but not essential; the beaches and downtown are
easily explored by bicycle or on foot. Visit the Santa Barbara Car Free
website for bike-route and walking-tour maps, suggestions for car-free
vacations, and transportation discounts.

Santa Barbara Metropolitan Transit District's Line 22 bus serves major
tourist sights. Several bus lines connect with the very convenient electric shuttles that cruise the downtown and waterfront every 10 to 15
minutes (50¢ each way).

Santa Barbara Trolley Co. operates a motorized San Francisco–style
cable car that loops past major hotels, shopping areas, and attractions
from 10 to 4. Get off whenever you like, and pick up another trolley
(they come every hour) when you're ready to move on. The fare is $22
for the day.

TOURS

Land and Sea Tours. This outfit conducts 90-minute narrated tours in an amphibious 49-passenger vehicle nicknamed the Land Shark. The adventure begins with a drive through the city, followed by a plunge into the harbor for a cruise along the coast. ⊠ *10 E. Cabrillo Blvd., at Stearns Wharf* ☎ *805/683–7600* ⊕ *out2seesb.com* ⊠ *From $30* ⊗ *Tours May–Oct., daily noon, 2, and 4; Nov.–Apr., daily noon and 2.*

ESSENTIALS

Transportation Contacts Santa Barbara Car Free ☎ *805/696–1100* ⊕ *santabarbaracarfree.org.* **Santa Barbara Metropolitan Transit District** ☎ *805/963–3366* ⊕ *sbmtd.gov.* **Santa Barbara Trolley Co.** ☎ *805/965–0353* ⊕ *www.sbtrolley.com.*

Visitor Information Santa Barbara Visitor Center ⊠ *1 Garden St., at Cabrillo Blvd.* ☎ *805/965–3021, 805/568–1811* ⊕ *www.sbchamber.org* ⊗ *Feb.–Oct., Mon.–Sat. 9–5, Sun. 10–5; Nov.–Jan., Mon.–Sat. 9–4, Sun. 10–4.* **Visit Santa Barbara** ⊠ *500 E. Montecito St.* ☎ *805/966–9222* ⊕ *www.santabarbaraca.com.*

EXPLORING

Santa Barbara's waterfront is beautiful, with palm-studded promenades and plenty of sand. In the few miles between the beaches and the hills are downtown, Mission Santa Barbara, and the Santa Barbara Botanic Garden.

TOP ATTRACTIONS

El Presidio State Historic Park. Founded in 1782, El Presidio was one of four military strongholds established by the Spanish along the coast of California. The park encompasses much of the original site in the heart of downtown. El Cuartel, the adobe guardhouse, is the oldest building in Santa Barbara and the second oldest in California. ∎**TIP→ Admission is free for children 16 and under.** ⊠ *123 E. Canon Perdido St., at Anacapa St.* ☎ *805/965–0093* ⊕ *www.sbthp.org* ⊠ *$5* ⊗ *Daily 10:30–4:30.*

FAMILY
Fodor'sChoice
★
Lotusland. The 37-acre estate called Lotusland once belonged to the Polish opera singer Ganna Walska, who purchased it in the late 1940s and lived here until her death in 1984. Many of the exotic trees and other subtropical flora were planted in 1882 by horticulturist R. Kinton Stevens. On the two-hour guided tour—the only option for visiting unless you're a member (reserve well ahead in summer)—you'll see an outdoor theater, a topiary garden, a lotus pond, and a huge collection of rare cycads, an unusual plant genus that has been around since the time of the dinosaurs. ∎**TIP→ Child-friendly family tours are available for groups with children under the age of 10; contact Lotusland for scheduling.** ⊠ *695 Ashley Rd., off Sycamore Canyon Rd. (Hwy. 192), Montecito* ☎ *805/969–9990* ⊕ *lotusland.org* ⊠ *$45* ⊗ *Mid-Feb.–mid-Nov., Wed.–Sat. at 10 and 1:30 by appointment only.*

Fodor'sChoice
★
Mission Santa Barbara. Widely referred to as the "Queen of Missions," this is one of the most beautiful and frequently photographed buildings in coastal California. Dating to 1786, the architecture evolved from adobe-brick buildings with thatch roofs to more permanent edifices as the mission's population burgeoned. An earthquake in 1812

Continued on page 64

CALIFORNIA'S MISSIONS

Their soul may belong to Spain, their heart to the New World, but the historic missions of California, with their lovely churches, beckon the traveler on a soulful journey back to the very founding of the American West.

by Cheryl Crabtree and Robert I.C. Fisher

California history changed forever in the 18th century when Spanish explorers founded a series of missions along the Pacific coast. Believing they were following God's will, they wanted to spread the gospel and convert as many natives as possible. The process produced a collision between the Hispanic and California Indian cultures, resulting in one of the most striking legacies of Old California: the Spanish mission churches. Rising like mirages in the middle of desert plains and rolling hills, these historic sites transport you back to the days of the Spanish colonial period.

GOD AND MAN IN CALIFORNIA

The Alta California territory came under pressure in the 1760s when Spain feared foreign advances into the territory explorer Juan Rodríguez Cabrillo had claimed for the Spanish crown back in 1542. But how could Spain create a visible and viable presence halfway around the world? They decided to build on the model that had already worked well in Spain's Mexico colony. The plan involved establishing a series of missions, to be operated by the Catholic Church and protected by four of Spain's *presidios* (military outposts). The native Indians— after quick conversion to Christianity—would provide the labor force necessary to build mission towns.

FATHER OF THE MISSIONS

Father Junípero Serra is an icon of the Spanish colonial period. At the behest of the Spanish government, the diminutive padre—then well into his fifties, and despite a chronic leg infection— started out on foot from Baja California to search for suitable mission sites, with a goal of reaching Monterey. In 1769 he helped establish Alta California's first mission in San Diego and continued his travels until his death, in 1784, by which time he had founded eight more missions.

The system ended about a decade after the Mexican government took control of Alta California in the early 1820s and began to secularize the missions. The church lost horses and cattle, as well as vast tracts of land, which the Mexican government in turn granted to private individuals. They also lost laborers, as the Indians were for the most part free to find work and a life beyond the missions. In 1848, the Americans assumed control of the territory, and California became part of the United States. Today, these missions stand as extraordinary monuments to their colorful past.

Mission Santa Barbara Museum

MISSION ACCOMPLISHED

California's Mission Trail is the best way to follow in the fathers' footsteps. Here, below, are its 21 settlements, north to south.

Amazingly, all 21 Spanish missions in California are still visible—some in their pristine historic state, others with modifications made over the centuries. Many are found on or near the "King's Road"—El Camino Real—which linked these mission outposts. At the height of the mission system the trail was approximately 600 miles long, eventually extending from San Diego to Sonoma. Today the road is commemorated on portions of routes 101 and 82 in the form of roadside bell markers erected by CalTrans every one to two miles between San Diego and San Francisco.

San Francisco Solano, Sonoma (1823; this was the final California mission constructed.)

San Rafael, San Rafael (1817)

San Francisco de Asís (aka Mission Dolores), San Francisco (1776). Situated in the heart of San Francisco,

Mission Santa Clara de Asís

these mission grounds and nearby Arroyo de los Dolores (Creek of Sorrows) are home to the oldest intact building in the city.

Santa Clara de Asís, Santa Clara (1777). On the campus of Santa Clara University, this beautifully restored mission contains original paintings, statues, a bell, and hundreds of artifacts, as well as a spectacular rose garden.

San José, Fremont (1797)

Santa Cruz, Santa Cruz (1791)

San Juan Bautista, San Juan Bautista (1797). Immortalized in Hitchcock's *Vertigo,* this remarkably preserved pueblo contains the largest church of all the California missions, as well as 18th- and 19th-century buildings and a sprawling plaza.

San Carlos Borromeo del Río Carmelo, Carmel (1770). Carmel Mission was head-

quarters for the California mission system under Father Serra and the Father Presidents who succeeded him; the on-site museum includes Serra's tiny sleeping quarters (where he died in 1784).

Nuestra Señora de la Soledad, Soledad (1791)

San Antonio de Padua, Jolon (1771)

San Miguel Arcángel, San Miguel (1797). San Miguel boasts the only intact original interior wall painting in any of the missions, painted in 1821 by Native American converts under the direction of Spanish artist Esteban Muras.

Painting from 1818, San Juan Bautista.

Mission Santa Inés

San Luis Obispo de Tolosa, San Luis Obispo (1772). Bear meat from grizzlies captured here saved the Spaniards from starving, which helped convince Father Serra to establish a mission.

La Purísima Concepción, Lompoc (1787). La Purísima is the nation's most completely restored mission complex. It is now a living-history museum with a church and nearly forty craft and residence rooms.

Santa Inés, Solvang (1804). Home to one of the most significant pieces of religious art created by a California mission Indian.

Santa Bárbara, Santa Barbara (1786). The "Queen of the Missions" has twin bell towers, gorgeous gardens with heirloom plant varietals, a massive collection of rare artworks and artifacts, and lovely stonework.

San Buenaventura, Ventura (1782). This was the last mission founded by Father Serra; it is still an active parish in the Archdiocese of Los Angeles.

Mission San Fernando Rey de España

San Fernando Rey de España, Mission Hills (1797)

San Gabriel Arcángel, San Gabriel (1771)

San Luis Rey de Francia, Oceanside (1798)

San Juan Capistrano, San Juan Capistrano (1776). This mission is famed for its Saint Joseph's Day (March 19) celebration of the return of swallows in the springtime. The mission's adobe walls enclose acres of lush gardens and historic buildings.

San Diego de Alcalá, San Diego (1769). This was the first California missions constructed, although the original was destroyed in 1775 and rebuilt over a number of years.

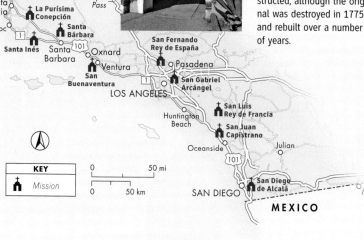

Coalinga

Paso Robles

† San Miguel Arcángel

McKittrick

San Luis Obispo
San Luis Obispo de Tolosa

Tejon Pass

Santa Maria   † La Purísima Conepción

Lompoc

† Santa Bárbara

Santa Inés   Santa Barbara

Oxnard

Ventura

San Buenaventura

San Fernando Rey de España

Pasadena

LOS ANGELES

San Gabriel Arcángel

Huntington Beach

San Luis Rey de Francia

San Juan Capistrano

Oceanside

Julian

San Diego de Alcalá

SAN DIEGO

MEXICO

KEY

† ⚑ Mission

0   50 mi

0   50 km

SPANISH MISSION STYLE

(left) Mission San Luis Rey de Francia; (right) Mission San Antonio de Padua

The Spanish mission churches derive much of their strength and enduring power from their extraordinary admixture of styles. They are spectacular examples of the combination of races and cultures that bloomed along Father Serra's road through Alta California.

SPIRIT OF THE PLACE

In building the missions, the Franciscan padres had to rely on available resources. Spanish churches back in Europe boasted marble floors and gilded statues. But here, whitewashed adobe walls gleamed in the sun and floors were often merely packed earth.

However simple the structures, the art within the mission confines continued to glorify the Church. The padres imported much finery to decorate the churches and perform the mass—silver, silk and lovely paintings to teach the life of Christ to the Indians and soldiers and settlers. Serra himself commissioned

fine artists in Mexico to produce custom works using the best materials and according to exact specifications. Sculptures of angels, Mary, Joseph, Jesus and the Franciscan heroes and saints—and of course the Stations of the Cross—adorned all the missions.

AN ENDURING LEGACY

Mission architecture reflects a gorgeous blend of European and New World influences. While naves followed the simple forms of Franciscan Gothic, cloisters (with beautiful arcades) adopted aspects of the Romanesque style, and ornamental touches of the Spanish Renaissance—including red-tiled roofs and wrought-iron grilles—added even more elegance. In the 20th century, the Mission Revival Style had a huge impact on architecture and design in California, as seen in examples ranging from San Diego's Union Station to Stanford University's main quadrangle.

Father Junípero Serra statue at Mission San Gabriel

FOR WHOM THE BELLS TOLLED

Perhaps the most famous architectural motif of the Spanish Mission churches was the belltower. These took the form of either a campanile—a single tower called a campanario—or, more spectacularly, of an open-work espedaña, a perforated adobe wall housing a series of bells (notable examples of this form are at San Juan Capistrano and San Diego de Alcalá). Bells were essential to maintaining the routines of daily life at the missions.

MISSION LIFE
Morning bells summoned residents to chapel for services; noontime bells introduced the main meal, while the evening bells sounded the alert to gather around 5 pm for mass and dinner. Many of the natives were happy with their new faith, and even enjoyed putting in numerous hours a week working as farmers, soapmakers, weavers, and masons.

Others were less willing to abandon their traditional culture, but were coerced to abide by the new Spanish laws and mission rules. Natives were sometimes mistreated by the friars, who used a system of punishments typical of the times to enforce submission to the new culture.

NATIVE TRAGEDY
In the end, mission life proved extremely destructive to the Native Californian population. European diseases and contaminated water caused the death of nearly a third, with some tribes—notably the Chumash—suffering disproportionately.

Despite these losses, small numbers did survive. After the Mexican government secularized the missions in 1833, a majority of the native population was reduced to poverty. Some stayed at the missions, while others went to live in the pueblos, ranchos, and countryside.

Many Native Californian people today still work and live near the missions that are monuments to their artistry skills.

FOR MORE INFORMATION

California Missions Foundation
☎ 805/963-1633
🌐 www.california missionsfoundation.org

Top, Mission San Gabriel Arcángel
Bottom, Mission San Miguel Arcángel

3

IN FOCUS CALIFORNIA'S MISSIONS

destroyed the third church built on the site. Its replacement, the present structure, is still a functioning Catholic church. Mission Santa Barbara has a splendid Spanish/Mexican colonial art collection, as well as Chumash sculptures and the only Native American–made altar and tabernacle left in the California missions. Docents lead 60-minute tours ($9 adult) Thursday and Friday at 11 and Saturday at 10:30. ✉ *2201 Laguna St., at E. Los Olivos St.* ☎ *805/682–4149 gift shop, 805/682–4713* ⊕ *www.santabarbaramission.org* 🎫 *$7* ⊙ *Daily 9–4:15 (4:30 in summer).*

> **BEST VIEWS**
>
> Drive along Alameda Padre Serra, a hillside road that begins near the mission and continues to Montecito, to feast your eyes on spectacular views of the city and the Santa Barbara Channel.

Santa Barbara Botanic Garden. Five miles of scenic trails meander through the garden's 78 acres of native plants. The Mission Dam, built in 1806, stands just beyond the redwood grove and above the restored aqueduct that once carried water to Mission Santa Barbara. More than a thousand plant species thrive in various themed sections, including mountains, deserts, meadows, redwoods, and Channel Islands. ■TIP➔ **A conservation center dedicated to rare and endangered plant species opens in 2016.** ✉ *1212 Mission Canyon Rd., north of Foothill Rd. (Hwy. 192)* ☎ *805/682–4726* ⊕ *www.sbbg.org* 🎫 *$10* ⊙ *Mar.–Oct., daily 9–6; Nov.–Feb., daily 9–5. Guided tours weekends at 11 and 2, Mon. at 2.*

Fodor's Choice ★   **Santa Barbara County Courthouse.** Hand-painted tiles and a spiral staircase infuse the courthouse, a national historic landmark, with the grandeur of a Moorish palace. This magnificent building was completed in 1929. An elevator rises to an arched observation area in the tower that provides a panoramic view of the city. Before or after you take in the view, you can (if it's open) visit an engaging gallery devoted to the workings of the tower's original, still operational Seth Thomas clock. The murals in the ceremonial chambers on the courthouse's second floor were painted by an artist who did backdrops for some of Cecil B. DeMille's films. ✉ *1100 Anacapa St., at E. Anapamu St.* ☎ *805/962–6464* ⊕ *www.santabarbaracourthouse.org* ⊙ *Weekdays 8–4:45, weekends 10–4:45. Free guided tours weekdays at 10:30, daily at 2.*

QUICK BITES

Jeannine's. Take a break from State Street shopping at Jeannine's, revered locally for its wholesome sandwiches, salads, and baked goods, made from scratch with organic and natural ingredients. Pick up a turkey cranberry or chicken pesto sandwich to go, and picnic in the courthouse gardens a block away. ✉ *La Arcada, 15 E. Figueroa St., at State St.* ☎ *805/966–1717* ⊕ *jeannines.com/restaurants* ⊙ *Daily 6:30–3.*

Santa Barbara Museum of Art. The highlights of this museum's permanent collection include ancient sculpture, Asian art, impressionist paintings, contemporary art, photography, and American works in several mediums. ✉ *1130 State St., at E. Anapamu St.* ☎ *805/963–4364* ⊕ *sbma.*

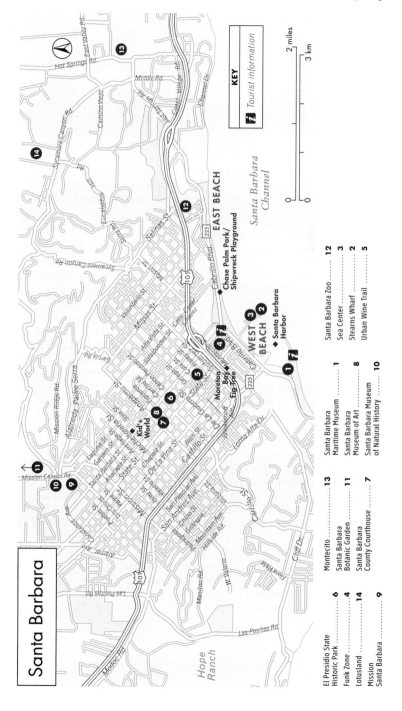

Santa Barbara

KEY

Tourist information

2 miles

3 km

*Santa Barbara
Channel*

EAST BEACH

Chase Palm Park/
Shipwreck Playground

WEST BEACH

Santa Barbara
Harbor

3

net ✉ *$10, free Thurs. 5–8* ☉ *Tues., Wed., Fri., and weekends 11–5, Thurs. 11–8.*

FAMILY   **Santa Barbara Museum of Natural History.** The gigantic blue whale skeleton greets you at the entrance to this complex whose major draws include its planetarium, space lab, and gem and mineral display. Startlingly alive-looking stuffed specimens, complete with nests and eggs, roost in the bird hall, and a room of dioramas illustrates Chumash Indian history and culture. Outdoors, nature trails wind through the serene oak-studded grounds. ■TIP➜ A Nature Pass, available at the museum and the associated Sea Center, is good for discounted admission to both facilities. ✉ *2559 Puesta del Sol Rd., off Mission Canyon Rd.* ☎ *805/682–4711* ⊕ *sbnature.org* ✉ *$12; free 3rd Sun. of month Sept.–Apr.* ☉ *Daily 10–5.*

FAMILY   **Santa Barbara Zoo.** This compact zoo's gorgeous grounds shelter elephants, gorillas, exotic birds, and big cats. For small children, there's a scenic railroad and barnyard petting zoo. Three high-tech dinosaurs perform in live stage shows (free with admission), daily in summer and on weekends the rest of the year. ■TIP➜ The palm-studded lawns on a hilltop overlooking the beach are perfect spots for family picnics. ✉ *500 Niños Dr., off El Cabrillo Blvd.* ☎ *805/962–5339 main line, 805/962–6310 information* ⊕ *santabarbarazoo.org* ✉ *Zoo $15, parking $6* ☉ *Daily 10–5.*

FAMILY   **Sea Center.** A branch of the Santa Barbara Museum of Natural History, the center specializes in Santa Barbara Channel marine life and conservation. Though small compared to aquariums in Monterey and Long Beach, this is a fascinating, hands-on marine science laboratory that lets you participate in experiments, projects, and exhibits, including touch pools. The two-story glass walls here open to stunning ocean, mountain, and city views. ■TIP➜ Purchase a Nature Pass, available here, for discounted admission to the center and the natural history museum. ✉ *211 Stearns Wharf* ☎ *805/962–2526* ⊕ *sbnature.org* ✉ *$8* ☉ *Daily 10–5.*

Stearns Wharf. Built in 1872, Stearns Wharf is Santa Barbara's most visited landmark. Expansive views of the mountains, cityscape, and harbor unfold from every vantage point on the three-block-long pier. Although it's a nice walk from the Cabrillo Boulevard parking areas, you can also park on the pier and then wander through the shops or stop for a meal at one of the wharf's restaurants. ✉ *Cabrillo Blvd. and State St.* ⊕ *stearnswharf.org.*

WORTH NOTING

Funk Zone. A formerly run-down industrial neighborhood near the waterfront and train station, the Funk Zone has evolved into a hip hangout filled with wine-tasting rooms, arts-and-crafts studios, murals, breweries, restaurants, and small shops. It's fun to poke around the three-square-block district. ■TIP➔ **Street parking is limited, so leave your car in a nearby city lot and cruise up and down the alleys on foot.** ⊠ *Between State and Garden Sts. and Cabrillo Blvd. and U.S. 101* ⊕ *funkzone.net.*

Montecito. Since the late 1800s the tree-studded hills and valleys of this town have attracted the rich and famous: Hollywood icons, business tycoons, tech moguls, and old-money families who installed themselves years ago. Shady roads wind through the community, which consists mostly of gated estates. Swank boutiques line **Coast Village Road,** where well-heeled residents such as Oprah Winfrey sometimes browse for truffle oil, picture frames, and designer jeans. Residents also hang out in the Upper Village, a chic shopping area with restaurants and cafés at the intersection of San Ysidro and East Valley roads.

FAMILY **Santa Barbara Maritime Museum.** California's seafaring history is the focus here. High-tech, hands-on exhibits, such as a sportfishing activity that lets participants haul in a "big one" and a local surfing history retrospective, make this a fun stop for families. The museum's shining star is a rare, 17-foot-tall Fresnel lens from the historic Point Conception Lighthouse. ■TIP➔ **Ride the elevator to the fourth-floor observation area for great harbor views.** ⊠ *113 Harbor Way, off Shoreline Dr.* ☎ *805/962–8404* ⊕ *www.sbmm.org* ⊠ *$7* ⊙ *June–Aug., Thurs.–Tues. 10–6; Sept.–May, Thurs.–Tues. 10–5.*

Urban Wine Trail. Nearly two-dozen winery tasting rooms form the Urban Wine Trail; most are within walking distance of the waterfront and the lower State Street shopping and restaurant district. **Santa Barbara Winery,** at 202 Anacapa Street, and **Au Bon Climat,** at 813 Anacapa Street, are good places to start your oenological trek. ⊕ *urbanwinetrailsb.com.*

BEACHES

FAMILY
Fodor's Choice
★
East Beach. The wide swath of sand at the east end of Cabrillo Boulevard is a great spot for people-watching. East Beach has sand volleyball courts, summertime lifeguard and sports competitions, and arts-and-crafts shows on Sunday and holidays. You can use showers, a weight room, and lockers (bring your own towel) and rent umbrellas and boogie boards at the Cabrillo Bathhouse. Next door, there's an elaborate jungle-gym play area for kids. Hotels line the boulevard across from the beach. **Amenities:** food and drink; lifeguards in summer; parking (fee); showers; toilets; water sports. **Best for:** walking; swimming; surfing. ⊠ *1118 Cabrillo Blvd., at Ninos Dr.* ☎ *805/897–2680.*

Santa Barbara's downtown is attractive, but be sure to also visit its beautiful—and usually uncrowded—beaches.

WHERE TO EAT

$$$ JAPANESE 🍴 **Arigato Sushi.** You might have to wait for a table at this two-story restaurant and sushi bar—locals line up early for the wildly creative combination rolls and other delectables. Fans of authentic Japanese food sometimes disagree about the quality of the seafood, but all dishes are fresh and artfully presented. The menu includes traditional dishes as well as innovative creations such as jalapeño yellowtail sashimi and ahi carpaccio. [$] *Average main: $30* ✉ *1225 State St., near W. Victoria St.* ☎ *805/965–6074* 🌐 *www.arigatosb.com* ✍ *Reservations not accepted* ⌚ *No lunch.*

$$ SEAFOOD 🍴 **Brophy Bros.** The outdoor tables at this casual harborside restaurant have perfect views of the marina and mountains. Staffers serve enormous, exceptionally fresh fish dishes—don't miss the seafood salad and chowder—and provide guests with a pager if there's a long wait for a table. Stroll along the waterfront until the beep lets you know your table's ready. Hugely popular, Brophy Bros. can be crowded and loud, especially on weekend evenings. [$] *Average main: $22* ✉ *119 Harbor Way, off Shoreline Dr.* ☎ *805/966–4418* 🌐 *brophybros.com.*

$$$ MODERN AMERICAN Fodor's Choice ★ 🍴 **The Lark.** Shared dining—small plates and larger—and a seasonal menu showcasing local ingredients are the focus at this urban-chic restaurant named for an overnight all-Pullman train that chugged into the nearby railroad station for six decades. Sit at the 24-seat communal table set atop vintage radiators, or at tables and booths crafted from antique Spanish church pews and other repurposed or recycled materials. Drink options range from classic and handcrafted locavore cocktails to wines curated by the master sommelier at the adjacent Les Marchands wine bar. [$] *Average main: $23* ✉ *131 Anacapa St., at E. Yanonali St.* ☎ *805/284–0370* 🌐 *www.thelarksb.com* ⏲ *Closed Mon. No lunch.*

$$$$ ITALIAN 🍴 **Olio e Limone.** Sophisticated Italian cuisine (with an emphasis on Sicily) is served at this restaurant near the Arlington Center. The juicy veal chop is popular, but surprises abound here; be sure to try unusual dishes such as ribbon pasta with quail and sausage in a mushroom ragout, or the duck ravioli. Tables are placed close together, so this may not be the best spot for intimate conversations. Next door are the more casual Olio Pizzeria, a combination pizzeria and wine bar, and Olio Crudo, a raw bar. [$] *Average main: $31* ✉ *17 W. Victoria St., at State St.* ☎ *805/899–2699* 🌐 *www.olioelimone.com* ⏲ *No lunch Sun.*

TAKE THE KIDS

Two playful playgrounds provide welcome interludes for the young set. Children love tooling around **Kids' World** (✉ *Garden and Micheltorena Sts.*), a public playground with a castle-shape maze of climbing structures, slides, and tunnels. At **Shipwreck Playground** (✉ *Chase Palm Park, E. Cabrillo Blvd., east of Garden St.*), parents take as much pleasure in the waterfront views as the kids do in the nautical-theme diversions and the antique carousel.

$$$ SOUTHERN 🍴 **Palace Grill.** Mardi Gras energy, team-style service, lively music, and great food have made the Palace a Santa Barbara icon. Acclaimed for its Cajun and creole dishes such as blackened redfish and jambalaya with dirty rice, the Palace also serves Caribbean fare, including a delicious coconut-shrimp dish. Be prepared to wait for a table on Friday and Saturday nights (when reservations are taken for a 5:30 seating only), though the live entertainment and free appetizers, sent out front when the line is long, will whet your appetite for the feast to come. [$] *Average main: $29* ✉ *8 E. Cota St., at State St.* ☎ *805/963–5000* 🌐 *palacegrill.com.*

$$$$ AMERICAN Fodor's Choice ★ 🍴 **The Stonehouse.** The elegant Stonehouse is inside a century-old granite former farmhouse at the San Ysidro Ranch resort. Executive chef Matt Johnson creates outstanding regional cuisine centered on top-quality local ingredients complemented by herbs and vegetables from the on-site garden. The menu changes constantly, but might include pan-seared abalone or classic steak Diane flambéed tableside. Dine on the radiant-heated oceanview deck, next to a fountain under a canopy of loquat trees, or in the romantic, candlelit dining room overlooking a creek. ■ **TIP→ The Plow & Angel pub, downstairs, serves casual bistro fare.** [$] *Average main: $49* ✉ *900 San Ysidro La., off San Ysidro Rd., Montecito* ☎ *805/565–1700* 🌐 *www.sanysidroranch.com* ✍ *Reservations essential* ⏲ *No lunch Mon. and Tues.*

$$$ ITALIAN Fodor's Choice ★ 🍴 **Toma.** Seasonal, locally sourced ingredients and softly lit muted-yellow walls evoke the flavors and charms of Tuscany and the Mediterranean at this rustic-romantic restaurant across from the harbor and West Beach. Ahi sashimi tucked in a crisp sesame cone is a popular appetizer, after which you can proceed to a house-made pasta dish or rock shrimp gnocchi. Mains of note include the tender braised beef

short ribs and savory cioppino. Central Coast and Italian wines figure prominently on the carefully selected wine list. $ *Average main: $26* ⊠ *324 W. Cabrillo Blvd., near Castillo St.* ☎ *805/962–0777* ⊕ *www. tomarestaurant.com* ☯ *No lunch.*

$$$
AMERICAN

✕ **Wine Cask.** A reinvention of a same-named local favorite that closed a few years back, the Wine Cask serves bistro-style meals in a comfortable and classy dining room. The dishes are paired with wines from Santa Barbara's most extensive wine list. The more casual bar-café, Intermezzo, across the courtyard, serves pizzas, salads, small plates, wines, and cocktails and is open late. $ *Average main: $29* ⊠ *El Paseo, 813 Anacapa St., at E. De La Guerra St.* ☎ *805/966–9463* ⊕ *winecask. com* ⌂ *Reservations essential.*

WHERE TO STAY

$$$$
RESORT
Fodor'sChoice
★

▦ **Bacara Resort & Spa.** A luxury resort with four restaurants and a 42,000-square-foot spa and fitness center with 36 treatment rooms, the Bacara provides a gorgeous setting for relaxing retreats. **Pros:** serene natural setting; nature trails; first-rate spa; three zero-edge pools; in-room iPads for quick service orders and lighting and climate control. **Cons:** pricey; not close to downtown; sand on beach not pristine enough for some. $ *Rooms from: $450* ⊠ *8301 Hollister Ave., Goleta* ☎ *805/968–0100, 855/817–9782* ⊕ *www.bacararesort.com* ⇆ *313 rooms, 45 suites* ⑩ *No meals.*

$$$$
HOTEL
Fodor'sChoice
★

▦ **Belmond El Encanto.** Following years of extensive renovations by Orient-Express, this Santa Barbara icon lives on to thrill a new generation of guests with its relaxed-luxe bungalow rooms, lush gardens, and personalized service. **Pros:** revitalized historic landmark; stellar spa facility; drinks and dining with stunning views; friendly and personal service; free use of electric bikes. **Cons:** long walk to downtown; pricey; guests staying for more than a few days may find the restaurant menus limited. $ *Rooms from: $650* ⊠ *800 Alvarado Pl.* ☎ *805/845–5800, 800/393–5315* ⊕ *belmond.com/elencanto* ⇆ *70 rooms, 22 suites* ⑩ *No meals.*

$$$$
HOTEL

▦ **Canary Hotel.** The only full-service hotel in the heart of downtown, this Kimpton property blends a casual, beach-getaway feel with urban sophistication. **Pros:** easy stroll to museums, shopping, dining; friendly, attentive service; adjacent fitness center. **Cons:** across from transit center; a mile from the beach. $ *Rooms from: $400* ⊠ *31 W. Carrillo St.* ☎ *805/884–0300, 877/468–3515* ⊕ *www.canarysantabarbara.com* ⇆ *77 rooms, 20 suites* ⑩ *No meals.*

$$$$
RESORT
Fodor'sChoice
★

▦ **Four Seasons Resort The Biltmore Santa Barbara.** Surrounded by lush, perfectly manicured gardens and across from the beach, Santa Barbara's grande dame has long been a favorite for quiet, California-style luxury. **Pros:** first-class resort; historic Santa Barbara character; personal service; steps from the beach. **Cons:** back rooms are close to train tracks; expensive. $ *Rooms from: $545* ⊠ *1260 Channel Dr.* ☎ *805/969–2261, 805/332–3442 reservations* ⊕ *www.fourseasons.com/santabarbara* ⇆ *181 rooms, 26 suites* ⑩ *No meals.*

$$
HOTEL

▦ **Franciscan Inn.** A block from the harbor and West Beach, the family-owned Franciscan has spacious, beach-theme rooms. **Pros:** near waterfront and harbor; friendly staff; good value; family-friendly. **Cons:** busy lobby; pool can be crowded. [$] *Rooms from: $175* ✉ *109 Bath St.* ☎ *805/963–8845* 🌐 *www.franciscaninn.com* 🛏 *33 rooms, 20 suites* 🍴 *Breakfast.*

$$$ HOTEL 🏨 **Hotel Indigo.** The closest hotel to the train station, artsy Hotel Indigo is a fine choice for travelers who appreciate contemporary art and want easy access to dining, nightlife, and the beach. **Pros:** multilingual staff; a block from Stearns Wharf; great value for location. **Cons:** showers only (no bathtubs); train whistles early morning; rooms on small side. [$] *Rooms from: $189* ✉ *121 State St.* ☎ *805/966–6586, 877/270–1392 toll-free* 🌐 *www.indigosantabarbara.com* 🛏 *41 rooms* 🍴 *No meals.*

$ HOTEL 🏨 **Motel 6 Santa Barbara Beach.** A half block from East Beach amid fancier hotels sits this basic but comfortable motel—the first Motel 6 in existence, and the first in the chain to transform into a contemporary Euro-style abode. **Pros:** very close to zoo and beach; friendly staff; clean. **Cons:** no frills; motel-style rooms; no breakfast. [$] *Rooms from: $119* ✉ *443 Corona Del Mar Dr.* ☎ *805/564–1392, 800/466–8356* 🌐 *motel6.com* 🛏 *51 rooms* 🍴 *No meals.*

$$$$ RESORT Fodor'sChoice ★ 🏨 **San Ysidro Ranch.** At this romantic hideaway on a historic property in the Montecito foothills—where John and Jackie Kennedy spent their honeymoon and Oprah sends her out-of-town visitors—guest cottages are scattered among groves of orange trees and flower beds. **Pros:** ultimate privacy; surrounded by nature; celebrity hangout; pet-friendly. **Cons:** very expensive; too remote for some. [$] *Rooms from: $695* ✉ *900 San Ysidro La., Montecito* ☎ *805/565–1700, 800/368–6788* 🌐 *www.sanysidroranch.com* 🛏 *23 rooms, 4 suites, 14 cottages* 🍴 *No meals* ☞ *2-day minimum stay on weekends, 3 days on holiday weekends.*

$$$$ B&B/INN Fodor'sChoice ★ 🏨 **Simpson House Inn.** If you're a fan of traditional bed-and-breakfast inns, this property, with its beautifully appointed Victorian main house and acre of lush gardens, is for you. **Pros:** elegant; impeccable landscaping; within walking distance of downtown. **Cons:** some rooms in main building are small; two-night minimum stay on weekends. [$] *Rooms from: $255* ✉ *121 E. Arrellaga St.* ☎ *805/963–7067, 800/676–1280* 🌐 *www.simpsonhouseinn.com* 🛏 *11 rooms, 4 cottages* 🍴 *Breakfast.*

$$$$ B&B/INN 🏨 **The Upham.** Built in 1871, this downtown Victorian in the arts and culture district has been restored as a full-service hotel. **Pros:** 1-acre garden; easy walk to theaters; on-site restaurant; many room choices. **Cons:** some rooms are small; not near beach or waterfront. [$] *Rooms from: $275* ✉ *1404 De la Vina St.* ☎ *805/962–0058, 800/727–0876* 🌐 *www.uphamhotel.com* 🛏 *46 rooms, 4 suites* 🍴 *Breakfast* ☞ *2-night minimum stay on weekends.*

NIGHTLIFE AND PERFORMING ARTS

The bar, club, and live-music scene centers on lower State Street, between the 300 and 800 blocks. The arts district, with theaters, restaurants, and cafés, starts around the 900 block of State and continues north to the 1300 block. To see what's scheduled around town, pick up the free weekly *Santa Barbara Independent* newspaper or visit its website, 🌐 *www.independent.com.*

NIGHTLIFE

James Joyce. A good place to have a few beers and while away an evening, the James Joyce sometimes hosts folk and rock performers. ⊠ *513 State St., at W. Haley St.* ☎ *805/962–2688* ⊕ *sbjamesjoyce.com.*

Joe's Cafe. Steins of beer and stiff cocktails accompany hearty bar food at Joe's. It's a fun, if occasionally rowdy, collegiate scene. ⊠ *536 State St., at E. Cota St.* ☎ *805/966–4638* ⊕ *joescafesb.com.*

Les Marchands. Brian McClintic, one of four real-life candidates trying to achieve master sommelier status in the 2013 film *Somm* (he succeeded), co-owns and operates this combination wine bar, store, and eatery in the Funk Zone. ■TIP➔ **From Friday through Sunday, you can combine your wine tasting with ramen slurping.** ⊠ *131 Anacapa St., at Yananoli St.* ☎ *805/284–0380* ⊕ *www.lesmarchandswine.com.*

SOhO. A hip restaurant, bar, and music club, SOhO books bands, from jazz to blues to rock. ⊠ *1221 State St., at W. Victoria St.* ☎ *805/962–7776* ⊕ *www.sohosb.com.*

PERFORMING ARTS

Arlington Theatre. This Moorish-style auditorium presents touring performers and films throughout the year. ⊠ *1317 State St., at Arlington Ave.* ☎ *805/963–4408* ⊕ *thearlingtontheatre.com.*

The Granada Theatre. A restored, modernized landmark that dates from 1924, the Granada hosts Broadway touring shows and dance, music, and other cultural events. ⊠ *1214 State St., at E. Anapamu St.* ☎ *805/899–2222* ⊕ *granadasb.org.*

Lobero Theatre. A state landmark, the Lobero hosts community theater groups and touring professionals. ⊠ *33 E. Canon Perdido St., at Anacapa St.* ☎ *805/963–0761* ⊕ *www.lobero.com.*

Fodor'sChoice ★ **Old Spanish Days Fiesta.** The city celebrates its Spanish, Mexican, and Chumash heritage in early August with events that include music, dancing, an all-equestrian parade, a carnival, and a rodeo. ⊕ *oldspanishdaysfiesta.org.*

Fodor'sChoice ★ **Santa Barbara International Film Festival.** The 12-day festival in late January and early February attracts film enthusiasts and major stars to downtown venues for screenings, panels, and tributes. ⊕ *sbiff.org.*

SPORTS AND THE OUTDOORS

BIKING

Cabrillo Bike Lane. The level, two-lane, 3-mile Cabrillo Bike Lane passes the Santa Barbara Zoo, the Andree Clark Bird Refuge, beaches, and the harbor. There are restaurants along the way, and you can stop for a picnic along the palm-lined path looking out on the Pacific.

Wheel Fun Rentals. You can rent bikes, quadricycles, and skates here. ⊠ *23 E. Cabrillo Blvd.* ☎ *805/966–2282* ⊕ *wheelfunrentalssb.com.*

BOATS AND CHARTERS

Channel Islands Outfitters. A full-service paddle-sports center in the harbor, this outfit rents kayaks, stand-up paddleboards, surfboards, boogie boards, and water-sports gear, and conducts guided tours and excursions. ✉ *117 B Harbor Way, off Shoreline Dr.* ☎ *805/899–4925 tours, 805/617–3425 rentals* ⊕ *www.channelislandso.com.*

Fodor's Choice
★

Condor Express. From SEA Landing, the *Condor Express*, a 75-foot high-speed catamaran, whisks up to 149 passengers toward the Channel Islands on whale-watching excursions and sunset and dinner cruises. ✉ *301 W. Cabrillo Blvd.* ☎ *805/882–0088, 888/779–4253* ⊕ *condorexpress.com.*

Santa Barbara Sailing Center. The center offers sailing instruction; rents and charters sailboats, kayaks, and stand-up paddleboards; and organizes dinner and sunset champagne cruises, island excursions, and whale-watching trips. ✉ *Santa Barbara Harbor launching ramp* ☎ *805/962–2826* ⊕ *www.sbsail.com.*

Truth Aquatics. Truth runs kayaking, paddleboarding, hiking, and scuba excursions to the National Marine Sanctuary and Channel Islands National Park. ✉ *Departures from SEA Landing, Santa Barbara Harbor* ☎ *805/962–1127* ⊕ *truthaquatics.com.*

SHOPPING

CLOTHING

Diani. This upscale, European-style women's boutique dresses clients in designer clothing from around the world. Sibling shoe and home-and-garden shops are nearby. ✉ *1324 State St., at Arlington Ave.* ☎ *805/966–3114, 805/966–7175 shoe shop* ⊕ *dianiboutique.com.*

Surf N Wear's Beach House. This shop carries surf clothing, gear, and collectibles; it's also the home of Santa Barbara Surf Shop and the exclusive local dealer of Surfboards by Yater. ✉ *10 State St., at Cabrillo Blvd.* ☎ *805/963–1281* ⊕ *surfnwear.com.*

Wendy Foster. This store sells casual-chic women's fashions. ✉ *833 State St., at W. Canon Perdido St.* ☎ *805/966–2276* ⊕ *wendyfoster.com.*

FOOD AND WINE

Santa Barbara Public Market. A dozen food and beverage vendors occupy this spacious arts district galleria that opened in 2014. Stock up on fresh seafood, meats, pastas, and other gourmet goodies; sip on handcrafted wines and beers; and nosh on locally made noodles, ice cream, and baked goods. ✉ *38 W. Victoria St., at Chapala St.* ☎ *805/770–7702* ⊕ *sbpublicmarket.com.*

SHOPPING AREAS

Fodor's Choice
★

El Paseo. Wine tasting rooms, shops, art galleries, and studios share the courtyard and gardens of El Paseo, a historic arcade. ✉ *Canon Perdido St., between State and Anacapa Sts.*

EARTH DAY

In 1969, 200,000 gallons of crude oil spilled into the Santa Barbara Channel, causing an immediate outcry from residents. The day after the spill, Get Oil Out (GOO) was established; the group helped lead the successful fight for legislation to limit and regulate offshore drilling in California. The Santa Barbara spill also spawned Earth Day, which is still celebrated across the nation today.

3

Fodor's Choice ★ **State Street.** Between Cabrillo Boulevard and Sola Street, State Street is a shopper's paradise. Chic malls, quirky storefronts, antiques emporia, elegant boutiques, and funky thrift shops abound. You can shop on foot or ride a battery-powered trolley (50¢) that runs between the waterfront and the 1300 block. Nordstrom and Macy's anchor **Paseo Nuevo**, an open-air mall in the 700 block. Shops, restaurants, galleries, and fountains line the tiled walkways of **La Arcada**, a small complex of landscaped courtyards in the 1100 block designed by architect Myron Hunt in 1926.

NORTHERN SANTA BARBARA COUNTY

The Santa Ynez Mountains divide Santa Barbara County geographically; U.S. 101 passes through a mountain tunnel leading inland. Northern Santa Barbara County used to be known for sprawling ranches and strawberry and broccoli fields. Today its 200-plus wineries and 22,000 acres of vineyards dominate the landscape from the Santa Ynez Valley in the south to Santa Maria in the north. Though more than 50 grape varietals are grown in the county, more than half the vineyards are planted to Chardonnay, Pinot Noir, and Syrah.

GETTING HERE AND AROUND

Two-lane Highway 154 over San Marcos Pass is the shortest and most scenic route from Santa Barbara into the Santa Ynez Valley. You can also drive along U.S. 101 north 43 miles to Buellton, then 7 miles east through Solvang to Santa Ynez. Santa Ynez Valley Transit shuttle buses serve Santa Ynez, Los Olivos, Ballard, Solvang, and Buellton. COLT Wine Country Express buses connect Lompoc, Buellton, and Solvang on weekdays except holidays.

ESSENTIALS

Bus Contacts COLT Wine Country Express ✉ Lompoc ☎ 805/736–7666 ⊕ cityoflompoc.com/transit. **Santa Ynez Valley Transit** ☎ 805/688–5452 ⊕ syvt.com.

Visitor Information Santa Barbara Vintners ☎ 805/688–0881 ⊕ www. sbcountywines.com. **Visit Santa Barbara** ⊕ www.santabarbaraca.com. **Visit the Santa Ynez Valley** ⊕ www.visitsyv.com.

SANTA YNEZ

31 miles north of Goleta.

Founded in 1882, the tiny town of Santa Ynez still has many of its original frontier buildings. You can walk through the three-block downtown area in a few minutes, shop for antiques, and hang around the old-time saloon. At some of the Santa Ynez Valley's best restaurants, you just might bump into one of the celebrities who own nearby ranches.

GETTING HERE AND AROUND

Take Highway 154 over San Marcos Pass or U.S. 101 north 43 miles to Buellton, then 7 miles east.

EXPLORING

Gainey Vineyard. The 1,800-acre Gainey Ranch, straddling the banks of the Santa Ynez River, includes about 100 acres of organic vineyards: Sauvignon Blanc, Merlot, Cabernet Sauvignon, and Cabernet Franc. The winery also makes wines from Chardonnay, Pinot Noir, and Syrah grapes from the Santa Rita Hills. You can taste the latest releases—the estate Pinot Noir is especially good—in a Spanish-style hacienda overlooking the ranch. ✉ *3950 E. Hwy. 246* ☎ *805/688–0558* 🌐 *www.gaineyvineyard.com* 🎟 *Tasting $15* 🕒 *Daily 10–5.*

WHERE TO EAT AND STAY

$$$ ITALIAN 🍴 **Santa Ynez Kitchen.** The owners of Toscana, a popular eatery in L.A.'s Brentwood neighborhood, run this rustic-chic restaurant with an Italy-meets-California Wine Country vibe. Chef and co-owner Luca Crestanelli, a native of Verona, Italy, typically offers about 10 seasonal daily specials. Menu regulars include Spanish-octopus salad, nettle ricotta gnocchi, wood-fired pizzas, and oak-grilled entrées such as salmon puttanesca and organic chicken. Save room for the gelatos or the "not-so-classic" tiramisu, served in small Mason jars. A big draw is the full bar, where resident mixologist Alberto Battaglini crafts creative cocktails using fresh local ingredients. [$] *Average main: $23* ✉ *1110 Faraday St., at Sagunto St.* ☎ *805/691–9794* 🌐 *www.sykitchen.com* 🕒 *No lunch Mon. and Tues.*

$$ ITALIAN 🍴 **Trattoria Grappolo.** Authentic Italian fare, an open kitchen, and festive, family-style seating make this trattoria equally popular with celebrities from Hollywood and ranchers from the Santa Ynez Valley. Thin-crust pizza, homemade ravioli, risottos, and seafood linguine are among the menu favorites. The noise level tends to rise in the evening, so this isn't the best spot for a romantic getaway. [$] *Average main: $22* ✉ *3687-C Sagunto St.* ☎ *805/688–6899* 🌐 *trattoriagrappolo.com* 🕒 *No lunch Mon.*

$$$$ B&B/INN 🏨 **ForFriends Inn.** Four close friends—Jim and Debbie Campbell and Dave and Katie Pollock—own and operate this luxury bed-and-breakfast, designed as a social place where friends gather to enjoy good wine, food, and music in a casual backyard setting. **Pros:** relaxed, intimate setting; walk to restaurants; friendly innkeepers; "Friendship Pass" provides perks and savings at restaurants and wineries. **Cons:** not suitable for children; no pets allowed. [$] *Rooms from: $295* ✉ *1121 Edison St.* ☎ *805/693–0303* 🌐 *www.forfriendsinn.com* 🛏 *5 rooms, 2 cottages* 🍽 *Breakfast.*

SPORTS AND THE OUTDOORS

Santa Barbara Soaring. The outfit's scenic glider rides last from 10 to 50 minutes. Tour options include the Santa Ynez Valley, coastal mountains and the Channel Islands, and celebrity homes. ✉ *Santa Ynez Airport, 900 Airport Rd.* ☎ *805/688–2517* 🌐 *www.sbsoaring.com* 🎟 *$157–$419.*

LOS OLIVOS

4 miles north of Santa Ynez.

This pretty village was once on Spanish-built El Camino Real (Royal Road) and later a stop on major stagecoach and rail routes. Tasting rooms, art galleries, antiques stores, and country markets line Grand Avenue and intersecting streets for several blocks.

GETTING HERE AND AROUND

From U.S. 101 north or south, exit at Highway 154 and drive east about 8 miles. From Santa Barbara, travel 30 miles northwest on Highway 154.

3

EXPLORING

Blair Fox Cellars. Blair Fox, a Santa Barbara native, crafts small-lot Rhône-style wines made from organic grapes. The bar in his rustic Los Olivos tasting room, where you can sample exceptional vineyard-designated Syrahs and other wines, was hewn from Australian white oak reclaimed from an old Tasmanian schoolhouse. ✉ *2902–B San Marcos Ave.* ☎ *805/691–1678* 🌐 *www.blairfoxcellars.com* 🎟 *Tasting $12* ⏲ *Sept.–May, Thurs.–Sun. noon–5; June–Aug., Thurs.–Mon. noon–5.*

Daniel Gehrs Tasting Room. Heather Cottage, built in the early 1900s as a doctor's office, houses winemaker Gehrs's tasting room, where you can sample Port, Chardonnay, Gewürztraminer, Riesling, and other small-lot wines. ✉ *2939 Grand Ave.* ☎ *805/693–9686* 🌐 *danielgehrswines.com* 🎟 *Tastings $5–$10* ⏲ *Sun.–Fri. 11–5, Sat. 11–6.*

Firestone Vineyard. Heirs to the Firestone tire fortune developed (but no longer own) this winery known for Chardonnay, Gewürztraminer, Merlot, Riesling, and Syrah—and for the fantastic valley views from its tasting room and picnic area. The tour here is highly informative. ✉ *5017 Zaca Station Rd., off U.S. 101* ☎ *805/688–3940* 🌐 *www.firestonewine.com* 🎟 *Tastings $10–$15* ⏲ *Daily 10–5; tours 11:15, 1:15, and 3:15.*

WHERE TO EAT AND STAY

$$ AMERICAN 🍴 **Los Olivos Cafe.** Part wine store and part social hub, this café focuses on wine-friendly fish, pasta, and meat dishes, plus salads, pizzas, and burgers. Don't miss the homemade muffuletta and olive tapenade spreads. [$] *Average main: $21* ✉ *2879 Grand Ave.* ☎ *805/688–7265* 🌐 *www.losolivoscafe.com.*

$$$ AMERICAN 🍴 **Sides Hardware & Shoes: A Brothers Restaurant.** Inside a historic storefront they renovated, brothers Matt and Jeff Nichols serve comfort food prepared with panache. The Kobe-style burgers, especially the one with bacon and white cheddar, make a great lunch, and the dinner favorites include fried chicken, Scottish salmon, and lamb sirloin with goat cheese gnocchi. [$] *Average main: $28* ✉ *2375 Alamo Pintado Ave.* ☎ *805/688–4820* 🌐 *brothersrestaurant.com.*

$$$$ B&B/INN Fodor's Choice ★ 🏨 **The Ballard Inn & Restaurant.** Set among orchards and vineyards in the tiny town of Ballard, 2 miles south of Los Olivos, this inn makes an elegant wine-country escape. **Pros:** exceptional food; attentive staff; secluded. **Cons:** some baths could use updating. [$] *Rooms from: $265* ✉ *2436 Baseline Ave., Ballard* ☎ *805/688–7770, 800/638–2466* 🌐 *ballardinn.com* 🛏 *15 rooms* 🍽 *Breakfast.*

$$$$ ⌨ **Fess Parker's Wine Country Inn and Spa.** This luxury inn includes an
B&B/INN   elegant, tree-shaded French country–style main building and an equally
attractive annex across the street with a pool and day spa. **Pros:** convenient wine-touring base; walking distance from restaurants and galleries; well-appointed rooms. **Cons:** pricey; not pet-friendly. ⓢ *Rooms
from: $395 ⊠ 2860 Grand Ave. ☎ 805/688–7788, 800/446–2455
⊕ www.fessparkerinn.com ⇗ 15 rooms, 4 suites ⑩ Breakfast.*

SOLVANG

5 miles south of Los Olivos.

You'll know you've reached the town of Solvang when the architecture
suddenly changes to half-timber buildings and windmills. Danish educators settled the town in 1911—the flatlands and rolling green hills
reminded them of home. Solvang has attracted tourists for decades,
but it's lately become more sophisticated, with smorgasbords giving
way to galleries, upscale restaurants, and wine-tasting rooms by day
and wine bars by night. The visitor center, on Copenhagen Drive, has
walking-tour maps (also available online). The Sweet Treats tour covers
the town's Danish bakeries, confectionary stores, and ice-cream parlors.
The Olsen's and Solvang bakeries and Ingeborg's Danish Chocolates
are worth investigating.

GETTING HERE AND AROUND
Highway 246 West (Mission Drive) traverses Solvang, connecting with
U.S. 101 to the west and Highway 154 to the east. Alamo Pintado Road
connects Solvang with Ballard and Los Olivos to the north. Park your
car in one of the free public lots and stroll the town. Or take the bus:
Santa Ynez Valley Transit shuttles run between Solvang and nearby
towns.

ESSENTIALS
Visitor Information Solvang Conference & Visitors Bureau ⊠ *1639 Copenhagen Dr., at 2nd St.* ☎ *805/688–6144* ⊕ *www.solvangusa.com.*

EXPLORING
Mission Santa Inés. The mission holds an impressive collection of paintings, statuary, vestments, and Chumash and Spanish artifacts in a serene
bluff-top setting. You can tour the museum, sanctuary, and gardens.
⊠ *1760 Mission Dr., at Alisal Rd.* ☎ *805/688–4815* ⊕ *missionsantaines.
org* ⌚ *$5* ☉ *Daily 9–4:30.*

Rideau Vineyard. This winery celebrates its locale's rich history—the King
of Spain himself once owned this land, and the tasting room occupies
a former guest ranch inn—but fully embraces the area's wine-making
present. Wines made from the Rhône varietals Grenache, Mourvèdre,
Roussanne, Syrah, and Viognier are the specialty here. ⊠ *1562 Alamo
Pintado Rd., 2 miles north of Hwy. 246* ☎ *805/688–0717* ⊕ *rideauvineyard.com* ⌚ *Tastings $12–$15* ☉ *Daily 11–5.*

Sevtap. Winemaker Art Sevtap, an Istanbul native, is often on hand to
pour samples of his limited-production wines—mostly from Bordeaux
varietals but also Chardonnay, Sangiovese, and Syrah—in this artsy
wine bar that's decked out with Tibetan prayer flags and chalkboard

walls and has a stage where guests can pick up a guitar and strum away. ✉ *1576 Copenhagen Dr., Ste. 1, near Atterdag Rd.* ☎ *805/693–9200* 🌐 *www.sevtapwinery.com* 🎫 *Tasting $15* 🕒 *Sun., Mon., and Thurs. 11–8, Fri. and Sat. 11–9.*

WHERE TO EAT

$$$ AMERICAN Fodor's Choice ★ 🍴 **Root 246.** This chic restaurant's chefs tap local purveyors and shop for organic ingredients at farmers' markets before deciding on the day's menu. Depending on the season, you might feast on Dungeness crab, a savory cassoulet, Santa Maria–style tri-tip grilled over an oak fire, or seaweed-crusted steelhead trout in a smoky red wine broth. The 1,800-bottle wine selection includes many regional offerings. Root 246's gorgeous design incorporates wood, stone, tempered glass, and leather elements. [$] *Average main: $30* ✉ *Hotel Corque, 420 Alisal Rd., at Molle Way* ☎ *805/686–8681* 🌐 *www.root-246.com* 🕒 *Closed Mon. No lunch Tues.–Sat.*

$$$ AMERICAN 🍴 **Succulent Café.** Locals flock to this cozy café for its comfort cuisine and regional wines and craft beers. Order at the counter, and staffers will deliver your meal to the interior dining areas or the sunny outdoor patio. For breakfast—on weekends and holiday Mondays only—try the cinnamon-cumin pulled pork. Served on homemade biscuits, it's topped with bacon gravy and pineapple chutney. Buttermilk fried-chicken salad and the house-roasted turkey sandwich, both succulent indeed, are two top lunch choices; dinnertime favorites include artisanal cheese and charcuterie plates, and rack of lamb crusted with pumpkin seeds. [$] *Average main: $23* ✉ *1555 Mission Dr., at 4th Pl.* ☎ *805/691–9444* 🌐 *succulentcafe.com* 🕒 *Closed Tues. No breakfast weekdays except holiday Mon.*

WHERE TO STAY

$$$$ RESORT 🏨 **Alisal Guest Ranch and Resort.** Since 1946 this 10,000-acre ranch has been popular with celebrities and plain folk alike. **Pros:** Old West atmosphere; many activities; ultraprivate. **Cons:** isolated; not close to downtown. [$] *Rooms from: $525* ✉ *1054 Alisal Rd.* ☎ *805/688–6411, 800/425–4725* 🌐 *alisal.com* 🛏 *36 rooms, 37 suites* 🍽 *Some meals.*

$$$ HOTEL Fodor's Choice ★ 🏨 **Hotel Corque.** Owned by the Santa Ynez Band of Chumash Indians, the stunning three-story "Corque" provides a full slate of upscale amenities. **Pros:** front desk staff are trained concierges; short walk to shops, tasting rooms and restaurants; free Wi-Fi. **Cons:** no kitchenettes or laundry facilities; pricey. [$] *Rooms from: $239* ✉ *400 Alisal Rd.* ☎ *805/688–8000, 800/624–5572* 🌐 *hotelcorque.com* 🛏 *122 rooms, 10 suites* 🍽 *No meals.*

$$ B&B/INN 🏨 **Solvang Gardens Lodge.** The lush gardens with fountains and waterfalls and the cheery English-country-theme rooms make for a peaceful retreat just a few blocks—but worlds away—from Solvang's main tourist area. **Pros:** homey; family-friendly; colorful gardens. **Cons:** some rooms tiny; some need upgrades. [$] *Rooms from: $125* ✉ *293 Alisal Rd.* ☎ *805/688–4404, 888/688–4404* 🌐 *www.solvanggardens.com* 🛏 *16 rooms, 8 suites* 🍽 *Breakfast.*

PERFORMING ARTS

Solvang Festival Theater. Pacific Conservatory of the Performing Arts presents crowd-pleasing musicals *(My Fair Lady, Man of La Mancha)* and classic *(Cyrano de Bergerac)* and contemporary plays at this 700-seat outdoor amphitheater. ⊠ *420 2nd St., at Molle Way* ☎ *805/922–8313* ⊕ *pcpa.org* ⊗ *June–Oct.*

BUELLTON

3 miles west of Solvang.

A crossroads town at the intersection of U.S. 101 and Highway 246, Buellton has evolved from a sleepy gas and coffee stop into an enclave of wine-tasting rooms, beer gardens, and restaurants. It's also a gateway to Lompoc and the Santa Rita Hills Wine Trail to the west, and to Solvang, Santa Ynez, and Los Olivos to the east.

GETTING HERE AND AROUND

Driving is the easiest way to get to Buellton. From Santa Barbara, follow U.S. 101 north to the Highway 246 exit. Santa Ynez Valley Transit serves Buellton with shuttle buses from Solvang and nearby towns.

ESSENTIALS

Visitor Information Buellton Visitors Bureau ⊠ *597 Avenue of the Flags, No. 101* ☎ *805/688–7829, 800/324–3800* ⊕ *visitbuellton.com.* **Santa Rita Hills Wine Trail** ⊕ *santaritahillswinetrail.com.*

EXPLORING

Alma Rosa Winery. Winemaker Richard Sanford helped put Santa Barbara County on the international wine map with a 1989 Pinot Noir. For Alma Rosa, started in 2005, he crafts wines from grapes grown on 100-plus acres of certified organic vineyards in the Santa Rita Hills. The Pinot Noirs and Chardonnays are exceptional. ⊠ *181-C Industrial Way, off Hwy. 246, west of U.S. 101* ☎ *805/688–9090* ⊕ *almarosawinery.com* 🍷 *Tastings $10–$15* ⊗ *Sun.–Thurs. 11–4:30; Fri. and Sat. 11–6:30.*

Industrial Way. A half-mile west of U.S. 101, head south from Highway 246 on Industrial Way to explore a hip and happening collection of food and drink destinations. Top stops include **Industrial Eats** (a craft butcher shop and restaurant), **Figueroa Mountain Brewing Co.**, the **Alma Rosa Winery** tasting room *(⇨ see above)*, **Avant Tapas and Wine**, and the **Ascendant Spirits Distillery.** ⊠ *Industrial Way, off Hwy. 246.*

Lafond Winery and Vineyards. A rich, concentrated Pinot Noir is the main attention-getter at this winery that also produces noteworthy Chardonnays and Syrahs. Bottles with Lafond's SRH (Santa Rita Hills) label are an especially good value. The winery also has a tasting room at 111 East Yanonali Street in Santa Barbara's Funk Zone. ⊠ *6855 Santa Rosa Rd., west off U.S. 101 Exit 139* ☎ *805/688–7921* ⊕ *lafondwinery.com* 🍷 *Tasting $10 (includes logo glass)* ⊗ *Daily 10–5.*

WHERE TO EAT

$$$ ✕ **The Hitching Post II.** You'll find everything from grilled artichokes
AMERICAN   to quail at this casual eatery, but most people come for the smoky
Santa Maria–style barbecue. Be sure to try a glass of owner-chef-
winemaker Frank Ostini's signature Highliner Pinot Noir, a star in the
film *Sideways.* $ *Average main: $30* ✉ *406 E. Hwy. 246, off U.S. 101*
☎ *805/688–0676* ⊕ *hitchingpost2.com* ⊘ *No lunch.*

LOMPOC

3

20 miles west of Solvang.

Known as the flower-seed capital of the world, Lompoc is blanketed
with vast fields of brightly colored flowers that bloom from May
through August. Also home to a starkly beautiful mission, Lompoc has
emerged as a major Pinot Noir and Chardonnay grape-growing region.
Overlapping the Santa Rita Hills Wine Trail in parts, the Lompoc Wine
Trail includes wineries in the Wine Ghetto, a downtown industrial park,
and along Highway 246 and (to the south) Santa Rosa Road, which
form a loop between Lompoc and Buellton.

GETTING HERE AND AROUND

Driving is the easiest way to get to Lompoc. From Santa Barbara, fol-
low U.S. 101 north to Highway 1 exit off Gaviota Pass, or Highway
246 west at Buellton.

ESSENTIALS

**Visitor Information Lompoc Valley Chamber of Commerce & Visitors
Bureau** ✉ *111 S. I St., at Hwy. 246* ☎ *805/736–4567, 800/240–0999* ⊕ *lompoc.
com.*

EXPLORING

FAMILY   **La Purísima Mission State Historic Park.** The state's most fully restored mis-
sion, founded in 1787, stands in a stark and still remote location that
powerfully evokes the lives and isolation of California's Spanish settlers.
Docents lead tours every afternoon, and vivid displays illustrate the
secular and religious activities that formed mission life. ✉ *2295 Purí-
sima Rd., off Hwy. 246* ☎ *805/733–3713* ⊕ *www.lapurisimamission.
org* ⊞ *$6 per vehicle* ⊘ *Daily 9–5; tour daily at 1.*

Lompoc Wine Ghetto. Laid-back tasting rooms can be found in a down-
town industrial park. Taste of Sta. Rita Hills, Fiddlehead Cellars, and
Flying Goat are three rooms worth checking out here. ✉ *200 N. 9th
St.* ⊕ *lompoctrail.com* ⊞ *Tasting fees vary, some free* ⊘ *Most tasting
rooms open Thurs.–Sun., 11 or noon until 4 or 5; some also Mon. and
by appointment.*

SAN LUIS OBISPO COUNTY

San Luis Obispo County's pristine landscapes and abundant wildlife
areas, especially those around Morro Bay, have long attracted nature
lovers. In the south, Pismo Beach and other coastal towns have great
sand and surf; inland, a booming wine region stretches from the Edna,

Arroyo Grande, and Avila valleys and Nipomo in the south to Paso Robles in the north.

GETTING HERE AND AROUND

San Luis Obispo Regional Transit Authority operates buses in San Luis Obispo and serves Paso Robles as well as Pismo Beach and other coastal towns.

ESSENTIALS

Transportation Contact San Luis Obispo Regional Transit Authority ☎ 805/541–2228 ⊕ www.slorta.org.

VOLCANOES?

Those funny-looking, sawed-off peaks along the drive from Pismo Beach to Morro Bay are the Nine Sisters—a series of ancient volcanic plugs. Morro Rock, the northernmost sibling and a state historic monument, is the most famous and photographed of the clan.

Visitor Information Highway 1 Discovery Route ⊠ San Luis Obispo ⊕ highway1discoveryroute.com. **SLO Wine Country** ☎ 805/541–5868 ⊕ www.slowine.com. **Visit San Luis Obispo County** ⊠ 835 12th St., Ste. 204, Paso Robles ☎ 805/541–8000 ⊕ www.visitsanluisobispocounty.com.

PISMO BEACH

40 miles north of Lompoc.

About 20 miles of sandy shoreline—nicknamed the Bakersfield Riviera for the throngs of vacationers who come here from the Central Valley—begins at the town of Pismo Beach. The southern end of town runs along sand dunes, some of which are open to cars and off-road vehicles. Sheltered by the dunes, a grove of eucalyptus trees attracts thousands of migrating monarch butterflies from November through February. A long, broad beach fronts the center of town, where a municipal pier extends into the sea at the foot of shop-lined Pomeroy Street. To the north, hotels and homes perch atop chalky oceanfront cliffs. Fewer than 10,000 people live in this quintessential surfer haven, but Pismo Beach has a slew of hotels and restaurants with great views of the Pacific Ocean.

GETTING HERE AND AROUND

Pismo Beach straddles both sides of U.S. 101. If you're coming from the south and have time for a scenic drive, exit U.S. 101 in Santa Maria and take Highway 166 west for 8 miles to Guadalupe and follow Highway 1 north 16 miles to Pismo Beach. South County Area Transit (*SCAT*; ⊕ *www.slorta.org*) buses run throughout San Luis Obispo and connect the city with nearby towns. On summer weekends, the free Avila Trolley extends service to Pismo Beach.

ESSENTIALS

Visitor Information California Welcome Center ⊠ 333 Five Cities Dr. ☎ 805/773–7924. **Pismo Beach Visitors Information Center** ⊠ Dolliver St./Hwy. 1, at Hinds Ave. ☎ 800/443–7778, 805/773–4382 ⊕ classiccalifornia.com ⊗ Weekdays 9–5, Sat. 11–4, Sun. 10–2.

BEACHES

Fodor's Choice **Oceano Dunes State Vehicular Recreation Area.** Part of the spectacular Gua-
★ dalupe-Nipomo Dunes, this 3,600-acre coastal playground is one of
the few places in California where you can drive or ride off-highway
vehicles on the beach and sand dunes. Hike, ride horses, kiteboard,
join a Hummer tour, or rent an ATV or a dune buggy and cruise up
the white-sand peaks for spectacular views. At **Oso Flaco Lake Nature
Area**—3 miles west of Highway 1 on Oso Flaco Road—a 1½-mile
boardwalk over the lake leads to a platform with views up and down
the coast. Leashed dogs are allowed in much of the park except Oso
Flaco and Pismo Dunes Natural Reserve. **Amenities:** food and drink;
lifeguards (seasonal); parking (fee); showers; toilets; water sports. **Best
for:** sunset; surfing; swimming; walking. ⊠ *West end of Pier Ave., off
Hwy. 1, Oceano* ☎ *805/473–7220* ⊕ *www.parks.ca.gov* ⌦ *$5 per vehi-
cle* ⊙ *Daily 6 am–11 pm; Oso Flaco Lake sunrise–sunset.*

Pismo State Beach. Hike, surf, ride horses, swim, fish in a lagoon or off
the pier, and dig for Pismo clams at this busy state beach. One of the
day-use parking areas is off Highway 1 near the **Monarch Butterfly
Grove,** where from November through February monarch butterflies
nest in eucalyptus and Monterey pines. The other parking area is about
1½ miles south at Pier Avenue. **Amenities:** food and drink; lifeguards
(seasonal); parking (fee); showers; toilets; water sports. **Best for:** sunset; surfing; swimming; walking. ⊠ *555 Pier Ave., off Hwy. 1, 3 miles
south of downtown Pismo Beach, Oceano* ☎ *805/489–1869* ⊕ *www.
parks.ca.gov* ⌦ *Day use $5 per vehicle if parking at the beach* ⊙ *Day
use 6 am–11 pm.*

WHERE TO EAT

$$$ ✕ **Cracked Crab.** This traditional New England–style crab shack imports
SEAFOOD fresh seafood daily from Australia, Alaska, and the East Coast. Fish
is line-caught, much of the produce is organic, and everything is made
from scratch. For a real treat, don a bib and sample a bucket of steamed
shellfish with Cajun sausage, potatoes, and corn on the cob, all dumped
right onto your table. Ⓢ *Average main: $26* ⊠ *751 Price St., near Main
St.* ☎ *805/773–2722* ⊕ *www.crackedcrab.com* ⌦ *Reservations not
accepted.*

$ ✕ **Doc Burnstein's Ice Cream Lab.** The delectable ice creams are churned on-
AMERICAN site at this beloved old-fashioned parlor east of Pismo Beach. Top-selling
FAMILY flavors include the Elvis Special (banana and peanut butter) and Motor
Oil, a blend of dark chocolate and Kahlúa with a fudge swirl. Slip into
a wooden booth and watch an antique model train chug around a cir-
cular ceiling track. ■TIP➡ There's a second Lab in downtown San Luis
Obispo at 860 Higuera Street. Ⓢ *Average main: $6* ⊠ *114 W. Branch
St., at Nevada St., east off U.S. 101, Arroyo Grande* ☎ *805/474–4068*
⊕ *docburnsteins.com.*

$$ ✕ **Ember.** A barn-style restaurant with high ceilings and an open kitchen,
MODERN Ember enjoys a red-hot reputation for Italian-inflected dishes prepared
AMERICAN in an authentic Tuscan fireplace or a wood-burning oven. Chef-owner
Fodor's Choice Brian Collins, a native of Arroyo Grande, the town bordering Pismo
★ Beach, honed his culinary skills at Berkeley's legendary Chez Panisse
Restaurant. His seasonal menu changes monthly, but nearly always

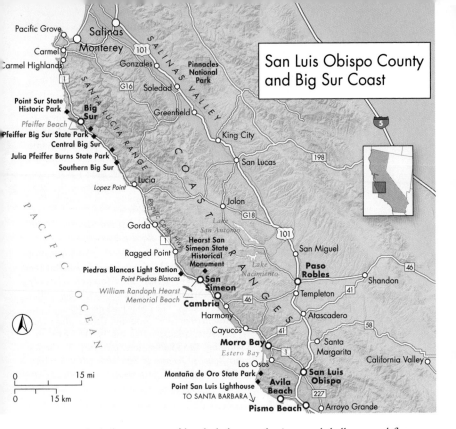

San Luis Obispo County and Big Sur Coast

includes a starter of local abalone and crispy pork belly, several flat-bread pizzas, grilled rib-eye steak, and chicken cooked under a brick on the hearth. ■TIP→ Ember doesn't accept reservations, so come before 6 or after 8 to avoid a wait. $ *Average main: $22* ✉ *1200 E. Grand Ave., at Brisco Rd., Arroyo Grande* ☎ *805/474–7700* ⊕ *www. emberwoodfire.com* ⚑ *Reservations not accepted* ⊗ *Closed Mon. and Tues. No lunch.*

$$$ ✕ **Giuseppe's Cucina Italiana.** The classic flavors of southern Italy are high-
ITALIAN lighted at this lively downtown spot. Most recipes originate from Bari, a seaport on the Adriatic; the menu includes breads and pizzas baked in the wood-burning oven, hearty dishes such as osso buco and lamb, and homemade pastas. The wait for a table can be long, but sometimes an accordion player gets the crowd singing. $ *Average main: $24* ✉ *891 Price St., at Pismo Ave.* ☎ *805/773–2870* ⊕ *giuseppesrestaurant.com* ⚑ *Reservations not accepted.*

WHERE TO STAY

$$$$ ⊡ **Dolphin Bay Resort & Spa.** On grass-covered bluffs overlooking Shell
RESORT Beach, this luxury resort looks and feels like an exclusive community of villas. **Pros:** lavish apartment units; killer views; walking distance from the beach. **Cons:** hefty price tag; vibe too upper-crust for some. $ *Rooms from: $405* ✉ *2727 Shell Beach Rd.* ☎ *805/773–4300,*

800/516–0112 reservations, 805/773–8900 restaurant ⊕ thedolphin-bay.com ⌇ 60 suites ⁄○⁄ No meals.

$$$$ 🛏 **Pismo Lighthouse Suites.** Each of the well-appointed two-room, two-
HOTEL bath suites at this oceanfront resort has a private balcony or patio. **Pros:**
lots of space for families and groups; nice pool area. **Cons:** not easy to
walk to main attractions; some units are next to busy road. Ⓢ *Rooms
from: $259 ⊠ 2411 Price St. ☎ 805/773–2411, 800/245–2411 ⊕ www.
pismolighthousesuites.com ⌇ 70 suites ⁄○⁄ Breakfast.*

AVILA BEACH

3

4 miles north of Pismo Beach.

FAMILY Because the village of Avila Beach and the sandy, cove-front shoreline
for which it's named face south into the Pacific Ocean, they get more
sun and less fog than any other stretch of coast in the area. With its
fortuitous climate and protected waters, Avila's public beach draws
sunbathers and families; summer weekends are very busy. Downtown
Avila Beach has a lively seaside promenade and some shops and hotels,
but for real local color, head to the far end of the cove and watch the
commercial fishers offload their catch on the old Port San Luis wharf.
On Friday from mid-April through mid-September, a fish and farmers'
market livens up the beach area with music, fresh local produce and
seafood, and children's activities.

GETTING HERE AND AROUND

Exit U.S. 101 at Avila Beach Drive and head 3 miles west to reach the
beach. The free Avila Trolley operates weekends year-round, plus Friday
afternoon and evening from April to September. The minibuses connect
Avila Beach and Port San Luis to Shell Beach, with multiple stops along
the way. Service extends to Pismo Beach in summer.

ESSENTIALS

Visitor Information Avila Beach Tourism Alliance ⊕ *visitavilabeach.com.*

EXPLORING

FAMILY **Avila Valley Barn.** An old-fashioned, family-friendly country store jam-
packed with local fruits and vegetables, prepared foods, and gift items,
Avila Valley Barn also gives visitors a chance to experience rural American traditions. You can pet farm animals and savor homemade ice
cream and pies daily, and on weekends ride a hay wagon out to the fields
to pick your own produce. ⊠ *560 Avila Beach Dr., San Luis Obispo*
☎ *805/595–2816 ⊕ avilavalleybarn.com ⊗ Daily 9–5 ⊗ Closed Tues.
and Wed. Jan.–Mar.*

Central Coast Aquarium. You'll learn all about local marine plants and animals from the hands-on exhibits at this science center next to the main
beach. ⊠ *50 San Juan St., at 1st St., off Avila Beach Dr. ☎ 805/595–
7280 ⊕ www.centralcoastaquarium.com ⊠ $8 ⊗ June–Aug., Tues.–
Sun. 10–5; Sept.–May, weekends 10–4 and holiday breaks.*

FAMILY **Point San Luis Lighthouse.** Docents lead hikes along scenic Pecho Coast
Trail (3½ miles round-trip) to see the historic 1890 lighthouse and its
rare Fresnel lens. ■TIP➜ **If you'd prefer a lift out to the lighthouse,
join a trolley tour. Hikes and tours require reservations.** ⊠ *Point San*

Luis, 1¾ miles west of Harford Pier, Port San Luis ☎ *855/533–7843, 805/528–8758 hikes reservations* 🌐 *sanluislighthouse.org* 🎟 *Trolley tours $20; hikes free ($5 to enter lighthouse)* 🕒 *Trolley tours Wed. at noon, Sat. at noon, 1, and 2; hikes Wed. and Sat. at 9.*

BEACHES

FAMILY **Avila State Beach.** At the edge of a sunny cove next to downtown shops and restaurants, Avila's ½-mile stretch of white sand is especially family-friendly, with a playground, barbecue and picnic tables, volleyball and basketball courts, and lifeguards on watch in summer and on many holiday weekends. The free beachfront parking fills up fast, but there's a nearby pay lot ($5 for the day, $1 after 4 pm). Dogs aren't allowed on the beach from 10 to 5. **Amenities:** food and drink; lifeguards (seasonal); parking (free); showers; toilets; water sports. **Best for:** sunset; surfing; swimming; walking. ✉ *Avila Beach Dr., at 1st St.* 🌐 *visitavilabeach.com* 🎟 *Free* 🕒 *Daily 6 am–10 pm.*

WHERE TO EAT AND STAY

$$$ SEAFOOD 🍴 **Ocean Grill.** Across from the promenade, beach, and pier, Ocean Grill serves up fresh seafood to diners who typically arrive before sunset to enjoy the views. Boats anchored in the bay provide much of the seafood, which pairs well with the mostly regional wines on the list. Southern California craft beers are also well represented. Along with fish and shellfish, the chefs prepare wood-fired pizzas and land-based entrées such as steaks and chops, and there are gluten-free and vegetarian options. [$] *Average main: $28* ✉ *268 Front St.* ☎ *805/595–4050* 🌐 *www.oceangrillavila.com* 🕒 *No lunch Mon.–Thurs.*

$$$$ HOTEL 🏨 **Avila La Fonda.** Modeled after a village in early California's Mexican period, Avila La Fonda surrounds guests with rich jewel tones, fountains, and upscale comfort. **Pros:** one-of-a-kind theme and artwork; flexible room combinations; a block from the beach. **Cons:** pricey; most rooms don't have an ocean view. [$] *Rooms from: $329* ✉ *101 San Miguel St.* ☎ *805/595–1700* 🌐 *avilalafondahotel.com* 🛏 *28 rooms, 1 suite* 🍽 *No meals.*

$$$ HOTEL 🏨 **Avila Lighthouse Suites.** Families, honeymooners, and business travelers all find respite at this two-story, all-suites luxury hotel. **Pros:** directly across from sand; easy walk to restaurants and shops; free underground parking. **Cons:** noise from passersby can be heard in room; some ocean-view rooms have limited vistas. [$] *Rooms from: $229* ✉ *550 Front St.* ☎ *805/627–1900, 800/372–8452* 🌐 *www.avilalighthousesuites.com* 🛏 *54 suites* 🍽 *Breakfast.*

$$ RESORT 🏨 **Sycamore Mineral Springs Resort.** This wellness resort's hot mineral springs bubble up into private outdoor tubs on an oak-and-sycamore-forest hillside. **Pros:** great place to rejuvenate; nice hiking; incredible spa services. **Cons:** rooms vary in quality; 2½ miles from the beach. [$] *Rooms from: $169* ✉ *1215 Avila Beach Dr., San Luis Obispo* ☎ *805/595–7302* 🌐 *www.sycamoresprings.com* 🛏 *26 rooms, 46 suites* 🍽 *No meals.*

SAN LUIS OBISPO

8 miles north of Avila Beach.

About halfway between San Francisco and Los Angeles, San Luis Obispo spreads out below gentle hills and rocky extinct volcanoes. Its main appeal lies in its architecturally diverse, pedestrian-friendly downtown, which bustles with shoppers, restaurant goers, and students from California Polytechnic State University, known as Cal Poly.

> **DEEP ROOTS**
>
> Way back in the 1700s, the Spanish padres who accompanied Father Junípero Serra planted grapevines from Mexico along California's Central Coast, and began using European wine-making techniques to turn the grapes into delectable vintages.

GETTING HERE AND AROUND

U.S. 101/Highway 1 traverses the city for several miles. From the north, Highway 1 merges with U.S. 101 when it reaches the city limits. The wineries of the Edna Valley and Arroyo Grande Valley wine regions lie south of town off Highway 227, the parallel (to the east) Orcutt Road, and connecting roads.

SLO City Transit buses operate daily; Regional Transit Authority (SLORTA) buses connect with north county towns. The Downtown Trolley provides evening service to the city's hub every Thursday, on Friday from June to early September, and on Saturday from April through October.

ESSENTIALS

Visitor Information San Luis Obispo Chamber of Commerce ✉ *895 Monterey St.* ☎ *805/781–2777* ⊕ *www.visitslo.com.* **San Luis Obispo City Visitor Information** ⊕ *www.sanluisobispovacations.com.*

EXPLORING

TOP ATTRACTIONS

Mission San Luis Obispo de Tolosa. Sun-dappled Mission Plaza fronts the fifth mission established in 1772 by Franciscan friars. A small museum exhibits artifacts of the Chumash Indians and early Spanish settlers. ✉ *751 Palm St., at Chorro St.* ☎ *805/543–6850* ⊕ *www.missionsanluisobispo.org* ✍ *$3* ☉ *Early Mar.–early Nov., daily 9–5; early Nov.–early Mar., daily 9–4.*

Fodor'sChoice **Talley Vineyards.** Acres of Chardonnay and Pinot Noir, plus smaller
★ parcels of Sauvignon Blanc, Syrah, and other varietals blanket Talley's mountain-ringed dell in the Arroyo Grande Valley. The estate tour ($40), worth a splurge, includes wine and cheese, a visit to an 1860s adobe, and barrel-room tastings of upcoming releases. ✉ *3031 Lopez Dr., off Orcutt Rd., Arroyo Grande* ☎ *805/489–0446* ⊕ *talleyvineyards. com* ✍ *Tastings $8–$15; tours $15–$40* ☉ *Daily 10:30–4:30; tours by appointment.*

WORTH NOTING

Edna Valley Vineyard. For sweeping valley views and crisp Sauvignon Blancs and Chardonnays, head to the modern tasting bar here. ■ **TIP→** The reserve tasting ($15) is the best option here. ✉ *2585 Biddle*

Ranch Rd., off Edna Rd. ☎ *805/544–5855* 🌐 *www.ednavalleyvineyard.com* 🎫 *Tastings $10–$15* 🕒 *Daily 10–5.*

Niven Family Wine Estates. A refurbished 1909 schoolhouse serves as tasting room for six Niven Family wineries: Baileyana, Cadre, Tangent, Trenza, True Myth, and Zocker. The winemaker for all these labels is Christian Roguenant, whose Cadre Pinot Noirs are worth checking out. ✉ *5828 Orcutt Rd., at Righetti Rd.* ☎ *805/269–8200* 🌐 *www.nivenfamilywines.com* 🎫 *Tasting $12* 🕒 *Daily 10–5.*

Old Edna. This peaceful, 2-acre site once *was* the town of Edna. Nowadays you can peek at the vintage 1897 and 1908 farmhouse cottages, taste Sextant wines, pick up sandwiches at the gourmet deli, and stroll along Old Edna Lane. ✉ *1655 Old Price Canyon Rd., at Hwy. 227* ☎ *805/710–3701 Old Edna Townsite, 805/542–0133 tasting room and deli* 🌐 *oldedna.com.*

FAMILY **San Luis Obispo Children's Museum.** Activities at this facility geared to kids under age eight include an "imagination-powered" elevator that transports visitors to a series of underground caverns. Elsewhere, simulated lava and steam sputter from an active volcano. Kids can pick rubber fruit at a farmers' market and race in a fire engine to fight a fire. ✉ *1010 Nipomo St., at Monterey St.* ☎ *805/544–5437* 🌐 *www.slocm.org* 🎫 *$8* 🕒 *May–Aug., Mon.–Wed. 10–3, Thurs.–Sat. 10–5, Sun. and some holidays 1–5; Sept.–Apr., Tues. and Wed. 10–3, Thurs.–Sat. 10–5, Sun. and some holidays 1–5.*

Wolff Vineyards. Syrah, Petite Sirah, and Riesling join the expected Pinot Noir and Chardonnay as the stars at this family-run winery 6 miles south of downtown. The pourers are super-friendly, and you'll often meet one of the owners or their children in the tasting room. With its hillside views, the outdoor patio is a great place to enjoy an afternoon picnic. ✉ *6238 Orcutt Rd., near Biddle Ranch Rd.* ☎ *805/781–0448* 🌐 *www.wolffvineyards.com* 🎫 *Tasting $10* 🕒 *Daily 11–5.*

WHERE TO EAT

$$ ECLECTIC 🍴 **Big Sky Café.** Family-friendly Big Sky turns local and organically grown ingredients into global dishes, starting with breakfast. Just pick your continent: Brazilian churrasco chicken breast, Thai catfish, North African vegetable stew, Maryland crab cakes. Vegetarians have ample choices. [$] *Average main: $17* ✉ *1121 Broad St., at Higuera St.* ☎ *805/545–5401* 🌐 *bigskycafe.com* ✍ *Reservations not accepted.*

$$ NORTHERN ITALIAN 🍴 **Café Roma.** At this Railroad Square restaurant you can dine on authentic northern Italian cuisine in the warmly lit dining room or out on the covered patio. Menu favorites include ricotta-filled squash blossoms, and beef tenderloin glistening with porcini butter and a Pinot Noir reduction. [$] *Average main: $20* ✉ *1020 Railroad Ave., at Osos St.* ☎ *805/541–6800* 🌐 *www.caferomaslo.com* 🕒 *No lunch weekends.*

$$$ MODERN AMERICAN 🍴 **Foremost Wine Company.** A hip combination restaurant, wine bar, lounge, and wineshop in the Creamery building, a former dairy, Foremost focuses on community-linked food and wine and sustainable practices. The bar, dining areas, and wine store occupy a huge interior space with copper-topped tables and other furnishings made with repurposed materials. Native Parisienne chef Julie Simon oversees a seasonal menu

that typically includes small plates and dishes to share: grilled octopus, lamb tartare, roast duck crostini, and pappardelle in a duck-pork Bolognese sauce. Vegan and vegetarian options are plentiful. $ *Average main: $28* ⊠ *570 Higuera St., near Nipomo St.* ☎ *805/439–3410* ⊕ *foremostwineco.com* ⌕ *Reservations not accepted* ⊘ *Closed Mon.*

$$$
INTERNATIONAL

✕ **Luna Red.** A spacious, contemporary space with a festive outdoor patio, this restaurant near Mission Plaza serves creative tapas and cocktails. The small plates include lamb sausage flatbread, avocado-tuna ceviche, and *piquillo* peppers stuffed with goat cheese. Turkey confit in mole sauce and coconut milk-braised pork shoulder are two large plates of note. $ *Average main: $25* ⊠ *1023 Chorro St., at Monterey St.* ☎ *805/540–5243* ⊕ *www.lunaredslo.com.*

$$
ECLECTIC

✕ **Novo Restaurant & Lounge.** In the colorful dining room or on the large creek-side deck, this animated downtown eatery will take you on a culinary world tour. The salads, small plates, and entrées come from nearly every continent. The wine and beer list also covers the globe and includes local favorites. $ *Average main: $20* ⊠ *726 Higuera St., at Broad St.* ☎ *805/543–3986* ⊕ *www.novorestaurant.com.*

WHERE TO STAY

$$$
HOTEL

🏨 **Apple Farm.** Decorated to the hilt with floral bedspreads and watercolors by local artists, this Wine Country–theme hotel is highly popular. **Pros:** flowers everywhere; convenient to Cal Poly and U.S. 101; creekside setting. **Cons:** hordes of tourists during the day; some rooms too floral for some people's tastes. $ *Rooms from: $219* ⊠ *2015 Monterey St.* ☎ *800/255-2040, 805/544-2040* ⊕ *www.applefarm.com* ⤳ *104 rooms* ⦿ *No meals.*

$$$
HOTEL

🏨 **Granada Hotel & Bistro.** Built in 1922 and sparkling again after renovations completed in 2012, the Granada is the only full-service hotel in the heart of downtown. **Pros:** free parking; easy walk to downtown; luxurious rooms and amenities. **Cons:** some rooms are tiny; sometimes noisy near restaurant kitchen. $ *Rooms from: $249* ⊠ *1126 Morro St.* ☎ *805/544–9100* ⊕ *granadahotelandbistro.com* ⤳ *17 rooms* ⦿ *No meals.*

$$$
HOTEL

🏨 **Madonna Inn.** From its rococo bathrooms to its pink-on-pink froufrou steak house, the Madonna Inn is fabulous or tacky, depending on your taste. **Pros:** fun, one-of-a-kind experience; on-site horseback riding for all levels. **Cons:** rooms vary widely; must appreciate kitsch. $ *Rooms from: $189* ⊠ *100 Madonna Rd.* ☎ *805/543–3000, 800/543–9666* ⊕ *www.madonnainn.com* ⤳ *106 rooms, 4 suites* ⦿ *No meals.*

$$$
B&B/INN

🏨 **Petit Soleil.** A cobblestone courtyard, country-French custom furnishings, and Gallic music piped through the halls evoke a Provençal mood at this cheery inn. **Pros:** French details throughout; scrumptious breakfasts; cozy rooms. **Cons:** sits on a busy avenue; cramped parking. $ *Rooms from: $179* ⊠ *1473 Monterey St.* ☎ *805/549–0321, 800/676–1588* ⊕ *psslo.com* ⤳ *15 rooms, 1 suite* ⦿ *Breakfast.*

NIGHTLIFE AND PERFORMING ARTS
SLO's club scene is centered on Higuera Street, off Monterey Street.

Koberl at Blue. A trendy crowd hangs out at this upscale restaurant's slick bar to sip on exotic martinis and the many local and imported beers and wines. ⊠ *998 Monterey St., at Osos St.* ☎ *805/783–1135* ⊕ *epkoberl.com.*

Linnaea's. A mellow java joint, Linnaea's sometimes hosts poetry readings, as well as blues, jazz, and folk music performances. ⊠ *1110 Garden St., at Higuera St.* ☎ *805/541–5888* ⊕ *linnaeas.com.*

Mother's Tavern. Chicago-style MoTav draws crowds with good pub food and live entertainment in a turn-of-the-20th-century setting, complete with antique U.S. flags and a wall-mounted moose head. ⊠ *725 Higuera St., at Broad St.* ☎ *805/541–8733* ⊕ *www.motherstavern.com.*

SLO Brew. Handcrafted microbrews and live music most nights make for a winning combination at this downtown watering hole and restaurant that opened in new digs in 2015. ⊠ *1119 Garden St.* ☎ *805/543–1843* ⊕ *slobrewingco.com.*

Performing Arts Center, San Luis Obispo. A truly great performance space, the center hosts live theater, dance, and music. ⊠ *Cal Poly, 1 Grand Ave., off U.S. 101* ☎ *805/756–4849* ⊕ *www.pacslo.org.*

MORRO BAY

14 miles north of San Luis Obispo.

Commercial fishermen slog around Morro Bay in galoshes, and beat-up fishing boats bob in the bay's protected waters. Nature-oriented activities take center stage here: kayaking, hiking, biking, fishing, and wildlife-watching around the bay and national marine estuary and along the state beach.

GETTING HERE AND AROUND

From U.S. 101 south or north, exit at Highway 1 in San Luis Obispo and head west. Scenic Highway 1 passes through the eastern edge of town. From Atascadero, two-lane Highway 41 West treks over the mountains to Morro Bay. San Luis Obispo RTA Route 12 buses travel year-round between Morro Bay, San Luis Obispo, Cayucos, Cambria, San Simeon, and Hearst Castle. The Morro Bay Shuttle picks up riders throughout the town from Friday through Monday in summer ($1.25 one-way, $3 day pass).

ESSENTIALS

Visitor Information Morro Bay Visitors Center ⊠ *255 Morro Bay Blvd., at Morro Ave.* ☎ *805/225–1633, 800/231–0592* ⊕ *www.morrobay.org* ⊗ *Daily 9–5.*

EXPLORING

Embarcadero. The center of Morro Bay action on land is the Embarcadero, where vacationers pour in and out of souvenir shops and seafood restaurants and stroll or bike along the scenic half-mile Harborwalk to Morro Rock. From here, you can get out on the bay in a kayak or tour boat. ⊠ *On waterfront from Beach St. to Tidelands Park.*

FAMILY **Morro Bay State Park Museum of Natural History.** The museum's entertaining interactive exhibits explain the natural environment and how to preserve it—in the bay and estuary and on the rest of the planet. ■TIP→ **Kids age 16 and under are admitted free.** ⊠ *State Park Rd.,* *south of downtown* ☎ *805/772–2694* ⊕ *www.ccnha.org/morrobay* 🎫 *$3* ⊗ *Daily 10–5.*

Morro Rock. At the mouth of Morro Bay stands 576-foot-high Morro Rock, one of nine small volcanic peaks, or morros, in the area. A short walk leads to a breakwater, with the harbor on one side and crashing ocean waves on the other. You may not climb the rock, where endangered falcons and other birds nest. Sea lions and otters often play in the water below the rock. ⊠ *Northern end of Embarcadero.*

WHERE TO EAT

$$
SEAFOOD
✕ **Dorn's Original Breakers Cafe.** This restaurant overlooking the harbor has satisfied local appetites since 1942. In addition to straight-ahead dishes such as cod or shrimp fish-and-chips or calamari tubes sautéed in butter and wine, Dorn's serves breakfast. 🈺 *Average main: $22* ⊠ *801 Market Ave., at Morro Bay Blvd.* ☎ *805/772–4415* ⊕ *dornscafe.com.*

$
SOUTHWESTERN
✕ **Taco Temple.** This family-run diner serves some of the freshest food around. The seafood-heavy menu includes salmon burritos, superb fish tacos with mango salsa, and other dishes hailing from somewhere between California and Mexico. 🈺 *Average main: $15* ⊠ *2680 Main St., at Elena St., just north of Hwy. 1/Hwy. 41 junction* ☎ *805/772–4965* 🚫 *Reservations not accepted* ▭ *No credit cards* ⊗ *Closed Tues.*

$$$
SEAFOOD
✕ **Windows on the Water.** Diners at this second-floor restaurant view the sunset through giant picture windows. Meanwhile, fresh fish and other dishes based on local ingredients emerge from the wood-fired oven in the open kitchen, and oysters on the half shell beckon from the raw bar. The California-centric wine list includes about 20 selections poured by the glass. 🈺 *Average main: $30* ⊠ *699 Embarcadero, at Pacific St.* ☎ *805/772–0677* ⊕ *www.windowsmb.com* ⊗ *No lunch.*

WHERE TO STAY

$$$
B&B/INN
Fodor's Choice
★
🏨 **Anderson Inn.** Friendly, personalized service and an oceanfront setting keep loyal patrons returning to this Embarcadero inn. **Pros:** walk to restaurants and sights; spacious rooms; attentive service. **Cons:** not low-budget; waterfront area can get crowded. 🈺 *Rooms from: $249* ⊠ *897 Embarcadero* ☎ *805/772–3434, 866/950–3434 toll-free reservations* ⊕ *andersoninnmorrobay.com* 🛏 *8 rooms* 🍽 *No meals.*

$$$$
B&B/INN
🏨 **Cass House.** In tiny Cayucos, 4 miles north of Morro Bay, a shipping pioneer's 1867 home is now a luxurious bed-and-breakfast surrounded by rose and other gardens. **Pros:** historic property; some ocean views; excellent meals. **Cons:** away from nightlife and attractions; not good for families. 🈺 *Rooms from: $265* ⊠ *222 N. Ocean Ave., Cayucos* ☎ *805/995–3669* ⊕ *casshouseinn.com* 🛏 *4 rooms* 🍽 *Breakfast.*

$$$
HOTEL
🏨 **Embarcadero Inn.** The rooms at this waterfront hotel are cheery and welcoming, and many have fireplaces. **Pros:** across from waterfront. **Cons:** tiny lobby; no pool. 🈺 *Rooms from: $185* ⊠ *456 Embarcadero* ☎ *805/772–2700, 800/292–7625* ⊕ *www.embarcaderoinn.com* 🛏 *29 rooms, 4 suites* 🍽 *Breakfast.*

SPORTS AND THE OUTDOORS

Kayak Horizons. This outfit rents kayaks and paddleboards and gives lessons and guided tours. ⊠ *551 Embarcadero, near Marina St.* ☎ *805/772–6444* ⊕ *kayakhorizons.com.*

Sub-Sea Tours & Kayaks. You can view sea life aboard this outfit's glass-bottom boat, watch whales from its catamaran, or rent a kayak or canoe. ⊠ *699 Embarcadero* ☎ *805/772–9463* ⊕ *subseatours.com.*

Virg's Landing. Virg's conducts deep-sea-fishing and whale-watching trips. ⊠ *1169 Market Ave.* ☎ *805/772–1222* ⊕ *virgslanding.com.*

PASO ROBLES

30 miles north of San Luis Obispo; 25 miles northwest of Morro Bay.

In the 1860s, tourists began flocking to this ranching outpost to "take the cure" in a bathhouse fed by underground mineral hot springs. An Old West town emerged, and grand Victorian homes went up, followed in the 20th century by Craftsman bungalows. These days, the wooded hills of Paso Robles west of U.S. 101 and the flatter, more open land to the freeway's east hold more than 250 wineries, many with tasting rooms. Hot summer days, cool nights, and varied soils and microclimates allow growers to cultivate an impressive array of Bordeaux, Rhône, and other grape types. Cabernet Sauvignon grows well in the Paso Robles AVA—32,000 of its 600,000-plus acres are planted to grapes—as do Petit Verdot, Grenache, Syrah, Viognier, and Zinfandel. In recognition of the diverse growing conditions, the AVA was divided into 11 subappellations in 2014. Pick up a wine-touring map at lodgings, wineries, and attractions around town. The fee at most tasting rooms is between $5 and $15; many lodgings pass out discount coupons.

Upmarket restaurants, bars, antiques stores, and little shops fill the streets around oak-shaded City Park, where special events of all kinds—custom car shows, an olive festival, Friday-night summer concerts—take place on many weekends. Despite its increasing sophistication, Paso (as the locals call it) retains a small-town vibe. The city celebrates its cowboy roots in late July and early August with the two-week California Mid-State Fair, complete with livestock auctions, carnival rides, and corn dogs.

GETTING HERE AND AROUND

U.S. 101 runs north–south through Paso Robles. Highway 46 West links Paso Robles to Highway 1 and Cambria on the coast. Highway 46 East connects Paso Robles with Interstate 5 and the San Joaquin Valley. Public transit is not convenient for wine touring and sightseeing.

Visitor Information Paso Robles CAB Collective ☎ *888/963–9934* ⊕ *pasoroblescab.com.* **Paso Robles Wine Country Alliance** ☎ *805/239-8463, 800/549-9463* ⊕ *www.pasowine.com.* **Rhone Rangers/Paso Robles** ⊕ *rhonerangers.org/pasorobles.* **Paso Robles Visitor Center** ⊠ *1225 Park St., near 12th St.* ☎ *805/238-0506* ⊕ *travelpaso.com.*

EXPLORING

TOP ATTRACTIONS

Fodor'sChoice ★ **Calcareous Vineyard.** Elegant wines, a stylish tasting room, and knockout hilltop views make for a winning experience at this winery along winding Peachy Canyon Road. Cabernet Sauvignon, Syrah, and Zinfandel grapes thrive in the summer heat and limestone soils of the two vineyards near the tasting room, and a third vineyard on cooler York Mountain produces Pinot Noir, Chardonnay, and a Cabernet with a completely different character from the Peachy Canyon edition. ■TIP➔ The picnic area's expansive eastward views invite lingering. ⊠ 3430 Peachy Canyon Rd. ☎ 805/239-0289 ⊕ calcareous.com ✆ Tasting $10; tour and tasting (reservations required) $35 ⊙ Daily 11–5.

FAMILY **Estrella Warbirds Museum.** An entertaining homage to fighter planes, flyboys, and flygirls, this museum maintains indoor exhibits about wartime aviation and displays retired specimens (of planes) outdoors and in repair shops. Bonus attraction: a huge building with spruced-up autos, drag racers, and "funny cars." ⊠ 4251 Dry Creek Rd., off Airport Rd., north off Hwy. 46E ☎ 805/227-0440 ⊕ ewarbirds.org ✆ $10 ⊙ Thurs.–Sun. and Mon. legal holidays 10–4.

Firestone Walker Brewing Company. At this working craft brewery you can sample medal-winners such as the Double Barrel Ale and learn about the beer-making process on 30-minute guided tours of the brew house and cellar. ⊠ 1400 Ramada Dr., east side of U.S. 101; exit at Hwy. 46 W/Cambria, but head east ☎ 805/225-5911 ⊕ www.firestonebeer.com ✆ Tastings $1.50–$3 per sample, tour free ⊙ Daily 10–5; tours on the half hr Fri.–Sun. 10:30–4:30, Mon.–Thurs. by appointment.

Halter Ranch Vineyard. A good place to learn about contemporary Paso Robles wine making, this ultramodern operation produces high-quality wines from estate-grown Bordeaux and Rhône grapes grown in sustainably farmed vineyards. The gravity-flow winery, which you can view on tours, is a marvel of efficiency. Ancestor, the flagship wine, a potent Bordeaux-style blend of Cabernet Sauvignon, Petit Verdot, and Malbec, is named for the ranch's huge centuries-old coast oak tree. ⊠ 8910 Adelaida Rd., at Vineyard Dr. ☎ 888/367-9977 ⊕ www.halterranch.com ✆ Tasting $10 ⊙ Daily 11–5; winery/cave tour weekends at 11, noon, and 1 (reservations required), weekdays by appointment.

Fodor'sChoice ★ **HammerSky Vineyards.** Owner Doug Hauck bucks a few trends by focusing on Merlot and Zinfandel, two varietals of variable popularity in recent years. Hauck makes excellent small lots of each, along with a Merlot-heavy Bordeaux-style blend; on the lighter side are Sauvignon Blanc and a Rosé of Zinfandel. Set amid rolling hills of vineyards punctuated by a huge oak, HammerSky's bright-white contemporary structure houses both the tasting and barrel-aging rooms; an outdoor patio has views of the estate vines. ⊠ 7725 Vineyard Dr., at Jensen Rd. ☎ 805/239-0930 ⊕ www.hammersky.com ✆ Tasting $10 ⊙ Thurs.–Sun. 11–5 (closes on some summer days at 3:30 for weddings).

Fodor'sChoice ★ **Jada Vineyard & Winery.** Winemaker David Galzignato, formerly of the Napa Valley's Charles Krug Winery, crafts Jada's nuanced, highly structured wines. Two worth checking out are Jack of Hearts, starring Petit

Verdot, and Passing By, a Cabernet-heavy blend. Galzignato also shines with Tannat and with Rhône-style wines, particularly Grenache. At tastings, the wines are paired with gourmet cheeses or organic chocolates. ✉ *5620 Vineyard Dr., north of Hwy. 46 W* ☎ *805/226–4200* ⊕ *jadavineyard.com* ✎ *Tastings $10–$15* ⊙ *Daily 11–5.*

Fodor'sChoice ★ **Justin Vineyards & Winery.** Suave Justin built its reputation—and, claim some, the Paso Robles wine region's as well—on Isosceles, a hearty Bordeaux blend, usually of Cabernet Sauvignon, Cabernet Franc, and Merlot. Justin's Cabernet Sauvignon is also well regarded, as is the Right Angle blend of Cab and three

> ## SIP CERTIFICATION
>
> Many wineries in Paso Robles take pride in being SIP (Sustainability in Practice) Certified, for which they undergo a rigorous third-party audit of their entire operations. Water and energy conservation practices are reviewed, along with pest management and other aspects of farming. Also considered are the wages, benefits, and working conditions of the employees, and the steps taken to mitigate the impact of grape growing and wine production on area habitats.

other varietals. Tastings here take place in an expansive room whose equally expansive windows provide views of Justin's hillside vineyards. ✉ *11680 Chimney Rock Rd., 15 miles west of U.S. 101's Hwy 46 E exit; take 24th St. west and follow road (name changes along the way) to Chimney Rock Rd.* ☎ *805/238–6932, 800/726–0049* ⊕ *justinwine.com* ✎ *Tasting $15, tour and tasting $20* ⊙ *Daily 10–4:30; tours 10 and 2:30 (reservations recommended).*

Fodor'sChoice ★ **Pasolivo.** While touring the idyllic west side of Paso Robles, take a break from wine tasting by stopping at Pasolivo. Find out how the artisans here make their Tuscan-style olive oils on a high-tech Italian press, and test the acclaimed results. ✉ *8530 Vineyard Dr., west off U.S. 101 (Exit 224) or Hwy. 46 W (Exit 228)* ☎ *805/227–0186* ⊕ *www.pasolivo.com* ✎ *Free* ⊙ *Daily 11–5.*

Tablas Creek Vineyard. Tucked in the western hills of Paso Robles, Tablas Creek is known for its blends of organically grown, hand-harvested Rhône varietals. Roussanne and Viognier are the standout whites; the Mourvèdre-heavy blend called Panoplie (it also includes Grenache and Syrah) has received high praise in recent years. ■TIP→ **There's a fine picnic area here.** ✉ *9339 Adelaida Rd., west of Vineyard Dr.* ☎ *805/237–1231* ⊕ *www.tablascreek.com* ✎ *Tasting $10 (reserve $40 by appointment), tour free* ⊙ *Daily 10–5; tour 10:30 and 2 by appointment.*

WORTH NOTING

Paso Robles Pioneer Museum. The delightful museum's one-room schoolhouse and its displays of ranching paraphernalia, horse-drawn vehicles, hot-springs artifacts, and photos evoke Paso's rural heritage. ✉ *2010 Riverside Ave., at 21st St.* ☎ *805/239–4556* ⊕ *www.pasoroblespioneermuseum.org* ✎ *Free* ⊙ *Thurs.–Sun. 1–4.*

Villa San-Juliette Vineyard & Winery. Two *American Idol* producers established this winery northeast of Paso Robles. With a cast that includes Petit Verdot, a fine Grenache, and a perky Albariño (a Spanish white varietal), their stylish operation is no flash in the pan. From 11 to 4 you can order snacks, panini, pizzas, soup and salad, and cheese and charcuterie plates to enjoy with your wine in the tasting room or on the view-filled outdoor terrace. ⊠ *6385 Cross Canyons Rd., at Ranchita Canyon Rd., San Miguel* ☎ *805/467–0014* ⊕ *www.villasanjuliette.com* ▤ *Tasting $10* ⊙ *Daily 11–5.*

WHERE TO EAT

$$$ ✕**Artisan.** Innovative variations on traditional American comfort cuisine
AMERICAN and an urban vibe have made this bistro a hit with winemakers, locals, and tourists. Chef Chris Kobayashi uses regional, organic, wild-caught ingredients to put a fresh spin on dishes such as rabbit Stroganoff, boar tenderloin with fennel risotto, and wild king salmon with succotash and bacon. There's often a fine wood-fired pizza with duck confit, kale, and charred onions. ■TIP➔ **Save room for home-style desserts that include sundaes, puddings, cakes, and cookies.** $ *Average main: $30* ⊠ *843 12th St., at Pine St.* ☎ *805/237–8084* ⊕ *artisanpasorobles.com.*

$$$ ✕**Bistro Laurent.** Owner-chef Laurent Grangien's handsome, welcoming
FRENCH French bistro occupies an 1890s brick building across from City Park. He focuses on traditional dishes such as duck confit, rack of lamb, and onion soup, but always prepares a few au courant daily specials as well. The wines, sourced from the adjacent wineshop, come from around the world. $ *Average main: $28* ⊠ *1202 Pine St., at 12th St.* ☎ *805/226–8191* ⊕ *www.bistrolaurent.com* ⊙ *Closed Sun. and Mon.*

$$$ ✕**Il Cortile.** One of two Paso establishments owned by chef Santos Mac-
MODERN ITALIAN Donal and his wife, Carole, this Italian restaurant entices diners with
Fodor'sChoice complex flavors and a contemporary space with art-deco overtones.
★ Consistent crowd-pleasers often on the menu include beef carpaccio with white truffle cream sauce and shaved black truffles; pork osso buco, perhaps served with Parmesan herb risotto; and braised beef cheeks over white polenta. ■TIP➔ **Carole selected the Central Coast and Italian wines here specifically to pair with Santos's dishes; it's worth asking her or your waiter for suggestions.** $ *Average main: $26* ⊠ *608 12th St., near Spring St.* ☎ *805/226–0300* ⊕ *ilcortileristorante. com* ⊙ *Closed Tues. No lunch.*

$$$ ✕**La Cosecha.** At barlike, tin-ceilinged La Cosecha (Spanish for "the har-
SOUTH vest"), Honduran-born chef Santos MacDonal faithfully re-creates dishes
AMERICAN from Spain and South America that pair well with the restaurant's craft
Fodor'sChoice beers, cocktails, and white-wine sangria and other wines. Noteworthy
★ starters include *pastelitos catracho*, Honduran-style empanadas in a light tomato sauce served with *queso fresco* (fresh cheese) and micro cilantro. If it's on the menu, consider trying the *moqueca*, a Brazilian seafood stew in a piquant coconut-milk base. $ *Average main: $29* ⊠ *835 12th St., near Pine St.* ☎ *805/237–0019* ⊕ *lacosechabr.com* ⊙ *Closed Mon.*

$$$ ✕**McPhee's Grill.** Just south of Paso Robles in tiny Templeton, this casual
AMERICAN chophouse in an 1860s wood-frame storefront serves sophisticated, contemporary versions of traditional Western fare such as oak-grilled filet mignon and fresh seafood tostadas. The house-label wines, made especially for the restaurant, are quite good. $ *Average main: $25* ⊠ *416 S. Main St., at 5th St., Templeton* ☎ *805/434–3204* ⊕ *mcphees-grill.com* ⊙ *No lunch Sun.*

$$ FRENCH 🍴 **Panolivo Family Bistro.** Affordable French fare draws patrons to this café north of the town square. For breakfast, try a fresh pastry or quiche, or build your own omelet. Lunch and dinner choices include sandwiches, salads, and fresh pastas—including cannelloni stuffed with vegetables or stewed beef—along with traditional dishes such as snails baked in garlic-butter sauce and beef bourguignon. ■ **TIP→ At $30, the three-course prix-fixe dinner option is a good value.** [$] *Average main: $20* ✉ *1344 Park St., at 14th St.* ☎ *805/239–3366* 🌐 *www.panolivo.com.*

$$ MODERN AMERICAN Fodor's Choice ★ 🍴 **Thomas Hill Organics Market Bistro & Wine Bar.** Chef Christopher Manning, whose previous stops include the Napa Valley restaurant of sparkling-wine maker Domaine Chandon, brings French flair and finesse to this brick-walled downtown favorite. The menu might include seared scallops flavorfully matched with pork belly and served on creamy polenta; tender pan-roasted duck with braised fennel, pomegranate, and persimmon; and beef tenderloin with a Cabernet Sauvignon bordelaise. The wine list celebrates local wines. With many by the half-glass, you can sample a good cross-section. [$] *Average main: $17* ✉ *1313 Park St., at 13th St.* ☎ *805/226–5888* 🌐 *thomashillorganics.com.*

WHERE TO STAY

$$$$ HOTEL Fodor's Choice ★ 🏨 **Hotel Cheval.** Equestrian themes surface throughout this intimate, European-style boutique hotel a half-block from the main square and near some of Paso's best restaurants. **Pros:** near downtown restaurants; sophisticated; personal service. **Cons:** views aren't great; no pool or hot tub. [$] *Rooms from: $330* ✉ *1021 Pine St.* ☎ *805/226–9995, 866/522–6999* 🌐 *www.hotelcheval.com* 🛏 *16 rooms* 🍽 *Breakfast.*

$$$ HOTEL 🏨 **La Bellasera Hotel & Suites.** The swankest full-service hotel for miles around, La Bellasera caters to those looking for high-tech amenities and easy access to major Central Coast roadways. **Pros:** convenient to highways; tons of amenities. **Cons:** far from downtown; at a major intersection. [$] *Rooms from: $199* ✉ *206 Alexa Ct.* ☎ *805/238–2834, 866/782–9669* 🌐 *labellasera.com* 🛏 *35 rooms, 25 suites* 🍽 *No meals.*

$$ HOTEL 🏨 **La Quinta Inn & Suites.** A good value for Paso Robles, this three-story chain property attracts heavy repeat business with its upbeat staff and slew of perks. **Pros:** quiet; well maintained; upbeat staff; good for leisure or business travelers; pet-friendly; free weekday wine-tasting sessions. **Cons:** conventional decor. [$] *Rooms from: $155* ✉ *2615 Buena Vista Dr.* ☎ *805/239–3004, 800/753–3757* 🌐 *www.laquintapasorobles.com* 🛏 *101 rooms and suites* 🍽 *Breakfast.*

$$ HOTEL 🏨 **Paso Robles Inn.** On the site of an old spa hotel of the same name, the inn is built around a lush, shaded garden with a pool. **Pros:** private spring-fed hot tubs; historic property; across from town square. **Cons:** fronts a busy street; rooms vary in size and amenities. [$] *Rooms from: $139* ✉ *1103 Spring St.* ☎ *805/238–2660, 800/676–1713* 🌐 *pasoroblesinn.com* 🛏 *92 rooms, 6 suites* 🍽 *No meals.*

$$$$ B&B/INN Fodor's Choice ★ 🏨 **SummerWood Inn.** Easygoing hospitality, vineyard-view rooms, and elaborate breakfasts make this inn a mile west of U.S. 101 worth seeking out. **Pros:** convenient wine-touring base; accommodating staff; elaborate breakfasts; complimentary tastings at associated winery. **Cons:**

some noise from nearby highway during the day. [$] *Rooms from: $275* ✉ *2130 Arbor Rd., 1 mile west of U.S. 101, at Hwy. 46W* ☎ *805/227–1111* 🌐 *www.summerwoodwine.com/inn* 🛏 *9 rooms* 🍴 *Breakfast.*

PERFORMING ARTS

Vina Robles Amphitheatre. At this 3,300-seat, Mission-style venue with good food, wine, and sight lines, you can enjoy acclaimed musicians in concert. ✉ *Vina Robles winery, 3800 Mill Rd., off Hwy. 46* ☎ *805/227–4812* 🌐 *vinarobles.com* 🕒 *May–Nov.*

CAMBRIA

28 miles west of Paso Robles; 20 miles north of Morro Bay.

Cambria, set on piney hills above the sea, was settled by Welsh miners in the 1890s. In the 1970s the isolated setting attracted artists and other independent types; the town now caters to tourists, but it still bears the imprint of its bohemian past. Both of Cambria's downtowns, the original East Village and the newer West Village, are packed with art and crafts galleries, antiques shops, cafés, restaurants, and bed-and-breakfasts.

Two diverting detours lie between Morro Bay and Cambria. In the laid-back beach town of **Cayucos,** 4 miles north of Morro Bay, you can stroll the long pier, feast on chowder (at Duckie's), and sample the namesake delicacies of the Brown Butter Cookie Co. Over in **Harmony,** a cute former dairy town 7 miles south of Cambria, you can take in the glassworks, pottery, and other artsy enterprises.

GETTING HERE AND AROUND

Highway 1 leads to Cambria from the north and south. Highway 246 West curves from U.S. 101 through the mountains to Cambria. San Luis Obispo RTA Route 12 buses stop in Cambria (and Hearst Castle).

ESSENTIALS

Visitor Information Cambria Chamber of Commerce ☎ *805/927–3624* 🌐 *cambriachamber.org.*

EXPLORING

Fiscalini Ranch Preserve. Walk along a mile-long coastal bluff trail to spot migrating whales, otters, and shore birds at this 450-acre public open space. Miles of additional scenic trails crisscross the protected habitats of rare and endangered species of flora and fauna, including a Monterey pine forest, western pond turtles, monarch butterflies, and burrowing owls. Dogs are permitted on-leash everywhere and off-leash on all trails except the bluff. ✉ *Hwy. 1, between Cambria Rd. and Main St. to the north, and Burton Dr. and Warren Rd. to the south; access either end of bluff trail off Windsor Blvd.* ☎ *805/927–2856* 🌐 *ffrpcambria.org.*

Leffingwell Landing. A state picnic ground, the landing is a good place for examining tidal pools and watching otters as they frolic in the surf. ✉ *North end of Moonstone Beach Dr., Cambria* ☎ *805/927–2070.*

Moonstone Beach Drive. The drive runs along a bluff above the ocean, paralleled by a 3-mile boardwalk that winds along the beach. On this photogenic walk you might glimpse sea lions and sea otters, and perhaps a gray whale during winter and spring. Year-round, birds fly about, and tiny creatures scurry amid the tidepools. ✉ *Off Hwy. 1.*

WHERE TO EAT

$$ MODERN AMERICAN 🍴 **Centrally Grown.** A collection of sustainably conscious spaces fashioned from repurposed materials, Centrally Grown encompasses a deli and market, exotic gardens, and a second-floor restaurant with fantastic views of San Simeon Bay and the Big Sur Coast. At the market and deli (open daily from 8 to 7), you can pick up organic and natural food to go or to enjoy in the gardens. The restaurant, decorated in a "planet-friendly chic" style that includes a driftwood archway, serves classic California cuisine with global influences. The colorful gardens, dense with native and water-wise plants and exotic varietals, are well worth a stroll. [$] *Average main: $18* ✉ *7432 Exotic Garden Dr., off Hwy. 1, Cambria* ☎ *800/717–4379* 🌐 *centrallygrown.com.*

$$ AMERICAN FAMILY 🍴 **Linn's Restaurant.** Homemade olallieberry pies, soups, potpies, and other farmhouse comfort foods share the menu at this spacious East Village restaurant with fancier farm-to-table dishes such as organic, free-range chicken topped with raspberry-orange-cranberry sauce. Also on-site are a bakery, a café serving more casual fare (take-out available), and a gift shop that sells gourmet foods. [$] *Average main: $21* ✉ *2277 Main St., at Wall St., Cambria* ☎ *805/927–0371* 🌐 *www.linnsfruitbin.com.*

$$ ECLECTIC 🍴 **Robin's.** A multiethnic, vegetarian-friendly dining experience awaits you at this cozy East Village cottage. Dinner choices include wild prawn enchiladas, Moroccan-spiced grilled salmon, Japanese scallops, and short ribs. Lunchtime's extensive salad and sandwich menu embraces burgers and tofu alike. ■ **TIP→ Unless it's raining, ask for a table on the secluded (heated) garden patio.** [$] *Average main: $22* ✉ *4095 Burton Dr., at Center St., Cambria* ☎ *805/927–5007* 🌐 *robinsrestaurant.com.*

$$$ SEAFOOD Fodor's Choice ★ 🍴 **Sea Chest Oyster Bar and Restaurant.** Cambria's best place for seafood fills up soon after it opens at 5:30. Those in the know grab seats at the oyster bar and take in spectacular sunsets while watching the chefs broil fresh halibut, steam garlicky clams, and fry crispy calamari steaks. If you arrive to a wait, play cribbage or checkers in the game room. [$] *Average main: $28* ✉ *6216 Moonstone Beach Dr., near Weymouth St., Cambria* ☎ *805/927–4514* 🌐 *www.seachestrestaurant.com* ✍ *Reservations not accepted* 💳 *No credit cards* 🕒 *Closed Tues. mid-Sept.–May. No lunch.*

WHERE TO STAY

$ HOTEL 🏨 **Bluebird Inn.** This sweet motel in Cambria's East Village sits amid beautiful gardens along Santa Rosa Creek. **Pros:** excellent value; well-kept gardens; friendly staff. **Cons:** few frills; basic rooms; on Cambria's main drag; not on beach. [$] *Rooms from: $90* ✉ *1880 Main St., Cambria* ☎ *805/927–4634, 800/552–5434* 🌐 *bluebirdmotel.com* 🛏 *37 rooms* 🍽 *No meals.*

$$ RESORT 🏨 **Cambria Pines Lodge.** This 25-acre retreat up the hill from the East Village is a good choice for families. **Pros:** short walk from downtown; many recreational facilities; verdant gardens; spacious grounds. **Cons:** service and housekeeping not always top-quality; some units need updating. [$] *Rooms from: $149* ✉ *2905 Burton Dr., Cambria*

☎ *805/927–4200, 800/966–6490* 🌐 *www.cambriapineslodge.com* 🛏 *77 rooms, 75 suites* 🍴 *Breakfast.*

$$$ B&B/INN 🏨 **J. Patrick House.** Monterey pines and flower gardens surround this Irish-theme inn, which sits on a hilltop above Cambria's East Village. **Pros:** fantastic breakfasts; friendly innkeepers; quiet neighborhood. **Cons:** few rooms; fills up quickly. [$] *Rooms from: $185* ✉ *2990 Burton Dr., Cambria* ☎ *805/927–3812, 800/341–5258* 🌐 *jpatrickhouse.com* 🛏 *8 rooms* 🍴 *Breakfast.*

$$ HOTEL 🏨 **Moonstone Landing.** This up-to-date motel's amenities, reasonable rates, and accommodating staff make it a Moonstone Beach winner. **Pros:** sleek furnishings; across from the beach; cheery lounge. **Cons:** narrow property; some rooms overlook a parking lot. [$] *Rooms from: $125* ✉ *6240 Moonstone Beach Dr., Cambria* ☎ *805/927–0012, 800/830–4540* 🌐 *www.moonstonelanding.com* 🛏 *29 rooms* 🍴 *Breakfast.*

SAN SIMEON

9 miles north of Cambria; 65 miles south of Big Sur.

Whalers founded San Simeon in the 1850s, but had virtually abandoned it by 1865, when Senator George Hearst began purchasing most of the surrounding ranch land. Hearst turned San Simeon into a bustling port, and his son, William Randolph Hearst, further developed the area while erecting Hearst Castle. Today San Simeon is basically a strip of unremarkable gift shops and so-so motels that straddle Highway 1 about 4 miles south of the castle's entrance, but **Old San Simeon,** right across from the entrance, is worth a peek. Julia Morgan, William Randolph Hearst's architect, designed some of the village's Mission Revival–style buildings.

GETTING HERE AND AROUND

Highway 1 is the only way to reach San Simeon. Connect with the highway off U.S. 101 directly or via rural routes such as Highway 41 West (Atascadero to Morro Bay) and Highway 46 West (Paso Robles to Cambria).

EXPLORING

TOP ATTRACTIONS

Fodor's Choice ★ **Hearst Castle.** Officially known as "Hearst San Simeon State Historical Monument," Hearst Castle sits in solitary splendor atop La Cuesta Encantada (the Enchanted Hill). Its buildings and gardens spread over 127 acres that were the heart of newspaper magnate William Randolph Hearst's 250,000-acre ranch. Hearst commissioned renowned California architect Julia Morgan to design the estate, but he was very much involved with the final product, a blend of Italian, Spanish, and Moorish styles. The 115-room main structure and three huge "cottages" are connected by terraces and staircases and surrounded by pools, gardens, and statuary. In its heyday the castle, whose buildings hold about 22,000 works of fine and decorative art, was a playground for Hearst and his guests—Hollywood celebrities, political leaders, scientists, and other well-known figures. Construction began in 1919 and was never officially completed. Work was halted in 1947 when Hearst had to leave San Simeon because of failing health. The Hearst Corporation donated the property to the State of California in 1958, and it is now part of the state park system.

Access to the castle is through the visitor center at the foot of the hill, where you can view educational exhibits and a 40-minute film about Hearst's life and the castle's construction. Buses from the center zigzag up to the hilltop estate, where guides conduct four daytime tours, each with a different focus: Grand Rooms, Upstairs Suites, Designing the Dream, and Cottages and Kitchen. These tours take about three hours and include the movie and time at the end to explore the castle's exterior and gardens. In spring and fall, docents in period costume portray Hearst's guests and staff for the Evening Tour, which begins around sunset. Reservations are recommended for all tours, which include a ½-mile walk and between 150 and 400 stairs. ⊠ *San Simeon State Park, 750 Hearst Castle Rd.* ☎ *800/444-4445* ⊕ *www.hearstcastle.org* 🎫 *Daytime tours $25, evening tours $36* ☉ *Tours daily 9–3:20, later in summer; additional tours take place most Fri. and Sat. evenings Mar.–May and Sept.–Dec.*

FAMILY **Piedras Blancas Elephant Seal Rookery.** A large colony of elephant seals (at last count 17,000 members) gathers every year at Piedras Blancas Elephant Seal Rookery, on the beaches near Piedras Blancas Lighthouse. The huge males with their pendulous, trunklike noses typically start appearing on shore in late November, and the females begin to arrive in December to give birth—most babies are born in the last two weeks of January. The newborn pups spend about four weeks nursing before their mothers head out to sea, leaving them on their own; the "weaners" leave the rookery when they are about 3½ months old. The seals return in the spring and summer months to molt or rest, but not en masse as in winter. You can watch them from a boardwalk along the bluffs just a few feet above the beach; do not attempt to approach them, as they are wild animals. The nonprofit Friends of the Elephant Seal runs a small visitor center and gift shop at 250 San Simeon Avenue in San Simeon. ⊠ *Off Hwy. 1, 4½ miles north of Hearst Castle, just south of Piedras Blancas Lighthouse* ☎ *805/924-1628* ⊕ *elephantseal.org.*

Piedras Blancas Light Station. If you think traversing craggy, twisting Highway 1 is tough, imagine trying to navigate a boat up the rocky coastline (*piedras blancas* means "white rocks" in Spanish) near San Simeon before lighthouses were built. Captains must have cheered wildly when the beam began to shine here in 1875. Try to time a visit to include a morning tour (reservations not required). ■TIP➜ **Do not meet at the gate to the lighthouse—you'll miss the tour. Meet your guide instead at the former Piedras Blancas Motel, a mile and a half north of the light station.** ☎ *805/927-7361* ⊕ *piedrasblancas.org* 🎫 *$10* ☉ *Tour at 9:45, mid-June–Aug. Mon.–Sat.; Sept.–mid-June Tues., Thurs., and Sat.; no tour on national holidays* ☞ *No pets allowed.*

WORTH NOTING

Hearst Ranch Winery. Old whaling equipment and Hearst Ranch and Hearst Castle memorabilia decorate this winery's casual Old San Simeon outpost. The tasting room occupies part of Sebastian's, a former whaling store built in 1852 and moved by oxen to its present location in 1878. The flagship wines include a Bordeaux-style red blend with Petite Sirah added to round out the flavor, and Rhône-style white and red blends. Malbec and Tempranillo are two other strong suits. ■TIP→ Templeton chef Ian McPhee serves burgers and other lunch items at the adjacent deli, whose outdoor patio is a delight in good weather. ⊠ *442 SLO San Simeon Rd., off Hwy. 1* ☎ *805/467–2241* ⊕ *www.hearstranchwinery.com* ☕ *Tasting $10* ☉ *Daily 11–5.*

BEACHES

William Randolph Hearst Memorial Beach. This wide, sandy beach edges a protected cove on both sides of San Simeon Pier. Fish from the pier or from a charter boat, picnic and barbecue on the bluffs, or boogie board or bodysurf the relatively gentle waves. In summer you can rent a kayak and paddle out into the bay for close encounters with marine life and sea caves. The NOAA Coastal Discovery Center, next to the parking lot, has interactive exhibits and hosts educational activities and events. **Amenities:** food and drink; parking; toilets; water sports. **Best for:** sunset; swimming; walking. ⊠ *750 Hearst Castle Rd., off Hwy. 1, west of Hearst Castle entrance* ☎ *805/927–2020, 805/927–6575 Coastal Discovery Center* ⊕ *www.parks.ca.gov* ☕ *Free* ☉ *Beach daily sunrise–sunset; Discovery Center Fri.–Sun. and holidays 11–5.*

WHERE TO STAY

$$$ ⌂ **Best Western Cavalier Oceanfront Resort.** Reasonable rates, an ocean-
HOTEL front location, evening bonfires, and well-equipped rooms—some with wood-burning fireplaces and private patios—make this motel a great choice. **Pros:** on the bluffs; fantastic views; close to Hearst Castle. **Cons:** room amenities and sizes vary; pools are small and sometimes crowded. Ⓢ *Rooms from: $189* ⊠ *9415 Hearst Dr.* ☎ *805/927–4688, 800/826–8168* ⊕ *www.cavalierresort.com* ⤳ *90 rooms* ⦿*No meals.*

BIG SUR COASTLINE

Long a retreat of artists and writers, Big Sur is a place of ancient forests and rugged shoreline, stretching 90 miles from San Simeon to Carmel. Residents have protected it from overdevelopment, and much of the region lies within several state parks and the more than 165,000-acre Ventana Wilderness, itself part of the Los Padres National Forest.

ESSENTIALS

Visitor Information Big Sur Chamber of Commerce ☎ *831/667–2100* ⊕ *bigsurcalifornia.org.*

SOUTHERN BIG SUR

Hwy. 1 from San Simeon to Julia Pfeiffer Burns State Park.

This especially rugged stretch of oceanfront is a rocky world of mountains, cliffs, and beaches.

GETTING HERE AND AROUND

Highway 1 is the only major access route from north or south. From the south, access Highway 1 from U.S. 101 in San Luis Obispo. From the north, take rural route Highway 46 West (Paso Robles to Cambria) or

Highway 41 West (Atascadero to Morro Bay). Nacimiento-Fergusson Road snakes through mountains and forest from U.S. 101 at Jolon about 25 miles to Highway 1 at Kirk Creek, about 4 miles south of Lucia; this curving, at times precipitous road is a motorcyclist favorite, not recommended for the faint of heart or during inclement weather.

EXPLORING

Fodor's Choice ★ **Highway 1.** One of California's most spectacular drives, Highway 1 snakes up the coast north of San Simeon. Numerous pullouts along the way offer tremendous views and photo ops. On some of the beaches huge elephant seals lounge nonchalantly, seemingly oblivious to the attention of rubberneckers. Heavy rain sometimes causes mudslides that block the highway north and south of Big Sur. 🌐 *www.dot.ca.gov.*

Fodor's Choice ★ **Julia Pfeiffer Burns State Park.** The park provides fine hiking, from an easy ½-mile stroll with marvelous coastal views to a strenuous 6-mile trek through redwoods. The big draw here, an 80-foot waterfall that drops into the ocean, gets crowded in summer; still, it's an astounding place to contemplate nature. Migrating whales, harbor seals, and sea lions can sometimes be spotted just offshore. ✉ *Hwy. 1, 15 miles north of Lucia* ☎ *831/667–2315* 🌐 *www.parks.ca.gov* 🎫 *$10* 🕒 *Daily sunrise–sunset.*

WHERE TO STAY

$$ HOTEL 🏨 **Ragged Point Inn.** At this cliff-top resort—the only inn and restaurant for miles around—glass walls in most rooms open to awesome ocean views. **Pros:** on the cliffs; good food; idyllic views. **Cons:** busy road stop during the day; often booked for weekend weddings. [$] *Rooms from: $169* ✉ *19019 Hwy. 1, 20 miles north of San Simeon, Ragged Point* ☎ *805/927–4502, 805/927–5708 restaurant* 🌐 *raggedpointinn.com* 🛏 *39 rooms* 🍴 *No meals.*

$$$ RESORT 🏨 **Treebones Resort.** Perched on a hilltop, surrounded by national forest and stunning, unobstructed ocean views, this yurt resort provides a stellar back-to-nature experience along with creature comforts. **Pros:** 360-degree views; spacious pool area; comfortable beds. **Cons:** steep paths; no private bathrooms; not good for families with young children. [$] *Rooms from: $225* ✉ *71895 Hwy. 1, Willow Creek Rd., 32 miles north of San Simeon, 1 mile north of Gorda* ☎ *805/927–2390, 877/424–4787* 🌐 *www.treebonesresort.com* 🛏 *16 yurts, 5 campsites, 1 human nest w/campsite* 🍴 *Breakfast* ☞ *2-night minimum.*

CENTRAL BIG SUR

Hwy. 1, from Partington Cove to Bixby Bridge.

The countercultural spirit of Big Sur—which instead of a conventional town is a loose string of coast-hugging properties along Highway 1—is alive and well today. Its few residents include the very wealthy, the enthusiastically outdoorsy, and the thoroughly evolved: since the 1960s the Esalen Institute, a center for alternative education and East–West philosophical study, has attracted seekers of higher consciousness and devotees of the property's hot springs. Today posh and rustic resorts hidden among the redwoods cater to visitors drawn from near and far by the extraordinary scenery and serene isolation.

GETTING HERE AND AROUND

From the north, follow Highway 1 south from Carmel. From the south, continue the drive north from Julia Pfeiffer Burns State Park *(above)* on Highway 1. Monterey-Salinas Transit operates the Line 22 Big Sur bus from Monterey and Carmel to Central Big Sur (the last stop is Nepenthe), daily from late May to early September and weekends only the rest of the year.

Bus Contact Monterey-Salinas Transit ☎ *888/678–2871* ⊕ *mst.org.*

EXPLORING

Bixby Creek Bridge. The graceful arc of Bixby Creek Bridge is a photographer's dream. Built in 1932, the bridge spans a deep canyon, more than 100 feet wide at the bottom. From the north-side parking area you can admire the view or walk the 550-foot structure. ⊠ *Hwy. 1, 6 miles north of Point Sur State Historic Park, 13 miles south of Carmel.*

Pfeiffer Big Sur State Park. Among the many hiking trails at Pfeiffer Big Sur, a short route through a redwood-filled valley leads to a waterfall. You can double back or continue on the more difficult trail along the valley wall for views over miles of treetops to the sea. ⊠ *47225 Hwy. 1* ☎ *831/667–2315* ⊕ *www.parks.ca.gov* ⊠ *$10 per vehicle* ⊙ *Daily sunrise–sunset.*

Point Sur State Historic Park. An 1889 lighthouse at this state park still stands watch from atop a large volcanic rock. Four lighthouse keepers lived here with their families until 1974, when the light station became automated. Their homes and working spaces are open to the public only on 2½- to 3-hour ranger-led tours. Considerable walking, including up two stairways, is involved. Strollers are not allowed. ⊠ *Hwy. 1, 7 miles north of Pfeiffer Big Sur State Park* ☎ *831/625–4419* ⊕ *www.pointsur. org* ⊠ *$12* ⊙ *Tours generally Nov.–Mar., weekends at 10, Wed. at 1; Apr.–Oct., Sat. and Wed. at 10 and 2, Sun. at 10; July–Aug. additional tour at 10; call to confirm.*

BEACHES

Pfeiffer Beach. Through a hole in one of the gigantic boulders at secluded Pfeiffer Beach, you can watch the waves break first on the sea side and then on the beach side. Keep a sharp eye out for the unsigned, ungated road to the beach: it branches west of Highway 1 between the post office and Pfeiffer Big Sur State Park. The 2-mile, one-lane road descends sharply. **Amenities:** parking (fee); toilets. **Best for:** solitude; sunset. ⊠ *Off Hwy. 1, 1 mile south of Pfeiffer Big Sur State Park* ⊠ *$10 per vehicle* ⊙ *Daily 9–8.*

WHERE TO EAT

$$$ ✕ **Big Sur Roadhouse.** The chef at this colorful bistro perks up Califor-
ECLECTIC   nia favorites with seasonal Big Sur ingredients such as lemons, grapefruit, chanterelles, and locally sourced meats. Popular dishes include duck confit, vegetarian pastas, Dungeness crab salad on brioche toast, and breaded pork loin with wild mushroom spaetzle, caramelized fennel, and sauerkraut. The roadhouse serves breakfast, lunch, and dinner. ■TIP➔ Save room for house-made ice cream or a sorbet float.

[$] *Average main: $27* ✉ *Hwy. 1, 1 mile north of Pfeiffer Big Sur State Park* ☎ *831/667–2370* 🌐 *bigsurroadhouse.com.*

$$$ AMERICAN Fodor's Choice ★ 🍴 **Deetjen's Big Sur Inn.** The candle-lighted, creaky-floor restaurant in the main house at the historic inn of the same name is a Big Sur institution. It serves spicy seafood paella, grass-fed filet mignon, and rack of lamb for dinner and flavorful eggs Benedict for breakfast. The chef sources most ingredients from purveyors known for sustainable practices. [$] *Average main: $30* ✉ *Hwy. 1, 3½ miles south of Pfeiffer Big Sur State Park* ☎ *831/667–2378* 🌐 *deetjens.com* ⏲ *No lunch.*

$$$ AMERICAN 🍴 **Nepenthe.** It may be that no other restaurant between San Francisco and Los Angeles has a better coastal view than Nepenthe. The food and drink are overpriced but good; there are burgers, sandwiches, and salads for lunch, and fresh fish and hormone-free steaks for dinner. For the real show, settle on the terraced deck in the late afternoon, order a glass from the extensive wine list, and watch the sun slip into the Pacific Ocean. The less expensive, outdoor Café Kevah serves brunch and lunch. [$] *Average main: $30* ✉ *48510 Hwy. 1, 2½ miles south of Big Sur Station* ☎ *831/667–2345* 🌐 *nepenthebigsur.com.*

$$$$ AMERICAN Fodor's Choice ★ 🍴 **The Restaurant at Ventana.** The Ventana Inn's restaurant sits high on a ridge, and a magnificent terrace offers stunning ocean views. The redwood, copper, and cedar elements indoors complement the natural setting outside, but the design flourishes and gleaming fixtures place the facility firmly in the 21st century. So, too, does chef Paul Corsentino's menu, which might include creative dishes such as quail tempura, grilled octopus, or a New York strip steak served with barley and wild mushrooms. Regional and international wines on a comprehensive list pair well with these dishes, many of whose ingredients are sourced from local purveyors, and the bar serves seasonal specialty cocktails and California craft beers. The restaurant is open for breakfast, lunch, and dinner. [$] *Average main: $36* ✉ *48123 Hwy. 1, 1½ miles south of Pfeiffer Big Sur State Park* ☎ *831/667–4242* 🌐 *www.ventanainn.com* ✍ *Reservations essential.*

$$$$ AMERICAN Fodor's Choice ★ 🍴 **Sierra Mar.** Ocean-view dining doesn't get much better than this. At cliff's edge 1,200 feet above the Pacific at the ultra-chic Post Ranch Inn, Sierra Mar serves cutting-edge American cuisine made from mostly organic, seasonal ingredients, some from the on-site chef's garden. The four-course prix-fixe option always shines. The nine-course Taste of Big Sur menu centers on ingredients grown or foraged on the property or sourced locally. The restaurant's wine list is among the nation's most extensive. **■ TIP→ If you're unable to reserve a table for dinner, you can sit at the bar, which opens at 5:30 (first-come, first-served), or opt for the abbreviated prix-fixe ($55 and $95) lunch.** [$] *Average main: $125* ✉ *Hwy. 1, 1½ miles south of Pfeiffer Big Sur State Park* ☎ *831/667–2800* 🌐 *postranchinn.com/dining* ✍ *Reservations essential.*

WHERE TO STAY

$$$ HOTEL 🏨 **Big Sur Lodge.** The lodge's modern, motel-style cottages with Mission-style furnishings and vaulted ceilings sit in a meadow, surrounded by redwood trees and flowering shrubbery. **Pros:** secluded setting near trailheads; good camping alternative; rates include state parks pass. **Cons:** basic rooms; walk to main lodge. [$] *Rooms from: $204* ✉ *Pfeiffer*

Big Sur State Park, 47225 Hwy. 1 ☎ *831/667–3100, 800/424–4787* 🌐 *www.bigsurlodge.com* 🛏 *61 rooms* 🍴 *No meals.*

$$$ B&B/INN 🏨 **Big Sur River Inn.** The main draws of this rustic property are the lawns and wooded grounds fronting the Big Sur River. **Pros:** riverside setting; next to a restaurant and small market; outdoor pool. **Cons:** thin walls in some rooms; no phone in rooms. [$] *Rooms from: $200* ✉ *Hwy. 1, 2 miles north of Pfeiffer Big Sur State Park* ☎ *831/667–2700, 800/548–3610* 🌐 *bigsurriverinn.com* 🛏 *14 rooms, 6 suites* 🍴 *No meals.*

$$ B&B/INN 🏨 **Deetjen's Big Sur Inn.** This historic 1930s Norwegian-style property is endearingly rustic, especially if you're willing to go with a camplike flow. **Pros:** tons of character; wooded grounds. **Cons:** thin walls; some rooms don't have private baths; no TVs or Wi-Fi; limited cell phone access. [$] *Rooms from: $170* ✉ *Hwy. 1, 3½ miles south of Pfeiffer Big Sur State Park* ☎ *831/667–2377* 🌐 *deetjens.com* 🛏 *20 rooms, 15 with bath* 🍴 *No meals* ☞ *2-night minimum stay on weekends.*

$$$ HOTEL 🏨 **Glen Oaks Big Sur.** At this rustic-modern cluster of adobe-and-redwood buildings, you can choose between motel-style rooms, cabins, and cottages in the woods. **Pros:** in the heart of town; walking distance of restaurants. **Cons:** near busy road and parking lot; no TVs. [$] *Rooms from: $225* ✉ *Hwy. 1, 1 mile north of Pfeiffer Big Sur State Park* ☎ *831/667–2105* 🌐 *www.glenoaksbigsur.com* 🛏 *16 rooms, 2 cottages, 7 cabins* 🍴 *No meals.*

$$$$ RESORT Fodor's Choice ★ 🏨 **Post Ranch Inn.** This luxurious retreat, designed exclusively for adult getaways, has remarkably environmentally conscious architecture. **Pros:** world-class resort; spectacular views; gorgeous property with hiking trails. **Cons:** expensive; austere design; not a good choice if heights scare you. [$] *Rooms from: $675* ✉ *Hwy. 1, 1½ miles south of Pfeiffer Big Sur State Park* ☎ *831/667–2200, 800/527–2200* 🌐 *www.postranchinn.com* 🛏 *39 rooms, 1 house* 🍴 *Breakfast.*

$$$$ HOTEL Fodor's Choice ★ 🏨 **Ventana.** Hundreds of celebrities, from Oprah Winfrey to Sir Anthony Hopkins, have escaped to Ventana, a romantic resort on 243 tranquil acres 1,200 feet above the Pacific. **Pros:** secluded; nature trails everywhere; rates include daily guided hike, yoga, wine and cheese hour. **Cons:** expensive; some rooms lack an ocean view. [$] *Rooms from: $650* ✉ *Hwy. 1, almost 1 mile south of Pfeiffer Big Sur State Park* ☎ *831/667–2331, 800/628–6500* 🌐 *www.ventanainn.com* 🛏 *28 rooms, 31 suites* 🍴 *Breakfast.*

THE MONTEREY BAY AREA

From Carmel to Santa Cruz

WELCOME TO THE MONTEREY BAY AREA

TOP REASONS TO GO

★ **Marine life:** Monterey Bay is the location of the world's third-largest marine sanctuary, home to whales, otters, and other underwater creatures.

★ **Getaway central:** For more than a century, urbanites have come to the Monterey Bay area to unwind, relax, and have fun. It's a great place to browse unique shops and galleries, ride a giant roller coaster, or play a round of golf on a world-class course.

★ **Nature preserves:** More than the sea is protected here: the region boasts nearly 30 state parks, beaches, and preserves—fantastic places for walking, jogging, hiking, and biking.

★ **Wine and dine:** The area's rich agricultural bounty translates into abundant fresh produce, great wines, and fabulous dining. It's no wonder more than 300 culinary events take place here every year.

★ **Small-town vibes:** Even the cities here are friendly, walkable places where you'll feel like a local.

1 Carmel and Pacific Grove. Exclusive Carmel-by-the-Sea and Carmel Valley Village burst with historic charm, fine dining, and unusual boutiques that cater to celebrity residents and well-heeled visitors. Nearby 17-Mile Drive—quite possibly the prettiest stretch of road you'll ever travel—runs between Carmel-by-the-Sea and Victorian-studded Pacific Grove, home to thousands of migrating monarch butterflies between October and February.

2 Monterey. A former Spanish military outpost, Monterey's well-preserved historic district is a hands-on history lesson. Cannery Row, the center of Monterey's once-thriving sardine industry, has been reborn as a tourist attraction with shops, restaurants, hotels, and the Monterey Bay Aquarium.

3 Around Monterey Bay. Much of California's lettuce, berries, artichokes, and brussels sprouts is grown in Salinas and other towns. Salinas is also home to the National Steinbeck Center, and Moss Landing encompasses pristine wildlife wetlands. Aptos, Capitola, and Soquel are former lumber towns that became popular seaside resorts more than a century ago. Today they're filled with antiques shops, restaurants, and wine-tasting rooms; you'll also find some of the bay's best beaches along the shore here.

4 Santa Cruz. Santa Cruz shows its colors along an old-time beach boardwalk and municipal wharf. A University of California campus imbues the town with arts and culture and a liberal mind-set.

GETTING ORIENTED

North of Big Sur the coastline softens into lower bluffs, windswept dunes, pristine estuaries, and long, sandy beaches, bordering one of the world's most amazing marine environments— Monterey Bay. On the Monterey Peninsula, at the southern end of the bay, are Carmel-by-the-Sea, Pacific Grove, and Monterey; Santa Cruz sits at the northern tip of the crescent. In between, Highway 1 cruises along the coastline, passing windswept beaches piled high with sand dunes. Along the route are wetlands and artichoke and strawberry fields.

4

Updated
by Cheryl
Crabtree

Natural beauty is at the heart of the Monterey Bay area's enormous appeal—it's everywhere, from the redwood-studded hillsides to the pristine shoreline with miles of walking paths and bluff-top vistas. Nature even takes center stage indoors at the world-famous Monterey Bay Aquarium, but history also draws visitors, most notably to Monterey's well-preserved waterfront district. Quaint, walkable towns and villages such as Carmel-by-the-Sea and Carmel Valley Village lure with smart restaurants and galleries, while sunny Aptos, Capitola, Soquel, and Santa Cruz, with miles of sand and surf, attract surfers and beach lovers.

Monterey Bay life centers on the ocean. The bay itself is protected by the Monterey Bay National Marine Sanctuary, the nation's largest undersea canyon—bigger and deeper than the Grand Canyon. On-the-water activities abound, from whale-watching and kayaking to sailing and surfing. Bay cruises from Monterey and Moss Landing almost always encounter other enchanting sea creatures, among them sea otters, sea lions, and porpoises.

Land-based activities include hiking, zip-lining in the redwood canopy, and wine tasting along urban and rural trails. Golf has been an integral part of the Monterey Peninsula's social and recreational scene since the Del Monte Golf Course opened in 1897. Pebble Beach's championship courses host prestigious tournaments, and though the green fees at these courses can run up to $500, elsewhere on the peninsula you'll find less expensive options. And, of course, whatever activity you pursue, natural splendor appears at every turn.

PLANNING

WHEN TO GO

Summer is peak season; mild weather brings in big crowds. In this coastal region a cool breeze generally blows and fog often rolls in from offshore; you will frequently need a sweater or windbreaker. Off-season, from November through April, fewer people visit and the mood is mellower. Rainfall is heaviest in January and February. Fall and spring days are often clearer than those in summer.

GETTING HERE AND AROUND

AIR TRAVEL

Monterey Regional Airport, 3 miles east of downtown Monterey off Highway 68, is served by Alaska, Allegiant, American, United, and US Airways. Taxi service costs from $18 to $20 to downtown, and from $26 to $35 to Carmel. Monterey Airbus service between the region and the San Jose and San Francisco airports starts at $40; the Early Bird Airport Shuttle costs from $80 to $190 ($195 from Oakland).

Airport Contacts Monterey Regional Airport (MRY) ⊠ *200 Fred Kane Dr., at Olmsted Rd., off Hwy. 68, Monterey* ☎ *831/648–7000* ⊕ *www.monterey airport.com.*

Ground Transportation Central Coast Cab Company ☎ *831/626–3333.* **Early Bird Airport Shuttle** ☎ *831/462–3933* ⊕ *www.earlybirdairportshuttle. com.* **Monterey Airbus** ☎ *831/373–7777* ⊕ *www.montereyairbus.com.* **Yellow Cab** ☎ *831/333–1234.*

BUS TRAVEL

Greyhound serves Santa Cruz and Salinas from San Francisco and San Jose. The trips take about 3 and 4½ hours, respectively. Monterey-Salinas Transit (MST) provides frequent service in Monterey County (from $1.50 to $3.50; day pass $10), and Santa Cruz METRO ($2; day pass from $6 to $10) buses operate throughout Santa Cruz County. You can switch between the lines in Watsonville.

Bus Contacts Greyhound ☎ *800/231–2222* ⊕ *www.greyhound.com.* **Monterey-Salinas Transit** ☎ *888/678–2871* ⊕ *mst.org.* **Santa Cruz METRO** ☎ *831/425–8600* ⊕ *scmtd.com.*

CAR TRAVEL

Highway 1 runs south–north along the coast, linking the towns of Carmel-by-the-Sea, Monterey, and Santa Cruz; some sections have only two lanes. The freeway, U.S. 101, lies to the east, roughly parallel to Highway 1. The two roads are connected by Highway 68 from Pacific Grove to Salinas; Highway 156 from Castroville to Prunedale; Highway 152 from Watsonville to Gilroy; and Highway 17 from Santa Cruz to San Jose. ⚠ **Traffic near Santa Cruz can crawl to a standstill during commuter hours. In the morning, avoid traveling between 7 and 9; in the afternoon avoid traveling between 4 and 7.**

The drive south from San Francisco to Monterey can be made comfortably in three hours or less. The most scenic way is to follow Highway 1 down the coast. A generally faster route is Interstate 280 south to Highway 85 to Highway 17 to Highway 1. The drive from the Los

Angeles area takes five or six hours. Take U.S. 101 to Salinas and head west on Highway 68. You can also follow Highway 1 up the coast.

TRAIN TRAVEL

Amtrak's *Coast Starlight* runs between Los Angeles, Oakland, and Seattle. From the train station in Salinas you can connect with buses serving Carmel and Monterey, and from the train station in San Jose with buses to Santa Cruz.

Train Contacts Amtrak ☎ *800/872-7245* ⊕ *amtrak.com.*

RESTAURANTS

The Monterey Bay area is a culinary paradise. The surrounding waters are full of fish, wild game roams the foothills, and the inland valleys are some of the most fertile in the country—local chefs draw on this bounty for their fresh, truly Californian cuisine. Except at beachside stands and inexpensive eateries, where anything goes, casual but neat dress is the norm.

HOTELS

Accommodations in the Monterey area range from no-frills motels to luxurious hotels. Pacific Grove, amply endowed with ornate Victorian houses, is the region's bed-and-breakfast capital; Carmel also has charming inns. Lavish resorts cluster in exclusive Pebble Beach and pastoral Carmel Valley.

High season runs from May through October. Rates in winter, especially at the larger hotels, may drop by 50% or more, and smaller inns often offer midweek specials. Whatever the month, some properties require a two-night stay on weekends. *Hotel reviews have been shortened. For full information, visit Fodors.com.* ⚠ **Many of the fancier accommodations aren't suitable for children; if you're traveling with kids, ask before you book.**

WHAT IT COSTS			
	$	$$	$$$	$$$$
Restaurants	under $16	$16–$22	$23–$30	over $30
Hotels	under $120	$120–$175	$176–$250	over $250

Restaurant prices are the average cost of a main course at dinner or, if dinner is not served, at lunch, excluding sales tax of 8¼%–9½% (depending on location). Hotel prices are the lowest cost of a standard double room in high season, excluding service charges and 10%–10½% tax.

TOUR OPTIONS

Ag Venture Tours & Consulting. Crowd-pleasing half- and full-day winetasting, sightseeing, and agricultural tours are Ag Venture's specialty. Tastings are at Monterey and Santa Cruz Mountains wineries; sightseeing opportunities include the Monterey Peninsula, Big Sur, and Santa Cruz; and the agricultural forays take in the Salinas and Pajaro valleys. Customized itineraries can be arranged. ☎ *831/761-8463* ⊕ *agventure tours.com* ✉ *From $75.*

California Parlor Car Tours. This outfit operates motor-coach tours from San Francisco that include one or two days in Monterey and Carmel. The company's three-day San Francisco–Los Angeles tours include stops in Monterey and Carmel. ☎ *415/474–7500, 800/227–4250* ⊕ *www. calpartours.com* ✉ *From $80 (day) and $267 (overnight).*

Monterey Guided Wine Tours. The company's guides lead customized wine tours in Monterey, Carmel, and Carmel Valley, along with the Santa Lucia Highlands, the Santa Cruz Mountains, and the Paso Robles area. Tours, which typically last from four to six hours, take place in a town car, a stretch limo, or a party bus. ☎ *831/920–2792* ⊕ *montereyguided winetours.com* ✉ *From $85.*

VISITOR INFORMATION

Contacts Monterey County Convention & Visitors Bureau ☎ *888/221–1010* ⊕ *www.seemonterey.com.* **Monterey Wine Country** ☎ *831/375–9400* ⊕ *www. montereywines.org.* **Santa Cruz County Conference & Visitors Council** ✉ *303 Water St., No. 100, Santa Cruz* ☎ *831/425–1234, 800/833–3494* ⊕ *santacruz. org.* **Santa Cruz Mountain Winegrowers Association** ✉ *725 Front St., No. 112, Santa Cruz* ☎ *831/685–8463* ⊕ *www.scmwa.com.*

CARMEL AND PACIFIC GROVE

As Highway 1 swings inland about 30 miles north of Big Sur, historic Carmel-by-the Sea anchors the southern entry to the Monterey Peninsula—a gorgeous promontory at the southern tip of Monterey Bay. Just north of Carmel along the coast, the legendary 17-Mile Drive wends its way through private Pebble Beach and the town of Pacific Grove. Highway 1 skirts the peninsula to the east with more direct access to Pebble Beach and Pacific Grove.

CARMEL-BY-THE-SEA

26 miles north of Big Sur.

Even when its population quadruples with tourists on weekends and in summer, Carmel-by-the-Sea, commonly referred to as Carmel, retains its identity as a quaint village. Self-consciously charming, the town is populated by many celebrities, major and minor, and has its share of quirky ordinances. For instance, women wearing high heels do not have the right to pursue legal action if they trip and fall on the cobblestone streets, and drivers who hit a tree and leave the scene are charged with hit-and-run.

Buildings have no street numbers—street names are written on discreet white posts—and consequently no mail delivery. One way to commune with the locals: head to the post office. Artists started this community, and their legacy is evident in the numerous galleries.

GETTING HERE AND AROUND

From north or south follow Highway 1 to Carmel. Head west at Ocean Avenue to reach the main village hub. In summer the MST Carmel-by-the-Sea Trolley loops around town to the beach and mission every 30 minutes or so.

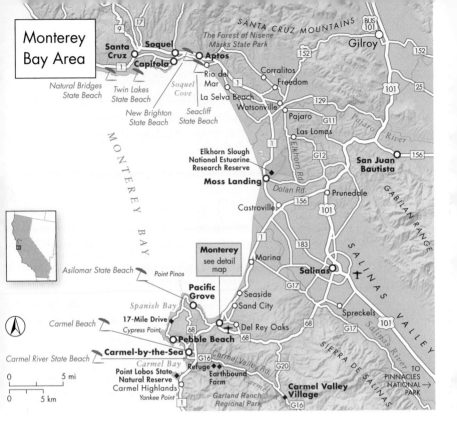

TOURS

Carmel Walks. For insight into Carmel's history and culture, join one of these guided two-hour ambles through hidden courtyards, gardens, and pathways. Tours depart from the Pine Inn courtyard, on Lincoln Street. Call to reserve a spot. ⌧ *Lincoln St. at 6th Ave.* ☎ *831/223–4399* ⊕ *carmelwalks.com* 🎫 *From $25* 🕙 *Tues.–Fri. 10, Sat. 10 and 2.*

ESSENTIALS

Visitor Information Carmel Chamber of Commerce ⌧ *Visitor Center, San Carlos, between 5th and 6th* ☎ *831/624–2522, 800/550–4333* ⊕ *carmelcalifornia.org* 🕙 *Daily 10–5.*

EXPLORING

TOP ATTRACTIONS

Carmel Mission. Long before it became a shopping and browsing destination, Carmel was an important religious center during the establishment of Spanish California. That heritage is preserved in the Mission San Carlos Borroméo del Rio Carmelo, more commonly known as the Carmel Mission. Founded in 1771, it served as headquarters for the mission system in California under Father Junípero Serra. Adjoining the stone church is a tranquil garden planted with California poppies. Museum rooms at the mission include an early kitchen, Serra's spartan sleeping quarters and burial shrine, and the first college library in California. ✉ *3080 Rio Rd., at Lasuen Dr.* ☎ *831/624–1271* ⊕ *carmelmission.org* 🖭 *$6.50* ⊗ *May–Aug., daily 9:30–6:45; Sept.–Apr., daily 9:30–4:45.*

Fodor'sChoice
★
Ocean Avenue. Downtown Carmel's chief lure is shopping, especially along its main street, Ocean Avenue, between Junipero Avenue and Camino Real. The architecture here is a mishmash of ersatz Tudor, Mediterranean, and other styles.

Fodor'sChoice
★
Point Lobos State Natural Reserve. A 350-acre headland harboring a wealth of marine life, the reserve lies a few miles south of Carmel. The best way to explore here is to walk along one of the many trails. The Cypress Grove Trail leads through a forest of Monterey cypress (one of only two natural groves remaining) that clings to the rocks above an emerald-green cove. Sea Lion Point Trail is a good place to view sea lions. From those and other trails, you might also spot otters, harbor seals, and (in winter and spring) migrating whales. An additional 750 acres of the reserve is an undersea marine park open to qualified scuba divers. No pets are allowed. ■TIP→ **Arrive early (or in late afternoon) to avoid crowds; the parking lots fill up.** ✉ *Hwy. 1* ☎ *831/624–4909, 831/624–8413 water sports reservations* ⊕ *www.pointlobos.org* 🖭 *$10 per vehicle* ⊗ *Daily 8 am–½ hr after sunset.*

WORTH NOTING

Carmel Wine Walk By-the-Sea. If you purchase a Wine Walk Passport, you can park the car and sample local wines at any nine of 14 tasting rooms, all within a few blocks of each other in downtown Carmel. Individual passports be used by two or more people at the same tasting room, and they entitle holders to free corkage at some local restaurants. ✉ *Carmel Chamber of Commerce Visitor Center, San Carlos St., between 5th and 6th Aves.* ☎ *831/624–2522, 800/550–4333* ⊕ *carmelcalifornia.org* 🖭 *$65.*

Dawson Cole Fine Art. Amazing images of dancers, athletes, and other humans in motion come to life in this gallery that is devoted to the artworks of Monterey Bay resident Richard MacDonald, one of the most famed figurative sculptors of our time. ✉ *Lincoln St., at 6th Ave.* ☎ *800/972–5528* ⊕ *dawsoncolefineart.com* 🖭 *Free* ⊗ *Mon.–Sat. 10–6, Sun. 10–5:30.*

Tor House. Scattered throughout the pines of Carmel-by-the-Sea are houses and cottages originally built for the writers, artists, and photographers who discovered the area decades ago. Among the most impressive dwellings is Tor House, a stone cottage built in 1919 by poet Robinson Jeffers on a craggy knoll overlooking the sea. Portraits, books, and unusual art objects fill the low-ceilinged rooms. The highlight of the small estate is Hawk Tower, a detached edifice set with stones from the Carmel coastline—as well as one from the Great Wall

4

of China. The docents who lead tours (six people maximum) are well informed about the poet's work and life. ■TIP➜ To reserve a tour, which is recommended, email *thf@torhouse.org*. ✉ *26304 Ocean View Ave.* ☎ *831/624–1813, 831/624–1840 direct docent office line, Fri. and Sat. only* ⊕ *www.torhouse.org* ▨ *$10* ⊙ *Hourly tours Fri. and Sat. 10–3* ☞ *No children under 12.*

BEACHES

Carmel Beach. Carmel-by-the-Sea's greatest attraction is its rugged coastline, with pine and cypress forests and countless inlets. Carmel Beach, an easy walk from downtown shops, has sparkling white sands and magnificent sunsets. ■TIP➜ Dogs are allowed to romp off-leash here. **Amenities:** parking (no fee); toilets. **Best For:** sunset; surfing; walking. ✉ *End of Ocean Ave.*

Carmel River State Beach. This sugar-white beach, stretching 106 acres along Carmel Bay, is adjacent to a bird sanctuary, where you might spot pelicans, kingfishers, hawks, and sandpipers. Dogs are allowed on leash. **Amenities:** parking (no fee); toilets. **Best For:** sunrise; sunset; walking. ✉ *Off Scenic Rd., south of Carmel Beach* ☎ *831/649–2836* ⊕ *www.parks.ca.gov* ▨ *Free* ⊙ *Spring–fall, daily 8–7; winter, daily 8 am–½ hr after sunset.*

WHERE TO EAT

$$$$
EUROPEAN

✕ **Anton and Michel.** Carefully prepared European cuisine is the draw at this airy restaurant. The rack of lamb is carved at the table, the grilled halloumi cheese and tomatoes are meticulously stacked and served with basil and Kalamata olive tapenade, and the desserts are set aflame before your eyes. ■TIP➜ For lighter fare with a worldwide flair, head to the bar, where small plates such as Dungeness crab ravioli and brochette of filet mignon with chimichurri sauce are served. Ⓢ *Average main: $32* ✉ *Mission St. and 7th Ave.* ☎ *831/624–2406* ⊕ *antonand michel.com* ⌕ *Reservations essential.*

$$$$
AMERICAN
Fodor'sChoice
★

✕ **Aubergine.** To eat and sleep at luxe L'Auberge Carmel is an experience in itself, but even those staying elsewhere can splurge at the inn's intimate restaurant. Chef Justin Cogley's prix-fixe regular menu ($110) includes four or five courses—perhaps chilled Dungeness crab with pumpkin seeds and spaghetti squash, yellowtail with seaweed and hibiscus, dry-aged rib eye grilled over *binchotan* (white charcoal), milk chocolate tart with pear and walnut, and an optional artisanal cheese plate. You can also choose the tasting menu ($145), for which the chefs assemble surprise courses. The well-informed sommelier helps diners navigate the wine list—Aubergine's cellar holds 2,500 bottles—and offers wine pairings for your courses (from $75 to $175). Ⓢ *Average main: $110* ✉ *Monte Verde, at 7th Ave.* ☎ *831/624–8578* ⊕ *aubergine carmel.com* ⌕ *Reservations essential* ⊙ *No lunch.*

$$$
MODERN
AMERICAN
Fodor'sChoice
★

✕ **Basil.** Eco-friendly Basil was Monterey County's first restaurant to achieve a green dining certification, recognition of chef-owner Soerke Peters's commitment to using organic, sustainably cultivated ingredients in his cuisine. Peters grows many of his own herbs, which find their way into creative dishes such as black squid linguine with sea urchin sauce, creamy duck liver–pear pâté, and smoked venison and other house-made charcuterie. The grass-fed burger is a good lunch choice, as are, in season, the crab sliders. French toast with poached eggs and truffled mushrooms is a Sunday brunch staple. You can dine in the eight-table interior or on the outdoor covered patio, where heaters and blankets provide warmth year-round. [$] *Average main: $23* ✉ *Paseo Square, San Carlos St., between Ocean Ave. and 7th Ave.* ☎ *831/636–8226* 🌐 *basilcarmel.com* ✍ *Reservations essential.*

$$$$ MEDITERRANEAN 🍴 **Casanova.** This restaurant inspires European-style celebration and romance: accordions hang from the walls, and tiny party lights flicker along the low ceilings. Dishes from southern France and northern Italy—game hen, osso buco, Wagyu beef tartare—predominate. Private dining and a special tasting menu are offered at Van Gogh's Table, a relic from France's Auberge Ravoux, the artist's final residence. [$] *Average main: $32* ✉ *5th Ave., between San Carlos and Mission Sts.* ☎ *831/625–0501* 🌐 *www.casanovarestaurant.com* ✍ *Reservations essential.*

4

$ AMERICAN 🍴 **The Cottage Restaurant.** This family-friendly spot serves sandwiches, pizzas, and homemade soups at lunch, but the best meal is breakfast (good thing it's served all day). The menu offers six variations on eggs Benedict, and all kinds of sweet and savory crepes. [$] *Average main: $15* ✉ *Lincoln St., between Ocean and 7th Aves.* ☎ *831/625–6260* 🌐 *cottagerestaurant.com* 🕓 *No dinner.*

$$$$ AMERICAN 🍴 **Grasing's Coastal Cuisine.** Chef Kurt Grasing draws from fresh Carmel Coast and Central Valley ingredients to whip up contemporary adaptations of European-provincial and American cooking. Longtime menu favorites include artichoke lasagna in a roasted tomato sauce, duck with fresh cherries in a red wine sauce, a savory paella, and grilled steaks and chops. [$] *Average main: $34* ✉ *6th Ave. and Mission St.* ☎ *831/624–6562* 🌐 *grasings.com* ✍ *Reservations essential.*

$$ TAPAS 🍴 **Mundaka.** The traditional Spanish-style tapas, made with fresh local ingredients, and the full bar attract legions of locals to this downtown spot. Longtime favorites include the chorizo slider with truffle fries, the authentic Valencian paella, and a charcuterie platter made in-house. At the adjacent Mundaka Cafe, the breakfast menu includes Spanish tortillas, Belgian waffles, and homemade baked goods; among the lunchtime choices are sandwiches, soups, and salads. Leashed dogs are welcome at the patio tables. [$] *Average main: $21* ✉ *San Carlos St., between Ocean and 7th Aves.* ☎ *831/624–7400* 🌐 *www.mundakacarmel.com.*

$$$ ITALIAN 🍴 **Vesuvio.** Chef and restaurateur Rich Pèpe heats up the night with this lively trattoria downstairs and swinging rooftop terrace, the Starlight Lounge 65°. Pèpe's elegant take on traditional Italian cuisine yields dishes such as wild-boar Bolognese pappardelle, lobster ravioli, and velvety limoncello mousse cake. Pizzas and small plates are served in the restaurant and two bars. Upstairs, relax in comfy chairs by fire pits and enjoy bird's-eye views of the village. On most nights in summer there's live music. [$] *Average main: $26* ✉ *6th and Junipero Aves.* ☎ *831/625–1766* 🌐 *vesuviocarmel.com* 🕓 *No lunch.*

WHERE TO STAY

$$$ B&B/INN 🏨 **Cypress Inn.** This luxurious inn has a fresh Mediterranean ambience with Moroccan touches. **Pros:** luxury without snobbery; popular lounge and restaurant; British-style afternoon tea on weekends. **Cons:**

Point Lobos Reserve State Park is home to one of the only two natural stands of Monterey cypress in the world.

not for the pet-phobic. $ *Rooms from: $250* ✉ *Lincoln St. and 7th Ave.* ☎ *831/624–3871, 800/443–7443* ⊕ *cypress-inn.com* ⇗ *39 rooms, 5 suites* ✦ *Breakfast.*

$$$$
HOTEL
🛏 **Hyatt Carmel Highlands.** High on a hill overlooking the Pacific, this place has superb views; accommodations include king rooms with fireplaces, suites with personal Jacuzzis, and full town houses with many perks. **Pros:** killer views; romantic getaway; great food. **Cons:** thin walls; must drive to Carmel. $ *Rooms from: $399* ✉ *120 Highlands Dr.* ☎ *831/620–1234, 800/233–1234* ⊕ *highlandsinn.hyatt.com* ⇗ *46 rooms, 2 suites.*

$$$$
B&B/INN
Fodor's Choice
★
🛏 **L'Auberge Carmel.** Stepping through the doors of this elegant inn is like being transported to a little European village. **Pros:** in town but off the main drag; four blocks from the beach; full-service luxury. **Cons:** touristy area; not a good choice for families. $ *Rooms from: $435* ✉ *Monte Verde at 7th Ave.* ☎ *831/624–8578* ⊕ *www.laubergecarmel. com* ⇗ *20 rooms* ✦ *Breakfast.*

$$$$
HOTEL
🛏 **La Playa Carmel.** A historic complex of lush gardens and Mediterranean-style buildings, La Playa has light and airy interiors done in Carmel Bay beach-cottage style. **Pros:** residential neighborhood; manicured gardens; two blocks from the beach. **Cons:** four stories (no elevator); busy lobby; some rooms are on the small side. $ *Rooms from: $458* ✉ *Camino Real, at 8th Ave.* ☎ *831/293–6100, 800/582–8900* ⊕ *laplayahotel.com* ⇗ *75 rooms* ✦ *Breakfast.*

$$
HOTEL
🛏 **Mission Ranch.** Movie star Clint Eastwood owns this sprawling property whose accommodations include rooms in a converted barn, and several cottages, some with fireplaces. **Pros:** farm setting; pastoral views;

great for tennis buffs. **Cons:** busy parking lot; must drive to the heart of town. [$] *Rooms from: $140* ✉ *26270 Dolores St.* ☎ *831/624–6436, 800/538–8221, 831/625–9040 restaurant* 🌐 *www.missionranchcarmel.com* 🛏 *31 rooms* 🍴 *Breakfast.*

$$$$ B&B/INN 🏨 **Tickle Pink Inn.** Atop a towering cliff, this inn has views of the Big Sur coastline, which you can contemplate from your private balcony. **Pros:** close to great hiking; intimate; dramatic views. **Cons:** close to a big hotel; lots of traffic during the day. [$] *Rooms from: $309* ✉ *155 Highland Dr.* ☎ *831/624–1244, 800/635–4774* 🌐 *ticklepink.com* 🛏 *23 rooms, 10 suites, 1 cottage* 🍴 *Breakfast.*

$$$ B&B/INN 🏨 **Tradewinds Carmel.** This converted motel with sleek decor inspired by the South Seas encircles a courtyard with waterfalls, a meditation garden, and a fire pit. **Pros:** serene; within walking distance of restaurants; friendly service. **Cons:** no pool; long walk to the beach. [$] *Rooms from: $250* ✉ *Mission St., at 3rd Ave.* ☎ *831/624–2776* 🌐 *tradewindscarmel.com* 🛏 *26 rooms, 2 suites* 🍴 *Breakfast.*

NIGHTLIFE

BARS AND PUBS

Barmel. Al Capone and other Prohibition-era legends once sidled up to this hip nightspot's carved wooden bar. Rock to DJ music and sit indoors, or head out to the pet-friendly patio. Some menu items pay homage to California's early days, and you can order Spanish tapas and wines from the adjacent Mundaka restaurant, which is under the same ownership. ✉ *San Carlos St., between Ocean and 7th Aves.* ☎ *831/626–3400* 🌐 *www.mundakacarmel.com* 💳 *No credit cards.*

Jack London's. Among the few Carmel restaurants that serve food late, this publike hangout, also open for lunch, is a good stop for a beer or cocktail or to watch sports on TV. On most weekends Jack London's hosts live music. The weekday happy hour (from 4 to 6) is a bargain. ✉ *Su Vecino Court, Dolores St., between 5th and 6th Aves.* ☎ *831/624–2336* 🌐 *jacklondonscarmel.com.*

SHOPPING

ART GALLERIES

Carmel Art Association. Carmel's oldest gallery, established in 1927, exhibits original paintings and sculptures by local artists. ✉ *Dolores St., between 5th and 6th Aves.* ☎ *831/624–6176* 🌐 *carmelart.org.*

Galerie Plein Aire. The gallery showcases the oil paintings of a group of local artists. ✉ *Dolores St., between 5th and 6th Aves.* ☎ *831/625–5686* 🌐 *galeriepleinaire.com.*

Gallery Sur. Fine art photography of the Big Sur Coast and the Monterey Peninsula, including scenic shots and golf images, is the focus here. ✉ *6th Ave., between Dolores and Lincoln Sts.* ☎ *831/626–2615* 🌐 *gallerysur.com.*

Weston Gallery. Run by the family of the late Edward Weston, this is hands down the best photography gallery around, with contemporary color photography and classic black-and-whites. ✉ *6th Ave., between Dolores and Lincoln Sts.* ☎ *831/624–4453* 🌐 *westongallery.com.*

CARMEL VALLEY

10 miles east of Carmel.

Carmel Valley Road, which heads inland from Highway 1 south of Carmel, is the main thoroughfare through this valley, a secluded enclave of horse ranchers and other well-heeled residents who prefer the area's sunny climate to coastal fog and wind. Once thick with dairy farms, the valley has evolved into an esteemed wine appellation. Carmel Valley Village has crafts shops, art galleries, and the tasting rooms of numerous local wineries.

GETTING HERE AND AROUND

From U.S. 101 north or south, exit at Highway 68 and head west toward the coast. Scenic, two-lane Laureles Grade winds west over the mountains to Carmel Valley Road north of the village.

TOURS

Carmel Valley Grapevine Express. An incredible bargain, the express—aka MST's Bus 24—travels between downtown Monterey and Carmel Valley Village, with stops near wineries, restaurants, and shopping centers. ☎ 888/678–2871 ⊕ *mst.org* ✉ *$10 all-day pass.*

EXPLORING

TOP ATTRACTIONS

Bernardus Tasting Room. At the tasting room of Bernardus, known for its Bordeaux-style red blend, called Marinus, and Chardonnays, you can sample current releases and library and reserve wines. ✉ *5 W. Carmel Valley Rd., at El Caminito Rd.* ☎ *831/298–8021, 800/223–2533* ⊕ *bernardus.com* ✉ *Tastings $12–$20* ☯ *Daily 11–5.*

Château Julien. The expansive winery, best known for its Chardonnays and Merlots, offers daily public tours and a range of private tours and tastings, available by appointment. Tours take in some of the 16-acre estate and its traditional French-style buildings, gardens, and vineyards. ✉ *8940 Carmel Valley Rd., at Schetter Rd., Carmel* ☎ *831/624–2600* ⊕ *chateaujulien.com* ✉ *Tasting $15 (includes tour), private tours $20–$100* ☯ *Winery weekdays 8–5, weekends 11–5; public tour (reservations encouraged) daily at 12:30 and 2:30.*

Cowgirl Winery. Cowgirl chic prevails in the main tasting building here, and it's just plain rustic at the outdoor tables, set amid chickens, a tractor, and a flatbed truck. The wines include Chardonnay, Cabernet Sauvignon, Rosé, and some blends. You can order a wood-fired pizza from sister business Corkscrew Café, and play boccie ball, horseshoes, or corn hole until your food arrives. ✉ *25 Pilot Rd., off W. Carmel Valley Rd.* ☎ *831/298–7030* ⊕ *cowgirlwinery.com* ✉ *Tasting $13* ☯ *Sun.–Fri. 11:30–5, Sat. until 6 (until 7 Apr.–Oct.).*

Holman Ranch Vineyards Tasting Room. Estate-grown Pinot Gris and Pinot Noir are among the standout wines made by Holman Ranch, which operates a tasting room in Carmel Valley village. If the Heather's Hill Pinot is being poured, be sure to try it. The ranch itself occupies rolling hills once part of the Carmel mission's land grant. You can book winery and vineyard tours by appointment, and the ranch welcomes overnight guests at its 10-room hacienda. ✉ *19 E. Carmel Valley Rd., Suite C* ☎ *831/659–2640*

🌐 *holmanranch.com* 🎟 *Tastings $8–$12* ⏲ *Late May–early Sept., Mon.–Thurs. 11–6, Fri.–Sun. noon–7; early Sept.–late May, daily 11–6.*

WORTH NOTING

Earthbound Farm. Pick up fresh vegetables, ready-to-eat meals, gourmet groceries, flowers, and gifts at Earthbound Farm, the world's largest grower of organic produce. You can also take a romp in the kid's garden, cut your own herbs, and stroll through the chamomile aromatherapy labyrinth. Special events, on Saturday from April through December, include bug walks and garlic-braiding workshops. ✉ *7250 Carmel Valley Rd., Carmel* ☎ *831/625–6219* 🌐 *www.ebfarm.com* 🎟 *Free* ⏲ *Mon.–Sat. 8–6:30, Sun. 9–6.*

WHERE TO EAT

$$ EUROPEAN 🍴 **Café Rustica.** European country cooking is the focus at this lively roadhouse. Specialties include roasted meats, seafood, pastas, and thin-crust pizzas from the wood-fired oven. It can get noisy inside; for a quieter meal, request a table outside. [$] *Average main: $21* ✉ *10 Delfino Pl., at Pilot Rd., off Carmel Valley Rd.* ☎ *831/659–4444* 🌐 *caferusticavillage.com* ✍ *Reservations essential* ⏲ *Closed Mon.*

$$ MODERN AMERICAN 🍴 **Corkscrew Café.** Farm-fresh food is the specialty of this casual, Old Monterey–style bistro. Herbs and seasonal produce come from the Corkscrew's own organic gardens, the catch of the day comes from local waters, and the meats are hormone-free. Popular dishes include the fish tacos, chicken salad, and wood-fired pizzas, which come with classic toppings and unusual ones such as Meyer lemon and prosciutto. You can dine indoors near the open kitchen, or outside in the garden patio. **■TIP→ Don't miss the collection of corkscrews from the 17th century to the present.** [$] *Average main: $22* ✉ *55 W. Carmel Valley Rd., at Pilot Rd.* ☎ *831/659–8888* 🌐 *corkscrewcafe.com.*

$$$ AMERICAN 🍴 **Will's Fargo.** Around since the 1920s, this restaurant calls itself a "dressed-up saloon." Steer horns and gilt-frame paintings adorn the walls of the Victorian-style dining room; you can also eat on the patios. The menu, for years mainly seafood and steaks, including a 20-ounce porterhouse, is evolving under new owners, the proprietors of Holman Ranch Vineyards. Their wines, along with those of other local vintners, dominate the extensive list. [$] *Average main: $28* ✉ *16 E. Carmel Valley Rd., at Via Contenta* ☎ *831/659–2774* 🌐 *wfrestaurant.com* ⏲ *No lunch Sept.–mid-May, no lunch weekdays mid-May.–Aug.*

WHERE TO STAY

$$$$ RESORT Fodor's Choice ★ 🏨 **Bernardus Lodge.** The spacious guest rooms at this luxury spa resort, which was completely remodeled before reopening in spring 2015, have vaulted ceilings, French oak floors, featherbeds, fireplaces, patios, and bathrooms with heated-tile floors and soaking tubs for two. **Pros:** exceptional personal service; outstanding food and wine. **Cons:** pricey; some guests can seem snooty. [$] *Rooms from: $475* ✉ *415 W. Carmel Valley Rd.* ☎ *831/658–3400* 🌐 *bernarduslodge.com* 🛏 *56 rooms, 1 suite.*

$$$$ RESORT Fodor's Choice ★ 🏨 **Carmel Valley Ranch.** The activity options at this luxury ranch are so varied that the resort provides a program director to guide you through them. **Pros:** stunning natural setting; tons of activities; state-of-the-art amenities. **Cons:** must drive several miles to shops and nightlife; pricey.

$ *Rooms from: $335* ✉ *1 Old Ranch Rd., Carmel* ☎ *831/625–9500* ⊕ *carmelvalleyranch.com* ⇱ *181 suites* ⦿*No meals.*

$$$ ⛺ **Quail Lodge & Golf Club.** A sprawling collection of ranch-style build-
HOTEL   ings on 850 acres of meadows, fairways, and lakes, Quail Lodge offers
FAMILY   luxury rooms and outdoor activities at surprisingly affordable rates.
Pros: on the golf course; on-site restaurant. **Cons:** extra fees for ath-
letic passes and some services; 5 miles from the beach and Carmel Val-
ley Village. $ *Rooms from: $195* ✉ *8205 Valley Greens Dr., Carmel*
☎ *831/624–2888, 866/675–1101 reservations* ⊕ *www.quaillodge.com*
⇱ *77 rooms, 16 suites* ⦿*Breakfast.*

$$$$ ⛺ **Stonepine Estate Resort.** Set on 330 pastoral acres, the former estate of
RESORT   the Crocker banking family has been converted to a luxurious inn. **Pros:**
Fodor'sChoice   supremely exclusive. **Cons:** difficult to get a reservation; far from the
★   coast. $ *Rooms from: $300* ✉ *150 E. Carmel Valley Rd.* ☎ *831/659–
2245* ⊕ *www.stonepineestate.com* ⇱ *10 rooms, 2 suites, 3 cottages*
⦿*No meals.*

SPORTS AND THE OUTDOORS
GOLF

Quail Lodge & Golf Club. Robert Muir Graves designed this championship
semiprivate 18-hole course next to Quail Lodge that provides challeng-
ing play for golfers of all skill levels. The course, which incorporates
five lakes, edges the Carmel River. For the most part flat, the walk-
able course is well maintained, with stunning views, lush fairways, and
ultrasmooth greens. ✉ *8000 Valley Greens Dr., Carmel* ☎ *831/620–
8808 golf shop, 831/620–8866 club concierge* ⊕ *www.quaillodge.com*
🎟 *$175 Apr.–Oct., $150 Nov.–Mar.* ⛳ *18 holes, 6500 yards, par 71.*

Rancho Cañada Golf Club. With two 18-hole courses at reasonable rates,
this public facility is a local favorite. The gently rolling fairways criss-
cross the Carmel River, and views of the tree-studded Santa Lucia
Mountains appear from nearly every vantage point. ✉ *4860 Carmel
Valley Rd., 1 mile east of Hwy. 1, Carmel* ☎ *831/624–0111, 800/536–
9459* ⊕ *ranchocanada.com* 🎟 *$70* ⛳ *East Course: 18 holes, 6125
yards, par 71; West Course: 18 holes, 6357 yards, par 71.*

SPA

Fodor'sChoice   **Refuge.** At this co-ed, European-style center on 2 serene acres you can
★   recharge without breaking the bank. Heat up in the eucalyptus steam
room or cedar sauna, plunge into cold pools, and relax indoors in zero-
gravity chairs or outdoors in Adirondack chairs around fire pits. Repeat
the cycle a few times, then lounge around the thermal waterfall pools.
Talk is not allowed, and bathing suits are required. ✉ *27300 Rancho
San Carlos Rd., south off Carmel Valley Rd., Carmel* ☎ *831/620–7360*
⊕ *refuge.com* 🎟 *$44* 🕐 *Daily 10–10* ☞ *$109 50-min massage (includes
Refuge admission), $12 robe rental, hot tubs (outdoor), sauna, steam
room. Services: Aromatherapy, hydrotherapy, massage.*

PEBBLE BEACH

Off North San Antonio Avenue in Carmel-by-the-Sea or off Sunset Drive in Pacific Grove.

Fodor's Choice ★ In 1919 the Pacific Improvement Company acquired 18,000 acres of prime land on the Monterey Peninsula, including the entire Pebble Beach coastal region and much of Pacific Grove. Pebble Beach Golf Links and The Lodge at Pebble Beach opened the same year, and the private enclave evolved into a world-class golf destination with three posh lodges, five golf courses, and some of the West Coast's ritziest homes.

GETTING HERE AND AROUND

If you drive south from Monterey on Highway 1, exit at 17-Mile Drive/Sunset Drive in Pacific Grove to find the northern entrance gate. Coming from Carmel, exit at Ocean Avenue and follow the road almost to the beach; turn right on North San Antonio Avenue to the Carmel Gate. You can also enter through the Highway 1 Gate off Highway 68. Monterey–Salinas Transit buses provide regular service in and around Pebble Beach.

EXPLORING

Fodor's Choice ★ **17-Mile Drive.** Primordial nature resides in quiet harmony with palatial, mostly Spanish Mission–style estates along 17-Mile Drive, which winds through an 8,400-acre microcosm of the Pebble Beach coastal landscape. Dotting the drive are rare Monterey cypresses, trees so gnarled and twisted that Robert Louis Stevenson described them as "ghosts fleeing before the wind." The most famous of these is the **Lone Cypress** (⇨ *see below*). Other highlights include **Bird Rock** and **Seal Rock,** home to harbor seals, sea lions, cormorants, and pelicans and other sea creatures and birds, and the **Crocker Marble Palace,** inspired by a Byzantine castle and easily identifiable by its dozens of marble arches.

Enter 17-Mile Drive at the Highway 1 Gate, at Highway 68; the Carmel Gate, off North San Antonio Avenue; the Pacific Grove Gate, off Sunset Drive; S.F.B. Morse Gate, Morse Drive off Highway 68; and Country Club Gate, at Congress Avenue and Forest Lodge Road. **■ TIP→ If you spend $30 or more on dining or shopping in Pebble Beach and show a receipt upon exiting, you'll receive a refund off the drive's $10 per car fee.** ✉ *Highway 1 Gate, 17-Mile Dr., west of Hwy. 1 and Hwy. 68 intersection* 🎟 *$10 per car, free for bicyclists.*

The Lone Cypress. The most-photographed tree along 17-Mile Drive is the weather-sculpted Lone Cypress, which grows out of a precipitous outcropping above the waves about 1½ miles up the road from Pebble Beach Golf Links. You can't walk out to the tree, but you can stop for a view of it at a small parking area off the road.

WHERE TO STAY

$$$$ RESORT Fodor's Choice ★ 🏨 **Casa Palmero.** This exclusive boutique hotel evokes a stately Mediterranean villa. **Pros:** ultimate in pampering; sumptuous decor; more private than sister resorts; right on the golf course. **Cons:** pricey; may be *too* posh for some. [$] *Rooms from: $910* ✉ *1518 Cypress Dr.* ☎ *831/622–6650, 800/654–9300* 🌐 *www.pebblebeach.com* 🛏 *20 rooms, 4 suites* 🍴 *Breakfast.*

$$$$ RESORT **The Inn at Spanish Bay.** This resort sprawls across a breathtaking stretch of shoreline, and has lush, 600-square-foot rooms. **Pros:** attentive service; many amenities; spectacular views. **Cons:** huge hotel; 4 miles from other Pebble Beach Resorts facilities. [$] *Rooms from: $650* ✉ *2700 17-Mile Dr.* ☎ *831/647–7500, 800/654–9300* 🌐 *www.pebblebeach.com* 🛏 *252 rooms, 17 suites.*

$$$$ RESORT **The Lodge at Pebble Beach.** Most rooms have wood-burning fireplaces and many have wonderful ocean views at this circa-1919 resort. **Pros:** world-class golf; borders the ocean and fairways; fabulous facilities. **Cons:** some rooms are on the small side; very pricey. [$] *Rooms from: $765* ✉ *1700 17-Mile Dr.* ☎ *831/624–3811, 800/654–9300* 🌐 *www.pebblebeach.com* 🛏 *142 rooms, 19 suites* 🍴 *No meals.*

SPORTS AND THE OUTDOORS

GOLF

Links at Spanish Bay. This course, which hugs a choice stretch of shoreline, was designed by Robert Trent Jones Jr., Tom Watson, and Sandy Tatum in the rugged manner of traditional Scottish links, with sand dunes and coastal marshes interspersed among the greens. A bagpiper signals the course's closing each day. ■ **TIP→ Nonguests of the Pebble Beach Resorts can reserve tee times up to two months in advance.** ✉ *17-Mile Dr., north end* ☎ *800/654–9300* 🌐 *www.pebblebeach.com* 🎟 *$270* ⛳ *18 holes, 6821 yards, par 72.*

Fodor's Choice ★ **Pebble Beach Golf Links.** Each February, show-business celebrities and golf pros team up at this course, the main site of the glamorous AT&T Pebble Beach National Pro-Am tournament. On most days the rest of the year, tee times are available to guests of the Pebble Beach Resorts who book a minimum two-night stay. Nonguests can reserve a tee time only one day in advance on a space-available basis; resort guests can reserve up to 18 months in advance. ✉ *17-Mile Dr., near The Lodge at Pebble Beach* ☎ *800/654–9300* 🌐 *www.pebblebeach.com* 🎟 *$495* ⛳ *18 holes, 6828 yards, par 72.*

Peter Hay. The only 9-hole, par-3 course on the Monterey Peninsula open to the public, Peter Hay attracts golfers of all skill levels. It's an ideal place for warm-ups, practicing short games, and for those who don't have time to play 18 holes. ✉ *17-Mile Dr. and Portola Rd.* ☎ *831/622–8723* 🌐 *www.pebblebeach.com* 🎟 *$30* ⛳ *9 holes, 725 yards, par 27.*

Poppy Hills. An 18-hole course designed in 1986 by Robert Trent Jones Jr., Poppy Hills reopened in 2014 after a yearlong renovation that Jones supervised. Each hole has been restored to its natural elevation along the forest floor, and all 18 greens have been rebuilt with bent grass. Individuals may reserve up to a month in advance. Chef Johnny De Vivo grows and sources organic ingredients that inspire the menus at the course's restaurant. ■ **TIP→ Poppy Hills, owned by a golfing nonprofit, represents good value for this area.** ✉ *3200 Lopez Rd., at 17-Mile Dr.* ☎ *831/622–8239* 🌐 *poppyhillsgolf.com* 🎟 *$210* ⛳ *18 holes, 7002 yards, par 73.5.*

Spyglass Hill. With three holes rated among the toughest on the PGA tour, Spyglass Hill, designed by Robert Trent Jones Sr. and Jr., challenges golfers with its varied terrain but rewards them with glorious views.

The first five holes border the Pacific, and the other 13 reach deep into the Del Monte Forest. Reservations are essential and may be made up to one month in advance (18 months for resort guests). ⊠ *Stevenson Dr. and Spyglass Hill Rd.* ☎ *800/654–9300* ⊕ *www.pebblebeach.com* ⊠ *$385* ⅃ *18 holes, 6960 yards, par 72.*

PACIFIC GROVE

3 miles north of Carmel-by-the-Sea.

This picturesque town, which began as a summer retreat for church groups more than a century ago, recalls its prim and proper Victorian heritage in its host of tiny board-and-batten cottages and stately mansions. However, long before the church groups flocked here the area received thousands of annual pilgrims—in the form of bright orange-and-black monarch butterflies. They still come, migrating south from Canada and the Pacific Northwest to take residence in pine and eucalyptus groves from October through March. In Butterfly Town USA, as Pacific Grove is known, the sight of a mass of butterflies hanging from the branches like a long, fluttering veil is unforgettable.

A prime way to enjoy Pacific Grove is to walk or bicycle the 3 miles of city-owned shoreline along Ocean View Boulevard, a cliff-top area landscaped with native plants and dotted with benches meant for sitting and gazing at the sea. You can spot many types of birds here, including the web-footed cormorants that crowd the massive rocks rising out of the surf. Two Victorians of note along Ocean View are the Queen Anne–style Green Gables, at No. 301—erected in 1888, it's now an inn—and the 1909 Pryor House, at No. 429, a massive, shingled, private residence with a leaded- and beveled-glass doorway.

GETTING HERE AND AROUND

Reach Pacific Grove via Highway 68 off Highway 1, just south of Monterey. From Cannery Row in Monterey, head north until the road merges with Ocean Boulevard and follow it along the coast. MST buses travel within Pacific Grove and surrounding towns.

EXPLORING

FAMILY **Lovers Point Park.** The coastal views are gorgeous from this waterfront park whose sheltered beach has a children's pool and a picnic area. The main lawn has a volleyball court and a snack bar. ⊠ *Ocean View Blvd. northwest of Forest Ave.* ☎ *831/648–5730.*

FAMILY **Monarch Grove Sanctuary.** The sanctuary is a reliable spot for viewing monarch butterflies between October and March. ■TIP➔ **The best time to visit is between noon and 3 pm.** ⊠ *250 Ridge Rd., off Lighthouse Ave.* ⊕ *www.pgmuseum.org/monarch-viewing.*

Pacific Grove Museum of Natural History. The museum, a good source for the latest information about monarch butterflies, has permanent exhibitions about the butterflies, birds of Monterey County, biodiversity, and plants. There's a native plant garden, and a display documents life in Pacific Grove's 19th-century Chinese fishing village. ⊠ *165 Forest Ave., at Central Ave.* ☎ *831/648–5716* ⊕ *pgmuseum.org* ⊠ *$9, free last Sat. of the month* ⊙ *Tues.–Sun. 10–5.*

FAMILY **Point Pinos Lighthouse.** At this 1855 structure, the West Coast's oldest continuously operating lighthouse, you can learn about the lighting and foghorn operations and wander through a small museum containing U.S. Coast Guard memorabilia. ✉ *Asilomar Ave., between Lighthouse Ave. and Del Monte Blvd.* ☎ *831/648–3176* 🌐 *pointpinoslighthouse.org* 🎟 *$2* 🕒 *Thurs.–Mon. 1–4.*

BEACHES

Asilomar State Beach. A beautiful coastal area, Asilomar State Beach stretches between Point Pinos and the Del Monte Forest. The 100 acres of dunes, tidal pools, and pocket-size beaches form one of the region's richest areas for marine life—including surfers, who migrate here most winter mornings. Leashed dogs are allowed on the beach. **Amenities:** none. **Best For:** sunrise; sunset; surfing; walking. ✉ *Sunset Dr. and Asilomar Ave.* ☎ *831/646–6440* 🌐 *www.parks.ca.gov.*

4

WHERE TO EAT

$$ MODERN AMERICAN

🍴 **Beach House.** Patrons of this blufftop perch sip classic cocktails, sample California fare, and watch the otters frolic on Lovers Point Beach below. Standouts among the appetizers include the crispy shrimp—tossed in a creamy, spicy sauce—and oysters Rockefeller on ciabatta crostini. Among the entrées worth a try are pan-roasted duck breast with brandy-persimmon wild rice, bacon-wrapped meat loaf, and crab-stuffed sole topped with saffron cream. The sunset discounts between 4 and 6 (reservations recommended) are a great value. **■ TIP→ For the best views of the beach and bay, sit on the heated outdoor patio.** [$] *Average main: $21* ✉ *620 Ocean View Blvd.* ☎ *831/375–2345* 🌐 *beachhousepg.com* 🕒 *No lunch.*

$$$ MEDITERRANEAN Fodor's Choice ★

🍴 **Fandango.** The menu here is mostly Mediterranean and southern French, with such dishes as osso buco and paella. The decor follows suit: stone walls and country furniture lend the restaurant the earthy feel of a European farmhouse. This is where locals come when they want to have a big dinner with friends, drink wine, have fun, and generally feel at home. [$] *Average main: $28* ✉ *223 17th St., south of Lighthouse Ave.* ☎ *831/372–3456* 🌐 *fandangorestaurant.com.*

$$$ ITALIAN

🍴 **Joe Rombi's La Mia Cucina.** Pasta, fish, steaks, and chops are the specialties at this modern trattoria, the best in town for Italian food. The look is spare and clean, with colorful antique wine posters decorating the white walls. Next door, the affiliated **La Piccola Casa** serves breakfast (baked goods) and lunch daily, plus early dinner from Wednesday through Sunday. [$] *Average main: $23* ✉ *208 17th St., at Lighthouse Ave.* ☎ *831/373–2416* 🌐 *lamiacucinaristorante.com* 🕒 *Closed Mon. and Tues. No lunch.*

$$$ MODERN AMERICAN Fodor's Choice ★

🍴 **Passionfish.** South American artwork and artifacts decorate Passionfish, and Latin and Asian flavors infuse the dishes. Chef Ted Walter shops at local farmers' markets several times a week to find the best produce, fish, and meat available, then pairs it with creative sauces. The menu might include sea scallops with a caper, raisin, and walnut relish, or banana walnut–bread pudding with honey-ginger ice cream. [$] *Average main: $24* ✉ *701 Lighthouse Ave., at Congress Ave.* ☎ *831/655–3311* 🌐 *passionfish.net* 🕒 *No lunch.*

$$ ✕ **Red House Café.** When it's nice out, sun pours through the big windows
AMERICAN   of this cozy restaurant and across tables on the porch; when fog rolls
in, the fireplace is lit. The American menu changes with the seasons but
grilled lamb chops atop mashed potatoes are often on offer for dinner,
and a grilled calamari steak might be served for lunch, either in a salad
or as part of a sandwich. Breakfast on weekends is a local favorite.
$ *Average main: $21* ⊠ *662 Lighthouse Ave., at 19th St.* ☎ *831/643–
1060* ⊕ *redhousecafe.com* ☾ *No dinner Mon.*

$$ ✕ **Taste Café and Bistro.** Grilled marinated rabbit, roasted half chicken,
AMERICAN   filet mignon, and other meats are the focus at Taste, which serves hearty
European-inspired food in a casual, open-kitchen setting. $ *Average
main: $21* ⊠ *1199 Forest Ave., at Prescott La.* ☎ *831/655–0324* ⊕ *taste
cafebistro.com* ☾ *Closed Sun. and Mon.*

WHERE TO STAY

$$ ⌂ **Green Gables Inn.** Stained-glass windows and ornate interior details
B&B/INN   compete with spectacular ocean views at this Queen Anne–style man-
Fodor's Choice   sion. **Pros:** exceptional views; impeccable attention to historic detail.
★   **Cons:** some rooms are small; thin walls. $ *Rooms from: $155* ⊠ *301
Ocean View Blvd.* ☎ *831/375–2095, 800/722–1774* ⊕ *www.green
gablesinnpg.com* ⇥ *10 rooms, 7 with bath; 1 suite* ⦿ *Breakfast.*

$$$ ⌂ **Martine Inn.** The glassed-in parlor and many guest rooms at this 1899
B&B/INN   Mediterranean-style villa have stunning ocean views. **Pros:** romantic;
exquisite antiques; fancy breakfast; ocean views. **Cons:** not child-
friendly; sits on a busy thoroughfare. $ *Rooms from: $209* ⊠ *255
Ocean View Blvd.* ☎ *831/373–3388, 800/852–5588* ⊕ *martineinn.com*
⇥ *25 rooms* ⦿ *Breakfast.*

MONTEREY

2 miles southeast of Pacific Grove; 2 miles north of Carmel.

Early in the 20th century Carmel Martin, the first mayor of the city of
Monterey, saw a bright future for his town: "Monterey Bay is the one
place where people can live without being disturbed by manufacturing
and big factories. I am certain that the day is coming when this will be
the most desirable place in the whole state of California." His Honor
was not far off the mark. Monterey is a scenic city filled with early
California history: adobe buildings from the 1700s, Colton Hall, where
California's first constitution was drafted in 1849, and Cannery Row,
made famous by author John Steinbeck. Thousands of visitors come
each year to mingle with otters and other sea creatures at the world-
famous Monterey Bay Aquarium and in the protected waters of the
national marine sanctuary that hugs the shoreline.

GETTING HERE AND AROUND

From San Jose or San Francisco, take U.S. 101 south to Highway 156
West at Prunedale. Head west about 8 miles to Highway 1 and follow
it about 15 miles south. From San Luis Obispo, take U.S. 101 north to
Salinas and drive west on Highway 68 about 20 miles.

Many MST bus lines connect at the Monterey Transit Center, at Pearl
Street and Munras Avenue. In summer (daily from 10 until at least 7),

the free MST Monterey Trolley travels from downtown Monterey along Cannery Row to the Aquarium and back.

TOURS

Monterey Movie Tours. Board a customized motor coach and relax while a film-savvy local takes you on a scenic tour of the Monterey Peninsula enhanced by film clips from the more than 200 movies shot in the area. The three-hour adventure travels a 32-mile loop through Monterey, Pacific Grove, and Carmel. ⊠ *Departs from Monterey Conference Center, 1 Portola Plaza* ☎ *831/240–0191, 866/846–0488* ⊕ *montereymovie tours.com* ✉ *$55* ⊙ *Daily at 1.*

Old Monterey Walking Tour. Learn all about Monterey's storied past by joining a guided walking tour through the historic district. Tours begin at Custom House Plaza, across from Fisherman's Wharf. ✉ *$5, includes admission to Custom House and Pacific House* ⊙ *Fri.–Sun. and Mon. holidays at 10:30, 12:30, and 2.*

ESSENTIALS

Visitor Information Monterey County Convention & Visitors Bureau ☎ *888/221–1010* ⊕ *seemonterey.com.*

EXPLORING

TOP ATTRACTIONS

Cannery Row. When John Steinbeck published the novel *Cannery Row* in 1945, he immortalized a place of rough-edged working people. The waterfront street, edging a mile of gorgeous coastline, once was crowded with sardine canneries processing, at their peak, nearly 200,000 tons of the smelly silver fish a year. During the mid-1940s, however, the sardines disappeared from the bay, causing the canneries to close. Through the years the old tin-roof canneries have been converted into restaurants, art galleries, and malls with shops selling T-shirts, fudge, and plastic sea otters. Recent tourist development along the row has been more tasteful, however, and includes stylish inns and hotels, wine tasting rooms, and upscale specialty shops. ⊠ *Cannery Row, between Reeside and David Aves.* ⊕ *www.canneryrow.com.*

Colton Hall. A convention of delegates met here in 1849 to draft the first state constitution. The stone building, which has served as a school, a courthouse, and the county seat, is a city-run museum furnished as it was during the constitutional convention. The extensive grounds outside the hall surround the Old Monterey Jail. ⊠ *570 Pacific St., between Madison and Jefferson Sts.* ☎ *831/646–5640* ⊕ *www.monterey.org/ museums* ✉ *Free* ⊙ *Daily 10–4 (Sun. and Tues. noon–3 in winter).*

FAMILY **Fisherman's Wharf.** The mournful barking of sea lions provides a steady soundtrack all along Monterey's waterfront, but the best way to actually view the whiskered marine mammals is to walk along one of the two piers across from Custom House Plaza. Lined with souvenir shops, the wharf is undeniably touristy, but it's lively and entertaining. At Wharf No. 2, a working municipal pier, you can see the day's catch being unloaded from fishing boats on one side and fishermen casting their lines into the water on the other. The pier has a couple of low-key

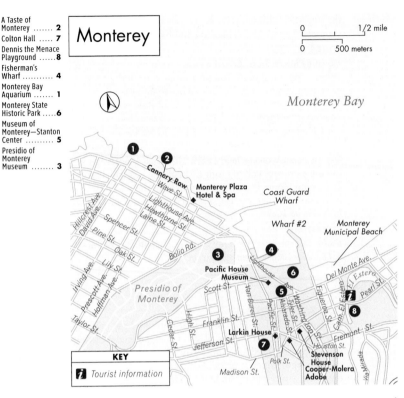

restaurants, from whose seats lucky customers might spot otters and harbor seals. ⊠ *At end of Calle Principal* ⊕ *www.montereywharf.com.*

FAMILY

Fodor's Choice

★

Monterey Bay Aquarium. Sea creatures surround you the minute you hand over your ticket at this extraordinary facility: right at the entrance dozens of them swim in a three-story-tall, sunlit kelp-forest tank. All the exhibits here provide a sense of what it's like to be in the water with the animals—sardines swim around your head in a circular tank, and jellyfish drift in and out of view in dramatically lighted spaces that suggest the ocean depths. A petting pool puts you literally in touch with bat rays, and the million-gallon Open Seas tank illustrates the variety of creatures, from sharks to placid-looking turtles, that live in the eastern Pacific. At the Splash Zone, which has 45 interactive bilingual exhibits, kids can commune with African black-footed penguins, potbellied seahorses, and other creatures. The only drawback to the aquarium experience is that it must be shared with the throngs that congregate daily, but most visitors think it's worth it. ■TIP→ **Through 2016, don't miss Tentacles: The Astounding Lives of Octopuses, Squid, and Cuttlefishes, a huge and fascinating exhibit of marine mollusks.** ⊠ *886 Cannery Row, at David Ave.* ☎ *831/648–4800 info, 866/963–9645 for advance tickets* ⊕ *montereybayaquarium.org* ⊠ *$40* ☾ *Mar.–June, daily 10–6; July–Aug., weekdays, 9:30–6, weekends 9:30–8; Nov.–Feb., daily 10–5.*

Fodor's Choice ★ **Monterey State Historic Park.** You can glimpse Monterey's early history in several well-preserved adobe buildings downtown. Some of the structures have gardens that are themselves worthy sights, and they're visitable even if the buildings, among them **Casa Soberanes,** the **Cooper-Molera Adobe,** the **Larkin House,** and the **Stevenson House,** are closed.

A good place to start is the **Pacific House Museum.** Once a hotel and saloon, this facility, also a visitor center, commemorates life in pioneer-era California with gold-rush relics and photographs of old Monterey. On the upper floor are Native American artifacts, including gorgeous baskets and pottery. In the same plaza is the **Custom House.** Built by the Mexican government in 1827, it's California's oldest standing public building.

■TIP→ Because of state budget cuts, some buildings may be closed when you visit, but 24/7 you can access a cell phone tour at ☎831/998–9498. ⊠ *Pacific House Museum visitor center, 10 Custom House Plaza* ☎ *831/649–7118* ⊕ *www.parks.ca.gov/mshp* ☜ *Free–$5* ☉ *Call or check website for hrs.*

Museum of Monterey—Stanton Center. The museum displays maritime artifacts, art, photography, and costumes from Monterey's earliest days to the present. The collection's jewel is the enormous Fresnel lens from the Point Sur Light Station. ⊠ *Stanton Center, 5 Custom House Plaza* ☎ *831/372–2608* ⊕ *www.museumofmonterey.org* ☜ *Free* ☉ *May–Aug., Tues.–Sat. 10–7, Sun. noon–5; Sept.–Apr., Wed.–Sat. 11–5, Sun. noon–5.*

WORTH NOTING

A Taste of Monterey. Without driving the back roads, you can taste the wines of nearly 100 area vintners (craft beers, too) while taking in fantastic bay views. Bottles are available for purchase, and food is served from noon until closing. ⊠ *700 Cannery Row, Suite KK* ☎ *831/646–5446, 888/646–5446* ⊕ *atasteofmonterey.com* ☜ *Tastings $10–$20* ☉ *Sun.–Wed. 11–7, Thurs.–Sat. 11–8.*

FAMILY **Dennis the Menace Playground.** The late cartoonist Hank Ketcham designed this play area. Its equipment is on a grand scale and made for Dennis-like daredevils: kid favorites include the roller slide, rock-climbing area, and clanking suspension bridge. You can rent a rowboat or a paddleboat for cruising around U-shaped Lake El Estero, populated with an assortment of ducks, mud hens, and geese. ⊠ *El Estero Park, Pearl St. and Camino El Estero* ☎ *831/646–3866* ⊕ *www.monterey.org/parks* ☉ *Closed Tues., Sept.–May.*

Trained "seals" that perform in circuses are actually California sea lions—intelligent, social animals that live (and sleep) close together in groups.

Presidio of Monterey Museum. This spot has been significant for centuries. Its first incarnation was as a Native American village for the Rumsien tribe. The Spanish explorer Sebastián Vizcaíno landed here in 1602, and Father Junípero Serra arrived in 1770. Notable battles fought here include the 1818 skirmish in which the corsair Hipólito Bruchard conquered the Spanish garrison that stood on this site and claimed part of California for Argentina. The indoor museum tells the stories; plaques mark the outdoor sites. ⊠ *Presidio of Monterey, Corporal Ewing Rd., off Lighthouse Ave.* ☎ *831/646–3456* ⊕ *www.monterey.org/museums* ⊠ *Free* ☉ *Mon. 10–1, Thurs.–Sat. 10–4, Sun. 1–4.*

WHERE TO EAT

$$
SEAFOOD
✕ **Monterey Fish House.** Casual yet stylish and always packed, this seafood restaurant is removed from the hubbub of the wharf. If the dining room is full, you can wait at the bar and savor plump oysters on the half shell. The bartenders and waitstaff will gladly advise you on the perfect wine to go with your poached, blackened, or oak-grilled seafood. Ⓢ *Average main: $22* ⊠ *2114 Del Monte Ave., at Dela Vina Ave.* ☎ *831/373–4647* ⌕ *Reservations essential* ☉ *No lunch weekends.*

$$$
AMERICAN
Fodor's Choice
★
✕ **Montrio Bistro.** This quirky converted firehouse, with its rawhide walls and iron indoor trellises, has a wonderfully sophisticated menu. Chef Tony Baker uses organic produce and meats and sustainably sourced seafood to create imaginative dishes that reflect the area's agriculture—fire-roasted artichokes with Mediterranean relish, for instance, and pesto-rubbed sirloin prepared with brussels sprouts, dates, and smoked bacon. Monterey wineries are well represented on the wine list, and

the signature cocktails are infused with local fruits, herbs, and vegetables. $ *Average main: $25* ⊠ *414 Calle Principal, at W. Franklin St.* ☎ *831/648–8880* ⊕ *montrio.com* ⚑ *Reservations essential* ⊙ *No lunch.*

$$$ ✕ **Old Fisherman's Grotto.** Otters and

SEAFOOD seals frolic in the water just below this nautical-theme Fisherman's Wharf restaurant famous for its creamy clam chowder. Seafood paella, sand dabs, filet mignon, teriyaki chicken, and several pastas are among the many entrée options. ■ TIP→ **Reserve a window-side table for the best views.** $ *Average main: $26* ⊠ *39 Fisherman's Wharf* ☎ *831/375–4604* ⊕ *oldfishermansgrotto.com.*

$ ✕ **Old Monterey Café.** Breakfast here gets constant local raves. The café's

AMERICAN fame rests on familiar favorites: a dozen kinds of omelets, and pancakes from blueberry to cinnamon-raisin-pecan. For lunch are good soups, salads, and sandwiches. $ *Average main: $13* ⊠ *489 Alvarado St., at Munras Ave.* ☎ *831/646–1021* ⚑ *Reservations not accepted* ⊙ *No dinner.*

$$$$ ✕ **Restaurant 1833.** Inside the two-story Stokes Adobe, built in 1833,

MODERN this popular restaurant and bar showcases the region's colorful history

AMERICAN and local bounty. Each of the seven dining rooms honors an era and

Fodor'sChoice characters from the adobe's past, which includes an early stint as an

★ apothecary. Sit in a leather booth on the Founder's Balcony for a bird's-eye view of the bustling bar scene below, or outdoors by the courtyard fire pits near giant oak, redwood, palm, and magnolia trees. Menu stars include whole roasted truffle chicken, pan-roasted sturgeon, and grilled prime château sirloin with duck-fat potatoes, cipollini onions, and bordelaise sauce. The extensive wine selection will appeal to connoisseurs. $ *Average main: $32* ⊠ *500 Hartnell St., at Polk St.* ☎ *831/643–1833* ⊕ *www.restaurant1833.com* ⊙ *No lunch.*

$$$ ✕ **Tarpy's Roadhouse.** Fun, dressed-up American favorites—a little some-

AMERICAN thing for everyone—are served in this renovated early-1900s stone farmhouse several miles east of town. The kitchen cranks out everything from Cajun-spiced prawns to meat loaf with marsala-mushroom gravy to grilled ribs and steaks. Eat indoors by a fireplace or outdoors in the courtyard. $ *Average main: $24* ⊠ *2999 Monterey–Salinas Hwy., Hwy. 68* ☎ *831/647–1444* ⊕ *tarpys.com.*

FORMER CAPITAL OF CALIFORNIA

In 1602 Spanish explorer Sebastián Vizcaíno stepped ashore on a remote California peninsula. He named it after the viceroy of New Spain—Count de Monte Rey. Soon the Spanish built a military outpost, and the site was the capital of California until the state came under American rule.

4

WHERE TO STAY

$$$ ⛱ **InterContinental The Clement Monterey.** Spectacular bay views, upscale

HOTEL amenities, assiduous service, and a superb location next to the aquarium propelled this luxury hotel to immediate stardom. **Pros:** a block from the aquarium; fantastic waterfront views from some rooms; great for families. **Cons:** a tad formal; pricey. $ *Rooms from: $229* ⊠ *750*

CLOSE UP

The Monterey Bay National Marine Sanctuary

Although Monterey's coastal landscapes are stunning, their beauty is more than equaled by the wonders that lie offshore. The Monterey Bay National Marine Sanctuary—which stretches 276 miles, from north of San Francisco almost down to Santa Barbara—teems with abundant life, and has topography as diverse as that aboveground.

The preserve's 5,322 square miles include vast submarine canyons, which reach down 10,663 feet at their deepest point. They also encompass dense forests of giant kelp—a kind of seaweed that can grow more than a hundred feet from its roots on the ocean floor. These kelp forests are especially robust off Monterey.

The sanctuary was established in 1992 to protect the habitat of the many species that thrive in the bay. Some animals can be seen quite easily from land. In summer and winter you might glimpse the offshore spray of gray whales as they migrate between their summer feeding grounds in Alaska and their breeding grounds in Baja. Clouds of marine birds—including white-faced ibis, three types of albatross, and more than 15 types of gull—skim the waves, or roost in the rock islands along 17-Mile Drive. Sea otters dart and gambol in the calmer waters of the bay; and of course, you can watch the sea lions—and hear their round-the-clock barking—on the wharves in Santa Cruz and Monterey.

The sanctuary supports many other creatures, however, that remain unseen by most on-land visitors. Some of these are enormous, such as the giant blue whales that arrive to feed on plankton in summer; others, like the more than 22 species of red algae in these waters, are microscopic. So whether you choose to visit the Monterey Bay Aquarium, take a whale-watch trip, or look out to sea with your binoculars, remember you're seeing just a small part of a vibrant underwater kingdom.

Cannery Row ☎ *831/375–4500, 866/781–2406 toll free* 🌐 *www.ictheclementmonterey.com* 🛏 *192 rooms, 16 suites* 🍴 *No meals.*

$$ HOTEL **Monterey Bay Lodge.** Its superior amenities and location bordering El Estero Park give this cheerful facility the edge over other area motels. **Pros:** within walking distance of the beach and a playground; quiet at night; good family choice. **Cons:** near a busy boulevard. [$] *Rooms from: $140* ✉ *55 Camino Aguajito* ☎ *831/372–8057, 800/558–1900* 🌐 *montereybaylodge.com* 🛏 *43 rooms, 3 suites* 🍴 *No meals.*

$$$ RESORT **Monterey Beach Resort.** One of the area's best values, this hotel has a great waterfront location—2 miles north of Monterey, with views of the bay and the city skyline—and offers a surprising array of amenities. **Pros:** on the beach; great value; family-friendly. **Cons:** several miles from major attractions; big-box mall neighborhood. [$] *Rooms from: $199* ✉ *2600 Sand Dunes Dr.* ☎ *831/394–3321, 800/242–8627* 🌐 *montereybeachresort.com* 🛏 *196 rooms* 🍴 *No meals.*

$$$$ HOTEL **Monterey Plaza Hotel & Spa.** Guests at this waterfront Cannery Row hotel can see frolicking sea otters from its wide outdoor patio and many room balconies. **Pros:** on the ocean; many amenities; attentive

service. **Cons:** touristy area; heavy traffic. $\boxed{\$}$ *Rooms from: $269* ⊠ *400 Cannery Row* ☎ *831/646–1700, 800/334–3999* ⊕ *www.montereyplaza hotel.com* ↝ *280 rooms, 10 suites* ⏵⊙⏴ *Multiple meal plans.*

$$$$
B&B/INN
Fodor's Choice
★

⏢ **Old Monterey Inn.** This three-story manor house was the home of Monterey's first mayor, and today it remains a private enclave within walking distance of downtown, set off by lush gardens shaded by huge old trees and bordered by a creek. **Pros:** gorgeous gardens; refined luxury; serene. **Cons:** must drive to attractions and sights; fills quickly. $\boxed{\$}$ *Rooms from: $289* ⊠ *500 Martin St.* ☎ *831/375–8284, 800/350–2344* ⊕ *www.old montereyinn.com* ↝ *6 rooms, 3 suites, 1 cottage* ⏵⊙⏴ *Breakfast.*

$$$
HOTEL

⏢ **Spindrift Inn.** This boutique hotel on Cannery Row has beach access and a rooftop garden that overlooks the water. **Pros:** close to aquarium; steps from the beach; friendly staff. **Cons:** throngs of visitors outside; can be noisy; not good for families. $\boxed{\$}$ *Rooms from: $209* ⊠ *652 Cannery Row* ☎ *831/646–8900, 800/841–1879* ⊕ *spindriftinn.com* ↝ *45 rooms* ⏵⊙⏴ *Breakfast.*

NIGHTLIFE AND PERFORMING ARTS

BARS

Turn 12 Bar & Grill. The motorcycles and vintage photographs at this downtown watering hole pay homage to nearby 11-turn Laguna Seca Raceway. The large-screen TVs, heated outdoor patio, happy-hour specials, and live entertainment keep the place jumpin' into the wee hours. ⊠ *400 Tyler St., at E. Franklin St.* ☎ *831/372–8876* ⊕ *turn12barand-grill.com.*

Peter B's Brewpub. Housemade beers, 15 HDTVs, a decent pub menu, and a pet-friendly patio ensure lively crowds at this craft brewery in back of the Portola Plaza Hotel. ⊠ *2 Portola Plaza* ☎ *831/649–2699* ⊕ *www.peterbsbrewpub.com.*

MUSIC FESTIVALS

Monterey Jazz Festival. The world's oldest jazz festival attracts top-name performers to the Monterey Fairgrounds on the third full weekend of September. ☎ *888/248–6499 ticket office, 831/373–3366* ⊕ *monterey jazzfestival.org.*

THEATER

Bruce Ariss Wharf Theater (*The New Wharf Theatre*). American musicals past and present are the focus here, with dramas and comedies also in the mix. ⊠ *One Fisherman's Wharf* ☎ *831/649–2332.*

SPORTS AND THE OUTDOORS

Monterey Bay waters never warm to the temperatures of their Southern California counterparts—the warmest they get is the low 60s. That's one reason why the marine life here is so diverse, which in turn brings out the fishers, kayakers, and whale-watchers. During the rainy winter, the waves grow larger, and surfers flock to the water. On land pretty much year-round, bikers find opportunities to ride, and walkers have plenty of waterfront to stroll.

BIKING

Adventures by the Sea. You can rent surreys plus tandem, standard, and electric bicycles from this outfit that also conducts bike and kayak tours and rents kayaks and standup paddleboards. ⊠ *299 Cannery Row* ☎ *831/372–1807, 800/979–3370 reservations* ⊕ *adventuresbythesea. com* ⊠ *Breakwater Cove, 32 Cannery Row* ⊠ *685 Cannery Row* ⊠ *Beach at Lovers Point, Pacific Grove* ⊠ *Stillwater Cove, 17-Mile Drive, Pebble Beach* ⊠ *210 Alvarado Mall.*

Bay Bikes. For bicycle and surrey rentals, visit Bay Bikes at one of its two Monterey shops. ■**TIP→ You can rent a bike on Cannery Row and drop it off at the company's Carmel location.** ⊠ *585 Cannery Row* ☎ *831/655–2453* ⊕ *www.baybikes.com* ⊠ *486 Washington St.* ⊠ *3600 The Barnyard, Carmel.*

FISHING

Randy's Fishing and Whale Watching Trips. In business since 1949, Randy's takes beginning and experienced fishers out to sea. ⊠ *66 Fisherman's Wharf* ☎ *831/372–7440, 800/251–7440* ⊕ *randysfishingtrips.com.*

KAYAKING

Fodor's Choice ★ **Monterey Bay Kayaks.** For many visitors the best way to see the bay is by kayak. This company rents equipment and conducts classes and natural-history tours. ⊠ *693 Del Monte Ave.* ☎ *831/373–5357, 800/649–5357* ⊕ *www.montereybaykayaks.com.*

WALKING

Monterey Bay Coastal Recreation Trail. From Custom House Plaza, you can walk along the coast in either direction on this 29-mile-long trail and take in spectacular views of the sea. The trail runs from north of Monterey in Castroville south to Pacific Grove, with sections continuing around Pebble Beach. Much of the path follows an old Southern Pacific Railroad route. ☎ *888/221–1010* ⊕ *seemonterey.com/things-to-do/ parks/coastal-trail.*

WHALE-WATCHING

Thousands of gray whales pass close by the Monterey Coast on their annual migration between the Bering Sea and Baja California, and a whale-watching cruise is the best way to see these magnificent mammals close up. The migration south takes place from December through March; January is prime viewing time. The whales migrate north from March through June. Blue whales and humpbacks also pass the coast; they're most easily spotted in late summer and early fall.

Fast Raft Ocean Safaris. Naturalists lead whale-watching and sightseeing tours of Monterey Bay aboard the 33-foot *Ranger,* a six-passenger, rigid-hull inflatable boat. The speedy craft slips into coves inaccessible to larger vessels; its quiet engines enable intimate marine experiences without disturbing wildlife. Children ages 12 and older are welcome to participate. ⊠ *32 Cannery Row, Suite F2* ☎ *800/979–3370* ⊕ *www. fastraft.com* ⊠ *$140.*

Monterey Bay Whale Watch. The marine biologists here lead three- to five-hour whale-watching tours. ⊠ *84 Fisherman's Wharf* ☎ *831/375–4658* ⊕ *montereybaywhalewatch.com.*

Princess Monterey Whale Watching. Tours are offered daily on a 150-passenger high-speed cruiser and a large 75-foot boat. ⊠ *96 Fisherman's Wharf* ☎ *831/372–2203, 831/205–2370 reservations, 888/223–9153 international reservations* ⊕ *montereywhalewatching.com.*

SHOPPING

Alvarado and nearby downtown streets are good places to start a Monterey shopping spree, especially if you're interested in antiques and collectibles.

Cannery Row Antique Mall. Bargain hunters can sometimes find little treasures at the mall, which houses more than 100 local vendors under one roof. ⊠ *471 Wave St.* ☎ *831/655–0264* ⊕ *canneryrowantiquemall.com* ⊙ *Weekdays 10–5:30, Sat. 10–6, Sun. 10–5.*

Old Monterey Book Co. Antiquarian books and prints are this shop's specialties. ⊠ *136 Bonifacio Pl., off Alvarado St.* ☎ *831/372–3111* ⊙ *Tues. 3–7, Wed.–Sat. 1–5.*

AROUND MONTEREY BAY

As Highway 1 follows the curve of the bay between Monterey and Santa Cruz, it passes through a rich agricultural zone. Opening right onto the bay, where the Salinas and Pajaro rivers drain into the Pacific, a broad valley brings together fertile soil, an ideal climate, and a good water supply to create optimum growing conditions for crops such as strawberries, artichokes, brussels sprouts, and broccoli. Several beautiful beaches line this part of the coast. Salinas and Moss Landing are in Monterey County; the other cities and towns covered here are in Santa Cruz County.

GETTING HERE AND AROUND

All the towns in this area are on or just off Highway 1. MST buses serve Monterey County destinations, connecting in Watsonville with Santa Cruz METRO buses, which operate throughout Santa Cruz County.

SALINAS

17 miles east of Monterey on Hwy. 68.

Salinas, a hard-working city surrounded by vineyards and fruit and vegetable fields, honors the memory and literary legacy of John Steinbeck, its most famous native, with the National Steinbeck Center. The facility is in Old Town Salinas, where renovated turn-of-the-20th-century stone buildings house shops and restaurants.

ESSENTIALS

Train Information Salinas Amtrak Station ⊠ *11 Station Pl., at W. Market St., Salinas* ☎ *800/872–7245* ⊕ *www.amtrak.com.*

Visitor Information California Welcome Center ⊠ *1213 N. Davis Rd., west of U.S. 101, exit 330, Salinas* ☎ *831/757–8687* ⊕ *visitcalifornia.com/attraction/ california-welcome-center-salinas* ⊙ *Open daily 9–5.*

EXPLORING

FAMILY **Monterey Zoo.** Exotic animals, many of them retired from film, television, and live production work or rescued from less than ideal environments, find sanctuary here. For an in-depth experience, stay in a safari bungalow at Vision Quest Safari B&B, where breakfast is delivered in a basket by an elephant. ⊠ *400 River Rd., off Hwy. 68, Salinas* ☎ *831/455–1901, 800/228–7382* ⊕ *www.montereyzoo.com* ☒ *Tours $10; optional posttour elephant feeding $5* ⊙ *Tours daily at 1, June–Aug. also at 3.*

National Steinbeck Center. The center's exhibits document the life of Pulitzer- and Nobel-prize winner John Steinbeck and the history of the nearby communities that inspired novels such as *East of Eden*. Highlights include reproductions of the green pickup-camper from *Travels with Charley* and the bunkroom from *Of Mice and Men*. **Steinbeck House**, the author's Victorian birthplace, at 132 Central Avenue, is two blocks from the center in a so-so neighborhood. Now a decent lunch spot, it displays memorabilia. ⊠ *1 Main St., at Central Ave., Salinas* ☎ *831/775–4721* ⊕ *steinbeck.org* ☒ *$15* ⊙ *Daily 10–5.*

PINNACLES NATIONAL PARK

38 miles southeast of Salinas.

Pinnacles may be the nation's newest national park, but Teddy Roosevelt recognized the uniqueness of this ancient volcano—its jagged spires and monoliths thrusting upward from chaparral-covered mountains—when he made it a national monument in 1908. Though only about two hours from the bustling Bay Area, the outside world seems to recede even before you reach the park's gates.

GETTING HERE AND AROUND

One of the first things you need to decide when visiting Pinnacles is which entrance—east or west—you'll use, because there's no road connecting the two rugged peaks separating them. Entering from Highway 25 on the east is straightforward. The gate is only a mile or so from the turnoff. From the west, once you head east out of Soledad on Highway 146, the road quickly becomes narrow and hilly, with many blind curves. Drive slowly and cautiously along the 10 miles or so before you reach the west entrance.

ESSENTIALS

Pinnacles Visitor Center. At the park's main visitor center, located at the eastern entrance, you can purchase admission passes, get maps, browse books, and buy gifts. The adjacent campground store sells snacks and drinks. ⊠ *Hwy. 146, 2 miles west of Hwy. 25, Paicines* ☎ *831/389–4485* ⊕ *www.nps.gov/pinn.*

West Pinnacles Visitor Center. This station is just past the park's western entrance, about 10 miles east of Soledad. Here you can get maps and information, watch a 13-minute film about Pinnacles, and view some displays. ■TIP➔ Food and drink aren't available here, so come prepared. ⊠ *Hwy. 146, off U.S. 101, Soledad* ☎ *831/389–4427* ⊕ *www. nps.gov/pinn* ⊙ *Daily 9–4:30, call or check website to confirm hrs.*

EXPLORING

FAMILY **Pinnacles National Park.** The many attractions at Pinnacles include talus caves, 30 miles of hiking trails, and hundreds of rock climbing routes. A mosaic of diverse habitats supports an amazing variety of wildlife species: 185 birds, 49 mammals, 70 butterflies, and nearly 400 bees. The park is also home to some of the world's remaining few hundred condors in captivity and release areas. Fourteen of California's 25 bat species live in caves and other habitats in the park. President Theodore Roosevelt declared this remarkable 26,000-acre geologic and wildlife preserve a national monument in 1908. President Barack Obama officially designated it a national park in 2013.

The pinnacles are believed to have been created when two major tectonic plates collided and pushed a smaller plate down beneath the earth's crust, spawning volcanoes in what's now called the Gabilan Mountains, southeast of Salinas and Monterey. After the eruptions ceased, the San Andreas Fault split the volcanic field in two, carrying part of it northward to what is now Pinnacles National Park. Millions of years of erosion left a rugged landscape of rocky spires and crags, or pinnacles. Boulders fell into canyons and valleys, creating talus caves and a paradise for modern-day rock climbers. Spring is the most popular time to visit, when colorful wildflowers blanket the meadows, and the light and scenery can be striking in fall and winter; the summer heat is often brutal. The park has two entrances—east and west—but they are not connected. The Pinnacles Visitor Center, Bear Gulch Nature Center, Park Headquarters, the Pinnacles Campground, and the Bear Gulch Cave and Reservoir are on the east side. The Chaparral Parking Area is on the west side, where you can feast on fantastic views of the Pinnacles High Peaks from the parking area. Dogs are not allowed on hiking trails. ■TIP→ The east entrance is 32 miles southeast of Hollister via Highway 25. The west entrance is about 12 miles east of Soledad via Highway 146. ⊠ *5000 Hwy. 146, Paicines* ☎ *831/389–4486, 831/389–4427 Westside* ⊕ *www.nps.gov/pinn* 🖃 *$10 per vehicle, $5 per visitor if biking or walking* ⊗ *West entrance, daily 7:30 am–8 pm; West Pinnacles Visitor Center, daily 9–4:30 depending on season (check website or Facebook page to confirm hrs). East entrance, daily 24 hrs; Pinnacles Visitor Center, daily 9:30–5.*

SPORTS AND THE OUTDOORS
HIKING

Hiking is the most popular activity at Pinnacles, with more than 30 miles of trails for every interest and level of fitness. Because there isn't a road through the park, hiking is also the only way to experience its interior, including the High Peaks, the talus caves, and the reservoir.

Balconies Cliffs-Cave Loop. Grab your flashlight before heading out from the Chaparral Trailhead parking lot for this 2.4-mile loop that takes you through the Balconies Caves. This trail is especially beautiful in spring, when an abundance of wildflowers carpets the canyon floor. About 0.6 mile from the start of the trail, turn left to begin ascending the Balconies Cliffs Trail, where you'll be rewarded with close-up views of Machete Ridge and other steep, vertical formations; you'll probably run across a few rock climbers testing their skills. *Easy.* ⊠ *Pinnacles National Park*

⊕ *From West Pinnacles Visitor Contact Station, drive about 2 miles to Chaparral Trailhead parking lot. Trail picks up on west side of lot.*

FAMILY   **Moses Spring-Rim Trail Loop.** This is perhaps the most popular hike at Pinnacles, as it's relatively short (2.2 miles) and fun for kids and adults. It takes you to the Bear Gulch cave system, and if your timing is right, you'll pass by several seasonal waterfalls inside the caves (if it's been raining, check with a ranger, as the caves could be flooded). ⚠ The upper side of the cave is usually closed in spring and early summer to protect the Townsend's big-ear bats and their pups. *Easy.* ⊕ *Trail begins just past Bear Gulch Nature Center, on the south side of overflow parking lot.*

SAN JUAN BAUTISTA

20 miles northeast of Salinas.

Much of the small town that grew up around Mission San Juan Bautista, still a working church, has been protected from development since 1933, when a state park was established here. Small antiques shops and restaurants occupy the Old West and art deco buildings that line 3rd Street.

GETTING HERE AND AROUND

From Highway 1 north or south, exit east onto Highway 156. MST buses do not serve San Juan Bautista.

EXPLORING

San Juan Bautista State Historic Park. With the low-slung, colonnaded **Mission San Juan Bautista** as its drawing card, this park 20 miles northeast of Salinas is about as close to early-19th-century California as you can get. Historic buildings ring the wide green plaza, among them an adobe home furnished with Spanish-colonial antiques, a hotel frozen in the 1860s, a blacksmith shop, a pioneer cabin, and a jailhouse. The mission's cemetery contains the unmarked graves of more than 4,300 Native American converts. ■ TIP → On the first Saturday of the month, costumed volunteers engage in quilting bees, tortilla making, and other frontier activities, and sarsaparilla and other nonalcoholic drinks are served in the saloon. ✉ *19 Franklin St., off Hwy. 156, east of U.S. 101* ☎ *831/623–4881* ⊕ *www.parks.ca.gov* ✍ *$3 park, $4 mission* ☾ *Daily 10–4:30.*

MOSS LANDING

17 miles north of Monterey; 12 miles north of Salinas.

Moss Landing is not much more than a couple of blocks of cafés and restaurants, art galleries, and studios, plus a busy fishing port, but therein lies its charm. It's a fine place to overnight or stop for a meal and get a dose of nature.

GETTING HERE AND AROUND

From Highway 1 north or south, exit at Moss Landing Road on the ocean side. MST buses serve Moss Landing.

TOURS

Elkhorn Slough Safari Nature Boat Tours. This outfit's naturalists lead two-hour tours of Elkhorn Sough aboard a 27-foot pontoon boat. Reservations are required. ✉ *Moss Landing Harbor* ☎ *831/633–5555* 🌐 *elkhornslough.com* 🎟 *$38.*

ESSENTIALS

Visitor Information

Moss Landing Chamber of Commerce ☎ *831/633–4501* 🌐 *mosslanding chamber.com.*

EXPLORING

Elkhorn Slough National Estuarine Research Reserve. The reserve's 1,400 acres of tidal flats and salt marshes form a complex environment that supports some 300 species of birds. A walk along the meandering waterways and wetlands can reveal hawks, white-tailed kites, owls, herons, and egrets. Also living or visiting here are sea otters, sharks, rays, and many other animals. ■ **TIP→ On weekends, guided walks from the visitor center begin at 10 and 1. On the first Saturday of the month, an early-bird tour departs at 8:30.** ✉ *1700 Elkhorn Rd., Watsonville* ☎ *831/728–2822* 🌐 *elkhornslough.org* 🎟 *$4 day use fee (credit card only)* 🕑 *Wed.–Sun. 9–5.*

4

WHERE TO EAT AND STAY

$$ SOUTH AMERICAN

🍴 **Haute Enchilada.** Part of a complex that includes art galleries and an events venue, the Haute (pronounced "hot") adds bohemian character to the seafaring village of Moss Landing. The inventive Latin American–inspired dishes include crab and black corn enchiladas topped with a citrus cilantro cream sauce, and roasted *pasilla* chilies stuffed with mashed plantains and caramelized onions. Gluten-free and vegan options are also on the menu. [$] *Average main: $22* ✉ *7902 Moss Landing Rd.* ☎ *831/633–5843* 🌐 *hauteenchilada.com.*

$$ SEAFOOD

🍴 **Phil's Fish Market & Eatery.** Exquisitely fresh, simply prepared seafood (try the cioppino) is on the menu at this warehouselike restaurant on the harbor; all kinds of glistening fish are for sale at the market in the front. ■ **TIP→ Phil's Snack Shack, a tiny sandwich-and-smoothie joint, serves quicker meals at the north end of town.** [$] *Average main: $19* ✉ *7600 Sandholdt Rd.* ☎ *831/633–2152* 🌐 *philsfishmarket.com.*

$$ B&B/INN

🏨 **Captain's Inn.** Commune with nature and pamper yourself with upscale creature comforts at this green-certified complex in the heart of town. **Pros:** walk to restaurants and shops; tranquil natural setting; free Wi-Fi and parking. **Cons:** rooms in historic building don't have water views; far from urban amenities; not appropriate for young children. [$] *Rooms from: $155* ✉ *8122 Moss Landing Rd.* ☎ *831/633–5550* 🌐 *www.captainsinn.com* 🛏 *10 rooms, 1 apartment* 🍽 *Breakfast.*

SPORTS AND THE OUTDOORS

KAYAKING

Monterey Bay Kayaks. Rent a kayak to paddle out into Elkhorn Slough for up-close wildlife encounters. ✉ *2390 Hwy. 1, at North Harbor* ☎ *831/373–5357, 800/649–5357 toll free* 🌐 *montereybaykayaks.com.*

APTOS

17 miles north of Moss Landing.

Backed by a redwood forest and facing the sea, downtown Aptos—known as Aptos Village—is a place of wooden walkways and false-fronted shops. Antiques dealers cluster along Trout Gulch Road, off Soquel Drive east of Highway 1.

GETTING HERE AND AROUND

Use Highway 1 to reach Aptos from Santa Cruz or Monterey. Exit at State Park Drive to reach the main shopping hub and Aptos Village. You can also exit at Freedom Boulevard or Rio del Mar. Soquel Drive is the main artery through town.

ESSENTIALS

Visitor Information Aptos Chamber of Commerce ✉ *7605-A Old Dominion Ct.* ☎ *831/688–1467* 🌐 *aptoschamber.com.*

BEACHES

FAMILY Fodor's Choice ★ **Seacliff State Beach.** Sandstone bluffs tower above popular Seacliff State Beach. You can fish off the pier, which leads out to a sunken World War I tanker ship built of concrete. Leashed dogs are allowed on the beach. **Amenities:** food and drink; lifeguards; parking (fee); showers; toilets. **Best For:** sunset; swimming; walking. ✉ *201 State Park Dr., off Hwy. 1* ☎ *831/685–6442* 🌐 *www.parks.ca.gov* 🎟 *$10 per vehicle* 🕒 *Daily 8 am–sunset.*

WHERE TO EAT AND STAY

$$$ MEDITERRANEAN 🍴 **Bittersweet Bistro.** A large old tavern with cathedral ceilings houses this popular bistro, where chef-owner Thomas Vinolus draws culinary inspiration from the Mediterranean. The menu changes seasonally, but regular highlights include paella, seafood puttanesca, and pepper-crusted rib-eye steak with Cabernet demi-glace. The chocolate desserts are not to be missed. Breakfast and lunch are available in the casual Bittersweet Café. Leashed dogs are welcome on the outdoor patio, where you can order meaty meals for them. [$] *Average main: $27* ✉ *787 Rio Del Mar Blvd., off Hwy. 1* ☎ *831/662–9799* 🌐 *www.bittersweetbistro.com.*

$$$ HOTEL FAMILY 🏨 **Best Western Seacliff Inn.** Families and business travelers like this 6-acre property near Seacliff State Beach that's more resort than hotel. **Pros:** walking distance to the beach; family-friendly; hot breakfast buffet. **Cons:** close to freeway; occasional nighttime bar noise. [$] *Rooms from: $180* ✉ *7500 Old Dominion Ct.* ☎ *831/688–7300, 800/367–2003* 🌐 *seacliffinn.com* 🛏 *139 rooms, 10 suites* 🍽 *Breakfast.*

$$$ B&B/INN 🏨 **Flora Vista.** Multicolor fields of flowers, strawberries, and veggies unfold in every direction at this luxury neo-Georgian inn on 2 acres south of Aptos. **Pros:** private; near Sand Dollar Beach; flowers everywhere. **Cons:** no restaurants or nightlife within walking distance; not a good place for kids. [$] *Rooms from: $195* ✉ *1258 San Andreas Rd., La Selva Beach* ☎ *831/724–8663, 877/753–5672* 🌐 *floravistainn.com* 🛏 *5 rooms* 🍽 *Breakfast.*

$$$ HOTEL 🏨 **Rio Sands Hotel.** A property-wide makeover completed in 2015 has made this casual two-building complex near the beach an even more exceptional value. **Pros:** two-minute walk to Rio Del Mar Beach

(Seacliff State Beach is also nearby); free parking and Wi-Fi; close to a deli and restaurants. **Cons:** some rooms and suites are small; neighborhood becomes congested in summer. $ *Rooms from: $179* ✉ *116 Aptos Beach Dr.* ☎ *831/688–3207, 800/826–2077* ⊕ *riosands.com* ⤳ *25 rooms, 25 suites* ⦿ *Breakfast.*

$$$$
RESORT
FAMILY

⊞ **Seascape Beach Resort.** It's easy to unwind at this full-fledged resort on a bluff overlooking Monterey Bay. **Pros:** time share–style apartments; access to miles of beachfront; superb views. **Cons:** far from city life; most bathrooms are small. $ *Rooms from: $300* ✉ *1 Seascape Resort Dr.* ☎ *831/688–6800, 800/929–7727* ⊕ *seascaperesort.com* ⤳ *285 suites* ⦿ *No meals.*

CAPITOLA AND SOQUEL

4 miles northwest of Aptos.

On the National Register of Historic places as California's first seaside resort town, the village of Capitola has been in a holiday mood since the late 1800s. Casual eateries, surf shops, and ice cream parlors pack its walkable downtown. Inland, across Highway 1, antiques shops line Soquel Drive in the town of Soquel. Wineries dot the Santa Cruz Mountains beyond.

GETTING HERE AND AROUND

From Santa Cruz or Monterey, follow Highway 1 to the Capitola/Soquel (Bay Avenue) exit about 7 miles south of Santa Cruz and head west to reach Capitola and east to access Soquel Village. On summer weekends, park for free in the lot behind the Crossroads Center, a block west of the freeway, and hop aboard the free Capitola Shuttle to the village.

ESSENTIALS

Visitor Information Capitola-Soquel Chamber of Commerce ✉ *716-G Capitola Ave., Capitola* ☎ *831/475–6522* ⊕ *capitolachamber.com.*

BEACHES

FAMILY
Fodor'sChoice
★

New Brighton State Beach. Once the site of a Chinese fishing village, New Brighton is now a popular surfing and camping spot. Its Pacific Migrations Visitor Center traces the history of the Chinese and other peoples who settled around Monterey Bay and documents the migratory patterns of the area's wildlife, such as monarch butterflies and gray whales. Leashed dogs are allowed in the park. New Brighton connects with Seacliff Beach, and at low tide you can walk or run along this scenic stretch of sand for nearly 16 miles south (though you might have to wade through a few creeks). ■ **TIP →** **The 1½-mile stroll from New Brighton to Seacliff's concrete ship is a local favorite. Amenities:** parking (fee); showers; toilets. **Best for:** sunset; swimming; walking. ✉ *1500 State Park Dr., off Hwy. 1, Capitola* ☎ *831/464–6330* ⊕ *www.parks. ca.gov* 🎫 *$10 per vehicle* ☉ *Day use daily 8 am–sunset.*

WHERE TO EAT

$
SEAFOOD
FAMILY

✕ **Carpo's.** Locals love this casual counter where seafood predominates, but you can also order burgers, salads, and steaks. Baskets of battered snapper are among the favorites, along with calamari, prawns, seafood kebabs, fish-and-chips, and home-made olallieberry pie. Many items cost less than $10. ■TIP→ **Come early for lunch or dinner to beat the crowds.** $ *Average main: $11* ✉ *2400 Porter St., at Hwy. 1, Soquel* ☎ *831/476–6260* ⊕ *carpos restaurant.com.*

$
CAFÉ
FAMILY
× **Gayle's Bakery & Rosticceria.** Whether you're in the mood for an orange-olallieberry muffin, a wild rice and chicken salad, or tri-tip on garlic toast, this bakery-deli's varied menu is likely to satisfy. Munch on your lemon meringue tartlet or chocolate brownie on the shady patio, or dig into the daily blue-plate dinner—Southwestern skirt steak with corn pudding, perhaps, or roast turkey breast with Chardonnay gravy—amid the whirl of activity inside. $ *Average main: $14* ✉ *504 Bay Ave., at Capitola Ave., Capitola* ☎ *831/462–1200* ⊕ *gayles bakery.com.*

$$$
AMERICAN
× **Michael's on Main.** Creative variations on classic comfort food draw lively crowds to this upscale but casual creekside eatery. Chef Michael Clark's menu changes seasonally, but might include pork osso buco in red-wine tomato-citrus sauce or pistachio-crusted salmon with mint vinaigrette. For a quiet conversation spot, ask for a table on the romantic patio overlooking the creek. The busy bar area hosts live music from Tuesday through Saturday. $ *Average main: $24* ✉ *2591 Main St., at Porter St., Soquel* ☎ *831/479–9777* ⊕ *michaelsonmain. net* ⊘ *Closed Mon.*

$$$$
EUROPEAN
× **Shadowbrook.** To get to this romantic spot overlooking Soquel Creek, you can take a cable car or walk the stairs down a steep, fern-lined bank beside a running waterfall. Dining room options include the rooftop Redwood Room, the wood-paneled Wine Cellar, the creekside, glass-enclosed Greenhouse, the Fireplace Room, and the airy Garden Room. Prime rib and grilled seafood are the simple menu's stars. Lighter, less expensive entrées are served in the lounge. $ *Average main: $32* ✉ *1750 Wharf Rd., at Lincoln Ave., Capitola* ☎ *831/475–1511* ⊕ *www. shadowbrook-capitola.com* ⊘ *No lunch.*

WHERE TO STAY

$$$$
B&B/INN
⊡ **Inn at Depot Hill.** This inventively designed bed-and-breakfast in a former rail depot views itself as a link to the era of luxury train travel. **Pros:** short walk to beach and village; historic charm; excellent service. **Cons:** fills quickly; hot-tub conversation audible in some rooms. $ *Rooms from: $299* ✉ *250 Monterey Ave., Capitola* ☎ *831/462–3376, 800/572–2632* ⊕ *www.innatdepothill.com* ⇗ *12 rooms* ⦿ *Breakfast.*

SANTA CRUZ

5 miles west of Capitola; 48 miles north of Monterey.

The big city on this stretch of the California coast, Santa Cruz (pop. 62,684) is less manicured than Carmel or Monterey. Long known for its surfing and its amusement-filled beach boardwalk, the town is a mix of grand Victorian-era homes and rinky-dink motels. The opening of the University of California campus in the 1960s swung the town sharply to the left politically, and the counterculture more or less lives on here. At the same time, the revitalized downtown and an insane real-estate market reflect the city's proximity to Silicon Valley and to a growing wine country in the surrounding mountains.

4

GETTING HERE AND AROUND

From the San Francisco Bay Area, take Highway 17 south over the mountains to Santa Cruz, where it merges with Highway 1. Use Highway 1 to get around the area. The Santa Cruz Transit Center is at 920 Pacific Avenue, at Front Street, a short walk from the Wharf and Boardwalk, with connections to public transit throughout the Monterey Bay and San Francisco Bay areas. You can purchase day passes for Santa Cruz METRO buses (⇨ *Bus Travel, in Planner*) here.

ESSENTIALS

Visitor Information Visit Santa Cruz County ✉ *303 Water St., No. 100* ☎ *831/425–1234, 800/833–3494* ⊕ *www.santacruz.org/regions/santa-cruz.php.*

EXPLORING

TOP ATTRACTIONS

Pacific Avenue. When you've had your fill of the city's beaches and waters, take a stroll in downtown Santa Cruz, especially on Pacific Avenue between Laurel and Water streets. Vintage boutiques and mountain-sports stores, sushi bars, and Mexican restaurants, day spas, and nightclubs keep the main drag and the surrounding streets hopping from mid-morning until late evening.

FAMILY

Fodor's Choice

★

Santa Cruz Beach Boardwalk. Santa Cruz has been a seaside resort since the mid-19th century. Along one end of the broad, south-facing beach, the Boardwalk has entertained holidaymakers for more than a century. Its Looff carousel and classic wooden Giant Dipper roller coaster, both dating from the early 1900s, are surrounded by high-tech thrill rides and easygoing kiddie rides with ocean views. Video and arcade games, a mini-golf course, and a laser-tag arena pack one gigantic building, which is open daily even if the rides aren't running. You have to pay to play, but you can wander the entire boardwalk for free while sampling delicacies such as corn dogs and garlic fries. ✉ *Along Beach St.* ☎ *831/423–5590 info line* ⊕ *beachboardwalk.com* 🎟 *$33 day pass for unlimited rides, or pay per ride* ☉ *Apr.–early Sept., daily; early Sept.–Mar., some rides open weekends and holidays, weather permitting; call for hrs.*

FAMILY

Santa Cruz Municipal Wharf. Jutting half a mile into the ocean near one end of the boardwalk, the century-old Municipal Wharf is lined with seafood restaurants, a wine bar, souvenir shops, and outfitters offering bay cruises, fishing trips, and boat rentals. A salty soundtrack drifts up from under the wharf, where barking sea lions lounge in heaps on the crossbeams. Docents from the Seymour Marine Discovery Center lead free 30-minute tours on spring and summer weekends at 1 and 3; meet at the stage on the west side of the wharf between Olitas Cantina and Marini's Candies. ⊠ *Beach St. and Pacific Ave.* 🕾 *831/459–3800 tour information* ⊕ *santacruzwharf.com.*

Santa Cruz Surfing Museum. This museum inside the Mark Abbott Memorial Lighthouse chronicles local surfing history. Photographs show old-time surfers, and a display of boards includes rarities such as a heavy redwood plank predating the fiberglass era and the remains of a modern board chomped by a great white shark. Surfer docents reminisce about the good old days. ⊠ *Lighthouse Point Park, 701 W. Cliff Dr., near Pelton Ave.* 🕾 *831/420–6289* ⊕ *santacruzsurfingmuseum.org* 🖃 *$2* ⊙ *Sept.–June, Thurs.–Mon. noon–4; July–Aug., Wed.–Mon. 10–5.*

Fodor'sChoice **West Cliff Drive.** The road that winds along an oceanfront bluff from
★ the municipal wharf to Natural Bridges State Beach makes for a spectacular drive, but it's even more fun to walk or bike the paved path that parallels the road. Surfers bob and swoosh in Monterey Bay at several points near the foot of the bluff, especially at a break known as **Steamer Lane.** Named for a surfer who died here in 1965, the nearby Mark Abbott Memorial Lighthouse stands at Point Santa Cruz, the cliff's major promontory. From here you can watch pinnipeds hang out, sunbathe, and frolic on Seal Rock.

WORTH NOTING

FAMILY **Monterey Bay National Marine Sanctuary Exploration Center.** The interactive and multimedia exhibits at this fascinating interpretive center reveal and explain the treasures of the nation's largest marine sanctuary. The two-story building, across from the main beach and municipal wharf, has films and exhibits about migratory species, watersheds, underwater canyons, kelp forests, and intertidal zones. The second-floor deck has stellar ocean views and an interactive station that provides real-time weather, surf, and buoy reports. ⊠ *35 Pacific Ave., near Beach St.* 🕾 *831/421–9993* ⊕ *montereybay.noaa.gov/vc/sec* 🖃 *Free* ⊙ *Wed.– Sun. 10–5.*

Mystery Spot. Hokey tourist trap or genuine scientific enigma? Since 1940, curious throngs baffled by the Mystery Spot have made it one of the most visited attractions in Santa Cruz. The laws of gravity and physics don't appear to apply in this tiny patch of redwood forest, where balls roll uphill and people stand on a slant. ■TIP➔ On weekends and holidays, it's wise to purchase tickets online in advance. ⊠ *465 Mystery Spot Rd., off Branciforte Dr. (north off Hwy. 1)* 🕾 *831/423–8897* ⊕ *mysteryspot.com* 🖃 *$6, parking $5* ⊙ *Late May–early Sept., daily 10–6; early Sept.–late May, weekdays 10–4, weekends 10–5.*

**OFF THE
BEATEN
PATH**

Surf City Vintners. A dozen tasting rooms of limited-production wineries occupy renovated warehouse spaces west of the beach. MJA, Storrs, and Equinox are good places to start. Also here are the Santa Cruz Mountain Brewing Company and El Salchicheroa, popular for its homemade sausages, jams, and pickled and candied vegetables. ✉ *Swift Street Courtyard, 334 Ingalls St., at Swift St., off Hwy. 1 (Mission St.)* 🌐 *surfcityvintners.com.*

UC Santa Cruz. The 2,000-acre University of California Santa Cruz campus nestles in the forested hills above town. Its sylvan setting, ocean vistas, and redwood architecture make the university worth a visit, as does its **arboretum** ($5, open daily from 9 to 5), whose walking path leads through areas dedicated to the plants of California, Australia, New Zealand, and South Africa. **■TIP→ Free shuttles help students and visitors get around campus, and you can join a guided tour (online reservation required).** ✉ *Main entrance at Bay and High Sts. (turn left on High for arboretum)* ☎ *831/459–0111* 🌐 *www.ucsc.edu/visit.*

4

BEACHES

FAMILY **Natural Bridges State Beach.** At the end of West Cliff Drive lies this stretch of soft sand edged with tide pools and sea-sculpted rock bridges. **■TIP→ From October to early March a colony of monarch butterflies roosts in a eucalyptus grove.** **Amenities:** lifeguards; parking (fee); toilets. **Best for:** sunrise; sunset; surfing; swimming. ✉ *2531 W. Cliff Dr.* ☎ *831/423–4609* 🌐 *www.parks.ca.gov* 🎫 *Beach free, parking $10* ⏲ *Beach: daily 8 am–sunset. Visitor center: Oct.–Jan., daily 10–4; Feb.–Sept., Fri.–Sun. 10–4.*

Twin Lakes State Beach. Stretching a half-mile along the coast on both sides of the small-craft jetties, Twin Lakes is one of Monterey Bay's sunniest beaches. It encompasses Seabright State Beach (with access in a residential neighborhood on the upcoast side) and Black's Beach on the downcoast side. Families often come here to sunbathe, picnic, and hike the nature trail around adjacent Schwann Lake. Parking is tricky on weekends from April through September, but you can park all day in the harbor pay lot and walk here. Leashed dogs are allowed. **Amenities:** food and drink; lifeguards (seasonal); parking; showers; toilets; water sports (seasonal). **Best for:** sunset; surfing; swimming; walking. ✉ *7th Ave., at East Cliff Dr.* ☎ *831/427–4868* 🌐 *www.parks.ca.gov.*

WHERE TO EAT

$$ MODERN AMERICAN 🍴 **Assembly.** Seasonal, sustainably farmed local ingredients inspire this downtown eatery's rustic California cuisine. The menu changes constantly, but you might find swordfish with preserved-lemon risotto, braised fennel, spinach, and avocado; potato gnocchi with braised chicken, black trumpets, and ricotta cheese; or a burger on a house-made brioche bun. An adjacent pop-up space hosts rising chefs who for two months or so create dishes with ingredients sourced from local purveyors before moving on. [$] *Average main: $19* ✉ *1108 Pacific Ave., at Cathcart St.* ☎ *831/824–6100* 🌐 *assembleforfood.com* ⏲ *Closed Mon. and Tues. during off-season; call to verify hrs.*

$$ SEAFOOD 🍴 **Crow's Nest.** A classic California beachside restaurant, the Crow's Nest sits right on the water in Santa Cruz Harbor. Vintage surfboards and local surf photography line the walls in the main dining room, and

nearly every table overlooks sand and surf. Breakfast favorites include crab-cake eggs Benedict and olallieberry pancakes. Seafood and steaks, served with locally grown vegetables, dominate the lunch and dinner menus; favorite appetizers include fried calamari and the chilled shrimp-stuffed artichoke. For sweeping ocean views and fish tacos, burgers, and other casual fare, head upstairs to the Breakwater Bar & Grill. ■ **TIP→ If you're in a hurry, pick up pizzas, sandwiches, soups, and salads at the on-site market.** $ *Average main: $21* ⊠ *2218 E. Cliff Dr., west of 7th Ave.* ☎ *831/476–4560* ⊕ *crowsnest-santacruz.com.*

$$

MEDITERRANEAN

Fodor's Choice

★

× **Laili Restaurant.** Exotic Mediterranean flavors with an Afghan twist take center stage at this artsy, stylish space with soaring ceilings. Traditional dishes range from Moroccan beet salad and apricot chicken flatbread to pomegranate eggplant and *maush-awa*, a soup with lentils, split peas, and lamb, topped with yogurt. The menus also include housemade pastas and numerous vegetarian options; fresh *naan* and delectable chutneys and dips accompany every meal. Evenings are especially lively, when locals come to relax over wine and soft jazz at the blue-concrete bar, the heated patio with twinkly lights, or at a communal table near the open kitchen. $ *Average main: $20* ⊠ *101–B Cooper St., near Pacific Ave.* ☎ *831/423–4545* ⊕ *lailirestaurant.com* ⊗ *Closed Mon.*

$$$

ITALIAN

× **La Posta.** Authentic Italian fare made with fresh local produce lures diners into cozy, modern-rustic La Posta. Nearly everything is made in-house, from the pizzas and breads baked in the brick oven to the pasta and the vanilla-bean gelato. The seasonal menu includes flavorful dishes such as wild-nettle lasagna, braised lamb shank with saffron-infused vegetables, and sautéed fish from local waters. $ *Average main: $24* ⊠ *538 Seabright Ave., at Logan St.* ☎ *831/457–2782* ⊕ *lapostarestaurant.com* ⊗ *Closed Mon. No lunch.*

$$$

EUROPEAN

× **Oswald.** Sophisticated yet unpretentious European-inspired California cooking is the order of the day at this intimate and stylish bistro. The menu changes seasonally, but might include such items as seafood risotto or crispy duck breast in a pomegranate reduction sauce. The creative concoctions poured at the slick marble bar include whiskey mixed with apple and lemon juice, and tequila with celery juice and lime. ■ **TIP→ On Wednesday, a three-course prix-fixe menu (at $29 a good value) is offered in lieu of the regular fare.** $ *Average main: $26* ⊠ *121 Soquel Ave., at Front St.* ☎ *831/423–7427* ⊕ *oswaldrestaurant.com* ⊗ *Closed Mon. No lunch Tues.–Thurs. and weekends.*

$$

MEDITERRANEAN

Fodor's Choice

★

× **Soif.** Wine reigns at this sleek bistro and wineshop that takes its name from the French word for thirst. The selections come from near and far, and you can order many of them by the taste or glass. Mediterranean-inspired small plates and entrées are served at the copper-top bar, the big communal table, and private tables. A jazz combo or solo pianist plays on some evenings. $ *Average main: $22* ⊠ *105 Walnut Ave., at Pacific Ave.* ☎ *831/423–2020* ⊕ *soifwine.com* ⊗ *No lunch.*

WHERE TO STAY

$$$ **Babbling Brook Inn.** Though it's in the middle of Santa Cruz, this bed-
B&B/INN and-breakfast has lush gardens, a running stream, and tall trees that
make you feel like you're in a secluded wood. **Pros:** close to UCSC;
within walking distance of downtown shops; woodsy feel. **Cons:** near
a high school; some rooms close to a busy street. $ *Rooms from:*
$229 ✉ *1025 Laurel St.* ☎ *831/427–2437, 800/866–1131* ⊕ *babbling*
brookinn.com ⤳ *13 rooms* ⦿ *Breakfast.*

$$ **Carousel Beach Inn.** Remodeled in 2014 in bold, retro seaside style,
HOTEL this basic but comfy motel across the street from the boardwalk is ideal
for travelers who want easy access to the sand and the amusement
park rides without spending a fortune. **Pros:** steps from Santa Cruz
Main Beach; affordable lodging rates and ride packages; free parking
and Wi-Fi. **Cons:** no pool or spa; no exercise room; not pet-friendly.
$ *Rooms from: $159* ✉ *110 Riverside Ave.* ☎ *831/425–7090* ⊕ *santa-*
cruzmotels.com/carousel.html ⤳ *34 rooms* ⦿ *Breakfast.*

$$$$ **Chaminade Resort & Spa.** Secluded on 300 hilltop acres of redwood and
RESORT eucalyptus forest with hiking trails, this Mission-style complex commands expansive views of Monterey Bay. **Pros:** far from city life; spectacular property; ideal spot for romance and rejuvenation. **Cons:** must
drive to attractions and sights; near a major hospital. $ *Rooms from:*
$269 ✉ *1 Chaminade La.* ☎ *800/283–6569 reservations, 831/475–5600*
⊕ *www.chaminade.com* ⤳ *112 rooms, 44 suites* ⦿ *No meals.*

$$$ **Hotel Paradox.** About a mile from the ocean and two blocks from
HOTEL Pacific Avenue, this stylish, forest-theme complex is among the few
full-service hotels in town. **Pros:** close to downtown and main beach;
alternative to beach-oriented lodgings; contemporary feel. **Cons:** pool
area can get crowded on warm-weather days; some rooms on the
small side. $ *Rooms from: $200* ✉ *611 Ocean St.* ☎ *831/425–7100,*
855/425–7200 ⊕ *www.thehotelparadox.com* ⤳ *164 rooms, 6 suites*
⦿ *No meals.*

$$$ **Pacific Blue Inn.** Green themes predominate in this three-story, eco-
B&B/INN friendly bed-and-breakfast, completed in 2009 on a sliver of prime
downtown property. **Pros:** free parking; free bicycles; downtown location. **Cons:** tiny property; not suitable for children. $ *Rooms from:*
$189 ✉ *636 Pacific Ave.* ☎ *831/600–8880* ⊕ *pacificblueinn.com* ⤳ *9*
rooms ⦿ *No meals.*

$$$$ **Santa Cruz Dream Inn.** A short stroll from the boardwalk and wharf,
HOTEL this full-service luxury hotel is the only lodging in Santa Cruz directly
Fodor's Choice on the beach. **Pros:** directly on the beach; easy parking; walk to board-
★ walk and downtown. **Cons:** expensive; area gets congested on summer
weekends. $ *Rooms from: $369* ✉ *175 W. Cliff Dr.* ☎ *831/426–4330,*
866/774–7735 reservations ⊕ *dreaminnsantacruz.com* ⤳ *149 rooms,*
16 suites ⦿ *No meals.*

$$$ **West Cliff Inn.** With views of the boardwalk and Monterey Bay, the
B&B/INN West Cliff perches on the bluffs across from Cowell Beach. **Pros:** killer
Fodor's Choice views; walking distance to the beach; close to downtown. **Cons:** board-
★ walk noise; street traffic. $ *Rooms from: $195* ✉ *174 West Cliff Dr.*
☎ *800/979–0910 toll free, 831/457–2200* ⊕ *www.westcliffinn.com* ⤳ *7*
rooms, 2 suites, 1 cottage ⦿ *Breakfast.*

4

O'Neill: A Santa Cruz Icon

O'Neill wet suits and beachwear weren't exactly born in Santa Cruz, but as far as most of the world is concerned, the O'Neill brand is synonymous with Santa Cruz and surfing legend.

The O'Neill wet-suit story began in 1952, when Jack O'Neill and his brother Robert opened their first Surf Shop in a garage across from San Francisco's Ocean Beach. While shaping balsa surfboards and selling accessories, the O'Neills experimented with solutions to a common surfer problem: frigid waters. Tired of being forced back to shore, blue-lipped and shivering, after just 20 or 30 minutes riding the waves, they played with

various materials and eventually designed a neoprene vest.

In 1959 Jack moved his Surf Shop 90 miles south to Cowell's Beach in Santa Cruz. It quickly became a popular surf hangout, and O'Neill's new wet suits began to sell like hotcakes. In the early 1960s, the company opened a warehouse for manufacturing on a larger scale. Santa Cruz soon became a major surf city, attracting wave riders to prime breaks at Steamer Lane, Pleasure Point, and the Hook. In 1965 O'Neill pioneered the first wet-suit boots, and in 1971 Jack's son invented the surf leash. By 1980, O'Neill stood at the top of the world wet-suit market.

NIGHTLIFE AND PERFORMING ARTS

NIGHTLIFE

Catalyst. This huge, grimy, and fun club books rock, indie rock, punk, death-metal, reggae, and other acts. ⊠ *1011 Pacific Ave.* ☎ *877/987–6487 tickets* ⊕ *catalystclub.com.*

Kuumbwa Jazz Center. The center draws top performers such as the Brubeck Brothers Quartet, Ladysmith Black Mambazo, and Chick Corea; the café serves meals an hour before most shows. ⊠ *320–2 Cedar St.* ☎ *831/427–2227* ⊕ *kuumbwajazz.org.*

PERFORMING ARTS

Tannery Arts Center. The former Salz Tannery now contains studios and live-work spaces for artists whose disciplines range from ceramics and glass to film and digital media. The social center is the **Artbar & Cafe,** which in the late afternoons and evenings hosts poets (Monday), all types of performers (Wednesday), and live music (from Thursday to Saturday). The center also hosts assorted arts events on weekends and occasionally on weekdays. ⊠ *1060 River St., at intersection of Hwys. 1 and 9* ☎ *831/428–8989* ⊕ *scartbar.com.*

SPORTS AND THE OUTDOORS

ADVENTURE TOURS

Mount Hermon Adventures. Zip-line through the redwoods at this adventure center in the Santa Cruz Mountains. On some summer weekends there's an aerial adventure course with obstacles and challenges in the redwoods. ■TIP➜ **To join a tour (reservations essential), you must be**

at least 10 years old and weigh between 75 and 250 pounds. ⊠ *17 Conference Dr., 9 miles north of downtown Santa Cruz near Felton, Mount Hermon* ☎ *831/430–4357* ⊕ *mounthermonadventures.com* ✉ *From $50.*

BICYCLING

Another Bike Shop. Mountain bikers should head here for tips on the best area trails and to browse cutting-edge gear made and tested locally. ⊠ *2361 Mission St., at King St.* ☎ *831/427–2232* ⊕ *www. anotherbikeshop.com.*

BOATS AND CHARTERS

Chardonnay II Sailing Charters. The 70-foot *Chardonnay II* departs year-round from Santa Cruz yacht harbor on whale-watching, sunset, and other cruises around Monterey Bay. Most regularly scheduled excursions cost $64; food and drink are served on many of them. Reservations are essential. ⊠ *Santa Cruz West Harbor, 790 Mariner Park Way* ☎ *831/423–1213* ⊕ *chardonnay.com.*

Stagnaro Sport Fishing, Charters, & Whale Watching Cruises. Stagnaro operates salmon, albacore, and rock-cod fishing expeditions; the fees include bait. The company (aka Santa Cruz Whale Watching) also runs whale-watching, dolphin, and sea-life cruises year-round. ⊠ *1718 Brommer St., near Santa Cruz Harbor* ☎ *831/427–0230, 888/237–7084 tickets, 831/205–2380 international tickets* ⊕ *stagnaros.com* ✉ *From $48.*

GOLF

Pasatiempo Golf Club. Designed by famed golf architect Dr. Alister MacKenzie in 1929, this semiprivate course, set amid undulating hills just above the city, is among the nation's top championship courses. Golfers rave about the spectacular views and challenging terrain. According to the club, MacKenzie, who designed Pebble Beach's exclusive Cypress Point course and Augusta National in Georgia, the home of the Masters Golf Tournament, declared this his favorite layout. ⊠ *20 Clubhouse Rd.* ☎ *831/459–9155* ⊕ *www.pasatiempo.com* ✉ *From $260* ⛳ *18 holes, 6125 yards, par 72.*

KAYAKING

Kayak Connection. From March through May, participants in this outfit's tours mingle with gray whales and their calves on their northward journey to Alaska. Throughout the year, the company rents kayaks and paddleboards and conducts tours of Natural Bridges State Beach, Capitola, and Elkhorn Slough. ⊠ *Santa Cruz Harbor, 413 Lake Ave., No. 3* ☎ *831/479–1121* ⊕ *kayakconnection.com* ✉ *From $60 for scheduled tours.*

Venture Quest Kayaking. Explore hidden coves and kelp forests on guided two-hour kayak tours that depart from Santa Cruz Wharf. The tours include a kayaking lesson. Venture Quest also rents kayaks (and wet suits and gear), and arranges tours at other Monterey Bay destinations, including Elkhorn Slough. ⊠ *2 Santa Cruz Wharf* ☎ *831/427–2267 kayak hotline, 831/425–8445 rental office* ⊕ *kayaksantacruz.com* ✉ *From $30 for rentals, $58 for tours.*

SURFING
EQUIPMENT AND LESSONS
Club-Ed Surf School and Camps. Find out what all the fun is about at Club-Ed. Your first private or group lesson ($90 and up) includes all equipment. ⊠ *Cowell's Beach, at Santa Cruz Dream Inn* ☎ *831/464–0177* ⊕ *club-ed.com.*

Cowell's Beach Surf Shop. This shop sells gear, clothing, and swimwear; rents surfboards, standup paddle boards, and wet suits; and offers lessons. ⊠ *30 Front St.* ☎ *831/427–2355* ⊕ *cowellssurfshop.com.*

SHOPPING

Bookshop Santa Cruz. In 2016 the town's best and most beloved independent bookstore celebrates its 50th anniversary of selling new, used, and remaindered titles. The children's section is especially comprehensive, and the shop's special events calendar is packed with readings, social mixers, book signings, and discussions. ⊠ *1520 Pacific Ave.* ☎ *831/423–0900* ⊕ *bookshopsantacruz.com.*

O'Neill Surf Shop. Local surfers get their wetties (wet suits) and other gear at this O'Neill store or the one in Capitola, at 1115 41st Avenue. There's also a satellite shop on the Santa Cruz Boardwalk. ⊠ *110 Cooper St.* ☎ *831/469–4377* ⊕ *www.oneill.com.*

The True Olive Connection. Taste your way through boutique extra-virgin olive oils and balsamic vinegars from around the world at this family-run shop. You can also pick up gourmet food products and olive-oil-based gift items. There's another location in Aptos. ⊠ *106 Lincoln St., at Pacific Ave.* ☎ *831/458–6457* ⊕ *trueoliveconnection.com* ⊠ *7960 Soquel Dr., Aptos* ☎ *831/612–6932.*

SAN FRANCISCO

WELCOME TO SAN FRANCISCO

TOP REASONS TO GO

★ **The bay:** It's hard not to gasp as you catch sight of sunlight dancing on the water when you crest a hill, or watch the Golden Gate Bridge vanish and reemerge in the summer fog.

★ **The food:** San Franciscans are serious about what they eat, and with good reason. Home to some of the nation's best chefs, top restaurants, and finest local produce, it's hard not to eat well here.

★ **The shopping:** Shopaholics visiting the city will not be disappointed: San Francisco is packed with browsing destinations, everything from quirky boutiques to massive malls.

★ **The good life:** A laid-back atmosphere, beautiful surroundings, and oodles of cultural, culinary, and aesthetic pleasures . . . if you spend too much time here, you might not leave.

★ **The great outdoors:** From Golden Gate Park to sidewalk cafés in North Beach, San Franciscans relish their outdoor spaces.

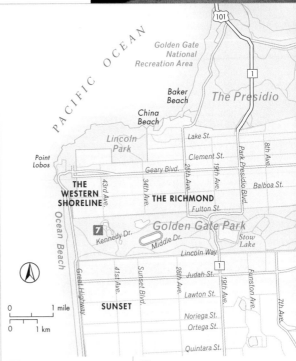

1 **Union Square and Chinatown.** Union Square has hotels, public transportation, and shopping; walking through Chinatown is like visiting a bustling street in Beijing.

2 **SoMa and Civic Center.** SoMa is anchored by SFMOMA and Yerba Buena Gardens; the city's performing arts venues are in Civic Center.

3 **Nob Hill and Russian Hill.** Nob Hill is old-money San Francisco; Russian Hill's steep streets have excellent eateries and shopping.

4 **North Beach.** The city's small Italian neighborhood makes even locals feel as if they're on holiday.

5 **On the Waterfront.** Wandering the shops and attractions of Fisherman's Wharf, Pier 39, and Ghirardelli Square, the only locals you'll meet will be the ones with visitors in tow.

6 **The Marina and the Presidio.** The Marina has trendy boutiques, restaurants, and cafés; the wooded Presidio offers great views of the Golden Gate Bridge.

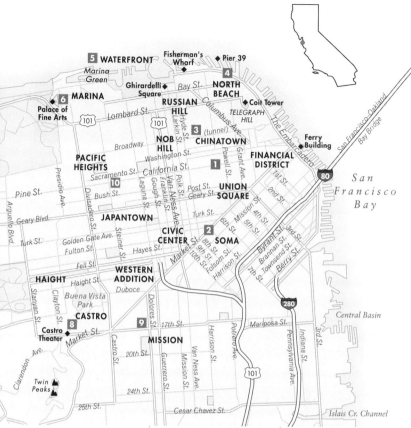

7 Golden Gate Park and the Western Shoreline. San Francisco's 1,000-acre backyard has sports fields, windmills, museums, and gardens; the windswept Western Shoreline stretches for miles.

8 The Haight, the Castro, and Noe Valley. After you've seen the blockbuster sights, come to these neighborhoods to see where the city's heart beats.

9 The Mission. When the sun sets, people descend on the Mission for destination restaurants, excellent bargain-price ethnic eateries, and the hippest bar scene around.

10 Pacific Heights and Japantown. Pacific Heights has some of the city's most opulent real estate; Japantown is packed with authentic Japanese shops and restaurants.

GETTING ORIENTED

San Francisco is a compact city; just 46.7 square miles. Essentially a tightly packed cluster of extremely diverse neighborhoods, the city clearly rewards walking. The areas that most visitors cover are easy (and safe) to reach on foot, but many have steep— make that *steep*—hills.

Updated by Michele Bigley, Christine Ciarmello, Denise Leto, Fiona Parrott, and Jerry James Stone

On a 46½-square-mile strip of land between San Francisco Bay and the Pacific Ocean, San Francisco has charms great and small. Residents cherish their city for the same reasons visitors do: the proximity to the bay, rows of Victorian homes clinging precariously to the hillsides, the sun setting behind the Golden Gate Bridge, the world-class cuisine. Locals and visitors alike spend hours exploring downtown, Chinatown, North Beach, the northern and western waterfronts, and Golden Gate Park, along with colorful neighborhoods like the Haight, the Mission murals, and the Castro.

The city's attraction, though, goes much deeper than its alluring physical space, from the diversity of its neighborhoods to its free-spirited tolerance. Take all these things together and you'll understand why many San Franciscans—despite the dizzying cost of living and the chilly summers—can't imagine calling any place else home.

You won't want to miss the City by the Bay's highlights, whether it's a cable car ride over Nob Hill; a walk down the Filbert Street Steps; gazing at the thundering Pacific from the cliffs of Lincoln Park; cheering the San Francisco Giants to *beat L.A.* in lively AT&T Park; or eating freshly shucked oysters at the Ferry Building. San Francisco is a beautiful metropolis packed with diverse wonders that inspire at every turn.

PLANNING

WHEN TO GO
You can visit San Francisco comfortably any time of year. Possibly the best time is September and October, when the city's summerlike weather brings outdoor concerts and festivals. The climate here always feels Mediterranean and moderate—with a foggy, sometimes chilly bite. The temperature rarely drops below 40°F, and anything warmer than 80°F

is considered a heat wave. Be prepared for rain in winter, especially December and January. Winds off the ocean can add to the chill factor. That old joke about summer in San Francisco feeling like winter is true at heart, but once you move inland, it gets warmer. (And some locals swear that the thermostat has inched up in recent years.)

GETTING HERE AND AROUND

AIR TRAVEL

The major gateway to San Francisco is San Francisco International Airport (SFO), 15 miles south of the city. It's off U.S. 101 near Millbrae and San Bruno. Oakland International Airport (OAK) is across the bay, not much farther away from downtown San Francisco (via I–80 east and I–880 south), but rush-hour traffic on the Bay Bridge may lengthen travel times considerably. San Jose International Airport (SJC) is about 40 miles south of San Francisco; travel time depends largely on traffic flow, but plan on an hour and a half with moderate traffic.

Airports San Francisco International Airport (SFO) ⊠ McDonnell and Link Rds. ☎ 800/435–9736, 650/821–8211 ⊕ www.flysfo.com. **Oakland International Airport** (OAK) ⊠ 1 Airport Dr., Oakland, California, United States ☎ 510/563–3300 ⊕ www.flyoakland.com. **San Jose International Airport** (SJC) ⊠ 1701 Airport Blvd., San Jose, California, United States ☎ 408/392–3600 ⊕ www.flysanjose.com.

Airport Transfers American Airporter ☎ 415/202–0733 ⊕ www.americanairporter.com. **BayPorter Express** ☎ 415/467–1800, 510/864–4000 ⊕ www.bayporter.com. **Caltrain** ☎ 800/660–4287 ⊕ www.caltrain.com. **East Bay Express Airporter** ☎ 877/526–0304 ⊕ www.eastbaytransportation.com. **GO Lorrie's Airport Shuttle** ☎ 415/334–9000 ⊕ www.gosfovan.com. **Marin Airporter** ☎ 415/461–4222 ⊕ www.marinairporter.com. **Marin Door to Door** ☎ 415/457–2717 ⊕ www.marindoortodoor.com. **SamTrans** ☎ 800/660–4287 ⊕ www.samtrans.com. **South and East Bay Airport Shuttle** ☎ 800/548–4664 ⊕ www.southandeastbayairportshuttle.com. **SuperShuttle** ☎ 800/258–3826 ⊕ www.supershuttle.com.

BART TRAVEL

BART (Bay Area Rapid Transit) trains, which run until midnight, travel under the bay via tunnel to connect San Francisco with Oakland, Berkeley, and other cities and towns beyond. Within San Francisco, stations are limited to downtown, the Mission, and a couple of outlying neighborhoods.

Trains travel frequently from early morning until evening on weekdays. After 8 pm weekdays and on weekends there's often a 20-minute wait between trains on the same line. Trains also travel south from San Francisco as far as Millbrae. BART trains connect downtown San Francisco to San Francisco International Airport; the ride costs $8.25.

Intracity San Francisco fares are $1.85; intercity fares are $3.80 to $11.65. BART bases its ticket prices on miles traveled and doesn't offer price breaks by zone. The easy-to-read maps posted in BART stations list fares based on destination, radiating out from your starting point of the current station.

Contact Bay Area Rapid Transit (BART) ☎ 415/989–2278 ⊕ www.bart.gov.

BOAT AND FERRY TRAVEL

Several ferry lines run out of San Francisco. Blue & Gold Fleet operates a number of routes, including service to Sausalito ($11 one-way) and Tiburon ($11 one-way). Tickets are sold at Pier 41 (between Fisherman's Wharf and Pier 39), where the boats depart. Alcatraz Cruises, owned by Hornblower Yachts, operates the ferries to Alcatraz Island ($30 including audio tour and National Park Service ranger-led programs) from Pier 33, about a half-mile east of Fisherman's Wharf ($3 shuttle buses serve several area hotels and other locations). Boats leave 10 times a day (14 times a day in summer), and the journey itself takes 30 minutes. Allow roughly 2½ hours for a round-trip jaunt. Golden Gate Ferry runs daily to and from Sausalito and Larkspur ($10.75 and $10 one-way), leaving from Pier 1, behind the San Francisco Ferry Building. The Alameda/Oakland Ferry operates daily between Alameda's Main Street Ferry Building, Oakland's Jack London Square, and San Francisco's Pier 41 and the Ferry Building ($6.25 one-way); some ferries go only to Pier 41 or the Ferry Building, so ask when you board. Purchase tickets on board.

Ferry Lines Alameda/Oakland Ferry ☏ 510/522–3300 ⊕ sanfranciscobayferry.com. **Alcatraz Cruises** ☏ 415/981–7625 ⊕ www.alcatrazcruises.com. **Blue & Gold Fleet** ☏ 415/705–8200 ⊕ www.blueandgoldfleet.com. **Golden Gate Ferry** ☏ 415/923–2000 ⊕ www.goldengateferry.org. **San Francisco Ferry Building** ✉ 1 Ferry Bldg., at foot of Market St. on Embarcadero ☏ 415/983–8030 ⊕ www.ferrybuildingmarketplace.com.

CABLE CAR TRAVEL

Don't miss the sensation of moving up and down some of San Francisco's steepest hills in a clattering cable car. Jump aboard as it pauses at a designated stop, and wedge yourself into any available space. Then just hold on.

The fare (for one direction) is $6 (Muni Passport holders only pay a $1 supplement). You can buy tickets on board (exact change isn't necessary) or at the kiosks at the cable-car turnarounds at Hyde and Beach streets and at Powell and Market streets.

The heavily traveled Powell–Mason and Powell–Hyde lines begin at Powell and Market streets near Union Square and terminate at Fisherman's Wharf; lines for these routes can be long, especially in summer. The California Street line runs east and west from Market and California streets to Van Ness Avenue; there's often no wait to board this route.

CAR TRAVEL

Driving in San Francisco can be a challenge because of the one-way streets, snarly traffic, and steep hills. The first two elements can be frustrating enough, but those hills are tough for unfamiliar drivers. ■TIP→ Remember to curb your wheels when parking on hills—turn wheels away from the curb when facing uphill, toward the curb when facing downhill. You can get a ticket if you don't do this.

MUNI TRAVEL

The San Francisco Municipal Railway, or Muni, operates light-rail vehicles, the historic F-line streetcars along Fisherman's Wharf and Market Street, trolley buses, and the world-famous cable cars. Light rail travels along Market Street to the Mission District and Noe Valley (J line), the Ingleside District (K line), and the Sunset District (L, M, and N lines); during peak hours (weekdays, 6 am–9 am and 3 pm–7 pm) the J line continues around the Embarcadero to the Caltrain station at 4th and King streets. The T-line light rail runs from the Castro, down Market Street, around the Embarcadero, and south past Hunters Point and Monster Park to Sunnydale Avenue and Bayshore Boulevard. Muni provides 24-hour service on select lines to all areas of the city.

On buses and streetcars the fare is $2.25. Exact change is required, and dollar bills are accepted in the fare boxes. For all Muni vehicles other than cable cars, 90-minute transfers are issued free upon request at the time the fare is paid. These are valid for two additional transfers in any direction. Cable cars cost $6 and include no transfers.

One-day ($15), three-day ($23), and seven-day ($29) Passports valid on the entire Muni system can be purchased at several outlets, including the cable-car ticket booth at Powell and Market streets and the visitor information center downstairs in Hallidie Plaza. A monthly ticket is available for $80, and can be used on all Muni lines (including cable cars) and on BART within city limits. The San Francisco CityPass ($86), a discount ticket booklet to several major city attractions, also covers all Muni travel for seven consecutive days.

The San Francisco Municipal Transit and Street Map ($5) is a useful guide to the extensive transportation system. You can buy the map at most bookstores and at the San Francisco Visitor Information Center, on the lower level of Hallidie Plaza at Powell and Market streets.

Muni Info **San Francisco Municipal Railway System** (*Muni*) ☎ *311, 415/701–3000* ⊕ *www.sfmta.com.*

TAXI TRAVEL

Taxi service is notoriously bad in San Francisco, and hailing a cab can be frustratingly difficult in some parts of the city, especially on weekends. Popular nightspots such as the Mission, SoMa, North Beach, the Haight, and the Castro have a lot of cabs but a lot of people looking for taxis, too. Midweek, and during the day, you shouldn't have much of a problem—unless it's raining. In a pinch, hotel taxi stands are an option, as is calling for a pickup. But be forewarned: taxi companies frequently don't answer the phone in peak periods. The absolute worst time to find a taxi is Friday afternoon and evening; plan well ahead, and if you're going to the airport, make a reservation or book a shuttle instead. Most taxi companies take reservations for airport and out-of-town runs but not in-town rides.

Taxis in San Francisco charge $3.50 for the first 0.5 mile (one of the highest base rates in the United States), 55¢ for each additional 0.5 mile, and 55¢ per minute in stalled traffic; a $2 surcharge is added for trips to the airport. There's no charge for additional passengers; there's no surcharge for luggage. For trips outside city limits, multiply the metered rate by 1.5; tolls and tip are extra.

Alternatively, you can download the Uber or Lyft apps to participate in the city's user-generated car services. You basically join the group and pay via a credit card on your app, then order a car to pick you up from your destination and deliver you anywhere in the city. Rates vary by company, but are generally comparable to taxi rates.

Taxi Companies DeSoto Cab ☎ *415/970–1300* ⊕ *www.desotosf.com.* **Luxor Cab** ☎ *415/282–4141* ⊕ *www.luxorcab.com.* **Veteran's Taxicab** ☎ *415/552–1300.* **Yellow Cab** ☎ *415/333–3333* ⊕ *yellowcabsf.com.*

Complaints San Francisco Police Department Taxi Complaints ☎ *415/701–4400.*

TRAIN TRAVEL

Amtrak trains travel to the Bay Area from some cities in California and the United States. San Francisco doesn't have an Amtrak train station but does have an Amtrak bus station, at the Ferry Building, from which shuttle buses transport passengers to trains in Emeryville, just over the Bay Bridge. Shuttle buses also connect the Emeryville train station with downtown Oakland, the Caltrain station, and other points in downtown San Francisco. You can buy a California Rail Pass, which gives you seven days of travel in a 21-day period for $159.

Caltrain connects San Francisco to Palo Alto, San Jose, Santa Clara, and many smaller cities en route. In San Francisco, trains leave from the main depot, at 4th and Townsend streets, and a rail-side stop at 22nd and Pennsylvania streets. One-way fares are $3.25 to $13.25, depending on the number of zones through which you travel; tickets are valid for four hours after purchase time. A ticket is $7.25 from San Francisco to Palo Alto, at least $9.25 to San Jose. You can also buy a day pass ($6.50–$26.50) for unlimited travel in a 24-hour period. It's worth waiting for an express train for trips that last from 1 to 1¾ hours. On weekdays, trains depart three or four times per hour during the morning and evening, twice per hour during daytime noncommute hours, and as little as once per hour in the evening. Weekend trains run once per hour. The system shuts down at midnight. There are no onboard ticket sales. You must buy tickets before boarding the train or risk paying a $250 fine for fare evasion.

Train Contacts Amtrak ☎ *800/872–7245* ⊕ *www.amtrak.com.* **Caltrain** ☎ *800/660–4287* ⊕ *www.caltrain.com.* **San Francisco Caltrain station** ✉ *700 4th St., at King St.* ☎ *800/660–4287.*

VISITOR INFORMATION

The San Francisco Convention and Visitors Bureau can mail you brochures, maps, and events listings. Once in town, you can stop by the bureau's info center near Union Square.

Contacts San Francisco Visitor Information Center ✉ *Hallidie Plaza, lower level, 900 Market St., at Powell St., Union Sq.* ☎ *415/391–2000 TDD* ⊕ *www. sanfrancisco.travel.*

EXPLORING SAN FRANCISCO

UNION SQUARE AND CHINATOWN

The Union Square area bristles with big-city bravado, while just a stone's throw away is a place that feels like a city unto itself, Chinatown. The two areas share a strong commercial streak, although manifested very differently. In Union Square—a plaza but also the neighborhood around it—the crowds zigzag among international brands, trailing glossy shopping bags. A few blocks north, people dash between small neighborhood stores, their arms draped with plastic totes filled with groceries or souvenirs.

UNION SQUARE

TOP ATTRACTIONS

Union Square. Ground zero for big-name shopping in the city and within walking distance of many hotels, Union Square is home base for many visitors. The Westin St. Francis Hotel and Macy's line two of the square's sides, and Saks, Neiman-Marcus, and Tiffany & Co. edge the other two. Four globular lamp sculptures by the artist R. M. Fischer preside over the landscaped, 2½-acre park, which has a café with outdoor seating, an open-air stage, and a visitor-information booth—along with a familiar kaleidoscope of characters: office workers sunning and brown-bagging, street musicians, shoppers taking a rest, kids chasing pigeons, and a fair number of homeless people. The constant clang of cable cars traveling up and down Powell Street helps maintain a festive mood.

The heart of San Francisco's downtown since 1850, the square takes its name from the violent pro-Union demonstrations staged here before the Civil War. At center stage, Robert Ingersoll Aitken's *Victory Monument* commemorates Commodore George Dewey's victory over the Spanish fleet at Manila in 1898. The 97-foot Corinthian column, topped by a bronze figure symbolizing naval conquest, was dedicated by Theodore Roosevelt in 1903 and withstood the 1906 earthquake. After the earthquake and fire of 1906, the square was dubbed "Little St. Francis" because of the temporary shelter erected for residents of the St. Francis Hotel. Actor John Barrymore (grandfather of actress Drew Barrymore and a notorious carouser) was among the guests pressed into volunteering to stack bricks in the square. His uncle, thespian John Drew, remarked, "It took an act of God to get John out of bed and the United States Army to get him to work."

The square sits atop a handy four-level garage, allegedly the world's first underground parking structure. Aboveground the convenient **TIX Bay Area** (*415/433–7827, www.tixbayarea.com*) provides half-price, day-of-performance tickets to performing-arts events, as well as regular full-price box-office services. ■ TIP→ Tired of shopping? Grab a coffee and pastry right in the square at Emporio Rulli, sit at a small outdoor table, and take in the action. ✉ *Bordered by Powell, Stockton, Post, and Geary Sts., Union Sq.*

The epicenter of high-end shopping, Union Square is lined with department stores.

WORTH NOTING

Maiden Lane. Known as Morton Street in the raffish Barbary Coast era, this former red-light district reported at least one murder a week during the late 19th century. Things cooled down after the 1906 fire destroyed the brothels, and these days Maiden Lane is a chic, boutique-lined pedestrian mall (favored by brides-to-be) stretching two blocks, between Stockton and Kearny streets. Wrought-iron gates close the street to traffic most days between 11 and 5, when the lane becomes a patchwork of umbrella-shaded tables.

At **140 Maiden Lane** you can see the only Frank Lloyd Wright building in San Francisco. Walking through the brick archway and recessed entry feels a bit like entering a glowing cave. The interior's graceful, curving ramp and skylights are said to have been his model for the Guggenheim Museum in New York. Xanadu Gallery, which showcases expensive Baltic, Latin American, and African folk art, occupies the space and welcomes Frank Lloyd Wright fans. ⊠ *Between Stockton and Kearny Sts., Union Sq.*

San Francisco Visitor Information Center. Head downstairs from the cable-car terminus to the visitor center, where multilingual staffers answer questions and provide maps and pamphlets. Muni Passports are sold here, and you can pick up discount coupons—the savings can be significant, especially for families. If you're planning to hit the big-ticket stops like the California Academy of Sciences and the Exploratorium and ride the cable cars, consider purchasing a CityPass (*www.citypass. com/san-francisco*) here. ■TIP➜ The CityPass ($86, $64 ages 5–11), good for nine days, including seven days of transit, will save you more than 40%. The pass is also available at the attractions it covers, though if you choose the pass that includes Alcatraz—an excellent deal—you'll have to buy it directly from Alcatraz Cruises *(⇨ see On the Waterfront, below)*. ⊠ *Hallidie Plaza, lower level, 900 Market St., at Market and Powell Sts., Union Sq.* ☏ *415/391–2000* ⊕ *www.sanfrancisco.travel* ⊙ *Weekdays 9–5, Sat. 9–3; also May–Oct., Sun. 9–3.*

Westin St. Francis Hotel. Built in 1904 and barely established as the most sumptuous hotel in town before it was ravaged by fire following the 1906 earthquake, this grande-dame hotel designed by Walter Danforth Bliss and William Baker Faville reopened in 1907 with the addition of a luxurious Italian Renaissance–style residence designed to attract loyal clients from among the world's rich and powerful. The hotel's checkered past includes the ill-fated 1921 bash in the suite of the silent-film superstar Fatty Arbuckle, at which a woman became ill and later died. Arbuckle endured three sensational trials for rape and murder before being acquitted, by which time his career was kaput. In 1975 Sara Jane Moore, standing among a crowd outside the hotel, attempted to shoot then-president Gerald Ford. Of course the grand lobby contains no plaques commemorating these events. Every November the hotel's pastry chef adds a new touch to his spectacular, rotating 12-foot-high gingerbread castle on display here; it's fun to compare it with the grand walk-through gingerbread house at the Fairmont. ■TIP➜ **Some visitors make the St. Francis a stop whenever they're in town, soaking up the lobby ambience or enjoying a cocktail in Clock Bar or a meal at Michael Mina's Bourbon Steak.** ⊠ *335 Powell St., at Geary St., Union Sq.* ☏ *415/397–7000* ⊕ *www.westinstfrancis.com.*

CHINATOWN
TOP ATTRACTIONS

Chinatown Gate. This is the official entrance to Chinatown. Stone lions flank the base of the pagoda-topped gate; the lions, dragons, and fish up top symbolize wealth, prosperity, and other good things. The four Chinese characters immediately beneath the pagoda represent the philosophy of Sun Yat-sen (1866–1925), the leader who unified China in the early 20th century. Sun Yat-sen, who lived in exile in San Francisco for a few years, promoted the notion of friendship and peace among all nations based on equality, justice, and goodwill. The vertical characters under the left pagoda read "peace" and "trust," the ones under the right pagoda "respect" and "love." The whole shebang telegraphs the internationally understood message of "photo op." Immediately beyond the gate, dive into souvenir shopping on Grant Avenue, Chinatown's tourist strip. ⊠ *Grant Ave. at Bush St., Chinatown.*

Kong Chow Temple. This ornate temple sets a somber, spiritual tone right away with a sign warning visitors not to touch *anything*. The god to whom the members of this temple pray represents honesty and trust. Chinese stores and restaurants often display his image because he's thought to bring good luck in business. Chinese immigrants established the temple in 1851; its congregation moved to this building in 1977. Take the elevator up to the fourth floor, where incense fills the air. You can show respect by placing a dollar or two in the donation

Union Square and Chinatown

CHINATOWN

Chinese Culture Center

Old St. Mary's Cathedral

Jackson Square Historic District

NOB HILL

Hallidie Building

MONTGOMERY ST.

Lotta's Fountain

UNION SQUARE

Pacific Telephone Bldg.

POWELL ST.

Yerba Buena Gardens

Moscone Convention Center

KEY

b *Bart Stop*

...... *Cable Car*

Old U.S. Mint

0   350 M

0   1,000 ft.

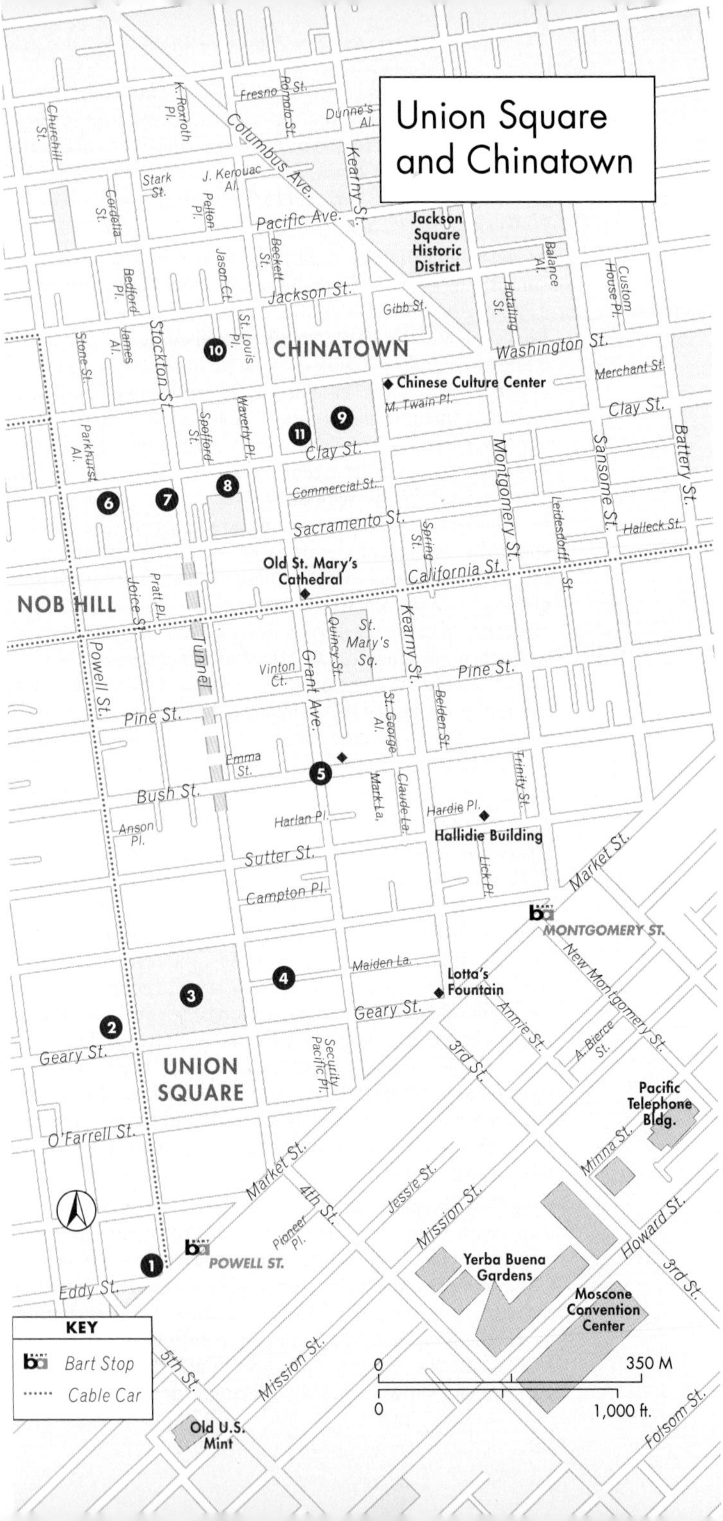

box and by leaving your camera in its case. Amid the statuary, flowers, and richly colored altars (red wards off evil spirits and signifies virility, green symbolizes longevity, and gold connotes majesty), a couple of plaques announce that "Mrs. Harry S. Truman came to this temple in June 1948 for a prediction on the outcome of the election . . . this fortune came true." ■TIP➔ **The temple's balcony has a good view of Chinatown.** ✉ *855 Stockton St., Chinatown* ✆ *Free* ⊘ *Mon.–Sat. 9–4.*

Fodor's Choice ★ **Tin How Temple.** Duck into the inconspicuous doorway, climb three flights of stairs, and be assaulted by the aroma of incense in this tiny, altar-filled room. In 1852, Day Ju, one of the first three Chinese to arrive in San Francisco, dedicated this temple to the Queen of the Heavens and the Goddess of the Seven Seas, and the temple looks largely the same today as it did more than a century ago. In the entryway, elderly ladies can often be seen preparing "money" to be burned as offerings to various Buddhist gods or as funds for ancestors to use in the afterlife. Hundreds of red-and-gold lanterns cover the ceiling; the larger the lamp, the larger its donor's contribution to the temple. Gifts of oranges, dim sum, and money left by the faithful, who kneel mumbling prayers, rest on altars to different gods. Tin How presides over the middle back of the temple, flanked by one red and one green lesser god. Take a good look around, since taking photographs is not allowed. ✉ *125 Waverly Pl., between Clay and Washington Sts., Chinatown* ✆ *Free, donations accepted* ⊘ *Daily 10–4.*

CABLE CAR TERMINUS

Two of the three cable-car lines begin and end their runs at Powell and Market streets, a couple blocks south of Union Square. These two lines are the most scenic, and both pass near Fisherman's Wharf, so they're usually clogged with first-time sightseers. The wait to board a cable car at this intersection is longer than at any other stop in the system. If you'd rather avoid the mob, board the less-touristy California line at the bottom of Market Street, at Drumm Street.

WORTH NOTING

Chinese Historical Society of America Museum and Learning Center. The displays at this small, light-filled gallery document the Chinese-American experience—from 19th-century agriculture to 21st-century food and fashion trends—and include a thought-provoking collection of racist games and toys. The facility also has temporary exhibits of works by contemporary Chinese-American artists. ✉ *965 Clay St., between Stockton and Powell Sts., Chinatown* ✆ *415/391–1188* ⊕ *www.chsa. org* ✆ *$5, free 1st Thurs. of month* ⊘ *Tues.–Fri. noon–5, Sat. 11–4.*

FAMILY **Golden Gate Fortune Cookie Factory.** Follow your nose down Ross Alley to this tiny but fragrant cookie factory. Workers sit at circular motorized griddles and wait for dollops of batter to drop onto a tiny metal plate, which rotates into an oven. A few moments later out comes a cookie that's pliable and ready for folding. It's easy to peek in for a moment, and hard to leave without a few free samples. A bagful of cookies—with mildly racy "adult" fortunes or more benign ones—costs under $5. You can also purchase the cookies "fortuneless" in their waferlike unfolded state, which makes snacking that much more efficient. ■TIP➔ **Photographing the cookie makers at work will set you back 50¢.** ⊠ *56 Ross Alley, off Washington or Jackson St. west of Grant Ave., Chinatown* ☎ *415/781–3956* 📧 *Free* ⊙ *Daily 9–8.*

Old Chinese Telephone Exchange. After the 1906 earthquake, many Chinatown buildings were rebuilt in Western style with pagoda roof and fancy balconies slapped on. This building—today East West Bank—is the exception, an example of top-to-bottom Chinese architecture. The intricate three-tier pagoda was built in 1909. To the Chinese, it's considered rude to refer to a person as a number, so the operators were required to memorize each subscriber's name. As the San Francisco Chamber of Commerce boasted in 1914: "These girls respond all day with hardly a mistake to calls that are given (in English or one of five Chinese dialects) by the name of the subscriber instead of by his number—a mental feat that would be practically impossible for most high-schooled American misses." ⊠ *EastWest Bank, 743 Washington St., Chinatown.*

Portsmouth Square. Chinatown's living room buzzes with activity. The square, with its pagoda-shape structures, is a favorite spot for morning tai chi; by noon dozens of men huddle around Chinese chess tables, engaged in competition. Kids scamper about the square's two grungy playgrounds (warning: the bathrooms are sketchy). Back in the late 19th century this land was near the waterfront. The square is named for the USS *Portsmouth*, the ship helmed by Captain John Montgomery, who in 1846 raised the American flag here and claimed the then-Mexican land for the United States. A couple of years later, Sam Brannan kicked off the gold rush at the square when he waved his loot and proclaimed, "Gold from the American River!" Robert Louis Stevenson, the author of *Treasure Island*, often dropped by, chatting up the sailors who hung out here. Some of the information he gleaned about life at sea found its way into his fiction. A bronze galleon sculpture, a tribute to Stevenson, anchors the square's northwest corner. A plaque marks the site of California's first public school, built in 1847. ⊠ *Bordered by Walter Lum Pl. and Kearny, Washington, and Clay Sts., Chinatown.*

SOMA, CIVIC CENTER, AND HAYES VALLEY

To a newcomer, SoMa (short for "south of Market") and the Civic Center may look like cheek-by-jowl neighbors—they're divided by Market Street. To locals, though, these areas are separate entities, especially since Market Street itself is considered such a strong demarcation line. Both neighborhoods have a core of cultural sights but more than their share of sketchy blocks. North of the Civic Center lies the western section of the frisky Tenderloin neighborhood, while to the east is hip Hayes Valley.

Continued on page 173

CHINATOWN

Chinatown's streets flood the senses. Incense and cigarette smoke mingle with the scents of briny fish and sweet vanilla. Rooflines flare outward, pagoda-style. Loud Cantonese bargaining and honking car horns rise above the sharp clack of mah-jongg tiles and the eternally humming cables beneath the street.

Most Chinatown visitors march down Grant Avenue, buy a few trinkets, and call it a day. Do yourself a favor and dig deeper. This is one of the largest Chinese communities outside Asia, and there is far more to it than buying a back-scratcher near Chinatown Gate. To get a real feel for the neighborhood, wander off the main drag. Step into a temple or an herb shop and wander down a flag-draped alley. And don't be shy: residents welcome guests warmly, though rarely in English.

Whatever you do, don't leave without eating something. Noodle houses, bakeries, tea houses, and dim sum shops seem to occupy every other storefront. There's a feast for your eyes as well: in the market windows on Stockton and Grant, you'll see hanging whole roast ducks, fish, and shellfish swimming in tanks, and strips of shiny, pink-glazed Chinese-style barbecued pork.

CHINATOWN'S HISTORY

Sam Brannan's 1848 cry of "Gold!" didn't take long to reach across the world to China. Struggling with famine, drought, and political upheaval at home, thousands of Chinese jumped at the chance to try their luck in California. Most came from the Pearl River Delta region, in the Guangdong province, and spoke Cantonese dialects. From the start, Chinese businesses circled around Portsmouth Square, which was conveniently central. Bachelor rooming houses sprang up, since the vast majority of new arrivals were men. By 1853, the area was called Chinatown.

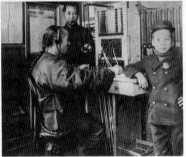

The Street of Gamblers (Ross Alley), 1898 (top). The first Chinese telephone operator in Chinatown (bottom).

COLD WELCOME

The Chinese faced discrimination from the get-go. Harrassment became outright hostility as first the gold rush, then the work on the Transcontinental Railroad petered out. Special taxes were imposed to shoulder aside competing "coolie labor." Laws forbidding the Chinese from moving outside Chinatown kept the residents packed in like sardines, with nowhere to go but up and down— thus the many basement establishments in the neighborhood. State and federal laws passed in the 1870s deterred Chinese women from immigrating, deeming them prostitutes. In the late 1870s, looting and arson attacks on Chinatown businesses soared.

The coup de grace, though, was the Chinese Exclusion Act, passed by the U.S.

Chinatown's Grant Avenue.

Women and children flooded into the neighborhood after the Great Quake.

Congress in 1882, which slammed the doors to America for "Asiatics." This was the country's first significant restriction on immigration. The law also prevented the existing Chinese residents, including American-born children, from becoming naturalized citizens. With a society of mostly men (forbidden, of course, from marrying white women), San Francisco hoped that Chinatown would simply die out.

OUT OF THE ASHES

When the devastating 1906 earthquake and fire hit, city fathers thought they'd seize the opportunity to kick the Chinese out of Chinatown and get their hands on that desirable piece of downtown real estate. Then Chinatown businessman Look Tin Eli had a brainstorm of Disneyesque proportions.

He proposed that Chinatown be rebuilt, but in a tourist-friendly, stylized, "Oriental" way. Anglo-American architects would design new buildings with pagoda roofs and dragon-covered columns. Chinatown would attract more tourists—the curious had been visiting on the sly

for decades—and add more tax money to the city's coffers. Ka-ching: the sales pitch worked.

PAPER SONS

For the Chinese, the 1906 earthquake turned the virtual "no entry" sign into a flashing neon "welcome!" All the city's immigration records went up in smoke, and the Chinese quickly began to apply for passports as U.S. citizens, claiming their old ones were lost in the fire. Not only did thousands of Chinese become legal overnight, but so did their sons in China, or "sons," if they weren't really related. Whole families in Chinatown had passports in names that weren't their own; these "paper sons" were not only a windfall but also an uncomfortable neighborhood conspiracy. The city caught on eventually and set up an immigration center on Angel Island in 1910. Immigrants spent weeks or months being inspected and interrogated while their papers were checked. Roughly 250,000 people made it through. With this influx, including women and children, Chinatown finally became a more complete community.

A GREAT WALK THROUGH CHINATOWN

■ Start at the Chinatown Gate and walk ahead on Grant Avenue, entering the souvenir gauntlet. (You'll also pass Old St. Mary's Cathedral.)

■ Make a right on Clay Street and walk to Portsmouth Square. Sometimes it feels like the whole neighborhood's here, playing chess and exercising.

■ Head up Washington Street to the Old Chinese Telephone Exchange building, now the EastWest Bank. Across Grant, look left for Waverly Place. Here Free Republic of China (Taiwanese) flags flap over some of the neighborhood's most striking buildings, including Tin How Temple.

■ At the Sacramento Street end of Waverly Place stands the First Chinese Baptist Church of 1908. Just across the way, the Clarion Music Center is full of unusual instruments, as well as exquisite lion-dance sets.

■ Head back to Washington Street and check out the many herb shops.

■ Follow the scent of vanilla down Ross Alley (entrance across from Superior Trading Company) to the Golden Gate Fortune Cookie Factory. Then head across the alley to Sam Bo Trading Co., where religious

items are stacked in the narrow space. Tell the owners your troubles and they'll prepare a package of joss papers, joss sticks, and candles, and tell you how and when to offer them up.

■ Turn left on Jackson Street; ahead is the real Chinatown's main artery, Stockton Street, where most residents do their

grocery shopping. Vegetarians will want to avoid Luen Fat Market (No. 1135), with tanks of live frogs, turtles, and lobster as well as chickens and ducks. Look toward the back of stores for Buddhist altars with offerings of oranges and grapefruit. From here you can loop one block east back to Grant.

SOMA

TOP ATTRACTIONS

California Historical Society. If you're not a history buff, the CHS might seem like an obvious skip—who wants to look at fading old photographs and musty artifacts?—but these airy galleries are worth a stop. The shows here draw from the society's vast repository of Californiana—hundreds of thousands of photographs, publications, paintings, and gold-rush paraphernalia. Special exhibits have included *A Wild Flight of the Imagination: The Story of the Golden Gate Bridge* and *Hobos to Street People: Artists' Responses to Homelessness from the New Deal to the Present.* ■TIP➡ From out front, take a look across the street: this is the best view of the Museum of the African Diaspora's three-story photo mosaic. ✉ *678 Mission St., SoMa* ☎ *415/357–1848* ⊕ *www.california historicalsociety.org* ✉ *$5* ⊙ *Tues.–Sun. noon–5; galleries close between exhibitions.*

LOOK UP!

When wandering around China-town, don't forget to look up! Above the chintziest souvenir shop might loom an ornate balcony or a curly pagoda roof. The best examples are on the 900 block of Grant Avenue (at Washington Street) and at Waverly Place.

Contemporary Jewish Museum. Daniel Liebeskind designed the postmodern CJM, whose impossible-to-ignore diagonal blue cube juts out of a painstakingly restored power substation. A physical manifestation of the Hebrew phrase *l'chaim* (to life), the cube may have obscure philosophical origins, but Liebeskind created a unique, light-filled space that merits a stroll through the lobby even if current exhibits don't entice you into the galleries. Be sure to check out the seam where old building meets new, and check the website for fun children's activities linked to exhibits. ■TIP➡ San Francisco's best Jewish deli, Wise Sons, recently opened a counter in the museum, giving you a chance to sample the company's wildly popular smoked trout. ✉ *736 Mission St., between 3rd and 4th Sts., SoMa* ☎ *415/655–7800* ⊕ *www.thecjm. org* ✉ *$12; $5 Thurs. after 5 pm, free 1st Tues. of month* ⊙ *Thurs. 1–8, Fri.–Tues. 11–5.*

Museum of the African Diaspora (MoAD). Dedicated to the influence that people of African descent have had all over the world, MoAD provokes discussion from the get-go with the question, "When did you discover you are African?" painted on the wall in the lobby. Recently renovated and reimagined for its 10th anniversary in 2015, MoAD is moving away from static historical displays toward temporary exhibits in its three new galleries over two upper floors. Its new status as a Smithsonian affiliate means access to resources, lecturers, and touring shows, and perhaps a higher profile for this institution, which has struggled to find its place. With floor-to-ceiling windows onto Mission Street, the museum fits perfectly into the cultural scene of Yerba Buena and is well worth a 30-minute foray. Happily, the museum retained its striking front-window exhibit: a three-story mosaic, made from thousands of photographs, that forms the image of a young girl's face. ■TIP➡ Walk up the stairs inside the museum to view the photographs

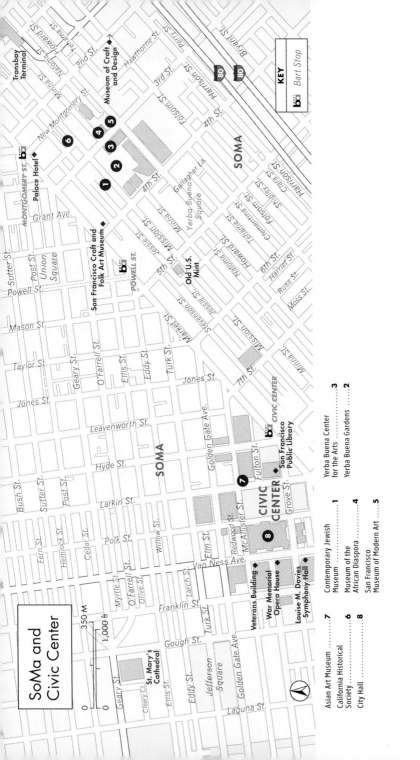

SoMa and Civic Center

KEY
🚇 Bart Stop

Transbay Terminal
Palace Hotel ◆
Museum of Craft and Design →◆

San Francisco Craft and Folk Art Museum ◆

Old U.S. Mint

Veterans Building ◆
War Memorial Opera House ◆
Louise M. Davies Symphony Hall ◆

St. Mary's Cathedral

San Francisco Public Library ◆

SOMA

CIVIC CENTER

Yerba Buena Square

Union Square

350 M
1,000 ft

Asian Art Museum 7
California Historical Society 6
City Hall 8

Contemporary Jewish Museum 1
Museum of the African Diaspora 4
San Francisco Museum of Modern Art 5

Yerba Buena Center for the Arts 3
Yerba Buena Gardens 2

up close—Malcolm X is there, Muhammad Ali, too, along with everyday folks—but the best view is from across the street. ⊠ *685 Mission St., SoMa* ☎ *415/358–7200* ⊕ *www.moadsf.org* ☜ *$10* ⊙ *Wed.–Sat. 11–6, Sun. noon–5.*

FAMILY

Fodor's Choice
★

Yerba Buena Gardens. There's not much south of Market Street that encourages lingering outdoors—or indeed walking at all—with this notable exception. These two blocks encompass the Center for the Arts, the Metreon, Moscone Convention Center, and the convention center's rooftop Children's Creativity Museum, but the gardens themselves are the everyday draw. Office workers escape to the green swath of the East Garden, the focal point of which is the memorial to Martin Luther King Jr. Powerful streams of water surge over large, jagged stone columns, mirroring the enduring force of King's words that are carved on the stone walls and on glass blocks behind the waterfall. Moscone North is behind the memorial, and an overhead walkway leads to Moscone South and its rooftop attractions. ■ TIP➔ The gardens are liveliest during the week and especially during the Yerba Buena Gardens Festival, from May through October (*www.ybgfestival.org*), with free performances of everything from Latin music to Balinese dance.

Atop the Moscone Convention Center perch a few lures for kids. The historic Looff carousel (*$4 for two rides*) twirls daily 10–5. South of the carousel is the Children's Creativity Museum (*415/820–3320, creativity. org*), a high-tech, interactive arts-and-technology center (*$12*) geared to children ages 3–12. Kids can make Claymation videos, work in a computer lab, check out new games and apps, and perform and record music videos. The museum is open year-round 10–4 from Wednesday through Sunday, and on Tuesday during the summer. Just outside, kids adore the excellent slides, including a 25-foot tube slide, at the play circle. Also part of the rooftop complex are gardens, an ice-skating rink, and a bowling alley. ⊠ *Bordered by 3rd, 4th, Mission, and Folsom Sts., SoMa* ⊕ *www.yerbabuenagardens.com* ☜ *Free* ⊙ *Daily sunrise–10 pm.*

WORTH NOTING

San Francisco Museum of Modern Art. SFMOMA closed for a massive expansion project in 2013 and is scheduled to reopen in 2016. Until then, the museum will draw from its collection to create joint exhibitions with the Asian Art Museum, the Yerba Buena Center for the Arts, and other institutions. SFMOMA's store—known for its fun gadgets, artsy doodads, and superb art and kids' books—is relocating temporarily to 51 Yerba Buena Lane, off Mission and Market streets near 4th Street. ⊠ *151 3rd St., SoMa* ☎ *415/357–4000* ⊕ *www.sfmoma.org.*

Yerba Buena Center for the Arts. You never know what's going to be on display at this facility in Yerba Buena Gardens, but whether it's an exhibit of Mexican street art (graffiti to laypeople), innovative modern dance, or a baffling video installation, it's likely to be memorable. The productions here, which lean toward the cutting edge, tend to draw a young, energetic crowd. ■ TIP➔ Present any public library card to receive a $2 discount. ⊠ *701 Mission St., SoMa* ☎ *415/978–2787* ⊕ *www.ybca.org* ☜ *Galleries $10, free 1st Tues. of month* ⊙ *Wed. noon–6, Thurs.–Sat. noon–8, Sun. noon–6, 1st Tues. of the month noon–8.*

5

CIVIC CENTER

Asian Art Museum. You don't have to be a connoisseur of Asian art to appreciate a visit to this museum whose monumental exterior conceals a light, open, and welcoming space. The fraction of the Asian's collection on display (about 2,500 pieces out of 15,000-plus total) is laid out thematically and by region, making it easy to follow historical developments.

Begin on the third floor, where highlights of Buddhist art in Southeast Asia and early China include a large, jewel-encrusted, exquisitely painted 19th-century Burmese Buddha and clothed rod puppets from Java. On the second floor you can find later Chinese works, as well as pieces from Korea and Japan. The joy here is all in the details: on a whimsical Korean jar, look for a cobalt tiger jauntily smoking a pipe, or admire the delicacy of the Japanese tea implements. The ground floor is devoted to temporary exhibits, often traveling shows such as recent ones about Balinese art, and the transformation of yoga. ■ TIP→ During spring and summer, visit the museum the first Thursday evening of the month for extended programs and sip drinks while a DJ spins tunes. ✉ *200 Larkin St., between McAllister and Fulton Sts., Civic Center* ☎ *415/581–3500* ⊕ *www.asianart.org* 🖅 *$15, free 1st Sun. of month; $10 Thurs. 5–9* ⊙ *Tues.–Sun. 10–5; Feb.–Oct., also Thurs. until 9.*

City Hall. This imposing 1915 structure with its massive gold-leaf dome—higher than the U.S. Capitol's—is about as close to a palace as you're going to get in San Francisco. (Alas, the metal detectors detract from the grandeur.) The classic granite-and-marble behemoth was modeled after St. Peter's Basilica in Rome. Architect Arthur Brown Jr., who also designed Coit Tower and the War Memorial Opera House, designed an interior with grand columns and a sweeping central staircase. San Franciscans were thrilled, and probably a bit surprised, when his firm built City Hall in just a few years. The 1899 structure it replaced had taken 27 years to erect, as corrupt builders and politicians lined their pockets with funds earmarked for it. That building collapsed in about 27 seconds during the 1906 earthquake, revealing trash and newspapers mixed into the construction materials.

City Hall was spruced up and seismically retrofitted in the late 1990s, but the sense of history remains palpable. Some noteworthy events that have taken place here include the marriage of Marilyn Monroe and Joe DiMaggio (1954); the hosing—down the central staircase—of civil-rights and freedom-of-speech protesters (1960); the murders of Mayor George Moscone and openly gay supervisor Harvey Milk (1978); the torching of the lobby by angry members of the gay community in response to the light sentence given to the former supervisor who killed both men (1979); and the registrations of scores of gay couples in celebration of the passage of San Francisco's Domestic Partners Act (1991). February 2004 has come to be known as the Winter of Love: thousands of gay and lesbian couples responded to Mayor Gavin Newsom's decision to issue marriage licenses to same-sex partners, turning City Hall into the site of raucous celebration and joyful nuptials for a month before the state Supreme Court ordered the practice stopped. That celebratory scene replayed during 2008, when scores of couples were wed between the court's June ruling that everyone enjoys the civil right to marry and the November passage of California's ballot proposition banning same-sex marriage. In 2013, the U.S. Supreme Court resolved the issue, ruling against the proposition.

On display in the South Light Court are artifacts from the collection of the **Museum of the City of San Francisco** (*www.sfmuseum.org*), including maps, documents, and photographs. That enormous, 700-pound iron head once crowned the *Goddess of Progress* statue, which topped the old City Hall building until it crumbled during the 1906 earthquake. City Hall's centennial in 2013 kicked off three years of exhibits—the same amount of time it took to raise the building.

Across Polk Street from City Hall is **Civic Center Plaza,** with lawns, walkways, seasonal flower beds, a playground, and an underground parking garage. This sprawling space is generally clean but somewhat grim. A large part of the city's homeless population hangs out here, so the plaza can feel dodgy. ⊠ *Bordered by Van Ness Ave. and Polk, Grove, and McAllister Sts., Civic Center* ☎ *415/554–6023 recorded tour info, 415/554–6139 tour reservations* ⊕ *sfgsa.org/index.aspx?page=1172* ▧ *Free* ⊙ *Weekdays 8–8 except holidays; free tours weekdays at 10, noon, and 2.*

HAYES VALLEY

SFJAZZ Center. Opened in 2013 to much fanfare, the center is devoted entirely to jazz. The debut week alone saw performances by McCoy Tyner, Joshua Redman, Regina Carter, Chick Corea, and Savion Glover, among others. Walk by and the street-level glass walls will make you feel as if you're inside; head indoors and the acoustics will knock your socks off. Celebrated artists Sandow Birk and Elyse Pignolet created the lobby murals. ∎**TIP→ Grab dinner at South, a rustic-Mexican restaurant developed by Charles Phan, the acclaimed chef of the Slanted Door; during showtime, you can listen to the musicians playing in the adjacent auditorium.** ⊠ *201 Franklin St., at Fell St., Hayes Valley* ☎ *866/920–5299* ⊕ *www.sfjazz.org.*

NOB HILL AND RUSSIAN HILL

In place of the quirky charm and cultural diversity that mark other San Francisco neighborhoods, Nob Hill exudes history and good breeding. Topped with some of the city's most elegant hotels, Gothic Grace Cathedral, and private blue-blood clubs, it's the pinnacle of privilege. One hill over, across Pacific Avenue, is another old-family bastion, Russian Hill. It may not be quite as wealthy as Nob Hill, but it's no slouch—and it's got jaw-dropping views.

NOB HILL

FAMILY **Cable Car Museum.** One of the city's best free offerings, this museum is an absolute must for kids. You can even ride a cable car here—all three lines stop between Russian Hill and Nob Hill. The facility, which is inside the city's last cable-car barn, takes the top off the system to let you see how it all works. Eternally humming and squealing, the massive powerhouse cable wheels steal the show. You can also climb aboard a vintage car and take the grip, let the kids ring a cable-car bell (briefly), and check out vintage gear dating from 1873.

The gift shop sells cable-car paraphernalia, including an authentic gripman's bell for $600—it'll sound like Powell Street in your house every day. For significantly less, you can pick up a key chain made from a piece of worn-out cable. ⊠ *1201 Mason St., at Washington St., Nob Hill* 🕾 *415/474–1887* ⊕ *www.cablecarmuseum.org* ⊠ *Free* ☉ *Oct.–Mar., daily 10–5; Apr.–Sept., daily 10–6.*

Grace Cathedral. Not many churches can boast an altarpiece by Keith Haring and not one, but two labyrinths. The seat of the Episcopal Church in San Francisco, this soaring Gothic-style structure, erected on the site of the 19th-century railroad baron Charles Crocker's mansion, took 53 years to build, wrapping up in 1964. The gilded bronze doors at the east entrance were taken from casts of Lorenzo Ghiberti's incredible Gates of Paradise, which are on the Baptistery in Florence, Italy. A black-and-bronze stone sculpture of St. Francis by Beniamino Bufano greets you as you enter.

The 35-foot-wide limestone labyrinth is a replica of the 13th-century stone maze on the floor of Chartres Cathedral. All are encouraged to walk the ¼-mile-long labyrinth, a ritual based on the tradition of meditative walking. There's also a terrazzo outdoor labyrinth on the church's north side. The AIDS Interfaith Chapel, to the right as you enter Grace, contains a metal triptych by the late artist Keith Haring and panels from the AIDS Memorial Quilt. ■TIP→ Especially dramatic times to view the cathedral are during Thursday-night evensong (5:15 pm) and during special holiday programs. ⊠ *1100 California St., at Taylor St., Nob Hill* 🕾 *415/749–6300* ⊕ *www.gracecathedral.org* ⊠ *Free; tours $25* ☉ *Weekdays 7–6, Sat. 8–6, Sun. 8–7; tour times vary.*

RUSSIAN HILL
TOP ATTRACTIONS

Fodor's Choice ★ **Ina Coolbrith Park.** If you make it all the way up here, you may have the place all to yourself, or at least feel like you do. The park's terraces are carved from a hill so steep that it's difficult to see if anyone else is there or not. Locals love this park because it feels like a secret no one else knows about—one of the city's magic hidden gardens, with a meditative setting and spectacular views of the bay peeking out from among the trees. A poet, Oakland librarian, and niece of Mormon prophet Joseph Smith, Ina Coolbrith (1842–1928) introduced Jack London and Isadora Duncan to the world of books. For years she entertained literary greats in her Macondray Lane home near the park. In 1915 she was named poet laureate of California. ⊠ *Vallejo St. between Mason and Taylor Sts., Russian Hill.*

Lombard Street. The block-long "Crookedest Street in the World" makes eight switchbacks down the east face of Russian Hill between Hyde and Leavenworth streets. Residents bemoan the traffic jam outside their front doors, but the throngs continue. Join the line of cars waiting to drive down the steep hill, or avoid the whole mess and walk down the steps on either side of Lombard. You take in super views of North Beach and Coit Tower whether you walk or drive—though if you're

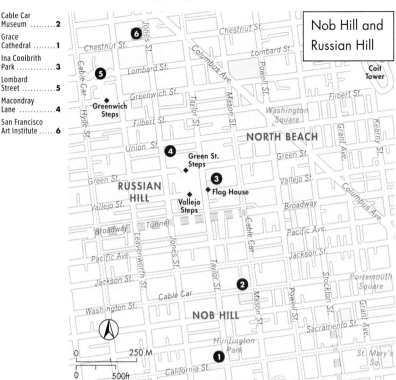

Nob Hill and
Russian Hill

the one behind the wheel, you'd better keep your eye on the road lest
you become yet another of the many folks who ram the garden barriers.
■ TIP→ **Can't stand the traffic? Thrill seekers of a different stripe may
want to head two blocks south of Lombard to Filbert Street. At a gradi-
ent of 31.5%, the hair-raising descent between Hyde and Leavenworth
streets is the city's steepest. Go slowly!** ⊠ *Lombard St. between Hyde
and Leavenworth Sts., Russian Hill.*

Fodor's Choice **Macondray Lane.** San Francisco has no shortage of impressive, grand
★ homes, but it's the tiny fairy-tale lanes that make most want to move
here, and Macondray Lane is the quintessential hidden garden. Enter
under a lovely wooden trellis and proceed down a quiet, cobbled pedestrian lane lined with Edwardian cottages and flowering plants and trees.
Watch your step—the cobblestones are quite uneven in spots. A flight
of steep wooden stairs at the end of the lane leads to Taylor Street—
on the way down you can't miss the bay views. If you've read any of
Armistead Maupin's *Tales of the City* books, you may find the lane
vaguely familiar. It's the thinly disguised setting for part of the series'
action. ⊠ *Between Jones and Taylor Sts., and Union and Green Sts.,
Russian Hill.*

WORTH NOTING

San Francisco Art Institute. A Moorish-tile fountain in a tree-shaded court-yard draws the eye as soon as you enter the institute. The number-one reason for a visit is Mexican master Diego Rivera's *The Making of a Fresco Showing the Building of a City* (1931), in the student gallery to your immediate left inside the entrance. Rivera himself is in the fresco—his broad behind is to the viewer—and he's surrounded by his assistants. They in turn are surrounded by a construction scene, laborers, and city notables such as sculptor Robert Stackpole and architect Timothy Pfleuger. *Making* is one of three San Francisco murals painted by Rivera. The number-two reason to come here is the café, or more precisely the eye-popping, panoramic view from the café, which serves surprisingly decent food for a song.

The older portions of the Art Institute, including the lovely Mission-style bell tower, were erected in 1926. To this day, otherwise pragmatic people claim that ghostly footsteps can be heard in the tower at night. Ansel Adams created the school's fine-arts photography department in 1946, and school directors established the country's first fine-arts film program. Notable faculty and alumni have included painter Richard Diebenkorn and photographers Dorothea Lange, Edward Weston, and Annie Leibovitz.

The **Walter & McBean Galleries** *(415/749–4563; Open Tues. 11–7, Wed.–Sat. 11–6)* exhibit the often provocative works of established artists. ✉ *800 Chestnut St., Russian Hill* ☎ *415/771–7020* ⊕ *www.sfai.edu* 🎟 *Galleries free* ⊙ *Hrs vary but building generally open Mon.–Sat. 9–7*

NORTH BEACH

San Francisco novelist Herbert Gold calls North Beach "the longest-running, most glorious, American bohemian operetta outside Greenwich Village." Indeed, to anyone who's spent some time in its eccentric old bars and cafés, North Beach evokes everything from the Barbary Coast days to the no-less-rowdy Beatnik era.

TOP ATTRACTIONS

Coit Tower. Whether or not you agree that it resembles a fire-hose nozzle, this 210-foot tower is among San Francisco's most distinctive skyline sights. Although the monument wasn't intended as a tribute to firemen, it's often considered as such because of the donor's special attachment to the local fire company. As the story goes, a young gold rush–era girl, Lillie Hitchcock Coit (known as Miss Lil), was a fervent admirer of her local fire company—so much so that she once deserted a wedding party and chased down the street after her favorite engine, Knickerbocker No. 5, while clad in her bridesmaid finery. She became the Knickerbocker Company's mascot and always signed her name "Lillie Coit 5." When Lillie died in 1929 she left the city $125,000 to "expend in an appropriate manner . . . to the beauty of San Francisco."

You can ride the elevator to the top of the tower—the only thing you have to pay for here—to enjoy the view of the Bay Bridge and the Golden Gate Bridge; due north is Alcatraz Island. Most visitors saunter

Continued on page 185

SAN FRANCISCO'S CABLE CARS

The moment it dawns on you that you severely underestimated the steepness of the San Francisco hills will likely be the same moment you look down and realize those tracks aren't just for show—or just for tourists.

Sure, locals rarely use the cable cars for commuting these days. (That's partially due to the $6 fare—hear that, Muni?) So you'll likely be packed in with plenty of fellow sightseers. You may even be approaching cable-car fatigue after seeing its image on so many souvenirs. But if you fear the magic is gone, simply climb on board, and those jaded thoughts will dissolve. Grab the pole and gawk at the view as the car clanks down an insanely steep grade toward the bay. Listen to the humming cable, the clang of the bell, and the occasional quip from the gripman. It's an experience you shouldn't pass up, whether on your first trip or your fiftieth.

HOW CABLE CARS WORK

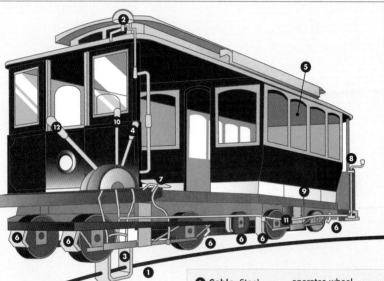

The mechanics are pretty simple: cable cars grab a moving subterranean cable with a "grip" to go. To stop, they release the grip and apply one or more types of brakes. Four cables, totaling 9 miles, power the city's three lines. If the gripman doesn't adjust the grip just right when going up a steep hill, the cable will start to slip and the car will have to back down the hill and try again. This is an extremely rare occurrence—imagine the ribbing the gripman gets back at the cable car barn!

Gripman: Stands in front and operates the grip, brakes, and bell. Favorite joke, especially at the peak of a steep hill: "This is my first day on the job folks…"

Conductor: Moves around the car, deals with tickets, alerts the grip about what's coming up, and operates the rear wheel brakes.

❶ Cable: Steel wrapped around flexible sisal core; 2 inches thick; runs at a constant 9½ mph.

❷ Bells: Used for crew communication; alerts other drivers and pedestrians.

❸ Grip: Vice-like lever extends through the center slot in the track to grab or release the cable.

❹ Grip Lever: Left-hand lever; operates grip.

❺ Car: Entire car weighs 8 tons.

❻ Wheel Brake: Steel brake pads on each wheel.

❼ Wheel Brake Lever: Foot pedal; operates wheel brakes.

❽ Rear Wheel Brake Lever: Applied for extra traction on hills.

❾ Track Brake: 2-foot-long sections of Monterey pine push down against the track to help stop the car.

❿ Track Brake Lever: Middle lever; operates track brakes.

⓫ Emergency Brake: 18-inch steel wedge, jams into street slot to bring car to an immediate stop.

⓬ Emergency Brake Lever: Right-hand lever, red; operates emergency brake.

ROUTES

Cars run at least every 15 minutes, from around 6 AM to about 1 AM.

Powell–Hyde line: Most scenic, with classic Bay views. Begins at Powell and Market streets, then crosses Nob Hill and Russian Hill before a white-knuckle descent down Hyde Street, ending near the Hyde Street Pier.

Powell–Mason line: Also begins at Powell and Market streets, but winds through North Beach to Bay and Taylor streets, a few blocks from Fisherman's Wharf.

California line: Runs from the foot of Market Street, at Drumm Street, up Nob Hill and back. Great views (and aromas and sounds) of Chinatown on the way up. Sit in back to catch glimpses of the Bay. ■TIP→ Take the California line if it's just the cable-car experience you're after—the lines are shorter, and the grips and conductors say it's friendlier and has a slower pace.

RULES OF THE RIDE

Tickets. There are ticket booths at all three turnarounds, or you can pay the conductor after you board (they can make change). Try not to grumble about the price—they're embarrassed enough as it is.

■TIP→ If you're planning to use public transit a few times, or if you'd like to ride back and forth on the cable car without worrying about the price, consider a one-day Muni passport. You can get passports online, at the Powell Street turnaround, the TIX booth on Union Square, or the Fisherman's Wharf cable-car ticket booth at Beach and Hyde streets.

All Aboard. You can board on either side of the cable car. It's legal to stand on the running boards and hang on to the pole, but keep your ears open for the gripman's warnings. ■TIP→ Grab a seat on the outside bench for the best views.

Most people wait (and wait) in line at one of the cable car turnarounds, but you can also hop on along the route. Board wherever you see a white sign showing a figure climbing aboard a brown cable car; wave to the approaching driver, and wait until the car stops.

Riding on the running boards can be part of the thrill.

CABLE CAR HISTORY

HALLIDIE FREES THE HORSES

In the 1850s and '60s, San Francisco's streetcars were drawn by horses. Legend has it that the horrible sight of a car dragging a team of horses downhill to their deaths roused Andrew Smith Hallidie to action. The English immigrant had invented the "Hallidie Ropeway," essentially a cable car for mined ore, and he was convinced that his invention could also move people. In 1873, Hallidie and his intrepid crew prepared to test the first cable car high on Russian Hill. The anxious engineer peered down into the foggy darkness, failed to see the bottom of the hill, and promptly turned the controls over to Hallidie. Needless to say, the thing worked . . . but rides were free for the first two days because people were afraid to get on.

SEE IT FOR YOURSELF

The **Cable Car Museum** is one of the city's best free offerings and an absolute must for kids. (You can even ride a cable car there, since all three lines stop between Russian Hill and Nob Hill.) The museum, which is inside the city's last cable-car barn, takes the top off the system to let you see how it all works.

Eternally humming and squealing, the massive powerhouse cable wheels steal the show. You can also climb aboard a vintage car and take the grip, let the kids ring a cable-car bell (briefly, please!), and check out vintage gear dating from 1873.

■ TIP→ The gift shop sells cable car paraphernalia, including an authentic gripman's bell for $600 (it'll sound like Powell Street in your house every day). For significantly less, you can pick up a key chain made from a piece of worn-out cable.

CHAMPION OF THE CABLE CAR BELL

Each September the city's best and brightest come together to crown a bell-ringing champion at Union Square. The crowd cheers gripmen and conductors as they stomp, shake, and riff with the rope. But it's not a popularity contest; the ringers are judged by former bell-ringing champions who take each ping and gong very seriously.

The Birds

While on Telegraph Hill, you might be startled by a chorus of piercing squawks and a rushing sound of wings. No, you're not about to have a Hitchcock bird-attack moment. These small, vivid green parrots with cherry red heads number in the hundreds; they're descendants of former pets that escaped or were released by their owners. (The birds dislike cages, and they bite if bothered—must've been some disillusioned owners along the way.)

The parrots like to roost high in the aging cypress trees on the hill, chattering and fluttering, sometimes taking wing en masse. They're not popular with some residents, but they did find a champion in local bohemian Mark Bittner, a former street musician. Bittner began chronicling their habits, publishing a book and battling the homeowners who wanted to cut down the cypresses. A documentary, *The Wild Parrots of Telegraph Hill*, made the issue a cause célèbre. In 2007 City Hall, which recognizes a golden goose when it sees one, stepped in and brokered a solution to keep the celebrity birds in town. The city would cover the homeowners' insurance worries and plant new trees for the next generation of wild parrots.

right past the 19 fabulous Depression-era murals inside the tower that depict California's economic and political life, but take the time to appreciate the first New Deal art project supported by taxpayer money. The federal government commissioned the paintings from 25 local artists, and ended up funding a controversy. The radical Mexican painter Diego Rivera inspired the murals' socialist-realist style, with its biting cultural commentary, particularly about the exploitation of workers. At the time the murals were painted, clashes between management and labor along the waterfront and elsewhere in San Francisco were widespread. The elements, the thousands of visitors that pass by them every year, and the lack of climate control in the tower have taken their toll on the murals, but restoration work done on the tower in 2013 should help protect them. ■ TIP➔ **The views from the tower's base are also expansive—and free. Parking at Coit Tower is limited; in fact, you may have to wait (and wait) for a space. Spare yourself the frustration and hike up, if you're in good shape, or take the 39 bus.** ✉ *Telegraph Hill Blvd. at Greenwich St. or Lombard St., North Beach* ☎ *415/362–0808* 🖥 *Free; elevator to top $7* ⏰ *Mar.–Sept., daily 10–5:30; Oct.–Feb., daily 9–4:30.*

Grant Avenue. Originally called Calle de la Fundación, Grant Avenue is the oldest street in the city, but it's got plenty of young blood. Here dusty bars such as the Saloon and perennial favorites like the Savoy Tivoli mix with hotshot boutiques, odd curio shops like the antique jumble that is Aria, atmospheric cafés such as the boho haven Caffè Trieste, and authentic Italian delis. While the street runs from Union Square through Chinatown, North Beach, and beyond, the fun stuff in this neighborhood is crowded into the four blocks between Columbus Avenue and Filbert Street. ✉ *North Beach.*

Telegraph Hill. Residents here have some of the city's best views, as well as the most difficult ascents to their aeries. The hill rises from the east end of Lombard Street to a height of 284 feet and is capped by Coit Tower. Imagine lugging your groceries up that! If you brave the slope, though, you can be rewarded with a "secret treasure" San Francisco moment. Filbert Street starts up the hill, then becomes the **Filbert Steps** when the going gets too steep. You can cut between the Filbert Steps and another flight, the **Greenwich Steps,** on up to the hilltop. As you climb, you can pass some of the city's oldest houses and be surrounded by beautiful, flowering private gardens. In some places the trees grow over the stairs so it feels like you're walking through a green tunnel; elsewhere, you'll have wide-open views of the bay. The cypress trees that grow on the hill are a favorite roost of local avian celebrities the wild parrots of Telegraph Hill; you'll hear the cries of the cherry-headed conures if they're nearby. And the telegraphic name? It comes from the hill's status as the first Morse code signal station back in 1853. ⊠ *Bordered by Lombard, Filbert, Kearny, and Sansome Sts., North Beach.*

Washington Square. Once the daytime social heart of Little Italy, this grassy patch has changed character numerous times over the years. The Beats hung out here in the 1950s, hippies camped out in the 1960s and early '70s, and nowadays you're more likely to see kids of Southeast Asian descent tossing a Frisbee than Italian folks reminiscing about the old country. In the morning, elderly Asians perform the motions of tai chi. Then and later you might see homeless people hanging out on the benches, and by midday young locals sunbathing or running their dogs. Lillie Hitchcock Coit, in yet another show of affection for San Francisco's firefighters, donated the statue of two firemen with a child they rescued. ■TIP➡ **The North Beach Festival, the city's oldest street fair, celebrates the area's Italian culture here each June.** ⊠ *Bordered by Columbus Ave. and Stockton, Filbert, and Union Sts., North Beach.*

WORTH NOTING

Beat Museum. "Museum" might be a stretch for this tiny storefront that's half bookstore, half memorabilia collection. You can see the 1949 Hudson from the movie version of *On the Road* and the shirt Neal Cassady wore while driving Ken Kesey's Merry Prankster bus, "Further." There are also manuscripts, letters, and early editions by Jack Kerouac, Allen Ginsberg, and Lawrence Ferlinghetti, but the true treasure here is the passionate and well-informed staff, which often includes the museum's founder, Jerry Cimino: your short visit may turn into an hours-long trip through the Beat era. ■TIP➡ **The excellent two-hour walking tour goes beyond the museum to take in favorite Beat watering holes and hangouts in North Beach.** ⊠ *540 Broadway, North Beach* ☎ *415/399–9626* ⊕ *www.thebeatmuseum.org* ⊒ *$8; walking tours $30* ⊗ *Sun.–Thurs. 10–7, Fri.–Sat. 10–10.*

Levi Strauss Headquarters. The carefully landscaped complex appears so collegiate that it's affectionately known as LSU—short for Levi Strauss University. Lawns complement the redbrick buildings, and gurgling fountains drown out the sounds of traffic, providing a perfect environment for brown-bag and picnic lunches. The Vault, the lobby exhibition

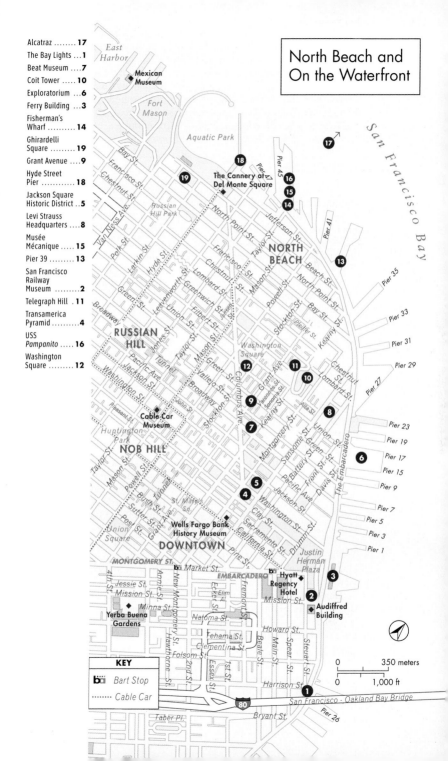

North Beach and On the Waterfront

space, has displays focusing on the history of the company, including jeans that saw the gold rush, videos about Levi's marketing and textile restoration, and temporary displays such as the jeans made for celebs like Lady Gaga and Elton John. ∎TIP→ **You can purchase Levi's and Dockers straight from the source at the cozy lobby boutique.** The wonderful Filbert Steps to Coit Tower are across the street. ⊠ *Levi's Plaza, 1155 Battery St., North Beach* ☎ *415/501–6000* ⊕ *www.levistrauss. com* ⊠ *Free* ☯ *Weekdays 9–6, weekends noon–5.*

ON THE WATERFRONT

San Francisco's waterfront neighborhoods have fabulous views and utterly different personalities. Kitschy, overpriced Fisherman's Wharf struggles to maintain the last shreds of its existence as a working wharf, while Pier 39 is a full-fledged consumer circus. The Ferry Building draws well-heeled locals with its culinary pleasures, firmly connecting the Embarcadero and downtown. Between the Ferry Building and Pier 39 a former maritime no-man's-land is filling in with the recently relocated Exploratorium, a new $90-million cruise-ship terminal, Alcatraz Landing, fashionable waterfront restaurants, and restored, pedestrian-friendly piers.

TOP ATTRACTIONS

FAMILY **Alcatraz.** Thousands of visitors come every day to walk in the footsteps of Alcatraz's notorious criminals. The stories of life and death on "the Rock" may sometimes be exaggerated, but it's almost impossible to resist the chance to wander the cell block that tamed the country's toughest gangsters and saw daring escape attempts of tremendous desperation. Fewer than 2,000 inmates ever did time on the Rock, and though they weren't the worst criminals, they were definitely the worst prisoners, including Al "Scarface" Capone, Robert "The Birdman" Stroud, and George "Machine Gun" Kelly.

Some tips for escaping to Alcatraz: 1) Buy your ticket in advance. Visit the website for Alcatraz Cruises (*www.alcatrazcruises.com*) to scout out available departure times for the ferry. Prepay by credit card and keep a receipt record; the ticket price covers the boat ride and the audio tour. Pick up your ticket at the "will call" window at Pier 33 up to an hour before sailing. 2) Dress smart. Bring a jacket to ward off the chill from the boat ride and wear comfortable shoes. 3) Go for the evening tour. You'll get even more out of your Alcatraz experience at night. The evening tour has programs not offered during the day, the bridge-to-bridge view of the city twinkles at night, and your "prison experience" will be amplified as darkness falls. 4) Be mindful of scheduled and limited-capacity talks. Some programs are only given once a day (the schedule is posted in the cell house) and have limited seating, so keep an eye out for a cell-house staffer handing out passes shortly before the start time.

The boat ride to the island is brief (15 minutes), but affords beautiful views of the city, Marin County, and the East Bay. The audio tour, highly recommended, includes observations by guards and prisoners about life in one of America's most notorious penal colonies. Plan your schedule to allow at least three hours for the visit and boat rides combined. Not

Thousands of visitors take ferries to Alcatraz each day to walk in the footsteps of the notorious criminals who were held on "The Rock."

inspired by the prison? Wander around the lovely native plant gardens and (if the tide is cooperating) the tide pools on the north side of the island. ✉ *Pier 33, Embarcadero* ☎ *415/981–7625* ⊕ *www.nps.gov/alca* 📷 *$30, including audio tour; $37 evening tour, including audio* ⏱ *Ferry departs every 30–45 mins Sept.–late May, daily 9:30–2:15, 4:20 for evening tour Thurs.–Mon. only; late May–Aug., daily 9:30–4:15, 6:30 and 7:30 for evening tour.*

The Bay Lights. Adored by romance seekers, local families, and tourists alike, installation artist Leo Villareal's jaw-dropping LED light sculpture on the San Francisco–Oakland Bay Bridge has become an iconic San Francisco experience. As you travel west into the city along the bridge's upper deck you can view the sculpture's 25,000 lights dancing across its western span, but this installation is best seen from the Embarcadero. Initially intended as a temporary installation, a permanent fixture is planned for early 2016 in collaboration with the state of California. ✉ *Embarcadero* ⊕ *thebaylights.org.*

FAMILY
Fodor's Choice
★

Exploratorium. Walking into this fascinating "museum of science, art, and human perception" is like visiting a mad-scientist's laboratory. Most of the exhibits are supersize, and you can play with everything. After moving into larger digs on the Embarcadero in 2013, the Exploratorium has even more space for its signature experiential exhibits, including a brand-new Tinkering Studio and a glass Bay Observatory building, where the exhibits inside help visitors better understand what they see outside.

Quintessential exhibits remain: Get an *Alice in Wonderland* feeling in the distortion room, where you seem to shrink and grow as you walk across the slanted, checkered floor. In the shadow room, a powerful flash freezes an image of your shadow on the wall; jumping is a favorite pose. "Pushover" demonstrates cow-tipping, but for people: stand on one foot and try to keep your balance while a friend swings a striped panel in front of you (trust us, you're going to fall).

More than 650 other exhibits focus on sea and insect life, computers, electricity, patterns and light, language, the weather, and more. "Explainers"—usually high-school students on their days off—demonstrate cool scientific tools and procedures, like DNA sample-collection and cow-eye dissection. One surefire hit is the pitch-black, touchy-feely Tactile Dome ($15 extra; reservations required). In this geodesic dome strewn with textured objects, you crawl through a course of ladders, slides, and tunnels, relying solely on your sense of touch. Lovey-dovey couples sometimes linger in the "grope dome," but be forewarned: the staff will turn on the lights if necessary. ■TIP➡ Patrons must be at least seven years old to enter the Tactile Dome, and the space is not for the claustrophobic. ⊠ *Piers 15–17, Embarcadero* ☎ *415/561–0360 general information, 415/561–0362 Tactile Dome reservations* ⊕ *www. exploratorium.edu* ⊠ *$29* ⊘ *Tues.–Sun. 10–5; Thurs. 6 pm–10 pm ages 18 and over only.*

F-line. The city's system of vintage electric trolleys, the F-line, gives the cable cars a run for their money as a beloved mode of transportation. The beautifully restored streetcars—some dating from the 19th century—run from the Castro District down Market Street to the Embarcadero, then north to Fisherman's Wharf. Each car is unique, restored to the colors of its city of origin, from New Orleans and Philadelphia to Moscow and Milan. ■TIP➡ Purchase tickets on board; exact change is required. ⊕ *www.streetcar.org* ⊠ *$2.25.*

Fodor's Choice
★

Ferry Building. The jewel of the Embarcadero, erected in 1896, is topped by a 230-foot clock tower modeled after the campanile of the cathedral in Seville, Spain. On the morning of April 18, 1906, the tower's four clock faces, powered by the swinging of a 14-foot pendulum, stopped at 5:17—the moment the great earthquake struck—and stayed still for 12 months.

Today San Franciscans flock to the street-level marketplace, stocking up on supplies from local favorites such as Acme Bread, Scharffen Berger Chocolate, Cowgirl Creamery, Blue Bottle Coffee, and Humphry Slocombe ice cream. Slanted Door, the city's beloved high-end Vietnamese restaurant, is here, along with highly regarded Bouli Bar. The seafood bar at Hog Island Oyster Company has fantastic bay view panoramas. On the plaza side, the outdoor tables at Gott's Roadside offer great people-watching with their famous burgers. On Saturday morning the plazas outside the building buzz with an upscale farmers' market where you can buy exotic sandwiches and other munchables. Extending south from the piers north of the building all the way to the Bay Bridge, the waterfront promenade out front is a favorite among joggers and picnickers, with a front-row view of sailboats plying the bay. True to its name the Ferry Building still serves actual ferries: from its eastern flank they sail to Sausalito, Larkspur, Tiburon, and the East

Bay. ✉ *At foot of Market St., Embarcadero* ☎ *415/983–8030* ⊕ *www. ferrybuildingmarketplace.com.*

QUICK BITES

Buena Vista Café. At the end of the Hyde Street cable-car line, the Buena Vista packs 'em in for its famous Irish coffee—which, according to owners, was the first served stateside (in 1952). The place oozes nostalgia, drawing devoted locals as well as out-of-towners relaxing after a day of sightseeing. It's narrow and can get crowded, but this spot provides a fine alternative to the overpriced tourist joints nearby. ✉ *2765 Hyde St., at Beach St., Fisherman's Wharf* ☎ *415/474–5044* ⊕ *www.thebuenavista.com.*

FAMILY

Fodor's Choice

★

Hyde Street Pier. Cotton candy and souvenirs are all well and good, but if you want to get to the heart of the Wharf—boats—there's no better place to do it than at this pier, one of the Wharf area's best bargains. Depending on the time of day, you might see boatbuilders at work or children pretending to man an early-1900s ship.

Don't pass up the centerpiece collection of historic vessels, part of the **San Francisco Maritime National Historic Park,** almost all of which can be boarded. The *Balclutha,* an 1886 full-rigged three-masted sailing vessel that's more than 250 feet long, sailed around Cape Horn 17 times. Kids especially love the *Eureka,* a side-wheel passenger and car ferry, for her onboard collection of vintage cars. The *Hercules* is a steam-powered tugboat, and the *C.A. Thayer* is a beautifully restored three-masted schooner.

Across the street from the pier and a museum in itself is the maritime park's **Visitor Center** (*499 Jefferson St., 415/447–5000; Open June– Aug., daily 9:30–5:30; Sept.–May, daily 9:30–5*), whose fun, large-scale exhibits make it an engaging stop. See a huge First Order Fresnel lighthouse lens and a shipwrecked boat. Then stroll through time in the exhibit "The Waterfront," where you can touch the timber from a gold rush–era ship recovered from below the Financial District, peek into 19th-century storefronts, and see the sails of an Italian fishing vessel. ✉ *Hyde and Jefferson Sts., Fisherman's Wharf* ☎ *415/561–7100* ⊕ *www.nps.gov/safr* 🚢 *Ships $5 (ticket good for five days)* ☉ *June– Aug., daily 9:30–5:30; Sept.–May, daily 9:30–5.*

Jackson Square Historic District. This was the heart of the Barbary Coast of the Gay '90s—the 1890s, that is. Although most of the red-light district was destroyed in the fire that followed the 1906 earthquake, the remaining old redbrick buildings, many of them now occupied by advertising agencies, law offices, and antiques firms, retain hints of the romance and rowdiness of San Francisco's early days.

With its gentrified gold rush–era buildings, the 700 block of **Montgomery Street** just barely evokes the Barbary Coast days, but this was a colorful block in the 19th century and on into the 20th. Writers Mark Twain and Bret Harte were among the contributors to the spunky *Golden Era* newspaper, which occupied No. 732 (now part of the building at No. 744). From 1959 to 1996 the late ambulance-chaser extraordinaire, lawyer Melvin Belli, had his headquarters at Nos. 722 and 728–730. There was never a dull moment in Belli's world; he represented clients

5

from the actress Mae West to Gloria Sykes (who in 1964 claimed that a cable-car accident turned her into a nymphomaniac) to the disgraced televangelists Jim and Tammy Faye Bakker. Whenever he won a case, he fired a cannon and raised the Jolly Roger. Belli was also known for receiving a letter from the never-caught Zodiac killer.

Restored 19th-century brick buildings line Hotaling Place, which connects Washington and Jackson streets. The lane is named for the head of the **A.P. Hotaling Company whiskey distillery** (*451 Jackson St., at Hotaling Pl.*), the largest liquor repository on the West Coast in its day. (Anchor Distillery still makes an occasional Hotaling whiskey in the city, by the way; look for this single malt for a sip of truly local flavor.) ■TIP➜ **The exceptional City Guides (415/557-4266, www.sfcityguides. org) Gold Rush City walking tour covers this area and brings its history to life.** ✉ *Bordered by Columbus Ave., Broadway, and Washington and Sansome Sts., Jackson Square.*

FAMILY **Musée Mécanique.** Once a staple at Playland-at-the-Beach, San Francisco's early-20th-century amusement park, the antique mechanical contrivances at this time-warped arcade—including peep shows and nickelodeons—make it one of the most worthwhile attractions at the Wharf. Some favorites are the giant and rather creepy "Laffing Sal," an arm-wrestling machine, the world's only steam-powered motorcycle, and mechanical fortune-telling figures that speak from their curtained boxes. Note the depictions of race that betray the prejudices of the time: stoned Chinese figures in the "Opium-Den" and clown-faced African Americans eating watermelon in the "Mechanical Farm." ■TIP➜ **Admission is free, but you'll need quarters to bring the machines to life.** ✉ *Pier 45, Shed A, Fisherman's Wharf* ☎ *415/346–2000* ⊕ *www.musee mechanique.org* ☞ *Free* ⊗ *Weekdays 10–7, weekends 10–8.*

Fodor's Choice
★

FAMILY **Pier 39.** The city's most popular waterfront attraction draws millions of visitors each year who come to browse through its shops and concessions hawking every conceivable form of souvenir. The pier can be quite crowded, and the numerous street performers may leave you feeling more harassed than entertained. Arriving early in the morning ensures you a front-row view of the sea lions that bask here, but if you're here to shop—and make no mistake about it, Pier 39 wants your money—be aware that most stores don't open until 9:30 or 10 (later in winter).

Brilliant colors enliven the double-decker **San Francisco Carousel** (*$3 per ride*), decorated with images of such city landmarks as the Golden Gate Bridge and Lombard Street.

Follow the sound of barking to the northwest side of the pier to view the **sea lions** that flop about the floating docks. During the summer, orange-clad naturalists answer questions and offer fascinating facts about the playful pinnipeds—for example, that most of the animals here are males.

At the **Aquarium of the Bay** (*415/623–5300 or 888/732–3483, www. aquariumofthebay.org; $19.95, hours vary but at least 10–6 daily*), moving walkways transport you through a space surrounded on three sides by water filled with indigenous San Francisco Bay marine life, from fish and plankton to sharks. Many find the aquarium overpriced; if you can, take advantage of the family rate (*$64 for two adults and two kids under 12*).

Parking is across the street at the **Pier 39 Garage** (*with validation from a Pier 39 restaurant, one hour free before 6 pm, two hours after 6 pm*), off Powell Street at the Embarcadero; look for the mural of the gray whales to spot it. ⊠ *Beach St. at Embarcadero, Fisherman's Wharf* ⊕ *www.pier39.com.*

WORTH NOTING

FAMILY **Fisherman's Wharf.** It may be one of the city's best-known attractions, but the Wharf is a no-go zone for most locals, who shy away from the tourist crowds, overpriced food, and cheesy shops. If you can't resist a visit, come early to avoid the crowds and get a sense of the Wharf's functional role—it's not just an amusement park replica. Two delights amid the tackiness, both at Pier 45, are the Museé Mécanique, a repository of old-fashioned but still working penny-arcade entertainments, and the World War II–era sub the USS *Pampanito*. ⊠ *Jefferson St. between Leavenworth St. and Pier 39, Fisherman's Wharf* ⊕ *www. fishermanswharf.org.*

Ghirardelli Square. Most of the redbrick buildings in this early-20th-century complex were once part of the Ghirardelli factory. Now tourists come here to pick up the famous chocolate, though you can purchase it all over town and save yourself a trip to what is essentially a mall. But this is the only place to watch the cool chocolate manufactory in action. Placards throughout the square describe the factory's history. ⊠ *900 North Point St., Fisherman's Wharf* ☎ *415/775–5500* ⊕ *www. ghirardellisq.com.*

FAMILY **San Francisco Railway Museum.** A labor of love brought to you by the same vintage-transit enthusiasts responsible for the F-line's revival, this one-room museum and store celebrates the city's streetcars and cable cars with photographs, models, and artifacts. The permanent exhibit includes the replicated end of a streetcar with a working cab—complete with controls and a bell—for kids to explore; the cool, antique Wiley birdcage traffic signal; and models and display cases to view. Right on the F-line track, just across from the Ferry Building, this is a great quick stop. ⊠ *77 Steuart St., Embarcadero* ☎ *415/974–1948* ⊕ *www.streetcar. org* 🎫 *Free* 🕐 *Daily 10–6; closed Mon. in winter.*

Transamerica Pyramid. It's neither owned by Transamerica nor is it a pyramid, but this 853-foot-tall obelisk *is* the most photographed of the city's high-rises. Excoriated in the design stages as "the world's largest architectural folly," the icon was quickly hailed as a masterpiece when it opened in 1972. Today it's probably the city's most recognized structure after the Golden Gate Bridge. Visit the small, street-level visitor center to see the virtual view from the top, watch videos about the building's history, and perhaps pick up a T-shirt. ■TIP➡ A fragrant redwood grove along the east side of the building, replete with benches and a cheerful fountain, is a placid patch in which to unwind. ⊠ *600 Montgomery St., Financial District* ⊕ *www.thepyramidcenter.com.*

USS *Pampanito*. Get an intriguing, if mildly claustrophobic, glimpse into life on a submarine during World War II on this small, 80-man sub, which sank six Japanese warships and damaged four others. ■TIP➜ There's not much in the way of interpretive signs, so opt for the audio tour to learn about what you're seeing. ✉ *Pier 45, Fisherman's Wharf* ☎ *415/775–1943* ⊕ *www.maritime.org/pamphome.htm* 🖭 *$12 (family pass $25)* ⊙ *Oct.–late May, Sun.–Thurs. 9–6, Fri. and Sat. 9–8; late May–Sept., daily 9–8.*

THE MARINA, COW HOLLOW, AND THE PRESIDIO

Yachts bob at their moorings, satisfied-looking folks jog along the Marina Green, and multimillion-dollar homes overlook the bay in the picturesque, if somewhat sterile, Marina neighborhood. Does it all seem a bit too perfect? Well, it got this way after the hard knock of Loma Prieta—the current pretty face was put on after hundreds of homes collapsed in the 1989 earthquake. Just west of this waterfront area is a more natural beauty: the Presidio. Once a military base, this beautiful, sprawling park is mostly green space, with hills, woods, and the marshlands of Crissy Field. Between old-money Pacific Heights and the well-heeled, postcollegiate Marina lies comfortably upscale Cow Hollow.

THE MARINA

Fodor'sChoice ★ **Palace of Fine Arts.** At first glance this stunning, rosy rococo palace seems to be from another world, and indeed, it's the sole survivor of the many tinted-plaster structures (a temporary classical city of sorts) built for the 1915 Panama-Pacific International Exposition, the world's fair that celebrated San Francisco's recovery from the 1906 earthquake and fire. The expo buildings originally extended about a mile along the shore. Bernard Maybeck designed this faux–Roman classic beauty, which was reconstructed in concrete and reopened in 1967. A victim of the elements, the Palace required a piece-by-piece renovation that was completed in 2008.

The pseudo-Latin language adorning the Palace's exterior urns continues to stump scholars. The massive columns (each topped with four "weeping maidens"), great rotunda, and swan-filled lagoon have been used in countless fashion layouts, films, and wedding photo shoots. After admiring the lagoon, look across the street to the house at 3460 Baker Street. If the maidens out front look familiar, they should—they're original casts of the "garland ladies" you can see in the Palace's colonnade.

Inside the palace is a performance venue favored by local community groups and international musicians. ✉ *3301 Lyon St., at Beach St., Marina* ☎ *415/561–0364 Palace history tours* ⊕ *www.palaceoffinearts. org* 🖭 *Free* ⊙ *Daily 24 hrs.*

COW HOLLOW

Octagon House. This eight-sided home sits across the street from its original site on Gough Street; it's one of two remaining octagonal houses in the city (the other is on Russian Hill), and the only one open to the public. White quoins accent each of the eight corners of the pretty blue-gray exterior, and a colonial-style garden completes the picture. The house is full of antique American furniture, decorative arts (paintings, silver, rugs), and documents from the 18th and 19th centuries, including the contents of a time capsule left by the original owners in 1861 that was discovered during a 1950s renovation. A deck of Revolutionary-era hand-painted playing cards takes an antimonarchist position: in place of kings, queens, and jacks, the American upstarts substituted American statesmen, Roman goddesses, and Indian chiefs. ⌧ *2645 Gough St., near Union St., Cow Hollow* ☎ *415/441–7512* ⌧ *Free, donations encouraged* ⊗ *Feb.–Dec., 2nd Sun. and 2nd and 4th Thurs. of month noon–3; group tours weekdays by appointment.*

THE PRESIDIO

TOP ATTRACTIONS

Fodor's Choice ★ **Golden Gate Bridge.** With its simple but powerful art-deco design, the 1.7-mile suspension span that connects San Francisco and Marin County was built to withstand winds of more than 100 mph. It's also not a bad place to be in an earthquake: designed to sway almost 28 feet, the Golden Gate Bridge (unlike the Bay Bridge) was undamaged by the 1989 Loma Prieta quake. If you're on the bridge when it's windy, stand still and you can feel it swaying a bit.

Crossing the Golden Gate Bridge under your own power is exhilarating—a little scary, and definitely chilly. From the bridge's eastern-side walkway, the only side pedestrians are allowed on, you can take in the San Francisco skyline and the bay islands; look west for the wild hills of the Marin Headlands, the curving coast south to Lands End, and the Pacific Ocean. On sunny days, sailboats dot the water, and brave windsurfers test the often-treacherous tides beneath the bridge. A vista point on the Marin County side provides a spectacular city panorama.

A structural engineer, dreamer, and poet named Joseph Strauss worked tirelessly for 20 years to make the bridge a reality, first promoting the idea of it and then overseeing design and construction. Though the final structure bore little resemblance to his original plan, Strauss guarded his legacy jealously, refusing to recognize the seminal contributions of engineer Charles A. Ellis. In 2007, the Golden Gate Bridge district finally recognized Ellis's role, though Strauss, who died less than a year after opening day in 1937, would doubtless be pleased with the inscription on his statue, which stands sentry in the southern parking lot: "The Man Who Built the Bridge."

You won't see it on a T-shirt, but the bridge is perhaps the world's most publicized suicide platform, with an average of one jumper about every 10 days. Signs on the bridge refer the disconsolate to special telephones, and officers patrol the walkway and watch by security camera to spot potential jumpers. Funding has finally been approved for a suicide barrier, an unobtrusive net not unlike the one that saved 19 workers during the bridge's construction.

While at the bridge you can grab a healthy snack at the art deco–style Bridge Café. The recently erected Bridge Pavilion sells attractive, high-quality souvenirs and has a small display of historical artifacts. At the outdoor exhibits, you can see the bridge rise before your eyes on

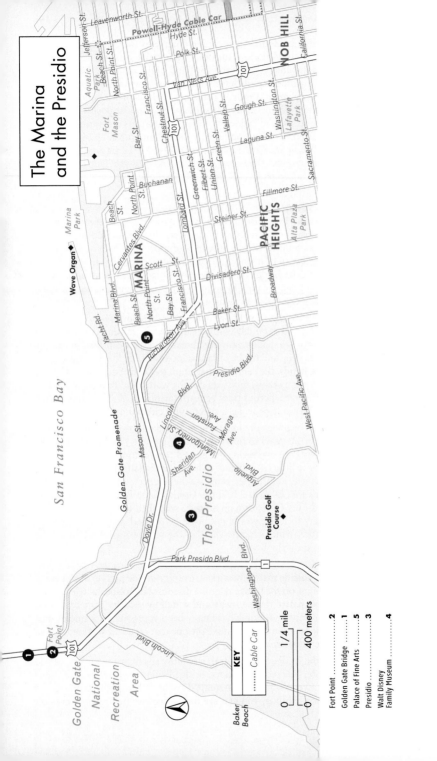

The Marina and the Presidio

San Francisco Bay

Golden Gate National Recreation Area

Fort Point

Baker Beach

The Presidio

Presidio Golf Course

MARINA

PACIFIC HEIGHTS

NOB HILL

Fort Mason

Marina Park

Aquatic Park

Lafayette Park

Alta Plaza Park

Wave Organ

Powell-Hyde Cable Car

Golden Gate Promenade

Leavenworth St.
Jefferson St.
Beach St.
North Point St.
Hyde St.
Polk St.
Powell St.
Francisco St.
Bay St.
Chestnut St.
Van Ness Ave.
Gough St.
Vallejo St.
Green St.
Laguna St.
Washington St.
Sacramento St.
California St.
Buchanan
North Point St.
Beach St.
Fillmore St.
Steiner St.
Greenwich St.
Filbert St.
Union St.
Tombard St.
Divisadero St.
Broadway
Baker St.
Lyon St.
Cervantes Blvd.
Scott St.
North Point St.
Bay St.
Francisco St.
Beach St.
Marina Blvd.
Yacht Rd.
Richardson Ave.
Presidio Blvd.
West Pacific Ave.
Lincoln Blvd.
Funston Ave.
Moraga Ave.
Montgomery St.
Sheridan Ave.
Arguello Blvd.
Mason St.
Doyle Dr.
Park Presidio Blvd.
Washington Blvd.
Lincoln Blvd.

KEY

------- Cable Car

0   1/4 mile

0   400 meters

Fort Point **2**
Golden Gate Bridge **1**
Palace of Fine Arts **5**
Presidio **3**
Walt Disney
Family Museum **4**

hologram panels, learn about the features that make it art deco, and read about the personalities behind its design and construction. City Guides offers free walking tours of the bridge every Thursday and Sunday at 11 am. ⊠ *Lincoln Blvd. near Doyle Dr. and Fort Point, Presidio* ☎ *415/921–5858* ⊕ *www.goldengatebridge.org* 🖼 *Free* ☉ *Pedestrians Mar.–Oct., daily 5 am–9 pm; Nov.–Feb., daily 5 am–6 pm; hrs change with daylight saving time. Bicyclists daily 24 hrs.*

Fodor'sChoice ★ **Presidio.** When San Franciscans want to spend a day in the woods, they come here. The Presidio has 1,400 acres of hills and majestic woods, two small beaches, and stunning views of the bay, the Golden Gate Bridge, and Marin County. Famed environmental artist Andy Goldsworthy's work greets visitors at the Arguello Gate entrance. The 100-plus-foot *Spire*, made of 37 cypress logs reclaimed from the Presidio, looks like a rough, natural version of a church spire. ■ TIP→ The Presidio's best lookout points lie along Washington Boulevard, which meanders through the park.

Part of the **Golden Gate National Recreation Area,** the Presidio was a military post for more than 200 years. Don Juan Bautista de Anza and a band of Spanish settlers first claimed the area in 1776. It became a Mexican garrison in 1822, when Mexico gained its independence from Spain; U.S. troops forcibly occupied the Presidio in 1846. The U.S. Sixth Army was stationed here until 1994.

The Presidio is now a thriving community of residential and nonresidential tenants, who help to fund its operations by rehabilitating and leasing its more than 700 buildings. In 2005 Bay Area filmmaker George Lucas opened the **Letterman Digital Arts Center,** his 23-acre digital studio "campus," along the eastern edge of the land. Seventeen of those acres are exquisitely landscaped and open to the public. If you have kids in tow or are a *Star Wars* fan yourself, sidle over to the **Yoda Fountain** (Letterman Drive at Dewitt Road), between two of the arts-center buildings, then take your picture with the life-size Darth Vader statue in the lobby, open to the public on weekdays.

The Presidio Trust, created to manage the Presidio and guide its transformation from military post to national park, has now turned its focus to rolling out the welcome mat to the public. The Presidio's visitor-serving tenants, such as the Asian-theme SenSpa, the House of Air Trampoline Park, Planet Granite climbing gym, the Walt Disney museum, a fabulous lodge at the Main Post, the newly reopened Officers' Club, and a handful of restaurants have helped with this goal. With old military housing now repurposed as apartments and homes with rents up to $13,000 a month, the Presidio is a very popular place to live and boasts a much higher rate of families with children than the rest of San Francisco (36% vs 16% in the rest of the city). Still, the $6 million that Lucas Film Ltd.—since 2012 a subsidiary of the Walt Disney Company—shells out annually for rent does plant a lot of saplings.

The Presidio also has a golf course, a visitor center, and picnic sites; the views from the many overlooks are sublime.

Especially popular is **Crissy Field,** a stretch of restored marshland along the sand of the bay. Kids on bikes, folks walking dogs, and joggers share

5

the paved path along the shore, often winding up at the Warming Hut, a combination café and fun gift store at the end of the path, for a hot chocolate in the shadow of the Golden Gate Bridge. Midway along the Golden Gate Promenade that winds along the shore is the Gulf of the Farallones National Marine Sanctuary Visitor Center, where kids can get a close-up view of small sea creatures and learn about the rich ecosystem offshore. Just across from the Palace of Fine Arts, Crissy Field Center offers great children's programs and has cool science displays. West of the Golden Gate Bridge is sandy **Baker Beach**, beloved for its spectacular views and laid-back vibe (read: you'll see naked people here). This is one of those places that inspires local pride. ⊠ *Between Marina and Lincoln Park, Presidio* ⊕ *www.presidio.gov.*

Walt Disney Family Museum. This beautifully refurbished brick barracks house is a tribute to the man behind Mickey Mouse, the Disney Studios, and Disneyland. The smartly organized displays include hundreds of family photos, and well-chosen videos play throughout. Disney's legendary attention to detail becomes particularly evident in the cels and footage of *Fantasia, Sleeping Beauty,* and other animation classics. "The Toughest Period in My Whole Life" exhibit sheds light on lesser-known bits of history: the animators' strike at Disney Studios, the films Walt Disney made for the U.S. military during World War II, and his testimony before the House Un-American Activities Committee during its investigation of Communist influence in Hollywood. The glass-walled gallery showcasing Disney's wildlife films takes full advantage of the museum's location, with a lovely view of Presidio trees and the Golden Gate Bridge in the background. The liveliest exhibit and the largest gallery documents the creation of Disneyland with a fun, detailed model of what Disney imagined the park would be. Teacups spin, the Matterhorn looms, and that world-famous castle leads the way to Fantasyland. You won't be the first to leave humming "It's a Small World." In the final gallery, titled simply "December 16, 1966," a series of sweet cartoons chronicles the world's reaction to Disney's sudden death. The one-way flow of the galleries deposits you near the attractive gift shop, which carries cool Disney-related stuff, and a café serving sandwiches, salads, and drinks. The downstairs theater shows Disney films (free with admission, $7 without) most days. ⊠ *Main Post, 104 Montgomery St., off Lincoln Blvd., Presidio* ☎ *415/345–6800* ⊕ *www.waltdisney.org* ⌚ *$20* ☺ *Wed.–Mon. 10–6.*

WORTH NOTING

FAMILY **Fort Point.** Dwarfed today by the Golden Gate Bridge, this brick fortress constructed between 1853 and 1861 was designed to protect San Francisco from a Civil War sea attack that never materialized. It was also used as a coastal-defense fortification post during World War II, when soldiers stood watch here. This National Historic Site is now a sprawling museum of military memorabilia. The building, which surrounds a lonely, windswept courtyard, has a gloomy air and is suitably atmospheric. It's usually chilly, too, so bring a jacket. The top floor affords a unique angle on the bay. ■TIP➜ Take care when walking along the front side of the building, as it's slippery, and the waves have a dizzying effect.

On the days when Fort Point is staffed (on Friday and weekends), guided group tours and cannon drills take place. The popular, guided candlelight tours, available only in winter, book up in advance, so plan ahead. Living-history days take place throughout the year, when Union soldiers perform drills, a drum-and-fife band plays, and a Civil War–era doctor shows his instruments and describes his surgical technique (gulp). ✉ *Marine Dr. off Lincoln Blvd., Presidio* ☎ *415/556–1693* ⊕ *www.nps.gov/fopo* ⌚ *Free* ☉ *Fri.–Sun. 10–5.*

GOLDEN GATE PARK AND THE WESTERN SHORELINE

More than 1,000 acres, stretching from the Haight all the way to the windy Pacific coast, Golden Gate Park is a vast patchwork of woods, trails, lakes, lush gardens, sports facilities, museums—even a herd of buffalo. There's more natural beauty beyond the park's borders, along San Francisco's wild Western Shoreline.

GOLDEN GATE PARK

TOP ATTRACTIONS

FAMILY

Fodor's Choice

★

California Academy of Sciences. With its native plant–covered living roof, retractable ceiling, three-story rain forest, gigantic planetarium, living coral reef, and frolicking penguins, the California Academy of Sciences is one of the city's most spectacular treasures. Dramatically designed by Renzo Piano, it's an eco-friendly, energy-efficient adventure in biodiversity and green architecture. The roof's large mounds and hills mirror the local topography, and Piano's audacious design completes the dramatic transformation of the park's Music Concourse. Moving away from a restrictive role as a museum that catalogued natural history, the academy these days is all about sustainability and the future. The locally beloved dioramas in African Hall have survived the transition, however.

By the time you arrive, hopefully you've decided which shows and programs to attend, looked at the academy's floor plan, and designed a plan to cover it all in the time you have. And if not, here's the quick version: Head left from the entrance to the wooden walkway over otherworldly rays in the Philippine Coral Reef, then continue to the Swamp to see Claude, the famous albino alligator. Swing through African Hall and gander at the penguins, take the elevator up to the living roof, then return to the main floor and get in line to explore the Rainforests of the World, ducking free-flying butterflies and watching for other live surprises. You'll end up below ground in the Amazonian Flooded Rainforest, where you can explore the academy's other aquarium exhibits. Phew.

■ TIP→ Considering the hefty price of admission here, start out early and take advantage of in-and-out privileges to take a break. ✉ *55 Music Concourse Dr., Golden Gate Park* ☎ *415/379–8000* ⊕ *www. calacademy.org* ⌚ *$34.95, save $3 if you bike, walk, or take public transit here; free 1 Sun. per quarter* ☉ *Mon.–Sat. 9:30–5, Sun. 11–5.*

Conservatory of Flowers. Whatever you do, be sure to at least drive by the Conservatory of Flowers—it's too darn pretty to miss. The gorgeous, white-framed 1878 glass structure is topped with a 14-ton glass dome.

Armed with only helmets, safety harnesses, and painting equipment, a full-time crew of 38 painters keeps the Golden Gate Bridge clad in International Orange.

Stepping inside the giant greenhouse is like taking a quick trip to the rain forest, with its earthy smell and humid warmth. The undeniable highlight is the Aquatic Plants section, where lily pads float and carnivorous plants dine on bugs to the sounds of rushing water. On the east side of the conservatory (to the right as you face the building), cypress, pine, and redwood trees surround the Dahlia Garden, which blooms in summer and fall. Adding to the allure are temporary exhibits such as a past one devoted to prehistoric plants; an annual model-train display punctuated with mini buildings, found objects, and dwarf plants; and a butterfly garden that returns periodically. To the west is the **Rhododendron Dell,** which contains 850 varieties, more than any other garden in the country. It's a favorite local Mother's Day picnic spot. ⊠ *John F. Kennedy Dr. at Conservatory Dr., Golden Gate Park* ☎ *415/666–7001* ⊕ *www.conservatoryofflowers.org* ✆ *$8, free 1st Tues. of month* ☉ *Tues.–Sun. 10–4:30* ☞ *No strollers allowed inside.*

de Young Museum. It seems that everyone in town has a strong opinion about the de Young Museum: Some adore its striking copper facade, while others just hope that the green patina of age will mellow the effect. Most maligned is the 144-foot tower, but the view from its ninth-story observation room, ringed by floor-to-ceiling windows and free to the public, is worth a trip here by itself. The building almost overshadows the de Young's respected collection of American, African, and Oceanic art. The museum also plays host to major international exhibits, such as 100 works from Paris's Musée National Picasso and a collection of the work of Jean Paul Gaultier from the Montreal Museum of Fine Arts; there's often an extra admission charge for these. The annual Bouquet

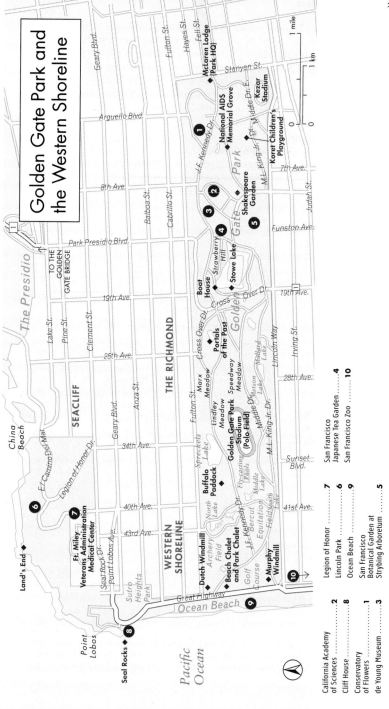

Golden Gate Park and the Western Shoreline

McLaren Lodge (Park HQ)
National AIDS Memorial Grove
Shakespeare Garden
Kezar Stadium
Koret Children's Playground
Strawberry Hill
Boat House
Stowe Lake
Cross Over Dr.
Portals of the Past
Marx Meadow
Speedway Meadow
Lindley Meadow
Golden Gate Park Stadium (Polo Field)
Buffalo Paddock
Fly-casting Pools
Dutch Windmill
Beach Chalet and Park Chalet
Murphy Windmill
Fort Miley
Veterans Administration Medical Center
Legion of Honor Dr.
Seal Rocks
Point Lobos
Land's End
China Beach
Sutro Heights Park
Ocean Beach
Great Highway
Pacific Ocean

The Presidio
TO THE GOLDEN GATE BRIDGE
SEACLIFF
THE RICHMOND
WESTERN SHORELINE
Golden Gate Park

1 mile
1 km

California Academy
of Sciences **2**
Cliff House **8**
Conservatory
of Flowers **1**
de Young Museum **3**
Legion of Honor **7**
Lincoln Park **6**
Ocean Beach **9**
San Francisco
Botanical Garden at
Strybing Arboretum **5**
San Francisco
Japanese Tea Garden **4**
San Francisco Zoo **10**

des Art is a fanciful tribute to the museum's collection by notable Bay Area floral designers. ■TIP➜ On many Friday evenings, the museum hosts fun, free, family-centered events, with live music, art projects for children, and a wine and beer bar (the café stays open late, too). ⊠ *50 Hagiwara Tea Garden Dr., Golden Gate Park* ☎ *415/750–3600* ⊕ *deyoung.famsf.org* ⊠ *$10, good for same-day admittance to the Legion of Honor; free 1st Tues. of month* ⊙ *Tues.–Sun. 9:30–5:15; mid-Jan.– Nov., Fri. until 8:45.*

WORTH NOTING

San Francisco Japanese Tea Garden. As you amble through the manicured landscape, past Japanese sculptures and perfect miniature pagodas, and over ponds of carp, you may feel transported to a more peaceful plane. Or maybe the shrieks of kids clambering over the almost vertical "humpback" bridges will keep you firmly in the here and now. Either way, this garden is one of those tourist spots that's truly worth a stop (a half hour will do). And at 5 acres, it's large enough that you'll always be able to find a bit of serenity, even when the tour buses drop by. The garden is especially lovely in March and April, when the cherry blossoms are in bloom. ⊠ *Hagiwara Tea Garden Dr., off John F. Kennedy Dr., Golden Gate Park* ☎ *415/752–4227* ⊕ *www.japaneseteagardensf. com* ⊠ *$8, free Mon., Wed., and Fri. if you enter by 10 am* ⊙ *Mar.– Oct., daily 9–6; Nov.–Feb., daily 9–4:45.*

San Francisco Botanical Garden at Strybing Arboretum. One of the best picnic spots in a very picnic-friendly park, the 55-acre arboretum specializes in plants from areas with climates similar to that of the Bay Area. Walk the Eastern Australian garden to see tough, pokey shrubs and plants with cartoon-like names, such as the hilly-pilly tree. You don't have to go to Muir Woods to see the largest living things on earth: the garden has a 4-acre redwood grove in the heart of the city. Kids gravitate toward the large shallow fountain and the pond with ducks, turtles, and egrets. Free tours leave the main gate daily at 1:30 and, from spring to fall, from the Friend Gate Friday through Sunday at 2. ⊠ *Lincoln Way and 9th Ave. entrance, Golden Gate Park* ☎ *415/661–1316* ⊕ *www. sfbotanicalgarden.org* ⊠ *$7, free 2nd Tues. of month and daily 7:30 am–9 am* ⊙ *Mid-Mar.–Sept., 7:30–6; Oct.–early Nov., 7:30–5; early Nov.–Jan., 7:30–4; Feb.–mid-Mar., 7:30–5; garden closes one hour after last entry.*

THE WESTERN SHORELINE
TOP ATTRACTIONS

Cliff House. A meal at the Cliff House isn't just about the food—the spectacular ocean view is what brings folks here—but the cuisine won't leave you wanting. The vistas, which include offshore Seal Rock (the barking marine mammals who reside there are actually sea lions), can be 30 miles or more on a clear day—or less than a mile on foggy days. ■TIP➜ Come for drinks just before sunset; then head back into town for dinner.

Three buildings have occupied this site since 1863. The current building dates from 1909; a 2004 renovation has left a strikingly attractive

restaurant and a squat concrete viewing platform out back. The complex, owned by the National Park Service, includes a gift shop.

Sitting on the observation deck is the **Giant Camera,** a camera obscura with its lens pointing skyward housed in a cute yellow-painted wooden shack. Built in the 1940s and threatened many times with demolition, it's now on the National Register of Historic Places. Step into the dark, tiny room inside (for a $3 fee); a fascinating 360-degree image of the surrounding area—which rotates as the "lens" on the roof rotates—is projected on a large, circular table. ■TIP➔ In winter and spring you may also glimpse migrating gray whales from the observation deck.

To the north of the Cliff House lie the ruins of the once grand glass-roof **Sutro Baths,** which you can explore on your own (they look a bit like water-storage receptacles). Adolf Sutro, eccentric onetime San Francisco mayor and Cliff House owner, built the bath complex, including a train out to the site, in 1896, so that everyday folks could enjoy the benefits of swimming. Six enormous baths (some freshwater and some seawater), more than 500 dressing rooms, and several restaurants covered 3 acres north of the Cliff House and accommodated 25,000 bathers. Likened to Roman baths in a European glass palace, the baths were for decades the favorite destination of San Franciscans in search of entertainment. The complex fell into disuse after World War II, was closed in 1952, and burned down (under questionable circumstances) during demolition in 1966. ⊠ *1090 Point Lobos Ave., Richmond* ☎ *415/386–3330* ⊕ *www.cliffhouse.com* ✉ *Free* ☉ *Weekdays 9 am–9:30 pm, weekends 9 am–10 pm.*

Fodor's Choice ★ **Legion of Honor.** The old adage of real estate—location, location, location—is at full force here. You can't beat the site of this museum of European art atop cliffs overlooking the ocean, the Golden Gate Bridge, and the Marin Headlands. A pyramidal glass skylight in the entrance court illuminates the lower-level galleries, which exhibit prints and drawings, English and European porcelain, and ancient Assyrian, Greek, Roman, and Egyptian art. The 20-plus galleries on the upper level display the permanent collection of European art (paintings, sculpture, decorative arts, and tapestries) from the 14th century to the present day.

The noteworthy Auguste Rodin collection includes two galleries devoted to the master and a third with works by Rodin and other 19th-century sculptors. An original cast of Rodin's *The Thinker* welcomes you as you walk through the courtyard. As fine as the museum is, the setting and view outshine the collection and also make a trip here worthwhile.

The **Legion Café,** on the lower level, serves tasty light meals (soup, sandwiches, grilled chicken) inside and on a garden terrace. (Unfortunately, there's no view.) Just north of the museum's parking lot is George Segal's *The Holocaust,* a stark white installation that evokes life in concentration camps during World War II. It's haunting at night, when backlighted by lights in the Legion's parking lot. ■TIP➔ Admission to the Legion is also good for same-day admission to the de Young Museum in Golden Gate Park. ⊠ *34th Ave. at Clement St., Richmond* ☎ *415/750–3600* ⊕ *legionofhonor.famsf.org* ✉ *$10, $2 off with proof of Bay Area public transit, free 1st Tues. of month* ☉ *Tues.–Sun. 9:30–5:15.*

5

Fodor'sChoice   **Lincoln Park.** Although many of the city's green spaces are gentle and
★   welcoming, Lincoln Park is a wild, 275-acre park in the Outer Rich-
mond with windswept cliffs and panoramic views. The newly renovated
Coastal Trail, the park's most dramatic one, leads out to **Lands End;**
pick it up west of the Legion of Honor (at the end of El Camino del
Mar) or from the parking lot at Point Lobos and El Camino del Mar.
Time your hike to hit Mile Rock at low tide, and you might catch a
glimpse of two wrecked ships peeking up from their watery graves.
⚠ Be careful if you hike here; landslides are frequent, and people have
fallen into the sea by standing too close to the edge of a crumbling
bluff top.

On the tamer side, large Monterey cypresses line the fairways at Lincoln
Park's 18-hole golf course, near the Legion of Honor. At one time this
land was the Golden Gate Cemetery, where the dead were segregated
by nationality; most were indigent and interred without ceremony in
the potter's field. In 1900 the Board of Supervisors voted to ban burials
within city limits, and all but two city cemeteries (at Mission Dolores
and the Presidio) were moved to Colma, a small town just south of San
Francisco. When digging has to be done in the park, bones occasionally surface again. ⊠ *Entrance at 34th Ave. at Clement St., Richmond.*

WORTH NOTING
Ocean Beach. Stretching 3 miles along the western side of the city from
the Richmond to the Sunset, this sandy swath of the Pacific coast is good
for jogging or walking the dog—but not for swimming. The water is so
cold that surfers wear wet suits year-round, and riptides are strong, so
only brave the waves if you are a strong swimmer or surfer—drownings
are not infrequent. As for sunbathing, it's rarely warm enough here;
think meditative walking instead of sun worshipping.

Paths on both sides of the Great Highway lead from Lincoln Way to
Sloat Boulevard (near the zoo); the beachside path winds through landscaped sand dunes, and the paved path across the highway is good for
biking and in-line skating (though you have to rent bikes elsewhere).
The **Beach Chalet** restaurant and brewpub is across the Great Highway
from Ocean Beach, about five blocks south of the Cliff House. ⊠ *Along
Great Hwy. from Cliff House to Sloat Blvd. and beyond.*

FAMILY   **San Francisco Zoo.** Occupying prime oceanfront property, the zoo is touting its metamorphosis into the "New Zoo," a wildlife-focused recreation center that inspires visitors to become conservationists. Integrated
exhibits group different species of animals from the same geographic
areas together in enclosures that don't look like cages. More than 250
species reside here, including endangered species such as the snow leop-
ard, Sumatran tiger, grizzly bear, and a Siberian tiger.

The zoo's superstar exhibit is **Grizzly Gulch,** where orphaned grizzly
bear sisters Kachina and Kiona enchant visitors with their frolicking
and swimming. When the bears are in the water, the only thing between
you and them is (thankfully thick) glass. Grizzly feedings are at 11:30
am daily.

The **Lemur Forest** has four varieties of the bug-eyed, long-tailed primates from Madagascar. You can help hoist food into the lemurs'

feeding towers and watch the fuzzy creatures climb up to chow down. African Kikuyu grass carpets the circular outer area of **Gorilla Preserve,** one of the largest and most natural gorilla habitats of any zoo in the world. Trees and shrubs create communal play areas.

Ten species of rare primates—including black howler monkeys, emperor tamarins, and lion-tailed macaques—live and play at the two-tier **Primate Discovery Center,** which contains 23 interactive learning exhibits on the ground level.

Magellanic penguins waddle about the rather sad concrete **Penguin Island,** splashing and frolicking in its 200-foot pool. Feeding times are 10:30 and 3:30. Koalas peer out from among the trees in **Koala Crossing,** and kangaroos and wallabies headline the **Australian Walkabout** exhibit. The 7-acre **Puente al Sur** (Bridge to the South) re-creates habitats in South America, replete with giant anteaters and capybaras.

An **African Savanna** exhibit mixes giraffes, zebras, kudus, ostriches, and many other species, all living together in a 3-acre section with a central viewing spot accessed by a covered passageway.

The 6-acre **Children's Zoo** has about 300 mammals, birds, and reptiles, plus an insect zoo, a meerkat and prairie-dog exhibit, a nature trail, a nature theater, a huge playground, a restored 1921 Dentzel carousel, and a mini steam train. A ride on the train costs $5, and you can hop astride one of the carousel's 52 hand-carved menagerie animals for $3. ⊠ *Sloat Blvd. and 47th Ave., Sunset* ☎ *415/753–7080* ⊕ *www.sfzoo.org* ✉ *$17, $1 off with Muni transfer (take Muni L–Taraval streetcar from downtown)* ⊙ *Mid-Mar.–Oct., daily 10–5; Nov.–mid-Mar., daily 10–4.*

THE HAIGHT, THE CASTRO, AND NOE VALLEY

These distinct neighborhoods wear their personalities large and proud, and all are perfect for just strolling around. Like a slide show of San Franciscan history, you can move from the Haight's residue of 1960s counterculture to the Castro's connection to 1970s and '80s gay life to 1990s gentrification in Noe Valley. Although historic events thrust the Haight and the Castro onto the international stage, both are anything but stagnant—they're still dynamic areas well worth exploring.

THE HAIGHT

Haight-Ashbury Intersection. On October 6, 1967, hippies took over the intersection of Haight and Ashbury streets to proclaim the "Death of Hip." If they thought hip was dead then, they'd find absolute confirmation of it today, what with the only tie-dye in sight on the famed corner being a Ben & Jerry's storefront.

Everyone knows the Summer of Love had something to do with free love and LSD, but the drugs and other excesses of that period have tended to obscure the residents' serious attempts to create an America that was more spiritually oriented, more environmentally aware, and less caught up in commercialism. The Diggers, a radical group of actors and populist agitators, for example, operated a free shop a few blocks off Haight Street. Everything really was free at the free shop; people brought in things they didn't need and took things they did.

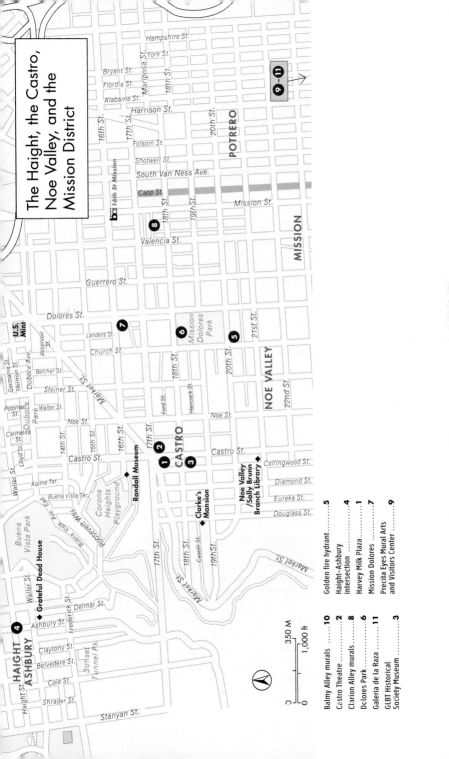

The Haight, the Castro, Noe Valley, and the Mission District

Hampshire St.
York St.
Bryant St.
Florida St.
Alabama St.
Harrison St.
Mariposa St.
18th St.
16th St.
17th St.
Folsom St.
Shotwell St.
South Van Ness Ave.
Capp St.
18th St.
19th St.
Mission St.
Valencia St.

16th St Mission

POTRERO
20th St.

MISSION

Guerrero St.
Dolores St.
Landers St.
Church St.

Mission Dolores Park

21st St.

NOE VALLEY
20th St.
22nd St.

U.S. Mint
Reservoir St.
Belcher St.
Steiner St.
Germania St.
Herman St.
Duboce Ave.
Potomac St.
Walter St.
Carmelita St.
Lloyd St.
Park

Market St.

14th St.
15th St.
16th St.
Noe St.
17th St.
Ford St.
Hancock St.
18th St.
Noe St.

Waller St.

Castro St.
Alpine Ter.
Buena Vista Ter.

CASTRO
Castro St.
Collingwood St.

Randall Museum

Corona Heights Playground

Clarke's Mansion

Noe Valley /Sally Brunn Branch Library
Diamond St.
Eureka St.
Douglass St.

Buena Vista Park

Grateful Dead House
Waller St.
Ashbury St.
Frederick St.
Delmar St.
Clayton St.
Belvedere St.
Cole St.
Shrader St.
Stanyan St.

Roosevelt Way
Buena Vista Ave. East
Buena Vista Ave.

Sunset Tunnel Park

17th St.
18th St.
19th St.
Caselli St.

Market St.

HAIGHT ASHBURY 4

350 M
1,000 ft

Balmy Alley murals 10
Castro Theatre 2
Clarion Alley murals......8
Dolores Park 6
Galeria de la Raza 11
GLBT Historical
Society Museum 3

Golden fire hydrant 5
Haight-Ashbury
intersection 4
Harvey Milk Plaza 1
Mission Dolores 7
Precita Eyes Mural Arts
and Visitors Center 9

A colorful mosaic mural in the Castro

Among the folks who hung out in or near the Haight during the late 1960s were writers Richard Brautigan, Allen Ginsberg, Ken Kesey, and Gary Snyder; anarchist Abbie Hoffman; rock performers Marty Balin, Jerry Garcia, Janis Joplin, and Grace Slick; LSD champion Timothy Leary; and filmmaker Kenneth Anger. If you're keen to feel something resembling the hippie spirit these days, there's always Hippie Hill, just inside the Haight Street entrance of Golden Gate Park. Think drum circles, guitar players, and whiffs of pot smoke. ⊠ *Haight.*

THE CASTRO

Fodor's Choice ★ **Castro Theatre.** Here's a classic way to join in the Castro community: grab some popcorn and catch a flick at this 1,500-seat art-deco theater; opened in 1922, it's the grandest of San Francisco's few remaining movie palaces. The neon marquee, which stands at the top of the Castro strip, is the neighborhood's great landmark. The Castro was the fitting host of 2008's red-carpet preview of Gus Van Sant's film *Milk*, starring Sean Penn as openly gay San Francisco supervisor Harvey Milk. The theater's elaborate Spanish baroque interior is fairly well preserved. Before many shows the theater's pipe organ rises from the orchestra pit and an organist plays pop and movie tunes, usually ending with the Jeanette McDonald standard "San Francisco" (go ahead, sing along). The crowd can be enthusiastic and vocal, talking back to the screen as loudly as it talks to them. Classics such as *Who's Afraid of Virginia Woolf?* take on a whole new life, with the assembled beating the actors to the punch and fashioning even snappier comebacks for Elizabeth Taylor. Head here to catch sing-along classics like *Mary Poppins*, a Fellini film

retrospective, or the latest take on same-sex love. ⌂ *429 Castro St., Castro* ☎ *415/621–6120* ⊕ *www.castrotheatre.com.*

GLBT Historical Society Museum. The two-gallery Gay, Lesbian, Bisexual, and Transgender (GLBT) Historical Society Museum, the first of its kind, presents multimedia exhibits from its vast holdings covering San Francisco's queer history. In the remodeled main gallery, you might hear the audiotape Harvey Milk made for the community in the event of his assassination; explore artifacts from "Gayborhoods," lost landmarks of the city's gay past; or flip through a memory book with pictures and thoughts on some of the more than 20,000 San Franciscans lost to AIDS. Though certainly not for the faint of heart (those offended by sex toys and photos of lustily frolicking naked people may, well, be offended), the museum offers an inside look at these communities so integral to the fabric of San Francisco life. ⌂ *4127 18th St., near Castro St., Castro* ☎ *415/621–1107* ⊕ *www.glbthistory.org* ⌂ *$5, free 1st Wed. of the month* ⊙ *Mon. and Wed.–Sat. 11–7, Sun. noon–5.*

Harvey Milk Plaza. An 18-foot-long rainbow flag, the symbol of gay pride, flies above this plaza named for the man who electrified the city in 1977 by being elected to its Board of Supervisors as an openly gay candidate. In the early 1970s Milk had opened a camera store on the block of Castro Street between 18th and 19th streets. The store became the center for his campaign to open San Francisco's social and political life to gays and lesbians.

The liberal Milk hadn't served a full year of his term before he and Mayor George Moscone, also a liberal, were shot in November 1978 at City Hall. The murderer was a conservative ex-supervisor named Dan White, who had recently resigned his post and then became enraged when Moscone wouldn't reinstate him. Milk and White had often been at odds on the board, and White thought Milk had been part of a cabal to keep him from returning to his post. Milk's assassination shocked the gay community, which became infuriated when the infamous "Twinkie defense"—that junk food had led to diminished mental capacity—resulted in a manslaughter verdict for White. During the so-called White Night Riot of May 21, 1979, gays and their allies stormed City Hall, torching its lobby and several police cars.

Milk, who had feared assassination, left behind a tape recording in which he urged the community to continue the work he had begun. His legacy is the high visibility of gay people throughout city government; a bust of him was unveiled at City Hall on his birthday in 2008, and the 2008 film *Milk* gives insight into his life. A plaque at the base of the flagpole lists the names of past and present openly gay and lesbian state and local officials. ⌂ *Southwest corner of Castro and Market Sts., Castro.*

NOE VALLEY

Golden fire hydrant. When all the other fire hydrants went dry during the fire that followed the 1906 earthquake, this one kept pumping. Noe Valley and the Mission District were thus spared the devastation wrought elsewhere in the city, which explains the large number of prequake homes here. Every year on April 18th (the anniversary of the quake) folks gather here to share stories about the earthquake, and the

famous hydrant gets a fresh coat of gold paint. ⊠ *Church and 20th Sts., southeastern corner, across from Dolores Park, Noe Valley.*

CASTRO AND NOE WALK

The Castro and Noe Valley are both neighborhoods that beg to be walked— or ambled through, really, without time pressure or an absolute destination. Hit the Castro first, beginning at **Harvey Milk Plaza** under the gigantic rainbow flag. If you're going on to Noe Valley, first head east down **Market Street** for the cafés, bistros, and shops, then go back to **Castro Street** and head south, past the glorious art-deco **Castro Theatre**, checking out boutiques and cafés along the way (Cliff's Variety, at 479 Castro Street, is a must). To tour Noe Valley, go east down **18th Street** to Church (at Dolores Park), and then either strap on your hiking boots and head south over the hill or hop the J–Church to **24th Street**, the center of this rambling neighborhood.

MISSION DISTRICT

The Mission has a number of distinct personalities: it's the Latino neighborhood, where working-class folks raise their families and where gangs occasionally clash; it's the hipster hood, where tattooed and pierced twenty- and thirtysomethings hold court in the coolest cafés and bars in town; it's a culinary epicenter, with the strongest concentration of destination restaurants and affordable ethnic cuisine; it's the face of gentrification, where high-tech money prices out longtime commercial and residential renters; and it's the artists' quarter, where murals adorn literally blocks of walls long after the artists have moved to cheaper digs. It's also the city's equivalent of the Sunshine State—this neighborhood's always the last to succumb to fog.

TOP ATTRACTIONS

Balmy Alley murals. Mission District artists have transformed the walls of their neighborhood with paintings, and Balmy Alley is one of the best-executed examples. Many murals adorn the one-block alley, with newer ones continually filling in the blank spaces. In 1971, artists began teaming with local children to create a space to promote peace in Central America, community spirit, and (later) AIDS awareness; since then dozens of artists have added their vibrant works. ■ TIP→ Be alert here: the 25th Street end of the alley adjoins a somewhat dangerous area. ⊠ *24th St. between and parallel to Harrison and Treat Sts., alley runs south to 25th St., Mission.*

Fodor's Choice ★ **Dolores Park.** A two-square-block microcosm of life in the Mission, Dolores Park is one of San Francisco's liveliest green spaces: dog lovers and their pampered pups congregate, kids play at the extravagant, recently reconstructed playground, and hipsters hold court, drinking beer on sunny days. During the summer, the park hosts movie nights; performances by Shakespeare in the Park, the San Francisco Mime Troupe, and the San Francisco Symphony; and any number of pop-up events and impromptu parties. Spend a warm day here—maybe sitting at the top of the park with a view of the city and the Bay Bridge—surrounded by

locals and that laid-back San Francisco energy, and you may well find yourself plotting your move to the city. The park continues to be well visited during a major renovation expected to continue through 2015. ⊠ *Between 18th and 20th Sts. and Dolores and Church Sts., Mission.*

Mission Dolores. Two churches stand side by side here, including the small adobe **Mission San Francisco de Asís,** which, along with the Presidio's Officers' Club, is the oldest standing structure in San Francisco. Completed in 1791, it's the sixth of the 21 California missions founded by Franciscan friars in the 18th and early 19th centuries. Its ceiling depicts original Ohlone Indian basket designs, executed in vegetable dyes. The tiny chapel includes frescoes and a hand-painted wooden altar.

There's a hidden treasure here, too. In 2004 an archaeologist and an artist crawling along the ceiling's rafters opened a trapdoor behind the altar and rediscovered the mission's original mural, painted with natural dyes by Native Americans in 1791. The centuries have taken their toll, so the team photographed the 20-by-22-foot mural and began digitally restoring the photographic version. Among the images is a dagger-pierced Sacred Heart of Jesus.

The small museum here covers the mission's founding and history, and the pretty little cemetery—which appears in Alfred Hitchcock's film *Vertigo*—contains the graves of mid-19th-century European immigrants. (The remains of an estimated 5,000 Native Americans lie in unmarked graves.) Services are held in both the old mission and next door in the handsome multidome basilica. ⊠ *Dolores and 16th Sts., Mission* ☎ *415/621–8203* ⊕ *www.missiondolores.org* 🖃 *$5, audio tour $7* ⊙ *Nov.–Apr., daily 9–4; May–Oct., daily 9–4:30.*

WORTH NOTING

Clarion Alley murals. Inspired by the work in Balmy Alley, a new generation of muralists began creating a fresh alley-cum-gallery here in 1992. The works by the loosely connected artists of the Clarion Alley Mural Project (CAMP) represent a broad range of styles and imagery, an exuberant, flowery exhortation to Tax the Rich; a lesbian celebration including donkey heads, skirts, and rainbows; and some of the first black-and-white murals in the city. The alley's murals offer a quick but dense glimpse at the Mission's contemporary art scene. ⊠ *Between Valencia and Mission Sts. and 17th and 18th Sts., Mission.*

Galería de la Raza. San Francisco's premier showcase for contemporary Latino art, the gallery exhibits the works of mostly local artists. Events include readings and spoken word by local poets and writers, screenings of Latin American and Spanish films, and theater works by local minority theater troupes. The gallery may close between exhibits, so call ahead. Just across the street, murals and mosaics festoon the 24th Street/York Street Minipark, a tiny urban playground. A mosaic-covered Quetzalcoatl serpent plunges into the ground and rises, creating hills for little ones to clamber over, and mural-covered walls surround the space. ⊠ *2857 24th St., at Bryant St., Mission* ☎ *415/826–8009* ⊕ *www.galeriadelaraza.org* ⊙ *Gallery Wed.–Sat. noon–6, Sun. noon–5.*

Precita Eyes Mural Arts and Visitors Center. The muralists of this nonprofit arts organization design and create murals and lead guided walks of area

murals. The Classic Mission Mural Walk ($20) starts with a 45-minute slide presentation before participants head outside to view murals on Balmy Alley and 24th Street. The Mission Trail Mural Walk ($15) includes some of the same murals and impressive ones at Cesar Chavez Elementary School. You can pick up a map of 24th Street's murals at the center and buy art supplies, T-shirts, postcards, and other mural-related items. ⊠ *2981 24th St., Mission* ☎ *415/285–2287* ⊕ *www.precitaeyes.org* 🖃 *Center free, tours $15–$20* ⊙ *Center weekdays 10–5, Sat. 10–4, Sun. noon–4; walks: weekends at 1:30 (Classic), Sat. at 11 (Mission Trail).*

DOGPATCH

East of the Mission District and Potrero Hill and a short T-Third Muni light-rail ride from SoMa, the Dogpatch neighborhood has been on the rise for the last decade. Artisans, designers, and craftspeople eager to protect the area's historical industrial legacy have all moved here in recent years, providing a solid customer base for shops, galleries, and boutique restaurants and artisanal food producers. The Museum of Craft and Design moved to Dogpatch in 2013 and instantly became the neighborhood's cultural anchor.

Museum of Craft and Design. Right at home in this once-industrial neighborhood now bursting with creative energy, this small, four-room space—definitely a quick view—mounts temporary art and design exhibitions. The focus might be sculpture, metalwork, furniture, or jewelry—or industrial design, architecture, or other topics. The MakeArt Lab gives kids the opportunity to create their own exhibit-inspired work, and the beautifully curated shop sells tempting textiles, housewares, jewelry, and other well-crafted items. ⊠ *2569 3rd St., near 22nd St., Dogpatch* ☎ *415/773–0303* ⊕ *sfmcd.org* 🖃 *$8, free 1st Tues. of month* ⊙ *Tues.–Sat. 11–6 (Thurs. until 7), Sun. noon–5.*

PACIFIC HEIGHTS AND JAPANTOWN

Pacific Heights and Japantown are something of an odd couple: privileged, old-school San Francisco and the workaday commercial center of Japanese American life in the city, stacked virtually on top of each other. The sprawling, extravagant mansions of Pacific Heights gradually give way to the more modest Victorians and unassuming housing tracts of Japantown. The most interesting spots in Japantown huddle in the Japan Center, the neighborhood's two-block centerpiece, and along Post Street. You can find plenty of authentic Japanese treats in the shops and restaurants.

PACIFIC HEIGHTS

TOP ATTRACTIONS

Haas-Lilienthal House. A small display of photographs on the bottom floor of this elaborate, gray 1886 Queen Anne house makes clear that despite its lofty stature and striking, round third-story tower, the house was modest compared with some of the giants that fell victim to the 1906 earthquake and fire. The Foundation for San Francisco's Architectural Heritage operates the home, whose carefully kept rooms provide a

glimpse into late-19th-century life through period furniture, authentic details (antique dishes in the kitchen built-in), and photos of the family that occupied the house until 1972. ■TIP→ You can admire hundreds of gorgeous San Francisco Victorians from the outside, but this is the only one that's open to the public, and it's worth a visit. Volunteers conduct one-hour house tours three days a week, and informative two-hour walking tours of Pacific Heights on Sunday afternoon (call or check website for schedule). ⊠ *2007 Franklin St., between Washington and Jackson Sts., Pacific Heights* ☎ *415/441–3004* ⊕ *www.sfheritage.org* ✉ *Tours $8* ⊗ *1-hr tour Wed. and Sat. noon–3, Sun. 11–4; 2-hr tour Sun. at 12:30.*

Spreckels Mansion. Shrouded behind tall juniper hedges at the corner of winding, redbrick Octavia Street, overlooking Lafayette Park, the estate was built for sugar heir Adolph Spreckels and his wife Alma. Mrs. Spreckels was so pleased with her house that she commissioned George Applegarth to design another building in a similar vein: the Legion of Honor. One of the city's great iconoclasts, Alma Spreckels was the model for the bronze figure atop the Victory Monument in Union Square. These days an iconoclast of another sort owns the mansion: romance novelist Danielle Steel, whose dust-up with local columnists over the size of those hedges entertained aficionados of local gossip in 2014. ⊠ *2080 Washington St., at Octavia St., Pacific Heights.*

WORTH NOTING

FAMILY **Alta Plaza Park.** Golden Gate Park's longtime superintendent, John McLaren, designed Alta Plaza in 1910, modeling its terracing on that of the Grand Casino in Monte Carlo, Monaco. From the top you can see Marin to the north, downtown to the east, Twin Peaks to the south, and Golden Gate Park to the west. ■TIP→ Kids love the many play structures at the large, enclosed playground at the top; everywhere else is dog territory. ⊠ *Bordered by Clay, Steiner, Jackson, and Scott Sts., Pacific Heights.*

Franklin Street buildings. The three blocks south of the Haas-Lilienthal House contain a few curiosities of interest to architecture buffs. What at first looks like a stone facade on the **Golden Gate Church** (*1901 Franklin St.*) is actually redwood painted white. A handsome Georgian-style residence built in the early 1900s for a coffee merchant sits at 1735 Franklin. On the northeast corner of Franklin and California streets is a **Christian Science church**; built in the Tuscan revival style, it's noteworthy for its terra-cotta detailing. The **Coleman House** (*1701 Franklin St.*) is an impressive twin-turret Queen Anne mansion that was built for a gold-rush mining and lumber baron. Don't miss the large, brilliant-purple stained-glass window on the house's north side. ⊠ *Franklin St. between Washington and California Sts., Pacific Heights.*

JAPANTOWN

Japan Center. Cool and curious trinkets, noodle houses and sushi joints, a destination bookstore, and a peek at Japanese culture high and low await at this 5-acre complex designed in 1968 by noted American architect Minoru Yamasaki. The Japan Center includes the shop- and restaurant-filled Kintetsu and Kinokuniya buildings; the excellent

DID YOU KNOW?

These soft-color Victorian homes in Pacific Heights are closer to the original hues sported back in the 1900s. It wasn't until the 1960s that the bold, electric colors now seen around San Francisco gained popularity. Before that, the most typical house paint color was a standard gray.

Kabuki Springs & Spa; the Hotel Kabuki; and the Sundance Kabuki, Robert Redford's fancy, reserved-seating cinema/restaurant complex.

The Kinokuniya Bookstore, in the Kinokuniya Building, has an extensive selection of Japanese-language books, *manga* (graphic novels), books on design, and English-language translations and books on Japanese topics. Just outside, follow the Japanese teenagers to Pika Pika, where you and your friends can step into a photo booth and then use special effects and stickers to decorate your creation. On the bridge connecting the center's two buildings, check out Shige Antiques for *yukata* (lightweight cotton kimonos) for kids and lovely silk kimonos, and Asakichi and its tiny incense shop for tinkling wind chimes and display-worthy teakettles. Continue into the Kintetsu Building for a selection of Japanese restaurants.

Between the Miyako Mall and Kintetsu Building are the five-tier, 100-foot-tall **Peace Pagoda** and the Peace Plaza, where seasonal festivals are held. The pagoda, which draws on the 1,200-year-old tradition of miniature round pagodas dedicated to eternal peace, was designed in the late 1960s by Yoshiro Taniguchi to convey the "friendship and goodwill" of the Japanese people to the people of the United States. The plaza itself is a shadeless, unwelcoming space with little seating. Continue into the Miyako Mall to Ichiban Kan, a Japanese dollar store

where you can pick up fun Japanese kitchenware, tote bags decorated with hedgehogs, and erasers shaped like food. ⊠ *Bordered by Geary Blvd. and Fillmore, Post, and Laguna Sts., Japantown.*

Fodor'sChoice **Kabuki Springs & Spa.** This serene spa is one Japantown destination that
★ draws locals from all over town, from hipster to grandma, Japanese-American or not. Balinese urns decorate the communal bath area of this house of tranquillity.

The massage menu has also expanded well beyond traditional shiatsu technique. The experience is no less relaxing, however, and the treatment regimen includes facials, salt scrubs, and mud and seaweed wraps. You can take your massage in a private room with a bath or in a curtained-off area.

The communal baths ($25) contain hot and cold tubs, a large Japanese-style bath, a sauna, a steam room, and showers. Bang the gong for quiet if your fellow bathers are speaking too loudly. The clothing-optional baths are open for men only on Monday, Thursday, and Saturday; women bathe on Wednesday, Friday, and Sunday. Bathing suits are required on Tuesday, when the baths are coed.

Men and women can reserve private rooms daily. An 80-minute massage-and-private-bath package costs $125 weekdays, $140 weekends; a package that includes a 50-minute massage and the use of the communal baths costs $105 weekdays, $114 weekends. ⊠ *1750 Geary Blvd., Japantown* ☎ *415/922–6000* ⊕ *www.kabukisprings.com* ⊗ *Daily 10–10.*

New People. The kids' counterpart to the Japan Center, this fresh shopping center combines a cinema, a tea parlor, and shops with a successful synergy. The downstairs cinema shows classic and cutting-edge Asian (largely Japanese) films and is home to the San Francisco Film Society. Upstairs you can peruse Japanese pop-culture items and anime-inspired fashion, like handmade, split-toe shoes at Sou Sou and Lolita fashion at Baby, the Stars Shine Bright. ⊠ *1746 Post St., Japantown* ⊕ *www. newpeopleworld.com* ⊗ *Mon.–Sat. noon–7, Sun. noon–6.*

WHERE TO EAT

Make no mistake, San Francisco is one of America's top food cities. Some of the biggest landmarks are restaurants; and for some visitors, chefs like Daniel Patterson are just as big a draw as Alcatraz. In fact, on a Saturday, the Ferry Building—a temple to local eating—may attract more visitors than the Golden Gate Bridge: cheeses, breads, "salty pig parts," homemade delicacies, and sensory-perfect vegetables and fruits attract rabidly dedicated aficionados. You see, San Franciscans are a little loco about their edibles. If you ask them what their favorite season is, don't be surprised if they respond, "tomato season."

Some renowned restaurants are booked weeks or even months in advance. But you can get lucky at the last minute if you're flexible—and friendly. Most restaurants keep a few tables open for walk-ins and VIPs. Show up for dinner early (5:30 pm) or late (after 9 pm) and politely inquire about any last-minute vacancies or cancellations. *Use the coordinate (⊕ A1) at the end of each listing to locate a site on the corresponding map.*

	WHAT IT COSTS			
	$	$$	$$$	$$$$
Restaurants	under $15	$15–$22	$23–$30	over $30

Restaurant prices are the average cost of a main course at dinner or, if dinner is not served, at lunch.

UNION SQUARE AND CHINATOWN

$ JAPANESE 🍴 **Katana-Ya.** From the moment it opens, there's a line in front of this hole-in-the-wall ramen house across from the American Conservatory Theater. Hand-drawn pictures of specials punctuate a colorful interior with too-close tables and a couple of stools around the bar. There's nothing fancy, but the ramen is among the most authentic in town, and the place stays open late (till 2 am). Add a couple sushi rolls and gyozas to your order and be on your way. [$] *Average main: $8* ✉ *430 Geary St., Union Sq.* ☎ *415/771–1280* ✍ *Reservations not accepted* ⊕ *E4.*

$$ CHINESE FAMILY 🍴 **R&G Lounge.** Cravings for salt-and-pepper Dungeness crab are deliciously sated at this bright, three-level Cantonese eatery that excels in the crustacean. A menu with photographs will help you sort through other HK specialties, including Peking duck and shrimp-stuffed tofu. Much of the seafood is fresh from the tank. Expect a packed dining room during peak hours. Dim sum is also served. **■ TIP→ Crab portions are easily splittable by three, especially when accompanied by appetizers and another dish.** [$] *Average main: $16* ✉ *631 Kearny St., Chinatown* ☎ *415/982–7877* ⊕ *F3.*

SOMA

$$$$ MODERN AMERICAN Fodor's Choice ★ 🍴 **Benu.** Chef Corey Lee's modern Californian Mecca is a must-stop for those who hop from city to city, collecting memorable meals. Each dish in the 15- to 19-course tasting menu is a marvel of textures and flavors, presented meticulously enough to make this one of only two restaurants in the city to earn three Michelin stars (the other is Saison). Lee, formerly of French Laundry, handles Asian ingredients—a thousand-year-old quail egg, *xiao long bao* dumplings, and sea cucumber—with a Western touch. You may find dishes like Hokkaido sea cucumber stuffed with lobster, pork belly, eggplant, fermented pepper or eel. An extremely professional staff is behind the quick pacing and on-point wine pairings. Bare-wood tables and a minimalistic interior guarantees concentration on the plate. The tasting menu is mandatory. [$] *Average main: $195* ✉ *22 Hawthorne St., SoMa* ☎ *415/685–4860* 🌐 *www.benusf.com* ✍ *Reservations essential* ⏲ *Closed Sun. and Mon. No lunch* ⊕ *G5.*

$$$ MODERN AMERICAN 🍴 **The Cavalier.** This Anna Weinberg–Jennifer Puccio production is no different than the two others (Marlowe and Park Tavern): insanely popular and loud, yet deliciously comforting. Chef Puccio gives British

Pub grub a Nor Cal makeover (fresh ingredients rightly cooked). The darkly painted space, with high ceilings and large arched windows, is decorated with stuffed animal heads, horses, and clusters of paintings imparting a decidedly British temperament that attracts the clubby tech crowd. The gin-based cocktails pair well with starters such as deviled quail eggs, brussels sprouts chips, and hearty mains like the Sunday chicken—bathed in a bacon-mustard *jus*. $ *Average main: $23* ⊠ *Hotel Zetta, 360 Jessie St., SoMa* ☎ *415/321–6000* ⊕ *thecavaliersf.com* ✛ *E5.*

$$ ✕**Citizen's Band.** This fresh take on the classic American diner always
DINER seems to pack its coveted 40 seats. The draw: one of the city's tastiest versions of mac and cheese (topped with onion rings), and fried chicken with red-eye gravy. Other "fine diner" dishes—among them seasonal salads and pan-roasted rock cod—further reveal chef-owner Chris Beerman's experience in upscale restaurants. The vibe is very SoMa, with an edgy and eclectic crowd that can match the rock-and-roll playing (sometimes loudly) on the stereo or at the club next door, but the well-chosen wine list keeps things elevated. The restaurant shares restrooms with the rock club next door. $ *Average main: $22* ⊠ *1198 Folsom St., at 8th St., SoMa* ☎ *415/556–4901* ⊕ *www.citizensbandsf.com* ✛ *E6.*

$$$ ✕**Marlowe.** A new location doubles the number of diners who can get a
AMERICAN piece of chef Jennifer Puccio's hearty American bistro fare, like roasted
Fodor's Choice chicken, steak tartare, and one of the city's best burgers. In hip SoMa,
★ near the main Caltrain station, this spot has a lighter, airy touch with white penny tile floors, marble countertops, and butcher paper emblazoned with the day's specials—including cocktails like the tequila-based la cuchilla. An outdoor patio is jam-packed in good weather. Chief pastry chef Emily Luchetti takes care of the kitchen's sweet side, and makes us wonder why no one has thought of a farmers' market sundae till now. ■TIP➔ Avoid the crowds and order a burger off the bar menu. $ *Average main: $24* ⊠ *500 Brannan St., SoMa* ☎ *415/777–1413* ⊕ *www. marlowesf.com* ⊗ *No lunch weekends* ✛ *G6.*

$$$ ✕**Trou Normand.** Walk through the door of the 1925 Timothy Pflueger-
ITALIAN designed building and it's like entering the art deco period, greeted
Fodor's Choice as you are with soaring ceilings, marble, and an enormous painted
★ illustration of a nude. Welcome to the Roaring 2010s. Thad Vogler's latest endeavor (Bar Agricole was the first) delivers on a fun boozy evening, introducing the French tradition known as *trou normand*— drinking a brandy between courses to settle your stomach. There are also about 40 house-cured salumi and charcuterie. Arancini, seasonal salads and pickles, and mains of pasta and roasted black cod round out offerings. An enclosed patio reads like a Parisian garden conservatory. Unfortunately, noise is a real issue out there, since it's an after-work escape. ■TIP➔ A small café within the restaurant serves up espresso and breakfast sandwiches in the mornings. $ *Average main: $25* ⊠ *140 New Montgomery St., SoMa* ☎ *415/975–0876* ⊕ *www.trounormandsf. com* ⌕ *Reservations essential* ⊗ *Closed Sun.* ✛ *G4.*

5

HOW TO EAT LIKE A LOCAL

San Francisco may well be the most piping-red-hot dining scene in the nation now. After all, with a booming tech industry, there are mouths to feed. Freedom to do what you want. Innovation. Eccentricity. These words define the culture, the food, and the cuisine of the city by the bay. Get in on what locals know by enjoying their favorite foods.

FOOD TRUCKS

This is where experimentation begins, where the overhead is low, and risk-taking is fun. From these mobile kitchens careers are launched. A food meet-up called "Off the Grid" happens in season at Fort Mason where you can do a progressive dinner among the 25 or so trucks. Year-round the convoy roams to different locations, selling things like Korean poutine, Indian burritos, and Vietnamese burgers. Each dish seems to reflect a refusal to follow the norm.

DIM SUM

The tradition of dim sum took hold in San Francisco when Chinese immigrants from Guangdong Province arrived with Cantonese cuisine. These earlier settlers eventually established teahouses and bakeries that sold dim sum, like the steamed dumplings stuffed with shrimp (*har gow*) or pork (*shao mai*). Now carts roll from table to table in Chinatown restaurants—and other parts of the city. Try the grilled and fried bite-size savories but also the sweets like *dan tat*, an egg custard tart.

BARBECUE

Whaaa? San Francisco barbecue? And what would that be? You can bet it's meat from top purveyors nearby. The city is surrounded by grazing lands, where the animals and their minders, the ranchers, are king. Until now, meats came simply plated. Now it's messy, with smokiness, charred crusts, and gorgeous marbling. But you may never hear of a San-Fran-style barbecue because, in the words of one chef, we're "nondenominational." You'll see it all: Memphis, Texas, Carolina, and Kansas City.

ICE CREAM

How ice cream became so popular in a place that spends many of its 365 days below the 75 degree mark is a mystery. But the lines attest to the popularity of the frozen dessert that gets its own San Francisco twist. This is the vanilla-bean vanilla and Tcho chocolate crowd. Bourbon and cornflakes? Reposado tequila? Cheers to that. Diversity and local produce is blended into flavors like ube (purple yam), yuzu, and Thai latte. Vegans, we got you covered, too.

BURRITOS

This stuffed tortilla got its Bay Area start in the 1960s in the Mission District. Because the size and fillings distinguish it from other styles, it became known as the Mission burrito. Look for rice (Southern Californians are cringing), beans, salsa, and enough meat in the burrito for two meals. The aluminum foil keeps the interior neat, in theory. Popular choices are *carne asada* (beef) and *carnitas* (pork). But then

there's *lengua* (beef tongue) and *birria* (goat). This is a hands-on meal. No utensils, please.

COFFEE

Coffee roasters here are like sports teams in other cities. You pick one of the big five or six to be loyal to, and defend it tirelessly. San Francisco favorites source impeccably and blend different beans as if they were wine-making. In addition, a few of the big names—Four Barrel, Sightglass, Ritual, Blue Bottle—roast their own to control what they grind and pour at their outlets across the city—and now nationally and internationally.

FARMERS' MARKETS

These are our new grocery stores. They're the places to discover the latest in fruits, vegetables, and dried beans—much of it grown within a 60-mile radius. Cheeses, cured salami, breads, and nuts are sampled. Then there are the local ready-to-eat snacks, like pizza and *huevos rancheros*. The most popular market is the one on Saturday at the Ferry Plaza.

Top left: Several farmers' markets occupy the Ferry Building; top right: dim sum; bottom right: the food truck

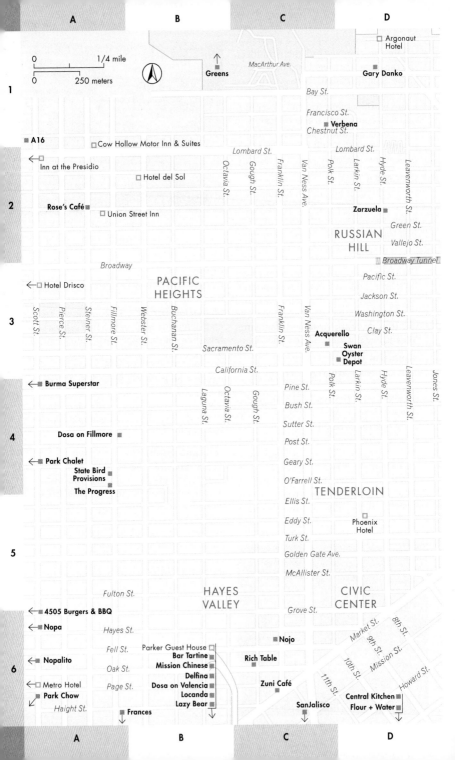

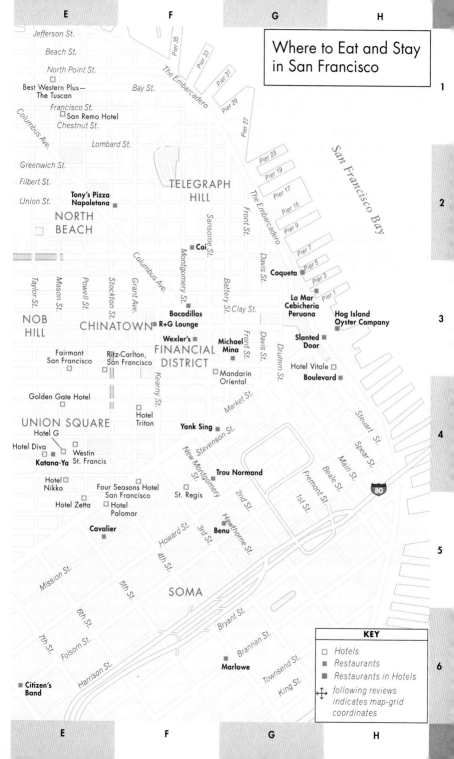

HAYES VALLEY

$$ JAPANESE 🍴 **Nojo.** For a little bonhomie before the symphony, this buzzy yakitori and izakaya spot serves stellar Japanese pub food, made from Bay Area ingredients. The menu is divided into items "on a stick" and "not on a stick." Much of the "stick" is *yakitori* (grilled chicken), like chicken skin with matcha sea salt and *tsukune* (a chicken meatball) with egg yolk sauce. Not on a stick is the savory, rich custard, *chawan mushi*, with Dungeness crabmeat and shiitake mushrooms. Seating is at bamboo tables in a mod-Japanese-slash-San Franciscan setting with windows overlooking Hayes Valley's main thoroughfare of Franklin. There are 20 sakes by the glass. ■ **TIP→ Nojo requires a credit card number to hold a reservation.** [$] *Average main: $20* ✉ *231 Franklin St., Hayes Valley* ☎ *415/896–4587* 🌐 *www.nojosf.com* 🕒 *Closed Tues. No lunch.* ✥ *C6.*

$$$ MODERN AMERICAN Fodor's Choice ★ 🍴 **Rich Table.** To leave co-chefs Evan and Sarah Rich's popular place without ordering the porcini doughnuts, served with a raclette béchamel sauce, is a dining sin. That and the sardines in chip format are the two most popular bites, and you should wander to the mains half of the menu for one of the half-dozen pastas or proteins, like a seared black cod with crunchy skin. The room's weathered-wood wallboards repurposed from a Northern California sawmill give it a homey vibe. There's a nice selection of wines by the glass and artisanal cocktails. All seats are by reservation only and are not an easy acquisition. ■ **TIP→ Ten bar seats are available for walk-ins.** [$] *Average main: $30* ✉ *199 Gough St., at Oak St., Hayes Valley* ☎ *415/355–9085* 🌐 *www.richtablesf.com* ✍ *Reservations essential* 🕒 *No lunch* ✥ *C6.*

$$$ MEDITERRANEAN Fodor's Choice ★ 🍴 **Zuni Café.** After one bite of Zuni's succulent brick-oven-roasted whole chicken with Tuscan bread salad, you'll understand why the two-floor café is a perennial star. At the long copper bar a disparate mix of patrons communes over oysters on the half shell and cocktails and wine. Nearly as famous as the chicken are the Caesar salad with house-cured anchovies and the chocolatey flourless *gâteau Victoire*. The most cheerful spot to sit is at the tip of the "pyramid window" near the bar, easier to score if you plan a late lunch. Zuni's world-famous chef-owner, Judy Rodgers, passed away in 2013, but thanks to her strong guidance, the food remains outstanding. [$] *Average main: $28* ✉ *1658 Market St., Hayes Valley* ☎ *415/552–2522* 🌐 *www.zunicafe.com* 🕒 *Closed Mon.* ✥ *C6.*

FINANCIAL DISTRICT

$$ SPANISH 🍴 **Bocadillos.** The name means "sandwiches," but that's only half the story here. You'll find a baker's dozen bocadillos at lunchtime: plump rolls (pick two for $12) filled with everything from Serrano ham to Catalan sausage with arugula. At night are two-dozen choices of tapas, including roasted Monterey Bay squid, bavette empanadas, and corn fritters with house-made chorizo. There are ample wines by the glass but also a few sherries. A youngish crowd typically piles into the red-brick dining space, whose aesthetic includes wire chairs and small, square light fixtures. ■ **TIP→ Breakfast is served here, too.** [$] *Average main: $18* ✉ *710 Montgomery St., Financial District* ☎ *415/982–2622*

🌐 *www.bocasf.com* ✍ *Reservations not accepted* ⏲ *Closed Sun. No lunch Sat.* ✥ *F3.*

$$$$ ECLECTIC 🍴 **Michael Mina.** The refined flagship outpost for this acclaimed chef remains a treat, with luxurious renditions of shabu-shabu (boiled beef) and lobster potpie with Meyer lemons and smoked potatoes. There's a prix fixe–only menu for dinner, while lunch is the time to sample the mastery of Mina at half the price. [$] *Average main: $38* ✉ *252 California St., Financial District* ☎ *415/397–9222* 🌐 *www.michaelmina.net* ⏲ *No lunch weekends* ✥ *G3*

$$ BARBECUE 🍴 **Wexler's.** Four words: bourbon banana cream pie. Of course, there's a slew of tempting barbecue items that threaten whether you'll have room at the end of the meal. The interior is chic minimalist, with a couple of red chandeliers to liven up the place. Barbecue traditionalists should come with an open mind. The crispy Scotch eggs, fork-tender short ribs, and smoked wings (with Point Reyes blue cheese dressing) wander into more creative territory—chef Charlie Kleinman earns accolades. [$] *Average main: $22* ✉ *568 Sacramento St., Financial District* ☎ *415/983–0102* 🌐 *www.wexlerssf.com* ⏲ *Closed Sun. No dinner Mon. No lunch weekends* ✥ *F3.*

5

$$ CHINESE FAMILY 🍴 **Yank Sing.** This granddaddy of teahouses in a quiet location on Stevenson Street—there's also a big, brassy branch in the Rincon Center—serves some of San Francisco's best dim sum to office workers on weekdays and boisterous families on weekends. The several dozen varieties prepared daily include both the classic (steamed pork buns, shrimp dumplings, egg custard tartlets) and the creative (scallion-skewered prawns tied with bacon, lobster and *tobiko* roe dumplings, basil seafood dumplings). The tab can rise quickly, so pace yourself. The take-out counter makes a meal on the run a satisfying compromise when office duties—or touring—won't wait. ■ **TIP→ The Shanghai soup dumplings are perfection.** [$] *Average main: $16* ✉ *49 Stevenson St., Financial District* ☎ *415/541–4949* 🌐 *www.yanksing.com* ⏲ *No dinner* ✥ *F4.*

NOB HIL AND RUSSIAN HILL

$$ TAPAS 🍴 **Swan Oyster Depot.** Half fish market and half diner, this small, slim, family-run seafood operation, open since 1912, has no tables, just a narrow marble counter with about a dozen-and-a-half stools. Most people come in to buy perfectly fresh salmon, halibut, crabs, and other seafood to take home. Everyone else hops onto one of the rickety stools to enjoy a dozen oysters, other shellfish, or a bowl of clam chowder—the only hot food served. It's all served up with a side of big personality from the jovial folks behind the counter who make you feel like a regular. ■ **TIP→ Come before 11 am or after 2 pm to avoid a long wait, and bring a full wallet: old-school Swan only takes cash.** [$] *Average main: $18* ✉ *1517 Polk St., Nob Hill* ☎ *415/673–1101* ✍ *Reservations not accepted* 💳 *No credit cards* ⏲ *Closed Sun. No dinner* ✥ *D3.*

🍴 **Zarzuela.** Full-blooded Spaniards swear by the paella at this tiny Old World–style bistro, complete with matador art on the wall, not far from the crookedest street in the world (Lombard). Also not to be missed is the homemade sangria—or the goat cheese baked in tomato sauce

Eating with Kids

Kids can be fussy eaters, and parents can be, too. Fortunately, there are plenty of excellent options in the city that will satisfy both.

Barney's Gourmet Burgers. With locations all over the Bay Area, including this one not far from Fort Mason, this chain caters to older kids and their parents with mile-high burgers and giant salads. But Barney's doesn't forget "kids under 8," who have their own menu featuring a burger, an all-beef frank, and chicken strips. And they don't forget parents, offering a nice selection of wines by the glass and beer on tap. ⊠ *3344 Steiner St., near Union St.* ☎ *415/563–0307* ⊕ *www.barneyshamburgers.com* ✚ *3:C6.*

City View Restaurant. Nearby in Chinatown, City View Restaurant serves a varied selection of dim sum, with tasty pork buns for kids and more-exotic fare for adults. ⊠ *662 Commercial St., near Kearny St.* ☎ *415/398–2838* ✚ *1:E4.*

The Ferry Building (✚ *1:G4*) on the Embarcadero has plenty of kid-friendly options, from **Mijita Cocina Mexicana,** which has its own kids' menu, to **Gott's Roadside,** for burgers, shakes, and more. (And the outdoor access can help keep the little ones entertained.)

Park Chalet. Finally, both kids and adults love to be by the ocean, and the Park Chalet, hidden behind the two-story Beach Chalet, offers pizza, mac and cheese, sticky ribs, and a big banana split. ⊠ *1000 Great Hwy., at Fulton St.* ☎ *415/386–8439* ✚ *3:A3.*

Rosamunde Sausage Grill. In Lower Haight, the small Rosamunde Sausage Grill serves just that—a slew of different sausages, from Polish to duck to *Weisswurst* (Bavarian veal). You get your choice of two toppings, like grilled onions, sauerkraut, and chili, and since there are only six stools, plan on take-out. ■TIP➔ Head to nearby Duboce Park, with its cute playground. ⊠ *545 Haight St., between Steiner and Fillmore Sts.* ☎ *415/437–6851* ✚ *3:D3.*

---

or poached octopus, all prepared by chef Lucas Gasco, who grew up in Madrid. Arched windows overlook Hyde Street and the cable cars rolling by. Riding the Powell–Hyde line to and from dinner adds to the romance of the evening and saves you the nightmare of parking in this neighborhood. Ⓢ *Average main: $21* ⊠ *2000 Hyde St., Russian Hill* ☎ *415/346–0800* ⚑ *Reservations not accepted* ☉ *Closed Sun. and Mon. No lunch* ✚ *D2.*

VAN NESS/POLK

$$$$
ITALIAN
Fodor'sChoice
★

✕**Acquerello.** Devotees of chef-owner Suzette Gresham-Tognetti's high-end but soulful Italian cooking have swooned for years over her Parmesan *budino* (pudding). Classics pepper the menu but there are also some cutting-edge touches, techniques, and flavors. Dinners are prix-fixe, with three, four, or five courses and at least four choices within each course. Co-owner Giancarlo Paterlini oversees the service and his son Gianpaolo presides over the roughly 1,900-bottle list of Italian wines.

The room, in a former chapel, with vaulted ceiling and terra-cotta and pale-ocher palette, is refined but never stuffy. This true San Francisco dining gem is worth every penny. [$] *Average main: $87* ✉ *1722 Sacramento St., Van Ness/Polk* ☎ *415/567–5432* 🌐 *www.acquerello.com* ✍ *Reservations essential* ⏲ *Closed Sun. and Mon. No lunch* ✥ *C3.*

NORTH BEACH

$$$$ MODERN AMERICAN Fodor's Choice ★ 🍴 **Coi.** Chef Daniel Patterson is one of the biggest names in the food circuit, and his destination restaurant shows you, via an eight-course tasting, just how he's gotten a golden reputation. Highly seasonal ingredients are obsessively sourced—some of it foraged. One example: the Dungeness crab raviolo with sheep sorrel and butter crab broth. A more casual front dining room is followed by a formal space, with natural linens, soft lighting, and handcrafted pottery. Patterson is always brining, curing, and innovating, including Coi's pay-in-advance, nonrefundable ticketing system for reservations. **■ TIP→ A vegetarian tasting menu is available with advance notice. Couldn't get a reservation? Call. Tables do open up.** [$] *Average main: $195* ✉ *373 Broadway, North Beach* ☎ *415/393–9000* 🌐 *www.coirestaurant.com* ✍ *Reservations essential* ⏲ *Closed Mon. No lunch* ✥ *F2.*

$$ PIZZA FAMILY 🍴 **Tony's Pizza Napoletana.** Locals hotly debate who makes the city's best pizza, and for many Tony Gemignani takes the prize. His reputation extends well beyond the city: at the World Pizza Cup in Naples he eclipsed the Italians for the title of World Champion Pizza Maker. The dough at his restaurant is flavorful and fired just right, with multiple wood-burning ovens in his casual, modern pizzeria turning out many different pies—the famed Neapolitan-style Margherita, but also Sicilian, Romana, and Detroit styles. Salads, antipasti, homemade pastas, and calzone, round out the menu. You can grab a slice next door. **■ TIP→ If you're dining with kids, ask for some pizza dough to keep them entertained.** [$] *Average main: $20* ✉ *1570 Stockton St., North Beach* ☎ *415/835–9888* 🌐 *www.tonyspizzanapoletana.com* ✍ *Reservations not accepted* ⏲ *Closed Tues.* ✥ *E2.*

ON THE WATERFRONT

FISHERMAN'S WHARF

$$$$ MODERN AMERICAN 🍴 **Gary Danko.** In high season plan on reserving two months ahead at Chef Danko's namesake restaurant—his legion of fans typically keep the reservation book full. The cost of a meal is pegged to the number of courses, from three to five, and the menu spans a classic yet Californian style that changes seasonally. Dishes might include risotto with lobster and rock shrimp, or herb-crusted lamb loin. A diet-destroying chocolate soufflé with two sauces is usually among the desserts. The wine list is the size of a small-town phone book, and the banquette-lined rooms, with beautiful wood floors and stunning (but restrained) floral arrangements, are as memorable as the food and impeccable service. [$] *Average main: $76* ✉ *800 N. Point St., Fisherman's Wharf* ☎ *415/749–2060* 🌐 *www.garydanko.com* ✍ *Reservations essential* 👔 *Jacket required* ⏲ *No lunch* ✥ *D1.*

5

EMBARCADERO

$$$$ ✕**Boulevard.** Two local restaurant celebrities—chef Nancy Oakes and
AMERICAN designer Pat Kuleto—are behind this high-profile, high-priced eatery
in the 1889 Audiffred Building, a Parisian look-alike that survived the
1906 quake. The Belle-Époque interior and sophisticated American
food with a French accent attract well-dressed locals and flush out-
of-towners. Count on generous portions of mains such as grilled king
salmon, Maine lobster ravioli, and a wood-grilled pork prime rib chop.
Save room for one of the dynamite desserts, among them the dark-
chocolate brioche custard. There's counter seating for folks too hungry
to wait for a table, and an American Wagyu beef burger with Cowgirl Creamery cheese at lunchtime. Ⓢ *Average main: $36* ⌗ *1 Mission
St., Embarcadero* ☎ *415/543–6084* ⊕ *www.boulevardrestaurant.com*
⌂ *Reservations essential* ⊗ *No lunch weekends* ✛ *H4.*

$$$ ✕**Coqueta.** With its Embarcadero perch, Bay Bridge views, and stellar
SPANISH Spanish tapas, celebrity chef Michael Chiarello's San Francisco debut
has been an instant hit. Equal parts rustic and chic, his dining room's
bold decor—stained wooden beams, cowhide rugs, marble bar—sends
out the visual message that Chiarello is on top of his game, and it's fun
to see him mingling with diners as they enjoy toothpicked *pintxos* (small
snacks) such as quail egg with Serrano ham. The real draws, though, are
the inventive cocktails, luscious paella, and dazzling variation on the
cut of pork *secreto Ibérico* (Iberian secret). The desserts are also small
bites, so you'll likely have room to end your experience on a sweet note.
■TIP→ Book well in advance for dinner. Ⓢ *Average main: $30* ⌗ *Pier
5, near Broadway, Embarcadero* ☎ *415/704–8866* ⊕ *coquetasf.com*
⌂ *Reservations essential* ⊗ *No lunch Mon.* ✛ *G3.*

$$ ✕**Hog Island Oyster Company.** A thriving oyster farm north of San Fran-
SEAFOOD cisco in Tomales Bay serves up its harvest at this newly expanded raw
bar and restaurant in the Ferry Building. Devotees come here for impeccably fresh oysters and clams on the half shell. Other mollusk-centered
options include a first-rate oyster stew, baked oysters, clam chowder,
and "steamer" dishes atop of a bed of local greens. The bar also turns
out one of the city's best grilled-cheese sandwiches, made with three
artisanal cheeses on artisanal bread. Ⓢ *Average main: $20* ⌗ *Ferry
Bldg., Embarcadero at Market St., Embarcadero* ☎ *415/391–7117*
⊕ *www.hogislandoysters.com* ⌂ *Reservations not accepted* ✛ *H3.*

$$$ ✕**La Mar Cebicheria Peruana.** Right on the water's edge, this casually chic
PERUVIAN outpost, the chain's first outside Peru, imports real Peruvian flavors to
San Francisco. Your waiter will start you out with a pile of potato and
plantain chips with three dipping sauces, but after that you're on your
own, choosing from a long list of ceviches, can't-miss *causas* (whipped
potatoes topped with a choice of fish, shellfish, or vegetable salads),
and everything from crisp, lightly fried fish and shellfish to soups and
stews. The view of the water is especially enjoyable during lunch or a
warm evening. Ⓢ *Average main: $25* ⌗ *Pier 1½, between Washington
and Jackson Sts., Embarcadero* ☎ *415/397–8880* ⊕ *lamarsf.com* ✛ *G3.*

$$$ ✕**Slanted Door.** If you're looking for homey Vietnamese food served
VIETNAMESE in a down-to-earth dining room at a decent price, *don't* stop here.
Celebrated chef-owner Charles Phan has mastered the upmarket,

Western-accented Vietnamese menu. To showcase his cuisine, he built a big space with sleek wooden tables and chairs, a cocktail lounge, a bar, and an enviable bay view. His popular dishes include green-papaya salad, daikon rice cakes, cellophane crab noodles, chicken clay pot, and shaking beef (tender beef cubes with garlic and onion). They don't come cheap, but they're made with quality ingredients. ■TIP➔ **To avoid the midday and evening crowds, dine at the bar, drop by for afternoon tea (2:30–4:30), or visit Out the Door, Phan's take-out counter around the corner, which is less expensive.** $ *Average main: $29* ⊠ *Ferry Bldg., Embarcadero at Market St., Embarcadero* ☎ *415/861–8032* ⊕ *www. slanteddoor.com* ⌂ *Reservations essential* ✦ *H3.*

THE MARINA

$$$ ✕**A16.** Marina residents—and, judging from the crowds, everybody
ITALIAN else—gravitate to this trattoria named for a highway that runs past Naples into surrounding Campania and specializing in the food from that region, done very, very well. Rustic pasta favorites such as *maccaronara* with *ragu napoletana* and house-made salted ricotta might show up on the menu, and for an entrée perhaps petrale sole with crispy black trumpet mushrooms. The pizzas are also a highlight. The selection of primarily southern Italian wines, augmented by some California vintages, supports the food perfectly, and there's a substantial beer list. ■TIP➔ **The animated bar scene near the door sets the tone; for a quieter time request a table in the alcove or try for the patio.** $ *Average main: $27* ⊠ *2355 Chestnut St., Marina* ☎ *415/771–2216* ⊕ *www. a16sf.com* ⌂ *Reservations essential* ⊘ *No lunch Mon. and Tues.* ✦ *A1.*

$$ ✕**Greens.** Owned and operated by the San Francisco Zen Center, this
VEGETARIAN nonprofit vegetarian restaurant gets some of its fresh produce from the center's organic Green Gulch Farm. Despite the lack of meat, hearty dishes from chef Annie Somerville—shepherd's pie with wild mushrooms, for example, or the vegetable brochette plate—really satisfy. An à la carte menu is offered on Sunday and weeknights, but on Saturday a four-course prix-fixe dinner is served. Floor-to-ceiling windows give diners a sweeping view of the Marina and the Golden Gate Bridge. ■TIP➔ **A small counter by the front door stocks sandwiches, soups, and sweets for easy takeout, open in the morning.** $ *Average main: $19* ⊠ *Bldg. A, Fort Mason, off Marina Blvd., Marina* ☎ *415/771–6222* ⊕ *www.greensrestaurant.com* ⌂ *Reservations essential* ⊘ *No lunch Mon.* ✦ *B1.*

COW HOLLOW

$$$ ✕**Rose's Café.** Sleepy-headed locals turn up for the breakfast pizza of
ITALIAN smoked ham, eggs, and fontina; poached eggs with Yukon Gold potato
FAMILY and mushroom hash; and soft polenta with mascarpone and jam. Midday is time for pizza with wild nettles, or linguine with clams. Evening hours find customers eating their way through more pizza and pasta, or skirt steak and a glorious roasted chicken. The ingredients are top-notch, the service is friendly, and the seating is in comfortable booths and at tables and a counter. Heaters above the outdoor tables keep

5

things toasty when the temperature dips. ■TIP➔ Expect long lines for Sunday brunch. $ *Average main: $27* ✉ *2298 Union St., Cow Hollow* ☎ *415/775–2200* ⊕ *www.rosescafesf.com* ✛ *A2.*

THE CASTRO

$$$ ✕**Frances.** Still one of the hottest tickets in town, this small space belts
FRENCH   out a delicious bacon beignet. You come to see what chef/owner Melissa Perello will execute. Standouts on the California-French menu are the savory bavette steak, duck confit, and baked clams with bacon cream. The apple galette for dessert hits all the right notes. The space is simply designed with a limited number of tables, so it can be extraordinarily difficult to get a reservation, except at 10 pm. Service is professional and warm. $ *Average main: $27* ✉ *3870 17th St., Castro* ☎ *415/621–3870* ⊕ *www.frances-sf.com* ⌂ *Reservations essential* ⊗ *Closed Mon. No lunch* ✛ *A6.*

THE MISSION

$$$ ✕**Bar Tartine.** An offshoot of the cultlike Tartine Bakery, this artsy space
MODERN   provides a way to taste the bakery's famed (and nearly always sold-
AMERICAN   out) country loaf. Flavor-packed cuisine is eclectic, influenced by Eastern Europe, Scandinavia, and Japan with California sensibility. The menu includes many house-pickled items, tempting *langos* (fried potato bread), and seasonal salads such as smoked potatoes with black garlic. Chicken *paprikas* and fisherman's stew are among the homey dishes. Weekend brunch is one of the city's more distinct offerings in that category, with buckwheat blintzes, and a beef-brisket hash with celery root, parsnip, Yukon Gold potatoes, and fried eggs. $ *Average main: $25* ✉ *561 Valencia St., Mission* ☎ *415/487–1600* ⊕ *www.bartartine. com* ⊗ *Closed for lunch weekdays* ✛ *B6.*

$$$ ✕**Central Kitchen.** Californian cuisine in all of its freshness is on display
MODERN   in this offshoot of Flour + Water. You might taste raw hamachi topped
AMERICAN   with fennel, or one of chef Thomas McNaughton's famous pastas. A
Fodor's Choice   planked-and-concrete tea-light strung courtyard, with a retractable
★   awning, shares space with Salumeria (a deli and larder) and Trick Dog (an energetic cocktail bar). $ *Average main: $30* ✉ *3000 20th St., Mission* ☎ *415/826–7004* ⊕ *www.centralkitchensf.com* ⊗ *No lunch weekdays* ✛ *D6.*

$$$ ✕**Delfina.** "Irresistible." That's how countless die-hard fans describe
ITALIAN   Craig and Anne Stoll's Northern Italian spot. Don't even think about an
Fodor's Choice   eye roll should we recommend you order the spaghetti with plum toma-
★   toes. It's been dialed to perfection. If Piemontese fresh white truffles have made their way to San Francisco, you are likely to find hand-cut tagliarini dressed with butter, cream, and the pricey aromatic fungus on the menu. The panna cotta is the best in its class. Tables are squeezed into an urban interior, with hardwood floors, aluminum-top tables, and a tile bar, that seems to radiate with happiness. $ *Average main: $25* ✉ *3621 18th St., Mission* ☎ *415/552–4055* ⊕ *www.delfinasf.com* ⌂ *Reservations essential* ⊗ *No lunch* ✛ *B6.*

$$ INDIAN Fodor's Choice ★ 🍴 **Dosa on Valencia.** If you like Indian food but crave more than chicken tikka masala and naan, this cheerful temple of South Indian cuisine is for you. Aside from the large, thin savory namesake pancake, the kitchen also prepares curries, *uttapam* (open-face pancakes), and various starters, breads, rice dishes, and chutneys. Dosa fillings range from traditional potatoes, onions, and cashews to spinach and fennel stems. Tamil lamb curry with fennel and tomatoes and poppy seed prawns are popular, as are the Indian street-food additions, among them *vada pav* (a vegetarian slider). A second, splashier branch is in Japantown. [$] *Average main: $18* ✉ *995 Valencia St., at 21st St., Mission* ☎ *415/642–3672* 🌐 *www.dosasf.com* ⏲ *No lunch weekdays* ✣ *B6.*

$$$ ITALIAN 🍴 **Flour + Water.** Diners used to flood into this hot spot for the blistery thin-crust Neapolitan pizza, but these days it's the pasta that holds attention. The grand experience here is the seven-course pasta-tasting menu (extra for wine pairings). The homemade mustard tagliatelle with smoked lamb's tongue is surprisingly zippy, with lemon zest lifting and extracting flavors. A whimsical interior includes tabletop beakers as candleholders, a moth-wing wall mural, and a cabinet of taxidermy in the bathroom. Expect a noisy, boisterous scene. Trying to get a reservation at Flour + Water is one of the longest-running jokes in town. Your best bet is to come when the doors open. [$] *Average main: $26* ✉ *2401 Harrison St., Mission* ☎ *415/826–7000* 🌐 *www.flourandwater.com* ⏲ *No lunch* ✣ *D6.*

$$$$ MODERN AMERICAN 🍴 **Lazy Bear.** There's no end to the buzz of chef David Barzelay's pop-up turned permanent restaurant, or the quest for a ticket to one of his modern American dinners. A reservation for the 12- to 18-course prix-fixe menu that changes monthly is required. You might see Delta crawfish, hen *jus*, or duck with cracklins. An ode to the Western lodge, the two-level dining room includes a modern fireplace, charred wood walls, wooden rafters and tables made of American elm. You're basically going to a dinner party for 40, with cocktails and bites enjoyed upstairs and dinner downstairs at two communal tables. Everyone is thoughtfully given a passbook for writing notes. [$] *Average main: $120* ✉ *3416 19th St., Mission* ☎ *415/874–9921* 🌐 *Closed Tues. and Wed. No lunch* ✍ *Reservations essential* ⏲ *www.lazybearsf.com* ✣ *B6.*

$$$ ITALIAN 🍴 **Locanda.** The owners of lauded Delfina have bestowed another culinary gift on the city. Only this time the muse for the menu is Rome. An addictive starter is pizza bianca: chewy, hot bread that holds mini puddles of olive oil and is sprinkled with sea salt. The peppery and creamy pasta, *tonnarelli cacio e pepe*, is a signature. A good strategy here is to double down on pastas and antipasti, then share a main. Finely made cocktails arrive at dark-wood tables on a candlelit tray, and white Heath wall tiles lend a Mission vibe. This is a busy place with the bar stools constantly occupied. [$] *Average main: $26* ✉ *557 Valencia St., Mission* ☎ *415/863–6800* 🌐 *www.locandasf.com* ⏲ *No lunch* ✣ *B6.*

$ CHINESE 🍴 **Mission Chinese Food.** While the setting is somewhat one-star, the food draws throngs for its wildly different and bold take on Chinese. MCF has become so popular that it now has a satellite in New York. The kitchen pumps out some fine and superfiery kung pao pastrami as well as other Chinese dishes made with quality meats and ingredients, like salt cod fried rice with mackerel confit, and braised lamb cheek with shanghai noodles. Some of the dishes spike hot (ma po tofu) while milder dishes (Westlake rice porridge) are homey and satisfying. Because of long waits, we recommend lunchtime. Many locals rely on delivery for their fix. $ *Average main: $14 ⊠ 2234 Mission St., Mission* ☎ *415/863–2800* ⊕ *www.missionchinesefood.com* ⌂ *Reservations not accepted* ⊘ *Closed Wed.* ✛ *B6.*

$

MEXICAN
FAMILY

✕ **SanJalisco.** This old-time, sun-filled, colorful, family-run restaurant is a neighborhood gem, and not only because it serves breakfast all day—though the hearty *chilaquiles* hit the spot. On weekends, adventurous eaters may opt for *birria*, a spicy goat stew, or *menudo*, a tongue-searing soup made from tripe, calf's foot, and hominy. The latter is a time-honored hangover cure—but don't come expecting margaritas (though you will find beer and sangria). Bring plenty of change for the jukebox loaded with Latin hits. $ *Average main: $11 ⊠ 901 S. Van Ness Ave., Mission* ☎ *415/648–8383* ⊕ *www.sanjalisco.com* ✛ *C6.*

JAPANTOWN

$$

INDIAN
Fodor's Choice
★

✕ **Dosa on Fillmore.** As soon as the large door swings open to this happening two-level space, diners are greeted with a sexy atmosphere with bright colors, a lively bar, and the smell of spices in the air. This is the second location of the popular Dosa on Valencia, but it's definitely the glamorous younger sister, with an expanded menu and much more room. The menu entices with savory fish dishes, fall-off-the-bone pepper chicken, and papery dosas. The restaurant handles group dining often. At lunch, indulge in the Indian street-food selections, and the famed *pani puri* (little crisp puffs you fill with mint and tamarind water and pop all at once into your mouth). $ *Average main: $17 ⊠ 1700 Fillmore St., Japantown* ☎ *415/441–3672* ⊕ *www.dosasf.com* ⊘ *No lunch Mon. and Tues.* ✛ *A4.*

WESTERN ADDITION

$$

BARBECUE

✕ **4505 Burgers & BBQ.** Those who have ever wondered how a butcher would prepare meat will find the answer in the tender brisket here. The crust is deliciously charred, and the meat flavorful, spending 18 to 24 hours in a smoker as part of a process perfected by the butcher/owners. Every plate comes with two sides, and you should choose frankaroni as one of them. Possibly the work of the devil, this is macaroni-and-cheese with pieces of hot dog . . . deep-fried. You order at the counter in this chic-hipster shack on a rapidly evolving stretch of Divis that attracts long lines, though they move quickly. Seating is mostly outside at communal picnic tables. The restaurant's sign, "Pig N or Pig Out" truly means it. They do take-out and delivery (via Try Caviar). $ *Average main: $15 ⊠ 705 Divisadero, at Grove St., Western Addition* ☎ *415/231–6993* ✛ *A6.*

$$$

AMERICAN

✕ **Nopa.** This is the good-food granddaddy of the hot corridor of the same name (NoPa equals North of the Panhandle). The Cali-rustic fare includes an always winning flatbread topped with fennel sausage and caramelized onions; smoky, crisp-skin rotisserie chicken; and a juicy hamburger with thick-cut fries. This place is so lively—and high ceilings and concrete floors contribute to the noise factor—that raised voices are sometimes the only way to communicate. The weekend brunch is among the city's best. ■TIP➡ Late-night cravings can be satisfied until 1 am. Ⓢ *Average main: $24* ✉ *560 Divisadero St., Western Addition* ☎ *415/864–8643* ⊕ *www.nopasf.com* ☾ *No lunch weekdays* ⊹ *A6.*

$$
MEXICAN
FAMILY
Fodor's Choice
★

✕ **Nopalito.** Those in the mood for Mexican will get some of the most authentic flavors here—and at the same time, be surprised by the creativity and fresh ingredients on the plate. All the tortillas are made from organic house-ground *masa* (dough), and Mexico's peppers find their way into many of the offerings. The spicy beef empanada and succulent pork carnitas are skillfully prepared—not a goopy mess. The casual atmosphere is popular with families yet pleasing to adults lured by the well-selected tequilas. Expect a substantial wait in the evening, though you can call ahead to be put on the list. If you're feeling truly impatient, order from the take-out window; or the second location in Inner Sunset may be less crowded. Ⓢ *Average main: $15* ✉ *306 Broderick St., Western Addition* ☎ *415/437–0303* ⊕ *www.nopalitosf.com* ⊹ *A6.*

$$$$
MODERN
AMERICAN

✕ **The Progress.** Tables are coveted at this restaurant by the chef-owners of the Michelin-starred State Bird Provisions, and for good reason: the inventive dishes, marrying Californian and Japanese cuisine, are a culinary adventure served family-style. Dumplings are filled with Mt. Tam cheese and porcini, and Cali beef comes with a mustard miso-oyster sauce, all served on eye-popping ceramics. For $65 per person, tables collectively decide on six items to get off the 18-item menu (which includes three desserts). Next door to the revered State Bird Provisions and equally signless, the space is airy with soaring ceilings, a mezzanine, and exposed beams and concrete. Foodies of all ages come out in droves. ■TIP➡ Nab one of the 12 bar stools, and you can forego the $65 prix-fixe menu, and order à la carte. Ⓢ *Average main: $65* ✉ *1525 Fillmore St., Western Addition* ☎ *415/673–1294* ⊕ *www.theprogress-sf. com* ☾ *No lunch* ⊹ *A4.*

$$$
MODERN
AMERICAN
Fodor's Choice
★

✕ **State Bird Provisions.** A reservation here is practically impossible to get, but if you do walk in and commit to a 90-plus minute wait you'll eventually be treated to a festive parade of bites that roll around on carts dim-sum style. Choices include half-dollar-size thick, savory pancakes stuffed with sauerkraut; giant nori chips topped with hamachi, radishes, and avocados; and about 15 or so other nightly creations, often with a Japanese slant. The colorful dining room with pegboard walls has a high-school art-room vibe. The staff remains super friendly, even though they turn away dozens. ■TIP➡ Get here an hour before opening and wait in line, or come at 5:30, leave your number, and the host will page you when the table is ready. Ⓢ *Average main: $30* ✉ *1529 Fillmore St., Western Addition* ☎ *415/795–1272* ⊕ *www.statebirdsf. com* ☾ *No lunch* ⊹ *A4.*

THE RICHMOND

$
ASIAN

✕ **Burma Superstar.** Locals make the trek to the "Avenues" for the extraordinary tea-leaf salad, a combo of spicy, salty, crunchy, and sour that is mixed table-side, with fermented tea leaves from Burma, fried garlic, and peanuts. Another hit is the hearty vegetarian *samusa* soup. The modestly decorated, no-reservations restaurant is small, so lines can be long during peak times. Leave your number and wait for the call. **■ TIP→ Walk a couple blocks east to B-Star, owned by the same people but lesser known and often less crowded.** [$] *Average main: $14* ✉ *309 Clement St., Richmond* ☎ *415/387–2147* 🌐 *www.burmasuperstar.com* ✍ *Reservations not accepted* ✣ *A4.*

$ AMERICAN FAMILY

🍴 **Park Chow.** What do spaghetti and meatballs, Thai noodles with chicken and shrimp, salads in three sizes, and big burgers have in common? They're all on the eclectic comfort-food menu here, and all are made with sustainable ingredients yet offered at unbeatable prices. This neighborhood standby is also known for its desserts: the fresh-baked pies and ginger cake with pumpkin ice cream are among the standouts. Kids get their own menu. In cool weather fires roar in the dining-room fireplaces; in warm weather, the outdoor tables are the place to be. There's another Chow in the Castro neighborhood. **■ TIP→ You can call ahead to put your name on the waiting list.** [$] *Average main: $13* ✉ *1240 9th Ave., Inner Sunset* ☎ *415/665–9912* 🌐 *www.chowfoodbar.com* ✣ *A6.*

WHERE TO STAY

San Francisco accommodations are diverse, ranging from cozy inns and kitschy motels, to chic little inns and true grande dames, housed in century-old structures and sleek high-rises. While the tech boom has skyrocketed the prices of even some of the most dependable low-cost options, luckily, some Fodor's faves still offer fine accommodations without the jaw-dropping prices to match those steep hills. In fact, the number of reasonably priced accommodations is impressive. *Hotel reviews have been shortened. For full information, visit Fodors.com. Use the coordinate (✣ A1) at the end of each listing to locate a site on the corresponding map.*

	WHAT IT COSTS			
	$	$$	$$$	$$$$
Hotels	under $150	$150–$249	$250–$350	over $350

Hotel prices are the lowest cost of a standard double room in high season.

UNION SQUARE

$ B&B/INN FAMILY Fodor's Choice ★

🏨 **Golden Gate Hotel.** Budget-seekers looking for accommodations around Union Square will enjoy this four-story Edwardian with bay windows, an original birdcage elevator, hallways lined with historical photographs, and rooms decorated with antiques, wicker pieces, and Laura Ashley bedding and curtains. **Pros:** friendly staff; free Wi-Fi; spotless rooms; comfortable bedding; good location if you're a walker. **Cons:** some rooms without private bath. [$] *Rooms from: $135* ✉ *775 Bush St., Union Sq.* ☎ *415/392–3702, 800/835–1118* 🌐 *www.goldengatehotel.com* 🛏 *25 rooms, 14 with bath* 🍽 *Breakfast* ✣ *E4.*

$$ ⬚ **Hotel Diva.** Entering this magnet for hip urbanites craving modern
HOTEL   decor requires stepping over footprints, handprints, and autographs
FAMILY embedded in the sidewalk by visiting stars; in the rooms, designer car-
Fodor'sChoice pets complement Harry Bertoia chairs and brushed-steel headboards
★   whose shape mimics that of ocean waves. **Pros:** punchy design; in
the heart of the theater district; accommodating service. **Cons:** few
frills; tiny bathrooms (but equipped with eco-friendly bath products).
$ *Rooms from: $199* ✉ *440 Geary St., Union Sq.* ☎ *415/885–0200,
800/553–1900* ⊕ *www.hoteldiva.com* ⇥ *115 rooms, 3 suites* ⦿ *No
meals* ⊹ *E4.*

$$ ⬚ **Hotel G.** Union Square's newest hotel manages to be both homey and
HOTEL   innovative, with an ensemble of woven Indian rugs, denim headboards,
black-and-white wallpapered closets, floating light fixtures, and throw
pillows shaped like the Golden State. **Pros:** fun design; on-site restaurants
and bars; great central location. **Cons:** new hotel is still working out some
kinks; wooden or concrete flooring can be loud. $ *Rooms from: $229*
✉ *386 Geary St., Union Sq.* ☎ *877/828–4478* ⊕ *www.hotelsanfrancisco.
com* ⇥ *121 rooms, 30 suites* ⦿ *No meals* ⊹ *E4.*

$$$$ ⬚ **Hotel Nikko, San Francisco.** The vast surfaces of gray-flecked white
HOTEL   marble that dominate the Nikko's neoclassical lobby have the starkness
FAMILY of an airport, but the crisply designed rooms please the business-traveler
Fodor'sChoice clientele with soothing muted tones, Bluetooth-enabled headboards,
★   and modern bathrooms with sinks atop granite bases. **Pros:** friendly
multilingual staff; tastefully designed rooms; large indoor pool; very
clean. **Cons:** lobby lacks color; atmosphere feels cold to some patrons;
expensive parking. $ *Rooms from: $399* ✉ *222 Mason St., Union Sq.*
☎ *415/394–1111, 800/248–3308* ⊕ *www.hotelnikkosf.com* ⇥ *510
rooms, 22 suites* ⦿ *No meals* ⊹ *E4.*

$$ ⬚ **Hotel Triton.** A spirit of fun has taken up full-time residence in this
HOTEL   Kimpton property with a youngish, super-friendly staff and smallish but
Fodor'sChoice colorful rooms that boast Chinese dragons stenciled over excerpts of
★   Beat literature, striking yellow headboards, vintage chairs, and chalk-
board doors donned with quotes from famed writers. **Pros:** attentive
service; refreshingly funky atmosphere; hip arty environs; good loca-
tion. **Cons:** rooms and baths are on the small side (with sinks positioned
outside the bathrooms). $ *Rooms from: $189* ✉ *342 Grant Ave., Union
Sq.* ☎ *415/394–0500, 800/800–1299* ⊕ *www.hoteltriton.com* ⇥ *133
rooms, 7 suites* ⦿ *No meals* ⊹ *F4.*

$$$ ⬚ **Westin St. Francis.** The survivor of two major earthquakes, some
HOTEL   headline-grabbing scandals, and even an attempted presidential assas-
Fodor'sChoice sination, this grande dame that dates to 1904 remains ever above the
★   fray—richly appointed, serenely elegant, and superbly located. **Pros:**
fantastic beds; prime Union Square location; spacious rooms, some with
great views. **Cons:** some guests comment on the long wait at check-in;
rooms in original building can be small. $ *Rooms from: $325* ✉ *335
Powell St., Union Sq.* ☎ *415/397–7000, 800/917–7458* ⊕ *www.westin
stfrancis.com* ⇥ *1,157 rooms, 38 suites* ⦿ *No meals* ⊹ *E4.*

5

SOMA

$$$$
HOTEL
Fodor's Choice
★
Four Seasons Hotel San Francisco. Occupying floors 5 through 17 of a skyscraper, these elegant rooms with contemporary artwork and fine linens have floor-to-ceiling windows overlooking either Yerba Buena Gardens or downtown; all have deep soaking tubs and glass-enclosed showers. **Pros:** near museums, galleries, restaurants, shopping, and clubs; terrific fitness facilities; luxurious rooms and amenities; MKT restaurant is worth the splurge. **Cons:** pricey; rooms can feel sterile. $\boxed{S}$ *Rooms from: $595* ✉ *757 Market St., SoMa* ☎ *415/633–3000, 800/332–3442, 800/819–5053* ⊕ *www.fourseasons.com/sanfrancisco* ⤳ *231 rooms, 46 suites* ⦵ *No meals* ✚ *F4.*

$$$
HOTEL
Fodor's Choice
★
Hotel Palomar San Francisco. Favored by celebrities, this lair on the top five floors of the green-tile 1908 Pacific Place Building offers a luxurious oasis above the busiest part of town, where spacious rooms offer muted alligator-pattern carpeting, drapes with bold taupe-and-cream stripes, and sleek furniture echoing a 1930s sensibility. **Pros:** in-room spa service available; much hyped restaurant and bar; good location; refuge from downtown. **Cons:** pricey. $\boxed{S}$ *Rooms from: $270* ✉ *12 4th St., SoMa* ☎ *415/348–1111, 866/373–4941* ⊕ *www.hotelpalomar-sf. com* ⤳ *184 rooms, 11 suites* ⦵ *No meals* ✚ *E5.*

$$$
HOTEL
Fodor's Choice
★
Hotel Zetta. With a playful lobby lounge, the lively Cavalier restaurant, and slick-yet-homey tech-friendly rooms, this trendy redo behind a stately 1913 neoclassical facade is a leader in the SoMa hotel scene. **Pros:** hip, arty design; eco-friendly; great location close to shopping and museums; fine restaurant and lounges; free basic Wi-Fi; state-of-the-art tech amenities. **Cons:** lots of hubbub and traffic; no bathtubs. $\boxed{S}$ *Rooms from: $289* ✉ *55 5th St., SoMa* ☎ *415/543–8555* ⊕ *www. viceroyhotelgroup.com/zetta* ⤳ *116 rooms, 1 suite* ⦵ *No meals* ✚ *E5.*

$$$$
HOTEL
Fodor's Choice
★
The St. Regis San Francisco. Across from Yerba Buena and the MOMA, the city's most luxurious property, favored by celebrities such as Lady Gaga and Al Gore, is at once luxurious and modern, pampering guests in rooms and suites with subdued cream colors, leather-textured walls, and window seats offering city views. **Pros:** tasteful, yet current; lap pool; good location; luxe spa; views; two on-site restaurants. **Cons:** very expensive; hallway noise; long waits for room service and valet parking. $\boxed{S}$ *Rooms from: $895* ✉ *125 3rd St., SoMa* ☎ *415/284–4000* ⊕ *www. stregis.com/sanfrancisco* ⤳ *214 rooms, 46 suites* ⦵ *No meals* ✚ *F4.*

THE TENDERLOIN

$
HOTEL
Phoenix Hotel. A magnet for the hip at heart and ultracool is a bit retro and low-key, with bamboo furniture, fresh white bedspreads, and original pieces by local artists, as well as modern amenities like iPad/iPod docking stations. **Pros:** boho atmosphere; cheeky design; popular with musicians; hip restaurant/bar; free parking. **Cons:** somewhat seedy location; no elevators; can be loud in the evening. $\boxed{S}$ *Rooms from: $149* ✉ *601 Eddy St., Tenderloin* ☎ *415/776–1380, 800/248–9466* ⊕ *www. thephoenixhotel.com* ⤳ *41 rooms, 3 suites* ⦵ *Breakfast* ✚ *D5.*

HAYES VALLEY

$ 🏨 **Metro Hotel.** These tiny rooms, with simple yet modern decor and
HOTEL equipped with private (though small) bathrooms, are within walking
Fodor's Choice ★ distance to the lively Haight, Hayes Valley, Panhandle, NoPa, and Castro districts. **Pros:** can't beat the price; great location for those wanting to be out of downtown; friendly staff. **Cons:** small rooms and bathrooms; street noise. [$] *Rooms from: $88* ✉ *319 Divisadero St., Hayes Valley* ☎ *415/861–5364* 🌐 *www.metrohotelsf.com* 🛏 *24 rooms* 🍴 *No meals* ✥ *A6.*

FINANCIAL DISTRICT

$$$$ 🏨 **Mandarin Oriental, San Francisco.** Two towers connected by glass-
HOTEL enclosed sky bridges compose the top 11 floors of one of San Francisco's tallest buildings, offering spectacular panoramas from every room; the windows open so you can hear that trademark San Francisco sound: the "ding ding" of the cable cars some 40 floors below (and rooms include binoculars). **Pros:** spectacular "bridge-to-bridge" views; attentive service; in the running for the most comfy beds in the city. **Cons:** in a business area that's quiet on weekends; extremely pricey. [$] *Rooms from: $595* ✉ *222 Sansome St., Financial District* ☎ *415/276–9600, 800/622–0404* 🌐 *www.mandarinoriental.com/sanfrancisco* 🛏 *151 rooms, 7 suites* 🍴 *No meals* ✥ *F3.*

NOB HILL

$$$$ 🏨 **Fairmont San Francisco.** Dominating the top of Nob Hill like a Euro-
HOTEL pean palace, the Fairmont is steeped in a rich history and pampers guests in luxury—rooms in the main building are done in conservative color schemes and have high ceilings, colorful Chinese porcelain lamps, decadent beds, and marble bathrooms; rooms in the newer Tower are generally larger and have better views. **Pros:** huge bathrooms; stunning lobby; great location. **Cons:** some guests have complained about spotty service; older rooms can be quite small; hills can be challenging for those on foot. [$] *Rooms from: $429* ✉ *950 Mason St., Nob Hill* ☎ *415/772–5000, 800/257–7544* 🌐 *www.fairmont.com/sanfrancisco* 🛏 *591 rooms, 65 suites* 🍴 *No meals* ✥ *E3.*

$$$$ 🏨 **Ritz-Carlton, San Francisco.** This stunning tribute to beauty and atten-
HOTEL tive, professional service offers a modern twist on that classic Ritz style
Fodor's Choice ★ with luxurious, fog-hued guest rooms that are geared to solid comforts, such as featherbeds outfitted with 300-thread-count, Egyptian-cotton Frette sheets, and down comforters. **Pros:** terrific service; all-day food available on Club Level; beautiful surroundings; fantastic new restaurant and Lobby Lounge; renovated fitness center. **Cons:** expensive; hilly location; no pool. [$] *Rooms from: $599* ✉ *600 Stockton St., at California St., Nob Hill* ☎ *415/296–7465* 🌐 *www.ritzcarlton.com* 🛏 *276 rooms, 60 suites* 🍴 *No meals* ✥ *E3.*

NORTH BEACH

$ **San Remo Hotel.** A few blocks from Fisherman's Wharf, this three-
HOTEL   story 1906 Italianate Victorian—once home to longshoremen and Beat
Fodor'sChoice   poets—has a narrow stairway from the street leading to the front desk
★   and labyrinthine hallways; rooms are small but charming, with lace
curtains, forest-green-painted wood floors, and brass beds and other
antique furnishings. **Pros:** inexpensive; historic; cozy. **Cons:** some rooms
are dark; only the penthouse suite has a private bath; spartan amenities.
$ *Rooms from: $104* ✉ *2237 Mason St., North Beach* ☎ *415/776–
8688, 800/352–7366* ⊕ *www.sanremohotel.com* ⇨ *64 rooms with
shared baths, 1 suite* ⦿ *No meals* ✛ *E1.*

FISHERMAN'S WHARF

$$$ **Argonaut Hotel.** These spacious guest rooms, many with a sofa bed in
HOTEL   the sitting areas, have exposed-brick walls, wood-beam ceilings, and
FAMILY   best of all, windows that open to the sea air and the sounds of the water-
Fodor'sChoice   front; many rooms enjoy views of Alcatraz and the Golden Gate Bridge.
★   **Pros:** bay views; near Hyde Street cable car; sofa beds; toys for the kids.
Cons: nautical theme isn't for everyone; cramped public areas; service
can be hit or miss; location requires a bit of a trek to many attractions.
$ *Rooms from: $309* ✉ *495 Jefferson St., at Hyde St., Fisherman's
Wharf* ☎ *415/563–0800, 866/415–0704* ⊕ *www.argonauthotel.com*
⇨ *239 rooms, 13 suites* ⦿ *No meals* ✛ *D1.*

$$$ **Best Western Plus–The Tuscan.** The redbrick facade of this hotel some
HOTEL   Fodors.com users describe as a "hidden treasure" barely hints at the
Tuscan country villa style that lies within—Italianate rooms feature
delightful bedding, kingly studded headboards, and wine-colored textiles. **Pros:** wine and beer hour; cozy feeling; great location near Fisherman's Wharf. **Cons:** congested touristy area; small rooms. $ *Rooms
from: $265* ✉ *425 North Point St., at Mason St., Fisherman's Wharf*
☎ *415/561–1100, 800/648–4626* ⊕ *www.tuscaninn.com* ⇨ *212 rooms,
12 suites* ⦿ *No meals* ✛ *E1.*

EMBARCADERO

$$$ **Hotel Vitale.** "Luxury, naturally," the theme of this eight-story, ter-
HOTEL   raced bay-front hotel, is apparent in every thoughtful detail: little vases
FAMILY   of lavender mounted outside each handsome room; limestone-lined
Fodor'sChoice   baths; the penthouse-level day spa with soaking tubs set in a roof-
★   top bamboo forest. **Pros:** family-friendly studios; great views of the
Bay Bridge, Embarcadero, Treasure Island, or the skyline; twice-daily
maid service. **Cons:** some rooms can feel cramped or be noisy; "urban
retreat fee" adds another charge to an already pricy property; some
guests report inconsistent service. $ *Rooms from: $350* ✉ *8 Mission
St., Embarcadero* ☎ *415/278–3700, 888/890–8688* ⊕ *www.hotelvitale.
com* ⇨ *190 rooms, 9 suites* ⦿ *No meals* ✛ *H3.*

THE MARINA, COW HOLLOW, AND THE PRESIDIO

$ **Cow Hollow Motor Inn and Suites.** The suites at this large, family-owned,
HOTEL   modern motel resemble typical San Francisco apartments and are more
Fodor'sChoice   spacious than average, featuring big living rooms, one or two bedrooms,
★   hardwood floors, sitting and dining areas, marble wood-burning fireplaces, and fully equipped kitchens. **Pros:** good for families; free covered parking in building for one vehicle. **Cons:** congested neighborhood has a college-rush-week feel; standard rooms are on a loud street. [$] *Rooms from: $120 ⊠ 2190 Lombard St., Marina ☎ 415/921–5800 ⊕ www. cowhollowmotorinn.com ⟿ 117 rooms, 12 suites ⓘⓞⓘ No meals ⊹ A1.*

$$ **Hotel Del Sol.** The proximity of this beach-themed, three-story 1950s
HOTEL   motor lodge to Fort Mason, the Walt Disney Family Museum, the Presi-
FAMILY   dio, Crissy Field, and Chestnut Street's munchkin-favored shops already qualify it as kid-friendly, but the toys, games, DVDs, outdoor saltwater heated pool with plenty of inflatable playthings, snow cones on summer weekends, and afternoon cookies and milk make it a real haven for little ones. **Pros:** kid-friendly; plenty of nearby places to eat and shop; recently renovated; relatively inexpensive parking. **Cons:** far from downtown and the landmark attractions around Fisherman's Wharf; faces a busy thoroughfare. [$] *Rooms from: $189 ⊠ 3100 Webster St., Cow Hollow ☎ 415/921–5520, 877/433–5765 ⊕ www.thehoteldelsol. com ⟿ 47 rooms, 10 suites ⓘⓞⓘ Breakfast ⊹ B2.*

$$ **The Inn at the Presidio.** Built in 1903 and opened as a hotel in 2012,
B&B/INN   this two-story, Georgian Revival–style building served as officers' quar-
Fodor'sChoice   ters in military days past and now has 26 guest rooms—17 of them
★   suites—complete with gas fireplaces and modern-meets-salvage-store finds, such as wrought-iron beds, industrial-inspired task lamps, historic black-and-white photos, and Pendleton blankets. **Pros:** playful design; only hotel in the Presidio; spacious rooms; views of Golden Gate Bridge. **Cons:** no on-site restaurant; no elevator; challenging to get a taxi; very far from downtown attractions. [$] *Rooms from: $220 ⊠ 42 Moraga Ave., Presidio ☎ 415/800–7356 ⊕ www.innatthepresidio.com ⟿ 8 rooms, 18 suites ⓘⓞⓘ Breakfast ⊹ A2.*

$$ **Union Street Inn.** Precious family antiques, unique artwork, and such
B&B/INN   touches as candles, fresh flowers, wineglasses, and fine linens make
Fodor'sChoice   rooms in this green-and-cream 1902 Edwardian popular with honey-
★   mooners and those looking for a romantic getaway with an English countryside ambience. **Pros:** personal service; Jane's excellent full breakfast; romantic setting. **Cons:** parking is difficult; no air-conditioning; no elevator. [$] *Rooms from: $249 ⊠ 2229 Union St., Cow Hollow ☎ 415/346–0424 ⊕ www.unionstreetinn.com ⟿ 6 rooms ⓘⓞⓘ Breakfast ⊹ A2.*

THE MISSION

$$ **The Parker Guest House.** Two yellow 1909 Edwardian houses enchant
B&B/INN   travelers wanting an authentic San Francisco experience; dark hall-
Fodor'sChoice   ways and steep staircases lead to bright earth-toned rooms with pri-
★   vate tiled baths (most with tubs), comfortable sitting areas and cozy linens. **Pros:** handsome affordable rooms; just steps from Dolores Park

5

and the vibrant Castro District on a Muni line; free Wi-Fi; elaborate gardens. **Cons:** stairs can be challenging for those with limited mobility. [$] *Rooms from: $169* ✉ *520 Church St., Mission* ☎ *415/621–4139* 🌐 *parkerguesthouse.com* 🛏 *21 rooms* 🍴 *Breakfast* ✥ *B6.*

PACIFIC HEIGHTS AND JAPANTOWN

$$$$ HOTEL Fodor's Choice ★ 🏨 **Hotel Drisco.** Pretend you're a resident of one of the wealthiest residential neighborhoods in San Francisco at this understated, elegant 1903 Edwardian hotel, where the pale yellow-and-white rooms are genteelly furnished and some have sweeping city views. **Pros:** great service and many amenities; comfortable rooms; quiet residential retreat; 24-hour room service. **Cons:** far from downtown (but free car service). [$] *Rooms from: $425* ✉ *2901 Pacific Ave., Pacific Heights* ☎ *415/346–2880, 800/634–7277* 🌐 *www.hoteldrisco.com* 🛏 *29 rooms, 19 suites* 🍴 *Breakfast* ✥ *A3.*

NIGHTLIFE

After hours, business folk and the working class give way to costume-clad partygoers, hippies and hipsters, downtown divas, frat boys, and those who prefer something a little more clothing-optional.

Entertainment information is printed in the "Datebook" section and the more calendar-based "96 Hours" section of the *San Francisco Chronicle* (🌐 *www.sfgate.com*). Also consult any of the free alternative weeklies, notably the *SF Weekly* (🌐 *www.sfweekly.com*), which blurbs nightclubs and music, and the *San Francisco Bay Guardian* (🌐 *www.sfbg.com*), which lists neighborhood, avant-garde, and budget events. SF Station (🌐 *www.sfstation.com*; online only) has an up-to-date calendar of entertainment goings-on.

You're better off taking public transportation or taxis on weekend nights, unless you're heading downtown (Financial District or Union Square) and are willing to park in a lot. There's only street parking in North Beach, the Mission, Castro, and the Haight, and finding a spot can be practically impossible. Muni stops running between 1 am and 5 am but has its limited Owl Service on a few lines—including the K, N, L, 90, 91, 14, 24, 38, and 22—every 30 minutes. Service cuts have put a dent in frequency; check 🌐 *www.sfmuni.com* for current details. You can sometimes hail a taxi on the street in well-trodden nightlife locations like North Beach or the Mission, but you can also call for one (☎ *415/626–2345 Yellow Cab, 415/648–3181 Arrow*). The best option by far is booking a taxi with a smartphone-based app (🌐 *www.uber.com, www.lyft.com*). ■ **TIP→ Cabs in San Francisco are more expensive than in other areas of the United States; expect to pay at least $15 to get anywhere within the city. Keep in mind that BART service across the bay stops shortly after midnight.**

UNION SQUARE

BARS

Cantina. Let the skull and crossbones over the entryway of this intimate Latin hangout provide fair warning, because the magic the bartenders perform here is pure voodoo. The drinks are handcrafted with fresh ingredients, homemade bitters, and even homegrown citrus fruits. Because of this the service can be slow during busy times; fortunately, many cocktails are served in pitchers. ■TIP→ **The most popular cocktail is the vibrant laughing buddha—vodka, lime, ginger, and Serrano chilies.** ⊠ *580 Sutter St., at Mason St., Union Sq.* ☎ *415/398–0195* ⊕ *www.cantinasf.com* ☾ *Closed Sun.*

Redwood Room. Opened in 1933 and updated by designer Philippe Starck in 2001, this lounge at the Clift Hotel is a San Francisco icon. The entire room, floor to ceiling, is paneled with the wood from a single redwood tree, giving the place a rich, monochromatic look. The gorgeous original art-deco sconces and chandeliers still hang, but bizarre video installations on plasma screens also adorn the walls. It's packed on weekend evenings after 10, when young scenesters swarm in; for maximum glamour, visit on a weeknight. ⊠ *Clift Hotel, 495 Geary St., at Taylor St., Union Sq.* ☎ *415/929–2372 for table reservations, 415/775–4700 for hotel* ⊕ *www.clifthotel.com.*

SOMA

BARS

City Beer Store. Called CBS by locals, this friendly tasting room cum liquor mart has a wine-bar's sensibility. Perfect for connoisseurs and the merely beer curious, CBS stocks more than 300 different bottled beers, and more than a dozen are on tap. The indecisive can mix and match six-packs to go. ■TIP→ **Come early: The small space fills up quickly on event nights.** ⊠ *1168 Folsom St., at 8th St., SoMa* ☎ *415/503–1033* ⊕ *www.citybeerstore.com.*

21st Amendment Brewery. This popular brewery is known for its range of beer types, with multiple taps going at all times. In the spring, the Hell or High Watermelon—a wheat beer—gets rave reviews. ■TIP→ **Serious beer drinkers should try the Back in Black, a black IPA-style beer this brewpub helped pioneer.** The space has an upmarket warehouse feel, though exposed wooden ceiling beams, framed photos, whitewashed brick walls, and hardwood floors make it feel cozy. It's a good spot to warm up before a Giants game and an even better place to party after they win. ⊠ *563 2nd St., between Federal and Brannan Sts., SoMa* ☎ *415/369–0900* ⊕ *www.21st-amendment.com.*

GAY NIGHTLIFE

The Stud. Glam drag queens, gay bears, tight-teed pretty boys, ladies and their ladies, and a handful of straight onlookers congregate here to dance to live DJ sounds and watch world-class drag performers on the small stage. The entertainment is often campy, pee-your-pants funny, and downright fantastic. Each night's music is different—from funk,

Built as a bordello in 1907, the Great American Music Hall now pulls in top-tier performers.

soul, and hip-hop to '80s tunes and disco favorites. ■TIP→ At Frolic, the Stud's most outrageous party (second Saturday of the month), club goers dance the night away dressed as bunnies, kittens, and even stranger creatures. ⊠ 1284 Harrison St., at 9th St., SoMa ☎ 415/863–6623 ⊕ www.studsf.com ☾ Closed Mon.

THE TENDERLOIN

BARS

Fodor'sChoice ★ **Bourbon & Branch.** The address and phone are unlisted, the black outer door unmarked, and when you make your reservation (required), you get a password for entry. In short, Bourbon & Branch reeks of Prohibition-era speakeasy cool. It's not exclusive, though: everyone is granted a password. The place has sex appeal, with tin ceilings, bordello-red silk wallpaper, intimate booths, and low lighting; loud conversations and cell phones are not allowed. The menu of expertly mixed cocktails and quality bourbon and whiskey is substantial, though the servers aren't always authorities. ■TIP→ Your reservation dictates your exit time, which is strictly enforced. There's also a speakeasy within the speakeasy called Wilson & Wilson, which is more exclusive, but just as funky. ⊠ 501 Jones St., at O'Farrell St., Tenderloin ⊕ www.bourbon andbranch.com.

MUSIC CLUBS

Fodor'sChoice ★ **Great American Music Hall.** You can find top-drawer entertainment at this eclectic nightclub. Acts range from the best in blues, folk, and jazz to up-and-coming college-radio and American-roots artists to indie rockers such as OK Go, Mates of State, and the Cowboy Junkies. The colorful marble-pillared emporium (built in 1907 as a bordello) also accommodates dancing at some shows. Pub grub is available on most nights. ⊠ *859 O'Farrell St., between Polk and Larkin Sts., Tenderloin* ☏ *415/885–0750* ⊕ *www.slimspresents.com.*

HAYES VALLEY

BARS

Hôtel Biron Wine Bar and Art Gallery. Sharing an alleylike block with the backs of Market Street restaurants, this tiny, cave-like (in a good way) spot displays artworks of the Mission School aesthetic on its brick walls. The well-behaved twenty- to thirtysomething clientele enjoys the off-the-beaten-path quarters, the wines from around the world, the soft lighting, and the hip music. ⊠ *45 Rose St., off Market St. near Gough St., Hayes Valley* ☏ *415/703–0403* ⊕ *www.hotelbiron.com.*

Fodor'sChoice ★ **Smuggler's Cove.** With the decor of a pirate ship and a slew of rum-based cocktails, you half expect Captain Jack Sparrow to sidle up next to you at this offbeat, Disney-esque hangout. But don't let the kitschy ambience fool you. The folks at Smuggler's Cove take rum so seriously they even make their own, which you can sample along with more than 200 other offerings, some of them vintage and very hard to find. A punch card is provided so you can try all 70 cocktails and remember where you left off without getting shipwrecked. The small space fills up quickly, so arrive early. ⊠ *650 Gough St., at McAllister St., Hayes Valley* ☏ *415/869–1900* ⊕ *www.smugglerscovesf.com.*

NORTH BEACH

BARS

Fodor'sChoice ★ **Vesuvio Cafe.** If you're only hitting one bar in North Beach, it should be this one. The low-ceiling second floor of this raucous boho hangout, little altered since its 1960s heyday (when Jack Kerouac frequented the place), is a fine vantage point for watching the colorful Broadway Street and Columbus Avenue intersection. Another part of Vesuvio's appeal is its diverse clientele, from older neighborhood regulars and young couples to Bacchanalian posses. ⊠ *255 Columbus Ave., at Broadway St., North Beach* ☏ *415/362–3370* ⊕ *www.vesuvio.com.*

CABARET

Fodor'sChoice ★ **Club Fugazi.** The claim to fame here is *Beach Blanket Babylon,* a wacky musical send-up of San Francisco moods and mores that has been going strong since 1974, making it the longest-running musical revue anywhere. Although the choreography is colorful, the singers brassy, and the satirical songs witty, the real stars are the comically exotic costumes and famous ceiling-high "hats"—which are worth the price of admission alone. The revue sells out as early as a month in advance, so order tickets as far ahead as possible. Those under 21 are admitted only to the Sunday matinee. ■TIP➜ **If you don't shell out the extra money for reserved seating, you won't have an assigned seat—so get your cannoli to go and arrive at least 30 minutes prior to showtime to get in line.**

⊠ *678 Green St., at Powell St., North Beach* ☎ *415/421–4222* ⊕ *www. beachblanketbabylon.com.*

MUSIC CLUBS

Bimbo's 365 Club. The plush main room and adjacent lounge of this club, here since 1951, retain a retro vibe perfect for the "Cocktail Nation" programming that keeps the crowds entertained. For a taste of the old-school San Francisco nightclub scene, you can't beat it. Indie low-fi and pop bands such as Stephen Malkmus and the Jicks and Camera Obscura play here. ⊠ *1025 Columbus Ave., at Chestnut St., North Beach* ☎ *415/474–0365* ⊕ *www.bimbos365club.com.*

EMBARCADERO

BARS

Hard Water. This waterfront restaurant and bar with stunning bay views pays homage to America's most iconic spirit—bourbon—with a wall of whiskeys and a lineup of specialty cocktails. The menu, crafted by Charles Phan of Slanted Door fame, includes spicy pork-belly cracklings, cornbread-crusted alligator, and other fun snacks. ⊠ *Pier 3, Suite 3–102, Embarcadero* ☎ *415/392–3021* ⊕ *www.hardwaterbar.com.*

THE WESTERN SHORELINE

BARS

Fodor'sChoice **Cliff House.** Classier than the nearby Beach Chalet, with a more impres-
★ sive view of Ocean Beach, this is our pick if you must choose just one oceanfront restaurant/bar. Sure, it's the site of many high-school prom dates, and you could argue that the food and drinks are overpriced, and some say the sleek facade seems more suitable for a mausoleum—but the views are terrific. The best window seats are reserved for diners, but there's a small upstairs lounge where you can watch gulls sail high above the vast blue Pacific. ■TIP➔ **Come before sunset.** ⊠ *1090 Point Lobos, at Great Hwy., Lincoln Park* ☎ *415/386–3330* ⊕ *www.cliffhouse.com.*

THE HAIGHT

Fodor'sChoice **Toronado.** You come to what may be the city's most popular dive bar
★ for one thing and one thing only: the reasonably priced beers, about four dozen of them on tap. The menu, which hangs from the ceiling, will put a kink in your neck as you try to decide. The bar opens in the late morning and has a good-size crowd by early afternoon, so show up early to sit at one of the highly coveted tables. ■TIP➔ **Don't worry about eating beforehand. It's okay to bring in outside food.** ⊠ *547 Haight St., at Fillmore St., Lower Haight* ☎ *415/863–2276* ⊕ *www.toronado.com.*

THE MISSION

BARS

Fodor'sChoice **El Rio.** A dive bar in the best sense has a calendar chock-full of events,
★ from free bands and films to Salsa Sunday (seasonal), all of which keep Mission kids coming back. Bands play several nights a week, and there

are plenty of other events. No matter what day you attend, expect to find a diverse gay-straight crowd. When the weather's warm, the large patio out back is especially popular and the midday dance parties are *the* place to be. ⊠ *3158 Mission St., between César Chavez and Valencia Sts., Mission* ☎ *415/282–3325* ⊕ *www.elriosf.com.*

Elbo Room. This popular two-story space has a little something for everyone. The main bar downstairs is quaint and swanky with tables, booths, and classic arcade games. Hit the upstairs to see up-and-coming artists before they hit the bigtime. The music includes Afro-Cuban, indie rock, jazz, and more. ⊠ *647 Valencia St., between 17th and 18th Sts., Mission* ☎ *415/552–7788* ⊕ *www.elbo.com.*

Zeitgeist. It's a bit divey, a bit rock and roll, but a good place to relax with a cold one or an ever-popular (and ever-strong) Bloody Mary in the large beer "garden" (there's not much greenery) on a sunny day. Grill food is available, and if you're lucky one of the city's most famous food-cart operators, the Tamale Lady, will drop by. If you own a trucker hat, a pair of Vans, and a Pabst Blue Ribbon T-shirt, you'll fit right in. ⊠ *199 Valencia St., at Duboce Ave., Mission* ☎ *415/255–7505* ⊕ *www. zeitgeistsf.com.*

GAY NIGHTLIFE

Martuni's. A mixed crowd enjoys cocktails in the semi-refined environment of this bar where the Castro, the Mission, and Hayes Valley intersect; variations on the martini are a specialty. In the intimate back room a pianist plays nightly, and patrons take turns boisterously singing show tunes. Martuni's often gets busy after symphony and opera performances—Davies Hall and the Opera House are both within walking distance. ■ TIP➔ **The Godiva Chocolate Martini is a crowd favorite.** ⊠ *4 Valencia St., at Market St., Mission* ☎ *415/241–0205.*

POTRERO HILL

MUSIC CLUBS

Bottom of the Hill. This is a great live-music dive—in the best sense of the word—and truly the epicenter for Bay Area indie rock. The club has hosted some great acts over the years, including the Strokes and Throwing Muses. Rap and hip-hop acts occasionally make it to the stage. ⊠ *1233 17th St., at Texas St., Potrero Hill* ☎ *415/621–4455* ⊕ *www.bottomofthehill.com.*

WESTERN ADDITION

MUSIC CLUBS

The Fillmore. This is *the* club that all the big names, from Coldplay to Clapton, want to play. San Francisco's most famous rock-music hall presents national and local acts: rock, reggae, grunge, jazz, folk, acid house, and more. Go upstairs to view the amazing collection of rock posters lining the walls. At the end of each show, free apples are set near the door, and staffers hand out collectible posters. ■ TIP➔ **Avoid steep service charges by purchasing tickets at the club's box office on Sunday**

from 10 to 4. ⊠ *1805 Geary Blvd., at Fillmore St., Western Addition* ☎ *415/346–6000* ⊕ *www.thefillmore.com.*

PERFORMING ARTS

Sophisticated, offbeat, and often ahead of the curve, San Francisco's performing arts scene supports world-class opera, ballet, and theater productions, along with alternative-dance events, avant-garde plays, groundbreaking documentaries, and a slew of spoken-word and other literary happenings.

The best guide to the arts is printed in the "Datebook" section and the "96 Hours" section of the *San Francisco Chronicle* (⊕ *www.sfgate. com*). Also check out the city's free alternative weeklies, including *SF Weekly* (⊕ *www.sfweekly.com*) and the *San Francisco Bay Guardian* (⊕ *www.sfbg.com*).

Online, SF Station (⊕ *www.sfstation.com*) has a frequently updated arts and nightlife calendar. *San Francisco Arts Monthly* (⊕ *www.sfarts. org*), which is published at the end of the month, has arts features and events listings, plus a helpful "Visiting San Francisco?" section. For offbeat, emerging-artist performances, consult CounterPULSE (⊕ *www. counterpulse.org*).

TICKETS

City Box Office. This charge-by-phone service sells tickets for many performances and lectures. You can also buy tickets online, or in person on weekdays from 9:30 to 5:30. ⊠ *180 Redwood St., Suite 100, off Van Ness Ave., between Golden Gate Ave. and McAllister St., Civic Center* ☎ *415/392–4400* ⊕ *www.cityboxoffice.com.*

San Francisco Performances. SFP brings an eclectic array of top-flight global music and dance talents to various venues—mostly the Yerba Buena Center for the Arts, Davies Symphony Hall, and Herbst Theatre. Artists have included Yo-Yo Ma, Edgar Meyer, the Paul Taylor Dance Company, and Midori. Tickets can be purchased in person through City Box Office, online, or by phone. ⊠ *500 Sutter St., Suite 710, Financial District* ☎ *415/392–2545* ⊕ *www.performances.org.*

TIX Bay Area. Half-price, same-day tickets for many local and touring shows go on sale (cash only) at the TIX booth in Union Square, which is open daily from 10 to 6. Discount purchases can also be made online. ⊠ *Powell St. between Geary and Post Sts., Union Sq.* ☎ *415/433–7827* ⊕ *www.tixbayarea.com.*

DANCE

Fodor's Choice
★

San Francisco Ballet. For ballet lovers the nation's oldest professional company is reason alone to visit the Bay Area. SFB's performances, for the past three decades under direction of Helgi Tomasson, have won critical raves. The primary season runs from February through May. The repertoire includes full-length ballets such as *Don Quixote* and *Sleeping Beauty*; the December presentation of *The Nutcracker* is truly spectacular. The company also performs bold new dances from star choreographers such as William Forsythe and Mark Morris, alongside modern classics by George Balanchine and Jerome Robbins. Tickets are available at the **War Memorial Opera House.** ⊠ *War Memorial Opera House, 301 Van Ness Ave., at Grove St., Civic Center* ☎ *415/865–2000* ⊕ *www.sfballet.org* ⊙ *Weekdays 10–4.*

FILM

Fodor's Choice **Castro Theatre.** A large neon sign marks the exterior of this 1,400-plus
★ seat art-deco movie palace whose exotic interior transports you back to 1922, when the theater first opened. High-profile festivals present films here, and classic revivals and foreign flicks also unfold. ■TIP➔ **Lines for the Castro's popular sing-along movie musicals often trail down the block.** ⊠ *429 Castro St., near Market St., Castro* ☎ *415/621–6350* ⊕ *www.castrotheatre.com.*

MUSIC

Fodor's Choice **San Francisco Symphony.** One of America's top orchestras performs from
★ September through May, with additional summer performances of light classical music and show tunes. The orchestra and its charismatic music director, Michael Tilson Thomas, known for his daring programming of 20th-century American works, often perform with soloists of the caliber of Andre Watts, Gil Shaham, and Renée Fleming. The symphony's adventurous projects include its collaboration with the heavy metal band Metallica. ■TIP➔ **Deep discounts on tickets are often available through Travelzoo, Groupon, and other vendors.** ⊠ *Davies Symphony Hall, 201 Van Ness Ave., at Grove St., Civic Center* ☎ *415/864–6000* ⊕ *www.sfsymphony.org.*

SFJAZZ Center. Jazz legends Branford Marsalis and Herbie Hancock have performed at the snazzy center, as have Rosanne Cash and world-music favorite Esperanza Spaulding. The sightlines and acoustics here impress. Shows often sell out quickly. ⊠ *201 Franklin St., Hayes Valley* ☎ *866/920–5299* ⊕ *www.sfjazz.org.*

MUSIC FESTIVALS

Fodor's Choice **Stern Grove Festival.** The nation's oldest continual free summer music
★ festival hosts Sunday-afternoon performances of symphony, opera, jazz, pop music, and dance. The amphitheater is in a beautiful eucalyptus grove, perfect for picnicking before the show. World-music favorites such as Ojos de Brujas, Seu Jorge, and Shuggie Otis get the massive crowds dancing. ■TIP➔ **Shows generally start at 2 pm, but arrive hours earlier if you want to see the performances up close—and dress for cool weather, as the fog often rolls in.** ⊠ *Sloat Blvd. at 19th Ave., Sunset* ☎ *415/252–6252* ⊕ *www.sterngrove.org.*

OPERA

Fodor's Choice **San Francisco Opera.** Founded in 1923, this internationally recognized
★ organization has occupied the War Memorial Opera House since the building's completion in 1932. From September through January and June through July, the company presents a dozen or so operas. SF

Opera frequently collaborates with European companies and presents unconventional, sometimes edgy projects designed to attract younger audiences. Translations are projected above the stage during most non-English productions. ⊠ *War Memorial Opera House, 301 Van Ness Ave., at Grove St., Civic Center* ☎ *415/864–3330 tickets* ⊕ *www. sfopera.com* ☞ *Box office: 199 Grove St., at Van Ness Ave.; open Mon. 10–5, Tues.–Fri. 10–6.*

PERFORMING ARTS CENTERS

Fodor's Choice ★ **War Memorial Opera House.** With its soaring vaulted ceilings and marble foyer, this elegant 3,146-seat venue, built in 1932, rivals the Old World theaters of Europe. Part of the San Francisco War Memorial and Performing Arts Center, which also includes Davies Symphony Hall and Herbst Theatre, this is the home of the San Francisco Opera and the San Francisco Ballet. ⊠ *301 Van Ness Ave., at Grove St., Civic Center* ☎ *415/621–6600* ⊕ *www.sfwmpac.org.*

Fodor's Choice ★ **Yerba Buena Center for the Arts.** Across the street from the San Francisco Museum of Modern Art and abutting a lovely urban garden, this performing arts complex schedules interdisciplinary art exhibitions, touring and local dance troupes, music, film programs, and contemporary theater events. You can depend on the quality of the productions at Yerba Buena. Film buffs often come here to check out the San Francisco Cinematheque (*www.sfcinematheque.org*), which showcases experimental film and digital media. And dance enthusiasts can attend concerts by a roster of city companies that perform here, including Smuin Ballet/SF (*www.smuinballet.org*), ODC/San Francisco (*www. odcdance.org*), the Margaret Jenkins Dance Company (*www.mjdc.org*), and Alonzo King's Lines Ballet (*www.linesballet.org*). The Lamplighters (*www.lamplighters.org*), an alternative opera that specializes in Gilbert and Sullivan, also performs here. ⊠ *3rd and Howard Sts., SoMa* ☎ *415/978–2787* ⊕ *www.ybca.org.*

THEATER

American Conservatory Theater. One of the nation's leading regional theater companies presents about eight plays a year, from classics to contemporary works, often in repertory. The season runs from early fall to late spring. In December ACT stages a beloved version of Charles Dickens's *A Christmas Carol.* ⊠ *415 Geary St., Union Sq.* ☎ *415/749–2228* ⊕ *www.act-sf.org.*

Fodor's Choice ★ **Teatro ZinZanni.** In a fabulous antique Belgian dance-hall tent, contortionists, chanteuses, jugglers, illusionists, and circus performers entertain audiences who dine on a surprisingly good five-course dinner. The show, which ran for 11 years on a waterfront pier, is scheduled to debut in its new permanent home in 2015. During summer and on most weekends, reservations are essential. ⊠ *Broadway and the Embarcadero, Northern Waterfront* ☎ *415/438–2668* ⊕ *www.zinzanni.org.*

SPORTS AND THE OUTDOORS

San Francisco's surroundings—the bay, ocean, mountains, and forests—make getting outdoors away from the city a no-brainer. Muir Woods, Point Reyes, and Stinson Beach in Marin County offer dozens of opportunities for exploring the natural beauty of the Bay Area. But the peninsular city—with its many green spaces, steep inclines, and breathtaking views—has plenty to offer itself.

BASEBALL

FAMILY **San Francisco Giants.** Three World Series titles (2010, 2012, and 2014)
Fodor's Choice and the classic design of AT&T Park lead to sellouts for nearly every
★ home game the National League team plays. ⊠ *AT&T Park, 24 Willie Mays Plaza, between 2nd and 3rd Sts., SoMa* ☎ *415/972–2000, 800/734–4268* ⊕ *sanfrancisco.giants.mlb.com.*

GETTING TICKETS
The park is small and there are 30,000 season-ticket holders (for 43,000 seats), so Giants tickets for popular games routinely sell out the day they go on sale. If tickets aren't available at Tickets.com, try the team-approved reseller StubHub! (⊕ *www.stubhub.com*) or even try showing up on game day—there are usually plenty of scalpers, some selling at reasonable prices.

BIKING

San Francisco Bicycle Coalition. The San Francisco Bicycle Coalition has extensive information about the policies and politics of riding and lists local events for cyclists on its website. You can download (but not print) a PDF version of the *San Francisco Bike Map and Walking Guide.* ⊠ *833 Market St., 10th fl.* ☎ *415/431–2453* ⊕ *www.sfbike.org.*

WHERE TO RENT
Bike and Roll. You can rent bikes at this national outfit's locations from $32 per day to $58; discounted weekly rates are available, and complimentary maps are provided. ⊠ *899 Columbus Ave., at Lombard St., North Beach* ☎ *415/229–2000* ⊕ *www.bikethegoldengate.com.*

Blazing Saddles. This outfitter with branches all around San Francisco rents bikes for $8 to $9 an hour ($32 to $60 a day), depending on the type of bike, and shares tips on sights to see along the paths. ⊠ *2715 Hyde St., at Beach St., Fisherman's Wharf* ☎ *415/202–8888* ⊕ *www.blazingsaddles.com.*

FOOTBALL

San Francisco 49ers. The city's NFL team recently debuted its new Levi's Stadium. The state-of-the-art facility, 44 miles south of San Francisco, has more than 13,000 square feet of HD video boards. The 49ers may have left town, but the team hasn't forgotten SF cuisine: restaurateur and season-ticket holder Michael Mina opened Tailgate, based on his Bourbon and Steak restaurants, within the stadium's towering walls.

Home games usually sell out far in advance. **Ticketmaster** (*www.ticketmaster.com*) and **StubHub!** (*www.stubhub.com*) are sources for single-game tickets. ⊠ *Levi's Stadium, 4949 Marie P. DeBartolo Way, Santa Clara ✛ from San Francisco, take U.S. 101 south to the Lawrence Expressway and follow signs* ☏ *800/745–3000 Ticketmaster, 866/788–2482 StubHub!, 415/464–9377 Santa Clara stadium* ⊕ *www.49ers.com*

HIKING

Hiking options in and around San Francisco include everything from the easygoing Golden Gate Promenade along the city's waterfront to the more rigorous sections of the Bay Area Ridge Trail. And there are plenty of great hikes to be had in the Presidio.

Bay Area Ridge Trail. Hills and mountains—including Mt. Tamalpais in Marin County and Mt. Diablo in the East Bay, which has the second-longest sight lines anywhere in the world after Mt. Kilimanjaro—form a ring around the Bay Area. The newest completed stretch of Ridge Trail connects the Pacific Overlook and the Golden Gate Overlook in the Presidio area of San Francisco, offering up the most spectacular views. The Bay Area Ridge Trail is an ongoing project to connect all of the region's ridgelines. The trail is currently more than 340 miles long, but when finished it will extend more than 550 miles, stretching from San Jose to Napa and encompassing all nine Bay Area counties. One of the trail's most impressive ridgelines can be found on Mt. Tamalpais, in Marin County. ⊕ *ridgetrail.org.*

FAMILY **Golden Gate National Recreation Area (GGNRA).** This huge, protected area encompasses the San Francisco coastline, the Marin Headlands, and Point Reyes National Seashore. It's veined with hiking trails, and many guided walks take place. You can find current schedules at visitor centers in the Presidio and Marin Headlands; they're also online at ⊕ *www.nps.gov/goga/parknews.* For descriptions of locations within the recreation area—along with rich color photographs, hiking information, and maps—pick up a copy of *Guide to the Parks,* available in local bookstores or online from the **Golden Gate National Parks Conservancy** (⊕ *www.parksconservancy.org).* ⊠ *Bldg. 201, Fort Mason* ☏ *415/561–4700* ⊕ *www.nps.gov/goga.*

FAMILY
Fodor's Choice
★
Golden Gate Promenade. This great walk passes through Crissy Field, taking in marshlands, kite-flyers, beachfront, and windsurfers, with the Golden Gate Bridge as a backdrop. The 3.3-mile walk is flat and easy—it should take about two hours round-trip. If you begin at Aquatic Park, you'll end up practically underneath the bridge at Fort Point Pier. ■TIP➜ **If you're driving, park at Fort Point and do the walk from west to east.** It can get blustery, even when it's sunny, so be sure to layer.

FAMILY **Presidio.** Hiking and biking trails wind through nearly 1,500 acres of woods and hills in the Presidio, past old redbrick military buildings and jaw-dropping scenic overlooks with bay and ocean views. Rangers and docents lead guided hikes and nature walks throughout the year. For a current schedule, pick up a copy of the quarterly *Park News* at the Presidio Visitor Center, in the park's Main Post area, or go online. The promenade at Crissy Field leads north past views of the Golden Gate

Bridge. If it's open, fortify yourself with coffee or snacks at the **Warming Hut** (⊠ *983 Marine Dr., off Long Ave.*) before following the paved road that continues on to the Civil War–era Fort Point, which sits under the bridge. ⊠ *Presidio Visitors Center, 105 Montgomery St. at Lincoln Blvd.* ☎ *415/561–4323* ⊕ *www.nps.gov/prsf.*

RUNNING

San Francisco is spectacular for running. There are more than 7 miles of paved trails in and around **Golden Gate Park**; circling **Stow Lake** and then crossing the bridge and running up the path to the top of Strawberry Hill is a total of 2½ miles. An enormously popular route is the 2-mile raised bike path that runs from Lincoln Way along the ocean, at the southern border of Golden Gate Park, to Sloat Boulevard, which is the northern border of the San Francisco Zoo. (Stick to the park's interior when it's windy, as ocean gusts can kick up sand.) From Sloat Boulevard you can pick up the **Lake Merced** bike path, which loops around the lake and the golf course, to extend your run another 5 miles.

The paved path along the **Marina** provides a 1½-mile (round-trip) run along a flat, well-paved surface and has glorious bay views. Start where Laguna Street crosses Marina Boulevard, then run west along the Marina Green toward the Golden Gate Yacht Club, which is close to the docks at the northern end of Marina Boulevard. On weekends beware: you'll have to wind through the crowds—but those views are worth it. You can extend your Marina run by jogging the paths through the restored wetlands of Crissy Field, just past the yacht harbor, then up the hill to the Golden Gate Bridge.

The *San Francisco Bike Map and Walking Guide*, which indicates hill grades on city streets by color, is a great resource. Online, check the **San Francisco Road Runners Club** site (⊕ *www.sfrrc.org*) for some recommended routes and links to several local running clubs.

SHOPPING

With its grand department stores and funky secondhand boutiques, San Francisco summons a full range of shopping experiences. From the anarchist bookstore to the mouthwatering specialty-food purveyors at the gleaming Ferry Building, the local shopping opportunities reflect the city's various personalities. Visitors with limited time often focus their energies on the high-density Union Square area, where several major department stores tower over big-name boutiques. But if you're keen to find unique local shops, consider moving beyond the square's radius.

Each neighborhood has its own distinctive finds, whether it's 1960s housewares, cheeky stationery, or vintage Levi's. If shopping in San Francisco has a downside, it's that real bargains can be few and far between. Sure, neighborhoods such as the Lower Haight and the Mission have thrift shops and other inexpensive stores, but you won't find many discount outlets in the city, where rents are sky-high and space is at a premium.

UNION SQUARE

ART GALLERIES

Fodor'sChoice
★
Fraenkel Gallery. This renowned gallery represents museum-caliber photographers or their estates, including Nicholas Nixon, Nan Goldin, Richard Misrach, and Garry Winogrand. Recent shows have included work by Robert Adams, Idris Khan, and Hiroshi Sugimoto. Most shows feature one or two artists, but the annual "Several Exceptionally Good Recently Acquired Pictures" showcases the range of works the gallery exhibits. ⊠ *49 Geary St., 4th fl., between Kearny St. and Grant Ave., Union Sq.* ☎ *415/981–2661* ⊕ *fraenkelgallery.com* ⊙ *Closed Sun. and Mon.*

Fodor'sChoice
★
John Berggruen Gallery. Twentieth-century American and European paintings are displayed throughout three airy floors. Some recent exhibitions have included the works of Robert Kelly and Isca Greenfield-Sanders. Look for thematic shows here too; past exhibits have had titles such as Summer Highlights and Four Decades. ⊠ *228 Grant Ave., at Post St., Union Sq.* ☎ *415/781–4629* ⊕ *www.berggruen.com* ⊙ *Closed Sun.*

CLOTHING: MEN AND WOMEN

Fodor'sChoice
★
Margaret O'Leary. If you can only buy one piece of clothing in San Francisco, make it a hand-loomed, cashmere sweater by this Irish-born local legend. The perfect antidote to the city's wind and fog, the sweaters are so beloved by San Franciscans that some of them never wear anything else. Pick up an airplane wrap for your trip home, or a media cozy to keep your iPod toasty. Another store is in Pacific Heights, at 2400 Fillmore Street. ⊠ *1 Claude La., at Sutter St., just west of Kearny St., Union Sq.* ☎ *415/391–1010* ⊕ *www.margaretoleary.com.*

Scotch & Soda. With clean tailored lines and deep solid colors, there is something elegant yet cutting-edge for every age here. Based on Amsterdam couture, and carrying European labels, this hive of a shop is cool but friendly; it also has an old but new feel to it. The Bodycon Peplum dress is a classic, as is the men's stretch wool blazer. This is a good place to visit if you're looking for a new pair of denims, or a cool shirt for a night out. ⊠ *59 Grant Ave., between Geary and O'Farrell Sts., Union Sq.* ☎ *415/644–8334* ⊕ *www.scotch-soda.com.*

DEPARTMENT STORES

Fodor'sChoice
★
Gump's. It's a San Francisco institution, dating to the 19th century, and it's a strikingly luxurious one. The airy store exudes a museumlike vibe, with its large decorative vases, sumptuous housewares, and Tahitian-pearl display. It's a great place to pick up gifts, such as the Golden Gate Bridge note cards or silver-plated butter spreaders in a signature Gump's box. ⊠ *135 Post St., near Kearny St., Union Sq.* ☎ *415/982–1616* ⊕ *www.gumps.com.*

Nordstrom. Somehow Nordstrom manages to be all things to all people, and this location, with spiral escalators circling a four-story atrium, is no exception. Whether you're an elegant lady of a certain age shopping for a new mink coat or a teen on the hunt for a Roxy hoodie, the salespeople are known for being happy to help. Nordstrom carries the best selections in town of designers such as Tory Burch, but its own brands

The Beat movement of the 1950s was born in San Francisco's most famous bookstore, City Lights.

have loyal followings, too. ■TIP→ **The café upstairs is a superb choice for a shopping break.** ⊠ *Westfield Shopping Centre, 865 Market St., at 5th St., Union Sq.* ☎ *415/243–8500* ⊕ *shop.nordstrom.com.*

FURNITURE, HOUSEWARES, AND GIFTS

Fodor's Choice
★
Diptyque. The original Diptyque boutique in Paris has attracted a long line of celebrities. You can find the full array of scented candles and fragrances in this chic shop that would be at home on the boulevard St-Germain. Trademark black-and-white labels adorn the popular L'eau toilet water, scented with geranium and sandalwood. Candles come in traditional and esoteric scents, including lavender, basil, leather, and fig tree. Also available are Mariage Frères teas. ⊠ *171 Maiden La., near Stockton St., Union Sq.* ☎ *415/402–0600* ⊕ *www.diptyqueparis.com.*

CHINATOWN

TOYS AND GADGETS

Chinatown Kite Shop. The kites sold here range from basic diamond shapes to box- and animal-shaped configurations. ■TIP→ **Colorful dragon kites make great souvenirs.** ⊠ *717 Grant Ave., near Sacramento St., Chinatown* ☎ *415/989–5182* ⊕ *www.chinatownkite.com.*

SOMA

BOOKS

Fodor's Choice
★
Chronicle Books. This local beacon of publishing produces inventively designed fiction, cookbooks, art books, and other titles, as well as diaries, planners, and address books—all of which you can purchase at

three airy and attractive spaces. The other stores are at 680 2nd Street, near AT&T Park, and 1846 Union Street, in Cow Hollow. ⌂ *Metreon Westfield Shopping Center, 165 4th St., near Howard St., SoMa* ☎ *415/369–6271* ⊕ *www.chroniclebooks.com.*

FOOD AND DRINK

K&L Wine Merchants. More than any other wine store, this one has an ardent cult following around town. The friendly staffers promise not to sell what they don't taste themselves, and weekly events—on Thursday from 5 pm to 6:30 pm and Saturday from noon to 3 pm—open the tastings to customers. The best-seller list for varietals and regions for both the under- and over-$30 categories appeals to the wine lover in everyone. ⌂ *638 4th St., between Brannan and Townsend Sts., SoMa* ☎ *415/896–1734* ⊕ *www.klwines.com.*

HAYES VALLEY

FOOD AND DRINK

Arlequin Wine Merchant. If you like the wine list at Absinthe Brasserie, you can walk next door and pick up a few bottles from its highly regarded sister establishment. This small, unintimidating shop carries hard-to-find wines from small producers. Why wait to taste? Crack open a bottle on the patio out back. ⌂ *384 Hayes St., at Gough St., Hayes Valley* ☎ *415/863–1104* ⊕ *www.arlequinwinemerchant.com.*

Miette Confiserie. There is truly nothing sweeter than a cellophane bag tied with blue-and-white twine and filled with malt balls or chocolate sardines from this European-style apothecary. Grab a gingerbread cupcake or a tantalizing macaron or some shortbread. The pastel-color cake stands make even window-shopping a treat. ⌂ *449 Octavia Blvd., between Hayes and Fell Sts., Hayes Valley* ☎ *415/626–6221* ⊕ *www. miette.com.*

NORTH BEACH

BOOKS

Fodor's Choice ★ **City Lights Bookstore.** The city's most famous bookstore is where the Beat movement of the 1950s was born. Neal Cassady and Jack Kerouac hung out in the basement, and now regulars and tourists while hours away in this well-worn space. The upstairs room holds impressive poetry and Beat literature collections. Poet Lawrence Ferlinghetti, the owner, remains involved in the workings of this three-story shop. City Lights Publishers, which issued the poet Allen Ginsberg's *Howl* in 1956, publishes a dozen new titles each year. ⌂ *261 Columbus Ave., at Broadway St., North Beach* ☎ *415/362–8193* ⊕ *www.citylights.com.*

FOOD AND DRINK

Fodor's Choice ★ **Molinari Delicatessen.** This store has been making its own salami, sausages, and cold cuts since 1896. Other homemade specialties include meat and cheese ravioli, tomato sauces, and fresh pastas. ■ **TIP→ Do like the locals: grab a made-to-order sandwich for lunch and eat it at one of the sidewalk tables or over at Washington Square Park.** ⌂ *373 Columbus Ave., at Vallejo St., North Beach* ☎ *415/421–2337.*

EMBARCADERO

FARMERS' MARKETS

Fodor's Choice ★ **Ferry Plaza Farmers' Market.** The partylike Saturday edition of the city's most upscale and expensive farmers' market places baked goods, gourmet cheeses, smoked fish, and fancy pots of jam alongside organic basil, specialty mushrooms, heirloom tomatoes, handcrafted jams, and juicy-ripe locally grown fruit. On Saturday about 100 vendors pack along three sides of the building, and sandwiches and other prepared foods are for sale in addition to fruit, vegetable, and other samples free for the nibbling. Smaller markets take place on Tuesday and Thursday. (The Thursday one doesn't operate from about late December through March.) ⊠ *Ferry Plaza, at Market St., Embarcadero* ☎ *415/291–3276* ⊕ *www. ferrybuildingmarketplace.com* ☉ *Tues. and Thurs. 10–2, Sat. 8–2.*

THE HAIGHT

MUSIC

Fodor's Choice ★ **Amoeba Music.** With more than 2.5 million new and used CDs, DVDs, and records at bargain prices, this warehouselike offshoot of the Berkeley original carries titles you can't find on Amazon. No niche is ignored—from electronica and hip-hop to jazz and classical—and the stock changes daily. ■ TIP→ Weekly in-store performances attract large crowds. ⊠ *1855 Haight St., between Stanyan and Shrader Sts., Haight* ☎ *415/831–1200* ⊕ *www.amoeba.com.*

THE MISSION

ART GALLERIES

Southern Exposure. An artist-run, nonprofit gallery, this is an established venue for cutting-edge art. In addition to exhibitions, lectures, performances, and film, video screenings take place. ⊠ *3030 20th St., at Alabama St., Mission* ☎ *415/863–2141* ⊕ *soex.org* ☉ *Closed Sun. and Mon.*

FURNITURE, HOUSEWARES, AND GIFTS

Fodor's Choice ★ **Paxton Gate.** Elevating gardening to an art, this serene shop offers beautiful earthenware pots, amaryllis and narcissus bulbs, decorative garden items, and coffee-table books such as *An Inordinate Fondness for Beetles*. The collection of taxidermy and preserved bugs provides more unusual gift ideas. A couple of storefronts away is too-cute Paxton Gate Curiosities for Kids, jam-packed with retro toys, books, and other stellar finds. ⊠ *824 Valencia St., between 19th and 20th Sts., Mission* ☎ *415/824–1872* ⊕ *www.paxtongate.com.*

PACIFIC HEIGHTS

BEAUTY

Benefit Cosmetics. You can find this locally based line of cosmetics and skin-care products at Macy's and Sephora, but it's much more fun to come to one of the eponymous boutiques. No-pressure salespeople dab you with whimsical makeup such as Ooh La Lift concealer and Tinted

Love, a stain for lips and cheeks. ✉ *2117 Fillmore St., between California and Sacramento Sts., Pacific Heights* ☎ *415/567–0242* ⊕ *www.benefitcosmetics.com.*

JAPANTOWN

BOOKS

Kinokuniya Bookstore. The selection of English-language books about Japanese culture—everything from medieval history to origami instructions—is one of the finest in the country. Kinokuniya is the city's biggest seller of Japanese-language books. Dozens of glossy Asian fashion magazines attract the young and trendy; the manga and anime books and magazines are wildly popular, too. ✉ *Kinokuniya Bldg., 1581 Webster St., at Geary Blvd., Japantown* ☎ *415/567–7625* ⊕ *www.kinokuniya.com/us.*

6

THE BAY AREA

WELCOME TO THE BAY AREA

TOP REASONS TO GO

★ **Bite into the "Gourmet Ghetto":** Eat your way through this area of North Berkeley, starting with a slice of perfect pizza from the Cheese Board (just look for the line).

★ **Find solitude at Point Reyes National Seashore:** Hike beautifully rugged—and often deserted—beaches at one of the most beautiful places on earth, period.

★ **Sit on a dock by the bay:** Admire the beauty of the Bay Area from the rocky, picturesque shores of Sausalito or Tiburon.

★ **Go bar-hopping in Oakland's hippest hood:** Spend an evening swinging through the watering holes of Uptown, Oakland's artsy-hip and fast-rising corner of downtown.

★ **Walk among giants:** Walking into Muir Woods, a mere 12 miles north of the Golden Gate Bridge, is like entering a cathedral built by God.

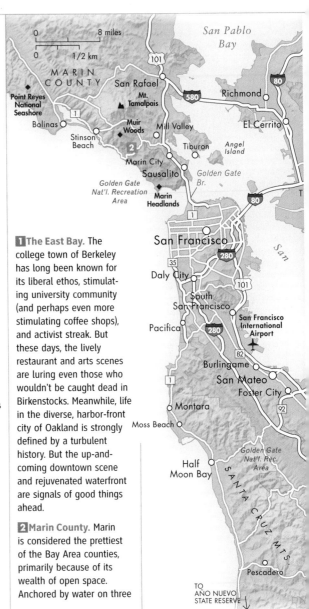

1 The East Bay. The college town of Berkeley has long been known for its liberal ethos, stimulating university community (and perhaps even more stimulating coffee shops), and activist streak. But these days, the lively restaurant and arts scenes are luring even those who wouldn't be caught dead in Birkenstocks. Meanwhile, life in the diverse, harbor-front city of Oakland is strongly defined by a turbulent history. But the up-and-coming downtown scene and rejuvenated waterfront are signals of good things ahead.

2 Marin County. Marin is considered the prettiest of the Bay Area counties, primarily because of its wealth of open space. Anchored by water on three

sides, the county is mostly parkland, including long stretches of undeveloped coastline. The picturesque small towns here—Sausalito, Tiburon, Mill Valley, and Bolinas among them—may sometimes look rustic, but they're mostly in a dizzyingly high tax bracket. There's a reason why people call BMWs "basic Marin wheels."

GETTING ORIENTED

East of the city, across the San Francisco Bay, lie Berkeley and Oakland, in what most Bay Area residents refer to as the East Bay. These two towns have distinct personalities, but life here feels more relaxed than in the city—though every bit as vibrant. Cross the Golden Gate Bridge and head north to reach Marin County's rolling hills and green expanses, where residents enjoy a haute-suburban lifestyle. Farther afield, the wild land-scapes of the Muir Woods, Mt. Tamalpais, Stinson Beach, and Point Reyes National Seashore await.

6

Berkeley

Redwood Regional Park

24

580

1

THE EAST BAY

Oakland

880

Oakland International Airport

San Leandro

Francisco

580

Hayward

92

Bay

880

Union City

680

Belmont

Fremont

101

84

San Francisco Bay National Wildlife Refuge

Redwood City

84

880

35

Palo Alto

Stanford University

101

Milpitas

Mountain View

237

280

85

Santa Clara

101

San Jose

280

TO BIG BASIN REDWOODS STATE PARK

85

Updated by
Denise M. Leto

It's rare for a metropolis to compete with its suburbs for visitors, but the view from any of San Francisco's hilltops shows that the Bay Area's temptations extend far beyond the city limits. East of town are two energetic urban centers, Berkeley and Oakland. Famously radical Berkeley is also comfortably sophisticated, while Oakland has an art and restaurant scene so hip that it pulls San Franciscans to this side of the bay. To the north is Marin County, the beauty queen, with dramatic coastal scenery of breathtaking beauty and chic, affluent villages like Tiburon and Mill Valley.

PLANNING

WHEN TO GO

As with San Francisco, you can visit the rest of the Bay Area comfortably at any time of year, and it's especially nice in late spring and fall. Unlike in San Francisco, though, the surrounding areas are reliably sunny in summer—it gets hotter as you head inland. Even the rainy season has its charms, as hills that are golden the rest of the year turn a rich green and wildflowers become plentiful. Precipitation is usually the heaviest between November and March. Berkeley is a university town, so the rhythm of the school year might affect your visit. It's easier to navigate the streets and find parking near the university between semesters, but there's also less buzz around town.

GETTING HERE AND AROUND

BART TRAVEL

Using public transportation to reach Berkeley or Oakland is ideal. The under- and aboveground BART (Bay Area Rapid Transit) trains make stops in both towns. Trips to either take about a half hour one-way from the center of San Francisco. BART does not serve Marin County.

Contacts BART ☎ 510/465–2278 ⊕ www.bart.gov.

BOAT AND FERRY TRAVEL

For sheer romance, nothing beats the ferry; there's service from San Francisco to Sausalito, Tiburon, and Larkspur in Marin County, and to Alameda and Oakland in the East Bay.

The Golden Gate Ferry crosses the bay to Sausalito from San Francisco's Ferry Building (⊠ *Market St. and the Embarcadero*). Blue & Gold Fleet ferries depart daily for Sausalito and Tiburon from Pier 41 at Fisherman's Wharf; weekday commuter ferries leave from the Ferry Building for Tiburon. The trip to Sausalito takes from 25 minutes to an hour; to Tiburon, it takes from 25 to 55 minutes.

The Angel Island–Tiburon Ferry sails to the island daily from April through October and on weekends the rest of the year.

The San Francisco Bay Ferry runs several times daily between San Francisco's Ferry Building or Pier 41 and Alameda, and Jack London Square in Oakland; one-way tickets cost $6.25. The trip lasts from 20 to 45 minutes, depending on your departure point, and leads to Oakland's waterfront shopping and restaurant district. Purchase tickets on board.

Boat and Ferry Lines Angel Island–Tiburon Ferry ☎ 415/435-2131 ⊕ www.angelislandferry.com. **Blue & Gold Fleet** ☎ 415/705-8200 ⊕ www.blueandgoldfleet.com. **Golden Gate Ferry** ☎ 511 ⊕ www.goldengateferry.org. **San Francisco Bay Ferry** ☎ 510/522-3300 ⊕ sanfranciscobayferry.com.

BUS TRAVEL

Golden Gate Transit buses travel to Sausalito, Tiburon, and Mill Valley from Folsom and Main streets—the Transbay Temporary Terminal—and from other points in San Francisco. For Mt. Tamalpais State Park and West Marin (Stinson Beach, Bolinas, and Point Reyes Station), take one of the many routes to Marin City and transfer there to the West Marin Stagecoach (schedules vary). San Francisco Muni bus 76X runs hourly from Sutter and Sansome streets to the Marin Headlands Visitor Center on weekends and major holidays only. The trip takes about 45 minutes.

Though much less convenient than BART, AC Transit buses run between the Transbay Temporary Terminal and the East Bay. AC Transit's F and FS lines stop near the university and 4th Street shopping, respectively, in Berkeley. Lines C and P travel to Piedmont in Oakland. The O bus stops at the edge of Chinatown near downtown Oakland.

Bus Lines AC Transit ☎ 511 ⊕ www.actransit.org. **Golden Gate Transit** ☎ 511 ⊕ www.goldengate.org. **San Francisco Muni** ☎ 311 ⊕ www.sfmta.com. **West Marin Stagecoach** ☎ 415/526-3239 ⊕ www.marintransit.org.

CAR TRAVEL

To reach the East Bay from San Francisco, take Interstate 80 East across the San Francisco–Oakland Bay Bridge. Head east from the University Avenue exit to reach U.C. Berkeley; there's a parking garage on Channing Way near the campus. For Oakland, take Interstate 580 off the Bay Bridge. To reach downtown and the waterfront, take Interstate 980 from Interstate 580 and exit at 12th Street. Both trips take about 30 minutes unless it's rush hour or a weekend afternoon, when you should count on an hour.

Head north on U.S.101 and cross the Golden Gate Bridge to reach all points in Marin by car, essential to visit the outer portions unless you want to spend all day on the bus. From San Francisco, the towns of Sausalito and Tiburon and the Marin Headlands and Point Reyes National Seashore are accessed off U.S. 101. The coastal route, Highway 1, also known as Shoreline Highway, can be accessed off U.S. 101 as well. Follow this road to Mill Valley, Muir Woods, Mt. Tamalpais State Park, Muir Beach, Stinson Beach, and Bolinas. From Bolinas, you can continue north on Highway 1 to Point Reyes. Depending on traffic, it takes from 20 to 45 minutes to get to the Marin Headlands, Sausalito, and Tiburon; driving directly to Point Reyes from San Francisco takes about 90 minutes in moderate traffic if you drive north on U.S. 101 and west on Sir Francis Drake Boulevard. Trips to Muir Woods take from 35 minutes to an hour from San Francisco. Add another 30 minutes for the drive to Stinson Beach (the curving roads make the going slower), 10 more if you continue on to Bolinas. The drive from Bolinas to Point Reyes takes an additional half hour.

RESTAURANTS

The Bay Area is home to popular, innovative restaurants such as Chez Panisse in Berkeley and Commis in Oakland—for which reservations must be made well in advance. Expect an emphasis on locally grown produce, hormone-free meats, and California wines. Many Marin cafés don't serve dinner, and dinner service ends on the early side. (No 10 pm reservations in that neck of the woods.)

HOTELS

Hotels in Berkeley and Oakland tend to be standard-issue, but many Marin hotels package themselves as cozy retreats. Summer in Marin is often booked well in advance, despite weather that can be downright chilly. Check for special packages during this season. *Hotel reviews have been shortened. For full information, visit Fodors.com.*

WHAT IT COSTS			
$	$$	$$$	$$$$
Restaurants	under $16	$16–$22	$23–$30	over $30
Hotels	under $151	$151–$199	$200–$250	over $250

Restaurant prices are the average cost of a main course at dinner or, if dinner is not served, at lunch. Hotel prices are the lowest cost of a standard double room in high season.

TOURS

Best Bay Area Tours. Morning and afternoon tours of Muir Woods and Sausalito include at least two hours in the redwoods—longer than most tours—before heading on to Sausalito. Tours also make a stop in the Marin Headlands on the way back to the city to enjoy fantastic views. Knowledgeable guides lead small tours in comfortable vans, and hotel pickup is included. ☎ *415/543–8687, 877/705–8687* ⊕ *bestbayareatours. com* ✉ *From $60.*

Dylan's Tours. Spend three hours exploring San Francisco with some of the friendliest local guides around, then head to Muir Woods for an hour among giant redwoods, with a stop in Sausalito on the way back. Groups are limited to 14 people; past patrons rave about the tour's in-the-know feel. ⊠ *782 Columbus Ave., North Beach, San Francisco* ☎ *415/932–6993* ⊕ *dylanstours.com* ✆ *From $75.*

Extranomical Tours. Take a combination Muir Woods–Sausalito tour with Extranomical, and you can choose to ferry back to San Francisco from Sausalito. Another tour combines a Muir Woods visit with a Wine Country excursion. ☎ *866/231–3752* ⊕ *www.extranomical.com* ✆ *From $77.*

Great Pacific Tour Co. Morning and afternoon tours to Muir Woods and Sausalito run 3½ hours, with hotel pickup, in 14-passenger vans. ☎ *415/626–4499* ⊕ *www.greatpacifictour.com* ✆ *From $65.*

THE EAST BAY

When San Franciscans refer to it, the East Bay often means nothing more than what you can see across the bay from the city—mainly Oakland and Berkeley. There's far more here—industrial-chic Emeryville, the wooded ranchland of Walnut Creek, and sprawling, urban Richmond, to name a few other communities—but Berkeley, anchored by its world-class university, and Oakland, which struggles with violence but has booming arts, nightlife, and restaurant scenes, are the magnets that draw folks across the bay.

BERKELEY

2 miles northeast of Bay Bridge.

The birthplace of the Free Speech Movement, the radical hub of the 1960s, the home of arguably the nation's top public university, and the city whose government condemned the bombing of Afghanistan—Berkeley is all of those things. The city of 100,000 facing San Francisco across the bay is also culturally diverse, a breeding ground for social trends, a bastion of the counterculture, and an important center for Bay Area writers, artists, and musicians. Berkeley residents, students, and faculty spend hours nursing various coffee concoctions while they read, discuss, and debate at any of the dozens of cafés that surround the campus. It's the quintessential university town, and many who graduated years ago still bask in daily intellectual conversation, great weather, and good food. Residents will walk out of their way to go to the perfect bread shop or consult with their favorite wine merchant.

Oakland may have Berkeley beat when it comes to cutting-edge arts, and the city may have forfeited some of its renegade 1960s spirit over the years, but unless a guy in a hot-pink satin body suit, skullcap, and cape rides a unicycle around *your* town, you'll likely find Berkeley offbeat indeed.

GETTING HERE AND AROUND

BART is the easiest way to get to Berkeley from San Francisco. Alight at the Downtown Berkeley (not North Berkeley) station, and walk a block up Center Street to get to the western edge of campus. AC Transit buses F and FS lines stop near the university and 4th Street shopping. By car, take I–80 east across the Bay Bridge then take the University Avenue exit through downtown Berkeley to the campus or take the Ashby Avenue exit and turn left on Telegraph Avenue. Once you arrive, explore on foot. Berkeley is very pedestrian-friendly.

ESSENTIALS

Visitor Information Visit Berkeley ⊠ *2030 Addison St., Suite 102, Berkeley* ☎ *510/549–7040* ⊕ *www.visitberkeley.com.*

EXPLORING
TOP ATTRACTIONS

4th Street. Several blocks centering on 4th Street north of University Avenue have evolved from light industrial uses into an upscale shopping and dining district. The compact area is busiest on bright weekend afternoons. Stained Glass Garden, Builders Booksource, and the Apple Store are among shoppers' favorites, along with a slew of boutiques and wonderful paper stores. ■TIP➜ A walk through the East Bay Vivarium, at 1827 5th Street, where turtles swim, Amazonian snakes slither, and baby mice (dinner) cower, is better than a walk through the reptile house at the zoo—and it's free. ⊠ *4th St., between University Ave. and Delaware Sts., Berkeley* ⊕ *www.fourthstreet.com.*

QUICK BITES

Cheese Board Pizza. With a jazz combo playing in the storefront and a long line snaking down the block, Cheese Board Pizza taps into the pulse of the Gourmet Ghetto. The cooperatively owned takeout spot and restaurant draws devoted customers with the smell of just-baked garlic, fresh vegetables, and perfect sauces: one pizza a day, always vegetarian. For just a nibble, the Cheese Board bakery–cheese shop next door sells cookies, muffins, scones, bialys, and the best sourdough baguettes in town. ⊠ *1504–1512 Shattuck Ave., at Vine St., Berkeley* ☎ *510/549–3055* ⊕ *cheeseboardcollective.coop/pizza* .

Fodor's Choice ★

Gourmet Ghetto. The success of Chez Panisse restaurant attracted other food-related enterprises to its stretch of Shattuck Avenue, and the area surrounding the intersection of Shattuck and Vine Street became known as the Gourmet Ghetto. Foodies will do well to spend a couple of hours here, poking around the food shops, grabbing a quick bite, or indulging in a full meal at one of the neighborhood's many excellent eateries.

The line stretches down the block in front of **Cheese Board Pizza,** at 1512 Shattuck, where live jazz bands sometimes serenade the diners that spill out onto the sidewalk and median. Next door is the **Cheese Board Collective**—worker owned since 1971—and its fabulous bakery and extensive cheese counter. Next door to Chez Panisse, César (No. 1515) wine bar and tapas house is a good place for an afternoon quaff or late-night drink.

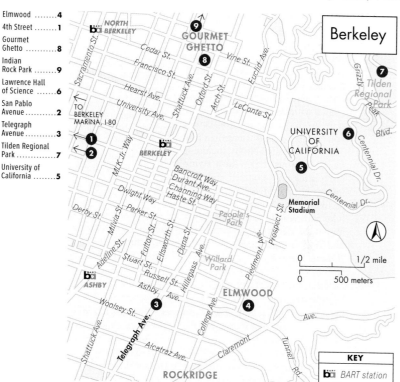

The small food stands of **Epicurious Garden,** at 1509–1513 Shattuck, sell everything from sushi to gelato. Out back, you can find a small terraced garden—the best place to sit—that winds up four levels and ends at the **Imperial Tea Court.** Around the corner just off Vine Street is **Love at First Bite,** a cupcakery that sells scrumptious confections. Across Vine, the **Vintage Berkeley** wine shop occupies the historic former pump house at No. 2113; the offerings here are shrewdly selected and reasonably priced. Coffee lovers of the **Peet's** persuasion may want to pay respects at No. 2124, where the famed roaster got its start; the small café includes a display chronicling Peet's history.

South of Cedar Street in the next block of Shattuck is the art-filled **Guerilla Cafe** (No. 1620), a breakfast and lunch spot beloved for its waffles (the Blue Bottle Coffee doesn't hurt). Also look for the **Local Butcher Shop** (No. 1600), with locally sourced meat and hearty made-to-order sandwiches. A former Ritz-Carlton chef brings white-linen quality to his to-go counter, **Grégoire,** around the corner on Cedar Street (No. 2109). In the block north of Vine Street on Shattuck are popular **Saul's** deli and restaurant and beautiful **Masse's Pastries.** On Thursday, an organic farmers' market thrives here. We could go on, but you get the idea. ⊠ *Shattuck Ave. between Cedar and Rose Sts., North Berkeley* ⊕ *www.gourmetghetto.org.*

FAMILY **Tilden Regional Park.** The **Regional Parks Botanic Garden** is the star of this 2,000-acre park in the hills east of the U.C. Berkeley campus. Botanically speaking, a stroll through the garden, which focuses on native plants of California, provides a whirlwind tour of the entire state. At the garden's visitors center, you can pick up information about Tilden's other attractions, including its picnic spots, Lake Anza swimming site, golf course, and hiking trails (the paved **Nimitz Way,** at Inspiration Point, is a popular hike with wonderful sunset views). ■TIP→ Children love Tilden Park's miniature steam trains; Little Farm, where kids can feed the animals; and the vintage carousel with wooden animals. ⊠ *Regional Parks Botanic Garden, Wildcat Canyon Rd. and South Park Dr., Tilden Park* ☎ *510/544–2747* ⊕ *www.ebparks.org/parks/tilden* ☝ *Free to park and botanic garden* ☉ *Park daily 5 am–10 pm; garden daily 8:30–5 (5:30 in summer).*

> ## A TASTING TOUR
>
> For an unforgettable foodie experience, take Lisa Rogovin's **Culinary Walking Tour** (☎ *415/806–5970* ⊕ *www.edibleexcursions.net*). You'll taste your way through the Gourmet Ghetto, learn some culinary history, and meet the chefs behind the food. Tours ($88) take place on Thursday from 11 to 2:15 and Saturday from 10 to 1.

University of California. Known simply as "Cal," the founding campus of California's university system is one of the leading intellectual centers in the United States and a major site for scientific research. Chartered in 1868, the university sits on 178 oak-covered acres split by Strawberry Creek. Bounded by Bancroft Way to the south, Hearst Avenue to the north, Oxford Street to the west, and Gayley Road to the east, Cal has more than 35,000 students and a full-time faculty of 1,600.

Below are a few places of note on campus:

Berkeley Art Museum & Pacific Film Archive. The museum's collection spans five centuries and is strong on mid-20th-century art, particularly abstract expressionist works. The archive is a major venue for foreign, independent, and avant-garde film. BAM/PFA is closed until 2016, when it reopens at a new location: ⊠ *Oxford St. at Center St.* ☎ *510/642–0808 museum, 510/642–1124 film info* ⊕ *www.bampfa. berkeley.edu.* ⊠ *Berkeley* ⊕ *www.berkeley.edu.*

Berkeley Visitor Information Center. You can get your bearings here and find out about campus events. Free 90-minute tours leave from here on weekdays. ⊠ *101 Sproul Hall, Bancroft Way at Telegraph Ave.* ☎ *510/642–5215* ⊕ *visitors.berkeley.edu* ☉ *Weekdays 8:30–4:30, tours at 10 am (also 1 pm in Apr.).*

Sather Tower. Weekend campus tours leave from this landmark, popularly known as the Campanile, at 10 am on Saturday and 1 pm on Sunday. The 307-foot structure, modeled on St. Mark's Tower in Venice, can be seen for miles. For a view of the campus and beyond, take the elevator up 175 feet, then walk another 38 steps to the observation deck. ☝ *Elevator $3* ☉ *Weekdays 10–4, Sat. 10–5, Sun. 10–1:30 and 3–5.*

Berkeley's Political History

Those looking for traces of Berkeley's politically charged past need go no further than Sather Gate. Both the Free Speech Movement and the fledgling political life of actor-turned-politician Ronald Reagan have their roots here. It was next to Sather Gate, on September 30, 1964, that a group of students defied the University of California–Berkeley chancellor's order that all organizations advocating "off-campus issues" (such as civil rights and nuclear disarmament) keep their information tables off campus. Citation of the tablers brought more than 400 sympathetic students into Sproul Hall that afternoon. They stayed until 3 am, setting a precedent of protest that would be repeated in the coming months, with students jamming Sproul Hall in greater numbers each time.

Conservative U.C. president Clark Kerr eventually backed down and allowed student groups to pass out information on campus. By then, the Free Speech Movement had gathered momentum, and the conflict had made a national hero of student leader Mario Savio. Political newcomer Ronald Reagan played on Californians' unease about the unruly Berkeley students in his successful 1966 bid for governor, promising to rein in the "unwashed kooks."

By the end of the 1960s, the cohesion of the groups making up the Free Speech Movement had begun to fray. Some members began questioning the efficacy of sit-ins and other nonviolent tactics that had, until then, been the hallmark of Berkeley student protests. The Black Panthers, headquartered just over the border in Oakland, were ascending into the national spotlight, and their "take no prisoners" approach appealed to some Berkeley activists who had seen little come of their efforts to affect national policy.

By 1969 both Robert Kennedy and Martin Luther King Jr. were dead, and the issue of the day—stopping the flow of troops heading to Vietnam—was not as easy as overpowering a school administration's resistance to free speech. But a more dramatic clash with the university came when it brought in police units to repossess People's Park, a university-owned plot of land at Telegraph Avenue and Haste Street that students and community members had adopted as a park. On the afternoon of May 15, 1969, nearly 6,000 students and residents moved to reclaim the park. In the ensuing riot, police and sheriff's deputies fired both tear gas and buckshot, blinding one observer and killing another. Governor Ronald Reagan ordered the National Guard into Berkeley. Despite a ban on public assembly, crowds continued to gather and march in the days after the first riot. The park changed hands several times in the following tear-gas-filled months, with the fence coming down for the last time in 1972.

A colorful mural on the side of Amoeba Records (Haste Street at Telegraph Avenue) offers the protestors' version of park history. Although the areas around People's Park and Sather Gate may seem quiet now, issues such as affirmative action and tuition increases still bring protests to the steps of Sproul. Protests over civil rights, war, and other inequities march through the center of the campus, though students also gather to rally for sports events, social gatherings, and shows of school spirit.

6

The University of California is the epicenter of Berkeley's energy and activism.

Sproul Plaza. The site of free-speech and civil-rights protests in the 1960s, the plaza remains a platform for political and social activists, musicians, and students. Preachers orate atop milk crates, amateur entertainers bang on makeshift drum sets, and protesters distribute leaflets about everything from marijuana to the Middle East. Walk through at noon for the liveliest show of student spirit. ✉ *Telegraph Ave. at Bancroft Way.*

University of California Botanical Garden. Thanks to Berkeley's temperate climate, about 13,500 species of plants from all over the world flourish in this 34-acre garden. Free tours are given on Thursdays and weekends at 1:30; the views are breathtaking. ✉ *200 Centennial Dr.* ☎ *510/643–2755* ⊕ *botanicalgarden.berkeley.edu* ✉ *$10, free 1st Wed. of month* ☉ *Daily 9–5, closed 1st Tues. of month.*

WORTH NOTING

Elmwood. Shops and cafés pack this pleasant neighborhood centered on College Avenue, just south of the U.C. campus. You'll know you're here when you see the logo for the beloved art-house cinema and performance space, the **Elmwood theater,** near College and Ashby avenues, though you're just as apt to see a line snaking outside nearby **Ici Ice Cream,** at 2948 College. All the treats here are made on the premises. While you're waiting, check out the architectural details of the nearby pre–World War II storefronts. Century-old shingled houses line the tree-shaded streets nearby. ✉ *College Ave. between Dwight Way and Alcatraz Ave., Elmwood, Berkeley.*

Indian Rock Park. An outcropping of nature in a sea of North Berkeley homes, this is an unbeatable spot for a sunset picnic. You know you've reached the rock when you see amateur rock climbers clinging precariously to its side. After-work walkers and cuddling couples, all watching the sun sinking beneath the Golden Gate Bridge, join you at the top. Come early to grab a spot on the rock while it's still light. ⊠ *950 Indian Rock Ave., at Shattuck Ave., Berkeley* ⚏ *Free* ⊙ *Daily 6 am–10 pm.*

Lawrence Hall of Science. At this hands-on science museum, kids can look at insects under microscopes, solve crimes using chemical forensics, and explore the physics of baseball. Out front they'll climb on Pheena, a life-size blue-whale model, and clamber over a giant strand of DNA. Out back, it's all about how earthquakes and water have shaped the bay, and from all vantage points sweeping views of the bay and beyond can be had. On weekends come special lectures, demonstrations, and planetarium shows. ⊠ *1 Centennial Dr., Berkeley* ☏ *510/642–5132* ⊕ *www. lawrencehallofscience.org* ⚏ *$12, planetarium $4 extra* ⊙ *Daily 10–5.*

San Pablo Avenue. Berkeley's diversity is front and center along this evolving north–south artery in West Berkeley, where the old and new stand side by side: sari shops and a Mexican grocery do business near a hipster dive bar, a bait-and-tackle store, a typewriter store, and a dozen cool boutiques, all cheek by jowl in an eight-block microhood that doesn't have a name . . . yet.

Start a block north of University Avenue at the **Albatross Pub** (No. 1822), a neighborhood favorite where grad students have been playing darts and eating free popcorn for 50 years. Tuck into solid Pakistani food at **Indus Village** (No. 1920) and stop by the **Halal Food Market** (No. 1964), then cross University Avenue. Duck into **Mi Tierra Foods** (No. 2082) for piñatas and chorizo—notice the Mission District–like mural—and **Middle East Market** (No. 2054) for rose water and rockin' baklava. **Café V** (No. 2056) has fresh, reliably good, and reasonably priced Vietnamese food, and pretty much everyone loves the thin-crust pies at **Lanesplitter Pizza & Pub** (No. 2033). The coffee at **Local 123** (No. 2049) is strong, delicious, and beautiful, and the back patio is a lovely surprise.

Old-fashioned, family-run **Country Cheese** (No. 2101) has hundreds of cheeses, of course, but it also carries great bulk foods and makes a heck of a sandwich to order. Or grab a table at industrial-cute **Gaumenkitzel** (No. 2121) and tuck in to schnitzel and other traditional German fare. The pierced-and-tattooed set loves **Acme Bar & Company** (No. 2115) for its Bloody Marys and whiskey selection.

As you move south, you'll pass lots of home-decor shops. Witness the reupholstering genius on display at **Mignonne Décor** (No. 2447). One of the Bay Area's oldest salvage shops, **Ohmega Salvage** (Nos. 2400–2407) makes for fun browsing, though its claw-foot tubs and Victorian window frames are pricey.

At the corner of Dwight Way, stop for more caffeine at **Caffè Trieste** (No. 2500), Berkeley's homey branch of North Beach's bohemian coffee bar. Arousing browsing can be had at sex-positive, woman-friendly **Good Vibrations** (No. 2504). Find wonderful gifts at **Juniper Tree**

6

Supplies (No. 2520), with everything for the soap and candle maker, and **Kiss My Ring** (No. 2522), which stocks jewelry designed by the owner. ✉ *San Pablo Ave., between Delaware and Parker Sts., Berkeley.*

Telegraph Avenue. Cafés, bookstores, poster shops, and street vendors line Berkeley's student-oriented thoroughfare, a bustling, if shabby, place to whiff the city's famed counterculture. T-shirt sellers and tarot-card readers come and go on a whim, but **Rasputin Music** (No. 2401), **Amoeba Music** (No. 2455), and **Moe's Books** (No. 2476) are neighborhood landmarks worth checking out. Allen Ginsberg wrote his acclaimed poem "Howl" at **Caffe Mediterraneum** (No. 2475), a relic of 1960s-era café culture that also lays claim to inventing the café latte. **■ TIP→ Panhandlers are omnipresent on Telegraph; take care at night, when things get edgier.** ✉ *South of university from Bancroft Way, Berkeley.*

WHERE TO EAT

Dining in Berkeley is a low-key affair; even in the finest restaurants, most folks dress casually. Late diners be forewarned: Berkeley is an "early to bed" kind of town.

$ SOUTHERN 🍴 **Angeline's Louisiana Kitchen.** The exposed brick walls, maps of Louisiana, ceiling fans, and New Orleans music create a festive atmosphere at Angeline's. Specialties include Voo Doo Shrimp with blue lake beans, crawfish étouffée, and buttermilk fried chicken. The Creole pecan pie is so good you'll be coming back for more. [$] *Average main: $15* ✉ *2261 Shattuck Ave., near Kittredge St., Berkeley* ☎ *510/548–6900* 🌐 *www.angelineskitchen.com* 🕘 *No lunch Mon.*

$ AMERICAN FAMILY 🍴 **Bette's Oceanview Diner.** Buttermilk pancakes are just one of the specialties at this 1930s-inspired diner complete with checkered floors and burgundy booths. Huevos rancheros and lox and eggs are other breakfast options; kosher franks, generous slices of pizza, and a slew of sandwiches are available for lunch. The wait for a seat at breakfast can be quite long; thankfully, 4th Street was made for strolling. **■ TIP→ If you're starving, head to Bette's to Go, next door, for takeout.** [$] *Average main: $10* ✉ *1807 4th St., near Delaware St., 4th Street, Berkeley* ☎ *510/644–3230* 🌐 *www.bettesdiner.com* ✍ *Reservations not accepted* 🕘 *No dinner.*

$$ SPANISH 🍴 **César.** In true Spanish style, dinners are served late at César, whose kitchen closes at 11:30 pm on Friday and Saturday and at 11 pm the rest of the week. Couples spill out from its street-level windows on warm nights, or rub shoulders at the polished bar or center communal table. Founded by a trio of former Chez Panisse chefs, César is like a first cousin to that stalwart eatery right next door, each restaurant recommending the other if there's a long wait ahead. For tapas and perfectly grilled *bocadillos* (small sandwiches), there's no better choice. The bar also makes a mean martini and has an impressive wine list. **■ TIP→ Come early to get seated quickly and to hear your tablemates; the room gets loud when the bar is in full swing.** [$] *Average main: $20* ✉ *1515 Shattuck Ave., at Vine St., North Berkeley* ☎ *510/883–0222* 🌐 *cesarberkeley.com* ✍ *Reservations not accepted.*

$$$$
AMERICAN
Fodor's Choice
★

✕ **Chez Panisse Café & Restaurant.** At Chez Panisse even humble pizza is reincarnated, with innovative toppings of the freshest local ingredients. The downstairs portion of Alice Waters's legendary eatery is noted for its formality and personal service. The daily-changing multicourse dinners are prix-fixe, with the cost slightly lower on weekdays. Upstairs, in the informal café, the crowd is livelier, the prices are lower, and the ever-changing menu is à la carte. The food is simpler, too: penne with new potatoes, arugula, and sheep's-milk cheese; fresh figs with Parmigiano-Reggiano cheese and arugula; and grilled tuna with savoy cabbage, for example. Legions of loyal fans insist that Chez Panisse lives up to its reputation and delivers a dining experience well worth the price. ■TIP➔ It's wise to make your reservation a few weeks ahead of your visit. $ *Average main: $100* ⊠ *1517 Shattuck Ave., at Vine St., North Berkeley* ☎ *510/548–5525 restaurant, 510/548–5049 café* ⊕ *www.chezpanisse.com* ⚱ *Reservations essential* ⊘ *Closed Sun. No lunch in the restaurant.*

$$
MODERN MEXICAN

✕ **Comal.** Relaxed yet trendy and surprisingly elegant for this university town, Comal draws a diverse, multigenerational, decidedly casual crowd for creative Mexican-influenced fare and well-crafted cocktails. The menu centers on small dishes that lend themselves to sharing: try the bright and subtle Dungeness crab with avocado, endive, and mandarins; tender and perfectly seasoned heritage pork enchiladas; or quesadillas with hen of the woods mushrooms. If you can't choose from among the more than 100 tequilas and mescals, four different flights offer samples from particular regions or family distilleries. $ *Average main: $16* ⊠ *2020 Shattuck Ave., near University Ave., Downtown, Berkeley* ☎ *510/926–6300* ⊕ *www.comalberkeley.com* ⊘ *No lunch.*

$$
TUSCAN

✕ **Corso Trattoria.** On the edge of Berkeley's Gourmet Ghetto, this lively spot serves up excellent Florentine cuisine in a spare but snazzy space. The open kitchen at the back dominates the room (which can get smoky at times), and the closely spaced tables add to the festivity of dining here. The seasonal menu might include pan-roasted sturgeon with Brussels sprouts or butter-roasted chicken breast. Side dishes are ordered separately; the baked polenta with mascarpone and Parmesan is a definite crowd pleaser. An extensive Italian wine list complements the menu; save room for the memorable panna cotta. $ *Average main: $20* ⊠ *1788 Shattuck Ave., at Delaware St., North Berkeley* ☎ *510/704–8004* ⊕ *www.trattoriacorso.com* ⊘ *No lunch.*

$$
AMERICAN

✕ **Gather.** Here organic, sustainable, and all things Berkeley reside harmoniously beneath one tasty roof. This vibrant, well-lit eatery boasts funky lighting fixtures, a variety of shiny wood furnishings, and banquettes made of recycled leather belts. Everything feels contemporary and local, especially the food. Locals foresee doom in the disappearance of the vegan "charcuterie," made of root vegetables, which put the restaurant on the national map; but the stinging nettles pizza is refreshing, and the grilled chicken is oh so juicy. This is a haven for vegetarian, vegan, and gluten-free eaters, but there's plenty for meat eaters to choose from, too. Desserts don't get much better than the chocolate semifreddo with Zinfandel-braised Mission figs and pine nuts.

6

Innovative Berkeley restaurant Chez Panisse focuses on seasonal local ingredients.

$ *Average main: $22* ✉ *2200 Oxford St., at Allston Way, Berkeley* ☎ *510/809–0400* ⊕ *www.gatherrestaurant.com.*

$$$
JAPANESE

✕ **Ippuku.** More Tokyo street chic than standard sushi house, this *izakaya*—the Japanese equivalent of a bar with appetizers—with bamboo-screen booths serves up surprising fare, from chicken tartare to wonderful *yakitori*, skewers such as bacon-wrapped enoki, bacon-wrapped mushrooms, and pork belly. (Anything skewered here is sure to please.) Dinner beats lunch at Ippuku, and savvy diners make reservations and arrive early for the best selection. The bar, which opens onto the street, pours an impressive array of sakes and *shōchū* (liquor distilled from sweet potatoes, rice, or barley). **$** *Average main: $23* ✉ *2130 Center St., Downtown, Berkeley* ☎ *510/665–1969* ⊕ *www. ippukuberkeley.com* ⊘ *No lunch.*

$$$
MEDITERRANEAN

✕ **Lalime's.** Inside a charming, flower-covered house, this restaurant serves dishes that reflect the entire Mediterranean region. The menu, constantly changing and unfailingly great, depends on the availability of fresh seasonal ingredients. Choices might include grilled ahi tuna, creamy Italian risotto, or grilled lamb chops. The two-level dining room is cheerful and light. Excellent and long-lived but not flashy, the restaurant has a legion of dedicated fans, many middle-aged and up. ■TIP➔ **Lalime's is a good second choice if Chez Panisse is booked up.** **$** *Average main: $27* ✉ *1329 Gilman St., at Tevlin St., North Berkeley* ☎ *510/527–9838* ⊕ *www.lalimes.com* ⌛ *Reservations essential* ⊘ *Closed Mon. No lunch.*

$ ✕**Picante.** A barnlike space full of cheerful Mexican tiles and folk-art
MEXICAN masks, Picante is a find for anyone seeking good, Cal-Mex food for a
FAMILY song. The masa is freshly ground for the tortillas and tamales (it's fun
to watch the tamale maker in action), the salsas are complex, and the
flavor combinations are inventive. Try tamales filled with butternut
squash and chilies or a simple taco of roasted poblanos and sautéed
onions; we challenge you to finish a plate of supernachos. Picante is
beloved of Berkeley families with raucous children, as they fit right in to
the festival-like atmosphere and are happily distracted by the fountain
on the back patio. $ *Average main: $12* ✉ *1328 6th St., near Camelia
St., Berkeley* ☎ *510/525–3121* ⊕ *www.picanteberkeley.com* ✐ *Reservations not accepted.*

$$ ✕**Rick & Ann's.** Haute comfort food is the focus at this cute diner across
AMERICAN from the Claremont hotel. The brunches are legendary for quality and
FAMILY value, and customers line up outside the door before the restaurant
opens on the weekend. If you come during prime brunch hours, expect
a long wait, but the soft-style eggs are worth it. Pancakes, waffles, and
French toast are more flavorful than usual, with variations such as
potato-cheese and orange–rice flour pancakes. Lunch and dinner offer
burgers, favorites such as Mom's macaroni and cheese, and chicken
potpie, but always with a festive twist. Reservations are accepted for
dinner and for lunch parties of six or more, but, alas, you can't reserve a
table for brunch. $ *Average main: $16* ✉ *2922 Domingo Ave., at Ashby
Ave., Claremont, Berkeley* ☎ *510/649–8538* ⊕ *www.rickandanns.com*
🕒 *No dinner Mon.*

$$$ ✕**Rivoli.** Italian-inspired dishes using fresh, mostly organic California
AMERICAN ingredients star on a menu that changes every three weeks. Typical
meals include line-caught fish, pastas, and inventive offerings such as
Rivoli's trademark portobello fritters with aioli. Desserts might include
pear granita with gingersnaps or a refreshing Meyer-lemon tart. A lovely
back garden and attentive service add to the overall appeal, though
some diners find the tables are too closely spaced. The small front bar
is a cozy spot for a drink and dessert, but it's standing-room-only on a
busy night. $ *Average main: $26* ✉ *1539 Solano Ave., at Neilson St.,
Berkeley* ☎ *510/526–2542* ⊕ *www.rivolirestaurant.com* ✐ *Reservations
essential* 🕒 *No lunch.*

$ ✕**Saul's.** Well known for its homemade sodas and enormous sand-
AMERICAN wiches, the Saul's of today uses sustainably sourced seafood, grass-fed
FAMILY beef, and organic eggs. The restaurant is a Berkeley institution, and its
loyal clientele swears by the pastrami sandwiches, stuffed-cabbage rolls,
and tuna melts. For breakfast, the challah French toast is so thick it's
almost too big to bite, and the deli omelets are served pancake style.
The high ceilings and red-leather booths add to the friendly, retro atmosphere. ■ **TIP➔ Don't overlook the glass deli case, where you can order
food to go.** $ *Average main: $15* ✉ *1475 Shattuck Ave., near Vine St.,
North Berkeley* ☎ *510/848–3354* ⊕ *www.saulsdeli.com* ✐ *Reservations
not accepted.*

6

WHERE TO STAY

For inexpensive lodging, investigate University Avenue, west of campus. The area can be noisy, congested, and somewhat dilapidated, but it does include a few decent motels and chain properties. All Berkeley lodgings, except for the swanky Claremont, are strictly mid-range.

$$ HOTEL **The Bancroft Hotel.** Lovingly remodeled in 2012, this green boutique hotel—across from the U.C. campus—is fresh, stylish, and completely eco-friendly. **Pros:** closest hotel in Berkeley to campus; friendly staff; many rooms have good views. **Cons:** some rooms are small; bathrooms small and need updating; no elevator. [$] *Rooms from: $155* ✉ *2680 Bancroft Way, Berkeley* ☎ *510/549–1000* 🌐 *bancrofthotel.com* 🛏 *22 rooms* 🍴 *Breakfast.*

$$$$ HOTEL FAMILY Fodor's Choice ★ **Claremont Resort and Spa.** Straddling the Oakland–Berkeley border, this amenities-rich resort—which celebrates its centennial in 2015—beckons like a gleaming white castle in the hills. **Pros:** amazing spa; supervised child care; solid business amenities; great bay views from some rooms. **Cons:** parking is pricey; resort charge for use of spa, tennis courts, pool, gym; additional fee for breakfast. [$] *Rooms from: $270* ✉ *41 Tunnel Rd., at Ashby and Domingo Aves., Claremont, Berkeley* ☎ *510/843–3000, 800/551–7266* 🌐 *www.claremontresort.com* 🛏 *249 rooms, 30 suites* 🍴 *No meals.*

$$ HOTEL **Holiday Inn Express.** Convenient to the freeway and 4th Street shopping, this peach-and-beige hotel provides good bang for the buck. **Pros:** good breakfast; short walk to restaurant options on San Pablo and University; free Internet in rooms. **Cons:** area can be noisy and congested with traffic during commute hours; neighborhood can feel sketchy after dark. [$] *Rooms from: $190* ✉ *1175 University Ave., at Curtis St., Berkeley* ☎ *510/548–1700, 866/548–1700* 🌐 *www.hiexberkeley.com* 🛏 *69 rooms, 3 suites* 🍴 *Breakfast.*

$$ HOTEL **Hotel Durant.** A mainstay of parents visiting their children at U.C. Berkeley, this boutique hotel is also a good option for those who want to be a short walk from Telegraph Avenue. **Pros:** convenient location to Cal and public transit; blackout shades; organic bathrobes. **Cons:** downstairs bar can get noisy during Cal games; parking can be pricey; service can be inept. [$] *Rooms from: $180* ✉ *2600 Durant Ave., at Bowditch St., Berkeley* ☎ *510/845–8981* 🌐 *www.hoteldurant.com* 🛏 *143 rooms* 🍴 *No meals.*

$$$ HOTEL Fodor's Choice ★ **Hotel Shattuck Plaza.** This historic boutique hotel sits amid Berkeley's downtown arts district, just steps from the U.C. campus and a short walk from the Gourmet Ghetto. **Pros:** central location; near public transit; modern facilities; good views; great restaurant. **Cons:** pricey parking; limited fitness center. [$] *Rooms from: $209* ✉ *2086 Allston Way, at Shattuck Ave., Downtown, Berkeley* ☎ *510/845–7300* 🌐 *www.hotelshattuckplaza.com* 🛏 *199 rooms, 17 suites* 🍴 *No meals.*

NIGHTLIFE AND PERFORMING ARTS

Berkeley Repertory Theatre. One of the region's highly respected resident professional companies, Berkeley Rep performs classic and contemporary plays. Well-known pieces such as *Crime and Punishment* and *The Arabian Nights* mix with edgier fare like Green Day's *American*

Idiot and Lemony Snicket's *The Composer Is Dead*. The theater's complex is in the heart of downtown Berkeley's arts district, near BART's Downtown Berkeley station. ⊠ *2025 Addison St., near Shattuck Ave., Berkeley* ☎ *510/647–2949* ⊕ *www.berkeleyrep.org.*

Berkeley Symphony Orchestra. The works of 20th-century composers are a focus of this prominent orchestra, but traditional pieces are also performed. BSO plays a handful of concerts each year, in Zellerbach Hall and other locations. ⊠ *1942 University Ave., Suite 207, Berkeley* ☎ *510/841–2800* ⊕ *www.berkeleysymphony.org.*

Cal Performances. The series, running from September through May at Zellerbach Hall and various other U.C. Berkeley venues, offers the Bay Area's most varied bill of internationally acclaimed artists in all disciplines, from classical soloists to the latest jazz, world-music, theater, and dance ensembles. Past performers include Mark Morris Dance Group, the Peking Acrobats, Arlo Guthrie, and Yo-Yo Ma. ⊠ *Zellerbach Hall, Telegraph Ave. and Bancroft Way, Berkeley* ☎ *510/642–9988* ⊕ *calperformances.org.*

Fodor's Choice ★ **Freight & Salvage Coffeehouse.** Some of the most talented practitioners of folk, blues, Cajun, and bluegrass perform in this alcohol-free space, one of the country's finest folk houses. Most tickets cost less than $30. ⊠ *2020 Addison St., between Shattuck Ave. and Milvia St., Berkeley* ☎ *510/644–2020* ⊕ *www.thefreight.org.*

SHOPPING

Fodor's Choice ★ **Amoeba Music.** Heaven for audiophiles, this legendary Berkeley favorite is *the* place to head for new and used CDs, records, cassettes, and DVDs. The dazzling stock includes thousands of titles for all music tastes. The store even has its own record label. There are branches in San Francisco and Hollywood, but this is the original. ⊠ *2455 Telegraph Ave., at Haste St., Berkeley* ☎ *510/549–1125* ⊕ *www.amoeba.com.*

Body Time. Founded in Berkeley in 1970, this local chain uses premium-quality ingredients to create its natural perfumes and skin-care and aromatherapy products. Sustainably harvested essential oils that you can combine and dilute to create your own personal fragrances are the specialty. The Citrus, Lavender-Mint, and China Rain scents are all popular. ⊠ *1950 Shattuck Ave., at Berkeley Way, Berkeley* ☎ *510/841–5818* ⊕ *www.bodytime.com.*

Kermit Lynch Wine Merchant. Credited with taking American appreciation of French wine to a higher level, this small shop is a great place to peruse as you educate your palate. The friendly salespeople can direct you to the latest French bargains. ⊠ *1605 San Pablo Ave., at Dwight Way, Berkeley* ☎ *510/524–1524* ⊕ *kermitlynch.com.*

Moe's Books. The spirit of Moe—the cantankerous, cigar-smoking late proprietor—lives on in this four-story house of books. Students and professors come here to browse the large selection of used books, including literary and cultural criticism, art titles, and literature in foreign languages. ⊠ *2476 Telegraph Ave., near Haste St., Berkeley* ☎ *510/849–2087* ⊕ *moesbooks.com.*

Fodor's Choice **Rasputin Music.** A huge selection of new music for every taste draws
★ crowds, and only in a town that also contained Amoeba Music could
Rasputin's stock of used CDs and vinyl be surpassed. ✉ *2403 Telegraph Ave., at Channing Way, Berkeley* ☎ *510/848–9004* ⊕ *www.rasputinmusic.com.*

OAKLAND

East of Bay Bridge.

Often overshadowed by San Francisco's beauty and Berkeley's storied
counterculture, Oakland's allure lies in its amazing diversity. Here you
can find a Nigerian clothing store, a beautifully renovated Victorian
home, a Buddhist meditation center, and a lively salsa club, all within
the same block.

Oakland's multifaceted nature reflects its colorful and often tumultuous
history. Once a cluster of Mediterranean-style homes and gardens that
served as a bedroom community for San Francisco, the city became a
hub of shipbuilding and industry almost overnight when the United
States entered World War II. New jobs in the city's shipyards and factories attracted thousands of workers, including some of the first female
welders, and the city's neighborhoods were imbued with a proud but
gritty spirit. In the 1960s and '70s this intense community pride gave
rise to such militant groups as the Black Panther Party and the Symbionese Liberation Army, but they were little match for the economic
hardships and racial tensions that plagued Oakland. In many neighborhoods the reality was widespread poverty and gang violence—subjects
that dominated the songs of such Oakland-bred rappers as the late
Tupac Shakur. The highly publicized protests of the Occupy Oakland
movement in 2011 and 2012 and the #BlackLivesMatter movement of
2014 and 2015 illustrated just how much Oakland remains a mosaic
of its past.

The affluent reside in the city's hillside homes, wooded enclaves like
Claremont and Montclair, which provide a warmer, more spacious,
and more affordable alternative to San Francisco, while a constant
flow of newcomers—many from Central America and Asia—ensures
continued diversity, vitality, and growing pains. Many neighborhoods
to the west and south of the city center remain run-down and unsafe,
but a renovated downtown area—sparking a vibrant arts scene—has
injected new energy into the city. Even San Franciscans, often loath to
cross the Bay Bridge, come to Uptown and Temescal for the crackling
arts and restaurant scenes there.

Everyday life here revolves around the neighborhood, with a main business strip attracting both shoppers and strollers. In some areas, such as
high-end Piedmont and Rockridge, you'd swear you were in Berkeley
or San Francisco's Noe Valley or Cow Hollow. Along Telegraph Avenue
just south of 51st Street, Temescal is pulsing with creative culinary
and design energy. These are perfect places for browsing, eating, or
just relaxing between sightseeing trips to Oakland's architectural gems,
rejuvenated waterfront, and numerous green spaces.

GETTING HERE AND AROUND

Driving from San Francisco, take Interstate 80 East across the Bay Bridge, then take Interstate 580 to the Grand Avenue exit for Lake Merritt. To reach downtown and the waterfront, take Interstate 980 from Interstate 580 and exit at 12th Street; exit at 18th Street for Uptown. For Temescal, take Interstate 580 to Highway 24 and exit at 51st Street.

By BART, use the Lake Merritt Station for the Oakland Museum and southern Lake Merritt; the Oakland City Center–12th Street Station for downtown, Chinatown, and Old Oakland; and the 19th Street Station for Uptown, the Paramount Theatre, and the north side of Lake Merritt.

By bus, take the AC Transit's C and P lines to get to Piedmont in Oakland. The O bus stops at the edge of Chinatown near downtown Oakland.

Oakland's Jack London Square is an easy hop on the ferry from San Francisco. Those without cars can take advantage of the free Broadway Shuttle, which runs from the square down Broadway through Chinatown/Old Oakland, downtown, Uptown, and Lake Merritt, all the way to 27th Street. The shuttle runs late on Friday and Saturday nights; its website has full schedule information.

Once you arrive, be aware of how quickly neighborhoods can change. Walking is safe downtown and in the Piedmont and Rockridge areas, but avoid walking west and southeast of downtown.

ESSENTIALS

Shuttle Contact Broadway Shuttle ⊠ *Oakland* ⊕ *www.meetdowntownoak. com.*

Visitor Information Visit Oakland ⊠ *Jack London Sq., 481 Water St., near Broadway, Oakland* ☎ *510/839–9000* ⊕ *visitoakland.org.*

EXPLORING

TOP ATTRACTIONS

FAMILY

Fodor'sChoice

★

Oakland Museum of California. The museum surveys the state's art, history, and natural wonders in three galleries of absorbing, detailed exhibits. You can travel through myriad ecosystems in the Gallery of California Natural Sciences, from the sand dunes of the Pacific to the coyotes and brush of the Nevada border. Kids love the lifelike wild-animal exhibits, especially the snarling wolverine and the big-eyed harbor seal. The rambling Gallery of California History includes everything from Spanish-era armor to a small but impressive collection of vintage vehicles, including a red, gold, and silver fire engine that battled the flames in San Francisco following the 1906 earthquake. Of particular interest in the Gallery of California Art are paintings by Richard Diebenkorn, Joan Brown, Elmer Bischoff, and David Park, all members of the Bay Area figurative school, which flourished here after World War II. Fans of Dorothea Lange won't want to miss the comprehensive collection of her photographs. ■TIP➔ **On Friday evening the museum is a lively scene, with live music, food trucks, and half-price admission.** ⊠ *1000 Oak St., at 10th St., Downtown, Oakland* ☎ *510/238–2200* ⊕ *www.museumca. org* ⛱*$15, $7.50 Thurs. 5–9, free 1st Sun. of month* ☉ *Wed.–Thurs. 11–5, Fri. 11–9, weekends 10–6.*

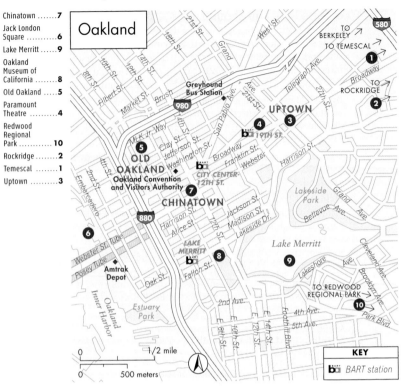

Fodor's Choice ★ **Paramount Theatre.** A glorious art-deco specimen, the Paramount operates as a venue for concerts and performances of all kinds, from the Oakland East Bay Symphony to Tom Waits and Elvis Costello. The popular monthly movie nights start off with a 30-minute Wurlitzer concert preceding classic films such as *Casablanca*. ■TIP➜ **The docent-led tours here are fun and informative.** ✉ *2025 Broadway, at 20th St., Uptown, Oakland* ☎ *510/465–6400* ⊕ *www.paramounttheatre.com* ➲ *Tour $5* ☉ *Tour 10 am on 1st and 3rd Sat. of month.*

Rockridge. This upscale neighborhood is one of Oakland's most desirable places to live. Explore the tree-lined streets that radiate out from **College Avenue** just north and south of the Rockridge BART station for a look at California bungalow architecture at its finest. By day College Avenue between Broadway and Alcatraz Avenue is crowded with shoppers buying fresh flowers, used books, and clothing; by night the same folks are back for dinner and locally brewed ales in the numerous restaurants and pubs. With its pricey specialty-food shops, **Market Hall,** an airy European-style marketplace at Shafter Avenue, is a hub of culinary activity. ✉ *Oakland* ⊕ *www.rockridgedistrict.com.*

Fodor's Choice ★ **Temescal.** Centering on Telegraph Avenue between Piedmont and South Berkeley, Temescal ("sweat house" in the language of the Aztec) is a low-pretension, moneyed-hipster hood with many young families and—gasp—middle-aged folks thrown into of the mix. A critical mass of excellent eateries, from veteran Doña Tomás and favorites Pizzaiola and Aunt Mary's to **Bakesale Betty** (⊠ *5098 Telegraph Ave.*), where folks line up for the fried-chicken sandwich on the one-item menu, and **Doughnut Dolly** (⊠ *482B 49th St.*), who fills her fried treats to order, draws folks from around the Bay Area. Old-time dive bars and check-cashing places share space with newer arrivals like crafty, local children's clothing shop **Ruby's Garden** (⊠ *5026 Telegraph Ave.*) and stalwart **East Bay Depot for Creative Reuse** (⊠ *4695 Telegraph Ave.*), where you might find a bucket of buttons or 1,000 muffin wrappers for $1 among birdcages, furniture, lunch boxes, and ribbon.

Around the corner, **Temescal Alley** (⊠ *49th St.*), a tucked-away lane of tiny storefronts, crackles with the creative energy of the craftspeople who have set up shop there. You can make some surprising finds at Crimson Horticultural Rarities and the fresh home-decor shop Bounty and Feast. ⊠ *Telegraph Ave., between 45th and 51st Sts., Temescal, Oakland* ⊕ *www.temescaldistrict.org.*

Uptown. This is where nightlife and cutting-edge art happens in Oakland, along the formerly gritty, currently crazy-cool Telegraph Avenue/ Broadway corridor north of downtown. Dozens of galleries cluster around Telegraph, showing everything from photography and video installations to glasswork and textile arts. On the first Friday of the month, thousands descend for the neighborhood's biggest happening, the gallery walk **Art Murmur** (⊕ *oaklandartmurmur.org*). In addition to galleries open late, Art Murmur has expanded into **First Friday,** a veritable festival featuring food trucks, street vendors, and live music along Telegraph Avenue. Less raucous and more intimate is the **Saturday Stroll,** with member galleries open on Saturday from 1 to 5, often with special events.

Lively restaurants with a distinctly urban vibe make the neighborhood a dining destination; favorites include friendly **Luka's Taproom and Lounge** (⊠ *2221 Broadway*); beautiful art-deco **Flora** (⊠ *1900 Telegraph Ave.*), one of the best brunch places in town; trendy, graffiti-walled **Hawker Fare** (⊠ *2300 Webster St.*), serving Asian street food; elegant **Picán** (⊠ *2295 Broadway*), for upscale Southern comfort food; and the sophisticated **Plum** (⊠ *2216 Broadway*) and its attached bar, just to name a few.

Toss in the bevy of bars, and there's plenty within walking distance to keep you busy for an entire evening: **Cafe Van Kleef** (⊠ *1621 Telegraph Ave.*), the friendly jumble that started it all Uptown; **Bar Three Fifty-Five** (⊠ *355 19th St.*), a house of great cocktails; strikingly beautiful but low-key **Dogwood** (⊠ *1644 Telegraph Ave.*), which has tasty nibbles; and **Somar** (⊠ *1727 Telegraph Ave.*), a bar, music lounge, and gallery in one. Uptown's shopping element is exploding as well, with local goods at the fore; stop by **Oaklandish** (⊠ *1444 Broadway*) for T-shirts, jeans, and everything Oaktown, and **OwlNWood** (⊠ *45 Grand Ave.*) for the coolest collection of vintage and locally designed clothing in town. The Paramount Theatre ⇨ *(see above)*, the Fox Theater ⇨ *(see Nightlife, below)*, and other art-deco architectural gems distinguish this neighborhood. ⊠ *Telegraph Ave. and Broadway from 16th to 26th Sts., Oakland.*

WORTH NOTING

Chinatown. A densely packed, bustling neighborhood, Oakland's Chinatown, unlike its San Francisco counterpart, makes no concessions to tourists. You won't find baskets of trinkets lining the sidewalk and souvenir displays in the shop windows, but supermarkets such as **Yuen Hop Noodle Company and Asian Food Products** (⊠ *824 Webster St.*), open since 1931, overflow with delicacies, and the line for sweets, breads, and towering cakes snakes out the door of **Napoleon Super Bakery** (⊠ *810 Franklin St.*). ⊠ *Between Broadway and Lakeside Dr. and between 6th and 12th Sts., Oakland* ⊕ *www.oakland-chinatown.info.*

Jack London Square. Shops, minor historic sites, restaurants, and the venerable Yoshi's jazz club line Jack London Square, named for the author of *The Call of the Wild, The Sea Wolf,* and other books. London, who was born in San Francisco, also lived in Oakland, where he spent many a day boozing and brawling in the waterfront area, most notably at the tiny **Heinold's First and Last Chance Saloon** (*48 Webster St., at Embarcadero W*). The wonderful saloon has been serving since 1883. Next door is the Klondike cabin in which London spent a summer in the late 1890s. The cabin was moved from Alaska and reassembled here in 1970.

Weekends at the square are lively, with diners filling the many outdoor patios, and shoppers perusing Sunday's farmers' market, from 9 am to 2 pm. ■TIP→ **The square is worth a peek if you've arrived on the ferry that docks here; but you'll get a better feel for Oakland checking out the Uptown, Rockridge, or Temescal neighborhoods.** ⊠ *Embarcadero W at Broadway, Oakland* ☎ *510/645–9292* ⊕ *www.jacklondonsquare.com.*

Lake Merritt. Joggers and power walkers charge along the 3-mile path that encircles this 155-acre natural saltwater lake in downtown Oakland. Crew teams often glide across the water, and boatmen guide snuggling couples in authentic Venetian gondolas (⊠ *fares start at $60 per couple for 30 minutes* ☎ *510/663–6603* ⊕ *gondolaservizio. com*). **Lakeside Park,** which surrounds the north side of Lake Merritt, has several outdoor attractions, including a small children's park and a waterfowl refuge. The lake is less an attraction than a pleasant backdrop to Oaklanders' everyday life. ■TIP→ **The nearby Grand Lake neighborhood, centering on the parallel commercial strips of Lakeshore Avenue and Grand Avenue, makes for good browsing and even better eating.** ⊠ *Lakeside Park, Bellevue and Grand Aves., Oakland* ⊕ *www. lakemerritt.org.*

Old Oakland. The restored Victorian storefronts lining four historic blocks, formerly Oakland's main business district, now contain restaurants, cafés, shops, galleries, and a three-block farmers' market that takes place on Friday morning. Architectural consistency distinguishes the area from surrounding streets, lending it a distinct neighborhood feel. Tuscany-inspired **Caffè 817** (⊠ *817 Washington St.*) serves excellent panini and bowls of café latte in an artsy atmosphere. Stop in for a deli sandwich at the Italian grocery **Ratto's International Market** (⊠ *827*

Washington St.), in business for more than a century, or head over to **Pacific Coast Brewing Company** (✉ *902 Washington St.*) for a microbrew on the patio. The **Trappist** (✉ *460 8th St.*) beer bar wins loyalty for its exhaustive selection of Belgian ales. Various pop-up boutiques and permanent shops throughout the neighborhood are reinvigorating the storefront scene. ✉ *Bordered by 7th, 10th, Clay, and Washington Sts., Oakland* 🌐 *old-oakland.com.*

Redwood Regional Park. *Sequoia sempervirens,* or coastal redwoods, grow to 150 feet tall in Redwood Regional Park, one of the few spots in the Bay Area that escaped timber-hungry loggers in the 19th century. The 1,836-acre park has forested picnic spots and dozens of hiking trails, including part of the 31-mile **Skyline National Trail,** which links Redwood to four other parks in the Berkeley–Oakland hills. From downtown Oakland take Interstate 580 east toward Hayward, exit at 35th Avenue/MacArthur Boulevard, and then take 35th Avenue east (which becomes Redwood Road). Watch for a park entrance on the left, 3 to 4 miles down the road. ✉ *7867 Redwood Rd., Oakland* ☎ *888/327–2757* 🌐 *www.ebparks.org/parks/redwood* 🎟 *Free; $5 per vehicle in season at some major entrances, $4 per trailered vehicle* ⏲ *Daily 5 am–10 pm.*

WHERE TO EAT

$$ MEDITERRANEAN 🍴 **À Côté.** This place for Mediterranean food is all about small plates, cozy tables, family-style eating—and truly excellent food. The butternut-squash ravioli, wild-boar chestnut sausage, and duck confit flatbread with apples and cantelet cheese are all fine choices, and you won't find a better plate of *pommes frites* (french fries) anywhere. The restaurant pours more than 40 wines by the glass. Among the tempting desserts here are the lemon pudding cake with lemon cream, huckleberries, and candied pistachios. Heavy wooden tables, cool tiles, and natural light make this a destination for students, families, couples, and the after-work crowd; the heated back patio is warm and welcoming in any weather. [$] *Average main: $20* ✉ *5478 College Ave., at Taft Ave., Rockridge, Oakland* ☎ *510/655–6469* 🌐 *www.acoterestaurant.com* ⏲ *No lunch.*

$ AMERICAN 🍴 **Brown Sugar Kitchen.** Chef and owner Tanya Holland turned an isolated corner in West Oakland into a breakfast and lunch destination. Influenced by her African-American heritage and her culinary education in France—and using local, organic, and seasonal products—she blends sweet and savory flavors like no one else and pairs her dishes with well-chosen wines. The dining room is fresh and bright, with a long, sleek counter, red-leather stools, and spacious booths and tables. ■ **TIP→ This is the place to come for chicken and waffles.** [$] *Average main: $15* ✉ *2534 Mandela Pkwy., at 26th St., West Oakland* ☎ *510/839–7685* 🌐 *www.brownsugarkitchen.com* ⏲ *Closed Mon. No dinner.*

$$$ AMERICAN 🍴 **Camino.** Chef-owner Russell Moore cooked at Chez Panisse for two decades before opening this restaurant with co-owner Allison Hopelain that focuses on simple, seasonal, straightforward dishes cooked in an enormous, crackling *camino* (Italian for "fireplace"). The nightly changing menu has only three entrées—each cooked over its own open fire—including one vegetarian option such as eggplant gratin. Everything is made with top-notch ingredients, including local sardines and smelts,

grilled lamb and sausage, and Dungeness crab (cooked in the fireplace with rutabagas). Camino is decorated in a Craftsman-meets-refectory style, with brick walls and two long redwood communal tables. **■ TIP→ A gin-based libation with house-made cherry and hibiscus bitters is among the perfectly crafted, seasonally inspired cocktails poured here.** [$] *Average main: $26* ✉ *3917 Grand Ave., at Boulevard Way, Grand Lake, Oakland* ☎ *510/547–5035* 🌐 *www.caminorestaurant.com* ⏲ *Closed Tues. No lunch (weekend brunch 10–2).*

$$ MODERN AMERICAN 🍴 **Chop Bar.** The walls and tables are made of reclaimed wood at this small, stylish space whose knowing, tattooed bartenders serve potent cocktails. A great neighborhood joint for every meal of the day (and brunch on weekends), Chop Bar serves upmarket gastropub grub, including favorites such as oxtail poutine, pork confit with polenta and kale, and burgers that rank among the Bay Area's best. On sunny days when the glass garage door is raised, extending the outdoor seating area out front, you'll feel like an insider who's stumbled upon an industrial neighborhood's cool secret. [$] *Average main: $20* ✉ *247 4th St., at Alice St., Jack London Square, Oakland* ☎ *510/834–2467* 🌐 *www.oaklandchopbar.com.*

$$$$ MODERN AMERICAN 🍴 **Commis.** A slender, unassuming storefront in Oakland's Piedmont neighborhood houses the only East Bay restaurant with a Michelin star. The room is simple and polished: nothing distracts from the artistry of the fixed multicourse meals ($95, wine pairing $55 additional) chef James Syhabout creates based on the season and his distinctive vision. Dishes might include poached egg yolk with smoked dates and alliums (members of the onion/garlic family) in malt vinegar, or duck roasted on the bone over charcoal with renderings, walnut, and persimmon. Diners don't see the menu until after the meal, the chef's way of ensuring that everyone comes to the table with an open mind. **■ TIP→ This isn't a place to grab a quick bite: meals last about three hours. The service is excellent.** [$] *Average main: $95* ✉ *3859 Piedmont Ave., at Rio Vista Ave., Piedmont, Oakland* ☎ *510/653–3902* 🌐 *commisrestaurant.com* ✍ *Reservations essential* ⏲ *Closed Mon. and Tues. No lunch.*

$$ MEXICAN 🍴 **Doña Tomás.** A neighborhood favorite, this spot in Oakland's hot Temescal District serves seasonal Mexican fare to a hip but low-key crowd. Mexican textiles and art adorn walls in two long rooms; there's also a vine-covered patio. Tuck into starters such as quesadillas filled with butternut squash and goat cheese and entrées such as *albondigas en sopa zanahoria* (pork-and-beef meatballs in carrot puree). Some mighty fine tequilas complement the offerings. Brunch is served on weekends. [$] *Average main: $19* ✉ *5004 Telegraph Ave., near 51st St., Temescal, Oakland* ☎ *510/450–0522* 🌐 *www.donatomas.com* ⏲ *Closed Mon. No lunch weekdays. No dinner Sun.*

$ VIETNAMESE 🍴 **Le Cheval Restaurant.** This cavernous restaurant, a lunchtime favorite, is a good place to sample *pho,* Hanoi-style beef noodle soup fragrant with star anise. Other entrées include lemon chicken, cubed beefsteak, and clay-pot snapper. It's hard to spend more than $20 for an entire meal unless you order the seven courses of beef ($28). The complimentary minibowls of soup that are placed on the table as soon as you sit down are a great balm to hungry diners, though the service is lightning-quick anyway. $ *Average main: $12* ⊠ *1019 Clay St., at 11th St., Old Oakland* ☎ *510/763–8495* ⊕ *www.lecheval.com* ⊙ *No lunch Sun.*

$$ ✕ **Luka's Taproom & Lounge.** Hip and urban, with an unpretentious vibe,
AMERICAN Luka's is a real taste of Uptown. Diners nibble on *frites* (fries) any Belgian would embrace and entrées such as crispy-skin salmon or gratinéed mac and cheese. The brews draw them in, too—a nice selection of Trappist ales complements plentiful beers on tap and international bottles—and the DJs in the adjacent lounge keep the scene going late. ■ **TIP→ Hungry night owls appreciate the late-night menu, served daily until midnight.** $ *Average main: $19* ⊠ *2221 Broadway, at West Grand Ave., Uptown, Oakland* ☎ *510/451–4677* ⊕ *www.lukasoakland.com.*

$$ ✕ **Pizzaiolo.** Apparently no length of a wait can discourage locals who
PIZZA persevere to enjoy the legendary thin-crust, wood-fired pizza served up by Chez Panisse alum Charlie Hallowell in this rustic-chic dining room. Diners—mostly neighborhood hipsters but also young families and foodies of all ages—perch in wooden chairs with red-leather backs; weathered wood floors and brick walls peeking through the plaster create an always-been-here feel. Seasonal pizza options might include wild nettles and pecorino, or rapini and house-made sausage; don't overlook nonpizza dishes such as wild steelhead salmon with fava greens, English peas, and Meyer-lemon butter. Except on Sunday, early risers get to skip the crowds and enjoy Blue Bottle Coffee and pastries from 8 until noon. $ *Average main: $20* ⊠ *5008 Telegraph Ave., at 51st St., Temescal, Oakland* ☎ *510/652–4888* ⊕ *www.pizzaiolooakland.com* ⊙ *Closed Sun. No lunch.*

$$ ✕ **Shakewell.** Two veterans of the *Top Chef* TV series opened this stylish
MEDITERRANEAN restaurant in the up-and-coming Lakeshore neighborhood, but hype aside, they're serving up creative and memorable small Mediterranean-influenced dishes. Favorites include the local squid and ink bomba (a paellalike dish baked in a wood-burning oven) and braised pork shoulder with pickled green tomatoes. The name implies an emphasis on cocktails, and you can enjoy a well-crafted one at the popular bar; also be sure to save room for dessert. Hard surfaces plus a lively crowd means the volume can get too high for some. $ *Average main: $20* ⊠ *3407 Lakeshore Ave., near Mandana Blvd., Lakeshore, Oakland* ☎ *510/251–0329* ⊕ *www.shakewelloakland.com* ⌂ *Reservations not accepted* ⊙ *Closed Mon. No lunch Tues.–Thurs.*

$$$ ✕ **Wood Tavern.** Expect a warm welcome and a lively atmosphere at this
AMERICAN longtime Rockridge favorite, a neighborhood gem with superb food and
Fodor's Choice refined service. Classic American fare includes standouts like the pork-
★ belly appetizer, anything marrow, perfect day boat scallops, and one of the best burgers around. For dessert the house-made Nutella–chocolate chip ice cream knocks it out of the park. It's wise to reserve well ahead here, but if you haven't you might score a seat at the bar. $ *Average main: $26* ⊠ *6317 College Ave., near 63rd St., Rockridge, Oakland* ☎ *510/654–6607* ⊕ *woodtavern.net* ⊙ *No lunch Sun.*

6

WHERE TO STAY

$$ HOTEL 🏨 **Best Western Plus Bayside Hotel.** Sandwiched between the serene and scenic Oakland Estuary on one side and train tracks and an eight-lane freeway on the other, this all-suites property has handsome accommodations with balconies or patios, many overlooking the water. **Pros:** attractive, budget-conscious choice; free parking; recently renovated; water views make city bustle seem far away. **Cons:** not near anything of interest; city-side rooms can be loud. [$] *Rooms from: $179* ✉ *1717 Embarcadero, off I–880, at 16th St. exit, Oakland* ☎ *510/356–2450* 🌐 *www.baysidehoteloakland.com* 🛏 *81 suites* 🍴 *Breakfast.*

$$$$ HOTEL 🏨 **Oakland Marriott City Center.** A good choice downtown for business travelers—and not bad for leisure ones, either—the Marriott, conveniently located near the Old Oakland and Uptown neighborhoods, provides comprehensive services and amenities. **Pros:** convenient location; ergonomically designed work areas; online discounts often available off-season and on weekends. **Cons:** low visual appeal; steep fee for Internet access. [$] *Rooms from: $269* ✉ *1001 Broadway, at 11th St., Downtown, Oakland* ☎ *510/451–4000* 🌐 *www.marriott.com* 🛏 *481 rooms, 8 suites* 🍴 *No meals.*

$$ HOTEL 🏨 **Waterfront Hotel.** The only bayfront hotel in town, this thoroughly modern, pleasantly appointed Joie de Vivre property sits among the appealing restaurants (including the hotel's own) of Jack London Square. **Pros:** great location; lovely views; dog-friendly. **Cons:** passing trains can be noisy on city side; parking is pricey; hotel is beginning to show its age. [$] *Rooms from: $159* ✉ *10 Washington St., Jack London Square, Oakland* ☎ *510/836–3800, 800/729–3638* 🌐 *www.jdvhotels.com* 🛏 *143 rooms* 🍴 *No meals.*

NIGHTLIFE AND PERFORMING ARTS

Artists have found relatively cheap rent and loft spaces in Oakland, giving rise to a cultural scene—visual arts, indie music, spoken word, film—that's definitely buzzing, especially in Uptown (which is pretty much downtown). Trendy bars and clubs seem to pop up by the week—everything from artisan breweries to all-out retro dives—and the beer-garden renaissance has come to Oakland in a big way. Whether you're an aficionado who likes to discuss the nose and mouthfeel of different brews or just someone who wants to enjoy a drink outside on a sunny day, you'll find something to suit you. Oakland's nightlife scene is less crowded and more intimate than what you'll find in San Francisco. Music is just about everywhere, though the most popular venues are downtown.

NIGHTLIFE

Beer Revolution. Hard-core beer geeks: with hundreds of bottled beers and 50 taps, Beer Revolution is for you. Tear yourself away from the beer lists and grab a table on the patio. ✉ *464 3rd St., at Broadway, Jack London Square, Oakland* ☎ *510/452–2337* 🌐 *www.beer-revolution.com.*

Brotzeit Lokal. If you want a water view with your brew, head to this spot east of Jack London Square and enjoy some wurst or Wiener schnitzel with your German, Belgian, or California beer. ✉ *1000 Embarcadero,* *near 10th Ave., Jack London Square, Oakland* ☎ *510/645–1905* ⊕ *brotzeitbiergarten.com* ⊘ *Closed Mon.*

Fodor'sChoice **Café Van Kleef.** Dutch artist Peter Van Kleef's candle-strewn, funky café-
★ bar crackles with creative energy. Van Kleef has a lot to do with the convivial atmosphere; the garrulous owner loves sharing tales about his quirky, floor-to-ceiling collection of pop-culture mementos. The café has a consistently solid calendar of live music, heavy on the jazz side. The drinks are among the stiffest in town. ⊠ *1621 Telegraph Ave., between 16th and 17th Sts., Uptown, Oakland* ☎ *510/763–7711* ⊕ *www.cafevankleef.com.*

Fox Theater. Willie Nelson, Counting Crows, Rebelution, and B.B. King have all played at this renovated Mediterranean Moorish–style stunner from 1928 that has good sight lines, a state-of-the-art sound system and acoustics, a bar, and other amenities. ⊠ *1807 Telegraph Ave., at 18th St., Uptown, Oakland* ☎ *510/548–3010* ⊕ *www.thefoxoakland.com.*

The Layover Music Bar and Lounge. Bright, bold, and very hip, this hang-out filled with recycled furniture is constantly evolving because everything is for sale, from the artwork to the pillows, rugs, and lamps. The busy bar serves up organic cocktails, and depending on the night, the entertainment might include comedy or live or DJ music. ⊠ *1517 Franklin St., near 15th St., Uptown, Oakland* ☎ *510/834–1517* ⊕ *www.oaklandlayover.com.*

Lost & Found. The diversions on the welcoming patio here include ping-pong, Hula-Hoops, and cornhole. The beers are great, the solid menu focuses on internationally inspired small bites, and there's a good selection of nonalcoholic drinks. ⊠ *2040 Telegraph Ave., at 21st St., Uptown, Oakland* ☎ *510/763–2040* ⊕ *www.lostandfound510.com* ⊘ *Closed Mon.*

Mua. Cuisine, cocktails, and culture—Mua puts it all together in a bright and airy former garage. The chefs serve up beautifully crafted meals like beef bone marrow and garlic prawns; the bartenders shake up elegant cocktails; and a lively crowd enjoys cultural offerings that include poetry readings, art shows, and DJ music. ⊠ *2442a Webster St., between 23rd St. and Grand Ave., Uptown, Oakland* ☎ *510/238–1100* ⊕ *www.muaoakland.com.*

The Trappist. Grand pillars, brick walls, soft lighting, and the buzz of conversation set a warm and mellow tone inside this Victorian space that's been renovated to resemble a traditional Belgian pub. The setting is definitely a draw, but the real stars are the artisan beers: more than a hundred Belgian, Dutch, and North American ones. The light fare includes panini made with organic ingredients. ⊠ *460 8th St., at Broadway, Old Oakland, Oakland* ☎ *510/238–8900* ⊕ *www.thetrappist.com.*

Telegraph. Hipsters hold court at Telegraph, where giant murals and bike wheel rims decorate the largely cement outdoor area, and great burgers pair with beers that change daily. ⊠ *2318 Telegraph Ave., at 23rd St., Uptown, Oakland* ☎ *510/444–8353* ⊕ *telegraphoakland.com.*

Fodor'sChoice **Yoshi's.** Omar Sosa and Charlie Hunter are among the musicians who
★ play at Yoshi's, one of the area's best jazz venues. Shows start at 8 pm

and 10 pm except on Sunday, when they're usually at 7 and 9. The cover runs from $20 to $60. ⊠ *510 Embarcadero St., between Washington and Clay Sts., Jack London Square, Oakland* ☎ *510/238–9200* ⊕ *www.yoshis.com.*

PERFORMING ARTS

California Shakespeare Theater. The Bay Area's largest outdoor theater event showcases three works by the Bard and one by another playwright. Performances take place east of Oakland in Orinda. ⊠ *Bruns Amphitheater, 100 California Shakespeare Theater Way, Orinda* ⊹ *From Oakland, take I–580 or Hwy. 13 to Hwy. 24 W toward Walnut Creek. Exit at Wilder Rd., and turn left* ☎ *510/548–9666 box office* ⊕ *www.calshakes.org* ☉ *Late May–early Oct.*

SPORTS AND THE OUTDOORS

BASEBALL

Oakland A's. Billy Beane of *Moneyball* fame is the general manager of the American League baseball team. Same-day tickets can usually be purchased at the **O.co Coliseum** box office (Gate D). To get to the game, take a BART train to the Coliseum station. ⊠ *O.co Coliseum, 7000 Coliseum Way, off I–880, north of Hegenberger Rd., Oakland* ☎ *510/638–4900* ⊕ *oakland.athletics.mlb.com.*

BASKETBALL

Golden State Warriors. The NBA team plays basketball at **Oracle Arena** from late October into April. BART trains serve the arena; get off at the Coliseum station. Purchase single tickets through Ticketmaster (*800/653–8000, www.ticketmaster.com*). ⊠ *Oracle Arena, 7000 Coliseum Way, off I–880, north of Hegenberger Rd., Oakland* ☎ *888/479–4667 tickets* ⊕ *www.nba.com/warriors.*

FOOTBALL

Oakland Raiders. The National Football League's brawling Oakland Raiders play at **O.co Coliseum.** Tickets are available through Ticketmaster. ⊠ *O.co Coliseum, 7000 Coliseum Way, off I–880, north of Hegenberger Rd., Oakland* ☎ *510/864–5000* ⊕ *www.raiders.com.*

SHOPPING

Pop-up shops and stylish, locally focused stores are proliferating in Old Oakland and Uptown, and Temescal's alleys are decidedly funky. The streets around Lake Merritt and Grand Lake have smaller, less fancy boutiques. College Avenue is great for upscale strolling, shopping, and people-watching.

Diesel. Wandering bibliophiles collect armfuls of the latest fiction and nonfiction at this revered shop. The loftlike space, with its high ceilings and spare design, encourages contemplation, and on chilly days a fire burns in the hearth. Past participants in the excellent authors' events have included Ian Rankin, Annie Leibovitz, Kareem Abdul-Jabbar, and Michael Moore. ⊠ *5433 College Ave., at Kales Ave., Rockridge, Oakland* ☎ *510/653–9965* ⊕ *www.dieselbookstore.com.*

Maison d'Etre. Close to the Rockridge BART station, this store epitomizes the Rockridge neighborhood's funky-chic shopping scene. Look for impulse buys like whimsical watches, imported fruit-tea blends, and funky slippers. ⊠ *5640 College Ave., at Keith Ave., Rockridge, Oakland* ☎ *510/658–2801* ⊕ *maisondetre.com.*

Fodor's Choice ★ **Oaklandish.** This is the place for Oaktown swag. What started out as a collective art project of local pride has become a celebrated brand around the Bay, and proceeds from hip Oaklandish brand T-shirts and accessories still go to support the group's free events and programs. It's good-looking stuff for a good cause. ⊠ *1444 Broadway, near 15th St., Uptown, Oakland* ☎ *510/251–9500* ⊕ *oaklandish.com.*

MARIN COUNTY

Marin is quite simply a knockout—some go so far as to call it spectacular and wild. This isn't an extravagant claim, since more than 40% of the county (180,000 acres), including the majority of the coastline, is parkland. The territory ranges from chaparral, grassland, and coastal scrub to broadleaf and evergreen forest, redwood, salt marsh, and rocky shoreline. It's well worth the drive over the Golden Gate Bridge to explore the Headlands and the stunning beauty of sprawling Point Reyes National Seashore, with more than 80 miles of shoreline.

Regardless of its natural beauty, what gave the county its reputation was Cyra McFadden's 1977 book *The Serial,* a literary soap opera that depicted the county as a bastion of hot-tubbing and "open" marriages. Indeed old-time bohemian, but also increasingly jet-set, Marinites still spend a lot of time outdoors, and surfing, cycling, and hiking are common after-work and weekend activities. Adrenaline junkies mountain bike down Mt. Tamalpais, and those who want solitude take a walk on one of Point Reyes's many empty beaches. The hot tub remains a popular destination, but things have changed since the boho days. Artists and musicians who arrived in the 1960s have set the tone for mellow country towns, but Marin is now undeniably chic, with BMWs supplanting VW buses as the cars of choice.

After exploring Marin's natural beauty, consider a stop in one of its lovely villages. Most cosmopolitan is Sausalito, the town just over the Golden Gate Bridge from San Francisco. Across the inlet from Sausalito, Tiburon and Belvedere are lined with grand homes that regularly appear on fund-raising circuits, and to the north, landlocked Mill Valley is a hub of wining and dining and tony boutiques. Book Passage, a noted bookseller in the next town, Corte Madera, hosts regular readings by top-notch authors, and Larkspur, San Anselmo, and Fairfax beyond have walkable downtown areas, each a bit folksier than the next but all with good restaurants and shops and a distinct sense of place.

In general, the farther west of U.S. 101 you go the more countrified things become, and West Marin is about as far as you can get from the big city, both physically and ideologically. Separated from the inland county by the slopes and ridges of giant Mt. Tamalpais, this territory beckons to mavericks, artists, ocean lovers, and other free spirits. Stinson Beach has tempered its isolationist attitude to accommodate out-of-towners, as have Inverness and Point Reyes Station. Bolinas, on the other hand, would prefer you not know its location.

VISITOR INFORMATION
Contact **Marin Convention & Visitors Bureau** ⊠ *1 Mitchell Blvd., Suite B, San Rafael* ☎ *415/925–2060* ⊕ *www.visitmarin.org.*

THE MARIN HEADLANDS

Due west of the Golden Gate Bridge's northern end.

The term *Golden Gate* may now be synonymous with the world-famous bridge, but it originally referred to the grassy, poppy-strewn hills flanking the passageway into San Francisco Bay. To the north of the gate lie the Marin Headlands, part of the Golden Gate National Recreation Area (GGNRA) and among the most dramatic scenery in these parts. Windswept hills plunge down to the ocean, and creek-fed thickets shelter swaying wildflowers.

GETTING HERE AND AROUND

Driving from San Francisco, head north on U.S. 101. Just after you cross the Golden Gate Bridge, take the Alexander Avenue exit. From there take the first left (signs read "San Francisco/U.S. 101 South"), go through the tunnel under the freeway, and turn right up the hill where the sign reads "Forts Barry and Cronkhite." Muni bus 76X runs hourly from Sutter and Sansome streets to the Marin Headlands Visitor Center on weekends and major holidays only. Once here, you can explore this beautiful countryside on foot.

EXPLORING

TOP ATTRACTIONS

FAMILY

Fodor's Choice
★

Marin Headlands. The headlands stretch from the Golden Gate Bridge to Muir Beach. Photographers perch on the southern headlands for spectacular shots of the city, with the bridge in the foreground and the skyline on the horizon. Equally remarkable are the views north along the coast and out to sea, where the Farallon Islands are visible on clear days.

The headlands' strategic position at the mouth of San Francisco Bay made them a logical site for World War II and cold-war military installations. Today you can explore the crumbling concrete batteries where naval guns protected the approaches from the sea. The headlands' main attractions are centered on Forts Barry and Cronkhite, which lie just across Rodeo Lagoon from each other. Fronting the lagoon is Rodeo Beach, a dark stretch of sand that attracts sand-castle builders and dog owners. The beaches at the Marin Headlands are not safe for swimming. ■TIP→ The giant cliffs are steep and unstable, so hiking down them can be dangerous. Stay on trails.

The visitor center is a worthwhile stop for its exhibits on the area's history and ecology, and kids enjoy the "please touch" educational sites and small play area inside. You can pick up guides to historic sites and wildlife at the center, as well as the park's newspaper, which has a schedule of guided walks. ⊠ *Visitor Center, Fort Barry Chapel, Fort Barry, Bldg. 948, Field and Bunker Rds., Sausalito* ☎ *415/331–1540* ⊕ *www.nps.gov/goga/marin-headlands.htm* ☉ *Park sunrise–sunset visitor center daily 9:30–4:30.*

FAMILY **Marine Mammal Center.** If you're curious about the rehabilitation of sea mammals from the Pacific—and the human practices that endanger them—stop by this facility for rescued seals, sea lions, dolphins, and otters. An observation area overlooks the pools where the animals convalesce, and nearby plaques describe what you're seeing. ■TIP➔ You'll learn even more—and get closer to the animals—on a worthwhile, docent-led tour. ⊠ *Fort Cronkhite, 2000 Bunker Rd., off U.S. 101's Alexander Ave. exit, Sausalito* ☎ *415/289–7325* ⊕ *www. marinemammalcenter.org* ✉ *Center free, tour $9* ☉ *Daily 10–5.*

Fodor's Choice
★
Nike Missile Site SF-88-L. The only accessible site of its kind in the United States provides a firsthand view of menacing cold war–era Hercules missiles and missile-tracking radar, the country's "last line of defense" against Soviet nuclear bombers. It's worth timing your visit to take the guided tour, whose highlight is a visit to the missile-launching bunker. ■TIP➔ On the first Saturday of the month the site holds an open house at which some of the docents leading walking tours are Nike veterans who describe their experiences. ⊠ *Field Rd., off Bunker Hill Rd.* ☎ *415/331–1453* ⊕ *www.nps.gov/goga/nike-missile-site.htm* ✉ *Free* ☉ *Thurs.–Sat. 12:30–3:30; guided tour at 12:45, 1:45, and 2:30* ☉ *Site sometimes closes during inclement weather.*

FAMILY **Point Bonita Lighthouse.** A restored beauty that still guides ships to safety with its original 1855 refractory lens, the lighthouse anchors the southern headlands. Half the fun of a visit is the steep ½-mile walk from the parking area through a rock tunnel, across a suspension bridge, and down to the lighthouse. Signposts along the way detail the bravado of surfmen, as the early lifeguards were called, and the tenacity of the "wickies," the first keepers of the light. ⊠ *End of Conzelman Rd.* ⊕ *www.nps.gov/goga/pobo.htm* ✉ *Free* ☉ *Sat.–Mon. 12:30–3:30.*

WORTH NOTING

Hawk Hill. Craggy Hawk Hill is the best place on the West Coast to watch the migration of eagles, hawks, and falcons as they fly south for winter: as many as 1,000 birds have been sighted in a single day. The main migration period is from September through November, and the viewing area is about 2 miles up Conzelman Road from U.S. 101; look for a Hawk Hill sign and parking right before the road becomes one way. In September and October, on rain- and fog-free weekends at noon, enthusiastic docents from the Golden Gate Raptor Observatory give free lectures on Hawk Hill, and a raptor-banding demonstration follows at 1 pm. ⊠ *Conzelman Rd., Sausalito* ⊕ *www.ggro.org.*

Headlands Center for the Arts. The center's main building, formerly the army barracks, exhibits contemporary art in a rustic natural setting; the downstairs "archive room" contains objects found and created by residents, such as natural rocks, interesting glass bottles filled with collected items, and unusual masks. Stop by the industrial gallery space, two flights up, to see what the resident visual artists are up to—most of the work is quite contemporary. ⊠ *Fort Barry, 944 Simmonds Rd., Sausalito* ☎ *415/331–2787* ⊕ *www.headlands.org* ☉ *Sun.–Thurs. noon–5.*

6

Kayakers enjoy a sunny day on the Sausalito waterfront.

SAUSALITO

2 miles north of Golden Gate Bridge.

Bougainvillea-covered hillsides and an expansive yacht harbor give Sausalito the feel of an Adriatic resort. The town sits on the northwestern edge of San Francisco Bay, where it's sheltered from the ocean by the Marin Headlands; the mostly mild weather here is perfect for strolling and outdoor dining. Nevertheless, morning fog and afternoon winds can roll over the hills without warning, funneling through the central part of Sausalito once known as Hurricane Gulch.

South on Bridgeway (toward San Francisco), which snakes between the bay and the hills, a waterside esplanade is lined with restaurants on piers that lure diners with good seafood and even better views. Stairs along the west side of Bridgeway climb the hill to wooded neighborhoods filled with both rustic and opulent homes. As you amble along Bridgeway past shops and galleries, you'll notice the absence of basic services. If you need an aspirin or some groceries (or if you want to see the locals), you'll have to head to Caledonia Street, which runs parallel to Bridgeway, north of the ferry terminus and inland a couple of blocks. The streets closest to the ferry landing flaunt their fair share of shops selling T-shirts and kitschy souvenirs. Venture into some of the side streets or narrow alleyways to catch a bit more of the town's taste for eccentric jewelry and handmade crafts.

■ TIP → The ferry is the best way to get to Sausalito from San Francisco; you get more romance (and less traffic) and disembark in the heart of downtown.

Sausalito developed its bohemian flair in the 1950s and '60s, when creative types, led by a charismatic Greek portraitist named Varda, established an artists' colony and a houseboat community here (this is Otis Redding's "Dock of the Bay"). Today more than 450 houseboats are docked in Sausalito, which has since also become a major yachting center. Some of these floating homes are ragged, others deluxe, but all are quirky (one, a miniature replica of a Persian castle, even has an elevator inside). For a close-up view of the community, head north on Bridgeway—Sausalito's main thoroughfare—from downtown, turn right on Gate Six Road, park where it dead-ends at the public shore, and enter through the unlocked gates. Keep a respectful distance; these are homes, after all, and the residents become a bit prickly from too much ogling.

GETTING HERE AND AROUND

From San Francisco by car or bike, follow U.S. 101 north across the Golden Gate Bridge and take the first exit, Alexander Avenue, just past Vista Point; continue down the winding hill to the water to where the road becomes Bridgeway. Golden Gate Transit buses 10 and 2 will drop you off in downtown Sausalito, and the ferries dock downtown as well. The center of town is flat, with plenty of sidewalks and bay views. It's a pleasure and a must to explore on foot.

ESSENTIALS

Visitor Information Sausalito Chamber of Commerce ⊠ *780 Bridgeway, Sausalito* ☎ *415/332–0505* ⊕ *www.sausalito.org.*

EXPLORING

FAMILY **Bay Area Discovery Museum.** Sitting at the base of the Golden Gate Bridge, this indoor-outdoor museum offers entertaining and enlightening hands-on exhibits for children under eight. Kids can fish from a boat at the indoor wharf, imagine themselves as marine biologists in the Wave Workshop, and play outdoors at Lookout Cove (made up of scaled-down sea caves, tidal pools, and even a re-created shipwreck). At Tot Spot, toddlers and preschoolers dress up in animal costumes and crawl through miniature tunnels. ■TIP→ From San Francisco, take U.S. 101's Alexander Avenue exit and follow signs to East Fort Baker. ⊠ *557 McReynolds Rd., at East Rd. off Alexander Ave., Sausalito* ☎ *415/339–3900* ⊕ *www.baykidsmuseum.org* ⊒ *$12, free 1st Wed. of month* ⊗ *Tues.–Sun. 9–5.*

FAMILY **Bay Model.** An anonymous-looking World War II shipyard building holds a great treasure: a sprawling (more than 1½ acres), walkable model of the entire San Francisco Bay and the San Joaquin–Sacramento River delta, complete with flowing water. The U.S. Army Corps of Engineers uses the model to reproduce the rise and fall of tides, the flow of currents, and the other physical forces at work on the bay. ⊠ *2100 Bridgeway, at Marinship Way, Sausalito* ☎ *415/332–3870 recorded information, 415/332–3871 operator assistance* ⊕ *www.spn.usace. army.mil* ⊒ *Free* ⊗ *Late May–early Sept., Tues.–Fri. 9–4, weekends 10–5; early Sept.–late May, Tues.–Sat. 9–4.*

Drinking Fountain. On the waterfront between the Hotel Sausalito and the Sausalito Yacht Club is an unusual historic landmark—a drinking

Marin
County

0   5 mi

0   5 km

fountain. It's inscribed with "Have a drink on Sally" in remembrance of Sally Stanford, the former San Francisco madam who became the town's mayor in the 1970s. Sassy Sally, as they called her, would have appreciated the fountain's eccentric custom attachment: a knee-level basin that reads "Have a drink on Leland," in memory of her beloved dog. ⊠ *Sausalito.*

QUICK
BITES

Hamburgers. Patrons queue up daily for a sandwich made from the hand-formed beef patties sizzling on the wheel-shaped grill here. Brave the line (it moves fast), get your food to go, and head to the esplanade to enjoy the sweeping views. ⊠ *737 Bridgeway, at Humboldt Ave., Sausalito* ☎ *415/332–9471* ⊘ *No dinner.*

Plaza Viña del Mar. The landmark Plaza Viña del Mar, named for Sausalito's sister city in Chile, marks the center of town. Flanked by two 14-foot-tall elephant statues (created in 1915 for the Panama-Pacific International Exposition), its fountain is a great setting for snapshots and people-watching. ⊠ *Bridgeway and Park St., Sausalito.*

Sausalito Visitors Center and Historical Exhibit. The local historical society operates the center, where you can get your bearings, learn some history, and find out what's happening in town. ⊠ *780 Bridgeway, at Bay*

St., Sausalito ☎ *415/332–0505* 🌐 *www.sausalitohistoricalsociety.com* 🕒 *Tues.–Sun. 11:30–4.*

WHERE TO EAT

$ INTERNATIONAL 🍴 **Avatar's.** "Purveyors of ethnic confusions," this Marin minichain offers Indian fusion combinations such as Punjabi burritos and pumpkin enchiladas that locals revere. The outgoing chef makes a big impression; tell him your preferences, sensitivities, and whims, and he'll create something spectacular and promise you'll want to lick the plate. The creativity of the food and the low prices more than make up for the uninspired space. [$] *Average main: $13* ✉ *2656 Bridgeway, at Coloma St., Sausalito* ☎ *415/332–8083* 🌐 *www.enjoyavatars.com* 🕒 *Closed Sun.*

$$ SEAFOOD FAMILY Fodor's Choice ★ 🍴 **Fish.** When locals want fresh seafood, they head to this gleaming dockside fish house a mile north of downtown. Order at the counter—cash only—and then grab a seat by the floor-to-ceiling windows or at a picnic table on the pier, overlooking the yachts and fishing boats. Most of the sustainably caught fish is hauled in from the owner's boats, docked right outside. Try the ceviche, crab Louis, cioppino, barbecue oysters, or anything fresh that's being grilled over the oak-wood fire. Outside, kids can doodle with sidewalk chalk on the pier. [$] *Average main: $20* ✉ *350 Harbor Dr., off Bridgeway, Sausalito* ☎ *415/331–3474* 🌐 *www.331fish.com* ✍ *Reservations not accepted* 💳 *No credit cards.*

6

$$$ FRENCH 🍴 **Le Garage.** Brittany-born Olivier Souvestre serves traditional French bistro fare in a relaxed, sidewalk café–style bayside setting. The menu is small, but the dishes are substantial in flavor and presentation. Standouts include frisée salad with poached egg, bacon, croutons, and pancetta vinaigrette; steak frites with a shallot confit and crispy fries; and a chef's selection of cheese or charcuterie with soup and mixed greens. The restaurant only seats 35 inside and 15 outside, so to avoid a long wait for lunch, arrive before 11:30 or after 1:30. [$] *Average main: $23* ✉ *85 Liberty Ship Way, off Marinship Way, Sausalito* ☎ *415/332–5625* 🌐 *www.legaragebistrosausalito.com* ✍ *Reservations essential* 🕒 *No dinner Sun.*

$ SCANDINAVIAN 🍴 **Lighthouse Cafe.** A cozy spot with a long coffee bar and dose of Scandinavian flair, this local establishment has been a favorite breakfast (served all day) and brunch destination for decades. The hearty Norwegian salmon omelet with spinach and cream cheese always hits the spot, as do the fruit pancakes and, for lunch, grilled burgers, sandwiches, and Danish specials such as meatballs with potato salad. Expect a wait. [$] *Average main: $12* ✉ *1311 Bridgeway, near Turney St., Sausalito* ☎ *415/331–3034* 🌐 *www.lighthouse-restaurants.com* ✍ *Reservations not accepted* 🕒 *No dinner.*

$$$ ITALIAN 🍴 **Poggio.** One of Sausalito's few restaurants to attract food-savvy locals and tourists, Poggio serves modern Tuscan-style cuisine in a handsome, open-wall space that spills onto the street. Expect dishes such as grilled chicken with roasted beets and sunchokes, braised artichokes with polenta, featherlight gnocchi, and pizzas from the open kitchen's wood-fired oven. Daily breakfast includes fresh-made pastries, house-made granola, and panini such as ham and eggs or prosciutto and provolone. [$] *Average main: $23* ✉ *777 Bridgeway, at Bay St.,*

Sausalito ☎ *415/332–7771* 🌐 *www.poggiotrattoria.com* ✍ *Reservations essential.*

$$$ JAPANESE Fodor's Choice ★ 🍴 **Sushi Ran.** Sushi aficionados swear that this stylish restaurant—in business for three decades—is the Bay Area's best option for raw fish, but don't overlook the excellent Pacific Rim fusions, a melding of Japanese ingredients and French cooking techniques, served up in unusual presentations. Because Sushi Ran is so highly ranked among area foodies, book from two to seven days in advance for dinner. Otherwise, expect a long wait, which you can soften by sipping one of the 45 by-the-glass sakes from the outstanding wine-and-sake bar. **■TIP→ If you arrive without a reservation and can't get a table, you can sometimes dine in the noisy bar.** [$] *Average main: $25* ✉ *107 Caledonia St., at Pine St., Sausalito* ☎ *415/332–3620* 🌐 *www.sushiran.com* ✍ *Reservations essential* ⏲ *No lunch weekends.*

WHERE TO STAY

$$$$ HOTEL 🏨 **Casa Madrona.** What began as a small inn in a 19th-century landmark mansion has expanded over the decades to include a contemporary section and hillside cottages, along with a full-service spa, all tiered down a hill in the center of Sausalito. **Pros:** elegant furniture; spacious rooms; central location. **Cons:** stairs required to access some cottages; breakfast is not included. [$] *Rooms from: $300* ✉ *801 Bridgeway, Sausalito* ☎ *415/332–0502, 800/567–9524* 🌐 *www.casamadrona.com* 🛏 *56 rooms, 1 suite, 7 cottages* 🍽 *No meals.*

$$$$ HOTEL 🏨 **Cavallo Point.** Set in the Golden Gate National Recreation Area, this luxury hotel and resort with a one-of-a-kind location on a former army post contains well-appointed eco-friendly rooms. **Pros:** stunning views; activities include a cooking classes, yoga classes, and nature walks; spa with a tea bar; art gallery; accommodating staff. **Cons:** isolated from urban amenities. [$] *Rooms from: $429* ✉ *601 Murray Circle, Fort Baker, Sausalito* ☎ *415/339–4700* 🌐 *www.cavallopoint.com* 🛏 *68 historic and 74 contemporary guest rooms* 🍽 *No meals.*

$$ B&B/INN 🏨 **Hotel Sausalito.** Handmade furniture and tasteful original art and reproductions give this well-run inn the feel of a small European hotel. **Pros:** great staff; central location; solid midrange hotel. **Cons:** no room service; some rooms feel cramped. [$] *Rooms from: $180* ✉ *16 El Portal, Sausalito* ☎ *415/332–0700, 888/442–0700* 🌐 *www.hotelsausalito.com* 🛏 *14 rooms, 2 suites* 🍽 *No meals.*

$$$$ B&B/INN 🏨 **The Inn Above Tide.** This is the only hotel in the Bay Area with balconies literally hanging over the water, and each of its rooms has a perfect-10 view that takes in wild Angel Island as well as the city lights across the bay. **Pros:** great complimentary breakfast; minutes from restaurants and attractions; central but tranquil setting. **Cons:** costly parking; some rooms are on the small side. [$] *Rooms from: $370* ✉ *30 El Portal, Sausalito* ☎ *415/332–9535, 800/893–8433* 🌐 *www.innabovetide.com* 🛏 *26 rooms, 5 suites* 🍽 *Breakfast.*

PERFORMING ARTS

Sausalito Art Festival. This annual juried fine-arts show, held over Labor Day weekend, attracts more than 30,000 people to the Sausalito waterfront; Blue & Gold Fleet ferries from San Francisco dock at the pier adjacent to the festival. ⊠ *Sausalito* ☎ *415/332–3555* ⊕ *www.sausalito artfestival.org* ⌲ *$25.*

SPORTS AND THE OUTDOORS
KAYAKING
Sea Trek Ocean Kayaking and SUP Center. The center (SUP stands for stand-up paddleboarding) offers guided half-day sea-kayaking trips underneath the Golden Gate Bridge and full- and half-day trips to Angel Island, both for beginners. Trips for experienced kayakers, classes, and rentals are also available. ■ TIP→ Starlight and full-moon paddles are particularly popular. ⊠ *Bay Model parking lot, off Bridgeway and Marinship Way, Sausalito* ☎ *415/332–8494* ⊕ *www.seatrek.com* ⌲ *From $20 per hr for rentals, $65 for 3-hr guided trip.*

SAILING
SF Bay Adventures. This outfit's expert skippers conduct sunset and full-moon sails around the bay, as well as fascinating eco- and whale-watching tours with the possibility of viewing great white sharks. If you're interested, the company can arrange for you to barbecue on Angel Island or even spend the night in a lighthouse. ⊠ *60 Liberty Ship Way, Suite 4, Sausalito* ☎ *415/331–0444* ⊕ *www.sfbayadventures.com.*

TIBURON

2 miles north of Sausalito, 7 miles north of Golden Gate Bridge.

On a peninsula that was called Punta de Tiburon (Shark Point) by the Spanish explorers, this beautiful Marin County community retains the feel of a village—it's more low-key than Sausalito—despite the encroachment of commercial establishments from the downtown area. The harbor faces Angel Island across Raccoon Strait, and San Francisco is directly south across the bay—which makes the views from the decks of harbor restaurants a major attraction. Since its incarnation, in 1884, when ferries from San Francisco connected the point with a railroad to San Rafael, the town has centered on the waterfront. ■ TIP→ The ferry is the most relaxing (and fastest) way to get here, particularly in summer, allowing you to skip traffic and parking problems. If visiting midweek, keep in mind that many shops close either Tuesday or Wednesday, or both.

GETTING HERE AND AROUND
Blue & Gold Fleet ferries travel between San Francisco and Tiburon daily. By car, head north from San Francisco on U.S. 101 and get off at CA 131/Tiburon Boulevard/East Blithedale Avenue (Exit 447). Turn right onto Tiburon Boulevard and drive just over 4 miles to downtown. Golden Gate Transit serves downtown Tiburon from San Francisco; except during evening rush hour you'll need to transfer in Mill Valley, making the bus an inconvenient option. Tiburon's Main Street is made for wandering, as are the footpaths that frame the water's edge.

ESSENTIALS
Visitor Information Tiburon ⊠ *Town Hall, 1505 Tiburon Blvd., Tiburon* ☎ *415/435–7373* ⊕ *www.townoftiburon.org.*

EXPLORING

Ark Row. Past the pink-brick bank building, Main Street is known as Ark Row and has a tree-shaded walk lined with antiques and specialty stores. Some of the buildings are actually old houseboats that floated in Belvedere Cove before being beached and transformed into stores. ■TIP→ If you're curious about architectural history, the Tiburon Heritage & Arts Commission has a self-guided walking-tour map, available online and at local businesses. ⊠ *Ark Row, parallel to Main St., Tiburon* ⊕ *tiburonheritageandarts.org.*

Old St. Hilary's Landmark and Wildflower Preserve. The architectural centerpiece of this attraction is a stark-white 1886 Carpenter Gothic church that overlooks the town and the bay from its hillside perch. Surrounding the church, which was barged over from Strawberry Point in 1957, is a wildflower preserve that's spectacular in May and June, when the rare black or Tiburon jewelflower blooms. Expect a steep walk uphill to reach the preserve. ■TIP→ The hiking trails behind the landmark wind up to a peak that has views of the entire Bay Area (great photo op). ⊠ *201 Esperanza St., off Mar West St. or Beach Rd., Tiburon* ☎ *415/435–1853* ⊕ *landmarkssociety.com* ✆ *Preserve free, $3 church tour* ⊙ *Preserve daily dawn–dusk; church Apr.–Oct., Sun. 1–4.*

WHERE TO EAT

$$$$
AMERICAN
✕ **The Caprice.** For more than 50 years this Tiburon landmark that overlooks the bay has been the place to come to mark special occasions. The views are spectacular, and soft-yellow walls and starched white tablecloths help to make the space bright and light. Elegant comfort food is the specialty, with choices like seared day-boat scallops or pan-roasted filet mignon. Polishing off the warm chocolate cake with almond ice cream while gazing out at the sunset and porpoises bobbing in the waves below is a near perfect end to the evening. Ⓢ *Average main: $31* ⊠ *2000 Paradise Dr., Tiburon* ☎ *415/435–3400* ⊕ *www.thecaprice.com* ⊙ *No lunch.*

$$
SICILIAN
✕ **Luna Blu.** This lively sliver of an Italian restaurant focusing on seafood has made a splash on the Tiburon dining scene, with locals raving about the food, the service, and the views. It's hard to beat a seat on the heated patio overlooking the bay, but the high-sided booths inside are appealing as well. Chef Renzo Azzarello's Sicilian childhood and training show in dishes such as spaghetti with sea urchin, sausage- and bell pepper-stuffed ravioli with porcini sauce, and braised veal shank; the towering burger served at lunch is a winner. Service is friendly, efficient, and informed. Ⓢ *Average main: $21* ⊠ *35 Main St., Tiburon* ☎ *415/789–5844* ⊙ *Closed Tues.*

$
AMERICAN
FAMILY
✕ **New Morning Cafe.** Omelets and scrambles are served all day long at this homey café. If you're past morning treats, choose from the many soups, salads, and sandwiches. The café is open from 6:30 until 2:30 on weekdays, until 4 on weekends. Ⓢ *Average main: $13* ⊠ *1696 Tiburon Blvd., near Main St., Tiburon* ☎ *415/435–4315* ⊙ *No dinner.*

$$$
AMERICAN
✕ **Sam's Anchor Cafe.** Open since 1921, this casual dockside restaurant with mahogany wainscoting is the town's most famous eatery. Most people flock to the deck here for beer, bay views, and seafood. The lunch menu has the usual suspects—burgers, sandwiches, salads, fried

fish with tartar sauce—and you'll sit on plastic chairs at tables covered with blue-and-white-checked oilcloths. At night you can find standard seafood dishes with vegetarian and meat options. Mind the seagulls; they know no restraint. ■TIP➔ Expect a wait for outside tables on sunny summer days or weekends; reservations aren't taken for deck seating or weekend lunch. Ⓢ *Average main: $23* ⊠ *27 Main St., Tiburon* ☎ *415/435–4527* ⊕ *www.samscafe.com.*

WHERE TO STAY

$$$$
HOTEL

⛅ **The Lodge at Tiburon.** A block from Main Street and framed by stone pillars and sloped rooftops, the Lodge at Tiburon has the feel of a winter ski chalet, though the outdoor pool and its cabanas provide a summery counterpoint. **Pros:** free parking; spacious work desks in each room; room service from the Tiburon Tavern. **Cons:** breakfast not included; some rooms have a few too many mirrors; no bay views. Ⓢ *Rooms from: $299* ⊠ *1651 Tiburon Blvd., at Beach St., Tiburon* ☎ *415/435–3133* ⊕ *lodgeattiburon.com* ⛆ *101 rooms, 2 suites* ⁋ *No meals.*

$$$$
B&B/INN

⛅ **Waters Edge Hotel.** Checking into this elegant hotel feels like tucking away into an inviting retreat by the water—the views are stunning and the lighting is perfect. **Pros:** complimentary wine and cheese for guests every evening; restaurants/sights are minutes away; free bike rentals for guests. **Cons:** downstairs rooms lack privacy and views; except for breakfast delivery, no room service; fitness center is off-site; not a great place to bring small children. Ⓢ *Rooms from: $279* ⊠ *25 Main St., off Tiburon Blvd., Tiburon* ☎ *415/789–5999, 877/789–5999* ⊕ *www.marinhotels.com* ⛆ *23 rooms* ⁋ *Breakfast.*

MILL VALLEY

2 miles north of Sausalito, 4 miles north of Golden Gate Bridge.

Chic and woodsy Mill Valley has a dual personality. Here, as elsewhere in the county, the foundation is a superb natural setting. Virtually surrounded by parkland, the town lies at the base of Mt. Tamalpais and contains dense redwood groves traversed by countless creeks. But this is no lumber camp. Smart restaurants and chichi boutiques line the streets, and more rock stars than one might suspect live here.

The rustic village flavor isn't a modern conceit but a holdover from the town's early days as a logging camp. In 1896 the Mill Valley and Mt. Tamalpais Scenic Railroad—called "the crookedest railroad in the world" because of its curvy tracks—began transporting visitors from Mill Valley to the top of Mt. Tam and down to Muir Woods, and the town soon became a vacation retreat for city slickers. The trains stopped running in the 1940s, but the old railway depot still serves as the center of town: the 1924 building has been transformed into the popular Depot Bookstore & Cafe, at 87 Throckmorton Avenue.

The small downtown area has the constant bustle of a leisure community; even at noon on a Tuesday, people are out shopping for fancy cookware and lacy pajamas.

GETTING HERE AND AROUND

By car from San Francisco, head north on U.S. 101 and get off at CA 131/Tiburon Boulevard/East Blithedale Avenue (Exit 447). Turn left onto East Blithedale and continue west to Throckmorton Avenue; turn left to reach Lytton Square, then park. Golden Gate Transit buses serve Mill Valley from San Francisco. Once here, explore the town on foot; it's great for strolling.

ESSENTIALS

Visitor Information Mill Valley Chamber of Commerce ⊠ *85 Throckmorton Ave., Mill Valley* ☎ *415/388-9700* ⊕ *www.enjoymillvalley.com.*

EXPLORING

FAMILY **Lytton Square.** Mill Valley locals congregate on weekends to socialize in the many coffeehouses near the town's central square (which is unmarked), but it bustles most any time of day. Shops, restaurants, and cultural venues line the nearby streets. ⊠ *Miller and Throckmorton Aves., Mill Valley.*

OFF THE
BEATEN
PATH

Marin County Civic Center. A wonder of arches, circles, and skylights about 8 miles north of Mill Valley, the civic center was Frank Lloyd Wright's last major architectural undertaking. Docent-led tours ($5) leave from the gift shop, on the second floor, on Wednesday morning at 10:30. The center's website has self-guided tour map that's also available at the gift shop. ■TIP➔ **Photographs on the first floor depict Marin County homes Wright designed.** ⊠ *3501 Civic Center Dr., off N. San Pedro Rd., San Rafael* ☎ *415/473-3762 for docent tour* ⊕ *www.marincounty.org/depts/cu/visitor-services* 🖾 *Free* ⊙ *Weekdays 8–5.*

WHERE TO EAT

$$$ ✕ **Buckeye Roadhouse.** This is Mill Valley's secret den of decadence,
AMERICAN   where house-smoked meats and fish, grilled steaks, and old-fashioned dishes such as brisket bring the locals coming back for more. The restaurant also serves beautiful organic salads and desserts so heavenly—like the s'more pie—you'll just about melt into the floor. The look of the 1937 roadhouse is decidedly hunting-lodge chic, with a river-rock fireplace, topped by a trophy fish, dominating one wall. The busy but cozy bar with elegant mahogany paneling and soft lighting is a good place to quench your thirst for a Marin martini or Napa Valley Merlot. 🖇 *Average main: $24* ⊠ *15 Shoreline Hwy., off U.S. 101, Mill Valley* ☎ *415/331-2600* ⊕ *buckeyeroadhouse.com* ⌾ *Reservations essential.*

$ ✕ **Joe's Taco Lounge.** A funky, bright lounge (and it really does feel like
MEXICAN   someone's lounge), this is a fun place to go for a casual, cheap, and deli-
FAMILY   cious Mexican meal. There are all sorts of colorful relics on the walls, and chili-pepper lights adorn the windows. The signature dishes are fish tacos and snapper burritos—which are generous in both size and flavor. The organic burger with spicy "firecracker" fries and the fire-grilled corn on the cob are also yummy. Choose from a wide selection of Mexican beers, or go for a refreshing agave wine margarita. Between 5 and 7 pm, Joe's is popular with families. 🖇 *Average main: $11* ⊠ *382 Miller Ave., and Montford Ave., Mill Valley* ☎ *415/383-8164* ⊕ *www. joestacolounge.com.*

$$$
MODERN
AMERICAN
✕ **Molina.** A suave yet homey design, a convivial vibe buoyed by an all-vinyl soundtrack, and vibrant, impeccable cuisine have turned this snug neighborhood spot into something approaching a destination restaurant. Owner-chef (and DJ) Todd Shoberg aims to please and usually succeeds, most especially with the food, a dozen small plates and five or so entrées that showcase local meat and produce. Smaller dishes have included heirloom broccoli with kumquats and farro, and game hen and king salmon from Bodega Bay have appeared as mains. Molina is on the small side and can get noisy when packed. Sunday brunch is also served. ⓢ *Average main: $26* ⊠ *17 Madrona St., near Throckmorton Ave., Mill Valley* ☎ *415/383–4200* ⊕ *molinarestaurant.com* ⊗ *No lunch.*

$
BURGER
FAMILY
✕ **Pearl's Phat Burgers.** Families, couples, and teenagers flock to Pearl's for juicy, grass-fed organic burgers stacked high with tomatoes, lettuce, bacon, and cheese; sweet-potato fries that are not too crispy and not too soft; and thick, creamy milk shakes. The food here is among the freshest, biggest, and fastest in town. No wonder there's always a line out the door. ⓢ *Average main: $14* ⊠ *8 E. Blithedale Ave., at Sunnyside Ave., Mill Valley* ☎ *415/381–6010.*

$
PIZZA
FAMILY
✕ **Tony Tutto Pizza.** Possibly the best pies in Marin—all vegetarian and mostly organic—are to be had in this simple, pleasant eatery where the focus is all on the food. The owner spent decades in the music business, which you'll see reflected in the menu. Try the Peter, Paul & Pesto, A Love Supreme (margherita), or Whiter Shade of Pale (three cheeses). Choose from the extensive beer list and good wine selection and grab an outdoor table under the heat lamps. Service is warm and welcoming. ⓢ *Average main: $13* ⊠ *246 E. Blithedale Ave., near Sycamore Ave., Mill Valley* ☎ *415/383–8646* ⊕ *www.tonytuttopizza.com* ⊟ *No credit cards* ⊗ *Closed Mon. and Tues.*

WHERE TO STAY

$$$$
B&B/INN
🛏 **Mill Valley Inn.** The only hotel in downtown Mill Valley has smart-looking rooms done up in Tuscan colors of ocher and olive, with hand-crafted beds, armoires, and lamps by local artisans. **Pros:** minutes from local shops and restaurants; great complimentary continental breakfast; free parking; free mountain bikes. **Cons:** some rooms are noisy; dark in winter because of surrounding trees; some rooms are not accessible via elevator. ⓢ *Rooms from: $279* ⊠ *165 Throckmorton Ave., near Miller Ave., Mill Valley* ☎ *415/389–6608, 800/595–2100* ⊕ *www.marinhotels.com* ⇥ *22 rooms, 1 suite, 2 cottages* ⏻ *Breakfast.*

$$$$
B&B/INN
Fodor'sChoice
★
🛏 **Mountain Home Inn.** Abutting 40,000 acres of state and national parks, the inn sits on the skirt of Mt. Tamalpais, where you can follow hiking trails all the way to Stinson Beach. **Pros:** amazing deck and views; peaceful, remote setting. **Cons:** nearest town is a 20-minute drive away; restaurant can get crowded on sunny weekend days; some complain the hotel and service don't live up to the views and price point. ⓢ *Rooms from: $279* ⊠ *810 Panoramic Hwy., at Edgewood Ave., Mill Valley* ☎ *415/381–9000* ⊕ *www.mtnhomeinn.com* ⇥ *10 rooms* ⏻ *Breakfast.*

6

NIGHTLIFE AND PERFORMING ARTS

NIGHTLIFE

Mill Valley Beerworks. A great place to rest your feet after shopping or hiking, Beerworks serves more than 100 local, national, and international beers, from ale to port to lager. For food, you'll find offerings such as a cheese plate, olives, grilled squid, and pappardelle. ⌂ *173 Throckmorton Ave., at Madrona St., Mill Valley* ☎ *415/888–8218* ⊕ *millvalley beerworks.com.*

PERFORMING ARTS

Sweetwater Music Hall. With the help of part-owner Bob Weir of the Grateful Dead, this renowned club reopened in an old Masonic Hall in 2012. Famous as well as up-and-coming bands play on most nights, and local stars such as Bonnie Raitt and Huey Lewis have been known to stop in for a pickup session. ⌂ *19 Corte Madera Ave., between Throckmorton and Lovell Aves., Mill Valley* ☎ *415/388–3850* ⊕ *www. sweetwatermusichall.com.*

MUIR WOODS NATIONAL MONUMENT

12 miles northwest of the Golden Gate Bridge.

Climbing hundreds of feet into the sky, *Sequoia sempervirens* are the tallest living things on Earth. One of the last remaining old-growth stands of these redwood behemoths, Muir Woods is nature's cathedral: imposing, awe-inspiring, reverence-inducing, and not to be missed.

GETTING HERE AND AROUND

Driving to Muir Woods, especially in summer and early fall, causes epic traffic jams around the tiny parking areas and miles-long walks to reach the entrance. Do yourself (and everyone else) a favor and take a shuttle instead, if you can. On weekends and holidays, Memorial Day through Labor Day, Marin Transit's Route 66 shuttle (☎ *$5 round-trip* ⊕ *www. marintransit.org*) is timed to meet boats at Sausalito's ferry landing four times daily en route to Muir Woods. The shuttle also runs every half hour from the Manzanita Park-and-Ride three miles north of the ferry. To get there, take the Highway 1 exit off U.S. 101 (look for the lot under the elevated freeway), or take connecting bus service from San Francisco with Golden Gate Transit. To drive directly from San Francisco by car, take U.S. 101 north across the Golden Gate Bridge to the Mill Valley/ Stinson Beach exit, then follow signs to Highway 1 north. Once here, you can wander by foot through this pristine patch of nature.

EXPLORING

FAMILY

Fodor's Choice

★

Muir Woods National Monument. Walking among some of the last old-growth redwoods on the planet, trees hundreds of feet tall and a millennium or more old, is magical, an experience like few others to clearly illustrate our tiny place in a bigger world. Ancestors of redwood and sequoia trees grew throughout what is now the United States 150,000,000 years ago. Today the *Sequoia sempervirens* can be found only in a narrow, cool coastal belt from Monterey to Oregon. The 550 acres of Muir Woods National Monument contain some of the most majestic redwoods in the world—some more than 250 feet tall. (To see the real giants, though, you'll have to head north to Humboldt County,

where the tallest redwood, in Redwood National Park, has been measured at 380 feet.) The Marin stand was saved from destruction in 1905, when it was purchased by a couple who donated it to the federal government. Three years later it was named after naturalist John Muir, whose environmental campaigns helped to establish the national park system. His response: "Saving these woods from the ax and saw is in many ways the most notable service to God and man I have heard of since my forest wandering began."

Muir Woods, part of the Golden Gate National Recreation Area, is a pedestrian's park. Old paved trails have been replaced by wooden walkways, and the trails vary in difficulty and length. Beginning from the park headquarters, an easy 2-mile, wheelchair-accessible **loop trail** crosses streams and passes ferns and azaleas, as well as magnificent redwood groves. Among the most famous are **Bohemian Grove** and the circular formation called **Cathedral Grove.** On summer weekends visitors oohing and aahing in a dozen languages line the trail. If you prefer a little serenity, consider the challenging **Dipsea Trail,** which climbs west from the forest floor to soothing views of the ocean and the Golden Gate Bridge. For a complete list of trails, check with rangers, who can also help you pick the best one for your ability level.

■ TIP → The weather in Muir Woods is usually cool and often wet—after all, these giants survive on fog drip—so wear warm clothes and shoes appropriate for damp trails. Picnicking and camping aren't allowed, and pets aren't permitted. Crowds can be large, especially from May through October, so try to come early in the morning or late in the afternoon. The **Muir Woods Visitor Center** has books and exhibits about redwood trees and the woods' history; the café here serves locally sourced, organic food, and the gift shop has plenty of souvenirs. ⊠ *1 Muir Woods Trail, off Panoramic Hwy., Mill Valley* ☎ *415/388–2595 park information, 415/526–3239 shuttle information* ⊕ *www.nps.gov/ muwo* ☞ *$7* ☾ *Daily 8 am–sunset.*

MT. TAMALPAIS STATE PARK

16 miles northwest of Golden Gate Bridge.

The view of Mt. Tamalpais from all around the bay can be a beauty, but that's nothing compared to the views *from* the mountain, which range from jaw-dropping to spectacular and take in San Francisco, the East Bay, the coast, and beyond—on a clear day, all the way to the Farallon Islands, 26 miles away.

GETTING HERE AND AROUND

By car, take the Highway 1–Stinson Beach exit off U.S. 101 and follow the road west and then north. From San Francisco, the trip can take from 30 minutes up to an hour, depending on traffic. By bus, take Golden Gate Transit's 10, 70 or 80 to Marin City; in Marin City transfer to the West Marin Stagecoach (☎ *415/226–0855* ⊕ *www. marintransit.org/stage.html*). Once here, the only way to explore is on foot or by bike.

EXPLORING

Mt. Tamalpais State Park. Although the summit of Mt. Tamalpais is only 2,571 feet high, the mountain rises practically from sea level, dominating the topography of Marin County. Adjacent to Muir Woods National Monument, Mt. Tamalpais State Park affords views of the entire Bay Area and the Pacific Ocean to the west. The mountain was sacred to Native Americans, who saw in its profile—as you can see today—the silhouette of a sleeping Indian maiden. Locals fondly refer to it as the "Sleeping Lady." For years the 6,300-acre park has been a favorite destination for hikers. There are more than 200 miles of trails, some rugged but many developed for easy walking through meadows, grasslands, and forests and along creeks. Mt. Tam, as it's called by locals, is also the birthplace (in the 1970s) of mountain biking, and today many spandex-clad bikers whiz down the park's winding roads.

The park's major thoroughfare, Panoramic Highway, snakes its way up from U.S. 101 to the **Pantoll Ranger Station.** The office is staffed sporadically, depending on funding. From the ranger station, Panoramic Highway drops down to the town of Stinson Beach. Pantoll Road branches off the highway at the station, connecting up with Ridgecrest Boulevard. Along these roads are numerous parking areas, picnic spots, scenic overlooks, and trailheads. Parking is free along the roadside, but there's a fee at the ranger station and at some of the other parking lots ($8).

The **Mountain Theater,** also known as the Cushing Memorial Amphitheatre, is a natural amphitheater with terraced stone seats (for nearly 4,000 people) constructed in its current form by the Civilian Conservation Corps in the 1930s.

The **Rock Spring Trail** starts at the Mountain Theater and gently climbs about 1¾ miles to the **West Point Inn,** once a stop on the Mt. Tam railroad route. Relax at a picnic table and stock up on water before forging ahead, via Old Railroad Grade Fire Road and the Miller Trail, to Mt. Tam's Middle Peak, about 2 miles uphill.

Starting from the Pantoll Ranger Station, the precipitous **Steep Ravine Trail** brings you past stands of coastal redwoods and, in the springtime, numerous small waterfalls. Take the connecting **Dipsea Trail** to reach the town of Stinson Beach and its swath of golden sand. ■TIP➜ If you're too weary to make the 3½-mile trek back up, Marin Transit Bus 61 takes you from Stinson Beach back to the ranger station. ✉ *Pantoll Ranger Station, 3801 Panoramic Hwy., at Pantoll Rd.* ☎ *415/388–2070* ⊕ *www.parks.ca.gov.*

PERFORMING ARTS

FAMILY **Mountain Play.** Every May and June, locals tote overstuffed picnic baskets to the Mountain Theater to see the Mountain Play, popular musicals such as *The Music Man* and *My Fair Lady.* ✉ *Mt. Tamalpais, Richardson Blvd. off Panoramic Hwy.* ☎ *415/383–1100* ⊕ *www.mountainplay. org* 💲 *$40.*

BEACH TOWNS

The winds whip wildly around Marin County's miles of coastline. If you've never heard sand "sing" as the wind rustles through it you're in for a treat—though when it lands in your sandwich you might not rejoice. But when the weather's calm and sunny as you stroll Stinson Beach—or you're communing with nature at rocky Muir Beach—you'll realize this landscape is ever so choice.

GETTING HERE AND AROUND

If you're driving, take the Highway 1–Stinson Beach exit off U.S. 101 and follow Highway 1, also signed as Shoreline Highway, west and then north. Public transit serves Stinson Beach and Bolinas but not Muir Beach.

MUIR BEACH

12 miles northwest of Golden Gate Bridge, 6 miles southwest of Mill Valley.

Except on the sunniest of weekends Muir Beach is relatively quiet. But this craggy cove has seen its share of history. Sir Francis Drake disembarked here five centuries ago, rock star Janis Joplin's ashes were scattered here among the sands, and this is where author Ken Kesey hosted the second of his famed Acid Tests.

GETTING HERE AND AROUND

A car is the best way to reach Muir Beach. From Highway 1, follow Pacific Way southwest ¼ mile.

EXPLORING

Green Gulch Farm Zen Center. Giant eucalyptus trees frame the long and winding road that leads to this tranquil retreat. Meditation programs, workshops, and various events take place here, and there's an extensive organic garden. Visitors are welcome to roam the acres of gardens that reach down toward Muir Beach. ■TIP→ Follow the main dirt road to a peaceful path (birds, trees, ocean breezes) that meanders to the beach. ⊠ *1601 Shoreline Hwy., at Green Gulch Rd., Muir Beach* ☎ *415/383–3134* ⊕ *www.sfzc.org* ✉ *Free* ☉ *Tues.–Sat. 9–noon and 2–4, Sun. 9–10 am.*

BEACHES

FAMILY   **Muir Beach.** Small but scenic, this beach—a rocky patch of shoreline off Highway 1 in the northern Marin Headlands—is a good place to stretch your legs and gaze out at the Pacific. Locals often walk their dogs here; families and cuddling couples come for picnicking and sunbathing. At one end of the sand are waterfront homes (and where nude sunbathers lay their towels), and at the other are the bluffs of the Golden Gate National Recreation Area. **Amenities:** parking (free); toilets. **Best for:** solitude; nudists; walking. ⊠ *190 Pacific Way, off Shoreline Hwy., Muir Beach* ⊕ *www.nps.gov/goga/planyourvisit/muirbeach.htm.*

Shutterbugs rejoice in catching a scenic Muir Beach sunset.

WHERE TO STAY

$$$
B&B/INN

Ⓣ **Pelican Inn.** From its slate roof to its whitewashed plaster walls, this inn looks so Tudor that it's hard to believe it was built in the 1970s, but the Pelican is English to the core, with its smallish guest rooms upstairs (no elevator), high half-tester beds draped in heavy fabrics, and bangers and grilled tomatoes for breakfast. **Pros:** five-minute walk to beach; great bar and restaurant; peaceful setting. **Cons:** 20-minute drive to nearby attractions; some rooms are quite small. Ⓢ *Rooms from: $222* ✉ *10 Pacific Way, off Hwy. 1, Muir Beach* ☎ *415/383–6000* ⊕ *www. pelicaninn.com* ⤴ *7 rooms* ⓄⅠ *Breakfast.*

STINSON BEACH

20 miles northwest of Golden Gate Bridge.

This laid-back hamlet is all about the beach, and folks come from all over the Bay Area to walk its sandy, often windswept shore. Ideal day trip: a morning Mt. Tam hike followed by lunch at one of Stinson's unassuming eateries and leisurely beach stroll.

GETTING HERE AND AROUND

If you're driving, take the Highway 1–Stinson Beach exit off U.S. 101 and follow the road west and then north. The journey from San Francisco can take from 35 minutes to more than an hour, depending on traffic. By bus, take the 10, 70, or 80 to Marin City; in Marin City transfer to the West Marin Stagecoach. The intimate town is perfect for casual walking.

BEACHES

FAMILY **Stinson Beach.** When the fog hasn't rolled in, this expansive stretch of sand is about as close as you can get in Marin to the stereotypical feel of a Southern California beach. There are several clothing-optional areas, among them a section called Red Rock Beach. ⚠ **Swimming at Stinson Beach is recommended only from early May through September, when lifeguards are on duty, because the undertow can be strong and shark sightings, although infrequent, aren't unheard of.** On any hot summer weekend, every road to Stinson is jam-packed, so factor this into your plans. The down-to-earth town itself—population 600, give or take—has a surfer vibe, with a few good eating options and pleasant hippie-craftsy browsing. **Amenities:** food and drink; lifeguards; parking (free); showers; toilets. **Best for:** nudists; sunset; surfing; swimming; walking. ✉ *Hwy. 1, Stinson Beach* 🌐 *www.stinsonbeachonline.com.*

WHERE TO EAT AND STAY

$$ AMERICAN FAMILY 🍴 **Parkside Cafe.** The Parkside is popular for its beachfront snack bar (cash only), but inside is Stinson Beach's best restaurant, with classic offerings such as clam chowder, Dungeness crab, and rock-shrimp risotto. Breakfast is served until 2 pm. Creeping vines on the sunny patio shelter diners from the wind; for a cozier ambience eat by the fire in the dining room. [$] *Average main: $20* ✉ *43 Arenal Ave., off Shoreline Hwy., Stinson Beach* ☎ *415/868–1272* 🌐 *www.parksidecafe.com.*

$$ AMERICAN 🍴 **Sand Dollar Restaurant.** The town's oldest restaurant still attracts all the old salts from Muir Beach to Bolinas, but these days they sip whiskey at an up-to-date bar or beneath market umbrellas on the spiffy deck. The food is good—try the fish tacos—but the big draw is the lively atmosphere. Musicians play on Sunday in summer, and on sunny afternoons the deck gets so packed that people sit on the fence rails sipping beer. [$] *Average main: $20* ✉ *3458 Shoreline Hwy., Stinson Beach* ☎ *415/868–0434* 🌐 *www.stinsonbeachrestaurant.com.*

$ B&B/INN FAMILY 🏨 **Sandpiper Lodging.** Recharge, rest, and enjoy the local scenery at this ultra-popular lodging that books up months, even years, in advance. **Pros:** bright rooms; lush gardens; minutes from the beach. **Cons:** walls are thin; some guests say motel rooms are overpriced. [$] *Rooms from: $145* ✉ *1 Marine Way, at Arenal Ave., Stinson Beach* ☎ *415/868–1632* 🌐 *www.sandpiperstinsonbeach.com* 🛏 *6 rooms, 4 cabins, 1 cottage* 🍽 *No meals.*

$ B&B/INN 🏨 **Stinson Beach Motel.** Built in the 1930s, this motel surrounds three courtyards that burst with flowering greenery, and rooms are clean, simple, and summery. **Pros:** minutes from the beach; cozy, unpretentious rooms; kitchenettes in cottages. **Cons:** smaller rooms are cramped. [$] *Rooms from: $140* ✉ *3416 Shoreline Hwy., Stinson Beach* ☎ *415/868–1712* 🌐 *www.stinsonbeachmotel.com* 🛏 *6 rooms, 2 cottages* 🍽 *No meals.*

EN ROUTE **Martin Griffin Preserve.** A 1,000-acre wildlife sanctuary along the Bolinas Lagoon, this Audubon Canyon Ranch preserve gets the most traffic during late spring, when great blue herons and egrets nest in the evergreens covering the hillside. It's spectacular to see these large birds in white and gray, dotting the tops of the trees. Quiet trails through the rest of the preserve offer tremendous vistas of the Bolinas Lagoon and

Stinson Beach—and fabulous birding. On weekends, "Ranch Guides" are posted throughout to point out nests—scopes are provided—and answer questions. During the week, check in at the small bookstore and take a self-guided tour. ✉ *4900 Shoreline Hwy. 1, between Stinson Beach and Bolinas, Stinson Beach* ☎ *415/868–9244* 🌐 *www.egret.org* 🎫 *Free* 🕒 *Closed mid-Dec.–mid-Mar.*

BOLINAS

7 miles north of Stinson Beach.

The tiny town of Bolinas wears its 1960s idealism on its sleeve, attracting potters, poets, and peace lovers to its quiet streets. With a funky gallery, a general store selling organic produce, a café, and an offbeat saloon, the main thoroughfare, Wharf Road, looks like a hippie-fied version of Main Street, USA.

GETTING HERE AND AROUND

Bolinas isn't difficult to find, though locals notoriously remove the street sign for their town from the highway: heading north from Stinson Beach, follow Highway 1 west and then north. Make a left at the first road just past the Bolinas Lagoon (✉ *Olema–Bolinas Rd.*), and then turn left at the stop sign. The road dead-ends smack-dab in the middle of town. By bus, take the 10, 70, or 80 to Marin City; in Marin City, transfer to the West Marin Stagecoach. Walking is the only way to see this small town.

6

WHERE TO EAT

$$ AMERICAN 🍴 **Coast Cafe.** Decked out in a nautical theme with surfboards and buoys, the dining room at the Coast serves dependably good American fare, including specials such as shepherd's pie, local fresh fish, grass-fed steaks, and gorgeous salads. Live music accompanies dinner on Thursday and Sunday. On weekends, the café is open for brunch. [$] *Average main: $16* ✉ *46 Wharf Rd., off Olema–Bolinas Rd., Bolinas* ☎ *415/868–2298* 🕒 *Closed Mon.*

POINT REYES NATIONAL SEASHORE

Bear Valley Visitor Center is 12 miles north of Bolinas.

With sandy beaches stretching for miles, a dramatic rocky coastline, a gem of a lighthouse, and idyllic, century-old dairy farms, Point Reyes National Seashore is one of the most varied and strikingly beautiful corners of the Bay Area.

GETTING HERE AND AROUND

From San Francisco, take U.S. 101 north, head west at Sir Francis Drake Boulevard (Exit 450B), and follow the road just under 20 miles to Bear Valley Road. From Stinson Beach or Bolinas, drive north on Highway 1 and turn left on Bear Valley Road. If you're going by bus, take one of several Golden Gate Transit buses to Marin City; in Marin City transfer to the West Marin Stagecoach (you'll switch buses in Olema). Once at the visitor center, the best way to get around is on foot.

EXPLORING

FAMILY **Bear Valley Visitor Center.** A life-size orca model hovers over the center's engaging exhibits about the wildlife and history of the Point Reyes National Seashore. The rangers at the barnlike facility are fonts of information about beaches, whale-watching, hiking trails, and camping. Winter hours may be shorter and summer weekend hours may be longer; call or check the website for details. ⊠ *Bear Valley Visitor Center Access Rd., west of Hwy. 1* ☎ *415/464–5100* ⊕ *www.nps.gov/pore/planyourvisit* ⊗ *Weekdays 10–5, weekends 9–5.*

FAMILY **Duxbury Reef.** Excellent tide pooling can be had along mile-long Duxbury Reef, the largest shale intertidal reef in North America. Look for sea stars, barnacles, sea anemones, purple urchins, limpets, sea mussels, and the occasional abalone. But check a tide table (⊕ *www.wrh.noaa.gov/mtr/marine.php*) or the local papers if you plan to explore the reef—it's accessible only at low tide. The reef is a 30-minute drive from the Bear Valley Visitor Center. Take Highway 1 south from the center, turn right at Olema–Bolinas Road (keep an eye peeled; the road is easy to miss), left on Horsehoe Hill Road, right on Mesa Road, left on Overlook Drive, and then right on Elm Road, which dead-ends at the Agate Beach County Park parking lot.

FAMILY **Point Blue Conservation Science.** Birders adore Point Blue, which lies in the southernmost part of Point Reyes National Seashore and is accessed through Bolinas. (Those not interested in birds might find it ho-hum.) The unstaffed Palomarin Field Station, open daily from sunrise to sunset, has excellent interpretive exhibits, including a comparative display of real birds' talons. The surrounding woods harbor more than 200 bird species. As you hike the quiet trails through forest and along ocean cliffs, you're likely to see biologists banding birds to aid in the study of their life cycles. ■TIP→ **Visit Point Blue's website to find out when banding will occur; it's a fun time to come here.** ⊠ *Mesa Rd., Bolinas* ☎ *415/868–0655* ⊕ *www.pointblue.org* ⧉ *Free* ⊗ *Daily sunrise–sunset.*

FAMILY **Point Reyes Lighthouse.** In operation since December 1, 1870, this light-
Fodor'sChoice house is one of the premier attractions of the Point Reyes National
★ Seashore. It occupies the tip of Point Reyes, 22 miles from the Bear Valley Visitor Center, a scenic 45-minute drive over hills scattered with longtime dairy farms. The lighthouse originally cast a rotating beam lighted by four wicks that burned lard oil. Keeping the wicks lighted and the 6,000-pound Fresnel lens soot-free in Point Reyes's perpetually foggy climate was a constant struggle that reputedly drove the early attendants to alcoholism and insanity.

■TIP→ **The lighthouse is one of the best spots on the coast for watching gray whales.** On both legs of their annual migration, the magnificent animals pass close enough to see with the naked eye. Southern migration peaks in mid-January, and the whales head back north in March; see the slower mothers and calves in late April and early May.

On busy whale-watching weekends (from late December through mid-April), buses shuttle visitors from the Drakes Beach parking lot to the top of the stairs leading down to the lighthouse (*Bus $7, admission free*) and the road is closed to private vehicles. However you've arrived, consider whether you have it in you to walk down—and up—the 308 steps to the lighthouse. The view from the bottom is worth the effort, but the whales are visible from the cliffs above the lighthouse. ⊠ *Visitor Center, Western end of Sir Francis Drake Blvd., Inverness* ☎ *415/669–1534* ☉ *Fri.–Mon. 10–4:30; weather lens room mid-Apr.–Dec., Fri.–Mon. 2:30–4 except during very windy weather.*

Fodor's Choice   **Point Reyes National Seashore.** One of the Bay Area's most spectacular
★   treasures and the only national seashore on the West Coast, the 66,500-acre Point Reyes National Seashore encompasses hiking trails, secluded beaches, and rugged grasslands as well as Point Reyes itself, a triangular peninsula that juts into the Pacific. The town of **Point Reyes Station** is a one-main-drag affair with some good places to eat and gift shops that sell locally made and imported goods.

When explorer Sir Francis Drake sailed along the California coast in 1579, he missed the Golden Gate and San Francisco Bay, but he did land at what he described as a convenient harbor. In 2012 the federal government finally officially recognized Drake's Bay, which flanks the point on the east, as that harbor, designating the spot a National Historic Landmark and silencing competing claims in the 433-year-old controversy. Today Point Reyes's hills and dramatic cliffs attract other kinds of explorers: hikers, whale-watchers, and solitude seekers.

The infamous San Andreas Fault runs along the park's eastern edge and up the center of Tomales Bay; take the short **Earthquake Trail** from the visitor center to see the impact near the epicenter of the 1906 earthquake that devastated San Francisco. A ½-mile path from the visitor center leads to **Kule Loklo,** a reconstructed Miwok village that sheds light on the daily lives of the region's first inhabitants. From here, trails also lead to the park's free, hike-in campgrounds (camping permits are required).

■ TIP→ In late winter and spring, take the short walk at Chimney Rock, just before the lighthouse, to the Elephant Seal Overlook. Even from the cliff, the male seals look enormous as they spar, growling and bloodied, for resident females.

You can experience the diversity of Point Reyes's ecosystems on the scenic **Coast Trail,** which starts at the Palomarin Trailhead, just outside Bolinas. From here, it's a 3-mile trek through eucalyptus groves and pine forests and along seaside cliffs to beautiful and tiny Bass Lake. To reach the Palomarin Trailhead, take Olema–Bolinas Road toward Bolinas, follow signs to Point Blue Conservation Science, and then continue until the road dead-ends.

The 4.7-mile-long (one-way) **Tomales Point Trail** follows the spine of the park's northernmost finger of land through a Tule Elk Preserve, providing spectacular ocean views from the high bluffs. Expect to see elk, but keep your distance from the animals. To reach the fairly easy hiking trail, look for the Pierce Point Road turnoff on the right, just north of the town of Inverness; park at the end of the road by the old ranch buildings. ⊠ *Bear Valley Visitor Center, Bear Valley Visitor Center Access Rd., off Hwy. 1, Point Reyes Station* ☎ *415/464–5100* ⊕ *www.nps.gov/pore.*

6

WHERE TO EAT

$ ECLECTIC 🍴 **Café Reyes.** In a triangular, semi-industrial room with glazed concrete floors and ceilings high enough to accommodate several full-size market umbrellas, you can mix and match Californian and international flavors. Wood-fired pizzas are the specialty, the sandwiches and salads come in generous portions, and regulars rave about the oysters. ■ **TIP→ On nice days, head for the outdoor patio.** [$] *Average main: $15* ✉ *11101 Hwy. 1, Point Reyes Station* ☎ *415/663–9493* 🕘 *Closed Mon. and Tues.*

$$ ITALIAN Fodor's Choice ★ 🍴 **Osteria Stellina.** The vaguely industrial-chic overtones of this West Marin star's otherwise rustic-contemporary decor hint at the panache that enlivens chef-owner Christian Caiazzo's "Point Reyes Italian" cuisine. The emphasis on locally sourced ingredients makes for ingenious combinations—oysters harvested a just a few miles away, for instance, anchor a pizza with leeks braised in cream from Marin and Sonoma cows and garnished with parsley and lemon thyme. Pastas and pizzas dominate the menu, which might contain as few as two entrées for lunch and a handful for dinner. The hit at lunch, tomato minestra, is a lightly spiced seafood concoction reminiscent of gumbo; dinner might include osso buco that pairs Niman Ranch veal with Marin-grown kale, or braised goat with greens from Stellina's own farm. [$] *Average main: $19* ✉ *11285 Hwy. 1, at 3rd St., Point Reyes Station* ☎ *415/663–9988* 🌐 *www.osteriastellina.com* 🕘 *Closed Thurs. in winter.*

$$$$ MODERN AMERICAN 🍴 **Sir and Star at the Olema.** With a decor that incorporates taxidermied animals, service that some Marinites find uneven if not indifferent, and outré menu items such as goat shin, Sir and Star elicits both rants and raves, often from diners sharing the same table. If you're up Point Reyes way, though, and ready for an indoor adventure to match your outdoor one, this restaurant by Margaret Gradé and Daniel DeLong, the owners of nearby Manka's Inverness Lodge, is worth checking out. The menu changes seasonally, and the ingredients are often so local a dish might be named A Neighbor's Quail (or duck) or Fritters of Coastal Kale. [$] *Average main: $35* ✉ *10000 Sir Francis Drake Blvd., at Hwy. 1, Olema* ☎ *415/663–1034* 🌐 *sirandstar.com* ✍ *Reservations essential* 🕘 *Closed Mon. and Tues. No lunch.*

$$ AMERICAN 🍴 **Station House Cafe.** In good weather, hikers fresh from the park fill the Station House's garden to enjoy alfresco dining, and on weekends there's not a spare seat on the banquettes in the dining room, so prepare for a wait. If you come for dinner, your meal will kick off with the café's signature popovers, then the focus is on local, seasonal, and sustainable food: oyster shooters, Niman Ranch braised lamb, Californian white sea bass, and sweet bread pudding are standbys. The place is also open for breakfast and lunch, and there's a full bar. [$] *Average main: $21* ✉ *11180 Hwy. 1, at 2nd St., Point Reyes Station* ☎ *415/663–1515* 🌐 *www.stationhousecafe.com* 🕘 *Closed Wed.*

$$$ AMERICAN FAMILY 🍴 **Tomales Bay Foods.** A renovated hay barn off the main drag houses this collection of upscale food shops, a favorite stopover among Bay Area foodies. Watch workers making Cowgirl Creamery cheese, then buy some at a counter that sells exquisite artisanal cheeses from around the world. Tomales Bay Foods showcases local organic fruits and vegetables

and premium packaged foods, and the **Cowgirl Cantina** turns the best ingredients into creative sandwiches, salads, and soups. You can eat at a small café table or the picnic areas outside. $ *Average main: $23* ✉ *80 4th St., at B St., Point Reyes Station* ☎ *415/663–9335 cheese shop* � *Closed Mon. and Tues. No dinner.*

WHERE TO STAY

$$
B&B/INN
FAMILY
🏨 **Cottages at Point Reyes Seashore.** Amid a 15-acre valley on the north end of town, this secluded getaway offers spacious one- and two-bedroom cabins with fireplaces and patios perfect for sunset barbecues and leisurely breakfasts. **Pros:** spacious accommodations; great place to bring kids. **Cons:** 3-plus miles from downtown Inverness; small pool. $ *Rooms from: $160* ✉ *13275 Sir Francis Drake Blvd., Inverness* ☎ *415/669–7250, 800/406–0405* ⊕ *www.cottagespointreyes.com* ⤳ *20 cabins* ⦿ *No meals.*

$$$$
B&B/INN
🏨 **Manka's Inverness Lodge.** Chef-owner Margaret Gradé takes rustic fantasy to extravagant heights in her 1917 hunting lodge and cabins, where mica-shaded lamps cast an amber glow, and bearskin rugs warm wide-planked floors. **Pros:** extremely romantic; remote and quiet. **Cons:** no on-site restaurant; sounds from neighboring rooms are easily heard; some question the value for the price. $ *Rooms from: $365* ✉ *30 Callendar Way, at Argyle Way, Inverness* ☎ *415/669–1034* ⊕ *www.mankas. com* ⤳ *5 rooms, 2 suites, 1 boathouse, 2 cabins* ⦿ *No meals.*

$$
B&B/INN
🏨 **Ten Inverness Way.** This is the kind of down-to-earth place where you sit around after breakfast and share tips for hiking Point Reyes or linger around the living room and its stone fireplace and library. **Pros:** great base for exploring the nearby wilderness; peaceful garden and friendly staff; exceptional breakfast. **Cons:** some rooms are on the small side; poor cell-phone reception. $ *Rooms from: $180* ✉ *10 Inverness Way, Inverness* ☎ *415/669–1648* ⊕ *www.teninvernessway.com* ⤳ *5 rooms* ⦿ *Breakfast.*

SPORTS AND THE OUTDOORS

HORSEBACK RIDING

Five Brooks Stable. Tour guides here lead private and group horse rides lasting from one to six hours; trails from the stable wind through Point Reyes National Seashore and along the beaches. ✉ *8001 Hwy. 1, north of town, Olema* ☎ *415/663–1570* ⊕ *www.fivebrooks.com* ⤳ *From $40.*

KAYAKING

Blue Waters Kayaking. This outfit rents kayaks and stand-up paddleboards and offers tours and lessons. Make a reservation for rentals to guarantee availability. ✉ *Tomales Bay Resort, 12944 Sir Francis Drake Blvd., Inverness* ☎ *415/669–2600* ⊕ *www.bwkayak.com* ⤳ *From $25.*

NAPA AND
SONOMA

WELCOME TO NAPA AND SONOMA

TOP REASONS TO GO

★ **Biking:** Cycling is one of the best ways to see the Wine Country—the Russian River and Dry Creek valleys, in Sonoma County, are particularly beautiful.

★ **Browsing the farmers' markets:** Many towns in Napa and Sonoma have seasonal farmers' markets, each rounding up an amazing variety of local produce.

★ **Wandering di Rosa:** Though this art and nature preserve is just off the busy Carneros Highway, it's a relatively unknown treasure. The galleries and gardens are filled with hundreds of artworks.

★ **Canoeing on the Russian River:** Trade in your car keys for a paddle and glide down the Russian River in Sonoma County. From May through October is the best time to be on the water.

★ **Touring wineries:** Let's face it: this is the reason you're here, and the range of excellent sips to sample would make any oeno-phile (or novice drinker, for that matter) giddy.

1 Napa Valley. You'll find big names all around, from high-profile wineries to world-renowned chefs. Napa, the valley's oldest town, sweet-life St. Helena, and down-to-earth Calistoga all make good home bases here. Calistoga has the extra draw of local thermal springs. Yountville has become a culinary boomtown, while the tiny communities of Oakville and Rutherford are home to historic wineries such as Robert Mondavi and Inglenook. Rutherford in particular is the source for outstanding Cabernet Sauvignon.

2 Sonoma Valley. Historic attractions and an unpretentious attitude prevail here. The town of Sonoma, with its picture-perfect central plaza, is rich with 19th-century buildings. Glen Ellen, meanwhile, has a special connection with author Jack London.

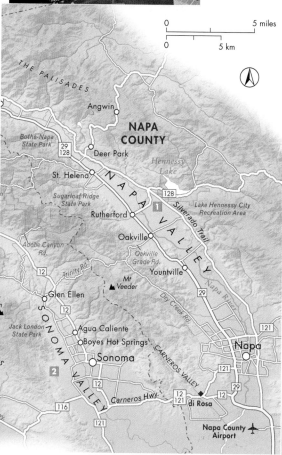

GETTING ORIENTED

The Napa and Sonoma valleys run roughly parallel, northwest to southeast, and are separated by the Mayacamas Mountains. Northwest of the Sonoma Valley are several more important viticultural areas in Sonoma County, including the Dry Creek, Alexander, and Russian River valleys. The Carneros region, which spans southern Sonoma and Napa counties, is just north of San Pablo Bay.

3 Elsewhere in Sonoma. The winding, rural roads here feel a world away from Napa's main drag. The Russian River, Dry Creek, and Alexander valleys are all excellent places to seek out Pinot Noir, Zinfandel, and Sauvignon Blanc. The small town of Healdsburg gets lots of attention, thanks to its terrific restaurants, bed-and-breakfasts, and chic boutiques.

Updated by
Daniel Mangin

Life is lived well in California's premiere wine region, where eating and drinking are cultivated as high arts, and the hotels, inns, and spas rival the world's top resorts for luxury and pampering. Ivy-draped wineries anchor highways and meandering back roads, and boutique operations flourish amid vineyard-blanketed hills. Marquee chefs preside over big-name restaurants whose dishes really *are* as gorgeous as they look in magazine spreads. There's so much to enjoy here: the natural setting is splendid, the architecture divine, the hospitality nearly always sublime.

The Wine Country is also rich in history. In Sonoma you can explore California's Spanish and Mexican pasts at the Sonoma Mission, and the origins of modern California wine making at Buena Vista Winery. Some wineries, among them St. Helena's Beringer and Rutherford's Inglenook, have cellars or tasting rooms dating to the late 1800s. Calistoga is a flurry of late-19th-century Steamboat Gothic architecture, though the town's oldest-looking building, the medieval-style Castello di Amorosa, is a 21st-century creation.

Tours at the Napa Valley's Beringer, Mondavi, and Inglenook—and at Buena Vista in the Sonoma Valley—provide an entertaining overview of Wine Country history. The tour at the splashy visitor center at St. Helena's Hall winery will introduce you to 21st-century wine-making technology, and over in Glen Ellen's Benziger Family Winery you can see how its vineyard managers apply biodynamic farming principles to grape growing. At numerous facilities you can play winemaker for a day at seminars in the fine art of blending wines. If that strikes you as too much effort, you can always pamper yourself at a luxury spa.

To delve further into the fine art of Wine Country living, pick up a copy of *Fodor's Napa and Sonoma*.

PLANNING

WHEN TO GO

High season extends from late May through October, with "crush"—the period when grapes are harvested and crushed—being the best time to see winery workers in action. Crush usually takes place in September and October, sometimes earlier or later depending on the weather. In summer expect hot and dry days, roads jammed with cars, and heavy traffic at tasting rooms. Wine auctions and art and food fairs occur from spring through November. During high season it's wise to book smaller hotels at least a month in advance. To avoid crowds, visit wineries during the week (Tuesday and Wednesday are usually the slowest days). Because many wineries close as early as 4 or 4:30—and only a handful are open past 5—you'll need to get a reasonably early start if you want to fit in more than one or two.

GETTING HERE AND AROUND
AIR TRAVEL

Wine Country regulars often bypass San Francisco and Oakland and fly into Santa Rosa's Charles M. Schulz Sonoma County Airport (STS) on Alaska Airlines, which has nonstop flights from San Diego, Los Angeles, Portland, and Seattle. Avis, Budget, Enterprise, Hertz, and National rent cars here. ■TIP→ Alaska allows passengers flying out of STS to check up to one case of wine for free.

BUS TRAVEL

Bus travel is an inconvenient way to explore the Wine Country, though it is possible. Take Golden Gate Transit from San Francisco to connect with Sonoma County Transit buses. VINE connects with BART commuter trains in the East Bay and the San Francisco Bay Ferry in Vallejo (⇨ see Ferry Travel, below). VINE buses serve the Napa Valley and connect the towns of Napa and Sonoma.

Bus Lines Golden Gate Transit ☎ 415/455–2000 ⊕ www.goldengatetransit. org. **Greyhound** ☎ 800/231–2222 ⊕ www.greyhound.com. **Sonoma County Transit** ☎ 707/576–7433, 800/345–7433 ⊕ www.sctransit.com. **VINE** ✉ Soscol Gateway Transit Center, 625 Burnell St., Napa ☎ 707/251–2800, 800/696–6443 ⊕ www.ridethevine.com.

CAR TRAVEL

Driving your own car is by far the most convenient way to get to and explore the Wine Country. In light traffic, the trip from San Francisco or Oakland to the southern portion of either Napa or Sonoma should take about an hour. Distances between Wine Country towns are fairly short, and in normal traffic you can drive from one end of the Napa or Sonoma valley to the other in less than an hour. Although this is a mostly rural area, the usual rush hours still apply, and high-season weekend traffic can often be slow.

Five major roads serve the region. U.S. 101 and Highways 12 and 121 travel through Sonoma County. Highway 29 and the parallel, more scenic, and often less crowded Silverado Trail travel north–south between Napa and Calistoga.

The easiest way to travel between the Napa Valley and Sonoma County is along Highway 12/121 to the south, or Highway 128 to the north. Travel between the middle sections of either area requires taking the slow, winding drive over the Mayacamas Mountains on the Oakville Grade, which links Oakville, in Napa, and Glen Ellen, in Sonoma.

■TIP➜ If you're wine tasting, either select a designated driver or be careful of your wine intake—the police keep an eye out for tipsy drivers.

From San Francisco to Napa: Cross the Golden Gate Bridge, then go north on U.S. 101. Head east on Highway 37 toward Vallejo, then north on Highway 121, aka the Carneros Highway. Turn left (north) when Highway 121 runs into Highway 29.

From San Francisco to Sonoma: Cross the Golden Gate Bridge, then go north on U.S. 101, east on Highway 37 toward Vallejo, and north on Highway 121. When you reach Highway 12, take it north to the town of Sonoma. For Sonoma County destinations north of Sonoma Valley stay on U.S. 101, which passes through Santa Rosa and Healdsburg.

From Berkeley and Oakland: Take Interstate 80 north to Highway 37 west, then on to Highway 29 north. For the Napa Valley, continue on Highway 29; to reach Sonoma County, head west on Highway 121.

FERRY TRAVEL
From late April through October the San Francisco Bay Ferry sails from the Ferry Building and Pier 41 in San Francisco to Vallejo, where you can board VINE Bus 11 to the town of Napa. Buses sometimes fill in for the ferries.

Contact San Francisco Bay Ferry ☎ 510/522–3300 ⊕ sanfranciscobayferry. com.

RESTAURANTS
Farm-to-table Modern American cuisine is the prevalent style in the Napa Valley and Sonoma County, but this encompasses both the delicate preparations of Thomas Keller's highly praised The French Laundry and the upscale comfort food served throughout the Wine Country. The quality (and hype) often means high prices, but you can also find appealing, inexpensive eateries, especially in the towns of Napa, Calistoga, Sonoma, and Santa Rosa, and many high-end delis prepare superb picnic fare. At pricey restaurants you can save money by having lunch instead of dinner.

With a few exceptions (noted in individual restaurant listings), dress is informal. Where reservations are indicated as essential, book a week or more ahead in summer and early fall.

HOTELS
The fanciest accommodations are concentrated in the Napa Valley towns of Yountville, Rutherford, St. Helena, and Calistoga; Sonoma County's poshest lodgings are in Healdsburg. The spas, amenities, and exclusivity of high-end properties attract travelers with the means and desire for luxury living. The cities of Napa and Santa Rosa are the best bets for budget hotels and inns, but even at a lower price point you'll still find a touch of Wine Country glamour. On weekends, two- or even three-night minimum stays are commonly required at smaller lodgings.

Book well ahead for stays at such places during the busy summer or fall season. If your party will include travelers under age 16, inquire about policies regarding younger guests; some smaller lodgings discourage (or discreetly forbid) children. *Hotel reviews have been shortened. For full information, visit Fodors.com.*

Accommodations Listings Napa Valley Hotels & Resorts ☎ *707/251–9188, 855/333–6272* ⊕ *www.visitnapavalley.com/napa_valley_hotels.htm.* **Sonoma Hotels & Lodging** ⊕ *www.sonomacounty.com/hotels-lodging.*

WHAT IT COSTS				
	$	$$	$$$	$$$$
Restaurants	under $16	$16–$22	$23–$30	over $30
Hotels	under $201	$201–$300	$301–$400	over $400

Restaurant prices are the average cost of a main course at dinner or, if dinner is not served, at lunch. Hotel prices are for the lowest cost of a standard double room in high season.

TASTINGS AND TOURS

Many wineries require reservations for tours, seminars, and tastings, which in most cases are made through booking websites such as Cellar-Pass and VinoVisit. A good scheduling strategy is to book appointment-only wineries in the morning, saving the ones that allow walk-ins until the afternoon. That way, if lunch or other winery visits take longer than expected you won't be stressed about having to arrive at later stops at a precise time.

Booking Websites CellarPass ☎ *707/255–4390* ⊕ *www.cellarpass.com.* **VinoVisit** ☎ *888/252–8990* ⊕ *www.vinovisit.com.*

Many visitors prefer to leave the scheduling and driving to seasoned professionals. Whether you want to tour wineries in a van or bus along with other passengers or spring for a private limo, there are plenty of operators who can accommodate you. Tours generally last from five to seven hours and stop at four or five wineries. Rates vary from $80 per person to $250 or more, depending on the vehicle and whether the tour includes other guests. On most tours, at least one stop includes a behind-the-scenes look at production facilities and the chance to meet winemakers or others involved in the wine-making process. Most tour operators will pick you up at your hotel or a specified meeting place. You can also book a car and driver by the hour for shorter trips. Rates for limo generally run from $50 to $85 per hour, and there's usually a two- or three-hour minimum. ■TIP→ **Some tours include lunch and tasting and other fees, but not all do, so ask.**

Fodor's Choice ★ **Perata Luxury Tours & Car Services.** Perata's customized private tours, led by well-trained, knowledgeable drivers, are tailored to its patrons' interests—you can create your own itinerary or have your guide craft one for you. Tours, in luxury SUVs, cover Napa and Sonoma. The options include exclusive, appointment-only boutique wineries. ☎ *707/227–8271* ⊕ *www.perataluxurycarservices.com* ▨ *From $325 per day, plus fuel surcharge ($25–$35), tasting fees, and 18% gratuity charge.*

Fodor's Choice **Platypus Wine Tours.** The emphasis at Platypus is on "fun" experiences at
★ off-the-beaten-path wineries. Expect intimate winery experiences with
jolly, well-informed guides. You can join an existing tour with other
guests or book a private one. ☎ 707/253–2723 ⊕ *www.platypustours.
com* ✉ *From $99, excluding tasting fees.*

Woody's Wine Tours. The amiable, well-informed Woody Guderian favors
small wineries but will customize a tour to suit your taste and budget. In addition to winery tours in both Napa and Sonoma, Woody
also conducts tours of local craft breweries. ☎ 707/396–8235 ⊕ *www.
woodyswinetours.com* ✉ *From $80 per hr, excluding tasting fees.*

VISITOR INFORMATION

Pretrip Planning Visit Napa Valley ☎ 707/251–5895 ⊕ www.visitnapavalley.
com. **Visit Sonoma** ☎ 707/522–5800, 800/576–6662 ⊕ www.sonomacounty.
com.

Visitor Centers California Welcome Center ✉ 9 4th St., at Wilson St., Santa
Rosa ☎ 800/404–7673 ⊕ www.visitcalifornia.com/california-welcome-centers/
santa-rosa. **Napa Valley Welcome Center** ✉ 600 Main St., at 5th St., Napa
☎ 707/251–5895 ⊕ www.visitnapavalley.com/welcome_centers.htm. **Sonoma
Valley Visitors Center** ✉ 453 1st St. E, east side of Sonoma Plaza, Sonoma
☎ 707/996–1090, 866/996–1090 ⊕ www.sonomavalley.com.

THE NAPA VALLEY

With more than 500 wineries and many of the biggest brands in the
business, the Napa Valley is the Wine Country's star. With a population
of about 79,000, Napa, the valley's largest town, lures with its cultural
attractions and (relatively) reasonably priced accommodations. A few
miles farther north, compact Yountville is densely packed with top-notch
restaurants and hotels, and Rutherford and Oakville are renowned for
their Cabernet Sauvignon–friendly soils. Beyond them, St. Helena teems
with elegant boutiques and restaurants, and casual Calistoga, known for
spas and hot springs, has the feel of an Old West frontier town.

NAPA

46 miles northeast of San Francisco.

Visitors who glimpse Napa's malls and big-box stores from Highway 29
often speed past the town on the way to the more seductive Yountville
or St. Helena. But Napa has evolved into a destination in its own right.
After spending many years as a blue-collar burg detached from the Wine
Country scene, Napa has reshaped its image. A walkway that follows
the Napa River has made downtown more pedestrian-friendly, and each
year high-profile new restaurants pop up. The nightlife options are arguably the valley's best, shopping is chic and varied, and the Oxbow Public
Market, a complex of high-end food purveyors, is popular with locals
and tourists. An magnitude 6.0 earthquake in August 2014 briefly slowed
Napa's momentum, but the town bounced back admirably and you'll see
little evidence of the damage (an estimated $380 million valley-wide) the
temblor caused. *Continued on page 328*

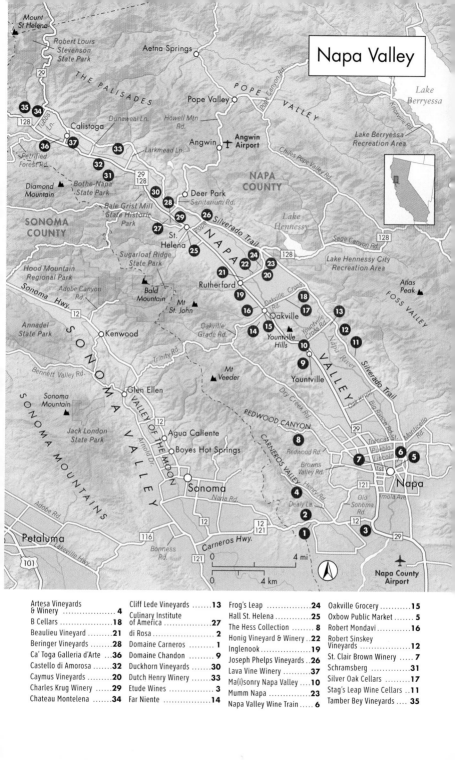

Napa Valley

WINE TASTING *in* NAPA *and* SONOMA

Whether you're a serious wine collector making your annual pilgrimage to Nothern California's Wine Country or a newbie who doesn't know the difference between a Merlot and Mourvèdre but is eager to learn, you can have a great time touring Napa and Sonoma wineries. Your gateway to the wine world is the tasting room, where staff members are happy to chat with curious guests.

VISITING WINERIES

Tasting rooms range from the grand to the humble, offering everything from a few sips of wine to in-depth tours of facilities and vineyards. Many are open for drop-in visits, usually daily from around 10 am to 5 pm. Others require guests to make reservations. First-time visitors frequently enjoy the history-oriented tours at Charles Krug and Inglenook, or ones at Mondavi and J Vineyards that highlight the process as well. The environments at some wineries reflect their founders' other interests: art and architecture at Artesa and Hall St. Helena, movie making at Francis Ford Coppola, and medieval history at the Castello di Amorosa.

Many wineries describe their pourers as "wine educators," and indeed some of them have taken online or other classes and have passed an exam to prove basic knowledge of appellations, grape varietals, vineyards, and wine-making techniques. The one constant, however, is a deep, shared pleasure in the experience of wine tasting. To prepare you for winery visits, we've covered the fundamentals: tasting rooms, fees and what to expect, and the types of tours wineries offer.

Fees. In the past few years, tasting fees have skyrocketed. Most Napa wineries charge $20 or $25 to taste four or so wines, though $35, $45 or even $65 fees aren't unheard of. Sonoma wineries are often a bit cheaper, in the $10 to $25 range, and you'll still find the occasional freebie.

Some winery tours are free, in which case you're usually required to pay a separate fee if you want to taste the wine. If you've paid a fee for the tour—generally from $20 to $40—your wine tasting is usually included in that price.

7

IN FOCUS WINE TASTING IN NAPA AND SONOMA

(opposite page) Carneros vineyards in autumn, Napa Valley. (top) Pinot Gris grapes. (bottom) Bottles from Far Niente winery.

MAKING THE MOST OF YOUR TIME

■Call ahead. Some wineries require reservations to visit or tour. It's wise to check before visiting.

■Come on weekdays. Especially between June and October, try to visit on weekdays to avoid traffic-clogged roads and crowded tasting rooms. For more info on the best times of year to visit, see this chapter's Planner.

■Get an early start. Tasting rooms are often deserted before 11 am or so, when most visitors are still lingering over a second cup of coffee. If you come early, you'll have the staff's undivided attention. You'll usually encounter the largest crowds between 3 and 5 pm.

■Schedule strategically. Visit appointment-only wineries in the morning and ones that allow walk-ins in the afternoon. It'll spare you the stress of being "on time" for later stops.

■Hit the Trail. Beringer, Mondavi, and other high-profile wineries line heavily trafficked Highway 29, but the going

(top) Sipping and swirling in the DeLoach tasting room. (bottom) Learning about barrel aging at Robert Mondavi Winery.

is often quicker on the Silverado Trail, which runs parallel to the highway to the east. You'll find famous names here, too, among them the sparkling wine house Mumm Napa Valley, but the traffic is often lighter and sometimes the crowds as well.

Domaine Carneros.

AT THE BAR

In most tasting rooms, you'll be handed a list of the wines available that day. The wines will be listed in a suggested tasting order, starting with the lightest-bodied whites, progressing to the most intense reds, and ending with dessert wines. If you can't decide which wines to choose, tell the server what types of wines you usually like and ask for a recommendation.

The server will pour you an ounce or so of each wine you select. As you taste it, feel free to take notes or ask questions. Don't be shy—the staff are there to educate you about the wine. If you don't like a wine, or you've simply tasted enough, feel free to pour the rest into one of the dump buckets on the bar.

TOURS

Tours tend to be the most exciting (and the most crowded) in September and October, when the harvest and crush-ing are underway. Tours typically last from 30 minutes to an hour and give you a brief overview of the winemaking process. At some of the older wineries, the tour guide might focus on the history of the property.

■ TIP → If you plan to take any tours, wear comfortable shoes, since you might be walking on wet floors or dirt or gravel pathways or stepping over hoses or other equipment.

MONEY-SAVING TIPS

■ Many hotels and B&Bs distribute coupons for free or discounted tastings to their guests—don't forget to ask.

■ If you and your travel partner don't mind sharing a glass, servers are happy to let you split a tasting.

■ Some wineries will refund all or part of the tasting fee if you buy a bottle. Usually one fee is waived per bottle purchased, though sometimes you must buy two or three.

■ Almost all wineries will also waive the fee if you join their wine club program. However, this typically commits you to buying a certain number of bottles on a regular basis, so be sure you really like the wines before signing up.

Preston of Dry Creek bottles only estate-grown grapes.

TOP 2-DAY ITINERARIES

First-Timer's Napa Tour

Start: Oxbow Public market, Napa. Get underway by browsing the shops selling wines, spices, locally grown produce, and other fine foods, for a taste of what the Wine Country has to offer.

Inglenook, Rutherford. The tour here is a particularly fun way to learn about the history

of Napa winemaking—and you can see the old, atmospheric, ivy-covered château.

Frog's Leap, Rutherford. Friendly, unpretentious, and knowledgeable staff makes this place great for wine newbies. (Make sure you get that reservation lined up.)

Dinner and Overnight: St. Helena. Splurge at Meadowood Napa Valley and you won't need to leave the property for

Domaine Carneros

121
12

di Rosa Preserve

Old Sonoma Rd.

Oxbow Public Market
Napa
29

NAPA COUNTY

Robert Mondavi

Far Niente

Yountville

Oakville

KEY
First-Timer's Napa Tour
Wine Buff's Tour

Silverado Trail

Stag's Leap Wine Cellars

Wine Buff's Tour

Start: Stag's Leap Wine Cellars, Yountville. Famed for its cabernet sauvignon and Bordeaux blends.

Beaulieu Vineyard, Rutherford. Pony up the extra fee to visit the reserve tasting room to try the flagship Cabernet Sauvignon.

Mumm Napa, Rutherford. Come for the bubbly—which is available in a variety of tastings—stay for the photography exhibits.

Dinner and Overnight: Yountville. Have dinner at one of the Thomas Keller restaurants. Splurge at Bardessono; save at

Maison Fleurie.

Next Day: Robert Mondavi, Oakville. Spring for the reserve room tasting so you can sip the top-of-the-line wines, especially the stellar Cabernet Sauvignon. Head across Highway 29 to the Oakville Grocery to pick up a picnic lunch.

an extravagant dinner at its restaurant. Save at El Bonita Motel with dinner at Gott's.

Next Day: Poke around St. Helena's shops, then drive to Yountville for lunch.

di Rosa, Napa. Call ahead to book a one- or two-hour tour of the acres of gardens and galleries, which

are chock-full of thousands of works of art.

Domaine Carneros, Napa. Toast your trip with a glass of outstanding bubbly.

Sonoma Backroads

Start: Iron Horse Vineyards, Russian River Valley.
Soak up a view of vine-covered hills and Mount St. Helena while sipping a sparkling wine or Pinot Noir at this beautifully rustic spot.

Hartford Family Winery, Russian River Valley.
A terrific source for Pinot Noir and Chardonnay, the stars of this valley.

Dinner and Overnight: Forestville. Go all out with a stay at the Farmhouse Inn, whose award-winning restaurant is one of the best in all of Sonoma.

Next Day: Westside Road, Russian River Valley.
This scenic route, which follows the river, is crowded with worthwhile wineries like Gary Farrell and Rochioli—but it's not crowded with visitors. Pinot fans will find a lot to love. Picnic at Rochioli and enjoy the lovely view.

Matanzas Creek Winery, near Santa Rosa.
End on an especially relaxed note with a walk through the lavender fields (best in June).

Far Niente, Oakville. You have to make a reservation and the fee for the tasting and tour is steep, but the

payoff is an especially intimate winery experience. You'll taste excellent Cabernet and Chardonnay, then end your trip on a sweet note with a dessert wine.

7

IN FOCUS WINE TASTING IN NAPA AND SONOMA

WINE TASTING 101

TAKE A GOOD LOOK.

Hold your glass by the stem, raise it to the light, and take a close look at the wine. Check for clarity and color. (This is easiest to do if you can hold the glass in front of a white background.) Any tinge of brown usually means that the wine is over the hill or has gone bad.

BREATHE DEEP.

1. Sniff the wine once or twice to see if you can identify any smells.

2. Swirl the wine gently in the glass. Aerating the wine this way releases more of its aromas. (It's called "volatilizing the esters," if you're trying to impress someone.)

3. Take another long sniff. You might notice that experienced wine tasters spend more time sniffing the wine than drinking it. This is because this step is where the magic happens. The number of scents you might detect is almost endless, from berries, apricots, honey, and wildflowers to leather, cedar, or even tar. Does the wine smell good to you? Do you detect any "off" flavors, like wet dog or sulfur?

Sniff

AT LAST! TAKE A SIP.

1. Swirl the wine around your mouth so that it makes contact with all your taste buds and releases more of its aromas. Think about the way the wine feels in your mouth. Is it watery or rich? Is it crisp or silky? Does it have a bold flavor, or is it subtle? The weight and intensity of a wine are called its body.

2. Hold the wine in your mouth for a few seconds and see if you can identify any developing flavors. More complex wines will reveal many different flavors as you drink them.

SPIT OR SWALLOW.

The pros typically spit, since they want to preserve their palate (and sobriety!) for the wines to come, but you'll find that swallowers far outnumber the spitters in the winery tasting rooms. Whether you spit or swallow, notice the flavor that remains after the wine is gone (the finish).

Sip

DODGE THE CROWDS

To avoid bumping elbows in the tasting rooms, look for wineries off the main drags of Highway 29 in Napa and Highway 12 in Sonoma. The back roads of the Russian River, Dry Creek, and Alexander valleys, all in Sonoma, are excellent places to explore. In Napa, try the northern end. Also look for wineries that are open by appointment only; they tend to schedule visitors carefully to avoid a big crush at any one time.

HOW WINE IS MADE

1. CRUSHING
Harvested grapes go into a stemmer-crusher, which separates stems from fruit and crushes the grapes to release "free-run" juice.

2. PRESSING
Remaining juice is gently extracted from grapes. Usually done by pressing grapes against the walls of a tank with an inflatable bladder.

3. FERMENTING
Extracted juice (and also grape skins and pulp, when making red wine) goes into stainless-steel tanks or oak barrels to ferment. During fermentation, sugars convert to alcohol.

4. AGING
Wine is stored in stainless-steel or oak casks or barrels, or sometimes in concrete vessels, to develop flavors.

5. RACKING
Wine is transferred to clean barrels; sediment is removed. Wine may be filtered and fined (clarified) to improve its clarity, color, and sometimes flavor.

6. BOTTLING
Wine is bottled either at the winery or at a special facility, then stored again for bottle-aging.

WHAT'S AN APPELLATION?

A specific region with a particular set of grape-growing conditions, such as soil type, climate, and elevation, is called an appellation. What makes things a little confusing is that appellations, which are defined by the Alcohol and Tobacco Tax and Trade Bureau, often overlap. California is an appellation, for example, but so is the Napa Valley. Napa and Sonoma counties are each county appellations, but they, too, are divided into even smaller regions, usually called subappellations or AVAs (American Viticultural Areas). You'll hear a lot about these AVAs from the staff in the tasting rooms; they might explain, for example, why the Russian River Valley AVA is such an excellent place to grow Pinot Noir grapes.

By law, if the label on a bottle of wine lists the name of an appellation, then at least 85% of the grapes in that wine must come from that appellation.

Wine and contemporary art find a home at di Rosa.

GETTING HERE AND AROUND

Downtown Napa lies a mile east of Highway 29—take the 1st Street exit and follow the signs. Ample parking, much of it free for the first three hours and some for the entire day, is available on or near Main Street. Several VINE buses serve downtown and beyond.

EXPLORING

TOP ATTRACTIONS

Fodor's Choice ★ **Artesa Vineyards & Winery.** From a distance the modern, minimalist architecture of Artesa blends harmoniously with the surrounding Carneros landscape, but up close its pools, fountains, and the large outdoor sculptures by resident artist Gordon Huether of Napa make a vivid impression. So, too, do the wines crafted by Mark Beringer, who focuses on Chardonnay and Pinot Noir but also produces Cabernet Sauvignon and other limited-release wines such as Albariño and Tempranillo. You can taste wines by themselves or paired with chocolate ($50), cheese ($60), and tapas ($60). ■TIP→ The main tour, conducted daily, explores wine making and the winery. A Friday-only tour covers the art, and from June through October there's a vineyard tour. ⊠ *1345 Henry Rd., off Old Sonoma Rd. and Dealy La., Napa* ☎ *707/224–1668* ⊕ *www.artesawinery.com* ⛃ *Tastings $20–$60, tours $30–$45* ⊙ *Daily 10–5, winery tour daily at 11 and 2, art tour Fri. at 10:30; reservations required for some tastings and tours.*

Fodor's Choice ★ **di Rosa.** About 2,000 works from the 1960s to the present by Northern California artists are displayed on this 217-acre art property. They can be found not only in galleries and in the former residence of its late founder, Rene di Rosa, but also on every lawn, in every courtyard, and even on the lake. Some works were commissioned especially for di Rosa, among them Paul Kos's meditative *Chartres Bleu,* a video installation in a chapel-like setting that replicates a stained-glass window from the cathedral in Chartres, France. ■TIP➜ **You can view the current temporary exhibition and a few permanent works at the Gatehouse Gallery, but to experience the breadth of this incomparable collection you'll need to book a tour.** ⊠ *5200 Sonoma Hwy./Hwy. 121, Napa* ☎ *707/226–5991* ⊕ *www.dirosaart.org* ⊠ *Gatehouse Gallery $5, tours $12–$15* ☉ *Wed.–Sun. 10–4.*

Fodor's Choice
★ **Domaine Carneros.** A visit to this majestic château is an opulent way to enjoy the Carneros District—especially in fine weather, when the vineyard views are spectacular. The château was modeled after an 18th-century French mansion owned by the Taittinger family. Carved into the hillside beneath the winery, the cellars produce delicate sparkling wines reminiscent of those made by Taittinger, using only Los Carneros AVA grapes. The winery sells full glasses, flights, and bottles of its wines, which also include Chardonnay, Pinot Noir, and other still wines. Enjoy them all with cheese and charcuterie plates, caviar, or smoked salmon. Seating is in the Louis XV–inspired salon or on the terrace overlooking the vines. The tour here covers traditional methods of making sparkling wines. ⊠ *1240 Duhig Rd., at Hwy. 121, Napa* ☎ *707/257–0101, 800/716–2788* ⊕ *www.domainecarneros.com* ⊠ *Tastings $10–$40, tour $40* ☉ *Daily 10–5:45; tour daily at 11, 1, and 3.*

Fodor's Choice
★ **The Hess Collection.** About 9 miles northwest of Napa, up a winding road ascending Mt. Veeder, this winery is a delightful discovery. The limestone structure, rustic from the outside but modern and airy within, contains Swiss owner Donald Hess's world-class art collection, including large-scale works by contemporary artists such as Andy Goldsworthy, Anselm Kiefer, and Robert Rauschenberg. Cabernet Sauvignon is a major strength, and the 19 Block Cuvée, Mount Veeder, a Cabernet blend, shows off the Malbec and other estate varietals. ■TIP➜ **Food-wine pairings include one with chocolates that go well with the Mount Veeder Cabernet Sauvignon.** ⊠ *4411 Redwood Rd., west off Hwy. 29 at Trancas St./Redwood Rd. exit, Napa* ☎ *707/255–1144* ⊕ *www. hesscollection.com* ⊠ *Art gallery free, tastings $20–$85* ☉ *Daily 10–5:30; guided tours daily 10:30–3:30.*

Fodor's Choice
★ **Oxbow Public Market.** The market's two dozen shops, wine bars, and artisanal food producers provide an introduction to Napa Valley's wealth of foods and wines. Swoon over decadent charcuterie at the Fatted Calf, slurp bivalves at Hog Island Oyster Company, or chow down on tacos with homemade tortillas at C Casa. Afterward, sip wine at Ca' Momi Enoteca or sample the barrel-aged cocktails and handcrafted vodka of the Napa Valley Distillery. The owner of C Casa also runs Cate & Co., a bakeshop that makes going gluten-free an absolute delight. ■TIP➜ **Locals head to Model Bakery around 3 pm for hot-from-the-oven "late bake" bread.** ⊠ *610 and 644 1st St., at McKinstry St., Napa* ⊕ *www. oxbowpublicmarket.com* ⊠ *Free* ☉ *Weekdays 9–9, weekends 10–9; merchants hrs vary.*

Climbing ivy and lily pads decorate the Hess Collection's rustic exterior.

Fodor's Choice **St. Clair Brown Winery.** Tastings at this women-run "urban winery" a few
★ blocks north of downtown take place in an intimate, light-filled greenhouse or the colorful culinary garden outside. Winemaker Elaine St. Clair,
well regarded for her stints at Domaine Carneros and Black Stallion, produces elegant wines—crisp yet complex whites and smooth, French-style
reds among whose stars are the Cabernet Sauvignon and a Syrah from
grapes grown in the Coombsville appellation. The wines are paired with
addictive appetizers that include almonds roasted with rosemary, cumin,
and Meyer lemon juice. ■TIP→ You can sip single wines by the glass or
half glass, or opt for the four-wine sampler. ⊠ *816 Vallejo St., off Soscol
Ave., Napa* ☎ *707/255–5591* ⊕ *www.stclairbrownwinery.com* ✉ *Tastings $4–$20* ⊘ *Daily 11–8.*

WORTH NOTING

Etude Wines. You're apt to see or hear hawks, egrets, Canada geese, and
other wildlife on the grounds of Etude, known for its sophisticated Pinot
Noirs. Though the winery and its light-filled tasting room are in Napa
County, the grapes for its flagship Carneros Estate Pinot Noir come from
the Sonoma portion of Los Carneros, as do the ones for the rarer Heirloom Carneros Pinot Noir. Chardonnay, Pinot Blanc, Pinot Noir, and
other wines made by Jon Priest are poured daily in the tasting room.
On Friday and the weekend, Pinot Noirs from California, Oregon, and
New Zealand are compared at seated The Study of Pinot Noir seminars
($45). ■TIP→ Single-vineyard Napa Valley Cabernets are another Etude
specialty; the Rutherford and Oakville ones are particularly good. ⊠ *1250
Cuttings Wharf Rd., 1 mile south of Hwy. 121, Napa* ☎ *877/586–9361*
⊕ *www.etudewines.com* ✉ *Tastings $15–$45* ⊘ *Daily 10–4:30; Study of
Pinot Noir tastings Fri.–Sun. at 10, 1, and 3 by appointment.*

Napa Valley Wine Train. Several century-old restored Pullman railroad cars and a two-story 1952 Vista Dome car with a curved glass roof travel a leisurely, scenic route between Napa and St. Helena. All trips include a well-made lunch or dinner; for all lunches and Saturday dinner you can combine your trip with a winery tour. Murder-mystery plays and dinners with vintners and winemakers are among the regularly scheduled special events. ■TIP➜ It's best to make this trip during the day, when you can enjoy the vineyard views. ⊠ *1275 McKinstry St., off 1st St., Napa* ☎ *707/253–2111, 800/427–4124* ⊕ *www.winetrain.com* ⊒ *From $124* ☉ *Lunch: Jan. and Feb., Fri.–Sun. 11:30; Mar.–Dec., daily 11:30. Dinner: May–Sept., Fri.–Sun. 6:30; Oct., Fri. and Sat. 6:30; Nov.–Mar., Sat. 6:30; Apr., Fri. and Sat. 6:30.*

WHERE TO EAT

$$ ✕ **The Boon Fly Café.** This small spot melds rural charm with industrial
MODERN   chic. Outside, swings occupy the porch of a modern red barn; inside,
AMERICAN   things get sleek with high ceilings and galvanized-steel tabletops. The
Fodor's Choice   menu of three squares a day updates American classics such as fried
★   chicken (free-range in this case), burgers (but with Kobe beef), and shrimp and grits. The flatbreads, including a super-creamy smoked salmon one made with fromage blanc, Parmesan, and lemon crème fraîche, are worth a try. Chicken and waffles and other daily specials draw locals, too, and there's a varied selection of wines by the glass. ■TIP➜ Open all day, The Boon Fly makes a convenient mid-morning or late-afternoon stop. Ⓢ *Average main: $22* ⊠ *Carneros Inn, 4048 Sonoma Hwy., Napa* ☎ *707/299–4870* ⊕ *www.boonflycafe.com.*

$$$ ✕ **Bounty Hunter Wine Bar & Smokin' BBQ.** A triple threat, Bounty Hunter is
AMERICAN   a wine store, wine bar, and restaurant in one. You can stop by for just a
Fodor's Choice   glass—about 40 choices are available in both 2- and 5-ounce pours—or
★   a bottle, but it's best to come with an appetite. Every dish on the small menu is a standout, including the pulled-pork and beef brisket sandwiches served with three types of barbecue sauce, the signature beer-can chicken (only Tecate will do), and meltingly tender St. Louis–style ribs. The space is whimsically rustic, with stuffed game trophies mounted on the wall and leather saddles standing in for seats at a couple of tables. Ⓢ *Average main: $26* ⊠ *975 1st St., near Main St., Napa* ☎ *707/226–3976* ⊕ *www.bountyhunterwinebar.com* ⌦ *Reservations not accepted.*

$$$$ ✕ **Cole's Chop House.** When only a thick, perfect steak will do, popular
STEAKHOUSE   Cole's is the best choice in town. The prime steaks—New York and
Fodor's Choice   porterhouse—are dry-aged by Allen Brothers of Chicago, purveyors to
★   America's top steak houses. New Zealand lamb chops are the house's non-beef favorite, and seasonal additions might include veal chops. Inside an 1886 stone building, Chops hews to tradition with the starters and sides. Expect oysters Rockefeller, creamed spinach, grilled asparagus with hollandaise, and other standbys, all prepared with finesse. The wine list is borderline epic, with the best of the Napa Valley amply represented. Ⓢ *Average main: $38* ⊠ *1122 Main St., at Pearl St., Napa* ☎ *707/224–6328* ⊕ *www.coleschophouse.com* ⌦ *Reservations essential* ☉ *No lunch.*

$$$$ MODERN AMERICAN Fodor's Choice ★ 🍴 **La Toque.** Chef Ken Frank's La Toque is the complete package: his imaginative Modern American cuisine is served in an elegant dining space, complemented by an astutely assembled wine lineup that in 2014 earned a coveted *Wine Spectator* Grand Award, bestowed on only 74 establishments worldwide. Built around seasonal local ingredients, the menu changes frequently, but Rosti potato with Israeli Russian Osetra caviar routinely appears as a starter, and Moroccan-spiced Liberty Farm duck breast and Wagyu beef served with Frank's variation on poutine are oft-seen entrées. Four-course ($80) and five-course ($98) tasting menus are offered, but for a memorable occasion consider letting the chef and sommelier surprise you via the chef's table tasting menu ($195, $95 additional for wine pairings). [$] *Average main: $80* ✉ *Westin Verasa Napa, 1314 McKinstry St., off Soscol Ave., Napa* ☎ *707/257–5157* 🌐 *www.latoque.com* ⏲ *No lunch.*

$$$$ JAPANESE 🍴 **Morimoto Napa.** *Iron Chef* star Masuharu Morimoto is the big name behind this downtown Napa hot spot. Organic materials such as twisting grapevines above the bar and rough-hewn wooden tables seem simultaneously earthy and modern, creating a fitting setting for the gorgeously plated Japanese fare, from sashimi served with grated fresh wasabi to elaborate concoctions that include sea-urchin carbonara, made with udon noodles. Everything's delightfully overdone, right down to the desserts. **■ TIP→ For the full experience, leave the choice up to the chef and opt for the omakase menu ($120–$160).** [$] *Average main: $44* ✉ *610 Main St., at 5th St., Napa* ☎ *707/252–1600* 🌐 *www.morimotonapa.com.*

$$$ MODERN AMERICAN Fodor's Choice ★ 🍴 **Torc.** *Torc* means "wild boar" in an early Celtic dialect, and chef Sean O'Toole occasionally incorporates his restaurant's namesake beast into dishes at his eclectic downtown restaurant. Bolognese sauce, for example, might include ground wild boar, tomato, lime, and cocoa. O'Toole has helmed kitchens at top New York City, San Francisco, and Yountville establishments. Torc is the first restaurant he's owned, and he crafts meals with style and precision that are reflected in the gracious service and classy, contemporary decor. **■ TIP→ The Bengali sweet potato–pakora appetizer, which comes with a dreamy-creamy yogurt-truffle dip, has been a hit since day one.** [$] *Average main: $25* ✉ *1140 Main St., at Pearl St., Napa* ☎ *707/252–3292* 🌐 *www.torcnapa.com* ⏲ *No lunch weekdays.*

$$$ SPANISH Fodor's Choice ★ 🍴 **ZuZu.** The focus at festive ZuZu is on tapas, paella, and other Spanish favorites. Diners down *cava* (Spanish sparkling wine) or sangria with dishes that might include white anchovies with boiled egg and rémoulade on grilled bread. Locals revere the paella, made with Spanish Bomba rice. Latin jazz on the stereo helps make this place a popular spot for get-togethers. In fall 2014, ZuZu's owners opened **La Taberna,** three doors south at 815 Main Street, a bar for *pintxos* (small bites) and cocktails. The signature dish: suckling pig, which goes well with the beers, wines, and other libations. [$] *Average main: $29* ✉ *829 Main St., near 3rd St., Napa* ☎ *707/224–8555* 🌐 *www.zuzunapa.com* ✍ *Reservations not accepted* ⏲ *No lunch weekends.*

WHERE TO STAY

$$$ HOTEL Fodor's Choice ★ 🏨 **Andaz Napa.** Part of the Hyatt family, this boutique hotel with an urban-hip vibe has luxurious rooms with flat-screen TVs, laptop-size safes, and white-marble bathrooms stocked with high-quality bath products. **Pros:** proximity to downtown restaurants, theaters, and tasting rooms; access

to modern fitness center; complimentary beverage upon arrival; complimentary snacks and nonalcoholic beverages in rooms. **Cons:** parking can be a challenge on weekends; unremarkable views from some rooms. $ *Rooms from: $309* ⊠ *1450 1st St., Napa* ☎ *707/687–1234* ⊕ *andaznapa.com* ⇥ *137 rooms, 4 suites* ⏹ *No meals.*

$$$$ ⊞ **Carneros Inn.** Freestanding board-and-batten cottages with rocking
RESORT chairs on each porch are simultaneously rustic and chic at this luxuri-
Fodor's Choice ous property. **Pros:** cottages have lots of privacy; beautiful views from
★ hilltop pool and hot tub; heaters on private patios; excellent Boon Fly Café is open all day. **Cons:** a long drive to destinations up-valley; small-ish rooms with limited seating options. $ *Rooms from: $600* ⊠ *4048 Sonoma Hwy./Hwy. 121, Napa* ☎ *707/299–4900, 888/400–9000* ⊕ *www.thecarnerosinn.com* ⇥ *76 cottages, 10 suites* ⏹ *No meals.*

$$ ⊞ **Inn on Randolph.** A few calm blocks from the downtown action, the
B&B/INN restored Inn on Randolph is a sophisticated haven celebrated for its
Fodor's Choice gluten-free breakfasts and snacks. **Pros:** quiet; gourmet breakfasts;
★ sophisticated decor; romantic setting. **Cons:** a bit of a walk from down-town. $ *Rooms from: $285* ⊠ *411 Randolph St., Napa* ☎ *707/257–2886* ⊕ *www.innonrandolph.com* ⇥ *5 rooms, 5 cottages* ⏹ *Breakfast.*

$$ ⊞ **Napa River Inn.** Part of a complex of restaurants, shops, a night-
B&B/INN club, and a spa, this waterfront inn is within easy walking distance of downtown hot spots. **Pros:** wide range of room sizes and prices; near downtown action; pet friendly. **Cons:** river views could be more scenic; some rooms get noise from nearby restaurants. $ *Rooms from: $249* ⊠ *500 Main St., Napa* ☎ *707/251–8500, 877/251–8500* ⊕ *www.napariverinn.com* ⇥ *65 rooms, 1 suite* ⏹ *Breakfast.*

$$$ ⊞ **Senza Hotel.** Exterior fountains, gallery-quality outdoor sculptures,
HOTEL and decorative rows of grapevines signal the Wine Country–chic aspira-
Fodor's Choice tions of this boutique hotel operated by the owners of Hall St. Helena
★ winery. **Pros:** high-style fixtures; fireplaces in all rooms; Wine Country–chic atmosphere. **Cons:** just off highway; little of interest within walking distance; some bathrooms have no tub. $ *Rooms from: $369* ⊠ *4066 Howard La., Napa* ☎ *707/253–0337* ⊕ *www.senzahotel.com* ⇥ *41 rooms* ⏹ *Breakfast.*

NIGHTLIFE AND PERFORMING ARTS

Fodor's Choice **1313 Main.** Cool, sexy 1313 Main attracts a youngish crowd for top-
★ drawer spirits and sparkling and still wines. The on-site **LuLu's Kitchen** serves bar food—past favorites have included coq au vin wings and corn and shiso fritters—and wild salmon, steak, and other entrées. ⊠ *1313 Main St., at Clinton St., Napa* ☎ *707/258–1313* ⊕ *www.1313main.com.*

City Winery Napa. A makeover transformed the 1879 Napa Valley Opera House into a combination wine bar, restaurant, and live-music venue that features top singer-songwriters and small acts. Many of the three dozen wines on tap are exclusive to the club from prestigious area wineries. ⊠ *1030 Main St., near 1st St., Napa* ☎ *707/260–1600* ⊕ *www.citywinery.com/napa.*

Uptown Theatre. This top-notch live-music venue, a former movie house, attracts Ziggy Marley, Ani DiFranco, Napa Valley resident and winery owner Boz Scaggs, and other performers. ⊠ *1350 3rd St., at Franklin St., Napa* ☎ *707/259–0123* ⊕ *www.uptowntheatrenapa.com.*

YOUNTVILLE

9 miles north of the town of Napa.

These days Yountville is something like Disneyland for food lovers. You could stay here for a week and not exhaust all the options—several of them owned by The French Laundry's Thomas Keller—and the tiny town is full of small inns and high-end hotels that cater to those who prefer to walk (not drive) after an extravagant meal. It's also well located for excursions to many big-name Napa wineries, especially those in the Stags Leap District, from which big, bold Cabernet Sauvignons helped make the Napa Valley's wine-making reputation.

GETTING HERE AND AROUND

Downtown Yountville sits just off Highway 29. Approaching from the south take the Yountville exit—from the north take Madison—and proceed to Washington Street, home to the major shops and restaurants. Yountville Cross Road connects downtown to the Silverado Trail, along which many noted wineries do business. The free Yountville Trolley serves the town daily from 10 am to 7 pm (on-call service until 11 except on Sunday).

Contact **Yountville Trolley** ✉ *Yountville* ☎ *707/944–1234 10 am–7 pm, 707/312–1509 7 pm–11 pm* ⊕ *www.ridethevine.com/yountville-trolley.*

EXPLORING

TOP ATTRACTIONS

Fodor'sChoice **Cliff Lede Vineyards.** Inspired by his passion for classic rock, owner and
★ construction magnate Cliff Lede named his Stags Leap vineyard blocks after hits by the Grateful Dead and other bands, but the vibe at his efficient, high-tech winery is anything but laid-back. It's worth taking the estate tour to learn about the agricultural science that informs vineyard management here, and to see the production facility in action. Architect Howard Backen designed the winery and its tasting room, where Lede's Sauvignon Blanc, Cabernet Sauvignons, and other wines, along with some from sister winery Fel, which produces much-lauded Anderson Valley Pinot Noirs, are poured. ■ TIP➔ **Walk-ins are welcome at the tasting bar, but appointments are required for the veranda outside and a nearby gallery that often displays rock-related art.** ✉ *1473 Yountville Cross Rd., off Silverado Trail, Yountville* ☎ *707/944–8642* ⊕ *cliffledevineyards.com* 🍷 *Tastings $25–$45; estate tour and tasting $75* ☉ *Daily 10–4.*

Domaine Chandon. On a knoll shaded by ancient oak trees, this French-owned maker of sparkling wines claims one of Yountville's prime pieces of real estate. Chandon is best known for bubblies, but the still wines—Cabernet Sauvignon, Chardonnay, Pinot Meunier, and Pinot Noir—are also worth a try. You can sip by the flight or the glass at the bar or begin there and sit at tables in the lounge and return to the bar as needed; in good weather, tables are set up outside. Tours, which cover Chandon's French and California histories and the basics of making sparkling wines, end with a seated tasting. For the complete experience, order a cheese board or other hors d'oeuvres on the lounge menu. ✉ *1 California Dr., off Hwy. 29, Yountville* ☎ *707/204–7530, 888/242–6366* ⊕ *www.chandon. com* 🍷 *Tastings $10–$22, tours $40* ☉ *Daily 10–5; tour times vary.*

Fodor's Choice
★
Ma(i)sonry Napa Valley. An art-and-design gallery that also pours the wines of two dozen limited-production wineries, Ma(i)sonry occupies an atmospheric stone manor house constructed in 1904. Tasting flights can be sampled in fair weather in the beautiful garden, in a private nook, or at the communal redwood table, and in any weather indoors among the contemporary artworks and well-chosen *objets*—which might include 17th-century furnishings, industrial lamps, or slabs of petrified wood. ■TIP➜ Walk-ins are welcome space permitting, but during summer, at harvesttime, and on weekends and holidays it's best to book in advance. ✉ 6711 *Washington St., at Pedroni St., Yountville* ☎ 707/944–0889 ⊕ *www.maisonry.com* ✆ *Tasting $15–$35* ⊗ *Sun.–Thurs. daily 10–6, Fri. and Sat. daily 10–7; check for later hrs in summer and early fall.*

WORTH NOTING

Fodor's Choice
★
Robert Sinskey Vineyards. Although the winery produces a well-regarded Stags Leap Cabernet Sauvignon, two supple red blends called Marcien and POV, and white wines, Sinskey is best known for its intense, brambly Carneros District Pinot Noirs. All the grapes are grown in organic, certified biodynamic vineyards. The influence of Robert's wife, Maria Helm Sinskey—a chef and cookbook author and the winery's culinary director—is evident during the tastings, which are accompanied by a few bites of food with each wine. ■TIP➜ The Perfect Circle Tour ($75) takes in the winery's gardens and ends with a seated pairing of food and wine. ✉ 6320 *Silverado Trail, at Yountville Cross Rd., Napa* ☎ 707/944–9090 ⊕ *www.robertsinskey.com* ✆ *Tasting $25, tour $75* ⊗ *Daily 10–4:30; tours by appointment weekdays at 11, weekends at 1.*

Stag's Leap Wine Cellars. A 1973 Stag's Leap Cabernet Sauvignon put this winery and the Napa Valley on the enological map by placing first in the famous Paris tasting of 1976. The grapes for that wine came from a vineyard visible from the new stone-and-glass Fay Outlook & Visitor Center, which opened in 2014. The tasting room has broad views of a second fabled Cabernet vineyard (Fay) and the promontory that gives both the winery and the Stags Leap District AVA their names. ■TIP➜ A $40 tasting includes the top-of-the-line estate-grown Cabernets, which sell for more than $100; a $25 tasting of more modestly priced wines is also available. ✉ 5766 *Silverado Trail, at Wappo Hill Rd., Napa* ☎ 707/944–2020, 866/422–7523 ⊕ *www.cask23.com* ✆ *Tastings $25–$40, tour with food and wine pairing $95* ⊗ *Daily 10–4:30; tours by appointment.*

WHERE TO EAT

$$$$
MODERN
AMERICAN
Fodor's Choice
★
✕ **Ad Hoc.** At this casual spot, superstar chef Thomas Keller offers a single, fixed-price menu ($52) nightly, with a small lineup of decadent brunch items served on Sunday. The dinner selection might include braised beef short ribs and creamy polenta, or a delicate panna cotta with a citrus glaze. The dining room is warmly low-key, with zinc-top tables, wine served in tumblers, and rock and jazz on the stereo. Call a day ahead to find out the next day's menu. ■TIP➜ From Thursday through Saturday, except in winter, you can pick up a boxed lunch to go—the buttermilk fried chicken one is delicious—at the on-site and aptly named Addendum. Ⓢ *Average main: $52* ✉ 6476 *Washington St., at Oak Circle, Yountville* ☎ 707/944–2487 ⊕ *www.adhocrestaurant.com* ⌘ *Reservations essential* ⊗ *No lunch Mon.–Sat. No dinner Tues. and Wed.*

$$$ FRENCH Fodor's Choice ★ 🍴 **Bistro Jeanty.** French classics and obscure delicacies tickle patrons' palates at chef Philippe Jeanty's genteel country bistro. Jeanty prepares the greatest hits—escargots, cassoulet, *daube de boeuf* (beef stewed in red wine)—with the utmost precision and turns out pike dumplings and lamb tongue with equal élan. Regulars often start with the extraordinary, rich tomato soup in a flaky puff pastry before proceeding to sole meunière, slow-roasted pork shoulder, or coq au vin (always choosing the simple, suggested side: thin egg noodles cooked with just the right amount of butter and salt). Chocolate pot de crème, warm apple tart tartin, and other authentic desserts complete the French sojourn. [$] *Average main: $27* ✉ *6510 Washington St., at Mulberry St., Yountville* ☎ *707/944–0103* 🌐 *www.bistrojeanty.com.*

$$$ ITALIAN 🍴 **Bottega.** The food at chef Michael Chiarello's trattoria is simultaneously soulful and inventive, transforming local ingredients into regional Italian dishes with a twist. The antipasti shine: you can order grilled short-rib meatballs, house-made charcuterie, or incredibly fresh fish. Potato gnocchi might be served with pumpkin *fonduta* (Italian-style fondue) and roasted root vegetables, and hearty main courses such as a grilled acorn-fed pork shoulder loin with a honey-mustard glaze might be accompanied by cinnamon stewed plums and crispy black kale. The vibe is festive, with exposed-brick walls and an open kitchen, but service is spot-on, and the wine list includes interesting choices from Italy and California. [$] *Average main: $26* ✉ *V Marketplace, 6525 Washington St., near Mulberry St., Yountville* ☎ *707/945–1050* 🌐 *www.botteganapavalley.com* 🕒 *No lunch Mon.*

$$$ FRENCH Fodor's Choice ★ 🍴 **Bouchon.** The team that created The French Laundry is also behind this place, where everything—the lively and crowded zinc-topped bar, the elbow-to-elbow seating, the traditional French onion soup—could have come straight from a Parisian bistro. Roast chicken with sautéed chicken livers and button mushrooms, and steamed mussels served with crispy, addictive *frites* (french fries) are among the dishes served. **■ TIP→ The adjacent Bouchon Bakery sells marvelous macaroons (meringue cookies) in many flavors, along with brownies, pastries, and other baked goods.** [$] *Average main: $27* ✉ *6534 Washington St., near Humboldt St., Yountville* ☎ *707/944–8037* 🌐 *www.bouchonbistro.com* ✍ *Reservations essential.*

$$ MODERN ITALIAN Fodor's Choice ★ 🍴 **Ciccio.** High-profile French and modern-American establishments may dominate the Yountville landscape, but recent arrival Ciccio instantly endeared itself with locals and visitors seeking inventive, reasonably priced—in this case, modern Italian—cuisine. Inside a remodeled former grocery store that retains a down-home feel, executive chef Polly Lappetito, formerly of the Culinary Institute of America, turns out pizzas and entrées, some of whose vegetables and herbs come from the garden of the owners, Frank and Karen Altamura. Seasonal growing cycles dictate the ever-changing menu; Tuscan kale and white-bean soup, wood-fired sardines with salsa verde, and a mushroom, Taleggio, and crispy-sage pizza are among the recent offerings. Frank and Karen own Altamura Vineyards, whose wines are featured here, but their Napa Valley neighbors are also represented, and there's a Negroni cocktail bar. [$] *Average main: $19* ✉ *6770 Washington St., at Madison*

St., Yountville ☎ *707/945–1000* 🌐 *www.ciccionapavalley.com* ✍ *Reservations not accepted* ⏲ *Closed Mon. and Tues. No lunch.*

$$$$ AMERICAN Fodor's Choice ★ 🍴 **The French Laundry.** An old stone building laced with ivy houses the most acclaimed restaurant in the Napa Valley—and, indeed, one of the most highly regarded in the country. The two nine-course prix-fixe menus (both $295), one of which highlights vegetables, vary, but "oysters and pearls," a silky dish of pearl tapioca with oysters and white sturgeon caviar, is a signature starter. Some courses rely on luxe ingredients like *calotte* (cap of the rib eye), while others take humble foods such as fava beans and elevate them to art. Many courses also offer the option of "supplements"—sea urchin, for instance, or black truffles. **TIP→ Reservations are hard-won here; to get one call two months ahead to the day at 10 am, on the dot.** [$] *Average main: $295* ✉ *6640 Washington St., at Creek St., Yountville* ☎ *707/944–2380* 🌐 *www.frenchlaundry.com* ✍ *Reservations essential* 👔 *Jacket required* ⏲ *No lunch Mon.–Thurs.*

$$$ AMERICAN 🍴 **Mustards Grill.** Cindy Pawlcyn's Mustards fills day and night with fans of her hearty cuisine. The menu mixes updated renditions of traditional American dishes (what Pawlcyn dubs "deluxe truck stop classics")—among them barbecued baby back pork ribs and a lemon-lime tart piled high with browned meringue—with more fanciful choices such as sweet corn tamales with tomatillo-avocado salsa and wild mushrooms. A black-and-white marble tile floor and upbeat artworks keep the mood jolly. [$] *Average main: $27* ✉ *7399 St. Helena Hwy./Hwy. 29, 1 mile north of Yountville, Napa* ☎ *707/944–2424* 🌐 *www.mustardsgrill.com.*

$$$ MODERN AMERICAN Fodor's Choice ★ 🍴 **Redd.** The minimalist dining room here seems a fitting setting for chef Richard Reddington's up-to-date menu. The culinary influences include California, Mexico, Europe, and Asia, but the food always feels modern and never fussy. The glazed pork belly with apple puree, set amid a pool of soy caramel, is a prime example of the East-meets-West style. The seafood preparations—among them petrale sole, clams, and chorizo poached in a saffron-curry broth—are deft variations on the original dishes. For the full experience, consider the five-course tasting menu ($80 per person, $125 with wine pairing). **TIP→ For a quick bite, order small plates and a cocktail and sit at the bar.** [$] *Average main: $30* ✉ *6480 Washington St., at Oak Circle, Yountville* ☎ *707/944–2222* 🌐 *www.reddnapavalley.com* ✍ *Reservations essential.*

$$ ITALIAN 🍴 **Redd Wood.** Chef Richard Reddington's casual restaurant specializes in thin-crust wood-fired pizzas and contemporary variations on rustic Italian classics. The nonchalance of the industrial decor mirrors the service, which is less officious than elsewhere in town, and the cuisine itself. A dish such as glazed beef short ribs, for instance, might seem like yet another fancy take on a down-home favorite until you realize how cleverly the sweetness of the glaze plays off the creamy polenta and the piquant splash of salsa verde. Redd Wood does for Italian comfort food what nearby Mustards Grill does for the American version: it spruces it up but retains its innate pleasures. [$] *Average main: $22* ✉ *North Block Hotel, 6755 Washington St., at Madison St., Yountville* ☎ *707/299–5030* 🌐 *www.redd-wood.com.*

WHERE TO STAY

$$$$
RESORT
Fodor's Choice
★

⌂ **Bardessono.** Although Bardessono bills itself as the "greenest luxury hotel in America," there's nothing spartan about its accommodations; arranged around four landscaped courtyards, the rooms have luxurious organic bedding, gas fireplaces, and huge bathrooms with walnut floors. **Pros:** large rooftop lap pool; exciting restaurant; excellent spa, with in-room treatments available; polished service. **Cons:** expensive; limited view from some rooms. $ *Rooms from: $650* ⌂ *6526 Yount St., Yountville* ☎ *707/204–6000* ⊕ *www.bardessono.com* ⇥ *56 rooms, 6 suites* ¶⊙¶ *No meals.*

$$
B&B/INN

⌂ **Lavender Inn.** On a quiet side street around the corner from The French Laundry restaurant, the Lavender Inn feels at once secluded and centrally located. **Pros:** reasonable rates for Yountville; in residential area but close to restaurants and shops; friendly staff. **Cons:** hard to book in high season; lacks amenities of larger properties. $ *Rooms from: $275* ⌂ *2020 Webber St., Yountville* ☎ *707/944–1388, 800/533–4140* ⊕ *www.lavendernapa.com* ⇥ *9 rooms* ¶⊙¶ *Breakfast.*

$$$
HOTEL

⌂ **Napa Valley Lodge.** Clean rooms in a convenient setting draw travelers willing to pay more than at comparable lodgings in the city of Napa to be within walking distance of Yountville's tasting rooms, restaurants, and shops. **Pros:** clean rooms; helpful staff; filling continental breakfast; large pool area; cookies, tea, and coffee in lobby. **Cons:** no elevator; lacks amenities of other Yountville properties. $ *Rooms from: $340* ⌂ *2230 Madison St., Yountville* ☎ *707/944–2468, 888/944–3545* ⊕ *www.napavalleylodge.com* ⇥ *54 rooms, 1 suite* ¶⊙¶ *Breakfast.*

$$$$
HOTEL

⌂ **North Block Hotel.** With a chic Tuscan style, this 20-room hotel has dark-wood furniture and soothing decor in brown and sage. **Pros:** extremely comfortable beds; attentive service; room service by Redd Wood restaurant. **Cons:** outdoor areas get some traffic noise. $ *Rooms from: $420* ⌂ *6757 Washington St., Yountville* ☎ *707/944–8080* ⊕ *northblockhotel.com* ⇥ *20 rooms* ¶⊙¶ *No meals.*

SPORTS AND THE OUTDOORS

BALLOONING

Napa Valley Aloft. Between 8 and 12 passengers soar over the Napa Valley in balloons that launch from downtown Yountville. The rates include preflight refreshments and a huge breakfast. ⌂ *V Marketplace, 6525 Washington St., near Mulberry St., Yountville* ☎ *707/944–4400, 855/944–4408* ⊕ *www.nvaloft.com* ⇥ *From $220.*

BIKING

Fodor's Choice
★

Napa Valley Bike Tours. With dozens of wineries within 5 miles, this shop makes a fine starting point for vineyard and wine-tasting excursions. The outfit also rents bikes. ⌂ *6500 Washington St., at Mulberry St., Yountville* ☎ *707/944–2953* ⊕ *www.napavalleybiketours.com* ⇥ *From $99.*

SPAS

Fodor's Choice
★

The Spa at Bardessono. Many of this spa's patrons are hotel guests who take their treatments in their rooms' large, customized bathrooms—all of them equipped with concealed massage tables—but the main facility is open to guests and nonguests alike. An in-room treatment popular with couples starts with massages in front of the fireplace and ends with a whirlpool bath and a split of sparkling wine. For the two-hour Yountville Signature treatment, which can be enjoyed in-room or at the spa, a shea butter–enriched sugar scrub is applied, followed by a massage with antioxidant Chardonnay grape seed oil and a hydrating hair and scalp treatment. The spa engages massage therapists skilled in Swedish, Thai, and several other techniques. In addition to massages, the services include facials, waxing, and other skin-care treatments as well as manicures and pedicures. ⊠ *Bardessono Hotel, 6526 Yount St., at Mulberry St., Yountville* ☎ *707/204–6050* ⊕ *www.bardessono.com/ spa* ⊠ *Treatments $65–$600* ⊗ *Spa 9–6, in-room service 8–8.*

SHOPPING

V Marketplace. The clothing boutiques, art galleries, and gift stores amid this vine-covered market include celebrity chef Michael Chiarello's **NapaStyle,** which sells cookbooks, kitchenware, and prepared foods that are perfect for picnics. The aromas alone will lure you into **Kollar Chocolates,** whose not-too-sweet, European-style chocolates are made on-site with imaginative ingredients. ⊠ *6525 Washington St., near Mulberry St., Yountville* ☎ *707/944–2451* ⊕ *www.vmarketplace.com.*

OAKVILLE

2 miles northwest of Yountville.

A large butte that runs east–west just north of Yountville blocks the cooling fogs from the south, facilitating the myriad microclimates of the Oakville AVA, home to several high-profile wineries.

GETTING HERE AND AROUND

Driving along Highway 29, you'll know you've reached Oakville when you see the Oakville Grocery on the east side of the road. You can reach Oakville from the Sonoma County town of Glen Ellen by heading east on Trinity Road from Highway 12. The twisting route, along the mountain range that divides Napa and Sonoma, eventually becomes the Oakville Grade. The views on this drive are breathtaking, though the continual curves make it unsuitable for those who suffer from motion sickness.

EXPLORING
TOP ATTRACTIONS

Fodor's Choice
★

B Cellars. The chefs hold center stage in this tasting room's large open kitchen, and with good reason: creating food-friendly wines is B Cellars's raison d'être. Founded in 2003, the winery moved from Calistoga to its new Oakville facility, all steel beams, corrugated metal, and plate glass, in 2014. The flagship wines are a Chardonnay, Sauvignon Blanc, and Viognier blend and three red blends. One of the latter is a robust "super Tuscan" made with Cabernet Sauvignon, Sangiovese, Petite Sirah, and Syrah. You can taste the blends and other wines—among them single-vineyard Cabernets whose grapes come from top Napa Valley vineyards—at appointment-only seated tastings involving good-size bites from the kitchen that prove just how admirably winemaker Kirk Venge fulfills the B Cellars mission. ⊠ *703 Oakville Cross Rd., west of Silverado Trail, Oakville* ☎ *707/709–8787* ⊕ *www.bcellars.com* ⊠ *Tastings $45–$125* ⊗ *Daily 10–5 by appointment.*

Far Niente's wine cellars have a touch of ballroom elegance.

Fodor's Choice
★

Far Niente. Though the fee for the combined tour and tasting is high, guests at Far Niente are welcomed by name and treated to a glimpse of one of the Napa Valley's most beautiful properties. Small groups are escorted through the historic 1885 stone winery, including some of the 40,000 square feet of aging caves, for a lesson on the labor-intensive method of making Far Niente's flagship wines: a Cabernet Sauvignon blend and a Chardonnay. The next stop is the Carriage House, which holds a gleaming collection of classic cars. The seated tasting of wines and cheeses that follows concludes on a sweet note with Dolce, a late-harvest wine made from Semillon and Sauvignon Blanc grapes. ✉ *1350 Acacia Dr., off Oakville Grade Rd., Oakville* ☎ *707/944–2861* ⊕ *www.farniente.com* ✉ *Tasting and tour $65* ☉ *Daily 10–3 by appointment.*

Fodor's Choice
★

Silver Oak Cellars. In what may been its decade's most addlepated prognostication, the first review of Silver Oak's Napa Valley Cabernet Sauvignon declared the debut 1972 vintage not all that good—and overpriced at $6 a bottle. Oops. The celebrated Bordeaux-style Cabernet blend, still the only Napa Valley wine bearing its winery's label each year, evolved into a cult favorite, and its only two creators, the late Justin Meyer and current winemaker Daniel Baron, received worldwide recognition for their artistry. At the august Oakville tasting room, constructed out of reclaimed stone and other materials from a 19th-century Kansas flour mill, you can sip the current Napa Valley vintage, the current 100% Cabernet from Silver Oak's Alexander Valley operation, and some library wines ($20). Tours, private tastings, and food-wine pairings elevate the experience. ✉ *915 Oakville Cross Rd., off Hwy. 29, Oakville* ☎ *707/942–7022* ⊕ *www.silveroak.com* ✉ *Tastings $20–$60, tour $30*

⊙ *Tasting Mon.–Sat.–5, Sun. 11–5; tour Mon.–Thurs. 10 and 1, Fri. and Sat. 10, 1, and 3, Sun. 11 and 1; no appointment required for current-release ($20) tasting; all other tastings and the tour by appointment.*

WORTH NOTING

Oakville Grocery. Built in 1881 as a general store, Oakville Grocery carries high-end groceries and prepared foods. On busy summer weekends the place is often packed with customers stocking up on picnic provisions: meats, cheeses, breads, and gourmet sandwiches. During the week this is a mellow pit stop where you can sit on a bench out front and sip an espresso or head out back and have a picnic. ■TIP➔ Patrons dropping by for savory breakfast burritos, scones and muffins, and hightest coffee drinks keep Oakville bustling until right before lunchtime. ⊠ *7856 St. Helena Hwy./Hwy. 29, at Oakville Cross Rd., Oakville* ☎ *707/944–8802* ⊕ *www.oakvillegrocery.com.*

Robert Mondavi Winery. The arch at the center of the sprawling Mission-style building frames the lawn and the vineyard behind, inviting a stroll under the arcades. You can head for one of the two tasting rooms, but if you've not toured a winery before, the 90-minute Signature Tour and Tasting ($30) is a good way to learn about enology, as well as the late Robert Mondavi's role in California wine making. Those new to tasting and mystified by all that swirling and sniffing should consider the 45-minute Wine Tasting Basics experience ($20). Serious wine lovers can opt for the one-hour $55 Exclusive Cellar tasting, during which a server pours and explains limited-production, reserve, and older-vintage wines. ■TIP➔ Concerts, mostly jazz and R&B, take place in summer on the lawn; call ahead for tickets. ⊠ *7801 St. Helena Hwy./Hwy. 29, Oakville* ☎ *888/766–6328* ⊕ *www.robertmondaviwinery.com* ⌑ *Tastings $20–$55, tours $20–$50* ⊙ *Daily 10–5; tour times vary.*

RUTHERFORD

2 miles northwest of Oakville.

With its singular microclimate and soil, Rutherford is an important viticultural center, with more big-name wineries than you can shake a corkscrew at. Cabernet Sauvignon is king here. The well-drained, loamy soil is ideal for those vines, and since this part of the valley gets plenty of sun, the grapes develop exceptionally intense flavors.

GETTING HERE AND AROUND

Wineries around Rutherford are dotted along Highway 29 and the parallel Silverado Trail north and south of Rutherford Road/Conn Creek Road, on which wineries can also be found.

EXPLORING

TOP ATTRACTIONS

Fodor's Choice
★

Caymus Vineyards. For a winery whose claims to fame include producing Special Selection Cabernet Sauvignon, the only two-time *Wine Spectator* Wine of the Year honoree, Caymus remains a remarkably accessible spot to taste current and past vintages of the celebrated wine. Chuck Wagner started making wine on this property in 1972 and still oversees Caymus production. His children craft most of the other wines in the

Wagner Family of Wines portfolio, including the oaked and unoaked Mer Soleil Chardonnays and the Belle Glos Pinot Noirs. ■TIP➔ You can sample Caymus and other wines at the often crowded tasting bar for $25—in good weather, wines are also poured outside—but to taste library wines and learn more about the winery's history, consider booking a private tasting. ✉ *8700 Conn Creek Rd., off Rutherford Rd., Rutherford* ☎ *707/967–3010* ⊕ *www.caymus.com* ☜ *Tastings $25–$40* ☺ *Daily 9:30–4:30, last tasting at 4; private tasting by appointment.*

FAMILY
Fodor'sChoice
★

Frog's Leap. John Williams, owner of Frog's Leap, maintains a sense of humor about wine that translates into an entertaining yet informative experience—if you're a novice, the tour here is a fun way to begin your education. You'll taste wines that might include Zinfandel, Merlot, Chardonnay, Sauvignon Blanc, and an estate-grown Cabernet Sauvignon. The winery includes a barn built in 1884, 5 acres of organic gardens, an eco-friendly visitor center, and a frog pond topped with lily pads. ■TIP➔ The tour is highly recommended, but you can also just sample wines either inside or on a porch overlooking the garden. ✉ *8815 Conn Creek Rd., Rutherford* ☎ *707/963–4704, 800/959–4704* ⊕ *www.frogsleap.com* ☜ *Tastings $15–$20, tour $20* ☺ *Tastings daily 10–4 by appointment only; tours weekdays at 10:30 and 2:30 by appointment.*

Inglenook. Filmmaker Francis Ford Coppola began his wine-making career in 1975, when he bought part of the historic Inglenook estate. Over the next few decades he reunited the original property acquired by Inglenook founder Gustave Niebaum, remodeled Niebaum's ivy-covered 1880s château, and purchased the rights to the Inglenook name. Various tours cover the estate's history, the local climate and geology, the sensory evaluation of wine, and the evolution of Coppola's signature wine, Rubicon, a Cabernet Sauvignon–based blend. Some tastings are held in an opulent, high-ceilinged room, others in a wine-aging cave. ■TIP➔ You can taste wines by the glass (or the bottle) at The Bistro, an on-site wine bar with a picturesque courtyard. ✉ *1991 St. Helena Hwy./Hwy. 29, Rutherford* ☎ *707/968–1100, 800/782–4266* ⊕ *www.inglenook.com* ☜ *Tastings $45–$60, tours $50–$85* ☺ *Daily 10–5; call for tour times.*

Mumm Napa. In well-known Mumm's light-filled tasting room or adjacent outdoor patio you can enjoy bubbly by the flute or the flight, but the sophisticated sparkling wines, elegant setting, and vineyard views aren't the only reasons to visit. An excellent gallery displays 27 original Ansel Adams prints and presents temporary exhibitions by acclaimed photographers. Winery tours cover the major steps making sparklers entails. For a leisurely tasting of several vintages of the top-of-the-line DVX wines, served with cheeses, nuts, and fresh and dried fruit, book an Oak Terrace tasting ($40; reservations recommended on Friday and weekends). ■TIP➔ Carlos Santana fans may want to taste the sparklers the musician makes in collaboration with Mumm's winemaker, Ludovic Dervin. ✉ *8445 Silverado Trail, 1 mile south of Rutherford Cross Rd., Rutherford* ☎ *707/967–7700, 800/686–6272* ⊕ *www.mummnapa.com* ☜ *Tastings $8–$40, tour $25 (includes tasting)* ☺ *Daily 10–4:45; tour daily at 10, 11, 1, and 3.*

Frog's Leap's picturesque country charm extends all the way to the white picket fence.

WORTH NOTING

Beaulieu Vineyard. The influential André Tchelistcheff (1901–94), who helped define the California style of wine making, worked his magic here for many years. BV, founded in 1900 by Georges de Latour and his wife, Fernande, is known for its widely distributed Chardonnay, Pinot Noir, and Cabernet Sauvignon wines, but many others are produced in small lots and are available only at the winery. The most famous of the small-lot wines is the flagship Georges De Latour Cabernet Sauvignon, first crafted by Tchelistcheff himself in the late 1930s. ■ TIP→ The engaging historic tour ($35) includes a peek at Prohibition-era artifacts and tastes of finished wines and ones still aging in their barrels. ⊠ *1960 St. Helena Hwy./Hwy. 29, Rutherford* ☎ *707/967–5233, 800/264–6918 Ext. 5233* ⊕ *www.bvwines.com* ☜ *Tastings $20–$75, tour $35* ⊘ *Daily 10–5.*

FAMILY **Honig Vineyard & Winery.** Sustainable farming is the big story at this family-run winery. Michael Honig, the grandson of founder Louis Honig, helped write the code of sustainable practices for the California Wine Institute and was a key player in developing the first certification programs for state wineries. The tour here, offered seasonally, focuses on the Honig family's environmentally friendly farming and production methods, which include the use of solar panels to generate a majority of the winery's power. The family produces only Cabernet Sauvignon and Sauvignon Blanc. You can taste whites and reds at a standard tasting for $20; the reserve tasting ($50) pairs single-vineyard Cabernets with small bites. ⊠ *850 Rutherford Rd., near Conn Creek Rd., Rutherford* ☎ *800/929–2217* ⊕ *www.honigwine.com* ☜ *Tastings $20–$50; tour $30* ⊘ *Daily 10:30–4:30 (reserve tasting daily Mon.–Sat.), tour spring–fall Mon.–Thurs. at 10; tastings and tour by appointment.*

WHERE TO EAT AND STAY

$$$$
MODERN
AMERICAN
Fodor'sChoice
★

✕ **Restaurant at Auberge du Soleil.** Possibly the most romantic roost for a dinner in all the Wine Country is a terrace seat at the Auberge du Soleil's illustrious restaurant, and the Mediterranean-inflected cuisine more than matches the dramatic vineyard views. The prix-fixe dinner menu ($105 for three courses, $125 for four; $150 for the six-course tasting menu), which relies largely on local produce, might include veal sweetbreads with hearts of palm and chanterelles in an orange glaze or prime beef pavé with white corn, potato croquettes, and a caramelized shallot sauce. The service is polished, and the wine list is comprehensive. ■TIP→ **With a menu that embraces everything from muffins and gnocchi to Cabernet-braised short rib and (in season) a Maine lobster omelet, the weekend brunch here is delightfully over-the-top.** $ *Average main: $105* ✉ *Auberge du Soleil, 180 Rutherford Hill Rd., off Silverado Trail, Rutherford* ☎ *707/963–1211, 800/348–5406* ⊕ *www.aubergedusoleil.com* ⚑ *Reservations essential.*

$$$
AMERICAN
Fodor'sChoice
★

✕ **Rutherford Grill.** Dark-wood walls, subdued lighting, and red-leather banquettes make for a perpetually clubby mood at this trusty Rutherford hangout. Many entrées—steaks, burgers, fish, succulent rotisserie chicken, and barbecued pork ribs—emerge from an oak-fired grill operated by master technicians. So, too, do starters such as the grilled jumbo artichokes and the iron-skillet corn bread, a ton of butter being the secret of success with both. The French dip sandwich is a local legend, and the wine list includes rare selections from Caymus and other celebrated producers at (for Napa) reasonable prices. You can also opt for a well-crafted cocktail. ■TIP→ **In good weather the patio, popular for its bar, fireplace, and rocking chairs, is open for full meal service or drinks and appetizers.** $ *Average main: $25* ✉ *1180 Rutherford Rd., at Hwy. 29, Rutherford* ☎ *707/963–1792* ⊕ *www.rutherfordgrill.com* ⚑ *Reservations essential.*

$$$$
RESORT
Fodor'sChoice
★

▥ **Auberge du Soleil.** Taking a cue from the olive-tree-studded landscape, this hotel with a renowned restaurant and spa cultivates a luxurious look that blends French and California style. **Pros:** stunning views over the valley; spectacular pool and spa areas; the most expensive suites are fit for a superstar. **Cons:** stratospheric prices; least expensive rooms get some noise from the bar and restaurant. $ *Rooms from: $850* ✉ *180 Rutherford Hill Rd., Rutherford* ☎ *707/963–1211, 800/348–5406* ⊕ *www.aubergedusoleil.com* ⚘ *31 rooms, 21 suites* ⋈ *Breakfast.*

ST. HELENA

2 miles northwest of Oakville.

Downtown St. Helena is a symbol of how well life can be lived in the Wine Country. Sycamore trees arch over Main Street (Highway 29), a funnel of outstanding restaurants and tempting boutiques. At the north end of town looms the hulking stone building of the Culinary Institute of America. Weathered stone and brick buildings from the late 1800s give off that gratifying whiff of history.

The town got its start in 1854, when Henry Still built a store. Still wanted company, so he donated land lots on his town site to anyone who wanted to erect a business. Soon he was joined by a wagon shop, a shoe shop, hotels, and churches. Dr. George Crane planted a vineyard in 1858, and was the first to produce wine in commercially viable quantities. A German winemaker named Charles Krug followed suit a couple of years later, and other wineries soon followed.

GETTING HERE AND AROUND

Downtown stretches along Highway 29, called Main Street here. Many wineries lie north and south of downtown along Highway 29. More can be found off Silverado Trail, and some of the most scenic spots are on Spring Mountain, which rises southwest of town.

EXPLORING

TOP ATTRACTIONS

Fodor'sChoice ★ **Charles Krug Winery.** A historically sensitive renovation of its 1874 Redwood Cellar Building transformed the former production facility of the Napa Valley's oldest operating winery into an epic hospitality center with a tasting room and a café. Charles Krug, a Prussian immigrant, established the winery in 1861 and ran it until his death in 1892. Italian immigrants Cesare Mondavi and his wife, Rosa, purchased Krug in 1943, and operated it with their sons Peter and Robert (who later opened his own winery). Krug, still run by Peter's family, specializes in small-lot Yountville and Howell Mountain Cabernet Sauvignons and makes Chardonnay, Merlot, Pinot Noir, Sauvignon Blanc, Zinfandel, and a Zinfandel Port. ■ TIP➜ The café sells food to eat inside or at oak-shaded picnic tables (reservations recommended). ✉ *2800 Main St./Hwy. 29, across from Culinary Institute of America, St. Helena* ☎ *707/967-2229* ⊕ *www.charleskrug.com* ✎ *Tastings $20–$50, tours $60 (includes tasting)* ☉ *Daily 10:30–5; tours by appointment Mon.– Thurs. 10:30 and 12:30, Fri.–Sun. 10:30.*

Duckhorn Vineyards. Merlot's moment in the spotlight may have passed, but you wouldn't know it at Duckhorn, whose fans gladly pay from $50 to nearly $100 a bottle for some of the world's finest wines from this varietal. You can taste Merlot, Sauvignon Blanc, Cabernet Sauvignon, and other wines in the airy, high-ceilinged tasting room, which looks like a sleek restaurant; you'll be seated at a table and served by staffers who make the rounds to pour. In fair weather, you may do your sipping on a fetching wraparound porch overlooking a vineyard. ■ TIP➜ You don't need a reservation on weekdays to taste the current releases ($30), but you do on weekends, and they're required all the time for private and semiprivate tastings. ✉ *1000 Lodi La., at Silverado Trail N, St. Helena* ☎ *707/963-7108* ⊕ *www.duckhorn.com* ✎ *Tastings $30–$75* ☉ *Daily 10–4.*

Fodor'sChoice ★ **Hall St. Helena.** The award-winning Cabernet Sauvignons, Merlots, and an impeccable Syrah produced here are works of art—and of up-to-the-minute organic-farming science and wine-making technology. A glass-walled tasting room allows you to see in action some of the high-tech equipment director of winemaking Steve Leveque employs to craft the wines, which also include Cabernet Franc and late-harvest Sauvignon Blanc. The main guided tour provides a closer-up look at the facility and covers the winery's history and architecture and the three-dozen works—inside and out—by Patrick Dougherty, John Baldessari, Jesús

7

Moroles, and other major contemporary artists. ■TIP➔ The well-conceived seminars here include ones about the artworks, demystifying food and wine, and collecting Cabernet Sauvignons. ⊠ *401 St. Helena Hwy./Hwy. 29, near White La., St. Helena* ☎ *707/967–2626* ⊕ *www.hallwines.com* ⊠ *Tastings $30–$100; tours $40–$75* ☉ *Daily 10–5:30.*

Fodor'sChoice **Joseph Phelps Vineyards.** An appointment is required for tastings at the
★ winery started by the legendary Joseph Phelps—his son Bill now runs the operation—but it's well worth the effort. Phelps makes fine whites, but the blockbuster wines are reds, particularly the Cabernet Sauvignon and the flagship Bordeaux-style blend called Insignia. The luscious-yet-subtle Insignia sells for more than $200 a bottle. Luckily, all tastings include the current vintage. The 90-minute seminars include one on wine-and-cheese pairing and another focusing on blending. Participants in the latter mix the various varietals that go into the Insignia blend. A new tasting room debuts in 2015 following a major renovation project. ⊠ *200 Taplin Rd., off Silverado Trail, St. Helena* ☎ *707/963–2745, 800/707–5789* ⊕ *www. josephphelps.com* ⊠ *Tastings and seminars $60–$150 by appointment* ☉ *Weekdays 10–4, weekends 10–3; tastings by appointment.*

WORTH NOTING

Beringer Vineyards. Arguably the Napa Valley's most beautiful winery, the 1876 Beringer Vineyards is also the oldest continuously operating property. In 1884 Frederick and Jacob Beringer built the Rhine House Mansion as Frederick's family home. Today it serves as the reserve tasting room, where you can sample wines surrounded by Belgian art-nouveau hand-carved oak and walnut furniture and stained-glass windows. The assortment includes a limited-release Chardonnay, a few big Cabernets, and a Sauterne-style dessert wine. A less expensive tasting takes place in the original stone winery. ■TIP➔ The one-hour Taste of Beringer tour ($40), which includes a tasting with small food bites, provides a good overview of the valley's wine-making history. ⊠ *2000 Main St./Hwy. 29, near Pratt Ave., St. Helena* ☎ *707/963–8989, 866/708–9463* ⊕ *www.beringer.com* ⊠ *Tastings $20–$50, tours $25– $40* ☉ *June–mid-Oct., daily 10–6; mid-Oct.–May, daily 10–5; many tours daily, call or check website for times.*

Culinary Institute of America. The West Coast headquarters of the country's leading school for chefs are in the 1889 Greystone Winery, an imposing building that once was the world's largest stone winery. On the ground floor you can check out the quirky Corkscrew Museum and browse a shop stocked with gleaming gadgets and many cookbooks. At the adjacent Flavor Bar you can sample various ingredients (for example, chocolate or olive oil). Plaques upstairs at the Vintners Hall of Fame commemorate winemakers past and present. Beguiling one-hour cooking demonstrations (reservations required) take place on weekends. The student-run Bakery Café by Illy serves soups, salads, sandwiches, and baked goods; the Institute also operates a full restaurant. ⊠ *2555 Main St./Hwy. 29, St. Helena* ☎ *707/967–1100* ⊕ *www.ciachef. edu* ⊠ *Museum and store free, cooking demonstrations $20, tastings $10–$15, tour $10* ☉ *Museum and store daily 10:30–6 (Mon.–Thurs. 11–5 in winter); tour 11:45, 2:45, 5.*

WHERE TO EAT

$$$
MODERN
AMERICAN
Fodor's Choice
★

X **Archetype.** Chef Ryder Zetts earned instant raves for his fancifully updated "Americana" cuisine at this establishment designed and owned by winery architect Howard Backen. The cream-color decor, twirling ceiling fans, and rattan settees and chairs set an upscale-homey tone in the main dining area and on the screened-in front porch. Seasonal appetizers might include textbook fried green tomatoes—but with burrata cheese—or peaches with Surryano ham served with creamily addictive mascarpone-pepper jelly. For lunch expect sandwiches such as smoked salmon pepped up by quick-pickled cucumbers. Dinner glides into a more serious realm with, perhaps, bacon-crusted Alaskan halibut or leg of lamb with lamb merguez sausage. ■TIP➔ **The $5 happy hour (daily from 5 to 7) and Monday burger night are popular with locals.** $ *Average main: $27* ⊠ *1429 Main St., near Adams St., St. Helena* ☎ *707/968–9200* ⊕ *www.archetypenapa.com.*

$$
MODERN
AMERICAN
Fodor's Choice
★

X **Cindy's Backstreet Kitchen.** At her St. Helena outpost, Cindy Pawlcyn serves variations on the comfort food she made popular at Mustards Grill, but spices things up with dishes influenced by Mexican, Central American, and occasionally Asian cuisines. Along with mainstays such as meat loaf with garlic mashed potatoes and beef and duck burgers served with flawless fries, the menu might include a rabbit tostada or chicken served with avocado salsa and a two-cheese stuffed green chili. Two dessert favorites are the high-style yet homey warm pineapple upside-down cake and the nearly ethereal parfait. $ *Average main: $22* ⊠ *1327 Railroad Ave., at Hunt St., 1 block east of Main St., St. Helena* ☎ *707/963–1200* ⊕ *www.cindysbackstreetkitchen.com.*

$$
MODERN
AMERICAN

X **Farmstead at Long Meadow Ranch.** Housed in a former barn, Farmstead revolves around an open kitchen where chef Stephen Barber cooks with as many local and organic ingredients as possible. Many of them—including grass-fed beef and lamb, fruits and vegetables, eggs, extra-virgin olive oil, wine, and honey—come from the property of parent company Long Meadow Ranch. Entrées might include grilled rainbow trout with wild mushrooms, or potato gnocchi with beef ragout, herbs, and Parmesan. Tuesday is the popular panfried chicken night—$37 for a three-course meal. ■TIP➔ **The weekday happy hour, from 4 to 6 (good eats, too), is often hoppin'.** $ *Average main: $20* ⊠ *738 Main St., at Charter Oak Ave., St. Helena* ☎ *707/963–4555* ⊕ *www. longmeadowranch.com/farmstead-restaurant.*

$$$
MODERN
AMERICAN
Fodor's Choice
★

X **Goose & Gander.** The pairing of food and drink at intimate Goose & Gander is as likely to involve cocktails as it is wine. Main courses such as wild king salmon with roasted delicata squash, lentils, applewood-smoked bacon, and celery root velouté work well with starters that in season might include cream of mushroom soup made from both wild and cultivated varieties. You can enjoy your meal with a top-notch Chardonnay or Pinot Noir—or a Manhattan made with three kinds of bitters and poured over a hand-carved block of ice. On cold days a fireplace warms the main dining room, and in good weather the outdoor patio is a fetching spot to dine alfresco. ■TIP➔ **Year-round the basement bar is a good stop for a drink.** $ *Average main: $25* ⊠ *1245 Spring St., at Oak St., St. Helena* ☎ *707/967–8779* ⊕ *www.goosegander.com.*

7

$ AMERICAN 🍴 **Gott's Roadside.** A 1950s-style outdoor hamburger stand goes upscale at this spot whose customers brave long lines to order breakfast sandwiches, juicy burgers, root-beer floats, and garlic fries. Choices not available a half century ago include the ahi tuna burger and the chili spice–marinated chicken breast served with Mexican slaw. ■ **TIP→ Arrive early or late for lunch, or all of the shaded picnic tables on the lawn might be filled.** A second branch does business at Napa's Oxbow Public Market. [$] *Average main: $12* ✉ *933 Main St./Hwy. 29, St. Helena* ☎ *707/963–3486* 🌐 *www.gotts.com* ✍ *Reservations not accepted* [$] *Average main: $12* ✉ *Oxbow Public Market, 644 1st St., at McKinstry St., Napa* ☎ *707/224–6900* ✍ *Reservations not accepted.*

$$$$ MODERN AMERICAN Fodor's Choice ★ 🍴 **Press.** Few taste sensations surpass the combination of a sizzling steak and a Napa Valley red, a union that the chef and sommeliers here celebrate with a reverence bordering on obsession. Beef from carefully selected local and international purveyors is the star—especially the rib eye for two—but chef Trevor Kunk also prepares pork chops and free-range chicken and veal on his cherry-and-almond-wood-fired grill and rotisserie. Kunk, hired in 2014, has added vegetarian offerings that include a roasted carrot "hot dog" and fried-green-tomato sandwiches. The cellar holds thousands of wines; if you recall having a great steak with a 1985 Mayacamas Mt. Veeder Cab, you'll be able to re-create, and perhaps exceed, the original event. Press's bartenders know their way around both rad and trad cocktails. [$] *Average main: $48* ✉ *587 St. Helena Hwy./Hwy. 29, at White La., St. Helena* ☎ *707/967–0550* 🌐 *www.presssthelena.com* ✍ *Reservations essential* ⏲ *Closed Tues. No lunch.*

$$$$ MODERN AMERICAN Fodor's Choice ★ 🍴 **The Restaurant at Meadowood.** Chef Christopher Kostow has garnered rave reviews—and three Michelin stars for several years running—for creating a unique dining experience. After you reserve your table, you'll have a conversation with a reservationist about your party's desired culinary experience and dietary restrictions. Inspired by this conversation, chef Kostow will transform seasonal local ingredients, some grown on or near the property, into an elaborate, multicourse experience. If you choose the Tasting Menu option ($225 per person, $450 with wine pairings), you'll enjoy your meal in the romantic dining room, its beautiful finishes aglow with warm lighting. Choose the Counter Menu ($500, $850 with wine pairings), and you and up to three guests can sit inside the kitchen and watch Kostow's team prepare your meal. ■ **TIP→ The restaurant also offers a limited, three-course menu ($90) at its bar.** [$] *Average main: $225* ✉ *900 Meadowood La., off Silverado Trail N, St. Helena* ☎ *707/967–1205, 800/458–8080* 🌐 *www.therestaurantatmeadowood.com* ✍ *Reservations essential* ⏲ *Closed Sun. No lunch.*

$$$$ MEDITERRANEAN Fodor's Choice ★ 🍴 **Terra.** For old-school romance and service, many diners return year after year to this quiet favorite in an 1884 fieldstone building. Chef Hiro Sone gives an unexpected twist to Italian and southern French cuisine, though for a few standouts, among them the signature sake-marinated black cod in a *shiso* broth, he draws on his Japanese background. Homey yet elegant desserts, courtesy of Sone's wife, Lissa Doumani, might include a chocolate mousseline with chocolate peanut butter crunch and toasted marshmallow. Meals here are prix-fixe—$78 for four courses where diners choose from the menu, $93 for five, and $105

for six. ■TIP→ Next door, Bar Terra serves cocktails, local wines, and a menu of lighter dishes—the succulent fried rock shrimp served with chive-mustard sauce is a local favorite. Ⓢ *Average main: $78* ✉ *1345 Railroad Ave., off Hunt Ave., St. Helena* ☎ *707/963–8931* ⊕ *www.terra restaurant.com* ⊘ *Closed Tues. No lunch.*

WHERE TO STAY

$ 🖳 **El Bonita Motel.** For budget-minded travelers the tidy rooms at this
HOTEL roadside motel are pleasant enough, and the landscaped grounds and picnic tables elevate this property over similar places. **Pros:** cheerful rooms; hot tub; microwaves and mini-refrigerators. **Cons:** road noise is a problem in some rooms. Ⓢ *Rooms from: $130* ✉ *195 Main St./Hwy. 29, St. Helena* ☎ *707/963–3216, 800/541–3284* ⊕ *www.elbonita.com* ↩ *48 rooms, 4 suites* ⦿ *Breakfast.*

$$$ 🖳 **Harvest Inn by Charlie Palmer.** Although this inn sits just off Highway
HOTEL 29, its patrons remain mostly above the fray, strolling 8 acres of land-
Fodor's Choice scaped gardens, enjoying views of the vineyards adjoining the prop-
★ erty, partaking in spa services, and drifting to sleep in beds adorned with fancy linens and down pillows. **Pros:** garden setting; spacious rooms; well-trained staff. **Cons:** some lower-priced rooms lack elegance; high weekend rates. Ⓢ *Rooms from: $359* ✉ *1 Main St., St. Helena* ☎ *707/963–9463, 800/950–8466* ⊕ *www.harvestinn.com* ↩ *69 rooms, 5 suites* ⦿ *Breakfast.*

$$$$ 🖳 **Meadowood Napa Valley.** Founded in 1964 as a country club, Meado-
RESORT wood has evolved into a five-star resort, a gathering place for Napa's
Fodor's Choice wine-making community, and a celebrated dining destination. **Pros:**
★ superb restaurant; pleasant hiking trails; gracious service. **Cons:** very expensive; far from downtown St. Helena. Ⓢ *Rooms from: $650* ✉ *900 Meadowood La., St. Helena* ☎ *707/963–3646, 800/458–8080* ⊕ *www. meadowood.com* ↩ *85 rooms, suites, and cottages* ⦿ *No meals.*

7

CALISTOGA

3 miles northwest of St. Helena.

With false-fronted, Old West–style shops and 19th-century inns and hotels lining its main drag, Lincoln Avenue, Calistoga comes across as more down-to-earth than its more polished neighbors. Don't be fooled, though. On its outskirts lie some of the Wine Country's swankest (and priciest) resorts and its most fanciful piece of architecture, the medieval-style Castello di Amorosa winery.

Calistoga was developed as a spa-oriented getaway from the start. Sam Brannan, a gold rush–era entrepreneur, planned to use the area's natural hot springs as the centerpiece of a resort complex. His venture failed, but old-time hotels and bathhouses—along with some glorious new spas—still operate. You can come for an old-school mud bath, or go completely 21st century and experience lavish treatments based on the latest innovations in skin and body care.

GETTING HERE AND AROUND

Highway 29 heads east (turn right) at Calistoga, where in town it is signed as Lincoln Avenue. If arriving via the Silverado Trail, head west at Highway 29/Lincoln Avenue.

EXPLORING
TOP ATTRACTIONS

Castello di Amorosa. An astounding medieval structure complete with drawbridge and moat, chapel, stables, and secret passageways, the Castello commands Diamond Mountain's lower eastern slope. Some of the 107 rooms contain replicas of 13th-century frescoes (cheekily signed [the-artist's-name].com), and the dungeon has an actual iron maiden from Nuremberg, Germany. You must pay for a tour to see most of Dario Sattui's extensive eight-level property, though basic tastings include access to part of the complex. Wines of note include several Italian-style wines, including La Castellana, a robust "super Tuscan" blend of Cabernet Sauvignon, Sangiovese, and Merlot; and Il Barone, a praiseworthy cab made largely from Diamond Mountain grapes. ■TIP→ **The two-hour food-and-wine pairing ($75) by sommelier Mary Davidek is among the Wine Country's best.** ⊠ *4045 N. St. Helena Hwy./Hwy. 29, near Maple La., Calistoga* ☎ *707/967–6272* ⊕ *www.castellodiamorosa.com* ➹ *Tastings $20–$30, tours (with tastings) $35–$75* ☉ *Mar.–Oct., daily 9:30–6; Nov.–Feb., daily 9:30–5; tours and food-wine pairings by appointment.*

Ca' Toga Galleria d'Arte. The boundless wit, whimsy, and creativity of the Venetian-born Carlo Marchiori, this gallery's owner-artist, finds expression in paintings, watercolors, ceramics, sculptures, and other artworks. Marchiori often draws on mythology and folktales for his inspiration. A stop at this magical gallery may inspire you to tour **Villa Ca' Toga,** the artist's fanciful Palladian home, a tromp l'oeil tour de force that can be toured from May through October on Saturday only, at 11 am. ⊠ *1206 Cedar St., near Lincoln Ave., Calistoga* ☎ *707/942–3900* ⊕ *www.catoga.com* ☉ *Closed Tues. and Wed.*

Chateau Montelena. Set amid a bucolic northern Calistoga landscape, this winery helped establish the Napa Valley's reputation for high-quality wine making. At the legendary Paris tasting of 1976, the Chateau Montelena 1973 Chardonnay took first place, beating out four white Burgundies from France and five other California Chardonnays. The 2008 movie *Bottle Shock* immortalized the event, and the winery honors its four decades of classic wine making with a special Beyond Paris & Hollywood tasting of the winery's Napa Valley Chardonnays ($40). You can also opt for a Current Release Tasting ($25) or a Limited Release Tasting ($50) that includes some stellar Cabernet Sauvignons. ⊠ *1429 Tubbs La., off Hwy. 29, Calistoga* ☎ *707/942–5105* ⊕ *www.montelena. com* ➹ *Tastings $20–$50, tours $40; appointment required and restrictions apply for some tastings and tours* ☉ *Daily 9:30–4.*

Fodor's Choice
★

Schramsberg. Founded in 1865, Schramsberg produces sparkling wines made using the *méthode traditionnelle,* also known as *méthode champenoise.* A fascinating tour precedes tastings. In addition to glimpsing the winery's historic architecture, you'll visit caves, some dug in late 19th century by Chinese laborers, where 2 million–plus bottles are stacked in gravity-defying configurations. Tastings include generous pours of very different bubblies. To learn more about them, consider the three-day **Camp Schramsberg,** held in fall and spring. Fall participants harvest grapes and learn about food and wine pairing, riddling (the process of turning the bottles every few days to nudge the sediment into the neck of the bottle), and other topics. In spring the focus is on blending. ⊠ *1400 Schramsberg Rd., off Hwy. 29, Calistoga* ☎ *707/942–4558, 800/877–3623* ⊕ *www.schramsberg.com* ✍ *Tasting and tour $60* ☉ *Tours at 10, 10:30, 11:30, 12:30, 1:30, and 2:30 by appointment.*

WORTH NOTING

Dutch Henry Winery. The casual style and lack of crowds at this pet-friendly winery make it a welcome change of pace from some of its overly serious neighbors. Towering oak barrels hold excellent Cabernet Sauvignon, Pinot Noir, Zinfandel, Syrah, and other single-varietal wines, along with a well-regarded Bordeaux blend called Argos. Dutch Henry also sells a Sauvignon Blanc and a charming Rosé. A current-release tasting will introduce you to these wines; you can also visit the wine caves on one of two tours that include tastings. ⊠ *4310 Silverado Trail, near Dutch Henry Canyon Rd., Calistoga* ☎ *707/942–5771* ⊕ *www.dutchhenry.com* ✍ *Tasting $25, tours $35–$50* ☉ *Daily 10–4:30, tours by appointment.*

Lava Vine Winery. The owners and staff of this jolly spot pride themselves on creating a family- and dog-friendly environment, and you're apt to hear rock, pop, and other tunes as you taste small-lot wines that include Cabernet Sauvignon, Chenin Blanc, Syrah, and Port. The wry Pete might even start playing the banjo. ■ **TIP→ If they're available and you like mighty reds, be sure to taste the Suisun Valley Petite Sirah and the Knights Valley Reserve Cabernet.** ⊠ *965 Silverado Trail N, Calistoga* ☎ *707/942–9500* ⊕ *www.lavavine.com* ✍ *Tasting $10* ☉ *Daily 10–5.*

Tamber Bey Vineyards. Endurance riders Barry and Jennifer Waitte share their passion for horses and wine at their glam-rustic winery north of Calistoga. Their 22-acre Sundance Ranch remains a working equestrian facility, but the site has been revamped to include a state-of-the-art winery with separate fermenting tanks for grapes from Tamber Bey's vineyards in Yountville, Oakville, and elsewhere. The winemakers produce two Chardonnays and a Sauvignon Blanc, but the winery's stars are several subtly powerful reds, including the flagship Cabernet Sauvignon, a Merlot, and blends dominated by Cabernet Franc, Cabernet Sauvignon, and Petit Verdot. ■ **TIP→ Appointments are required, but even on a few-minutes' notice they're generally easy to get.** ⊠ *1251 Tubbs La., at Myrtledale Rd., Calistoga* ☎ *707/942–2100* ⊕ *www.tamberbey.com* ✍ *Tastings $25–$55, tour and tasting $45* ☉ *Daily 10–5, by appointment only.*

WHERE TO EAT

$$$
ITALIAN
Fodor's Choice
★

✕ **Hotel D'Amici.** Italian and Italian-American influences abound at this restaurant operated by the Pestoni family, owners of Rutherford Grove Winery. A wall painted by San Francisco muralist Brian Barneclo riffs off Federico's Fellini's film 8½; photos of Pestonis making Napa Valley wine (since 1892) are everywhere; and, perhaps most importantly, chef Joe Venezia is a protégé of the late cookbook author Marcella Hazan. Like Hazan, Venezia seeks out top-quality ingredients, strives for simplicity, and cooks sauces and his meals' other components long enough to permit the flavors to meld. He prepares all the classics, including gnocchi, spaghetti with seafood, and veal scaloppine, with finesse. Pestoni and other California vintages dominate the wine list, and there

7

are Italian selections. $ *Average main: $24 ⊠ 1440 Lincoln Ave., near Washington St., Calistoga* ☎ *707/942–1400* ⊕ *www.hoteldamici.com.*

$$$ ✕ **Jolē.** Local produce plays a starring role at this modern American res-
MODERN taurant, not surprising as chef Matt Spector is one of the area's biggest
AMERICAN proponents of farm-to-table dining. Depending on when you visit, you
might enjoy roasted cauliflower served with almonds, dates, capers, and
balsamic; kale stew with Tasso ham, kabocha squash, and fingerling
potatoes; and molasses-glazed quail with farro risotto, roasted pumpkin,
and a maple-bourbon demi-glace. The menu is available à la carte, and
there are four-, five-, and six-course prix-fixe options. With about four
dozen wines by the glass, it's easy to find something to pair with each
course. There's also a full bar, with a happy hour daily from 4 pm to 6
pm. $ *Average main: $25 ⊠ Mount View Hotel, 1457 Lincoln Ave., near
Fair Way, Calistoga* ☎ *707/942–9538* ⊕ *jolerestaurant.com* ⊘ *No lunch.*

$$$$ ✕ **Solbar.** Chef Brandon Sharp is known around the region for his subtle
MODERN and sophisticated take on Wine Country cooking. As befits a restau-
AMERICAN rant at a spa resort, the menu here is divided into "healthy, lighter
Fodor's Choice dishes" and "hearty cuisine." On the lighter side, the lemongrass-
★ poached petrale sole comes with jasmine rice and hearts of palm. On
the heartier side you might find a rib-eye steak served with Kennebec
potatoes, creamed spinach, and sauce bordelaise. The service at Solbar
is uniformly excellent, and in good weather the patio is a festive spot
for breakfast, lunch, or dinner. $ *Average main: $31 ⊠ Solage Calis-
toga, 755 Silverado Trail, at Rosedale Rd., Calistoga* ☎ *877/684–9146*
⊕ *www.solagecalistoga.com/solbar.*

WHERE TO STAY

$$$$ ⛺ **Calistoga Ranch.** Spacious cedar-shingle lodges throughout this posh,
RESORT wooded property have outdoor living areas, and even the restaurant,
Fodor's Choice spa, and reception space have outdoor seating and fireplaces. **Pros:**
★ almost half the lodges have private hot tubs on the deck; lovely hiking
trails on the property; guests have reciprocal privileges at Auberge du
Soleil and Solage Calistoga. **Cons:** innovative indoor-outdoor organiza-
tion works better in fair weather than in rain or cold. $ *Rooms from:
$720 ⊠ 580 Lommel Rd., Calistoga* ☎ *707/254–2800, 800/942–4220*
⊕ *www.calistogaranch.com* ⚑ *50 guest lodges* ⚏ *No meals.*

$$ ⛺ **Indian Springs Resort and Spa.** Stylish Indian Springs—operating as
RESORT a spa since 1862—ably splits the difference between laid-back style
and ultrachic touches. **Pros:** palm-studded grounds with outdoor seating areas; on-site restaurant; stylish for the price; enormous mineral
pool; free touring bikes. **Cons:** lodge rooms are small; service could be
more polished. $ *Rooms from: $259 ⊠ 1712 Lincoln Ave., Calistoga*
☎ *707/942–4913* ⊕ *www.indianspringscalistoga.com* ⚑ *77 rooms, 18
suites, 18 cottages, 3 houses* ⚏ *No meals.*

$$ ⛺ **Luxe Calistoga.** Extravagant hospitality defines the Napa Valley's lux-
B&B/INN ury properties, but this inn takes the prize in the small-lodging category.
Fodor's Choice **Pros:** attentive owners; marvelous breakfasts; good restaurants, tasting
★ rooms, and shopping within walking distance. **Cons:** the hum (and
sometimes scent) of street traffic is ever-present. $ *Rooms from: $269*
⊠ *1139 Lincoln Ave., Calistoga* ☎ *707/942–9797* ⊕ *luxecalistoga.com*
⚑ *5 rooms* ⚏ *Breakfast.*

All it needs is a fair maiden: Castello di Amorosa's re-created castle.

$$ B&B/INN Fodor's Choice ★ [🏨] **Meadowlark Country House.** Two charming European gents run this laid-back but sophisticated inn on 20 wooded acres just north of downtown. **Pros:** charming innkeepers; tasty sit-down breakfasts; welcoming vibe that attracts diverse guests. **Cons:** clothing-optional pool policy isn't for everyone. [$] *Rooms from: $210* ✉ *601 Petrified Forest Rd., Calistoga* ☎ *707/942–5651, 800/942–5651* 🌐 *www.meadowlarkinn.com* 🛏 *5 rooms, 3 suites, 1 cottage, 1 guesthouse* 🍴 *Breakfast.*

$$$$ RESORT Fodor's Choice ★ [🏨] **Solage Calistoga.** The aesthetic at this 22-acre property is Napa Valley barn meets San Francisco loft, so the rooms have high ceilings, polished concrete floors, recycled walnut furniture, and all-natural fabrics in soothingly muted colors. **Pros:** great service; complimentary bikes; separate pools for kids and adults. **Cons:** the vibe may not suit everyone. [$] *Rooms from: $548* ✉ *755 Silverado Trail, Calistoga* ☎ *855/942–7442, 707/226–0800* 🌐 *www.solagecalistoga.com* 🛏 *83 rooms, 6 suites* 🍴 *No meals.*

SPAS

Fodor's Choice ★ **Spa Solage.** This eco-conscious spa has reinvented the traditional Calistoga mud and mineral water therapies. Case in point: the hour-long "Mudslide," a three-part treatment that includes a mud body mask (in a heated lounge), a soak in a thermal bath, and a power nap in a sound/vibration chair. The mud here is a mix of clay, volcanic ash, and essential oils. Traditional spa services—combination Shiatsu-Swedish and other massages, full-body exfoliations, facials, and waxes—are available, as are fitness and yoga classes. ✉ *755 Silverado Trail, at Rosedale Rd., Calistoga* ☎ *707/226–0825, 855/790–6023* 🌐 *www.solagecalistoga.com/spa* 🎫 *Treatments $98–$470* 🕐 *Daily 8–8.*

SPORTS AND THE OUTDOORS

Calistoga Bikeshop. Options here include regular and fancy bikes that rent for $18 an hour and up, and there's a self-guided Cool Wine Tour ($90) that includes tastings at three or four small wineries. ✉ *1318 Lincoln Ave., near Washington St., Calistoga* ☎ *707/942–9687* ⊕ *www. calistogabikeshop.net.*

THE SONOMA VALLEY

The birthplace of modern California wine making—Count Aragon Haraszthy opened Buena Vista Winery here in 1857—Sonoma Valley seduces with its unpretentious attitude and pastoral landscape. Tasting rooms, restaurants, and historical sites, among the latter the last mission established in California by Franciscan friars, abound near Sonoma Plaza. Beyond downtown Sonoma, the wineries and attractions are spread out along gently winding roads. Sonoma County's half of the Carneros District lies within Sonoma Valley, whose other towns of note include Glen Ellen and Kenwood. Sonoma Valley tasting rooms are often less crowded than those in Napa or northern Sonoma County, especially midweek, and the vibe here, though sophisticated, is definitely less sceney.

ESSENTIALS

Contact Sonoma Valley Visitors Bureau ☎ *707/996–1090, 866/996–1090* ⊕ *www.sonomavalley.com.*

SONOMA

14 miles west of Napa, 45 miles northeast of San Francisco.

One of the few towns in the valley with multiple attractions not related to food and wine, Sonoma has plenty to keep you busy for a couple of hours before you head out to tour the wineries. And you needn't leave town to taste wine. There are more than two dozen tasting rooms within steps of the plaza, some of which pour wines from more than one winery. The valley's cultural center, Sonoma, founded in 1835 when California was still part of Mexico, is built around a large, tree-filled plaza.

GETTING HERE AND AROUND

Highway 12 (signed as Broadway near Sonoma Plaza) heads north into Sonoma from Highway 121 and south from Santa Rosa into downtown Sonoma, where (signed as West Spain Street) it travels east to the plaza. Parking is relatively easy to find on or near the plaza, and you can walk to many restaurants, shops, and tasting rooms. Signs on East Spain Street and East Napa Street point the way to several wineries a mile or more east of the plaza.

EXPLORING

TOP ATTRACTIONS

Fodor's Choice ★ **Gundlach Bundschu.** Visitors may mispronounce this winery's name ("gun lock bun shoe" gets you close), but still they flock here to sample polished wines served by friendly pourers. Most of the winery's land has been in the Bundschu family since 1858. Cabernet Franc, Cabernet Sauvignon, Chardonnay, Merlot, and Tempranillo wines all are available in the standard $10 tasting. Add $10 to taste the signature Vintage Reserve red blend. For a more comprehensive experience, take the farm tour ($30), which ends with a cave tasting, or head into the vineyard ($50; available only between May and October). The Heritage Pairing ($75), involving gourmet bites and limited-release wines, takes place on weekends by appointment. ■TIP→ On summer Fridays and weekends you can taste at vineyard-view tables outdoors. ⊠ *2000 Denmark St., at Bundschu Rd., off 8th St. E, Sonoma* ☎ *707/938–5277* ⊕ *www.gunbun.com* ✉ *Tastings $10–$25, tours $30–$50; food-wine pairing $75* ☉ *June–mid-Oct., daily 11–5:30; mid-Oct.–May, daily 11–4:30; food-wine pairing weekends by appointment.*

Fodor's Choice ★ **Patz & Hall.** Sophisticated single-vineyard Chardonnays and Pinot Noirs are the trademark of this respected winery that relocated from Napa to Sonoma in 2014. It's a Wine Country adage that great wines are made in the vineyard—the all-star fields represented here include Hyde, Durell, and Gap's Crown—but winemaker James Hall routinely surpasses peers with access to the same fruit, proof that discernment and expertise (Hall is a master at oak aging) play a role, too. Seated tastings hosted by knowledgeable pourers take place in a fashionable single-story residence 3 miles southeast of Sonoma Plaza. You can taste at the bar and on some days on the vineyard-view terrace beyond it, but to learn how food friendly these wines are, consider the Salon Tasting, at which they're paired with gourmet bites crafted with equal finesse. ⊠ *21200 8th St. E, near Peru Rd., Sonoma* ☎ *707/265–7700* ⊕ *www.patzhall.com* ✉ *Tastings $25–$75* ☉ *Thurs.–Mon. 10–4, by appointment.*

Fodor's Choice ★ **Ram's Gate Winery.** Stunning views, ultrachic architecture, and wines made from grapes grown by acclaimed producers make a visit to Ram's Gate an event. The welcoming interior spaces—think Restoration Hardware with a dash of high-style whimsy—open up to the entire western Carneros. During fine weather you'll experience (in comfort) the cooling breezes that sweep through the area while sipping sophisticated wines, mostly Pinot Noirs and Chardonnays, but also Sauvignon Blanc, Cabernet Sauvignon, Syrah, late-harvest Zinfandel, and even a sparkler. With grapes sourced from the Sangiacomo, Hudson, and other illustrious vineyards, winemaker Jeff Gaffner focuses on creating balanced vintages that express what occurred in nature that year. One food-wine pairing ($60) includes tapas, wine tasting, and a winery tour; the other ($125; Thursday and Friday only) focuses on food and wine education. ⊠ *28700 Arnold Dr./Hwy. 121, Sonoma* ☎ *707/721–8700* ⊕ *www.ramsgatewinery.com* ✉ *Tasting $20–$125* ☉ *Thurs.–Mon. 10–6 by appointment.*

Fodor's Choice ★ **Scribe.** Andrew and Adam Mariani, sons of California walnut growers, established Scribe in 2007 on land first planted to grapes in 1858 by Emil Dresel, a German immigrant. Dresel's claims to fame include cultivating Sonoma's first Riesling and Sylvaner, an achievement the brothers honor by growing both these varietals on land he once farmed. Using natural wine-making techniques they craft bright, terroir-driven wines from those grapes, along with Chardonnay, Pinot Noir, Syrah, and Cabernet Sauvignon. Tastings take place at weathered picnic tables on an oak-shaded knoll overlooking some of Scribe's vineyards. A 1915 Mission Revival–style hacienda nearby is being restored for use as a

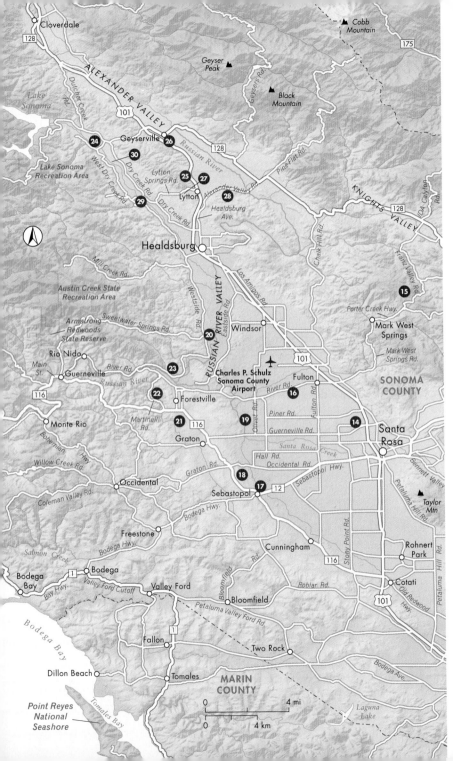

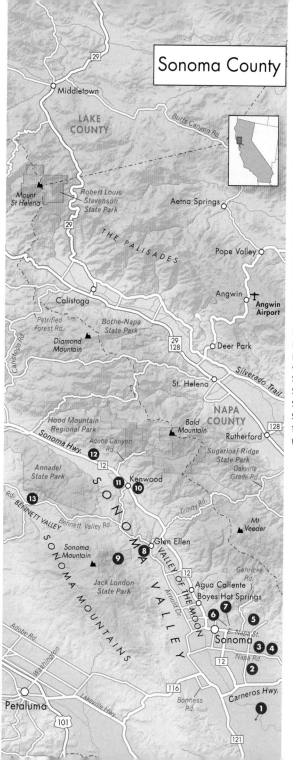

Sonoma County

tasting space. During Prohibition it served as a hideout for bootleggers, and its basement harbored a speakeasy, two of many intriguing tales associated with this historic property. ✉ *2100 Denmark St., off Napa Rd., Sonoma* ☎ *707/939–1858* ⊕ *scribewinery.com* 🍷 *Tasting price varies; contact winery* ⊗ *Daily by appointment.*

Sonoma Mission. The northernmost of the 21 missions established by Franciscan friars in California, Sonoma Mission was founded in 1823 as Mission San Francisco Solano. It serves as the centerpiece of **Sonoma State Historic Park,** which includes several other sites in Sonoma and nearby Petaluma. Some early mission structures were destroyed, but all or part of several remaining buildings date to the days of Mexican rule over California. These include the **Sonoma Barracks,** a half block west of the mission at 20 East Spain Street, which housed troops under the command of General Mariano Guadalupe Vallejo, who controlled vast tracks of land in the region. The modest museum contains displays about the missions and information about the other historic sites. ✉ *114 E. Spain St., at 1st St. E, Sonoma* ☎ *707/938–9560* ⊕ *www.parks.ca.gov/?page_id=479* 🍷 *$3, includes same-day admission to other historic sites* ⊗ *Daily 10–5.*

Fodor'sChoice **Walt Wines.** You could spend a full day sampling wines in the tasting
★ rooms bordering Sonoma Plaza, but one not to miss is Walt, which specializes in Pinot Noir and makes two Chardonnays. Fruit-forward yet subtle, the Pinots win over even the purists who pine for the genre's days of lighter, more perfumey vintages. Some of the Pinots come from Sonoma County grapes but others are from ones grown in Mendocino County (just north of Sonoma County), California's Central Coast, and Oregon's Willamette Valley. Critics routinely bestow high ratings on all these wines. ✉ *380 1st St. W, at W. Spain St., Sonoma* ☎ *707/933–4440* ⊕ *www.waltwines.com* 🍷 *Tastings $20* ⊗ *Daily 11–6.*

WORTH NOTING

Buena Vista Winery. The site where modern California wine making got its start has been transformed into an entertaining homage to the accomplishments of the 19th-century wine pioneer Count Agoston Haraszthy. Tours pass through the original aging caves dug deep into the hillside by Chinese laborers, and banners, photos, and artifacts inside and out convey the history made on this site. Reserve tastings ($40) include library and current wines, plus ones still aging in barrels. The stylish former press house (used for pressing grapes into wine), which dates to 1862, hosts the standard tastings. ■TIP➔ **Chardonnays and Pinot Noirs from Los Carneros AVA are this winery's strong suits.** ✉ *18000 Old Winery Rd., off E. Napa St., Sonoma* ☎ *800/926–1266* ⊕ *www.buenavistawinery.com* 🍷 *Tastings $15–$40; tours $10–$35* ⊗ *Daily 10–5; tours by appointment.*

WHERE TO EAT

$$$ ✕ **Cafe La Haye.** In a postage-stamp-size open kitchen, the skillful chef
AMERICAN turns out main courses that star on a small but worthwhile seasonal menu
Fodor'sChoice emphasizing local ingredients. Chicken, beef, pasta, and fish get deluxe
★ treatment without fuss or fanfare—the daily roasted chicken and the risotto specials are always good. Butterscotch pudding is a homey signature dessert. The dining room is compact, but the friendly owner, always

there to greet diners, maintains a particularly welcoming vibe. $ *Average main: $24* ⊠ *140 E. Napa St., at 1st St. E, Sonoma* ☎ *707/935–5994* ⊕ *www.cafelahaye.com* ⊙ *Closed Sun. and Mon. No lunch.*

$$$ ✕ **El Dorado Kitchen.** The visual delights at this winning restaurant include its clean lines and handsome decor, but the eye inevitably drifts westward to the open kitchen, where chef Armando Navarro and his diligent crew craft flavorful dishes full of subtle surprises. Focusing on locally sourced ingredients, the menu might include bomba-rice paella awash with seafood and linguica sausage, or duck confit accompanied by farro salad, kale, mushrooms, and almonds. Even a simple dish like truffle-oil fries, liberally sprinkled with Parmesan, charms with its combination of tastes and textures. The noteworthy desserts include profiteroles with toasted marshmallow and chocolate ganache, and cornbread French toast with strawberries and buttermilk sherbet. $ *Average main: $26* ⊠ *El Dorado Hotel, 405 1st St. W, at W. Spain St., Sonoma* ☎ *707/996–3030* ⊕ *www.eldoradosonoma.com/restaurant.*

MODERN AMERICAN
Fodor'sChoice
★

$$$ ✕ **Harvest Moon Cafe.** It's easy to feel like one of the family at this little restaurant with an odd, zigzagging layout. Diners seated at one of the two tiny bars chat with the servers like old friends, but the husband-and-wife team in the kitchen is serious about the food, much of which relies on local produce. The ever-changing menu might include homey dishes such as grilled pork loin with crispy polenta and artichokes, Niman Ranch rib-eye steak with a tomatillo salsa and Zinfandel reduction, or pan-seared Hawaiian Ono with jasmine rice, and eggplant. Everything is so perfectly executed and the vibe is so genuinely warm that a visit here is deeply satisfying. ■TIP➔ A spacious back patio with tables arranged around a fountain more than doubles the seating; a heated tent keeps this area warm in winter. $ *Average main: $25* ⊠ *487 1st St. W, at W. Napa St., Sonoma* ☎ *707/933–8160* ⊕ *www. harvestmooncafesonoma.com* ⊙ *Closed Tues. No lunch.*

AMERICAN
Fodor'sChoice
★

$$$ ✕ **LaSalette.** Born in the Azores and raised in Sonoma, chef-owner Manuel Azevedo serves dishes inspired by his native Portugal in this warmly decorated spot. The best seats are on a patio along an alleyway off Sonoma Plaza. Boldly flavored dishes such as pork tenderloin *recheado*, stuffed with olives and almonds and topped with a Port sauce, might be followed by a dish of rice pudding with Madeira-braised figs or a Port from the varied list. ■TIP➔ The daily seafood specials are well worth a try, especially the whole fish. $ *Average main: $24* ⊠ *452 1st St. E, near E. Spain St., Sonoma* ☎ *707/938–1927* ⊕ *www.lasalette-restaurant.com.*

PORTUGUESE

$$$$ ✕ **Oso.** Owner-chef David Bush, who achieved national recognition for his food and wine pairings at St. Francis Winery, struck out on his own in late 2014, opening this restaurant whose name, Spanish for "bear," acknowledges the nearby spot where rebels raised a flag depicting a bear and declared California's independence from Mexico. Bush serves tapas-size dishes à la carte and prepares a five-course tasting menu with optional wine pairings. An early menu included pickled shrimp with a red cabbage, kale, and peanut slaw à la carte and Syrah-braised short ribs for the tasting. Oso's contemporary barlike space's design incorporates materials reclaimed from previous incarnations of its building, erected in the 1890s as a livery stable. ■TIP➔ Reservations are required for the tasting

MODERN AMERICAN

7

but aren't accepted otherwise. $ *Average main: $32* ✉ *9 E. Napa St., at Broadway, Sonoma* ☎ *707/931–6926* 🌐 *ososonoma.com* ⏲ *No lunch.*

$$$$ AMERICAN Fodor's Choice ★ **Santé.** This elegant dining room has evolved into a destination restaurant through its focus on seasonal and locally sourced ingredients. The room is understated, with dark walls and soft lighting, but the food is anything but. Dishes such as the Sonoma Liberty duck breast and confit leg, served with pearl barley "risotto," sweet carrot puree, and maple duck jus, are sophisticated without being fussy. Others, like the sampler of Niman Ranch beef that includes a petite filet mignon, a skirt steak, and braised pavé beef à la bourguignonne, are pure decadence. The restaurant offers a seasonal tasting menu ($149). $ *Average main: $43* ✉ *Fairmont Sonoma Mission Inn & Spa, 100 Boyes Blvd./Hwy. 12, 2½ miles north of Sonoma Plaza, Boyes Hot Springs* ☎ *707/938–9000* 🌐 *www.santediningroom.com* ⏲ *No lunch.*

$ AMERICAN **Sunflower Caffé.** The food at this casual eatery, mostly salads and sandwiches, is simple but satisfying. Highlights include the smoked duck breast sandwich, served on a baguette and slathered with caramelized onions. A meal of soup and local cheeses is a good option if you just want to nibble. Both the pretty patio, which is in the back, and the sidewalk seating area facing Sonoma Plaza are equipped with heating lamps and get plenty of shade, so they're comfortable in all but the most inclement weather. Cheerful artworks brighten up the interior, where locals hunker over their computers and take advantage of the free Wi-Fi. Omelets and waffles are the stars at breakfast. $ *Average main: $13* ✉ *421 1st St. W, at W. Spain St., Sonoma* ☎ *707/996–6645* 🌐 *www.sonomasunflower.com* ⏲ *No dinner.*

WHERE TO STAY

$$ B&B/INN **Inn at Sonoma.** They don't skimp on the little luxuries here: wine and cheese is served every evening in the lobby, and the cheerfully painted rooms are warmed by gas fireplaces. **Pros:** last-minute specials are a great deal; free soda available in the lobby; free Wi-Fi. **Cons:** on a busy street rather than right on the plaza. $ *Rooms from: $220* ✉ *630 Broadway, Sonoma* ☎ *707/939–1340, 888/568–9818* 🌐 *www.innatsonoma.com* *27 rooms* 🍽 *Breakfast.*

$$$$ HOTEL Fodor's Choice ★ **MacArthur Place Hotel & Spa.** Guests at this 7-acre boutique property five blocks south of Sonoma Plaza bask in ritzy seclusion in plush accommodations set amid landscaped gardens. **Pros:** secluded garden setting; high-style furnishings; on-site steak house. **Cons:** a bit of a walk from the plaza; some traffic noise audible in street-side rooms. $ *Rooms from: $425* ✉ *29 E. MacArthur St., Sonoma* ☎ *707/938–2929, 800/722–1866* 🌐 *www.macarthurplace.com* *62 rooms, 2 cottage suites* 🍽 *Breakfast.*

$ B&B/INN FAMILY **Sonoma Creek Inn.** The small but cheerful rooms at this motel-style inn are individually decorated with painted wooden armoires, cozy quilts, and brightly colored contemporary artwork. **Pros:** clean, well-lighted bathrooms; lots of charm for the price; popular with bicyclists. **Cons:** office not staffed 24 hours a day; a 10-minute drive from Sonoma Plaza. $ *Rooms from: $145* ✉ *239 Boyes Blvd., off Hwy. 12, Sonoma* ☎ *707/939–9463, 888/712–1289* 🌐 *www.sonomacreekinn.com* *16 rooms* 🍽 *No meals.*

SPAS

Willow Stream Spa at Fairmont Sonoma Mission Inn & Spa. With 40,000 square feet and 30 treatment rooms, the Wine Country's largest spa provides every amenity you could possibly want, including pools and hot tubs fed by local thermal springs. Although the place bustles with patrons in summer and on some weekends, the vibe is always soothing. The signature bathing ritual includes an exfoliating shower, dips in two mineral-water soaking pools, an herbal steam, a dry sauna, and cool-down showers. Other popular treatments include the warm ginger-oil float, which involves relaxation in a weightless environment, and the perennially popular caviar facial. The most requested room among couples is outfitted with a two-person copper bathtub. ⊠ *100 Boyes Blvd./Hwy. 12, 2½ miles north of Sonoma Plaza, Boyes Hot Springs* ☎ *707/938–9000* ⊕ *www.fairmont.com/sonoma/willow-stream* ⌨ *Treatments $65–$485.*

SHOPPING

Sonoma Plaza is a shopping magnet, with tempting boutiques and specialty food purveyors facing the square or within a block or two.

Fodor's Choice ★ **Chateau Sonoma.** The fancy furniture, lighting fixtures, and objets d'art at this upscale shop make it a dangerous place to enter: after just a few minutes you may find yourself reconsidering your entire home's aesthetic. The owner's keen eye for style and sense of whimsy make a visit here a delight. ⊠ *153 W. Napa St., near 2nd St. W, Sonoma* ☎ *707/935–8553* ⊕ *www.chateausonoma.com.*

Fodor's Choice ★ **Sonoma Valley Certified Farmers Market.** To discover just how bountiful the Sonoma landscape is—and how talented its farmers and food artisans are—head to Depot Park, just north of the Sonoma Plaza, on Friday morning. From April through October, the market gets extra play on Tuesday evening in Sonoma Plaza. ⊠ *Depot Park, 1st St. W, at Sonoma Bike Path, Sonoma* ☎ *707/538–7023* ⊕ *www.svcfm.org.*

GLEN ELLEN

7 miles north of Sonoma.

Unlike its flashier Napa Valley counterparts, Glen Ellen eschews well-groomed sidewalks lined with upscale boutiques and restaurants, preferring instead its crooked streets, some with no sidewalks at all, shaded with stands of old oak trees. Jack London, who represents Glen Ellen's rugged spirit, lived in the area for many years; the town commemorates him with place names and nostalgic establishments. Hidden among sometimes-ramshackle buildings abutting Sonoma and Calabasas creeks are low-key shops and galleries worth poking through, and several fine dining establishments.

GETTING HERE AND AROUND

Glen Ellen sits just off Highway 12. From the north or south, take Arnold Drive west and follow it south less than a mile. The walkable downtown straddles a half-mile stretch of Arnold Drive.

EXPLORING

Fodor's Choice ★ **Benziger Family Winery.** One of the best-known Sonoma County wineries sits on a sprawling estate in a bowl with 360-degree sun exposure, the benefits of which are explored on popular tram tours that depart several times daily. Guides explain Benziger's biodynamic farming practices and give you a glimpse of the extensive cave system. The regular tram tour costs $25; another tour costing $50 concludes with a seated tasting. Noted for its Chardonnay, Cabernet Sauvignon, Merlot, Pinot Noir, and Sauvignon Blanc wines, the winery is a beautiful spot for a picnic. ■TIP➔ Reserve a seat on the tram tour through the winery's website or arrive early in the day on summer weekends and during harvest season. ✉ *1883 London Ranch Rd., off Arnold Dr., Glen Ellen* ☎ *707/935-3000, 888/490-2739* ⊕ *www.benziger.com* 🍷 *Tastings $15–$40, tours $25–$50* ⊘ *Daily 10–5; tours daily 11–3:30 except noon on the ½ hr (reservation recommended).*

Fodor's Choice ★ **Jack London State Historic Park.** The pleasures are both pastoral and intellectual at the late writer Jack London's beloved Beauty Ranch. You could easily spend the afternoon hiking the 20-plus miles of trails that loop through meadows and stands of oaks, redwoods, and other trees. Manuscripts and personal artifacts depicting London's travels are on view at the House of Happy Walls Museum, which provides a tantalizing overview of the author's life and literary passions. A short hike away lie the ruins of Wolf House, which mysteriously burned down just before the writer was to move in. Also open to the public are a few farm outbuildings and the completely restored Cottage, a wood-framed building where London penned many of his later works. He's buried on the property. ✉ *2400 London Ranch Rd., off Arnold Dr., Glen Ellen* ☎ *707/938-5216* ⊕ *www.jacklondonpark.com* 🅿 *Parking $10 ($5 walk-in or bike), includes admission to museum; cottage $4* ⊘ *Mar.–Nov., park daily 9:30–5, museum 10–5, cottage noon–4; Dec.–Feb., Thurs.–Mon. park 9:30–5, museum 10–5, cottage noon–4.*

WHERE TO EAT

$$ ✕ **Aventine Glen Ellen.** A Wine Country cousin to chef Adolfo Veronese's same-named San Francisco and Hollywood establishments, this Italian restaurant occupies an 1839 sawmill from California's Mexican period. Evidence of the building's early lives—in 1856 it was converted into a gristmill—can be seen in the old-redwood walls and exposed ceiling beams. Veronese's varied menu includes a half dozen pizzas (the seasonal one with black truffle honey, béchamel, and wild arugula is a savory masterpiece), an equal number of pasta dishes, a risotto of the day, and several meat and fish entrées. All are deftly constructed, and the chicken parmigiana has aroused envy among local Sicilian grandmothers. ■TIP➔ In good weather you can dine on a patio that overlooks Sonoma Creek, which powered the mill in days of yore. 💲 *Average main: $19* ✉ *Jack London Village, 14301 Arnold Dr., ¾ mile south of downtown, Glen Ellen* ☎ *707/934-8911* ⊕ *www.aventineglenellen.com* ⊘ *Closed Mon. No lunch.*

ITALIAN
Fodor's Choice
★

$$ ✕ **The Fig Cafe.** The compact menu at this cheerful bistro, a Glen Ellen fixture, focuses on California and French comfort food—pot roast and duck confit, for instance, as well as thin-crust pizza. Steamed mussels

FRENCH

Horseback riding tours loop around Jack London State Historic Park.

are served with terrific crispy fries, which also accompany the sirloin burger. Weekend brunch brings out locals and tourists for French toast, pizza with applewood-smoked bacon and poached eggs, corned-beef hash, and other delights. **■ TIP→ The unusual no-corkage-fee policy makes this a great place to drink the wine you discovered down the road.** [$] *Average main: $18* ✉ *13690 Arnold Dr., at O'Donnell La., Glen Ellen* ☎ *707/938–2130* 🌐 *www.thefigcafe.com* ✍ *Reservations not accepted* ⏲ *No lunch weekdays.*

$$ ECLECTIC Fodor's Choice ★

🍴 **Glen Ellen Star.** Chef Ari Weiswasser honed his craft at The French Laundry, Daniel, and other bastions of culinary finesse, but the goal at his Wine Country boîte is haute-rustic cuisine, much of which emerges from a wood-fired oven that burns a steady 600°F. Pizzas such as the crisp-crusted, richly sauced Margherita thrive in the torrid heat, as do root and other vegetables roasted in small iron skillets. Ditto for entrées that include juicy, tender roasted whole fish. Weiswasser signs each dish with a sauce, emulsion, or sly blend of spices that jazzes things up without upstaging the primary ingredient. The restaurant's decor is equally restrained, with an open-beam ceiling, exposed hardwood floors, and utilitarian seating. **■ TIP→ Many regulars perch on a stool at the kitchen-view counter to watch the chefs at work.** [$] *Average main: $22* ✉ *13648 Arnold Dr., at Warm Springs Rd., Glen Ellen* ☎ *707/343–1384* 🌐 *glenellenstar.com* ✍ *Reservations essential* ⏲ *No lunch.*

WHERE TO STAY

$$ B&B/INN Fodor's Choice ★

🏨 **Gaige House.** Asian objets d'art and leather club chairs cozied up to the lobby fireplace are just a few of the graceful touches in this luxurious but understated bed-and-breakfast. **Pros:** beautiful lounge areas; lots of privacy; excellent service; full breakfasts, afternoon wine and

Hitching a ride on the Benziger Family Winery tram tour

appetizers. **Cons:** sound carries in the main house; the least expensive rooms are on the small side. [$] *Rooms from: $275* ✉ *13540 Arnold Dr., Glen Ellen* ☎ *707/935–0237, 800/935–0237* 🌐 *www.gaige.com* 🛏 *10 rooms, 13 suites* 🍴 *Breakfast.*

$$ B&B/INN Fodor's Choice ★ 🏨 **Olea Hotel.** The husband-and-wife team of Ashish and Sia Patel operate this boutique lodging that's at once sophisticated and down-home country casual. **Pros:** beautiful style; welcoming staff; chef-prepared breakfasts; complimentary wine throughout stay. **Cons:** fills up quickly on weekends; minor road noise in some rooms. [$] *Rooms from: $288* ✉ *5131 Warm Springs Rd., west off Arnold Dr., Glen Ellen* ☎ *707/996–5131* 🌐 *www.oleahotel.com* 🛏 *10 rooms, 2 cottages* 🍴 *Breakfast.*

KENWOOD

3 miles north of Glen Ellen.

Tiny Kenwood consists of little more than a few restaurants and shops and a historic train depot. But hidden in this pretty landscape of meadows and woods at the north end of Sonoma Valley are several good wineries, most just off the Sonoma Highway (Highway 12).

GETTING HERE AND AROUND

To get to Kenwood from Glen Ellen, drive north on Highway 12.

EXPLORING

B Wise Vineyards Cellar. Although the stylish roadside tasting room of this producer of small-lot red wines sits on the valley floor in Kenwood, B Wise's winery and vineyards, 8½ miles to the southeast, occupy a prime spot high in the new Moon Mountain appellation. Owner-winemaker

Brion Wise made his name crafting big, bold Cabernets. One comes from Wise's mountain estate and another from the nearby Monte Rosso Vineyard, some of whose Cabernet vines are among California's oldest. These hearty mountain-fruit Cabs contrast pleasingly with a supplier one from the Napa Valley's Coombsville AVA. Wise also makes estate Syrah, Petite Sirah, Petit Verdot, and Zinfandel wines, along with Sonoma Coast and Willamette Valley (Oregon) Pinot Noirs and several red blends. ⊠ *9077 Sonoma Hwy., at Shaw Ave., Kenwood* ☎ *707/282–9169* ⊕ *www.bwisevineyards.com* 🖭 *Tastings $15–$25* ⊙ *Daily 10:30–5:30.*

Kunde Estate Winery & Vineyards. On your way into Kunde you pass a terrace flanked by fountains, virtually coaxing you to stay for a picnic with views over the vineyard. Best known for its toasty Chardonnays, the winery also makes well-regarded Sauvignon Blanc, Cabernet Sauvignon, Merlot, and Zinfandel wines. Among the Destination wines available only through the winery, the Dunfillan Cuvée, a blend of Cabernet and Syrah grapes, is worth checking out. The free basic tour of the grounds includes the caves, some of which stretch 175 feet below a vineyard. ■TIP➔ Reserve ahead for the Mountain Top Tasting, a popular tour that ends with a sampling of reserve wines ($40). ⊠ *9825 Sonoma Hwy./ Hwy. 12, Kenwood* ☎ *707/833–5501* ⊕ *www.kunde.com* 🖭 *Tastings $10–$40, tours free–$50* ⊙ *Daily 10:30–5, tours daily at various times.*

St. Francis Winery. Nestled at the foot of Mt. Hood, St. Francis has earned national acclaim for its food-and-wine pairings. With its red-tile roof and dramatic bell tower, the winery's California Mission–style visitor center occupies one of Sonoma's most scenic locations. The charm of the surroundings is matched by the wines, most of them red, including rich, earthy Zinfandels from the Dry Creek, Russian River, and Sonoma valleys. Chef Bryan Jones's five-course small bites and wine pairings ($50)—Liberty duck breast cassoulet with one of the Zins, for example— are offered from Thursday through Monday; pairings with cheeses and charcuterie ($30) are available daily. ⊠ *100 Pythian Rd., off Hwy. 12, Kenwood* ☎ *888/675–9463, 707/833–6146* ⊕ *www.stfranciswinery.com* 🖭 *Tastings $10–$50* ⊙ *Daily 10–5; tour Fri.–Sun at 11:30.*

WHERE TO EAT AND STAY

$ ✕ **Café Citti.** Classical music in the background, a friendly staff, and a
ITALIAN roaring fire when it's cold outside keep this roadside café from feeling too spartan. Order dishes such as roast chicken and slabs of tiramisu from the counter and they're delivered to your table, indoors or on an outdoor patio. The array of prepared salads and sandwiches means the café does a brisk business in takeout for picnic packers, but you can also choose pasta made to order. Ⓢ *Average main: $13* ⊠ *9049 Sonoma Hwy./Hwy. 12, Kenwood* ☎ *707/833–2690* ⊕ *www.cafecitti. com* 🖭 *Reservations not accepted.*

$$$$ 🛏 **Kenwood Inn and Spa.** Fluffy featherbeds, wood-burning fireplaces,
B&B/INN and French doors opening onto terraces or balconies give the uncom-
Fodor's Choice monly spacious guest rooms at this inn a particularly romantic air.
★ **Pros:** large rooms; lavish furnishings; excellent restaurant; rich full breakfast; romantic. **Cons:** road or lobby noise in some rooms; expensive. Ⓢ *Rooms from: $495* ⊠ *10400 Sonoma Hwy./Hwy. 12, Kenwood*

7

☎ *707/833–1293, 800/353–6966* ⊕ *www.kenwoodinn.com* ⌐ ⌐ *25 rooms, 4 suites* ☉ *Breakfast.*

ELSEWHERE IN SONOMA COUNTY

Sonoma County's northern and western reaches are a study in contrasts. Trendy hotels, restaurants, shops, and tasting rooms have transformed Healdsburg into a hot spot. Within a few miles, though, chic yields to bucolic, with only the occasional horse ranch, apple or peach orchard, or stand of oaks interrupting the rolling vineyard hills. The Russian River Valley is the grape-growing star, but Dry Creek and Alexander valleys and the Sonoma Coast also merit investigation. Office parks and tract housing diminish Santa Rosa's appeal, but wineries and cultural attractions, along with solid budget lodgings, can be found within its borders.

ESSENTIALS

Contacts **Sonoma County Tourism Bureau** ✉ *3637 Westwind Blvd., Santa Rosa* ☎ *707/522–5800, 800/576–6662* ⊕ *www.sonomacounty.com.*

SANTA ROSA

8 miles northwest of Kenwood, 55 miles north of San Francisco.

With more than 170,000 people, Santa Rosa, the Wine Country's largest city, isn't likely to charm you with its malls, office buildings, and frequent traffic snarls. Its moderately priced lodgings, however, can come in handy, especially since Santa Rosa is roughly equidistant from Sonoma, Healdsburg, and notable Russian River wineries.

The location of Santa Rosa's former Northwestern Pacific Railroad depot—built in 1903 by Italian stonemasons and immortalized in Alfred Hitchcock's coolly sinister 1943 film Shadow of a Doubt—provides the name for the revitalized Railroad Square Historic District west of U.S. 101. The depot is now a visitor center, and 4th Street between Wilson and Davis streets contains restaurants, bar, and antiques and thrift shops worth checking out, as do nearby lanes.

GETTING HERE AND AROUND

Santa Rosa straddles U.S. 101, the route to take (north) from San Francisco. From the Sonoma Valley, take Highway 12 north. Sonoma County Transit buses serve the city and surrounding area.

VISITOR INFORMATION

Contacts **Visit Santa Rosa** ✉ *9 4th St., at Wilson St., Santa Rosa, California, United States* ☎ *800/404–7673* ⊕ *www.visitsantarosa.com.*

EXPLORING

TOP ATTRACTIONS

Fodor's Choice
★ **Martinelli Winery.** In a century-old hop barn with the telltale triple towers, Martinelli has the feel of a traditional country store, but the sophisticated wines made here are anything but old-fashioned. The winery's reputation rests on its complex Pinot Noirs, Syrahs, and Zinfandels, including the $125-a-bottle Jackass Hill Vineyard Zin, made with

grapes from 130-year-old vines. You can sip these acclaimed wines—going back a decade or more—during a private Library Tasting ($50). A standard tasting ($10) focuses on current releases, a Chardonnay, three reds, and a Muscat that tastes like honeysuckle. Winemaker Helen Turley set the Martinelli style—fruit forward, easy on the oak, reined-in tannins—in the 1990s. The current winemaker Bryan Kvamme, a Turley protégé, continues the tradition. ⊠ *3360 River Rd., east of Olivet Rd., Windsor* ☎ *707/525–0570, 800/346–1627* ⊕ *www.martinelliwinery. com* ✉ *Tastings $10–$50* ⊗ *Daily 10–5; library tasting and wine-cheese pairing by appointment only with 48-hr notice.*

Fodor's Choice ★ **Matanzas Creek Winery.** The visitor center at Matanzas Creek sets itself apart with an understated Japanese aesthetic, extending to a tranquil fountain, a koi pond, and a vast field of lavender. The winery makes Sauvignon Blanc, Chardonnay, Merlot, and Pinot Noir wines under the Matanzas Creek name and three equally well-regarded wines—a Bordeaux red blend, a Chardonnay, and a Sauvignon Blanc—with the Journey label. All tours take in the beautiful estate and include tastings. The Signature tour concludes with tastings of limited-production and library wines paired with artisanal cheeses. ■ TIP➜ **An ideal time to visit is in May and June, when lavender perfumes the air.** ⊠ *6097 Bennett Valley Rd., Santa Rosa* ☎ *707/528–6464, 800/590–6464* ⊕ *www. matanzascreek.com* ✉ *Tastings $10–$25, tours $10–$35* ⊗ *Daily 10–4:30; estate tour ($10) daily at 10:30, others by appointment at least 48 hrs in advance.*

FAMILY **Safari West.** An unexpected bit of wilderness in the Wine Country, this African wildlife preserve covers 400 acres. A visit begins with a stroll around enclosures housing lemurs, cheetahs, giraffes, and rare birds such as the brightly colored scarlet ibis. Next, climb with your guide onto open-air vehicles that spend about two hours combing the expansive property, where more than 80 species—including gazelles, cape buffalo, antelope, wildebeests, and zebras—inhabit the hillsides. If you'd like to extend your stay, lodging in well-equipped tent cabins is available. ⊠ *3115 Porter Creek Rd., off Mark West Springs Rd., Santa Rosa* ☎ *707/579–2551, 800/616–2695* ⊕ *www.safariwest.com* ✉ *$70–$95 ($32–$35 ages 3–12)* ⊗ *Safaris mid-Mar.–early Sept., 9, 10, 1, 2, and 4; hrs vary rest of yr.*

WORTH NOTING

FAMILY **Charles M. Schulz Museum.** Fans of Snoopy and Charlie Brown will love this museum dedicated to the late Charles M. Schulz, who lived his last three decades in Santa Rosa. Permanent installations include a re-creation of the cartoonist's studio, and temporary exhibits often focus on a particular theme in his work. ■ TIP➜ **Children and adults can take a stab at creating cartoons in the Education Room.** ⊠ *2301 Hardies La., at W. Steele La., Santa Rosa* ☎ *707/579–4452* ⊕ *www.schulzmuseum. org* ✉ *$10* ⊗ *Labor Day–Memorial Day, Mon. and Wed.–Fri. 11–5, weekends 10–5; Memorial Day–Labor Day, weekdays 11–5, weekends 10–5.*

DeLoach Vineyards. Best known for its Russian River Valley Pinot Noirs, DeLoach also produces Chardonnays, old-vine Zinfandels, and a few

7

other wines. Some of the reds are made using open-top wood fermentation vats that have been used in France for centuries to intensify a wine's flavor. Tours focus on these and other wine-making techniques and include a stroll through organic gardens and vineyards. You can also take wine-blending a seminar, compare California and French Chardonnays and Pinot Noirs, or (on weekends only) relax with a wood-fired pizza and a glass of wine. ■ **TIP→ The sparklers and still wines of the JCB label, whose letters match the initials of its dapper creator, DeLoach's Burgundy-born owner, Jean-Charles Boisset, are poured in a separate tasting room.** ✉ *1791 Olivet Rd., off Guerneville Rd., Santa Rosa* ☎ *707/526–9111* 🌐 *www.deloachvineyards.com* 🎟 *Tastings $15–$100, tour $20* 🕒 *Daily 10–5, tour daily at noon.*

WHERE TO EAT AND STAY

$$$ ECLECTIC Fodor's Choice ★

🍴 **Willi's Wine Bar.** Don't let the name fool you: instead of a sedate spot serving wine and delicate nibbles, you'll find a cozy warren of rooms where boisterous crowds snap up small plates from the globe-trotting menu. Dishes such as the pork-belly pot stickers represent Asia, and duck prosciutto and Moroccan-style lamb chops are two of the Mediterranean-inspired foods. Several cheese and charcuterie plates are among the many using California-sourced ingredients. Wines are available in 2-ounce pours, making it easier to pair each of your little plates with a different glass. ■ **TIP→ It can get noisy inside on busy nights, so consider a table on the covered patio.** [$] *Average main: $28* ✉ *4404 Old Redwood Hwy., at Ursuline Rd., Santa Rosa* ☎ *707/526–3096* 🌐 *williswinebar.net* 🕒 *No lunch Sun. and Mon.*

$$ HOTEL Fodor's Choice ★

🏨 **Vintners Inn.** The owners of Ferrari-Carano Vineyards operate this oasis set amid 92 acres of vineyards that's known for its comfortable lodgings. **Pros:** spacious rooms with comfortable beds; jogging path through the vineyards; online deals pop up year-round. **Cons:** occasional noise from adjacent events center. [$] *Rooms from: $265* ✉ *4350 Barnes Rd., Santa Rosa* ☎ *707/575–7350, 800/421–2584* 🌐 *www.vintnersinn.com* 🛏 *38 rooms, 6 suites* 🍽 *No meals.*

RUSSIAN RIVER VALLEY

10 miles northwest of Santa Rosa.

The Russian River flows from Mendocino to the Pacific, but Russian River Valley wine making centers on a triangle with points at Healdsburg, Guerneville, and Sebastopol. Tall redwoods shade the two-lane roads of this scenic area, where, thanks to the cooling marine influence, Pinot Noir and Chardonnay are the king and queen of grapes.

GETTING HERE AND AROUND

Many Russian River Valley visitors base themselves in Healdsburg. You can find noteworthy purveyors of Pinots and Chards by heading west from downtown on Mill Street, which eventually becomes Westside Road. For Forestville and Sebastopol wineries, continue south and west along Westside until it intersects River Road and turn west. Turn south at Mirabel Road and follow it to Highway 116.

ESSENTIALS

Contacts Russian River Wine Road ☎ *707/433–4335, 800/723–6336* ⊕ *www.wineroad.com.*

EXPLORING

TOP ATTRACTIONS

Fodor's Choice
★
Hartford Family Winery. Pinot Noir lovers appreciate the subtle differences in the wines Hartford's Jeff Stewart crafts from grapes grown in Sonoma County's three top AVAs for the varietal—Los Carneros, Russian River Valley, and the Sonoma Coast—along with one from the Anderson Valley, just north in Mendocino County. The Pinot Noirs win praise from major wine critics, and Stewart also makes highly rated Chardonnays and old-vine Zinfandels. A reserve tasting ($15) includes a flight of six wines; a tour of the winery is part of the seated private library tasting ($40). ■TIP→ **If the weather's good and you've made a reservation, your reserve tasting can take place on the patio outside the opulent main winery building.** ⊠ *8075 Martinelli Rd., off Hwy. 116 or River Rd., Forestville* ☎ *707/887–8030, 800/588–0234* ⊕ *www.hartfordwines.com* 🍷 *Tastings $15–$40* ⊙ *Daily 10–4:30, tours by appointment.*

Fodor's Choice
★
Iron Horse Vineyards. A meandering one-lane road leads to this winery known for its sparkling wines and estate Chardonnays and Pinot Noirs. The sparklers have made history: Ronald Reagan served them at his summit meetings with Mikhail Gorbachev; George Herbert Walker Bush took some along to Moscow for treaty talks; and Barack Obama has included them at official state dinners. Despite Iron Horse's brushes with fame, a casual rusticity prevails at its outdoor tasting area (large heaters keep things comfortable on chilly days), which gazes out on acres of rolling, vine-covered hills. Regular tours ($25) take place on weekdays at 10 am. ■TIP→ **When his schedule permits, winemaker David Munksgard leads a private tour by truck ($50) at 10 am on Monday.** ⊠ *9786 Ross Station Rd., off Hwy. 116, Sebastopol* ☎ *707/887–1507* ⊕ *www.ironhorsevineyards.com* 🍷 *Tasting $20, tours $25–$50 (includes tasting)* ⊙ *Daily 10–4:30, tour (by appointment) weekdays at 10.*

Fodor's Choice
★
Merry Edwards Winery. Winemaker Merry Edwards describes the Russian River Valley as "the epicenter of great Pinot Noir," and she produces wines that express the unique characteristics of the soils, climates, and Pinot Noir clones from which they derive. (Edwards's research into Pinot Noir clones is so extensive that there's even one named after her.) The valley's advantages, says Edwards, are warmer-than-average daytime temperatures that encourage more intense fruit, and evening fogs that mitigate the extra heat's potential negative effects. Group tastings of the well-composed single-vineyard and blended Pinots take place throughout the day, and there are five sit-down appointment slots available except on Sunday. Edwards also makes a fine Sauvignon Blanc that's lightly aged in old oak. Tastings end, rather than begin, with this singular white wine so as not to distract guests' palates from the Pinot Noirs. ⊠ *2959 Gravenstein Hwy. N/Hwy. 116, near Oak Grove Ave., Sebastopol* ☎ *707/823–7466, 888/388–9050* ⊕ *www.merryedwards.*

7

com ✉ *Tasting free* ☉ *Daily 9:30–4:30; call for appointment or drop in and join next available tasting.*

Fodor'sChoice   **Rochioli Vineyards and Winery.** Claiming one of the prettiest picnic sites
★   in the area, with tables overlooking the vineyards, this winery has an airy little tasting room with an equally romantic view. Production is small and fans on the winery's mailing list snap up most of the bottles, but the winery is still worth a stop. Because of the cool growing conditions in the Russian River Valley, the flavors of the Chardonnay and Sauvignon Blanc are intense and complex, and the Pinot Noir, which helped cement the Russian River's status as a Pinot powerhouse, is consistently excellent. ✉ *6192 Westside Rd., Healdsburg* ☎ *707/433–2305* ⊕ *www.rochioliwinery.com* ✉ *Tasting $10* ☉ *Early Jan.–mid-Dec., Thurs.–Mon. 11–4, Tues. and Wed. by appointment.*

WORTH NOTING

Fodor'sChoice   **The Barlow.** On the site of a former apple cannery, this cluster of build-
★   ings celebrates Sonoma County's "maker" culture with an inspired combination production space and marketplace. The complex contains microbreweries and wine-making facilities, along with areas where people create or sell crafts, large-scale artworks, and artisanal food, herbs, and beverages. There's even a studio where artists using traditional methods are creating the world's largest *thangka* (Tibetan painting). Only club members can visit the anchor wine tenant, Kosta Browne, but La Follette, MacPhail, and other small producers have tasting rooms open to the public. Warped Brewing Company and Woodfour Brewing Company make and sell ales on-site, and you can have a nip of gin or bourbon at Spirit Works Distillery. ■TIP→ **From July through October the complex hosts a Thursday-night street fair, with live music and even more vendors.** ✉ *6770 McKinley St., at Morris St., off Hwy. 12, Sebastopol* ☎ *707/824–5600* ⊕ *www.thebarlow.net* ✉ *Free to complex; tasting fees at wineries, breweries, distillery* ☉ *Daily, hrs vary.*

Gary Farrell Winery. Pass through an impressive metal gate and wind your way up a steep hill to reach Gary Farrell, a spot with knockout views over the rolling hills and vineyards below. Though its Zinfandels and Chardonnays often excel, the winery is best known for its Russian River Valley Pinot Noirs, crafted these days by Theresa Heredia. At the tasting bar ($15) you can sample Sauvignon Blanc and other winery-only wines; depending on the weather, seated tastings ($25) focusing on single-vineyard Chardonnays and Pinot Noirs take place on an outdoor terrace or indoors near a fireplace. ■TIP→ **The Pinots from the Hallberg and Rochioli vineyards are worth checking out.** ✉ *10701 Westside Rd., Healdsburg* ☎ *707/473–2909* ⊕ *www.garyfarrellwinery. com* ✉ *Tastings $15–$25, tours $35–$75* ☉ *Daily 10:30–4:30, tours by appointment.*

WHERE TO EAT

$$$$ ✕ **The Farmhouse Inn.** From the sommelier who assists you with wine
FRENCH   choices to the servers who describe the provenance of the black truf-
Fodor'sChoice   fles shaved over the intricate pasta dishes, the staff matches the qual-
★   ity of this restaurant's French-inspired cuisine. The signature dish, "Rabbit Rabbit Rabbit," a trio of confit of leg, rabbit loin wrapped

in applewood-smoked bacon, and roasted rack of rabbit with a whole-grain mustard sauce, is typical of preparations that are both rustic and refined. The menu is prix-fixe (three courses $79, four $94). **TIP→ The inn is a favorite of wine-industry foodies, so reserve well in advance; if it's full, you might be able to dine in the small lounge.** [$] *Average main: $79* ✉ *7871 River Rd., at Wohler Rd., Forestville* ☎ *707/887–3300, 800/464–6642* 🌐 *www.farmhouseinn.com* ✍ *Reservations essential* ⏲ *Closed Tues. and Wed. No lunch.*

$$$ MODERN AMERICAN

🍴 **Zazu Kitchen + Farm.** "Know the face that feeds you" is the motto at Zazu, and some of the local ingredients in dishes here come from the owners themselves: executive chef Duskie Estes and her husband, John Stewart, the house salumist (specialist in all things pig). Small plates such as *chicharrones* (fried pork rinds), tamarind Petaluma chicken wings, and baby back ribs can add up to a meal, or you can sample a few appetizers before moving on to a bacon burger, porcini noodle and Sebastopol mushroom stroganoff, or a tomahawk steak for two and fries. In good weather the industrial-looking space's huge doors lift up to admit the breeze that often graces the open-air patio, which is surrounded by raised garden beds that supply produce and spices for diners' meals. [$] *Average main: $23* ✉ *The Barlow, 6770 McKinley St., No. 150, off Morris St., Sebastopol* ☎ *707/523–4814* 🌐 *www.zazukitchen.com* ⏲ *Closed Tues. No lunch Mon.*

WHERE TO STAY

$$$$ B&B/INN Fodor's Choice ★

🏨 **The Farmhouse Inn.** With a rustic-farmhouse-meets-modern-loft aesthetic, this low-key but upscale getaway with a pale-yellow exterior contains spacious rooms filled with king-size four-poster beds, whirlpool tubs, and hillside-view terraces. **Pros:** fantastic restaurant; luxury bath products; full-service spa. **Cons:** mild road noise audible in rooms closest to the street. [$] *Rooms from: $495* ✉ *7871 River Rd., Forestville* ☎ *707/887–3300, 800/464–6642* 🌐 *www.farmhouseinn.com* 🛏 *19 rooms, 6 suites* 🍽 *Breakfast.*

$ HOTEL FAMILY

🏨 **Sebastopol Inn.** The cheerful rooms clustered around this reasonably priced inn's courtyard are steps from The Barlow, a hip collection of restaurants, wine-tasting rooms, brewpubs, galleries, and other spaces. **Pros:** good rates; friendly staff; across from Barlow complex; near noteworthy wineries. **Cons:** no frills; bland decor. [$] *Rooms from: $129* ✉ *6751 Sebastopol Ave., Sebastopol* ☎ *707/829–2500* 🌐 *www.sebastopolinn.com* 🛏 *29 rooms, 2 suites* 🍽 *No meals.*

SPORTS AND THE OUTDOORS

CANOE TRIPS

Burke's Canoe Trips. You'll get a real feel for the Russian River's flora and fauna on a leisurely 10-mile paddle downstream from Burke's to Guerneville. A shuttle bus returns you to your car at the end of the journey, which is best taken from late May through mid-October and, in summer, on a weekday. Summer weekends can be crowded and raucous. ✉ *8600 River Rd., at Mirabel Rd., Forestville* ☎ *707/887–1222* 🌐 *www.burkescanoetrips.com* 🎟 *$65 per canoe.*

HEALDSBURG

17 miles north of Santa Rosa.

Just when it seems that the buzz about Healdsburg couldn't get any more intense, another feature story appears touting the chic hotel and restaurant scene here. Despite the hype, you needn't be a tycoon to enjoy this town. For every ritzy restaurant there's a bakery or grocery where you can find affordable gourmet eats, and luxe lodgings are matched by modest bed-and-breakfasts. The tin-roof bandstand on Healdsburg Plaza hosts free concerts, at which you might hear anything from bluegrass to Sousa marches. Add to that the plaza's fragrant magnolia trees and bright flower beds, and the whole ensemble seems right out of a Norman Rockwell painting. Healdsburg is ideally located at the confluence of the Dry Creek Valley, Russian River Valley, and Alexander Valley AVAs. Tucked behind groves of eucalyptus or hidden high on fog-shrouded hills, the winery buildings are often barely visible.

GETTING HERE AND AROUND

Healdsburg sits just off U.S. 101. Heading north, take the Central Healdsburg exit to reach Healdsburg Plaza; heading south, take the Westside Road exit and pass east under the freeway. Sonoma County Transit Bus 60 serves Healdsburg from Santa Rosa.

WHERE TO EAT

$$$
SPANISH
Fodor's Choice
★

✕ **Bravas Bar de Tapas.** Spanish-style tapas and an outdoor patio in perpetual party mode make this restaurant headquartered in a restored 1920s bungalow a popular downtown perch. Contemporary Spanish mosaics set a perky tone inside, but unless something's amiss with the weather nearly everyone heads out back for cocktails, sangrias, beers, or flights of sherry (a tapas-bar staple in Spain) to prep the palate for the onslaught of flavors. Reliable items include the paella, Spanish cured ham, *pan tomate* (tomato toast), farm-fried duck eggs, pork-cheek sliders, croquettes, skirt steak, and crispy fried chicken with pickled peppers. ■TIP➔ On a hot Healdsburg day, the watermelon salad or gazpacho will instantly reset your internal thermostat. $ *Average main: $26* ⊠ *420 Center St., near North St., Healdsburg* ☎ *707/433–7700* ⊕ *www.starkrestaurants.com/bravas.html.*

$$
ITALIAN
Fodor's Choice
★

✕ **Campo Fina.** Ari Rosen, the owner of popular Scopa, converted a storefront that once housed a bar notorious for boozin' and brawlin' into a second showcase for his contemporary-rustic Italian cuisine. Sandblasted red brick, satin-smooth walnut tables, and old-school lighting fixtures strike an appropriately retro note for a dinner menu built around pizzas and a few other Scopa gems such as Rosen's variation on his grandmother's tomato-braised chicken with creamy-soft polenta. Locals love Campo Fina for lunch, especially on the outdoor patio, beyond which lies a boccie court that looks out of a movie set. The Sally Peppers sandwich—house-made sausage, provolone, sweet and spicy peppers, and caramelized onions on a ciabatta roll—is a memorable medley. $ *Average main: $18* ⊠ *330 Healdsburg Ave., near North St., Healdsburg* ☎ *707/395–4640* ⊕ *www.campofina.com* ⚄ *Reservations essential.*

$$ MODERN AMERICAN Fodor's Choice ★ 🍴 **Chalkboard.** Unvarnished oak flooring, wrought-iron accents, and a vaulted white ceiling create a polished yet rustic ambience for the playfully ambitious cuisine of chef Shane McAnelly. Starters such as pork-belly biscuits might at first glance seem frivolous, but the silky flavor blend—maple glaze, pickled onions, and chipotle mayo playing off feathery biscuit halves—signals a supremely capable tactician at work. Likewise with vegetable sides such as fried brussels sprouts perched upon a perky kimchi puree, or moist and crispy buttermilk fried quail. House-made pasta dishes favor rich country flavors—the robust Sonoma lamb *sugo* (sauce) with Pecorino-Romano tickles the entire palate—while desserts named The Candy Bar and Donuts O' the Day aim to please (and do). The canny wine selections ably support McAnelly's cuisine. [$] *Average main: $19* ✉ *Hotel Les Mars, 29 North St., west of Healdsburg Ave., Healdsburg* ☎ *707/473–8030* 🌐 *chalkboardhealdsburg.com.*

$ BAKERY Fodor's Choice ★ 🍴 **Downtown Bakery & Creamery.** To catch the Healdsburg spirit, hit the plaza in the early morning to down a cup of coffee and a fragrant sticky bun or a too-darlin' *canelé,* a French-style pastry with a soft custard center surrounded by a dense caramel crust. Until 2 pm you can also go the full breakfast route: pancakes, granola, poached farm eggs on polenta, or perhaps the dandy bacon-and-egg pizza. For lunch there are sandwiches, pizzas, and calzones. [$] *Average main: $8* ✉ *308A Center St., at North St., Healdsburg* ☎ *707/431–2719* 🌐 *www.downtownbakery.net* ✍ *Reservations not accepted* ⏲ *No dinner.*

$$$ MODERN AMERICAN Fodor's Choice ★ 🍴 **Partake by K-J.** Kendall-Jackson's downtown restaurant opened with a novel wine-oriented tasting menu that has evolved into a more straightforward appetizers-salads-entrées format, but the emphasis on pairing top-tier Jackson-label wines and food remains. Much of chef Justin Wangler's produce finds its way from K-J's 3-acre Santa Rosa organic farm to diners' tables in a mere few hours. With ingredients this fresh, Wangler wisely displays a light touch: summertime heirloom-tomato dishes, for instance, might have no dressing at all, the same for salads of tender mixed baby greens. Popular appetizers include lamb sliders; duck breast and local salmon are consistent main-course favorites. **■ TIP→ Tempura maitake mushrooms, the tour de force side, are served with a sweet Korean soy sauce that plays well off the wafflelike notes in the tempura batter.** [$] *Average main: $23* ✉ *241 Healdsburg Ave., near Matheson St., Healdsburg* ☎ *707/433–6000* 🌐 *www.partakebykj.com* ⏲ *Restaurant closed Mon. and Tues. No lunch.*

$$ ITALIAN Fodor's Choice ★ 🍴 **Scopa.** At his tiny, deservedly popular eatery, chef Ari Rosen prepares rustic Italian specialties such as *sugo Calabrese* (tomato-braised beef and pork rib) and house-made ravioli stuffed with ricotta. Simple thin-crust pizzas, including one with mozzarella, figs, prosciutto, and arugula, make fine meals, too. Locals love the restaurant for its lack of pretension: wine is served in juice glasses, and the friendly hostess makes the rounds to ensure everyone is satisfied. You'll be packed in elbow-to-elbow with your fellow diners, but for a convivial evening over a bottle of Nebbiolo, there's no better choice. [$] *Average main: $20* ✉ *109A Plaza St., near Healdsburg Ave., Healdsburg* ☎ *707/433–5282* 🌐 *www.scopahealdsburg.com* ⏲ *No lunch.*

$$$ ✕ **Spoonbar.** Cantina doors that open onto Healdsburg Avenue make
MODERN this trendy eatery especially appealing in summer, when a warm breeze
AMERICAN wafts into the stylish space. Midcentury modern furnishings, concrete
walls, and a long communal table fashioned from rough-hewn aca-
cia wood create an urbane setting for contemporary American fare.
Chef Louis Maldonado, a 2014 finalist on Bravo TV's *Top Chef* and
a champion on the network's *Last Chance Kitchen,* divides his menu
into five sections, from which diners mix and match to create a meal.
The mains might include lamb rib-eye stuffed with merguez sausage
and escargots or barbecue-glazed flounder served with rock shrimp and
corn and scallion ragout. ■ **TIP→ The bar, known for inventive seasonal
and historical cocktails, is the real draw for many locals.** $ *Average
main: $25* ✉ *h2hotel, 219 Healdsburg Ave., at Vine St., Healdsburg*
☎ *707/433–7222* ⊕ *www.h2hotel.com/spoonbar* ☾ *No lunch.*

$$$ ✕ **Willi's Seafood & Raw Bar.** The festive crowd at Willi's likes to enjoy
SEAFOOD specialty cocktails at the full bar before sitting down to a dinner of
Fodor'sChoice small, mostly seafood-oriented plates. The warm Maine lobster roll
★ with garlic butter and fennel conjures up a New England fish shack,
while the ceviches and the scallops served with a ginger-lime aioli suggest Latin America. Gluten-, dairy-, nut-, and seed-free options are available for diners with dietary restrictions. Desserts are a big deal here,
with the key lime cheesecake and caramelized banana split among the
most popular. The wine list favors Sonoma County but also includes
entries from Australia, France, Greece, Portugal, and other locales.
$ *Average main: $25* ✉ *403 Healdsburg Ave., at North St., Healdsburg* ☎ *707/433–9191* ⊕ *www.willisseafood.net* ☞ *Reservations not
accepted Fri.–Sun.*

WHERE TO STAY

$ ⌂ **Best Western Dry Creek Inn.** Easy access to downtown restaurants,
HOTEL tasting rooms, and shopping as well as outlying wineries and bicycle
trails makes this Spanish Mission–style motel near U.S. 101 a good
budget option. **Pros:** laundry facilities; some pet-friendly rooms; frequent Internet discounts. **Cons:** thin walls; highway noise audible in
many rooms. $ *Rooms from: $172* ✉ *198 Dry Creek Rd., Healdsburg* ☎ *707/433–0300, 800/222–5784* ⊕ *www.drycreekinn.com* ⇗ *163
rooms* ⦿*Breakfast.*

$$$ ⌂ **h2hotel.** Eco-friendly touches abound at this hotel, from the plant-
B&B/INN covered "green roof" to wooden decks made from salvaged lumber.
Fodor'sChoice **Pros:** stylish modern design; popular bar; complimentary bikes. **Cons:**
★ least expensive rooms lack bathtubs; no fitness facilities. $ *Rooms
from: $313* ✉ *219 Healdsburg Ave., Healdsburg* ☎ *707/922–5251*
⊕ *www.h2hotel.com* ⇗ *28 rooms, 8 suites* ⦿*Breakfast.*

$$$ ⌂ **The Honor Mansion.** An 1883 Italianate Victorian houses this photo-
B&B/INN genic hotel; rooms in the main home preserve a sense of the building's
Fodor'sChoice heritage, whereas the larger suites are comparatively understated. **Pros:**
★ homemade sweets available at all hours; spa pavilions by pool avail-
able for massages in fair weather. **Cons:** almost a mile from Healdsburg
Plaza; walls can seem thin. $ *Rooms from: $325* ✉ *891 Grove St.,
Healdsburg* ☎ *707/433–4277, 800/554–4667* ⊕ *www.honormansion.*

com 🛏 *5 rooms, 7 suites, 1 cottage* ⏲ *Closed 2 wks around Christmas* 🍴 *Breakfast.*

$$$$ RESORT 🏨 **Hotel Healdsburg.** Across the street from the tidy town plaza, this spare, sophisticated hotel caters to travelers with an urban sensibility. **Pros:** several rooms overlook the town plaza; comfortable lobby with a small attached bar; extremely comfortable beds. **Cons:** exterior rooms get some street noise; rooms could use better lighting. [$] *Rooms from: $449* ✉ *25 Matheson St., Healdsburg* ☎ *707/431–2800, 800/889–7188* 🌐 *www.hotelhealdsburg.com* 🛏 *49 rooms, 6 suites* 🍴 *Breakfast.*

$$$$ HOTEL Fodor's Choice ★ 🏨 **Hôtel Les Mars.** This Relais & Châteaux property takes the prize for opulence with guest rooms spacious and elegant enough for French nobility, 18th- and 19th-century antiques and reproductions, canopy beds dressed in luxe linens, and gas-burning fireplaces. **Pros:** large rooms; just off Healdsburg's plaza; fancy bath products; room service by Chalkboard restaurant. **Cons:** very expensive. [$] *Rooms from: $675* ✉ *27 North St., Healdsburg* ☎ *707/433–4211* 🌐 *www.hotellesmars.com* 🛏 *16 rooms* 🍴 *Breakfast.*

SPAS

Fodor's Choice ★ **Spa Dolce.** Owner Ines von Majthenyi Scherrer has a good local rep, having run a popular nearby spa before opening this stylish facility just off Healdsburg Plaza. Spa Dolce specializes in skin and body care for men and women, and waxing and facials for women. Curved white walls and fresh-cut floral arrangements set a subdued tone for such treatments as the exfoliating Hauschka body scrub, which combines organic brown sugar with scented oil. There's a romantic room for couples to enjoy massages for two. ■ **TIP→ Many guests come just for the facials, which range from a straightforward cleansing to an anti-aging peel.** ✉ *250 Center St., at Matheson St., Healdsburg* ☎ *707/433–0177* 🌐 *www.spadolce.com* 🎫 *Treatments $55–$240* ⏲ *Tues.–Sun. 10–7.*

SPORTS AND THE OUTDOORS

Fodor's Choice ★ **Wine Country Bikes.** This shop in downtown Healdsburg is perfectly located for single or multiday treks into the Dry Creek and Russian River valleys. Bikes, including tandems, rent for $39 to $145 a day. One-day tours start at $149. ✉ *61 Front St., at Hudson St., Healdsburg* ☎ *707/473–0610, 866/922–4537* 🌐 *www.winecountrybikes.com.*

SHOPPING

Healdsburg is a pleasant spot to window shop, with dozens of art galleries, boutiques, and high-end design shops on or near the plaza.

Gallery Lulo. A collaboration between a local artist and jewelry maker and a Danish-born curator, this museumlike gallery presents changing exhibits of exquisite jewelry, sculpture, and objets d'art. ✉ *303 Center St., at Plaza St., Healdsburg* ☎ *707/433–7533* 🌐 *www.gallerylulo.com.*

Fodor's Choice ★ **The Shed.** Inside a glass-front, steel-clad variation on a traditional grange hall, this shop-cum-eatery celebrates local agriculture with specialty foods. It also stocks seeds and plants, gardening and farming implements, cookware, and everything a smart pantry should hold. ✉ *25 North St., west of Healdsburg Ave., Healdsburg* ☎ *707/431–7433* 🌐 *healdsburgshed.com.*

7

DRY CREEK AND ALEXANDER VALLEYS

With its diverse terrain and microclimates, the Dry Creek Valley supports an impressive range of varietals. Zinfandel grapes flourish on the benchlands, whereas the gravelly, well-drained soil of the valley floor is better known for Chardonnay and, in the north, Sauvignon Blanc. Pinot Noir, Syrah, and other cool-climate grapes thrive on eastern-facing slopes that receive less afternoon sun than elsewhere in the valley. The Alexander Valley, which lies northeast of Healdsburg, is similarly rustic. Wineries here are known for Zinfandels, Chardonnays, and Cabernet Sauvignons, though Cabernet Franc and other less high-profile wines are also made.

GETTING HERE AND AROUND

To reach the Dry Creek Valley from Healdsburg, drive north on Healdsburg Avenue and turn left on Dry Creek Road. West of U.S. 101, you'll see signs pointing the way to wineries on that road and West Dry Creek Road, which runs roughly parallel about a mile to the west. To get to the Alexander Valley from the plaza, drive north on Healdsburg Avenue and veer right onto Alexander Valley Road. Follow it to Highway 128, where many of this appellation's best wineries lie.

EXPLORING

TOP ATTRACTIONS

Fodor's Choice ★ **Jordan Vineyard and Winery.** A visit to this sprawling property north of Healdsburg revolves around an impressive estate built in the early 1970s to replicate a French château . A seated one-hour Library Tasting of the current Cabernet Sauvignon and Chardonnay releases takes place in the château itself, accompanied by small bites prepared by executive chef Todd Knoll. The tasting concludes with an older vintage Cabernet Sauvignon paired with cheese. The 90-minute Winery Tour & Tasting includes the above, plus a walk through part of the château. ■TIP→ For a truly memorable experience, splurge on the three-hour Estate Tour & Tasting, whose pièce de résistance is a Cabernet tasting at a 360-degree vista point overlooking 1,200 acres of vines, olive trees, and countryside. ⊠ *1474 Alexander Valley Rd., on Greco Rd., Healdsburg* ☎ *800/654–1213, 707/431–5250* ⊕ *www.jordanwinery.com* ⌨ *Library tasting $30, winery tour and tasting $40, estate tour and tasting $120* ☉ *Library tasting mid-Nov.–mid-Apr., Mon.–Sat. 10 and 2, mid-Apr.–mid-Nov., Mon.–Sat. 10 and 2, Sun. 11, 1, and 3; winery tour mid-Nov.–mid-Apr., Mon.–Sat. at 11, mid-Apr.–mid-Nov., Mon.–Sat. at 11, Sun. at 11; estate tour mid-Apr.–mid-Nov. at 9:45 Thurs.–Mon.*

Fodor's Choice ★ **Locals Tasting Room.** Though trending upscale, downtown Geyserville remains little more than a crossroads with a few shops and restaurants. But if you're serious about wine, Carolyn Lewis's tasting room is alone worth a trek. Connoisseurs come to sample the output of a dozen or so small wineries, most without tasting rooms of their own. There's no fee for tasting—a bargain for wines of this quality—and the extremely knowledgeable staff is happy to pour you a flight of several wines so you can compare, say, different Cabernet Sauvignons. ⊠ *21023A Geyserville Ave., at Hwy. 128, Geyserville* ☎ *707/857–4900* ⊕ *www.taste localwines.com* ⌨ *Tasting free* ☉ *Daily 11–6.*

Fodor's Choice **Ridge Vineyards.** Ridge stands tall among California wineries, and not
★ merely because one of its 1971 Cabernet Sauvignons placed first in a
2006 re-creation of the 1976 Judgment of Paris tasting. The winery
built its reputation on Cabernet Sauvignons, Zinfandels, and Chardonnays of unusual depth and complexity, but you'll also find blends of
Rhône varietals. Ridge makes wines using grapes from several California
locales—including the Dry Creek Valley, Sonoma Valley, Napa Valley,
and Paso Robles—but the focus is on single-vineyard estate wines such
as the exquisitely textured Lytton Springs Zinfandel blend from grapes
grown near the tasting room. In good weather you can taste outside,
taking in views of rolling vineyard hills while you sip. ■ TIP➜ The $20
tasting option includes a pour of the top-of-the-line Monte Bello Cabernet
Sauvignon blend from grapes grown in the Santa Cruz Mountains. ⊠ 650
Lytton Springs Rd., off U.S. 101, Healdsburg ☎ 707/433–7721 ⊕ www.
ridgewine.com ᐧ Tastings $5–$20, tours $30–$40 ⊙ June–Oct., Mon.–
Thurs. 11–4, Fri. and weekends 11–5; Nov.–May, daily 11–4.

Fodor's Choice **Truett Hurst Winery.** When the weather's fine, few experiences rate more
★ sublime ("pure magic," enthused one recent guest) than sitting on Truett
Hurst's sandy, tree-shaded Dry Creek shoreline, sipping a Green Valley
Pinot Noir or a Zinfandel Rosé, chatting with friends, and watching
the water flow by. In addition to the Rosé, Truett Hurst makes six Zinfandels, a few of which are always poured in the contemporary, high-ceilinged tasting room or on the outdoor patio. The winemaker blends
Petite Sirah into some of the Zins and makes a standalone Petite Sirah as
well. Picnickers are welcome creekside or on the patio; meats, smoked
fish, cheeses, and spreads are available for sale on-site. ■ TIP➜ Bands,
sometimes local, sometimes from beyond, liven things up in the tasting
room on weekend afternoons. ⊠ 5610 Dry Creek Rd., 2 miles south
of Canyon Rd., Healdsburg ☎ 707/433–9545 ⊕ www.truetthurst.com.

WORTH NOTING

Dry Creek Vineyard. Fumé Blanc is king at Dry Creek, where the refreshing white wine is made in the style of those in Sancerre, France. The
winery also makes well-regarded Zinfandels, a zesty dry Chenin Blanc,
a Pinot Noir, and a handful of Cabernet Sauvignon blends. Many wines
sell for less than $30 a bottle (and some even $20), making this a
popular stop for wine lovers looking to stock their cellars for a reasonable price. You can picnic on the lawn next to a flowering magnolia tree. Conveniently, a general store and deli is close by. ⊠ 3770
Lambert Bridge Rd., off Dry Creek Rd., Healdsburg ☎ 707/433–1000,
800/864–9463 ⊕ www.drycreekvineyard.com ᐧ Tastings $5–$50, tour
$20 ⊙ Daily 10:30–5, tour 11 and 1 by appointment.

FAMILY **Francis Ford Coppola Winery.** The film director's over-the-top fantasyland
is the sort of place the mid-level Mafiosi in his *The Godfather* saga
might declare had real class—the "everyday wines" poured here are
pretty much beside the point. The fun here is all in the excess, and you
may find it hard to resist having your photo snapped standing next to
Don Corleone's desk from *The Godfather* or beside memorabilia from
other Coppola films, including some directed by his daughter, Sofia. A
bandstand reminiscent of one in *The Godfather Part II* is the centerpiece
of a large pool area where you can rent a changing room, complete with

shower, and spend the afternoon lounging poolside, perhaps ordering food from the adjacent café. A more elaborate restaurant, Rustic, overlooks the vineyards. ✉ *300 Via Archimedes, off U.S. 101, Geyserville* ☎ *707/857–1400* 🌐 *www.franciscoppolawinery.com* 🎫 *Tastings free–$20, tours $20–$75, pool pass $30* 🕒 *Tasting room daily 11–6, restaurant daily 11–9; pool hrs vary seasonally.*

FAMILY Fodor's Choice ★ **Preston of Dry Creek.** The long driveway at convivial Preston, flanked by vineyards and punctuated by the occasional olive tree, winds down to farmhouses encircling a shady yard with picnic tables. Year-round a selection of organic produce grown in the winery's gardens is sold at a small shop near the tasting room; house-made bread and olive oil are also available. Owners Lou and Susan Preston are committed to organic growing techniques and use only estate-grown grapes in their wines, which include a perky Sauvignon Blanc (the best option for a picnic here), Barbera, Petite Sirah, Syrah, Viognier, and Zinfandel. ✉ *9282 W. Dry Creek Rd., at Hartsock Rd. No. 1, Healdsburg* ☎ *707/433–3372* 🌐 *www.prestonvineyards.com* 🎫 *Tasting $10* 🕒 *Daily 11–4:30.*

WHERE TO EAT AND STAY

$$ ITALIAN Fodor's Choice ★ 🍴 **Diavola Pizzeria & Salumeria.** A dining area with hardwood floors, a pressed-tin ceiling, and exposed-brick walls provides a fitting setting for the rustic cuisine at this Geyserville charmer. Chef Dino Bugica studied with several artisans in Italy before opening this restaurant that specializes in pizzas pulled from a wood-burning oven and several types of house-cured meats. A few salads and meaty main courses round out the menu. ■ **TIP→ If you're impressed by the antipasto plate, you can pick up some smoked pork belly, pancetta, or spicy Calabrese sausage to take home.** [$] *Average main: $19* ✉ *21021 Geyserville Ave., at Hwy. 128, Geyserville* ☎ *707/814–0111* 🌐 *www.diavolapizzeria.com* ✍ *Reservations not accepted.*

$ HOTEL 🏨 **Geyserville Inn.** Clever travelers give the Healdsburg hubbub and prices the heave-ho but still have easy access to outstanding Dry Creek and Alexander Valley wineries from this modest, well-run inn. **Pros:** pool; second-floor rooms in back have vineyard views; picnic area. **Cons:** occasional noise bleed-through from corporate and other events. [$] *Rooms from: $155* ✉ *21714 Geyserville Ave., Geyserville* ☎ *707/857–4343, 877/857–4343* 🌐 *www.geyservilleinn.com* 🛏 *41 rooms* 🍽 *No meals.*

THE NORTH COAST

From the Sonoma Coast to
Redwood National Park

WELCOME TO THE NORTH COAST

TOP REASONS TO GO

★ **Scenic coastal drives:** There's hardly a road here that *isn't* scenic.

★ **Wild beaches:** This stretch of California is one of nature's masterpieces. Revel in the unbridled, rugged coastline, without a building in sight.

★ **Dinnertime:** When you're done hiking the beach, refuel with delectable food; you'll find everything from burritos to bouillabaisse.

★ **Romance:** Here you can end almost every day with a perfect sunset.

★ **Wildlife:** Watch for migrating whales, sunbathing sea lions and huge Roosevelt elk with majestic antlers.

1 The Sonoma Coast. As you enter Sonoma County from the south on Highway 1, you pass first through gently rolling pastureland. North of Bodega Bay dramatic shoreline scenery takes over. The road snakes up, down, and around sheer cliffs and steep inclines—some without guardrails—where cows seem to cling precariously. Stunning vistas (or cottony fog) and hairpin turns make for an exhilarating drive.

2 The Mendocino Coast. The timber industry gave birth to most of the small towns along this stretch of coastline. Although tourism now drives the economy, the region has retained much of its old-fashioned charm. The beauty of the landscape, of course, has not changed. Inland lies the Anderson Valley, whose wineries mostly grow cool-climate grapes.

3 Redwood Country. There's a different state of mind in Humboldt County. Here, instead of spas, there are old-time hotels. Instead of wineries, there are breweries. The landscape is primarily thick redwood forest; the interior mountains get snow in winter and sizzle in summer while the coast sits covered in fog. Until as late as 1924 there was no road north of Willits; the coastal towns were reachable only by sea. That legacy is apparent in the communities of today: Eureka and Arcata, both former ports, are sizeable, but otherwise towns are tiny and nestled in the woods, and people have an independent spirit that recalls the original homesteaders. Coming from the south, Garberville is a good place to stop for picnic provisions and stretch your legs.

4 Redwood National and State Parks. For a pristine encounter with giant redwoods, make the trek to these coastal parks where even casual visitors have easy access to the trees. *Several inns near the parks occupy spruced-up Victorians.*

GETTING ORIENTED

It's all but impossible to explore the Northern California coast without a car. Indeed, you wouldn't want to—driving here is half the fun. The main road is Highway 1, two lanes that twist and turn (sometimes 180 degrees) up cliffs and down through valleys. Towns appear every so often, but this is mostly a land of green pasture, dense forest, and natural, undeveloped coastline. ■TIP→ Pace yourself: Most drivers stop frequently to appreciate the views, and you can't safely drive faster than 30 or 40 mph on many portions of the highway. Don't plan to drive too far in one day.

8

Updated by Christine Vovakes

The spectacular coastline between Marin County and the Oregon border defies expectations. The landscape is defined by the Pacific Ocean, but instead of boardwalks and bikinis there are ragged cliffs and pounding waves—and the sunbathers are mostly sea lions. Instead of strip malls and freeways, you'll find a single-lane road that follows a fickle shoreline. Although the towns along the way vary from deluxe spa retreat to hippie hideaway, all are reliably sleepy—and that's exactly why many Californians, especially those from the Bay Area, escape here to enjoy nature unspoiled by the agitations of daily life.

This stretch of Highway 1 is made up of numerous little worlds, each different from the last. From Point Reyes toward Bodega Bay, the land spreads out into green, rolling pastures and sandy beaches. The road climbs higher and higher as it heads north through Sonoma County, and in Mendocino County the coastline follows the ins and outs of lush valleys where rivers pour down from the forests and into the ocean. At Humboldt County the highway heads inland to the redwoods, and then returns to the shoreline at the tidal flats surrounding the ports of Eureka and Arcata. Heading north to the Oregon border, the coast is increasingly wild and lined with giant redwood trees.

PLANNING

WHEN TO GO

The North Coast is a year-round destination, though when you go determines what you will see. The migration of the Pacific gray whales is a wintertime phenomenon, which lasts roughly from mid-December to early April. Wildflowers follow the winter rain, as early as January in southern areas through June and July farther north. Summer is the high season for tourists, but spring, fall, and even winter are arguably better times to visit. The pace is slower, towns are quieter, and lodging is cheaper.

The coastal climate is similar to San Francisco's, although winter nights are colder than in the city. In July and August thick fog can drop temperatures to the high 50s, but fear not. You need only drive inland a few miles to find temperatures that are often 20 degrees higher.

GETTING HERE AND AROUND

AIR TRAVEL

The only North Coast airport with commercial air service, Arcata/Eureka Airport (ACV) receives United Express flights. The airport is in McKinleyville, which is 16 miles from Eureka. A taxi to Eureka costs about $50 and takes roughly 25 minutes. Door-to-door airport shuttles cost $20 to Arcata and Trinidad, $24 to Eureka, and $50 to Ferndale. All prices are for the first person, and go up $5 for each additional person.

Airport Contacts Arcata/Eureka Airport ✉ *3561 Boeing Ave., McKinleyville* ☎ *707/839–5401.*

Shuttle Contacts Door to Door Airport Shuttle ☎ *888/338–5497, 707/839–4186* ⊕ *www.doortodoorairporter.com.*

BUS TRAVEL

Greyhound buses travel along U.S. 101 from San Francisco to Garberville, Eureka, and Arcata. Humboldt Transit Authority connects Eureka, Arcata, and Trinidad.

Bus Contacts Greyhound ☎ *800/231–2222* ⊕ *www.greyhound.com.*
Humboldt Transit Authority ☎ *707/443–0826* ⊕ *www.hta.org.*

CAR TRAVEL

Although U.S. 101 has excellent services, long stretches separate towns along Highway 1, and services are even fewer and farther between on the smaller roads. ■**TIP➔ If you're running low on fuel and see a gas station, stop for a refill.** Twisting Highway 1 is the scenic route to Mendocino from San Francisco, but the fastest one is U.S. 101 north to Highway 128 west (from Cloverdale) to Highway 1 north. The quickest route to the far North Coast is a straight shot up U.S. 101, which runs inland until Eureka. Weather sometimes forces closure of parts of Highway 1, but it's rare.

Road Conditions Caltrans ☎ *800/427–7623* ⊕ *www.dot.ca.gov.*

RESTAURANTS

A few restaurants with national reputations, plus several more of regional note, entice palates on the North Coast. Even the smallest cafés take advantage of the abundant fresh seafood and locally grown vegetables and herbs. Attire is usually informal, though at pricier establishments dressy casual is the norm. Most kitchens close at 8 or 8:30 and few places serve past 9:30. Many restaurants close for a winter break in January or early February.

HOTELS

Restored Victorians, rustic lodges, country inns, and vintage motels are among the accommodations available here. Few have air-conditioning (the ocean breezes make it unnecessary), and many have no phones or

TVs in the rooms. Although several towns have only one or two places to spend the night, some of these lodgings are destinations in themselves. Budget accommodations are rare, but in winter you're likely to find reduced rates and nearly empty lodgings. In summer and on the weekends, though, make bed-and-breakfast reservations as far ahead as possible—rooms at the best inns often sell out months in advance. *Hotel reviews have been shortened. For full information, visit Fodors.com.*

WHAT IT COSTS			
$	$$	$$$	$$$$
RESTAURANTS under $16	$16–$22	$23–$30	over $30
HOTELS under $120	$120–$175	$176–$250	over $250

Restaurant prices are the average cost of a main course at dinner or, if dinner is not served, at lunch, excluding sales tax of 7.5–8¼%. Hotel prices are the lowest cost of a standard double room in high season, excluding service charges and 8%–11% tax.

VISITOR INFORMATION

Contacts Humboldt County Convention and Visitors Bureau ⊠ *322 1st St., Eureka* ☎ *707/443–5097, 800/346–3482* ⊕ *redwoods.info.* **Mendocino Coast Chamber of Commerce** ⊠ *217 S. Main St., Fort Bragg* ☎ *707/961–6300* ⊕ *mendocinocoast.com.* **Redwood Coast Chamber: Sonoma to Mendocino** ☎ *707/884–1080, 800/778–5252* ⊕ *www.redwoodcoastchamber.com.* **Sonoma County Tourism** ☎ *707/522–5800, 800/576–6662* ⊕ *www.sonomacounty.com.* **Visit Mendocino County** ⊠ *345 N. Franklin St., Ft. Bragg* ☎ *707/964–9010, 866/466–3636* ⊕ *www.visitmendocino.com.*

THE SONOMA COAST

BODEGA BAY

23 miles west of Santa Rosa.

From the busy harbor here, commercial boats pursue fish and Dungeness crab. There's nothing quaint about this working town without a center—it's just a string of businesses along several miles of Highway 1. But some tourists still come to see where Alfred Hitchcock shot *The Birds* in 1962. The Tides Wharf complex, an important location used for the movie, has been expanded and remodeled several times and is no longer recognizable. But a few miles inland, in Bodega, you can find Potter Schoolhouse, which is now a private residence.

GETTING HERE AND AROUND

To reach Bodega Bay, exit U.S. 101 at Santa Rosa and take Highway 12 west (it's called Bodega Highway west of Sebastopol) 23 miles to the coast. A scenic alternative is to take U.S. 101's East Washington Street/Central Petaluma exit and follow signs west to Bodega Bay; just after you merge onto Highway 1, you'll pass through down-home Valley Ford. Mendocino Transit Authority (*mendocinotransit.org*) Route 95 buses connect Bodega Bay with coastal towns and Santa Rosa.

Surfers check out the waves near Bodega Bay on the Sonoma Coast.

BEACHES

Fodor's Choice
★

Sonoma Coast State Park. The park's gorgeous sandy coves stretch for 17 miles from Bodega Head to 4 miles north of Jenner. **Bodega Head** is an especially popular perch for whale watchers, though if you're lucky you'll catch sight of migrating whales from any of the beaches. **Rock Point, Duncan's Landing,** and **Wright's Beach,** clustered at about the halfway mark, have picnic areas, as do several other spots. Rogue waves have swept people off the rocks at Duncan's Landing, so don't stray past signs warning you away. Relatively calmer **Shell Beach,** about 2 miles north, is known for beachcombing, tide pools, and fishing. About 2½ miles north of Shell Beach, near the mouth of the Russian River at Jenner, a long road leads from the highway to **Goat Rock.** Harbor seals lounge at the beach here; pupping season is from March through August. Bring binoculars and walk north from the parking lot to view the seals. During summer lifeguards are on duty at some beaches, but strong rip currents and heavy surf keep most would-be swimmers on shore. Wright's Beach and Bodega Dunes have developed campsites. **Amenities:** parking; toilets. **Best For:** solitude; sunset; walking. ⊠ *Park Headquarters/Salmon Creek Ranger Station, 3095 Hwy. 1, 2 miles north of Bodega Bay* ☎ *707/875–3483* ⊕ *www.parks.ca.gov* 🖃 *$8 per vehicle* ☉ *Daily 8 am–sunset (some beach hrs may be curtailed because of budget cuts).*

WHERE TO EAT AND STAY

$$

SEAFOOD

✕ **Sandpiper Restaurant.** A local favorite with big windows for bay views, this friendly café on the marina does a good job for a fair price. Peruse the board for the day's fresh catch or order a menu regular such as

8

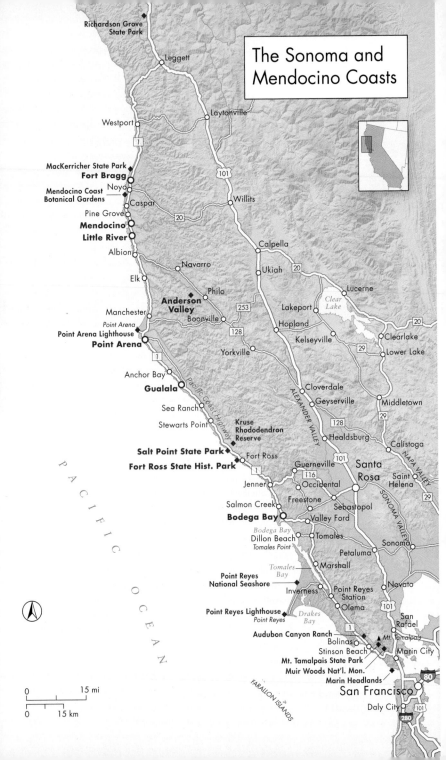

The Sonoma and Mendocino Coasts

Richardson Grove State Park

Leggett

Laytonville

Westport

MacKerricher State Park
Fort Bragg
Noyo
Mendocino Coast
Botanical Gardens
Caspar
Pine Grove
Mendocino
Little River
Albion

Willits

Calpella

Navarro

Ukiah

Elk

Philo
Anderson Valley
Boonville

Manchester
Point Arena
Point Arena Lighthouse
Point Arena

Yorkville

Anchor Bay

Gualala

Sea Ranch

Stewarts Point

Kruse
Rhododendron
Reserve

Salt Point State Park
Fort Ross State Hist. Park
Fort Ross

Cloverdale
Geyserville

Lucerne

Clear Lake

Lakeport

Hopland

Kelseyville

Clearlake
Lower Lake

Middletown

Healdsburg

Calistoga

Guerneville
Occidental
Freestone
Sebastopol

Santa Rosa

Saint Helena

Jenner

Salmon Creek
Bodega Bay
Bodega Bay
Dillon Beach
Tomales Point

Valley Ford
Tomales

Marshall

Tomales Bay

Petaluma

Sonoma

Novato

Point Reyes
National Seashore

Inverness

Point Reyes Lighthouse
Point Reyes

Point Reyes
Station
Olema

Drakes Bay

San Rafael

Audubon Canyon Ranch
Bolinas
Stinson Beach
Mt. Tamalpais State Park
Muir Woods Nat'l. Mon.
Marin Headlands

Mt. Tamalpais

Marin City

San Francisco

FARALLON ISLANDS

Daly City

PACIFIC OCEAN

Pacific Coast Highway

ALEXANDER VALLEY

NAPA VALLEY

SONOMA VALLEY

0   15 mi

0   15 km

101

1

20

101

20

253

128

29

20

29

128

29

101

116

101

1

80

101

280

crab stew, steak, or prawns; clam chowder is the house specialty. This is also a popular breakfast spot. [$] *Average main: $22* ✉ *1400 N. Hwy. 1* ☎ *707/875–2278* 🌐 *www.sandpiperbodegabay.com.*

$$$ HOTEL 🏨 **Bodega Bay Lodge.** Looking out to the ocean across a wetland, the lodge's shingle-and-river-rock buildings contain Bodega Bay's finest accommodations. **Pros:** most rooms have fireplaces and patios; variety of pampering treatments; ocean views. **Cons:** on the pricey side. [$] *Rooms from: $239* ✉ *103 Coast Hwy. 1* ☎ *707/875–3525, 888/875–2250* 🌐 *www.bodegabaylodge.com* 🛏 *78 rooms, 5 suites* 🍴 *No meals.*

SPORTS AND THE OUTDOORS

GOLF

The Links at Bodega Harbour. Robert Trent Jones II designed this Scottish-style, incredibly scenic, and fairly challenging 18-hole oceanfront course. Rates include a golf cart. ✉ *21301 Heron Dr.* ☎ *707/875–3538, 866/905–4657* 🌐 *www.bodegaharbourgolf.com* 🎟 *$60 for weekdays; $90 for weekends* ⛳ *18 holes, 6290 yards, par 70.*

WHALE-WATCHING

Bodega Bay Sportfishing. This outfit charters ocean-fishing boats, rents equipment, and conducts whale-watching trips from midwinter through spring. ✉ *1410 B Bay Flat Rd.* ☎ *707/875–3344* 🌐 *www.bodegabaysportfishing.com* 🎟 *Outings from $70.*

FORT ROSS STATE HISTORIC PARK

22 miles north of Bodega Bay.

With its reconstructed Russian Orthodox chapel, stockade, and officials' quarters, Fort Ross looks much the way it did after the Russians made it their major California coastal outpost in 1812. An excellent museum documents the fort's history.

GETTING HERE AND AROUND

From Santa Rosa, head west on Highway 116 about 33 miles to Jenner, then north 12 miles on Highway 1 to the park entrance. The Mendocino Transit Authority (*mendocinotransit.org*) Route 95 bus provides service between Fort Ross and other coastal towns.

EXPLORING

FAMILY **Fort Ross State Historic Park.** Russian settlers established Fort Ross in 1812 on land they leased from the native Kashia people. The Russians hoped to gain a foothold in the Pacific coast's warmer regions and to produce crops and other supplies for their Alaskan fur-trading operations. In 1841, with the local marine mammal population depleted and farming having proven unproductive, the Russians sold their holdings to John Sutter of gold-rush fame. The land was privately ranched for decades, and became a state park in 1909. One original Russian-era structure remains, as does a cemetery. The rest of the compound has been reconstructed to look much as it did during Russian times. An excellent small museum documents the history of the fort, the Kashia people, and the ranch and state-park eras. ✉ *19005 Hwy. 1, Jenner* ☎ *707/847–3437* 🌐 *www.fortross.org* 🎟 *$8 per vehicle* 🕒 *Hrs vary with season (call or check website), but usually open Fri.–Mon. 10–4:30* ☞ *No dogs allowed past parking lot and picnic area.*

8

SALT POINT STATE PARK

6 miles north of Fort Ross.

Enjoy dramatic views, forested acres, and a rocky, rugged shoreline along Highway 1's 5-mile route through this park. With 20 miles of hiking trails and a variety of picnicking, horseback riding, scuba diving, and fishing opportunities, you'll want to stay a while.

GETTING HERE AND AROUND

Exit U.S. 101 in Santa Rosa and travel west on Highway 116 about 33 miles to Jenner, then north 18 miles on Highway 1 to reach the park. Mendocino Transit Authority (*mendocinotransit.org*) Route 95 buses stop at Salt Point and connect with other North Coast towns.

EXPLORING

Salt Point State Park. For 5 miles, Highway 1 winds through this park, 6,000 acres of forest, meadows, and rocky shoreline. Heading north, the first park entrance (on the right) leads to forest hiking trails and several campgrounds. The next entrance—the park's main road—winds through meadows and along the wave-splashed coastline. This is also the route to the visitor center and **Gerstle Cove,** a favorite spot for scuba divers and sunbathing seals. Next along the highway is **Stump Beach Cove,** with picnic tables, toilets, and a ¼-mile walk to the sandy beach. The park's final entrance is at **Fisk Mill Cove,** where centuries of wind and rain erosion have carved unusual honeycomb patterns in the sandstone called "tafonis." A five-minute walk uphill from the parking lot leads to a dramatic view of Sentinel Rock, an excellent spot for sunsets.

Just up the highway, narrow, unpaved Kruse Ranch Road leads to the **Kruse Rhododendron State Reserve**, where each May thousands of rhododendrons bloom within a quiet forest of redwoods and tan oaks. ✉ *25050 Hwy. 1* ☎ *707/847–3221, 707/865–2391* 🌐 *www.parks.ca.gov* 🎟 *$8 per vehicle* 🕒 *Daily sunrise–sunset; some sections closed in winter, call ahead.*

WHERE TO STAY

$$$$ B&B/INN 🏨 **Sea Ranch Lodge.** Wide-open ocean-view vistas and minimalist design keep the focus on nature at this tranquil lodge 29 miles north of Jenner. **Pros:** all rooms are oceanfront; on-site spa; peaceful. **Cons:** remote. [$] *Rooms from: $279* ✉ *60 Sea Walk Dr., Sea Ranch* ☎ *707/785–2371, 800/732–7262* 🌐 *www.searanchlodge.com* 🛏 *19 rooms* 🍴 *Breakfast.*

THE MENDOCINO COAST

GUALALA

16 miles north of Salt Point State Park.

This former lumber port on the Gualala River has become a headquarters for exploring the coast. The busiest town on Highway 1 between Bodega Bay and Mendocino, it has all the basic services plus some galleries and gift shops.

GETTING HERE AND AROUND

From San Francisco, take U.S. 101 to the East Washington Street/Central Petaluma exit and follow signs west through Valley Ford (you're on Highway 1 by this point) to Bodega Bay. From there, continue north on Highway 1. From Ukiah, exit U.S. 101 at Highway 253, driving southwest to Boonville/Highway 128. From Boonville, turn west on Mountain View Road, which winds 24 miles to Highway 1; from there, drive south 18½ miles. Mendocino Transit Authority (*mendocinotransit.org*) Routes 75 and 95 buses connect Gualala with coastal and inland towns.

EXPLORING

Gualala Point Regional Park. This 195-acre park with picnic areas and a long, sandy beach is an excellent whale-watching spot from December through April. Opposite the beach, along the Gualala River estuary, redwoods shade two-dozen campsites. Dogs must be on a leash at all times throughout the park. ⚠ **Watch out for unpredictable sleeper waves, which are common along the North Coast.** ✉ *42401 Hwy. 1, 1 mile south of Gualala* ☎ *707/785–2377* 🌐 *www.sonoma-county.org/parks/pk_glala.htm* 🎟 *$7 per vehicle (day use)* 🕒 *Daily 8 am–sunset.*

WHERE TO EAT AND STAY

$$$$ AMERICAN

🍴 **St. Orres.** Resembling a traditional Russian dacha with two onion-dome towers, this intriguing lodge stands on 42 acres of redwood forest and meadow. In one of the towers is a spectacular atrium dining room. Here locally farmed and foraged ingredients appear in dishes such as garlic flan with black chanterelles and rack of venison medallions with wild huckleberries. The prix-fixe menu (from $45 to $50) includes soup and salad but no appetizer or dessert (available à la carte). Brunch and a bar menu are offered on weekends. [$] *Average main: $48* ✉ *36601 S. Hwy. 1, 3 miles north of Gualala* ☎ *707/884–3303 lodging, 707/884–3335 restaurant* 🌐 *www.saintorres.com* 🕒 *No lunch weekdays. Occasionally closed midweek in winter.*

$$$ HOTEL Fodor's Choice ★

🏨 **Mar Vista Cottages.** Escape to nature and retro-charm at these refurbished, gadget-free 1930s cottages. **Pros:** commune-with-nature solitude; peaceful retreat. **Cons:** no other businesses within walking distance. [$] *Rooms from: $185* ✉ *35101 S. Hwy 1, 5 miles north of Gualala* ☎ *707/884–3522, 877/855–3522* 🌐 *www.marvistamendocino.com* 🛏 *8 1-bedroom cottages, 4 2-bedroom cottages* 🍽 *No meals.*

$$ HOTEL

🏨 **Seacliff on the Bluff.** Wedged in back of a small shopping center, this motel is not much to look at, but you'll spend your time here staring at the Pacific panorama because all rooms have ocean views. **Pros:** budget choice; great views. **Cons:** limited dining options nearby. [$] *Rooms from: $150* ✉ *39140 S. Hwy. 1* ☎ *707/884–1213, 800/400–5053* 🌐 *www.seacliffmotel.com* 🛏 *16 rooms* 🍽 *No meals.*

POINT ARENA

15 miles north of Gualala.

Occupied by an eclectic mix of long-time locals and long-haired surfers, this former timber town on Highway 1 is part New Age, part rowdy, and always laid-back. The one road going west out of downtown will lead you to the harbor, where fishing boats unload sea urchins and salmon and there's almost always someone riding the waves.

GETTING HERE AND AROUND

To reach Point Arena from Santa Rosa, drive north on U.S. 101, exit at Cloverdale, and follow Highway 128 northwest 28 miles to Boonville. From Boonville take winding Mountain View Road west 24 miles to Highway 1. Point Arena is 4 miles south. From points north, exit U.S. 101 at Ukiah, take Highway 253 southwest to Boonville and follow Mountain View Road west to Highway 1 south. Mendocino Transit Authority (*mendocinotransit.org*) Routes 75 and 95 buses stop in Point Arena.

EXPLORING

Point Arena Lighthouse. For an outstanding view of the ocean and, in winter, migrating whales, take the marked road off Highway 1 north of town to the 115-foot lighthouse. It's possible to stay out here, in one of four rental units ($$), all of which have full kitchens. On weekends there's a two-night minimum. ⊠ *45500 Lighthouse Rd., off Hwy. 1* ☎ *707/882–2809, 877/725–4448* ⊕ *www.pointarenalighthouse.com* 🎫 *Tour $7.50* 🕐 *Late May–early Sept., daily 10–4:30; early Sept.–late May, daily 10–3:30.*

BEACHES

Manchester State Park. Before slipping into the sea, the northernmost segment of the San Andreas Fault cuts through this park beloved by locals for its 5 miles of sandy, usually empty shoreline and trails that wind through dunes and wetlands. Hiking, bird-watching, and beach strolling are the popular activities here. There's steelhead fishing at Brush and Alder creeks; beautiful coastal wildflowers bloom in early spring. Tundra swans overwinter in this area, and migrating whales are often spotted close to shore. Swimming and water sports are too dangerous because of the strong undertow. Dogs are not allowed on the beach. **Amenities:** parking (free). **Best for:** solitude; sunset; walking. ⊠ *Park entrance, 44500 Kinney La., off Hwy. 1, ½ mile north of Manchester, Manchester* ☎ *707/937–5804* ⊕ *www.parks.ca.gov* 🕐 *Call park for hrs; it's sometimes closed because of budget cuts.*

WHERE TO EAT

$ ✕ **Arena Market and Café.** The simple café at this all-organic grocery store
CAFÉ serves up hot soups, fine sandwiches, and has an ample salad bar. The market, which specializes in food from local farms, sells cheese, bread, and other picnic items. Ⓢ *Average main: $8* ⊠ *185 Main St.* ☎ *707/882–3663* ⊕ *www.arenaorganics.org* 🕐 *Mon.–Sat. 7–7, Sun. 8–6.*

$ ✕ **Franny's Cup and Saucer.** Aided by her mother Barbara, a former pastry
CAFÉ chef at Chez Panisse, Franny turns out baked goods that are sophisticated and inventive. Morning favorites include scones and sweet pastries as well as savory twists. Specialty cakes are dazzling concoctions such as champagne cake layered with raspberries and lemon curd, or rich chocolate almond tortes spread with marzipan and berry preserves and iced with dark chocolate ganache. More familiar options at this delightful spot include fruit tarts and strawberry-apricot crisps, plus a mouthwatering assortment of cookies, candy, jams, and jellies. Ⓢ *Average main: $5* ⊠ *213 Main St.* ☎ *707/882–2500* ⊕ *www.frannyscupandsaucer.com* ⊟ *No credit cards* 🕐 *Closed Sun.–Tues. No dinner.*

ANDERSON VALLEY

29 miles north of Point Arena.

At the town of Albion, Highway 128 leads southeast into the Anderson Valley, where warm summer weather lures those weary of the persistent coastal fog. Most of the first 13 miles wind through redwood forest along the Navarro River, then the road opens up to reveal farms and vineyards. While the community here is anchored in ranching, in the past few decades a progressive, gourmet-minded counterculture has taken root, and that is what defines most visitors' experiences. In the towns of Philo and Boonville, you'll find eclectic bed-and-breakfasts and small eateries.

Anderson Valley is best known to outsiders for its wineries. Tasting rooms here are more low-key than their counterparts in Napa; most are in farmhouses, and you're as likely to hear reggae as classical music as you sip. That said, Anderson Valley wineries produce world-class wines, particularly Pinot Noirs and Gewürztraminers, whose grapes thrive in the moderate coastal climate. Many wineries straddle Highway 128, mostly in Navarro and Philo with a few east of Boonville.

GETTING HERE AND AROUND

From the coast, pick up Highway 128 at Albion. From inland points south, take Highway 128 northwest from U.S. 101 at Cloverdale. From inland points north, exit U.S. 101 in Ukiah and take Highway 253 southwest 17 miles to Boonville. Mendocino Transit Authority (*mendocinotransit.org*) Route 75 buses serve the Anderson Valley between the coast and Ukiah.

EXPLORING

TOP ATTRACTIONS

Goldeneye Winery. The Napa Valley's well-respected Duckhorn Wine Company makes stellar Pinot Noirs here from local grapes, along with a Gewürztraminer, a Pinot Gris, a Chardonnay, and a blush Vin Gris of Pinot Noir. Leisurely tastings take place in either a restored farmhouse or on a patio with vineyard and redwood views. ✉ *9200 Hwy. 128, Philo* ☎ *800/208–0438, 707/895–3202* ⊕ *www.goldeneyewinery.com* 🍷 *Tastings $15–$35* ⊗ *Mar.–Dec., daily 10:30–4:30; Jan. and Feb., Thurs.–Mon. 10:30–4:30.*

Handley Cellars. International folk art collected by winemaker Milla Handley adorns the tasting room at this Anderson Valley pioneer whose lightly oaked Chardonnays and Pinot Noirs earn high praise from wine critics. The winery, which has a patio picnic area, also makes Gewürztraminer, Pinot Gris, Riesling, and very good sparkling wines. ✉ *3151 Hwy. 128, Philo* ☎ *707/895–3876, 800/733–3151* ⊕ *www.handleycellars.com* 🍷 *Tasting free* ⊗ *May–Oct., daily 10–6; Nov.–Apr., daily 10–5.*

Navarro River Redwoods State Park. Described by locals as the "11-mile-long redwood tunnel to the sea," this park that straddles Highway 128 is great for walks amid second-growth redwoods and for summer swimming in the gentle Navarro River. In late winter and spring, when the river is higher, you also can fish, canoe, and kayak. The two campgrounds (one on the river "beach") are quiet and clean. ✉ *Hwy. 128, 2 miles east of Hwy. 1, Navarro* ☎ *707/937–5804* 🌐 *www.parks.ca.gov.*

Navarro Vineyards. A visit to this family-run winery is a classic Anderson Valley experience. Make time if you can for a vineyard tour—the guides draw from years of hands-on experience to explain every aspect of production, from sustainable farming techniques to the choices made in aging and blending. Best known for Alsatian varietals such as Gewürztraminer and Riesling, Navarro also makes Chardonnay, Pinot Noir, and other wines. The tasting room sells cheese and charcuterie for picnickers. ✉ *5601 Hwy. 128, Philo* ☎ *707/895–3686, 800/537–9463* 🌐 *www.navarrowine.com* 🎟 *Tasting free* 🕒 *Apr.–Oct., daily 9–6; Nov.–Mar., daily 9–5; tour daily at 10:30 and 3 by appointment.*

Roederer Estate. The Anderson Valley is particularly hospitable to Pinot Noir and Chardonnay grapes, the two varietals used to create Roederer's well-regarded sparkling wines. The view of vineyards and rolling hills from the patio is splendid. ✉ *4501 Hwy. 128, Philo* ☎ *707/895–2288* 🌐 *www.roedererestate.com* 🎟 *Tasting $6* 🕒 *Daily 11–5.*

WORTH NOTING

Greenwood Ridge Vineyards. White Riesling is the specialty of this winery that also makes Pinot Noir, Syrah, and other wines. You can picnic here at tables on an island in the middle of a pond. ✉ *5501 Hwy. 128, Philo* ☎ *707/895–2002* 🌐 *www.greenwoodridge.com* 🎟 *Tasting $5* 🕒 *Daily 10–5.*

Husch Vineyards. A former pony barn houses the cozy tasting room of the Anderson Valley's oldest winery. Wines of note include Gewürztraminer, Chardonnay, Pinot Noir, and a Zinfandel that's made from old-vine grapes grown in the warmer Ukiah Valley. **■ TIP→ You can picnic on the deck here or at tables under grape arbors.** ✉ *4400 Hwy. 128, Philo* ☎ *800/554–8724* 🌐 *www.huschvineyards.com* 🎟 *Tasting free* 🕒 *May–Sept., daily 10–6; Oct.–Apr., daily 10–5.*

WHERE TO EAT AND STAY

$ CAFÉ

🍴 **The Boonville General Store.** The store's café menu includes innovative comfort-food specials whose ingredients often come from area farms. Sandwiches are served on freshly baked bread, and the beet salad comes with roasted pecans and local blue cheese. Breakfast options include granola and pastries, made in-house. [$] *Average main: $11* ✉ *14077A Hwy. 128, Boonville* ☎ *707/895–9477* 🕒 *No dinner.*

$$$$ AMERICAN Fodor's Choice ★

🍴 **Table 128.** The restaurant at the Boonville Hotel takes small-town dining into the 21st century. Proprietor Johnny Schmitt and his kitchen staff prepare one prix-fixe meal per night ($48 for three courses, $58 for four) and serve it family-style, with platters of food brought to the table to be shared. Expect an expertly grilled or roasted entrée (such as prosciutto-wrapped halibut, flank steak, or slow-roasted lamb), a sophisticated side dish (radicchio with polenta, perhaps, or curried cauliflower soup), and don't forget dessert (linzer torte with Chantilly cream; local blackberry tart). This is essentially home cooking done at a high level, and despite the limited menu—posted a few days in advance on the restaurant's website—most diners will leave satisfied. [$] *Average*

You'll find excellent vintages and great places to taste wine in the Anderson Valley—but it's much more laid-back than Napa.

main: $53 ✉ *14050 Hwy. 128, Boonville* ☎ *707/895–2210* 🌐 *www.boonvillehotel.com* 🕓 *No lunch. Closed Mon.–Thurs. Nov.–Apr., closed Tues. and Wed. May–Oct.*

$$$ HOTEL **Boonville Hotel.** From the street this looks like a standard small-town hotel, but once you cross the threshold you begin to sense the laid-back sophistication that makes the entire Anderson Valley so appealing. **Pros:** stylish but homey; beautiful gardens and grounds. **Cons:** friendly but straightforward service—don't expect to be pampered; two-night stay required on most weekends. [$] *Rooms from: $195* ✉ *14050 Hwy. 128, Boonville* ☎ *707/895–2210* 🌐 *www.boonvillehotel.com* 🛏 *8 rooms, 7 cottages* 🍴 *Breakfast.*

$$$ HOTEL Fodor's Choice ★ **The Philo Apple Farm.** Set in an orchard of organic heirloom apples, the three cottages and one guest room here are tasteful, inviting, and inspired by the surrounding landscape. **Pros:** country charm; back-to-nature, off-the-grid experience. **Cons:** occasionally hot in summer. [$] *Rooms from: $200* ✉ *18501 Greenwood Rd., Philo* ☎ *707/895–2333* 🌐 *www.philoapplefarm.com* 🛏 *1 room, 3 cottages* 🍴 *Breakfast.*

LITTLE RIVER

5 miles north of Anderson Valley.

The town of Little River is not much more than a post office and a convenience store; Albion, its neighbor to the south, is even smaller. Along this winding portion of Highway 1, though, you'll find numerous inns and restaurants, all of them quiet and situated to take advantage of the breathtaking ocean views.

GETTING HERE AND AROUND

From inland points south, exit U.S. 101 at Cloverdale and follow Highway 128 northwest about 56 miles to Highway 1, then head north 7 miles. From points north, exit U.S. 101 in Ukiah at Highway 253 and follow it west 17 miles to Boonville, where you'll pick up Highway 128 and drive northwest to Highway 1. Mendocino Transit Authority (*mendocinotransit.org*) Route 60 buses serve the area.

EXPLORING

Van Damme State Park. Best known for its beach, this park is a prime abalone diving spot. Upland trails lead through lush riparian habitat and the bizarre **Pygmy Forest,** where acidic soil and poor drainage have produced mature cypress and pine trees that are no taller than a person. The visitor center has displays on ocean life and the historical significance of the redwood lumber industry along the coast. ⊠ *Little River Park Rd., off Hwy. 1* ☎ *707/937–5804* ⊕ *www.parks.ca.gov.*

WHERE TO EAT AND STAY

$$$
FRENCH
Fodor'sChoice
★

✕ **Ledford House.** The only thing separating this bluff-top wood-and-glass restaurant from the Pacific Ocean is a great view. Entrées evoke the flavors of southern France and include hearty bistro dishes—stews, cassoulets, and pastas—and large portions of grilled meats and freshly caught fish (though the restaurant also is vegetarian friendly). The long bar, with its unobstructed water view, is a scenic spot for a sunset aperitif. Ⓢ *Average main: $25* ⊠ *3000 N. Hwy. 1, Albion* ☎ *707/937–0282* ⊕ *www.ledfordhouse.com* ☹ *Closed Mon. and Tues. and mid-Feb.–mid-Mar. No lunch.*

$$$
B&B/INN

🏠 **Albion River Inn.** Contemporary New England–style cottages at this inn overlook the dramatic bridge and seascape where the Albion River empties into the Pacific. **Pros:** great views; great bathtubs. **Cons:** newer buildings aren't as quaint as they could be. Ⓢ *Rooms from: $195* ⊠ *3790 N. Hwy. 1, Albion* ☎ *707/937–1919, 800/479–7944* ⊕ *albionriverinn.com* 🛏 *18 rooms, 4 cottages* ⦿ *Breakfast.*

MENDOCINO

3 miles north of Little River.

Many of Mendocino's original settlers came from the Northeast and built houses in the New England style. Thanks to the logging boom, the town flourished for most of the second half of the 19th century. As the timber industry declined, many residents left, but the town's setting was too beautiful to be ignored. Artists and craftspeople began flocking here in the 1950s, and Elia Kazan chose Mendocino as the backdrop for his 1955 film adaptation of John Steinbeck's *East of Eden*, starring James Dean. As the arts community thrived, restaurants, cafés, and inns sprang up. Today, the small downtown area consists almost entirely of places to eat and shop.

GETTING HERE AND AROUND

From U.S. 101, exit at Cloverdale and follow Highway 128 northwest about 56 miles and Highway 1 north 10 miles. You can also exit at Willits and drive west on Highway 20 about 33 miles to Highway 1, then south 8 miles. Mendocino Transit Authority (*mendocinotransit.org*) Route 60 buses serve the area.

EXPLORING

Ford House. The restored Ford House, built in 1854, serves as the visitor center for Mendocino Headlands State Park and the town. The house has a scale model of Mendocino as it looked in 1890, when it had 34 water towers and a 12-seat public outhouse. From the museum, you can head out on a 3-mile trail across the spectacular seaside cliffs that border the town. ✉ *45035 Main St., west of Lansing St.* ☎ *707/937–5397* 🌐 *mendoparks.org/mendocino-headlands-state-park-ford-house-museum* 🎟 *$2* 🕒 *Daily 11–4.*

Kelley House Museum. An 1861 structure holds this museum, whose artifacts include Victorian-era furniture and historical photographs of Mendocino coast's logging days. ✉ *45007 Albion St.* ☎ *707/937–5791* 🌐 *www.kelleyhousemuseum.org* 🎟 *$2* 🕒 *Fri.–Mon. 11–3.*

Mendocino Art Center. The center has an extensive program of workshops, mounts exhibits in its galleries, and is the home of the Mendocino Theatre Company. Artists from several states paint and sell their work during the center's plein air festival the second week of September. ✉ *45200 Little Lake St.* ☎ *707/937–5818, 800/653–3328* 🌐 *www.mendocinoart center.org* 🕒 *Daily 10–5.*

WHERE TO EAT AND STAY

$$$ AMERICAN 🍴 **Cafe Beaujolais.** The yellow Victorian cottage that houses this popular restaurant is surrounded by a garden of heirloom and exotic plantings. A commitment to the freshest possible organic and local ingredients guides the chef here. The menu is eclectic and ever evolving, but often includes free-range fowl, line-caught fish, and beef specialties. The bakery turns out delicious breads from a wood-fired oven. [$] *Average main: $29* ✉ *961 Ukiah St.* ☎ *707/937–5614* 🌐 *www.cafebeaujolais.com* 🕒 *No lunch Mon. and Tues.*

$$$$ B&B/INN Fodor's Choice ★ 🏨 **Brewery Gulch Inn.** The feel is modern yet tasteful at this smallish inn. **Pros:** luxury in tune with nature; peaceful ocean views; complimentary wine hour and buffet. **Cons:** must drive to town. [$] *Rooms from: $325* ✉ *9401 N. Hwy. 1, 1 mile south of Mendocino* ☎ *707/937–4752, 800/578–4454* 🌐 *www.brewerygulchinn.com* 🛏 *10 rooms, 1 suite* 🍽 *Breakfast.*

$$ B&B/INN Fodor's Choice ★ 🏨 **Glendeven Inn Mendocino.** If Mendocino is the New England village of the West Coast, then Glendeven is the local country manor with sea views. **Pros:** great ocean views; elegant; romantic. **Cons:** not within walking distance of town; on the main drag. [$] *Rooms from: $170* ✉ *8205 N. Hwy. 1* ☎ *707/937–0083, 800/822–4536* 🌐 *glendeven.com* 🛏 *6 rooms, 4 suites* 🍽 *Breakfast.*

$$ B&B/INN 🏨 **MacCallum House.** Set on two flower-filled acres in the middle of town, this inn is a perfect mix of Victorian charm and modern luxury. **Pros:** excellent breakfast; great central location. **Cons:** new luxury suites on a separate property are more modern. [$] *Rooms from: $159* ✉ *45020 Albion St.* ☎ *707/937–0289, 800/609–0492* 🌐 *www.maccallumhouse.com* 🛏 *12 rooms, 9 suites, 7 cottages* 🍽 *Breakfast.*

8

PERFORMING ARTS

THEATER

Mendocino Theatre Company. Dedicated to producing plays of substance and excitement, this well-established company mounts works by Pulitzer Prize winners and local and other contemporary playwrights. ✉ *Mendocino Art Center, 45200 Little Lake St.* ☎ 707/937–4477 ⊕ *mendocinotheatre.org.*

SPORTS AND THE OUTDOORS

Catch-A-Canoe and Bicycles Too. Rent kayaks and regular and outrigger canoes here year-round, as well as mountain and suspension bicycles. The outfit's tours, some by moonlight, explore Big River and its estuary. ✉ *Stanford Inn by the Sea, Comptche-Ukiah Rd., east of Hwy. 1* ☎ 707/937–0273 ⊕ *www.catchacanoe.com* 💰 *From $65.*

FORT BRAGG

10 miles north of Mendocino.

Fort Bragg is a working-class town that many feel is the most authentic place on the coast; it's certainly less expensive than its neighbors to the south. The declining timber industry has been steadily replaced by tourism, but the city maintains a local feel since most people who work at the area hotels and restaurants also live here, as do many artists. A stroll down Franklin Street, one block east of Highway 1, takes you past numerous bookstores, antiques shops, and boutiques.

GETTING HERE AND AROUND

From U.S. 101 at Willits follow Highway 20 west about 33 miles to Highway 1 and drive north 2 miles. Mendocino Transit Authority (*mendocinotransit.org*) Route 60 buses serve the town and region.

EXPLORING

Fodor's Choice
★

Mendocino Coast Botanical Gardens. Something beautiful is always abloom in these marvelous gardens. Along 3½ miles of trails, including pathways with ocean views and observation points for whale-watching, lies a splendid profusion of flowers. The rhododendrons are at their peak from April through June; the dahlias begin their spectacular show in August and last until October. In winter the heather and camellias add more than a splash of color. The main trails are wheelchair accessible. ✉ *18220 N. Hwy. 1, 2 miles south of Fort Bragg* ☎ 707/964–4352 ⊕ *www.gardenbythesea.org* 💰 *$14* ⏰ *Mar.–Oct., daily 9–5; Nov.–Feb., daily 9–4.*

Museum in the Triangle Tattoo Parlor. At the top of a steep staircase, this two-room museum pays homage to Fort Bragg's rough-and-tumble past with memorabilia that includes early 20th-century Burmese tattooing instruments, pictures of astonishing tattoos from around the world, and a small shrine to sword-swallowing sideshow king Captain Don Leslie. ✉ *356-B N. Main St.* ☎ 707/964–8814 ⊕ *www.triangletattoo. com* 💰 *Free* ⏰ *Daily noon–6.*

FAMILY **The Skunk Train.** In the 1920s, a fume-spewing gas-powered train car shuttled passengers along a rail line dating from the logging days of the 1880s. Nicknamed the Skunk Train, it traversed redwood forests

The North Coast is famous for its locally caught Dungeness crab; be sure to try some during your visit.

inaccessible to automobiles. A reproduction train now travels the same route, making a 3½–4 hour round-trip trek between Fort Bragg and the town of Northspur, 21 miles inland. The schedule varies depending on the season, and in summer includes evening barbecue excursions and wine parties for an additional fee. ✉ *Foot of Laurel St., west of Main St.* ☎ *707/964–6371, 866/457–5865* ⊕ *www.skunktrain.com* ✉ *$59–$79.*

BEACHES

Glass Beach. The ocean isn't visible from most of Fort Bragg, but a gravel path on Elm Street three blocks west of Main Street leads to wild coastline where you can walk for miles along the bluffs. The sandy coves nearest the road are called Glass Beach because here lies more sea glass than you've likely ever seen in one place (this area formerly served as the city dump, and the surf pulverized the trash into beautiful treasures). You can gaze at the dazzling colors, but don't take any glass with you; it's now against the law. No swimming at this beach either, for safety's sake. **Amenities:** parking (free); toilets. **Best For:** sunset; walking. ✉ *Elm St. and Old Haul Rd.* ⊕ *www.parks.ca.gov.*

MacKerricher State Park. This park begins at Glass Beach and stretches north for 9 miles, beginning with rocky headlands that taper into dunes and sandy beaches. The headland is a good place for whale-watching from December to mid-April. Fishing at Lake Cleone (a freshwater lake stocked with trout), canoeing, hiking, tidepooling, jogging, bicycling, beachcombing, camping, and harbor seal watching at Laguna Point are among the popular activities, many of which are accessible to the mobility-impaired. Rangers, who lead nature hikes in summer, discourage swimming in the treacherous surf and remind those on shore to be vigilant for rogue waves and to never turn their backs on the sea. Dogs must be leashed. **Amenities:** parking (fee); toilets. **Best for:** solitude; sunset; walking. ✉ *24100 MacKerricher Park Rd., off Hwy. 1, 3 miles north of Fort Bragg* ☎ *707/937–5804* 🌐 *www.parks.ca.gov* 🎟 *$8 per vehicle.*

WHERE TO EAT AND STAY

$$ AMERICAN FAMILY 🍴 **Mendo Bistro.** Everything on this menu is made from scratch, including the bread, pastas, and charcuterie. Though the chef doesn't tout it, his ingredients are nearly all organic, many of them local. In season, the roasted whole crab with three dipping sauces is sensational. A wide selection of pastas includes something for everyone—or, if not, there's the DIY menu: select your protein (beef, chicken, tofu), method of cooking, and sauce. This is a good place for upscale family dining. [$] *Average main: $22* ✉ *301 N. Main St.* ☎ *707/964–4974* 🌐 *www.mendobistro.com* 🕒 *No lunch.*

$ ITALIAN 🍴 **Piaci Pub and Pizzeria.** The seats are stools and your elbows might bang a neighbor's, but nobody seems to mind at this cozy spot that's hands down the area's most popular casual restaurant. The food is simple, mostly pizza and calzones, but everything is carefully prepared and comes out tasty. The well-chosen beers served here receive the same respect the wines do: the chalkboard list notes the origin, brewmaster, and alcohol content. Dogs and their owners are welcome at the tables outside. **TIP→ Piaci is a cash-only establishment.** [$] *Average main: $14* ✉ *120 W. Redwood Ave.* ☎ *707/961–1133* 🌐 *www.piacipizza.com* 💳 *No credit cards* 🕒 *No lunch Sun.*

$$ HOTEL 🏨 **Surf and Sand Lodge.** As its name implies, this hotel sits practically on the beach; pathways lead from the property down to the rock-strewn shore. **Pros:** beach location; gorgeous sunsets. **Cons:** motel style; no restaurants close by. [$] *Rooms from: $129* ✉ *1131 N. Main St.* ☎ *707/964–9383, 800/964–0184* 🌐 *www.surfsandlodge.com* 🛏 *30 rooms* 🍽 *No meals.*

$$$ B&B/INN 🏨 **Weller House Inn.** It's hard to believe that this house was abandoned and slated for demolition when it was purchased in 1994 and then carefully restored into the loveliest Victorian in Fort Bragg. **Pros:** handcrafted details; radiant heat in the wood floors; friendly innkeepers. **Cons:** some may find it too old-fashioned. [$] *Rooms from: $210* ✉ *524 Stewart St.* ☎ *707/964–4415* 🌐 *www.wellerhouse.com* 🛏 *9 rooms* 🍽 *Breakfast.*

SPORTS AND THE OUTDOORS

HORSEBACK RIDING

Ricochet Ridge Ranch. Come here for private and group trail rides through the redwood forest and on the beach. ✉ *24201 N. Hwy. 1* ☎ *707/964–7669, 888/873–5777* 🌐 *www.horse-vacation.com* 🎟 *From $50.*

WHALE-WATCHING

All Aboard Adventures. Captain Tim of All Aboard operates fishing excursions year-round and whale-watching trips from late December through April. ✉ *Noyo Harbor, 32410 N. Harbor Dr.* ☎ *707/964–1881* 🌐 *www.allaboardadventures.com* 🎟 *From $35.*

REDWOOD COUNTRY

HUMBOLDT REDWOODS STATE PARK

25 miles north of Garberville, 43 miles south of Eureka.

Conservationists banded together a century ago as the Save the Redwoods League and scored a key victory when a memorial grove was dedicated in 1921. That grove is now part of Humboldt Redwoods State Park, which these days has grown to nearly 53,000 acres, about a third of which are filled with untouched old-growth coast redwoods.

GETTING HERE AND AROUND

Access the park right off U.S. 101. *(See Bus Travel, at the beginning of this chapter, for Humboldt County public transportation information.)*

EXPLORING

FAMILY
Fodor'sChoice
★

Avenue of the Giants. Some of the tallest trees on Earth tower over this magnificent 32-mile stretch of two-lane blacktop, also known as Highway 254, that follows the south fork of the Eel River through Humboldt Redwoods State Park. The highway runs more or less parallel to U.S. 101 from Phillipsville in the south to the town of Pepperwood in the north. A brochure available at either end of the highway or the **visitor center**, 2 miles south of Weott, contains a self-guided tour, with short and long hikes through various redwood groves. A trail at **Founders Grove** passes by several impressive trees, among them the fallen 362-foot-long Dyerville Giant, whose root base points skyward 35 feet. The tree can be reached via a short trail that begins 4 miles north of the visitor center. About 6 miles north of the center lies **Rockefeller Forest.** The largest remaining old-growth coast redwood forest, it contains 40 of the 100 tallest trees in the world. ⊠ *Humboldt Redwoods State Park Visitor Center, Hwy. 254, Weott* ☎ *707/946–2263* ⊕ *www.parks.ca.gov* 🎟 *Free; $8 day-use fee for Williams Grove* ☉ *Visitor center Apr.–Sept., daily 9–5; Oct.–Mar., daily 10–4.*

FERNDALE

35 miles northwest of Weott; 57 miles northwest of Garberville.

Though gift shops and ice-cream stores comprise a fair share of the businesses here, Ferndale remains a fully functioning small town. There's a butcher, a small grocery, and a local saloon (the westernmost in the contiguous United States), and descendants of the Portuguese and Scandinavian dairy farmers who settled this town continue to raise dairy cows in the surrounding pastures. Ferndale is best known for its colorful Victorian architecture; many shops carry a self-guided tour map that highlights the town's most interesting historic buildings.

GETTING HERE AND AROUND

Ferndale is about 19 miles south of Eureka. Exit U.S. 101 at Highway 211 and follow it southwest 5 miles. There is no public transit service to Ferndale.

8

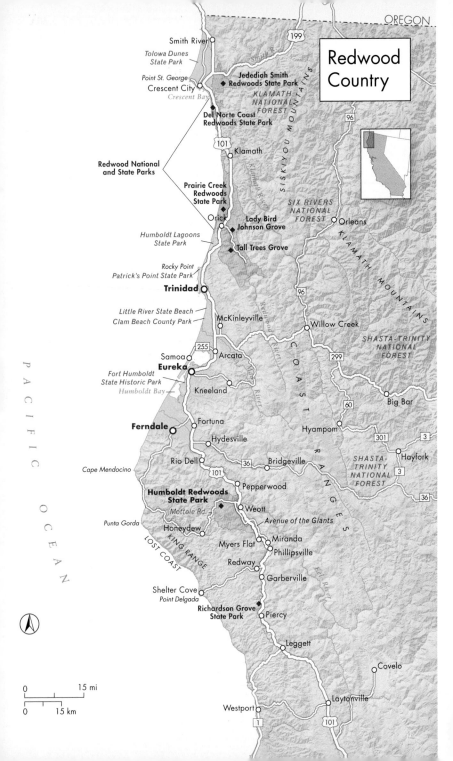

TOURS

Eel River Delta Tours. Bruce Slocum's engaging two-hour boat trips examine the wildlife and history of the Eel River's estuary and salt marsh. ✉ *285 Morgan Slough Rd.* ☎ *707/786–4902 leave message for call back* 💬 *From $25.*

EXPLORING

Ferndale Historic Cemetery. The worn, lovely gravestones at this cemetery on Ferndale's east side provide insight into the hard, often short lives of the European immigrants who cultivated this area in the mid-18th century. From the top of the hill here you can view the town, the surrounding farms, and the ocean. ✉ *Bluff St. and Craig St.*

Ferndale Museum. The main building of this museum exhibits Victoriana and historical photographs and has a display of an old-style barbershop and another of Wiyot Indian baskets. In the annex are a horse-drawn buggy, a re-created blacksmith's shop, and antique farming, fishing, and dairy equipment. Don't miss the historic Bosch-Omori seismograph, installed in 1933 in Ferndale; it's still checked daily for recordings of earthquake activity. ✉ *515 Shaw Ave.* ☎ *707/786–4466* ⊕ *www. ferndale-museum.org* 💬 *$1* ☉ *June–Sept., Tues.–Sat. 11–4, Sun. 1–4; Oct.–Dec. and Feb.–May, Wed.–Sat. 11–4, Sun. 1–4; closed Jan.*

WHERE TO STAY

$$
B&B/INN
🏨 **Gingerbread Mansion.** A dazzler that rivals San Francisco's "painted ladies," this Victorian mansion has detailed exterior spindle work, turrets, and gables. **Pros:** elegant; relaxing; friendly. **Cons:** some may find the place gaudy. 💲 *Rooms from: $165* ✉ *400 Berding St.* ☎ *707/786–4000, 855/786–4001* ⊕ *www.gingerbread-mansion.com* 💬 *7 rooms, 4 suites* 🍽 *Breakfast.*

EUREKA

19 miles north of Ferndale; 67 miles north of Garberville.

With a population of 27,000, Eureka is the North Coast's largest city. Over the past century, it has cycled through several periods of boom and bust—first with mining and later with timber and fishing—but these days tourism helps keep the local economy afloat. The town's nearly 100 Victorian buildings have inspired some to dub it "the Williamsburg of the West." Shops draw people to the renovated downtown, and a walking pier extends into the harbor.

GETTING HERE AND AROUND

U.S. 101 travels through Eureka. From Redding and Interstate 5, travel west along Highway 299 about 138 miles to U.S. 101; Eureka is 9 miles south. Eureka Transit (⊕ *www.eurekatransit.org*) buses serve the town and connect with regional transit.

EXPLORING

Blue Ox Millworks. This woodshop is among a handful in the country specializing in Victorian-era architecture, but what makes it truly unique is that its craftspeople use antique tools to do the work. The most modern tool here is a 1948 band saw. Lucky for curious craftspeople and history buffs, the shop doubles as a dusty historical park. Visitors can watch craftsmen use printing presses, lathes, and even a mill that pares down whole redwood logs into the ornate fixtures for Victorians like those around town. The museum is less interesting on Saturday, when most craftspeople take the day off. ✉ *1 X St.* ☎ *707/444–3437, 800/248–4259* 🌐 *www.blueoxmill.com* 🎫 *$10* 🕒 *Weekdays 9–5; Apr.–Nov., also Sat. 9–4.*

Clarke Historical Museum. The Native American Wing of this museum contains a beautiful collection of northwestern California basketry. Artifacts from Eureka's Victorian, logging, and maritime eras fill the rest of the space. ✉ *240 E St.* ☎ *707/443–1947* 🌐 *www.clarkemuseum.org* 🎫 *$3* 🕒 *Wed.–Sat. 11–4.*

Eureka Chamber of Commerce Visitor Center. The center has maps of self-guided driving tours of Eureka's Victorian architecture, and you can learn about organized tours. ✉ *2112 Broadway* ☎ *707/442–3738* 🌐 *www.eurekachamber.com* 🕒 *Weekdays 8:30–5, June–Aug., also Sat. 10–3.*

FAMILY **Fort Humboldt State Historic Park.** The structure that gives this park its name was built in response to conflicts between white settlers and Native Americans. It no longer stands, but on its grounds are some reconstructed buildings, fort and logging museums, and old logging locomotives. ✉ *3431 Fort Ave.* ☎ *707/445–6547* 🌐 *www.parks.ca.gov* 🎫 *Free* 🕒 *Daily 8–5.*

QUICK BITES

Lost Coast Brewery & Cafe. This bustling microbrewery is the best place in town to relax with a pint of ale or porter. Soups, salads, and light meals are served for lunch and dinner. ✉ ***617 4th St.*** ☎ ***707/445–4480*** 🌐 ***www.lostcoast.com.***

WHERE TO EAT AND STAY

$$$ AMERICAN Fodor's Choice ★

🍴 **Restaurant 301.** The elegant Restaurant 301, inside the Carter House, uses ingredients selected from the farmers' market, local cheese makers and ranchers, and the on-site gardens. Dishes are prepared with a delicate hand and a sensuous imagination. There's always a fresh seafood offering, and you can dine à la carte or choose the five-course prix-fixe menu ($62). **■ TIP→ The restaurant's praiseworthy wine selection includes many coveted older vintages.** [$] *Average main: $28* ✉ *301 L St.* ☎ *707/444–8062, 800/404–1390* 🌐 *carterhouse.com* 🕒 *No lunch.*

$$ AMERICAN FAMILY

🍴 **Samoa Cookhouse.** Waiters at this former cafeteria for local mill workers deliver family-style bowls—whatever is being served at the meal you've arrived for—to long, communal tables. For breakfast that means eggs, sausage, biscuits and gravy, and the like. Lunch and dinner usually feature soup, potatoes, salad, and pie, plus daily-changing entrées such as pot roast and pork loin. A museum in the back pays homage to logging culture, but the entire place is a tribute to the rough-and-tumble life and hard work that tamed this wild land. Dieters and vegetarians should look elsewhere for sustenance. [$] *Average main: $17* ✉ *908 Vance Ave., near Cookhouse Rd., Samoa* ☎ *707/442–1659* 🌐 *www.samoacookhouse.net.*

$$$ Abigail's Elegant Victorian Mansion. Innkeepers Doug and Lily Vieyra
HOTEL have devoted themselves to honoring this National Historic Landmark
Fodor'sChoice by decorating it in authentic, Victorian-era style. **Pros:** unique; lots of
★ character; delightful innkeepers. **Cons:** two-night minimum stay; down-
town is not within walking distance. $\boxed{S}$ *Rooms from: $225 ⊠ 1406 C
St.* ☎ *707/444–3144 ⊕ www.eureka-california.com* ↪ *4 rooms, 2 with
shared bath ═ No credit cards* ⦿ *No meals.*

$$$ Carter House. Owner Mark Carter says he trains his staff always to say
HOTEL yes; whether it's breakfast in bed or an in-room massage, someone here
Fodor'sChoice will get you what you want. **Pros:** elegant; every detail in place; aim-to-
★ please service. **Cons:** though kids are allowed, this is best for grown-ups.
$\boxed{S}$ *Rooms from: $189 ⊠ 301 L St.* ☎ *707/444–8062, 800/404–1390
⊕ carterhouse.com* ↪ *22 rooms, 8 suites, 2 cottages* ⦿ *Breakfast.*

SPORTS AND THE OUTDOORS
WHALE-WATCHING
Humboats Kayak Adventures. Kayak rentals and lessons are available here,
along with group kayaking tours, including whale-watching trips (from
December to June) that get you close enough for good photos of migrat-
ing gray whales and resident humpback whales. ⊠ *Dock A, Woodley
Island Marina* ☎ *707/443–5157 ⊕ www.humboats.com* ⧉ *From $50.*

SHOPPING
Eureka has several art galleries and numerous antiques stores in the
district running from C to I streets between 2nd and 3rd streets.

ART GALLERY
First Street Gallery. Run by Humboldt State University, this is the best
spot for contemporary art by local and regional artists, with some
national and international representation. ⊠ *422 1st St.* ☎ *707/443–
6363 ⊕ www.humboldt.edu/first.*

BOOKS
Eureka Books. Along with classics and bestsellers, this bibliophile's haven
has exceptional used books on all topics. ⊠ *426 2nd St.* ☎ *707/444–
9593 ⊕ eurekabooksellers.com.*

TRINIDAD

23 miles north of Eureka.

Trinidad got its name from the Spanish mariners who entered the bay
on Trinity Sunday, June 9, 1775. The town became a principal trading
post for the mining camps along the Klamath and Trinity rivers. Mining
and whaling have faded from the scene, and now Trinidad is a quiet
and genuinely charming community with ample sights and activities to
entertain low-key visitors.

GETTING HERE AND AROUND
Trinidad sits right off U.S. 101. To reach the town from Interstate 5,
head west from Redding on Highway 299 and turn north on U.S. 101
north of Arcata. Redwood Transit System (⊕ *www.redwoodtransit.
org*) provides bus service between Trinidad, Eureka, and nearby towns.

8

EXPLORING

Patrick's Point State Park. On a forested plateau almost 200 feet above the surf, the park has stunning views of the Pacific, great whale- and sea lion–watching, picnic areas, bike paths, and hiking trails through old-growth spruce forest. There are also tidal pools at Agate Beach, a re-created Yurok Indian village, and a small museum with natural-history exhibits. Because the park is far from major tourist hubs, there are few visitors (most are local surfers). It's sublimely quiet here. Three campgrounds amid spruce and alder trees have all amenities except RV hookups. Reservations are recommended in summer. Dogs are not allowed on trails or the beach. ✉ *U.S. 101, 5 miles north of Trinidad* ☎ *707/677–3570* 🌐 *www.parks.ca.gov* 🎟 *$8 per vehicle.*

BEACHES

FAMILY **Clam Beach County Park and Little River State Beach.** These two adjoining oceanfront areas stretch for several miles south of Trinidad. The sandy beach here is exceptionally wide, perfect for kids who need to get out of the car and burn off some energy. Beachcombing and savoring fabulous sunsets are favorite activities. The two parks share day-use facilities. **Amenities:** parking (free); toilets. **Best for:** solitude; sunset; walking. ✉ *Clam Beach Dr. & U.S. 101, 6 miles south of Trinidad* ☎ *707/445–7651* 🌐 *www.parks.ca.gov* 🕒 *5 am–midnight.*

WHERE TO EAT AND STAY

$ SEAFOOD 🍴 **Katy's Smokehouse.** This tiny operation has been doing things the same way since the 1940s, curing day-boat, line-caught fish with its original smokers. Albacore jerky, smoked scallops, and salmon cured with brown sugar are popular. Buy bread and drinks in town and walk to the waterside for fine alfresco snacking. [$] *Average main: $10* ✉ *740 Edwards St.* ☎ *707/677–0151* 🌐 *www.katyssmokehouse.com* 🕒 *No dinner.*

$$$ AMERICAN 🍴 **Larrupin' Cafe.** Set in a two-story house on a quiet country road north of town, this restaurant—locally considered one of the best places to eat on the North Coast—is often thronged with people enjoying fresh seafood, Cornish game hen, or mesquite-grilled ribs. The garden setting and candlelight stir thoughts of romance. [$] *Average main: $29* ✉ *1658 Patrick's Point Dr.* ☎ *707/677–0230* 🌐 *www.larrupin.com* 🕒 *No lunch.*

$$$$ B&B/INN 🏨 **Trinidad Bay Bed and Breakfast Inn.** Staying at this small Cape Cod–style inn perched above Trinidad Bay is like spending the weekend at a friend's vacation house. **Pros:** great location above bay; lots of light. **Cons:** if all rooms are full, the main house can feel a bit crowded. [$] *Rooms from: $275* ✉ *560 Edwards St., Box 849* ☎ *707/677–0840* 🌐 *www.trinidadbaybnb.com* 🛏 *4 rooms* 🍽 *Breakfast.*

$$$$ B&B/INN 🏨 **Turtle Rocks Oceanfront Inn.** This comfortable inn has the best view in Trinidad, and the builders have made the most of it, adding private, glassed-in decks to each room so that guests can fully enjoy the ocean and sunning sea lions. **Pros:** great ocean views; comfy king beds. **Cons:** no businesses within walking distance. [$] *Rooms from: $295* ✉ *3392 Patrick's Point Dr., 4½ miles north of town* ☎ *707/677–3707* 🌐 *www.turtlerocksinn.com* 🛏 *5 rooms, 1 suite* 🍽 *Breakfast.*

REDWOOD NATIONAL PARK

WELCOME TO REDWOOD NATIONAL PARK

TOP REASONS TO GO

★ **Giant trees:** These mature coastal redwoods are the tallest trees in the world.

★ **Hiking to the sea:** The park's trails wind through majestic redwood groves, and many connect to the Coastal Trail running along the western edge of the park.

★ **Rare wildlife:** Mighty Roosevelt elk favor the park's flat prairie and open lands; seldom-seen black bears roam the backcountry; trout and salmon leap through streams; and Pacific gray whales swim along the coast during their biannual migrations.

★ **Stepping back in time:** Hike Fern Canyon Trail and explore a prehistoric scene of lush vegetation and giant ferns.

★ **Cheeps, not beeps:** Amid the majestic redwoods you're out of range for cell-phone service—and in range for the soothing sounds of warblers and burbling creeks.

1 Del Norte Coast Redwoods State Park. The rugged terrain of this far northwest corner of California combines stretches of treacherous surf, steep cliffs, and forested ridges. On a clear day it's postcard-perfect; with fog, it's mysteriously mesmerizing.

2 Jedediah Smith Redwoods State Park. Gargantuan old-growth redwoods dominate the scenery here. The Smith River cuts through canyons and splits across boulders, carrying salmon to the inland creeks where they spawn.

3 Prairie Creek Redwoods State Park. The forests here give way to spacious, grassy plains where abundant wildlife thrives. Roosevelt elk are a common sight in the meadows and down to Gold Bluffs Beach.

4 Orick Area. The highlight of the southern portion of Redwood National and State Parks is the Tall Trees Grove. It's difficult to reach and requires a special pass, but it's worth the hassle—this section has the tallest coast redwood trees, with a new record holder discovered in 2006.

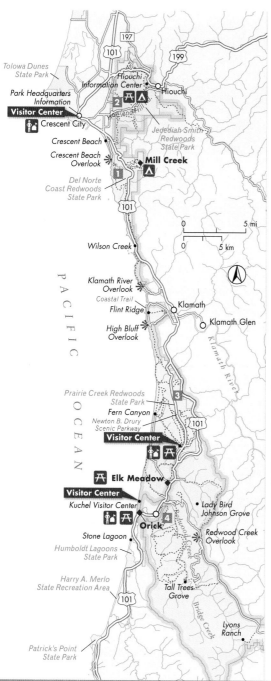

CALIFORNIA

GETTING ORIENTED

U.S. 101 weaves through the southern portion of the park, skirts around the center, and then slips back through redwoods in the north and on to Crescent City. Kuchel Visitor Center, Prairie Creek Redwoods State Park and Visitor Center, Tall Trees Grove, Fern Canyon, and Lady Bird Johnson Grove are all in the park's southern section. In the park's central section, where the Klamath River Overlook is the dominant feature, the narrow, mostly graveled Coastal Drive loop yields ocean vistas. To the north you'll find Mill Creek Trail, Enderts Beach, and Crescent Beach Overlook in Del Norte Coast Redwoods State Park as well as Jedediah Smith Redwoods State Park, Stout Grove, Little Bald Hills, and Simpson-Reed Grove.

9

Updated
by Christine
Vovakes

Soaring to more than 300 feet, the coastal redwoods that give this park its name are miracles of efficiency—some have survived hundreds of years (a few live for more than 2,000 years). These massive trees glean nutrients from the rich alluvial flats at their feet and from the moisture and nitrogen trapped in their uneven canopy. Their huge, thick-barked trunks can hold thousands of gallons of water, reservoirs that have helped them withstand centuries of firestorms.

REDWOOD PLANNER

WHEN TO GO

Campers and hikers flock to the park from mid-June to early September. Crowds disappear in winter, but you'll have to contend with frequent rains and nasty potholes on side roads. Temperatures fluctuate widely throughout the park: the foggy coastal lowland is much cooler than the higher-altitude interior.

The average annual rainfall here is 60 to 80 inches, and during dry summer months thick fog rolling in from the Pacific veils the forests.

GETTING HERE AND AROUND

CAR TRAVEL

U.S. 101 runs north–south along the park, and Highway 199 cuts east–west through its northern portion. Access routes off 101 include Bald Hills Road, Davison Road, Newton B. Drury Scenic Parkway, Coastal Drive loop, Requa Road, and Enderts Beach Road. From 199 take South Fork Road to Howland Hill Road. Many of the park's roads aren't paved, and winter rains can turn them into obstacle courses or close them completely. Motorhomes/RVs and trailers aren't permitted on some routes. ■TIP➜ **Park rangers say don't rely solely on GPS; closely consult park maps, available at the visitor information centers.**

PARK ESSENTIALS

PARK FEES AND PERMITS

Admission to Redwood National Park is free. There's an $8 day-use fee to enter one or all of Redwood's state parks; for camping at these state parks it's an additional $35. To visit Tall Trees Grove, you must get a free permit at the Kuchel Information Center in Orick. Permits also are needed to camp in all designated backcountry camps.

PARK HOURS

The park is open year-round, 24 hours a day.

VISITOR INFORMATION

PARK CONTACT INFORMATION

Redwood National and State Parks ⌂ *1111 2nd St., Crescent City* ☎ *707/465–7335* ⊕ *www.nps.gov/redw.*

VISITOR CENTERS

Crescent City Information Center. As the park's headquarters, this center is the main information stop if you're approaching the redwoods from the north. A gift shop and picnic area are here. ⌂ *Off U.S. 101, 1111 Second St., near K St., Crescent City* ☎ *707/465–7335* ⊕ *www.nps.gov/ redw* ☉ *Mid-May–mid-Oct., daily 9–5; mid-Oct.–mid-May, daily 9–4.*

Hiouchi Information Center. Located in Jedediah Smith Redwoods State Park, 2 miles west of Hiouchi and 9 miles east of Crescent City off U.S. 199, this seasonal center has a bookstore, film, and exhibits about the flora and fauna in the park. It's also a starting point for seasonal ranger programs. ⌂ *U.S. Hwy. 199* ☎ *707/458–3294, 707/465–7335* ⊕ *www. nps.gov/redw* ☉ *Late May–early Sept., daily 9–6.*

Jedediah Smith Visitor Center. Located off U.S. 199, adjacent to the Jedediah Smith Redwoods State Park main campground, this seasonal center has information about ranger-led walks and evening campfire programs in the summer. Also here are nature and history exhibits, a gift shop, and a picnic area. ⌂ *Off U.S.Hwy. 199,Hiouchi* ☎ *707/458–3496, 707/465–7335* ⊕ *www.parks.ca.gov* ☉ *Late May–early Sept., daily 9–5.*

Fodor's Choice ★ **Prairie Creek Visitor Center.** Housed in a redwood lodge, this center has wildlife displays and a massive stone fireplace that was built in 1933. Several trailheads begin here. Stretch your legs with an easy stroll along Revelation Trail, a short loop behind the lodge. Pick up information about summer programs in Prairie Creek Redwoods State Park. There's a nature museum, gift shop, picnic area, restrooms, and exhibits on flora and fauna. ■TIP➔ Roosevelt elk often roam in the vast field adjacent to the center. ⌂ *6 miles north of Orick, off the southern end of Newton B. Drury Scenic Pkwy., Orick* ☎ *707/488–2039* ⊕ *www.parks.ca.gov* ☉ *Mid-May–mid-Oct., daily 9–5; mid-Oct.–mid-May, Thurs.–Mon. 9–4.*

Thomas H. Kuchel Visitor Center. If you're approaching the park from the south end, stop here to get brochures, advice, and a free permit to drive up the access road to Tall Trees Grove. Whale-watchers find the deck of the visitor center an excellent observation point, and bird-watchers enjoy the nearby Freshwater Lagoon, a popular layover for migrating waterfowl. Many of the exhibits here are hands-on and kid-friendly. ⌂ *Off U.S. 101, Orick* ☎ *707/465–7765* ⊕ *www.nps.gov/redw* ☉ *Mid-May–mid-Oct., daily 9–5; mid-Oct.–mid-May, daily 9–4.*

9

Plants and Wildlife in Redwood

Coast redwoods, the world's tallest trees (a new record holder, topping out at 379 feet, was found within the park in 2006) grow in the moist, temperate climate of California's North Coast. These ancient giants thrive in an environment that exists in only a few hundred coastal miles along the Pacific Ocean. They commonly live 600 years—though some have been around for 2,000 years.

A healthy redwood forest is diverse and includes Douglas firs, western hemlocks, tan oaks, and madrone trees. The complex soils of the forest floor support a verdant profusion of ferns, mosses, and fungi, along with numerous shrubs and berry bushes. In spring, California rhododendron bloom throughout the forest, providing a dazzling purple and pink contrast to the dense greenery.

Redwood National and State Parks hold 45% of all California's old-growth redwood forests. Of the original 3,125 square miles (2 million acres) in the Redwoods Historic Range, only 4% remain following the logging that began in 1850; 1% is privately owned and managed, and 3% is on public land.

In the park's backcountry, you might spot mountain lions, black bears, black-tailed deer, river otters, beavers, and minks. Roosevelt elk roam the flatlands, and the rivers and streams teem with salmon and trout. Gray whales, seals, and sea lions cavort near the coastline. And thanks to the area's location along the Pacific Flyway, more than 400 species of birds have been recorded in the park.

EXPLORING

SCENIC DRIVES

Coastal Drive. This 8-mile, narrow and mostly unpaved road is closed to trailers and RVs and takes about one hour to drive. The slow pace alongside stands of redwoods offers close-up views of the Klamath River and expansive panoramas of the Pacific. From here you'll find access to the Flint Ridge section of the Coastal Trail. Recurring landslides have closed sections of the original road; this loop is all that remains. ⊠ *1 mile south of Klamath on U.S. 101, Klamath ✥ Take the Klamath Beach Rd. exit and follow signs to Coastal Dr.*

SCENIC STOPS

Crescent Beach Overlook. The scenery here includes ocean views and, in the distance, Crescent City and its working harbor. In balmy weather this is a great place for a picnic. From the overlook you can spot migrating gray whales going south November through December and returning north February through April. ⊠ *2 miles south of Crescent City off Enderts Beach Rd.*

Fodor's Choice
★
Fern Canyon. Enter another world and be surrounded by 30-foot canyon walls covered with sword, maidenhair, and five-finger ferns. Allow an

CLOSE UP

Best Campgrounds in Redwood

Within a 30-minute drive of Redwood National and State Parks there are nearly 60 public and private camping facilities. None of the four primitive areas in Redwood—DeMartin, Flint Ridge, Little Bald Hills, and Nickel Creek—is a drive-in site. You will need to get a free permit from any visitor center except Prairie Creek before camping in these campgrounds, and along Redwood Creek in the backcountry. Bring your own water, since drinking water isn't available in any of these sites. These campgrounds, plus Gold Bluffs Beach, are first-come, first-served.

If you'd rather drive than hike in, Redwood has four developed campgrounds—Elk Prairie, Gold Bluffs Beach, Jedediah Smith, and Mill Creek—that are within the state-park boundaries. None has RV hookups, and some length restrictions apply. Fees are $35 in state park campgrounds. For details and reservations, call ☎ 800/444-7275 or check ⊕ www.reserveamerica.com.

Elk Prairie Campground. Roosevelt elk frequent this popular campground adjacent to a prairie and old-growth redwoods. ⊠ *On Newton B. Drury Scenic Pkwy., 6 miles north of Orick in Prairie Creek Redwoods State Park* ☎ *800/444-7275.*

Gold Bluffs Beach Campground. You can camp in tents or RVs right on the beach at this Prairie Creek Redwoods State Park campground near Fern Canyon. ⊠ *At end of Davison Rd., 5 miles south of Prairie Creek Visitor Center off U.S. 101* ☎ *707/465-7335.*

Jedediah Smith Campground. This is one of the few places to camp—in tents or RVs—within groves of old-growth redwood forest. ⊠ *9 miles east of Crescent City on Hwy. 199* ☎ *800/444-7275.*

Mill Creek Campground. Mill Creek is the largest of the state-park campgrounds. ⊠ *East of U.S. 101, 7 miles southeast of Crescent City* ☎ *800/444-7275.*

Nickel Creek Campground. An easy hike gets you to this primitive site, which is near tide pools and has great ocean views. ⊠ *On Coastal Trail ½ mile from end of Enderts Beach Rd.* ☎ *707/465-7335.*

9

hour to explore the ¼-mile-long vertical garden along a 0.7-mile loop. From the north end of Gold Bluffs Beach it's an easy walk, although you'll have to wade across a small stream several times (in addition to driving across streams on the way to the parking area). But the lush surroundings are otherworldly, and worth a visit when creeks aren't running too high. Be aware that motorhomes/RVs and all trailers are prohibited here. ⊠ *10 miles from Prairie Creek Visitor Center, via Davison Rd. off U.S. 101, Orick* ⊕ *www.nps.gov/redw.*

Lady Bird Johnson Grove. This section of the park was dedicated by, and named for, the former first lady. A 1-mile nature loop follows an old logging road through a mature redwood forest. Allow 45 minutes to complete the trail. ⊠ *1 mile north of Orick off U.S. 101 onto Bald Hills Rd., Orick* ✛ *Turn onto Bald Hills Rd. for 2½ miles to trailhead* ⊕ *www.nps.gov/redw.*

Tall Trees Grove. From the Kuchel Visitor Center, you can get a free permit to make the steep 14-mile drive (the last 6.5 miles, on Tall Trees Access Road, are unpaved) to the grove's trailhead (trailers and RVs not allowed). Access to the popular grove is first-come, first-served, and a maximum of 50 permits are handed out each day. ⊠ *1 mile north of Orick off U.S. 101, Orick ✛ Turn right at Bald Hills Rd. and follow signs about 6.5 miles to access road, then drive 6.5 miles on unpaved road to trailhead. From there, take the approximately 4-mile round-trip hike to the grove.*

SPORTS AND THE OUTDOORS

HIKING

MODERATE
Coastal Trail. Although this easy-to-difficult trail runs along most of the park's length, smaller sections—of varying degrees of difficulty—are accessible via frequent, well-marked trailheads. The moderate-to-difficult DeMartin section leads past 6 miles of old growth redwoods and through prairie. If you're up for a real workout, you'll be well rewarded with the brutally difficult but stunning Flint Ridge section, a 4.5-mile stretch of steep grades and numerous switchbacks that leads past redwoods and Marshall Pond. The moderate 5.5-mile-long Klamath section, which connects the Wilson Creek picnic area with Hidden Beach tide pools and up to the Klamath Overlook, provides coastal views and whale-watching opportunities. *Moderate.* ⊠ *Flint Ridge trailhead: Douglas Bridge parking area, north end of Coastal Dr., Klamath* ⊕ *www.nps.gov/redw.*

KAYAKING

With many miles of often-shallow rivers and streams in the area, kayaking is a popular pastime in the park.

OUTFITTERS
Humboats Kayak Adventures. Kayak rental and lessons are available here, along with a variety of group kayak tours, including full-moon and sunset tours and popular whale-watching trips (October–June) that get you close enough for photos of migrating gray whales and resident humpback whales. ⊠ *601 Startare Dr., Dock A, Woodley Island Marina, Eureka* ☎ *707/443–5157* ⊕ *www.humboats.com* 🖅 *From $45.*

WHALE-WATCHING

Good vantage points for whale-watching include Crescent Beach Overlook, the Kuchel Visitor Center in Orick, points along the Coastal Trail, and the Klamath River Overlook. Late November through January are the best months to see their southward migrations; February through April they return and generally pass closer to shore.

THE SOUTHERN SIERRA

10

Around Sequoia, Kings Canyon,
and Yosemite National Parks

Visit Fodors.com for advice, updates, and bookings

WELCOME TO
THE SOUTHERN SIERRA

TOP REASONS TO GO

★ **Hiking:** Whether you walk the paved loops in the national parks or head off the beaten path into the backcountry, a hike through groves and meadows or alongside streams and waterfalls will allow you to see, smell, and feel nature up close.

★ **Winter Fun:** Famous for its incredible snow-pack—some of the deepest in the North American continent—the Sierra Nevada has something for every winter-sports fan.

★ **Live it up:** Mammoth Lakes is eastern California's most exciting resort area.

★ **Pamper yourself:** Tucked in the hills south of Oakhurst, the elegant Château du Sureau will make you feel as if you've stepped into a fairy tale.

★ **Go with the flow:** Three Rivers, the gateway to Sequoia National Park, is the launching pad for white-water trips down the Kaweah River.

1 South of Yosemite National Park. Several gateway towns to the south and west of Yosemite National Park, most within an hour's drive of Yosemite Valley, have food, lodging, and other services.

2 Mammoth Lakes. A jewel in the vast Eastern Sierra Nevada, the Mammoth Lakes area lies just east of the Sierra crest, on the backside of Yosemite and the Ansel Adams Wilderness. It's a place of rugged beauty, where giant sawtooth mountains drop into the vast deserts of the Great Basin. In winter, 11,053-foot-high Mammoth Mountain offers the finest skiing and snowboarding in California—sometimes as late as June or even July. Once the snows melt, Mammoth transforms itself into a warm-weather playground, with fishing, mountain biking, golfing, hiking, and horseback riding. Nine deep-blue lakes are spread throughout the Mammoth Lakes Basin, and another 100 lakes dot the surrounding countryside.

3 East of Yosemite National Park. The area to the east of Yosemite National Park includes some ruggedly handsome, albeit desolate, terrain, most notably around Mono Lake. The area is best visited by car, as distances are great and public transportation is negligible. U.S. 395 is the main north–south road on the eastern side of the Sierra Nevada, at the western edge of the Great Basin. It's one of California's most beautiful highways; plan to snap pictures at roadside pullouts.

GETTING ORIENTED

The transition between the Central Valley and the rugged Southern Sierra may be the most dramatic in California sightseeing; as you head into the mountains, your temptation to stop the car and gawk will increase with every foot gained in elevation. Although you should spend most of your time here in the nearby national parks, be sure to check out some of the mountain towns on the parks' fringes—in addition to being great places to stock up on supplies, they have worthy attractions, restaurants, and lodging options.

10

4 **South of Sequoia and Kings Canyon.** Scenic Three Rivers is the main gateway for Sequoia and Kings Canyon National Parks.

Updated by Cheryl Crabtree

The Southern Sierra's granite peaks and giant sequoias bedazzle heart and soul so completely that for many visitors the experience surpasses that at more famous urban attractions. Most of the Sierra's wonders lie within national parks, but outside them deep-blue Mono Lake and its tufa towers never cease to astound. The megaresort Mammoth Lakes, meanwhile, lures skiers and snowboarders in winter and hikers and mountain bikers in summer, and the town of Three Rivers delivers laid-back hospitality with a smile.

The national parks are accessed most easily via gateway towns that include Oakhurst, Fish Camp, and Lee Vining for Yosemite and Visalia and Three Rivers for Sequoia and Kings Canyon. Pristine lakes and rolling hills outside the parks offer year-round opportunities for rest and relaxation. Or not. In winter the thrill of the slopes—and their relative isolation compared to busy Lake Tahoe—draws a hearty breed of outdoor enthusiast. In summer a hike through groves and meadows or alongside streams and waterfalls allows you to see, smell, and feel nature up close.

PLANNING

GETTING HERE AND AROUND

AIR TRAVEL

Three main airports provide access to the Southern Sierra: Fresno Yosemite International (FAT), on the western side, and, on the eastern side, Mammoth-Yosemite (MMH), 6 miles east of Mammoth Lakes, and Reno–Tahoe (RNO), 130 miles north of Mammoth Lakes via U.S. 395. Alaska, Allegiant, American, Delta, Frontier, United, and a few other carriers serve Fresno and Reno. Alaska and United serve Mammoth Lakes.

Airports Fresno Yosemite International Airport (*FAT*) ⊠ *5175 E. Clinton Ave., Fresno* ☎ *800/244–2359 automated information, 559/454–2052 terminal info desk* ⊕ *www.flyfresno.com.* **Mammoth Yosemite Airport** ⊠ *1200 Airport Rd., Mammoth Lakes* ☎ *760/934–2712, 888/466–2666* ⊕ *www.visitmammoth. com.* **Reno-Tahoe International Airport** ⊠ *2001 E. Plumb La., Reno, Nevada* ☎ *775/328–6400* ⊕ *www.renoairport.com.*

BUS TRAVEL

Greyhound serves Fresno, Madera, and other Central Valley towns west of the Sierra. Madera County Connection buses travel between Madera and Oakhurst/Bass Lake. Eastern Sierra Transit Authority buses serve Mammoth Lakes and other eastern Sierra towns. YARTS (Yosemite Area Regional Transportation System) connects Yosemite National Park with surrounding towns, including Fresno, Merced, Oakhurst, Fish Camp, and Lee Vining; this is a good option during summer, when parking in Yosemite Valley and elsewhere in the park can be difficult.

Bus Contacts Eastern Sierra Transit Authority ☎ *760/872–1901 general, 760/914–1315 Mammoth Lakes* ⊕ *www.estransit.com.* **Greyhound** ☎ *800/231– 2222* ⊕ *www.greyhound.com.* **Madera County Connection** ⊠ *Madera* ☎ *559/661–3040* ⊕ *www.maderactc.org/public-transit.* **YARTS** ☎ *877/989– 2787, 209/388–9589* ⊕ *www.yarts.com.*

CAR TRAVEL

Interstate 5 and Highway 99 travel north–south along the western side of the Sierra Nevada. U.S. 395 follows a roughly parallel route on the eastern side.

From San Francisco: Head east on Interstate 80 to 580 to 205E to connect with Interstate 5 and Highway 99. To best reach the eastern side, take Interstate 80 to U.S. 395, then head south.

From Los Angeles: Head north on Interstate 5, continuing north on the interstate (or Highway 99) for the western side and exiting north onto Highway 14 and later onto U.S. 395.

■ TIP→ Gas stations are few and far between in the Sierra, so fill your tank when you can. Between October and May heavy snow may cover mountain roads. Always check road conditions before driving. Carry tire chains, and know how to install them. On Interstate 80 and U.S. 50 chain installers assist travelers (for $35), but elsewhere you're on your own.

Travel Reports Caltrans Current Highway Conditions ☎ *800/427–7623* ⊕ *www.dot.ca.gov.*

TRAIN TRAVEL

The Southern Sierra stops of Amtrak's daily *San Joaquin* train include Fresno and Merced, where you can connect to YARTS for travel to Yosemite National Park and smaller gateway towns.

Train Contact Amtrak ☎ *800/872–7245* ⊕ *www.amtrak.com.*

RESTAURANTS

Most small towns in the Sierra Nevada have at least one restaurant. Standard American fare is the norm, but you'll also find sophisticated cuisine. With few exceptions, dress is casual. Local grocery stores and

10

delis stock picnic fixings, good to have on hand should the opportunity for an impromptu meal under giant trees emerge.

HOTELS

The lodgings nearest the national parks generally fill up the quickest; book hotels in the western Sierra Nevada well in advance in summer. Booking far ahead is less crucial for Eastern Sierra accommodations, except in Mammoth Lakes. *Hotel reviews have been shortened. For full information, visit Fodors.com.*

Hotel Contacts Mammoth Reservations ⊠ *Mammoth Lakes* ☎ *800/223–3032* ⊕ *www.mammothreservations.com.*

WHAT IT COSTS			
$	$$	$$$	$$$$
Restaurants	under $16	$16–$22	$23–$30	over $30
Hotels	under $120	$120–$175	$176–$250	over $250

Restaurant prices are the average cost of a main course at dinner or, if dinner is not served, at lunch. Hotel prices are the lowest cost of a standard double room in high season.

TOUR OPERATORS

Discover Yosemite. This outfit operates daily tours to Yosemite Valley, Mariposa Grove, and Glacier Point in 14- and 29-passenger vehicles. The Highway 41 route stops in Bass Lake, Oakhurst, and Fish Camp, and the Highway 140 route departs from Mariposa, Midpines, and El Portal. Rates include lunch. Sunset tours to Sentinel Dome are additional summer options. ☎ *559/642–4400, 800/585–0565* ⊕ *www. discoveryosemite.com* ⌱ *From $124.*

Mammoth All Weather Shuttle. This outfit operates summer tours from Mammoth Lakes to Yosemite; north to June Lake, Mono Lake, and Bodie Ghost Town; and around the lakes region. The company also runs charters to Los Angeles, Reno, and Las Vegas airports—useful when inclement weather causes flight cancellations at Mammoth's airport. ⊠ *Mammoth Lakes* ☎ *760/709–2927* ⊕ *www.mawshuttle.com* ⌱ *From $60.*

VISITOR INFORMATION

Mammoth Lakes Tourism ⊠ *Mammoth Lakes* ☎ *760/934–2712, 888/466–2666* ⊕ *www.visitmammoth.com.*

Mono County Tourism ⊠ *Mammoth Lakes* ☎ *800/845–7922* ⊕ *mono county.org.*

SOUTH OF YOSEMITE NATIONAL PARK

People heading to Yosemite National Park, especially those interested in seeing the giant sequoias on the park's south side, pass through Oakhurst and Fish Camp on Highway 41.

OAKHURST

40 miles north of Fresno.

Motels, restaurants, gas stations, and small businesses line Highway 41 in Oakhurst, the last sizeable community before Yosemite National Park and a good spot to find provisions. The park's southern entrance is 23 miles north of Oakhurst on Highway 41.

GETTING HERE AND AROUND

At the junction of highways 41 and 49, Oakhurst is about an hour's drive north of Fresno. It's the southern gateway to Yosemite, so many people fly into Fresno and rent a car to get here and beyond.

ESSENTIALS

Visitor Information Yosemite Sierra Visitors Bureau ☎ *559/683–4636* 🌐 *www.yosemitethisyear.com.*

EXPLORING

Fresno Flats Historical Village and Park. For a dose of colorful foothills history, make a quick stop at this engaging local museum centered around two 1870s houses. ✉ *School Rd. and Indian Springs Rd.* ☎ *559/683–6570* 🌐 *www.fresnoflatsmuseum.org.*

Yosemite Gateway Gallery Row. Find out what mountain art is all about at this enclave of five galleries representing dozens of painters, sculptors, and other artists. ✉ *40982 Hwy. 41, 1¼ mile north of Hwy. 49* ☎ *559/683–5551* 🌐 *www.yosemitegatewaygalleryrow.com* 🎟 *Free* 🕓 *Daily 10–5 (days and hrs vary for some galleries).*

WHERE TO EAT

$$$$ EUROPEAN Fodor's Choice ★

🍴 **Erna's Elderberry House.** Erna Kubin-Clanin, the grande dame of Château du Sureau, created this culinary oasis, stunning for its understated elegance, gorgeous setting, and impeccable service. Earth-tone walls and wood beams accent the dining room's high ceilings, and arched windows reflect the glow of candles. The seasonal six-course prix-fixe dinner ($108) can be paired with superb wines, with each course delivered in perfect synchronicity by the elite waitstaff. **TIP→ Diners can also order à la carte, and a shorter bar menu is offered in the former wine cellar.** [$] *Average main: $48* ✉ *Château du Sureau, 48688 Victoria La., off Hwy. 41* ☎ *559/683–6800* 🌐 *www.elderberryhouse.com* ✍ *Reservations essential* 🕓 *No lunch Mon.–Sat.*

$ AMERICAN Fodor's Choice ★

🍴 **South Gate Brewing Company.** Locals pack this family-friendly, industrial-chic restaurant to socialize and savor small-lot beers, crafted on site, along with tasty meals. The creative pub fare runs a wide gamut, from shepherd's pie Wellington and thin-crust brick-oven pizzas to fish tacos, fish-and-chips, vegan black-bean burgers, and slow-roasted pulled-pork sandwiches. Save room for the house-made root-beer float or the brownie sundae, both topped with a scoop of locally made vanilla ice cream. When the weather's good, musicians perform on most weekends and on some weekday evenings. [$] *Average main: $13* ✉ *40233 Enterprise Dr., off Hwy. 49, north of Von's shopping center* ☎ *559/692–2739* 🌐 *southgatebrewco.com.*

10

WHERE TO STAY

$$ ⓣ **Best Western Plus Yosemite Gateway Inn.** Perched on 11 hillside acres,
HOTEL   Oakhurst's best motel has carefully tended landscaping and rooms with
FAMILY   stylish contemporary furnishings and hand-painted murals of Yosem-
ite. **Pros:** close to park's southern entrance; on-site restaurant; indoor
and outdoor swimming pools; frequent deer and wildlife sightings.
Cons: some rooms on the small side; Internet connection can be slow.
ⓢ *Rooms from: $150* ⊠ *40530 Hwy. 41, Oakhurst* ☎ *800/545–5462,
559/683–2378* ⊕ *www.yosemitegatewayinn.com* ↩ *133 rooms, 16
suites* †◯| *No meals.*

$$$$ ⓣ **Château du Sureau.** You'll feel pampered from the moment you drive
RESORT   through the wrought-iron gates of this fairy-tale castle. **Pros:** luxurious;
Fodor'sChoice   great views; sumptuous spa facility. **Cons:** expensive; cost might not
★   seem worth it to guests not spa-oriented. ⓢ *Rooms from: $385* ⊠ *48688
Victoria La., Oakhurst* ☎ *559/683–6860* ⊕ *www.chateausureau.com*
↩ *10 rooms, 1 villa* †◯| *Breakfast.*

$$$ ⓣ **Homestead Cottages.** Set on 160 acres of rolling hills that once held
B&B/INN   a Miwok village, these cottages (the largest sleeps six) have gas fire-
places, fully equipped kitchens, and queen-size beds. **Pros:** remote
location; quiet setting; friendly owners. **Cons:** might be too quiet for
some. ⓢ *Rooms from: $179* ⊠ *41110 Rd. 600, 2½ miles off Hwy. 49,
Ahwahnee* ☎ *559/683–0495* ⊕ *www.homesteadcottages.com* ↩ *6 cot-
tages* †◯| *Breakfast.*

NIGHTLIFE

Queen's Inn Wine Bar & Beer Garden. A combination wine bar, tasting
room, and small inn, this popular hangout on a bluff above the Fresno
River serves about 100 wines by the glass or flight, plus microbrews and
imported beers. At the tasting room, open from Wednesday through
Sunday between 11 and 5, you can sample ($5 tasting fee) Tempra-
nillo, Pinot Gris, and other limited-production wines. ⊠ *41139 Hwy.
41, Oakhurst* ☎ *559/683–4354* ⊕ *queensinn.com* ⊘ *Closed Sun.–Tues.*

SPORTS AND THE OUTDOORS

FAMILY   **Zip Yosemite.** Fly through ponderosa and sugar pine trees and gaze at
Fresno Dome and giant sequoias on a 1½-hour guided tour at this
Sierra National Forest complex. The progressively challenging course,
at elevation 5,000 feet, includes several zip lines, a suspension bridge,
and daring rope lowers from 100-foot-high platforms. Participants
should be at least 10 years old and weigh between 75 and 270 pounds.
⊠ *Calvin Crest Retreat Center, 45800 Calvin Crest Rd., 11 miles north-
east of Oakhurst via Highway 41 and Sierra Sky Ranch Rd. (632),
Oakhurst* ☎ *559/642–6688* ⊕ *zipyosemite.com* ⓔ *From $125* ⊘ *Closed
Dec.–Mar.*

FISH CAMP

14 miles north of Oakhurst.

As you climb in elevation along Highway 41 northbound, you see nothing but trees until you get to Fish Camp, where there's a post office and

general store, but no gasoline. (For gas, head 7 miles north to Wawona, in Yosemite, or 14 miles south to Oakhurst.)

GETTING HERE AND AROUND

Highway 41 is the main drag here. YARTS public transit stops in Fish Camp on its route between Fresno and Yosemite Valley.

EXPLORING

FAMILY **Yosemite Mountain Sugar Pine Railroad.** Travel back to a time when powerful steam locomotives hauled massive log trains through the Sierra. This 4-mile, narrow-gauge railroad excursion takes you near Yosemite's south gate. There's a moonlight special ($55), with dinner and entertainment, and you can pan for gold ($10) and visit the free museum. ✉ *56001 Hwy. 41, 8 miles south of Yosemite, Fish Camp* ☎ *559/683–7273* 🌐 *www.ymsprr.com* 🎫 *$22* 🕒 *May–Sept., daily; Apr. and Oct., weekends and selected weekdays.*

WHERE TO STAY

$$$ B&B/INN 🏨 **Narrow Gauge Inn.** The well-tended rooms at this family-owned property have balconies with views of the surrounding woods and mountains. **Pros:** close to Yosemite's south entrance; nicely appointed rooms; wonderful balconies. **Cons:** rooms can be a bit dark; dining options are limited, especially for vegetarians. [$] *Rooms from: $209* ✉ *48571 Hwy. 41, Fish Camp* ☎ *559/683–7720, 888/644–9050* 🌐 *www.narrowgaugeinn.com* 🛏 *26 rooms* 🍴 *Breakfast.*

$$$$ RESORT FAMILY Fodor's Choice ★ 🏨 **Tenaya Lodge.** One of the region's largest hotels, Tenaya Lodge is ideal for people who enjoy wilderness treks by day but prefer creature comforts at night. **Pros:** rustic setting with modern comforts; exceptional spa and exercise facility; close to Yosemite; activities for all ages. **Cons:** so big it can seem impersonal; pricey during summer. [$] *Rooms from: $295* ✉ *1122 Hwy. 41, Fish Camp* ☎ *559/683–6555, 888/514–2167* 🌐 *www.tenayalodge.com* 🛏 *282 rooms, 20 suites* 🍴 *No meals.*

$$$ B&B/INN 🏨 **Yosemite Lodging at Big Creek Inn.** A romantic bed-and-breakfast in a woodsy setting south of the park, the inn offers perks that place it ahead of the competition. **Pros:** friendly, knowledgeable innkeeper; hearty home-cooked breakfast; intimate setting. **Cons:** with only three rooms it books up quickly; no pets allowed. [$] *Rooms from: $239* ✉ *1221 Hwy. 41, Fish Camp* ☎ *559/641–2828* 🌐 *www.yosemiteinn.com* 🛏 *3 rooms* 🍴 *Breakfast.*

10

MAMMOTH LAKES

30 miles south of the eastern edge of Yosemite National Park.

International real-estate developers joined forces with Mammoth Mountain Ski Area to transform the once sleepy town of Mammoth Lakes (elevation 7,800 feet) into an upscale ski destination. Relatively sophisticated dining and lodging options can be found at the Village at Mammoth complex, and multimillion-dollar renovations to tired motels and restaurants have revived the "downtown" area of Old Mammoth Road. Also here is the hoppin' Mammoth Rock 'n' Bowl, a two-story

Twin Lakes, in the Mammoth Lakes region, is a great place to unwind.

activity, dining, and entertainment complex. Winter is high season at Mammoth; in summer, the room rates drop.

GETTING HERE AND AROUND
The best way to get to Mammoth Lakes is by car. The town is about 2 miles west of U.S. 395 on Highway 203, signed as Main Street in Mammoth Lakes and Minaret Road west of town. In summer and early fall (until the first big snow) you can drive to Mammoth Lakes east through Yosemite National Park on scenic Tioga Pass Road; signed as Highway 120 outside the park, the road connects to U.S. 395 north of Mammoth. In summer YARTS provides once-a-day public-transit service between Mammoth Lakes and Yosemite Valley. The shuttle buses of Eastern Sierra Transit Authority serve Mammoth Lakes and nearby tourist sites.

ESSENTIALS
Visitor Information Mammoth Lakes Visitor Center ⊠ *Welcome Center, 2510 Main St., near Sawmill Cutoff Rd.* ☎ *760/934-2712, 888/466-2666* ⊕ *www.visit mammoth.com.*

EXPLORING

TOP ATTRACTIONS

Fodor'sChoice
★
Devils Postpile National Monument. Volcanic and glacial forces sculpted this formation of smooth, vertical basalt columns. For a bird's-eye view, take the short, steep trail to the top of a 60-foot cliff. To see the monument's second scenic wonder, **Rainbow Falls,** hike 2 miles past Devils Postpile. A branch of the San Joaquin River plunges more than 100 feet over a lava ledge here. When the water hits the pool below, sunlight

turns the resulting mist into a spray of color. ■TIP→ From mid-June to early September, day-use visitors must ride the shuttle bus from the Mammoth Mountain Ski Area to the monument. ⊠ *13 miles southwest of Mammoth Lakes off Minaret Rd. (Hwy. 203)* ☎ *760/934–2289, 760/872–1901 shuttle* ⊕ *www.nps.gov/depo* ⊠ *$10 per vehicle (allowed early Sept.–mid-Oct.), $7 per person shuttle* ☉ *Park mid-June–mid-Oct.; shuttle mid-June–early Sept.*

Fodor's Choice ★
Mammoth Lakes Basin. Mammoth's seven main lakes are popular for fishing and boating in summer, and a network of multi-use paths connects them to the North Village. First comes Twin Lakes, at the far end of which is Twin Falls, where water cascades 300 feet over a shelf of volcanic rock. Also popular are Lake Mary, the largest lake in the basin; Lake Mamie; and Lake George. ■TIP→ Horseshoe Lake is the only lake in which you can swim. ⊠ *Lake Mary Rd., off Hwy. 203, southwest of town.*

Mammoth Rock 'n' Bowl. A sprawling complex with sweeping views of the Sherwin Mountains, Mammoth Rock 'n' Bowl supplies one-stop recreation, entertainment, and dining. Downstairs are 12 bowling lanes, a band stage and dance floor, Ping-Pong and foosball tables, dartboards, and a casual bar-restaurant ($$) serving burgers, pizzas, and small plates. The upstairs floor has three golf simulators, a pro shop, and Mammoth Rock Brasserie ($$$), an upscale dining room and lounge. ■TIP→ If the weather's nice, sit on the outdoor patio or the upstairs deck and enjoy the unobstructed vistas. ⊠ *3029 Chateau Rd., off Old Mammoth Rd.* ☎ *760/934–4200* ⊕ *mammothrocknbowl. com* ⊠ *Bowling: $7 per game per person evenings and weekends, $5 before 5 pm and after 10 pm; $3 shoe rental* ☉ *Hrs vary by venue; call or check website.*

FAMILY
Fodor's Choice ★
Panorama Gondola. Even if you don't ski, ride the gondola to see Mammoth Mountain, the aptly named dormant volcano that gives Mammoth Lakes its name. Gondolas serve skiers in winter and mountain bikers and sightseers in summer. The high-speed, eight-passenger gondolas whisk you from the chalet to the summit, where you can read about the area's volcanic history and take in top-of-the-world views. Standing high above the tree line, you can look west 150 miles across the state to the Coastal Range; to the east are the highest peaks of Nevada and the Great Basin beyond. You won't find a better view of the Sierra High Country without climbing. ■TIP→ The air is thin at the 11,053-foot summit; carry water, and don't overexert yourself. ⊠ *Boarding area at Main Lodge, off Minaret Rd. (Hwy. 203), west of village center* ☎ *760/934–2571* ⊠ *$25* ☉ *July 4–Oct., daily 9–4:30; Nov.–July 3, daily 8:30–4.*

WORTH NOTING

Minaret Vista. The glacier-carved sawtooth spires of the Minarets, the remains of an ancient lava flow, are best viewed from the Minaret Vista. Pull off the road, park your car in the visitors' viewing area, and walk along the path, which has interpretive signs explaining the spectacular peaks, ridges, and valleys beyond. ⊠ *Off Hwy. 203, 1¼ mile west of Mammoth Mountain Ski Area.*

10

Village at Mammoth. This huge complex of shops, restaurants, and luxury accommodations is the town's tourist center, and the venue for many special events—check the website for the weekly schedule. The complex is also the transfer hub for the free public transit system, with fixed routes throughout the Mammoth Lakes area. The free village gondola starts here and travels up the mountain to Canyon Lodge and back. ■TIP→ Unless you're staying in the village and have access to the on-site lots, parking can be very difficult here. ⊠ *100 Canyon Blvd.* ☎ *760/924–1575* ⊕ *villageatmammoth.com.*

WHERE TO EAT

$$$
STEAKHOUSE
FAMILY

✕ **The Mogul.** Come here for straightforward steaks—top sirloin, New York, filet mignon, and porterhouse. The only catch is that the waiters cook them, and the results vary depending on their experience. But generally things go well, and kids love the experience. The knotty-pine walls lend a woodsy touch, and suggest Mammoth before all the development. ■TIP→ There's an extensive salad bar—all you can eat, with hot bread included. Ⓢ *Average main: $24* ⊠ *1528 Tavern Rd., off Old Mammoth Rd., Mammoth Lakes* ☎ *760/934–3039* ⊕ *www.themogul. com* ⊗ *No lunch.*

$$$
AMERICAN

✕ **Petra's Bistro & Wine Bar.** The ambience at Petra's—quiet, dark, and warm (there's a great fireplace)—complements its seductive meat and seafood entrées and smart selection of mostly California-made wines. The service is top-notch. With its pub grub, whiskies, and craft beers and ales, the downstairs Clocktower Cellar bar provides a lively, if sometimes rowdy, alternative. Ⓢ *Average main: $28* ⊠ *Alpenhof Lodge, 6080 Minaret Rd.* ☎ *760/934–3500* ⊕ *www.petrasbistro.com* ⚏ *Reservations essential* ⊗ *Closed Mon. No lunch.*

$$$$
AMERICAN
Fodor'sChoice
★

✕ **Restaurant at Convict Lake.** The lake is one of the most spectacular spots in the Eastern Sierra, and the food here lives up to the view. Beef Wellington, rack of lamb, and pan-seared local trout, all beautifully prepared, are among the chef's specialties. The woodsy room has a vaulted knotty-pine ceiling and a copper-chimney fireplace. Natural light abounds in the daytime, but if it's summer, opt for a table outdoors under the white-barked aspens. Service is exceptional, as is the wine selection, which includes reasonably priced European and California bottlings. ■TIP→ The restaurant offers shuttle service from Mammoth Lakes for groups of four or more (reservations required). Ⓢ *Average main: $32* ⊠ *Convict Lake Rd. off U.S. 395, 4 miles south of Mammoth Lakes* ☎ *760/934–3803* ⊕ *www.convictlake.com* ⚏ *Reservations essential* ⊗ *No lunch early Sept.–mid-June.*

$$
AMERICAN

✕ **The Stove.** Down-to-earth, folksy cooking is the hallmark of this casual place known for hearty comfort—prime-rib hash, fried chicken, meat loaf, and other standbys. Breakfast is served all day; the mainstays include chicken and waffles. Save room for the pie, baked daily in-house. The dining room here is cozy, with gingham curtains and dark-wood booths, and the service is friendly. ■TIP→ Reservations are accepted for dinner only. Ⓢ *Average main: $16* ⊠ *644 Old Mammoth Rd., south off Meridian Blvd.* ☎ *760/934–2821* ⊕ *www.thestoverestaurantmammoth. com* ⊗ *No dinner occasionally during off-season; call for hrs.*

$$ MODERN AMERICAN FAMILY 🍴 **Toomey's.** A passionate baseball fan, chef Matt Toomey designed this casual space near the Village Gondola to resemble a dugout, and decorated it with baseball memorabilia. At breakfast, don't miss the coconut mascarpone pancakes. After a day outdoors, relax over lobster taquitos, giant chicken wings, fish tacos, and Angus beef sliders. Lunch and dinner entrées include buffalo meat loaf, seafood jambalaya, and a New Zealand elk rack chop. Save room for homemade, organic, gluten-free pie and other desserts. **TIP→ If you're in a hurry, phone in your order for curbside delivery to your car.** [$] *Average main: $20* ✉ *6085 Minaret Rd., at the Village* ☎ *760/924–4408* 🌐 *www.toomeyscatering.com.*

WHERE TO STAY

$$ B&B/INN 🏨 **Alpenhof Lodge.** Across from the Village at Mammoth, this mom-and-pop motel offers basic comforts and a few niceties such as the attractive pine furniture. **Pros:** convenient for skiers; reasonable rates. **Cons:** some bathrooms are small; rooms above pub can be noisy. [$] *Rooms from: $159* ✉ *6080 Minaret Rd., Box 1157* ☎ *760/934–6330, 800/828–0371* 🌐 *www.alpenhof-lodge.com* 🛏 *54 rooms, 3 cabins* 🍽 *Breakfast.*

$$$ RESORT Fodor's Choice ★ 🏨 **Double Eagle Resort and Spa.** Lofty pines tower over this very fine spa retreat on the June Lake Loop. **Pros:** pretty setting; spectacular indoor pool; 1½ mile from June Mountain Ski Area. **Cons:** expensive; remote. [$] *Rooms from: $249* ✉ *5587 Hwy. 158, June Lake* ☎ *760/648–7004* 🌐 *www.doubleeagle.com* 🛏 *17 2-bedroom cabins, 16 rooms, 1 3-bedroom house* 🍽 *No meals.*

$$$ RESORT 🏨 **Juniper Springs Resort.** Tops for slope-side comfort, these condominium-style units have full kitchens and ski-in ski-out access to the mountain. **Pros:** bargain during summer; direct access to the slopes; good views. **Cons:** no nightlife within walking distance; no air-conditioning. [$] *Rooms from: $199* ✉ *4000 Meridian Blvd.* ☎ *760/924–1102, 800/626–6684* 🌐 *www.juniperspringsmammoth.com* 🛏 *10 studios, 99 1-bedrooms, 92 2-bedrooms, 3 3-bedrooms* 🍽 *No meals.*

$$ RESORT 🏨 **Mammoth Mountain Inn.** If you want to be within walking distance of the Mammoth Mountain Main Lodge, this is the place. **Pros:** great location; big rooms; a traditional place to stay. **Cons:** can be crowded in ski season. [$] *Rooms from: $134* ✉ *1 Minaret Rd.* ☎ *760/934–2581, 800/626–6684* 🌐 *www.themammothmountaininn.com* 🛏 *124 rooms, 91 condos* 🍽 *No meals.*

$$$ RESORT 🏨 **Sierra Nevada Resort & Spa.** A full-service resort in the heart of Old Mammoth, the Sierra Nevada has it all: three restaurants, four bars, a dedicated spa facility, on-site ski and snowboard rentals, a pool and Jacuzzi, miniature golf, and room and suite options in three buildings. **Pros:** many on-site amenities; walk to restaurants on property or downtown; complimentary shuttle service. **Cons:** must drive or ride a bus or shuttle to the slopes; thin walls in older rooms. [$] *Rooms from: $189* ✉ *164 Old Mammoth Rd.* ☎ *760/934–2515, 800/824–5132* 📠 *760/934–7319* 🌐 *thesierranevadaresort.com* 🛏 *143 rooms, 6 townhomes* 🍽 *No meals.*

$$$ RESORT Fodor's Choice ★ 🏨 **Tamarack Lodge Resort & Lakefront Restaurant.** On the edge of the John Muir Wilderness Area, where cross-country ski trails lace the woods, this 1924 lodge looks like something out of a snow globe. **Pros:** rustic; eco-sensitive; many nearby outdoor activities. **Cons:** pricey; shared

10

bathrooms for some main lodge rooms. Ⓢ *Rooms from: $239* ✉ *Lake Mary Rd., off Hwy. 203* ☎ *760/934–2442, 800/626–6684* ⊕ *www. tamaracklodge.com* ⤳ *11 rooms, 35 cabins* ⦿ *No meals.*

$$$
RESORT

☷ **The Village Lodge.** With their exposed timbers and peaked roofs, these four-story condo buildings at the epicenter of Mammoth's dining and nightlife scene pay homage to Alpine style. **Pros:** central location; clean; big rooms; good restaurants nearby. **Cons:** pricey; can be noisy outside. Ⓢ *Rooms from: $239* ✉ *1111 Forest Trail* ☎ *760/934–1982, 800/626–6684* ⊕ *www.thevillagelodgemammoth.com* ⤳ *277 units* ⦿ *No meals.*

$$$$
RESORT

☷ **Westin Monache Resort.** On a hill just steps from the Village at Mammoth, the Westin provides full-service comfort and amenities close to restaurants, entertainment, and free public transportation. **Pros:** upscale amenities; prime location; free gondola to the slopes is across the street. **Cons:** long, steep stairway down to village; added resort fee. Ⓢ *Rooms from: $349* ✉ *50 Hillside Dr.* ☎ *760/934–0400, 888/627–8154 reservations* ⊕ *www.westinmammoth.com* ⤳ *109 rooms, 121 suites* ⦿ *No meals.*

SPORTS AND THE OUTDOORS

BIKING

Mammoth Mountain Bike Park. The park opens when the snow melts, usually by July, and has 100-plus miles of single-track trails—from mellow to super-challenging. Chairlifts and shuttles provide trail access, and rentals are available. ✉ *Mammoth Mountain Ski Area* ☎ *760/934–0677, 800/626–6684* ⊕ *www.mammothmountain.com* ✉ *$49 day pass.*

FISHING

The fishing season runs from the last Saturday in April until the end of October. Crowley Lake is the top trout-fishing spot in the area; Convict Lake, June Lake, and the lakes of the Mammoth Basin are other prime spots. One of the best trout rivers is the San Joaquin, near Devils Postpile. Hot Creek, a designated Wild Trout Stream, is renowned for fly-fishing (catch-and-release only).

Kittredge Sports. This outfit rents rods and reels and conducts guided trips. ✉ *3218 Main St., at Forest Trail* ☎ *760/934–7566* ⊕ *kittredgesports.com.*

Sierra Drifters Guide Service. To maximize your time on the water, get tips from local anglers, or better yet, book a guided fishing trip, contact Sierra Drifters. ☎ *760/935–4250* ⊕ *www.sierradrifters.com.*

HIKING

Hiking in Mammoth is stellar, especially along the trails that wind through alpine scenery around the Lakes Basin. Carry lots of water; and remember, the air is thin at 8,000-plus feet.

U.S. Forest Service Ranger Station. Stop at the ranger station, just east of the town of Mammoth Lakes, for an area trail map and permits for backpacking in wilderness areas. ✉ *2510 Main St., Hwy. 203* ☎ *760/924–5500* ⊕ *www.fs.usda.gov/main/inyo.*

HORSEBACK RIDING

Stables around Mammoth are typically open from June through September.

Mammoth Lakes Pack Outfit. This company runs day and overnight horseback trips and will shuttle you to the high country. ⊠ *Lake Mary Rd., between Twin Lakes and Lake Mary* ☎ *888/475–8747* ⊕ *www. mammothpack.com.*

McGee Creek Pack Station. These folks customize pack trips or will shuttle you to camp alone. ⊠ *2990 McGee Creek Rd., Crowley Lake* ☎ *760/935–4324 summer, 760/878–2207, 800/854–7407* ⊕ *www. mcgeecreekpackstation.com.*

SKIING

In winter, check the On the Snow website or call the Snow Report for information about Mammoth weather conditions.

FAMILY **June Mountain Ski Area.** Snowboarders especially dig June Mountain, a compact, low-key resort north of Mammoth Mountain. Three beginner-to-intermediate terrain areas—the Surprise Fun Zone, Mambo Playground, and Bucky's Adventure—are for both skiers and boarders. There's rarely a line for the lifts here: if you must ski on a weekend and want to avoid the crowds, this is the place to come, and in a storm it's better protected from wind and blowing snow than Mammoth is. (If it starts to storm, you can use your Mammoth ticket at June.) The services include a rental-and-repair shop, a ski school, and a sports shop. There's food, but the options are better at Mammoth. ■ TIP→ **Kids 12 and under ski and ride free.** ⊠ *3819 Hwy. 158/June Lake Loop, off U.S. 395, 22 miles northwest of Mammoth, June Lake* ☎ *760/648–7733, 888/586–3686* ⊕ *www.junemountain.com* 🎿 *From $72* 🎿 *35 trails on 1,400 acres, rated 35% beginner, 45% intermediate, 20% advanced. Longest run 2 miles, base 7,545 feet, summit 10,190 feet. Lifts: 7.*

Fodor's Choice **Mammoth Mountain Ski Area.** One of the West's largest and best ski areas, ★ Mammoth has more than 3,500 acres of skiable terrain and a 3,100-foot vertical drop. The views from the 11,053-foot summit are some of the most stunning in the Sierra. Below, you'll find a 6½-mile-wide swath of groomed boulevards and canyons, as well as pockets of tree-skiing and a dozen vast bowls. Snowboarders are everywhere on the slopes; there are three outstanding freestyle terrain parks of varying difficulty, with jumps, rails, tabletops, and giant super pipes—this is the location of several international snowboarding competitions, and, in summer, mountain-bike meets. Mammoth's season begins in November and often lingers into May. Lessons and equipment are available, and there's a children's ski and snowboard school. Mammoth runs free shuttle-bus routes around town and to the ski area, and the Village Gondola runs from the Village complex to Canyon Lodge. However, only overnight guests are allowed to park at the Village for more than a few hours. ⚠ **The main lodge is dark and dated, unsuited in almost every way for the crush of ski season.** ⊠ *Minaret Rd., west of Mammoth Lakes* ☎ *760/934–2571, 800/626–6684, 760/934–0687 shuttle* ⊕ *www.mammothmountain.com* 🎿 *From $95* 🎿 *150 trails on 3,500 acres, rated 25% beginner, 40% intermediate, 20% advanced, 15%*

10

expert. Longest run 3 miles, base 7,953 feet, summit 11,053 feet. Lifts: 28, including 11 high-speed and 3 gondolas.

Tamarack Cross Country Ski Center. Trails at the center, adjacent to Tamarack Lodge, meander around several lakes. Rentals are available. ✉ *Lake Mary Rd., off Hwy. 203* ☎ *760/934–5293, 760/934–2442* ⊕ *tamaracklodge.com* ✉ *$56 all-inclusive day rate.*

SKI RENTALS AND RESOURCES

Fodor's Choice
★

Black Tie Ski Rentals. Skiers and snowboarders love this rental outfit whose staffers will deliver and custom-fit equipment for free. They also offer slope-side assistance. ☎ *760/934–7009* ⊕ *mammothskis.com.*

Footloose. When the U.S. Ski Team visits Mammoth and needs boot adjustments, everyone heads to Footloose, the best place in town—and possibly all California—for ski-boot rentals and sales, as well as custom insoles. ✉ *3043 Main St., at Mammoth Rd.* ☎ *760/934–2400* ⊕ *www. footloosesports.com.*

Kittredge Sports. Advanced skiers should consider this outfit, which has been around since the 1960s. ✉ *3218 Main St.* ☎ *760/934–7566* ⊕ *kittredgesports.com.*

Mammoth Sporting Goods. This company rents good skis for intermediates and sells equipment, clothing, and accessories. ✉ *452 Old Mammoth Rd.* ☎ *760/934–3239* ⊕ *www.mammothoutdoorsports.com.*

OntheSnow.com ⊕ *www.onthesnow.com/california/mammoth-mountain-ski-area/ski-resort.html.*

Snow Report. For information on winter conditions around Mammoth, call the Snow Report. ☎ *760/934–7669, 888/766–9778.*

EAST OF YOSEMITE NATIONAL PARK

Most people enter Yosemite National Park from the west, having driven out from the Bay Area or Los Angeles. The eastern entrance on Tioga Pass Road (Highway 120), however, provides stunning, sweeping views of the High Sierra. Gray rocks shine in the bright sun, with scattered, small vegetation sprinkled about the mountainside. To drive from Lee Vining to Tuolumne Meadows is an unforgettable experience, but keep in mind that the road tends to be closed for at least seven months of the year.

LEE VINING

20 miles east of Tuolumne Meadows, 30 miles north of Mammoth Lakes.

Tiny Lee Vining is known primarily as the eastern gateway to Yosemite National Park (summer only) and the location of vast and desolate Mono Lake. Pick up supplies at the general store year-round, or stop here for lunch or dinner before or after a drive through the high country. In winter the town is all but deserted, except for the ice climbers who come to scale frozen waterfalls.

GETTING HERE AND AROUND

Lee Vining is on U.S. 395, north of the road's intersection with Highway 120 and on the south side of Mono Lake. In summer YARTS public transit can get you here from Yosemite Valley, but you'll need a car to explore the area.

ESSENTIALS

Visitor Information Lee Vining Chamber of Commerce ☎ *760/647-6629* 🌐 *www.leevining.com.* **Mono Basin National Forest Scenic Area Visitor Center** ✉ *Visitor Center Dr., off U.S. 395, 1 mile north of Hwy. 120* ☎ *760/647-3044* 🌐 *www.monolake.org/visit/vc* 🕒 *Mid-May–mid-Oct., daily 8–5; early Apr.–mid-May and mid-Oct.–Nov., Thurs.–Mon. 9–4:30.*

EXPLORING

Fodor's Choice ★ **Mono Lake.** Since the 1940s Los Angeles has diverted water from this lake, exposing striking towers of tufa, or calcium carbonate. Court victories by environmentalists have meant fewer diversions, and the lake is rising again. Although to see the lake from U.S. 395 is stunning, make time to visit South Tufa, whose parking lot is 5 miles east of U.S. 395 off Highway 120. There in summer you can join the naturalist-guided **South Tufa Walk,** which lasts about 90 minutes. The **Scenic Area Visitor Center,** off U.S. 395, is a sensational stop for its interactive exhibits and sweeping Mono Lake views. In town at U.S. 395 and 3rd Street, the **Mono Lake Committee Information Center & Bookstore,** open from 9 to 5 daily, has more information about this beautiful area. ✉ *Hwy. 120, east of Lee Vining, Lee Vining* ☎ *760/647–3044 visitor center, 760/647–6595 info center* 🌐 *www.monolake.org* 🎟 *Free* 🕒 *Visitor center early Apr.–Nov., daily 8–5; hrs vary at other times .*

EN ROUTE **June Lake Loop.** Heading south from Lee Vining, U.S. 395 intersects the June Lake Loop. This gorgeous 17-mile drive follows an old glacial canyon past Grant, June, Gull, and other lakes before reconnecting with U.S. 395 on its way to Mammoth Lakes. ■ **TIP→ The loop is especially colorful in fall.** ✉ *Hwy. 158 W.*

WHERE TO EAT AND STAY

$$ AMERICAN 🍴 **Tioga Gas Mart & Whoa Nelli Deli.** This might be the only gas station in the United States serving craft beers and lobster taquitos, but its appeal goes beyond novelty. Succulent fish tacos with mango salsa and barbecued ribs with a huckleberry glaze are among the many well-executed dishes. ■ **TIP→ Order at the counter and grab a seat inside, or sit at one of the picnic tables on the lawn outside and take in the distant view of Mono Lake.** [$] *Average main: $16* ✉ *Hwy. 120 and U.S. 395* ☎ *760/647–1088* 🌐 *www.whoanelliedeli.com* 🕒 *Closed early Nov.–late Apr.*

$ B&B/INN 🏨 **Lake View Lodge.** Enormous rooms and landscaping that includes several shaded sitting areas set this motel apart from its competitors in town. **Pros:** attractive; peaceful; clean; friendly staff. **Cons:** could use updating. [$] *Rooms from: $109* ✉ *51285 U.S. 395* ☎ *760/647–6543, 800/990–6614* 🌐 *www.lakeviewlodgeyosemite.com* 🛏 *76 rooms, 12 cottages* 🍽 *No meals.*

BODIE STATE HISTORIC PARK

31 miles northeast of Lee Vining.

The town of Bridgeport is the gateway to Bodie State Historic Park, and the only supply center for miles around. The scenery is spectacular, with craggy, snowcapped peaks looming over vast prairies. Bridgeport's claim to fame is that most of the 1947 film-noir classic *Out of the Past,* starring Robert Mitchum in his prime as a private eye whose past catches up with him, was filmed here. In winter, much of Bridgeport shuts down.

GETTING HERE AND AROUND

A car is the best way to reach this area. Bodie is on Highway 270 about 13 miles east of U.S. 395.

EXPLORING

Fodor's Choice **Bodie Ghost Town.** The mining village of Rattlesnake Gulch, abandoned
★ mine shafts, and the remains of a small Chinatown are among the sights at this fascinating ghost town. The town boomed from about 1878 to 1881, but by the late 1940s all its residents had departed. A state park was established here in 1962, with a mandate to preserve everything in a state of "arrested decay." Evidence of Bodie's wild past survives at an excellent museum, and you can tour an old stamp mill where ore was crushed into fine powder to extract gold and silver. Bodie lies 13 miles east of U.S. 395 off Highway 270. The last 3 miles are unpaved, and snow may close the highway from late fall through early spring. ■ TIP→ No food, drink, or lodging is available in Bodie. ⊠ *Bodie Rd., off Hwy. 270* ☎ *760/647–6445* ⊕ *www.parks.ca.gov/bodie* ☑ *$5* ⊗ *Mid-Apr.–Oct., daily 9–6; Nov.–mid-Apr., daily 9–4.*

SOUTH OF SEQUOIA AND KINGS CANYON

Numerous towns and cities tout themselves as "gateways" to Sequoia and Kings Canyon national parks, but one that merits the distinction is frisky Three Rivers, a foothills hamlet along the Kaweah River.

THREE RIVERS

7 miles south of Sequoia National Park's Foothills Visitor Center.

Close to Sequoia National Park's Ash Mountain and Lookout Point entrances, Three Rivers is a good spot to find a room when park lodgings are full. Either because residents here appreciate their idyllic setting or because they know that tourists are their bread and butter, you'll find them eager to share tips about the best spots for "Sierra surfing" the Kaweah's smooth, moss-covered rocks or where to find the best cell-phone reception (it's off to the cemetery for Verizon customers).

GETTING HERE AND AROUND

Driving is the easiest way to get to and around Three Rivers, which straddles a long stretch of Highway 198. In summer the Sequoia Shuttle connects Three Rivers to Visalia and Sequoia National Park.

BUS CONTACTS

Sequoia Shuttle ☎ *877/287–4453* ⊕ *www.sequoiashuttle.com* ☑ *$15 round-trip* ⊗ *Late May–early Sept.*

WHERE TO EAT AND STAY

$ CAFÉ **Antoinette's Coffee and Goodies.** For smoothies, well-crafted espresso drinks, and pumpkin chocolate-chip muffins and other homemade baked goods, stop for a spell at this convivial coffee shop next door to Sierra Subs and Salads. **TIP→ There's Wi-Fi here, too.** *Average main: $6 41727 Sierra Dr., Three Rivers 559/561–2253 www.antoinettescoffeeandgoodies.com Reservations not accepted Closed Tues. No dinner.*

$$$ AMERICAN **Gateway Restaurant and Lodge.** The view's the draw at this roadhouse that overlooks the Kaweah River as it plunges out of the high country. The Gateway serves everything from osso buco to shrimp in Thai chili sauce. Some menu items are pricey, but you can also order a pizza or a beef or salmon burger. For the best results, stick to the simpler preparations. Dinner reservations are essential on summer weekends. *Average main: $29 45978 Sierra Dr., Three Rivers 559/561–4133 www.gateway-sequoia.com.*

$ AMERICAN **Sierra Subs and Salads.** This well-run sandwichery satisfies carnivores and vegetarians alike with crispy-fresh ingredients prepared with panache. Depending on your preference, the centerpiece of the Bull's Eye sandwich, for instance, will be roast beef or a Portobello mushroom, but whichever you choose, the accompanying flavors—of ciabatta bread, horseradish-and-garlic mayonnaise, roasted red peppers, Havarti cheese, and spinach—will delight your palate. *Average main: $8 41717 Sierra Dr., Three Rivers 559/561–4810 www.sierrasubsandsalads.com Closed Mon. No dinner.*

$$ B&B/INN **Buckeye Tree Lodge.** Every room at this two-story motel has a patio facing a sun-dappled grassy lawn, right on the banks of the Kaweah River. **Pros:** near the park entrance; fantastic river views; friendly staff; kitchenette in some rooms. **Cons:** can fill up quickly in the summer; could use a little updating. *Rooms from: $139 46000 Sierra Dr., Hwy. 198, Three Rivers 559/561–5900 www.buckeyetree.com 11 rooms Breakfast 2-night minimum on summer weekends.*

$$ B&B/INN Fodor's Choice ★ **Rio Sierra Riverhouse.** Guests at Rio Sierra come for the river views, the sandy beach, and the proximity to Sequoia National Park (6 miles away), but invariably end up raving as much about the warm yet laid-back hospitality of proprietress Mars Roberts as they do about location. **Pros:** seductive beach; winning hostess; river views from all rooms; contemporary ambience; full kitchen in one room, kitchenette in another. **Cons:** books up quickly in summer; some road noise audible in rooms. *Rooms from: $170 41997 Sierra Dr., Hwy. 198, Three Rivers 559/561–4720 www.rio-sierra.com 5 rooms Closed Jan. No meals 2-night minimum stay on summer weekends.*

SPORTS AND THE OUTDOORS

RAFTING

Kaweah White Water Adventures. Kaweah's trips include a two-hour excursion (good for families) through Class III rapids, a longer paddle through Class IV rapids, and an extended trip (typically Class IV and V rapids). *40443 Sierra Dr. 559/740–8251, 800/229–8658 www.kaweah-whitewater.com $50–$140 per person.*

YOSEMITE
NATIONAL PARK

WELCOME TO YOSEMITE NATIONAL PARK

TOP REASONS TO GO

★ **Wet and wild:** An easy stroll brings you to the base of Lower Yosemite Falls, where roaring springtime waters make for misty lens caps and lasting memories.

★ **Tunnel vision:** Approaching Yosemite Valley, Wawona Road passes through a mountainside and emerges before one of the park's most heart-stopping vistas.

★ **Inhale the beauty:** Pause to smell the light, pristine air as you travel about the High Sierra's Tioga Pass and Tuolumne Meadows, where 10,000-foot granite peaks just might take your breath away.

★ **Walk away:** Leave the crowds behind—but do bring along a buddy—and take a hike somewhere along Yosemite's 800 miles of trails.

★ **Powder your nose:** Winter's hush floats into Yosemite on snowflakes. Lift your face to the sky and listen to the trees.

1 Yosemite Valley. At an elevation of 4,000 feet, in roughly the center of the park, beats Yosemite's heart. This is where you'll find the park's most famous sights and biggest crowds.

2 Wawona and Mariposa Grove. The park's southern tip holds Wawona, with its grand old hotel and pioneer history center, and the Mariposa Grove of Big Trees, filled with giant sequoias. These are closest to the South Entrance, 35 miles (a one-hour drive) south of Yosemite Village.

3 Tuolumne Meadows. The highlight of east-central Yosemite is this wildflower-strewn valley with hiking trails, nestled among sharp, rocky peaks. It's a 1½-hour drive northeast of Yosemite Valley along Tioga Road (closed mid-October through late May).

4 Hetch Hetchy. The most remote, least visited part of Yosemite accessible by automobile, this glacial valley is dominated by a reservoir and veined with wilderness trails. It's near the park's western boundary, about a half-hour drive north of the Big Oak Flat Entrance.

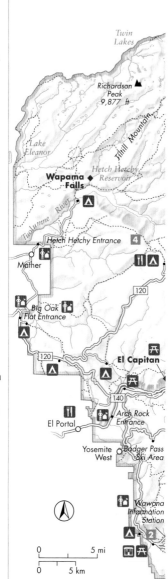

11

CALIFORNIA

GETTING ORIENTED

Yosemite is so large that you can think of it as five parks. Yosemite Valley, famous for waterfalls and cliffs, and Wawona, where the giant sequoias stand, are open all year. Hetch Hetchy, home of less-used backcountry trails, is most accessible from late spring through early fall. The subalpine high country, Tuolumne Meadows, is open for summer hiking and camping; in winter it's accessible via cross-country skis or snowshoes. Badger Pass Ski Area is open in winter only. Most visitors spend their time along the park's southwestern border, between Wawona and Big Oak Flat Entrance; a bit farther east in Yosemite Valley and Badger Pass Ski Area; and along the east–west corridor of Tioga Road, which spans the park north of Yosemite Valley and bisects Tuolumne Meadows.

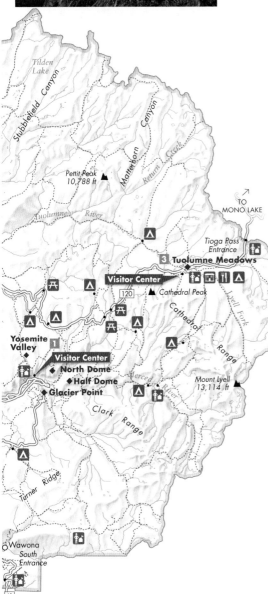

Updated by
Steve Pastorino

By merely standing in Yosemite Valley and turning in a circle, you can see more natural wonders in a minute than you could in a full day pretty much anywhere else. Half Dome, Yosemite Falls, El Capitan, Bridalveil Fall, Sentinel Dome, the Merced River, white-flowering dogwood trees, maybe even bears ripping into the bark of fallen trees or sticking their snouts into beehives—it's all in Yosemite Valley.

In the mid-1800s, when tourists were arriving to the area, the valley's special geologic qualities and the giant sequoias of Mariposa Grove 30 miles to the south so impressed a group of influential Californians that they persuaded President Abraham Lincoln to grant those two areas to the state for protection. On October 1, 1890—thanks largely to lobbying efforts by naturalist John Muir and Robert Underwood Johnson, the editor of *Century Magazine*—Congress set aside 1,500 square miles for Yosemite National Park.

YOSEMITE PLANNER

WHEN TO GO

During extremely busy periods—such as July 4—you will experience delays at the entrance gates. For smaller crowds, visit midweek. Or come mid-April through Memorial Day or mid-September through October, when the park is a bit less busy and the days usually are sunny and clear.

Summer rainfall is rare. In winter heavy snows occasionally cause road closures, and tire chains or four-wheel drive may be required on the roads that remain open. The road to Glacier Point beyond the turnoff for Badger Pass is closed after the first major snowfall; Tioga Road is closed from late October through May or mid-June. Mariposa Grove Road is typically closed for a shorter period in winter.

GETTING HERE AND AROUND
BUS TRAVEL

Once you're in Yosemite you can take advantage of the free shuttle buses, which operate on low emissions, have 21 stops, and run from 7 am to 10 pm year-round. Buses run about every 10 minutes in summer, a bit less frequently in winter. A separate (but also free) summer-only shuttle runs out to El Capitan. Also in summer, you can pay to take the morning "hikers' bus" from Yosemite Valley to Tuolumne or the bus up to Glacier Point. Bus service from Wawona is geared to people who are staying there and want to spend the day in Yosemite Valley. Free and frequent shuttles transport people between the Wawona Hotel and Mariposa Grove. During the snow season, buses run regularly between Yosemite Valley and Badger Pass Ski Area.

CAR TRAVEL

Roughly 200 miles from San Francisco, 300 miles from Los Angeles, and 500 miles from Las Vegas, Yosemite takes a while to reach—and its many sites and attractions merit much more time than what rangers say is the average visit: four hours. Most people arrive via automobile or tour bus, but public transportation (courtesy of Amtrak and the regional YARTS bus system) also can get you to the valley efficiently.

Of the park's four entrances, Arch Rock is the closest to Yosemite Valley. The road that goes through it, Route 140 from Merced and Mariposa, is a scenic western approach that snakes alongside the boulder-packed Merced River. Route 41, through Wawona, is the way to come from Los Angeles (or Fresno, if you've flown in and rented a car). Route 120, through Crane Flat, is the most direct route from San Francisco. The only way in from the east is Tioga Road, which may be the best route in terms of scenery—though due to snow accumulation it's open for a frustratingly short amount of time each year (typically early June through mid-October).

There are few gas stations within Yosemite (Crane Flat, Tuolumne Meadows, and Wawona; none in the valley), so fuel up before you reach the park. From late fall until early spring, the weather is especially unpredictable, and driving can be treacherous. You should carry chains.

PARK ESSENTIALS
PARK FEES AND PERMITS

The admission fee, valid for seven days, is $30 per vehicle (April through October), $25 during the off-season (November through March), or $10 per individual.

If you plan to camp in the backcountry or climb Half Dome, you must have a wilderness permit. Availability of permits depends upon trailhead quotas. It's best to make a reservation, especially if you will be visiting May through September. You can reserve two days to 24 weeks in advance by phone, mail, or fax (⌂ *Box 545, Yosemite, CA 95389* ☎ *209/372–0740* 🖷 *209/372–0739*); you'll pay $5 per person plus $5 per reservation if and when your reservation is confirmed. Requests must include your name, address, daytime phone, the number of people in your party, trip date, alternative dates, starting and ending trailheads, and a brief itinerary. Without a reservation, you may still get a free permit on a first-come, first-served basis at wilderness permit offices at Big Oak Flat, Hetch Hetchy, Tuolumne Meadows, Wawona, the Wilderness Center in Yosemite Village, and Yosemite Valley in summer. From fall to spring, visit the Valley Visitor Center.

PARK HOURS
The park is open 24/7 year-round. All entrances are open at all hours, except for Hetch Hetchy Entrance, which is open roughly dawn to dusk.

PRICES

WHAT IT COSTS			
$	$$	$$$	$$$$
Restaurants	under $12	$12–$20	$21–$30	over $30
Hotels	under $100	$100–$150	$151–$200	over $200

Restaurant prices are the average cost of a main course at dinner or, if dinner is not served, at lunch. Hotel prices are the lowest cost of a standard double room in high season, excluding taxes and service charges.

TOURS

Fodor's Choice ★ **Ansel Adams Photo Walks.** Photography enthusiasts shouldn't miss these 90-minute guided camera walks offered four mornings (Mon., Tues., Thurs., and Sat.) each week by professional photographers. All are free, but participation is limited to 15 people. Meeting points vary, and advance reservations are essential. ☎ 209/372–4413 ⊕ www.ansel adams.com ⌲ Free.

FAMILY **Wee Wild Ones.** Designed for kids under 7, this 45-minute program includes animal-theme games, songs, stories, and crafts. The event is held outdoors before the regular Yosemite Lodge or Curry Village evening programs in summer and fall; it moves to the Ahwahnee's big fireplace in winter and spring. All children must be accompanied by an adult. ☎ 209/372–8243 ⊕ www.yosemitepark.com ⌲ Free.

VISITOR INFORMATION

PARK CONTACT INFORMATION
Yosemite National Park ☎ 209/372–0200 ⊕ www.nps.gov/yose.

VISITOR CENTERS
Le Conte Memorial Lodge. This small but striking National Historic Landmark, with its granite walls and steeply pitched shingle roof, is Yosemite's first permanent public information center. Step inside to see the cathedral-like interior, which contains a library and environmental exhibits. To find out about evening programs, check the kiosk out front. ✉ Southside Dr., about ½ mile west of Curry Village ⊕ vault.sierraclub. org/education/leconte ☉ May–Sept., Wed.–Sun. 10–4.

Valley Visitor Center. Learn about Yosemite Valley's geology, vegetation, and human inhabitants at this visitor center, which is also staffed with helpful rangers and contains a bookstore with a wide selection of books and maps. Two films, including one by Ken Burns, alternate on the half-hour in the theater behind the visitor center. ✉ Yosemite Village ☎ 209/372–0200 ⊕ www.nps.gov/yose ☉ Late May–early Sept., daily 9–7; early Sept.–late May, daily 9–5.

11

CLOSE UP

Plants and Wildlife in Yosemite

Dense stands of incense cedar and Douglas fir—as well as ponderosa, Jeffrey, lodgepole, and sugar pines—cover much of the park, but the stellar standout, quite literally, is the *Sequoiadendron giganteum*, the giant sequoia. Sequoias grow only along the west slope of the Sierra Nevada between 4,500 and 7,000 feet in elevation. Starting from a seed the size of a rolled-oat flake, each of these ancient monuments assumes remarkable proportions in adulthood. In late May the valley's dogwood trees bloom with white, starlike flowers. Wildflowers, such as black-eyed Susan, bull thistle, cow parsnip, lupine, and meadow goldenrod, peak in June in the valley and in July at higher elevations.

The most visible animals in the park—aside from the omnipresent western gray squirrels, which fearlessly attempt to steal your food at every campground and picnic site—are

the mule deer. Though sightings of bighorn sheep are infrequent in the park itself, you can sometimes see them on the eastern side of the Sierra Crest, just off Route 120 in Lee Vining Canyon. You may also see the American black bear, which often has a brown, cinnamon, or blond coat. The Sierra Nevada is home to thousands of bears, and you should take all necessary precautions to keep yourself—and the bears—safe. Bears that acquire a taste for human food can become very aggressive and destructive, and often must be destroyed by rangers, so store all your food and even scented toiletries in the bear lockers located at many campgrounds and trailheads, or use bear-resistant canisters if you'll be hiking in the backcountry.

Watch for the blue Steller's jay along trails, near public buildings, and in campgrounds, and look for golden eagles soaring over Tioga Road.

EXPLORING

HISTORIC SITES

Ahwahneechee Village. This solemn smattering of structures, accessed by a short loop trail behind the Yosemite Valley Visitor Center, is a look at what Native American life might have been like in the 1870s. One interpretive sign points out that the Miwok people referred to the 19th-century newcomers as "Yohemite" and "Yohometuk," which have been translated as meaning "some of them are killers." ⊠ *Northside Dr., Yosemite Village* ⊒ *Free* ☉ *Daily sunrise–sunset.*

Pioneer Yosemite History Center. Some of Yosemite's first structures—those not occupied by Native Americans, that is—were relocated here in the 1950s and 1960s. You can spend a pleasurable and informative half-hour walking about them and reading the signs, perhaps springing for a self-guided-tour pamphlet (50¢) to further enhance the history lesson. Weekends and some weekdays in the summer, costumed docents conduct free blacksmithing and "wet-plate" photography demonstrations, and for a small fee you can take a stagecoach ride. ⊠ *Rte. 41, Wawona*

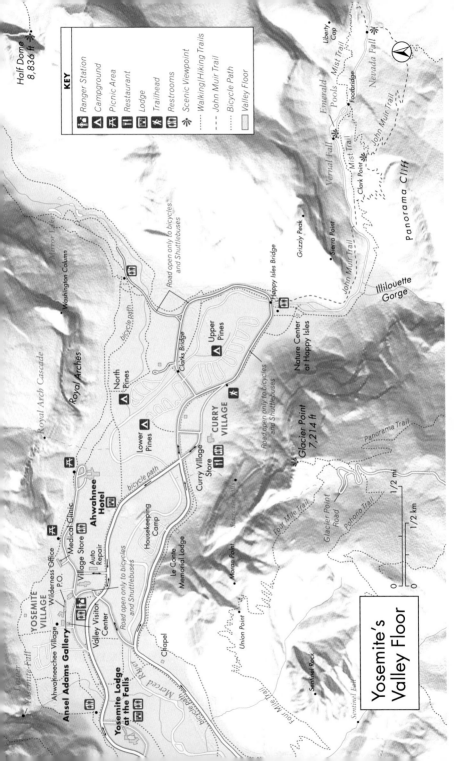

Yosemite's Valley Floor

Half Dome
8,836 ft

KEY

Ranger Station	
Campground	
Picnic Area	
Restaurant	
Lodge	
Trailhead	
Restrooms	
Scenic Viewpoint	
Walking/Hiking Trails	---
John Muir Trail	---
Bicycle Path	⋯
Valley Floor	

Liberty Cap

Emerald Pools

Vernal Fall

Nevada Fall

Footbridge

Mist Trail

Mist Trail

John Muir Trail

Clark Point

John Muir Trail

Panorama Cliff

Grizzly Peak

Sierra Point

Illilouette Gorge

Road open only to bicycles and shuttlebuses

Happy Isles Bridge

Upper Pines

Clarks Bridge

Nature Center at Happy Isles

North Pines

Royal Arches

Washington Column

Royal Arch Cascade

bicycle path

Lower Pines

Road open only to bicycles and shuttlebuses

Glacier Point
7,214 ft

CURRY VILLAGE

Curry Village Store

Panorama Trail

Ahwahnee Hotel

Medical Clinic

bicycle path

Housekeeping Camp

le Conte Memorial Lodge

Vernal Falls

Moran Point

Four Mile Trail

Glacier Point Road

Panono Trail

YOSEMITE VILLAGE

Ansel Adams Gallery

Ahwahneechee Village

Wilderness Office

P.O.

Village Store

Auto Repair

Valley Visitor Center

Road open only to bicycles and Shuttlebuses

Chapel

Union Point

Sentinel Rock

Sentinel Fall

Four Mile Trail

Yosemite Lodge at the Falls

Merced River

bicycle path

Yosemite Fall

Lower

1/2 mi

1/2 km

0

☎ *209/375–9531* ✆ *Free* ☉ *Building interiors are open mid-June–Labor Day, Wed. 2–5, Thurs.–Sun. 10–1 and 2–5.*

SCENIC STOPS

El Capitan. Rising 3,593 feet—more than 350 stories—above the valley, El Capitan is the largest exposed-granite monolith in the world. Since 1958, people have been climbing its entire face, including the famous "nose." You can spot adventurers with your binoculars by scanning the smooth and nearly vertical cliff for specks of color. ⊠ *Off Northside Dr., about 4 miles west of the Valley Visitor Center.*

Fodor's Choice ★ **Glacier Point.** If you lack the time, desire, or stamina to hike more than 3,200 feet up to Glacier Point from the Yosemite Valley floor, you can drive here—or take a bus from the valley—for a bird's-eye view. You are likely to encounter a lot of day-trippers on the short, paved trail that leads from the parking lot to the main overlook. Take a moment to veer off a few yards to the Geology Hut, which succinctly explains and illustrates what the valley looked like 10 million, 3 million, and 20,000 years ago. ⊠ *Glacier Point Rd., 16 miles northeast of Rte. 41* ☎ *209/372–0200* ☉ *Late May–late Oct.*

Fodor's Choice ★ **Half Dome.** Visitors' eyes are continually drawn to this remarkable granite formation that tops out at more than 4,700 feet above the valley floor. Despite its name, the dome is actually about three-quarters intact. You can hike to the top of Half Dome on an 8.5-mile (one-way) trail whose last 400 feet must be ascended while holding onto a steel cable. Permits are required (and checked on the trail), and available only by lottery. Call ☎ *209/372–0826* or visit ⊕ *www.recreation.gov* well in advance of your trip for details. Back down in the valley, see Half Dome reflected in the Merced River by heading to Sentinel Bridge just before sundown. The brilliant orange light on Half Dome is a stunning sight. ⊕ *www.nps.gov/yose/planyourvisit/halfdome.htm.*

Hetch Hetchy Reservoir. When Congress approved the O'Shaughnessy Dam in 1913, pragmatism triumphed over aestheticism. Some 2.5 million residents of the San Francisco Bay Area continue to get their water from this 117-billion-gallon reservoir. Although spirited efforts are being made to restore the Hetch Hetchy Valley to its former, pristine glory, three-quarters of San Francisco voters in 2012 ultimately opposed a measure to even consider draining the reservoir. Eight miles long, the reservoir is Yosemite's largest body of water, and one that can be seen up close from several trails. ⊠ *Hetch Hetchy Rd., about 15 miles north of the Big Oak Flat entrance station.*

Mariposa Grove of Big Trees. Mariposa Grove is closed until Spring 2017 for a restoration project. Check their website for details on the closure. Of Yosemite's three sequoia groves—the others being Merced and Tuolumne, both near Crane Flat well to the north—Mariposa is by far the largest and easiest to walk around. Grizzly Giant, whose base measures 96 feet around, has been estimated to be one of the largest in the world. Perhaps more astoundingly, it's about 1,800 years old. Up the hill, you'll find more sequoias, a small museum, and fewer people. Summer weekends are usually crowded here.

"This is us taking a break before conquering the top of Lembert Dome, while enjoying the beautiful view over Yosemite's high country." —photo by Rebalyn, Fodors.com member

Please note that due to major reconstruction the lower grove, which includes Grizzly Giant, Fallen Monarch, and the California Tunnel Tree, will be closed through November 2016. The upper grove may be open intermittently during this time. Shuttle service from Wawona will not be available in 2016. ■TIP→ Check the Yosemite website before visiting this area in 2016 or 2017. ⊠ *Rte. 41, 2 miles north of the South Entrance station* ⊕ *www.nps.gov/yose/planyourvisit/mariposa grove.htm.*

Tuolumne Meadows. The largest subalpine meadow in the Sierra (at 8,600 feet) is a popular way station for backpack trips along the Pacific Crest and John Muir trails. The setting is not as dramatic as Yosemite Valley, 56 miles away, but the almost perfectly flat basin, about 2½ miles long, is intriguing, and in July it's resplendent with wildflowers. The most popular day hike is up Lembert Dome, atop which you'll have breathtaking views of the basin below. Keep in mind that Tioga Road rarely opens before June and usually closes by mid-October. ⊠ *Tioga Rd. (Rte. 120), about 8 miles west of the Tioga Pass entrance station.*

WATERFALLS

Yosemite's waterfalls are at their most spectacular in May and June. When the snow starts to melt (usually peaking in May), streaming snowmelt spills down to meet the Merced River. By summer's end, particularly in recent drought years, some falls, including the mighty Yosemite Falls, trickle or dry up. Their flow may increase in late fall, and in winter they may be hung dramatically with ice. Even in drier months, the waterfalls can be breathtaking. If you choose to hike any

GOOD READS

■ *The Photographer's Guide to Yosemite,* by Michael Frye, is an insider's guide to the park, with maps for shutterbugs looking to capture perfect images.

■ John Muir penned his observations of the park he long advocated for in *The Yosemite.*

■ *Yosemite and the High Sierra,* edited by Andrea G. Stillman and John Szarkowski, features beautiful reproductions of landmark photographs by Ansel Adams,

accompanied by excerpts from the photographer's journals written when Adams traveled in Yosemite National Park in the early 20th century.

■ An insightful collection of essays accompanies the museum-quality artworks in *Yosemite: Art of an American Icon,* by Amy Scott.

■ Perfect for budding botanists, *Sierra Nevada Wildflowers,* by Karen Wiese, identifies more than 230 kinds of flora growing in the Sierra Nevada region.

of the trails to or up the falls, be sure to wear shoes with no-slip soles; the rocks can be extremely slick. Stay on trails at all times.

■ **TIP→** Visit the park during a full moon and you can stroll without a flashlight and still make out the ribbons of falling water, as well as silhouettes of the giant granite monoliths.

Bridalveil Fall. This 620-foot waterfall is often diverted dozens of feet one way or the other by the breeze. It is the first marvelous site you will see up-close when you drive into Yosemite Valley. ⊠ *Yosemite Valley, access from parking area off Wawona Rd.*

Nevada Fall. Climb Mist Trail from Happy Isles for an up-close view of this 594-foot cascading beauty. If you don't want to hike (the trail's final approach is quite taxing), you can see it—albeit distantly—from Glacier Point. ⚠ Stay safely on the trail, as there have been fatalities in recent years after visitors have fallen and been swept away by the water. ⊠ *Yosemite Valley, access via Mist Trail from Nature Center at Happy Isles.*

Ribbon Fall. At 1,612 feet, this is the highest single fall in North America. It's also the first waterfall to dry up in summer; the rainwater and melted snow that create the slender fall evaporate quickly at this height. Look just west of El Capitan for the best view of the fall from the base of Bridalveil Fall. ⊠ *Yosemite Valley, west of El Capitan Meadow.*

Vernal Fall. Fern-covered black rocks frame this 317-foot fall, and rainbows play in the spray at its base. You can get a distant view from Glacier Point, or hike to see it close up. You'll get wet, but the view is worth it. ⊠ *Yosemite Valley, access via Mist Trail from Nature Center at Happy Isles.*

Fodor's Choice ★ **Yosemite Falls.** Actually three falls, they together constitute the highest waterfall in North America and the fifth-highest in the world. The water from the top descends a total of 2,425 feet, and when the falls run hard, you can hear them thunder across the valley. If they dry up—that sometimes happens in late summer—the valley seems naked without the wavering tower of spray. ■TIP➔ If you hike the mile-long loop trail (partially paved) to the base of the Lower Falls in spring, prepare to get wet. You can get a good full-length view of the falls from the lawn of Yosemite Chapel, off Southside Drive. ⊠ *Yosemite Valley, access from Yosemite Lodge or trail parking area.*

EDUCATIONAL OFFERINGS

CLASSES AND SEMINARS

Art Classes. Professional artists conduct workshops in watercolor, etching, drawing, and other mediums. Bring your own materials or purchase the basics at the Art Activity Center, next to the Village Store. Children under 12 must be accompanied by an adult. ⊠ *Art Activity Center, Yosemite Village* ☎ *209/372–1442* ⊕ *www.yosemiteconservancy.org* ▨ *$10* ☯ *Early Apr.–early Oct., Mon.–Sat. 10–2.*

Yosemite Outdoor Adventures. Naturalists, scientists, and park rangers lead multi-hour to multiday educational outings on topics from woodpeckers to fire management to pastel painting. Most sessions take place spring through fall, but a few focus on winter phenomena. ☎ *209/379–2317* ⊕ *www.yosemiteconservancy.org* ▨ *From $99.*

RANGER PROGRAMS

Junior Ranger Program. Children ages 7 to 13 can participate in the informal, self-guided Junior Ranger program. A park activity handbook (about $4) is available at the Valley Visitor Center or the Nature Center at Happy Isles. Once kids complete the book, rangers present them with a certificate and a badge. ⊠ *Valley Visitor Center or the Nature Center at Happy Isles* ☎ *209/372–0299.*

Ranger-Led Programs. Rangers lead entertaining walks and give informative talks several times a day from spring to fall. The schedule is more limited in winter, but most days you can find a program somewhere in the park. In the evenings at Yosemite Lodge and Curry Village, lectures, slide shows, and documentary films present unique perspectives on Yosemite. On summer weekends, Camp Curry and Tuolumne Meadows Campground host sing-along campfire programs. Schedules and locations are posted on bulletin boards throughout the park as well as in the indispensable *Yosemite Guide*, which is distributed to visitors as they arrive at the park. ⊕ *www.yosemitepark.com.*

SPORTS AND THE OUTDOORS

BIKING

One enjoyable way to see Yosemite Valley is to ride a bike beneath its lofty granite monoliths. The eastern valley has 12 miles of paved, flat bicycle paths across meadows and through woods, with bike racks at convenient stopping points. For a greater challenge but at no small risk, you can ride on 196 miles of paved park roads—but bicycles are not allowed on hiking trails or in the backcountry. Kids under 18 must wear a helmet.

TOURS AND OUTFITTERS

Yosemite bike rentals. You can arrange for rentals from Yosemite Lodge and Curry Village bike stands. Bikes with child trailers, baby-jogger strollers, and wheelchairs are also available. The cost for bikes is $11.50 per hour, or $32 a day. ⊠ *Yosemite Lodge or Curry Village* ☎ *209/372– 1208* ⊕ *www.yosemitepark.com* ☉ *Apr.–Oct.*

BIRD-WATCHING

More than 250 bird species have been spotted in the park, including the sage sparrow, pygmy owl, blue grouse, and mountain bluebird. Park rangers lead free bird-watching walks in Yosemite Valley a few days each week in summer; check at a visitor center or information station for times and locations. Binoculars are sometimes available for loan.

HIKING

TOURS AND OUTFITTERS

Wilderness Center. This facility provides free wilderness permits, which are required for overnight camping (advance reservations are available for $5 per person plus $5 per reservation and are highly recommended for popular trailheads in summer and on weekends). The staff here also provides maps and advice to hikers heading into the backcountry, and rents bear-resistant canisters, which are required if you don't have your own. ⊠ *Between the Ansel Adams Gallery and the post office, Yosemite Village* ☎ *209/372–0308* ☉ *May–Oct., daily 8–5; permits at Valley Visitor's Center Nov.–Apr.*

Yosemite Mountaineering School and Guide Service. From April to November, you can learn to climb, hire a guide, or join a two-hour to full-day trek with Yosemite Mountaineering School. They also rent gear and lead backpacking and overnight excursions. Reservations are recommended. In winter, cross-country ski programs are available at Badger Pass. ⊠ *Yosemite Mountain Shop, Curry Village* ☎ *209/372–8344* ⊕ *yosemitemountaineering.com.*

EASY

Yosemite Falls Trail. This is the highest waterfall in North America. The upper fall (1,430 feet), the middle cascades (675 feet), and the lower fall (320 feet) combine for a total of 2,425 feet, and when viewed from the valley appear as a single waterfall. The ¼-mile trail leads from the parking lot to the base of the falls. Upper Yosemite Fall Trail, a strenuous 7.2-mile round-trip climb rising 2,700 feet, takes you above the top of the falls. Lower trail: *Easy.* Upper trail: *Difficult.* ⊠ *Trailhead off Camp 4, north of Northside Dr.*

MODERATE

Mist Trail. Except for Lower Yosemite Falls, more visitors take this trail (or portions of it) than any other in the park. The trek up to and back from Vernal Fall is 3 miles. Add another 4 miles total by continuing up to 594-foot Nevada Fall; the trail becomes quite steep and slippery in its final stages. The elevation gain to Vernal Fall is 1,000 feet, and to Nevada Fall an additional 1,000 feet. The Merced River tumbles down both falls on its way to a tranquil flow through the Valley. *Moderate.* ⊠ *Trailhead at Happy Isles.*

Fodor's Choice ★ **Panorama Trail.** Few hikes come with the visual punch that this 8½-mile trail provides. It starts from Glacier Point and descends to Yosemite Valley. The star attraction is Half Dome, visible from many intriguing angles, but you also see three waterfalls up close and walk through a manzanita grove. ⚠ **If you take the last bus from the valley floor to Glacier Point before starting your hike, you might run out of daylight before you finish.** *Moderate.* ⊠ *Trailhead at Glacier Point.*

DIFFICULT

Fodor's Choice ★ **John Muir Trail to Half Dome.** Ardent and courageous trekkers continue on from Nevada Fall to the top of Half Dome. Some hikers attempt this entire 10- to 12-hour, 16¾-mile round-trip trek in one day; if you're planning to do this, remember that the 4,800-foot elevation gain and the 8,842-foot altitude will cause shortness of breath. Another option is to hike to a campground in Little Yosemite Valley near the top of Nevada Fall the first day, then climb to the top of Half Dome and hike out the next day. Get your wilderness permit (required for a one-day hike to Half Dome, too) at least a month in advance. Be sure to wear hiking boots and bring gloves. The last pitch up the back of Half Dome is very steep—the only way to climb this sheer rock face is to pull yourself up using the steel cable handrails, which are in place only from late spring to early fall. Those who brave the ascent will be rewarded with an unbeatable view of Yosemite Valley below and the high country beyond. ⚠ **Only 300 hikers per day are allowed atop Half Dome, and they all must have permits, which are distributed by lottery, one in the spring before the season starts and another two days before the climb.** Contact www.recreation.gov for details. *Difficult.* ⊠ *Trailhead at Happy Isles* ⊕ *www.nps.gov/yose/planyourvisit/halfdome.htm.*

HORSEBACK RIDING

Reservations for guided trail rides must be made in advance at the hotel tour desks or by phone. Scenic trail rides range from two hours to a half day; four- and six-day High Sierra saddle trips are also available.

TOURS AND OUTFITTERS

Tuolumne Meadows Stables. Tuolumne Meadows Stables runs two- and four-hour trips that start at $65, as well as four- to six-day camping treks on mules that start at $1,000. Reservations are required at least one day in advance. ⊠ *Off Tioga Rd., 2 miles east of Tuolumne Meadows Visitor Center* ☎ *209/372–8427* ⊕ *www.yosemitepark.com.*

Wawona Stables. Two-hour rides at these stables start at $65, and half-day rides are $88.50. Reservations are recommended. ⊠ *Rte. 41, Wawona* ☎ *209/375–6502.*

Yosemite Valley Stables. You can tour the valley on two-hour and four-hour rides starting from the Yosemite Valley Stables. Reservations are strongly recommended for the trips, which start at $65. ⊠ *At entrance to North Pines Campground, 100 yards northeast of Curry Village* ☎ *209/372–8348* ⊕ *www.yosemitepark.com.*

RAFTING

Rafting is permitted only on designated areas of the Middle and South forks of the Merced River. Check with the Valley Visitor Center for closures and other restrictions.

OUTFITTERS

Curry Village raft stand. The per-person rental fee ($31) at Curry Village raft stand covers the four- to six-person raft, two paddles, and life jackets, plus a return shuttle at the end of your trip. ⊠ *South side of Southside Dr., Curry Village* ☎ *209/372–4386* ⊕ *www.yosemitepark. com* ⊠ *$31* ☺ *Late May–July.*

ROCK CLIMBING

Fodor's Choice ★   The granite canyon walls of Yosemite Valley are world-renowned for rock climbing. El Capitan, with its 3,593-foot vertical face, is the most famous, but there are many other options here for all skill levels.

TOURS AND OUTFITTERS

Yosemite Mountaineering School and Guide Service. The one-day basic lesson at Yosemite Mountaineering School and Guide Service includes some bouldering and rappelling, and three or four 60-foot climbs. Climbers must be at least 10 years old and in reasonably good physical condition. Intermediate and advanced classes include instruction in first aid, anchor building, multi-pitch climbing, summer snow climbing, and big-wall climbing. There's a nordic program in the winter. ⊠ *Yosemite Mountain Shop, Curry Village* ☎ *209/372–8344* ⊕ *www.yosemite mountaineering.com* ⊠ *From $148* ☺ *Apr.–Nov.*

WINTER SPORTS

ICE-SKATING

Curry Village Ice Rink. Winter visitors have skated at this outdoor rink for decades, and there's no mystery why: it's a kick to glide across the ice while soaking up views of Half Dome and Glacier Point. ⊠ *South side of Southside Dr., Curry Village* ☎ *209/372–8319* ⊠ *$10.50 per session, $4 skate rental* ☺ *Mid-Nov.–early Mar., hrs vary.*

SKIING AND SNOWSHOEING

Badger Pass Ski Area. California's first ski resort has five lifts and 10 downhill runs, as well as 90 miles of groomed cross-country trails. Free shuttle buses from Yosemite Valley operate between December and the end of March, weather permitting. Lessons, backcountry guiding, and cross-country tours are also available. You can rent downhill, telemark, and cross-country skis, plus snowshoes and snowboards. ⊠ *Badger Pass Rd., off Glacier Point Rd., 18 miles from Yosemite Valley* ☎ *209/372–8430* ⊕ *www.yosemitepark.com/BadgerPass.aspx* ⊠ *Lift tickets from $48.50.*

Yosemite Cross-Country Ski School. The highlight of Yosemite's cross-country skiing center is a 21-mile loop from Badger Pass to Glacier Point. You can rent cross-country skis for $25 per day at the Cross-Country

Ski School, which also rents snowshoes ($24 per day) and telemarking equipment ($29.50). ☎ *209/372–8444* 🌐 *www.yosemitepark.com.*

Yosemite Ski School. The gentle slopes of Badger Pass make Yosemite Ski School an ideal spot for children and beginners to learn downhill skiing or snowboarding for as little as $45.50 for a group lesson. ☎ *209/372–8430* 🌐 *www.yosemitepark.com.*

Yosemite Mountaineering School. This branch of the Yosemite Mountaineering School, open at the Badger Pass Ski Area during ski season only, conducts snowshoeing, cross-country skiing, telemarking, and skate-skiing classes starting at $35.50. ✉ *Badger Pass Ski Area* ☎ *209/372–8344* 🌐 *www.yosemitepark.com.*

WHERE TO EAT

In addition to the dining options listed here, you'll find fast-food grills and cafeterias, plus temporary snack bars, hamburger stands, and pizza joints lining park roads in summer. Many dining facilities in the park are open summer only.

$$$$ EUROPEAN Fodor's Choice ★

🍴 **Ahwahnee Hotel Dining Room.** Rave reviews about the dining room's appearance are fully justified—it features towering windows, a 34-foot-high ceiling with interlaced sugar-pine beams, and massive chandeliers. Although many continue to applaud the food, others have reported that they sense a dip in the quality both in the service and what is being served. Diners must spend a lot of money here, so perhaps that inflates the expectations and amplifies the disappointments. In any event, the lavish $45 Sunday brunch is a popular way to experience the grand room. Reservations are always advised, and the attire is "resort casual." [$] *Average main: $38* ✉ *Ahwahnee Hotel, Ahwahnee Rd., about ¾ mile east of Yosemite Valley Visitor Center, Yosemite Village* ☎ *209/372–1489* 🌐 *www.yosemitepark.com* ✍ *Reservations essential.*

$$$ AMERICAN Fodor's Choice ★

🍴 **Mountain Room.** Though good, the food becomes secondary when you see Yosemite Falls through this dining room's wall of windows—almost every table has a view. The chef makes a point of using locally sourced, organic ingredients whenever possible, so you can be assured of fresh vegetables to accompany the hearty main courses, such as steaks and seafood, as well as vegetarian and even vegan options. The Mountain Room Lounge, a few steps away in the Yosemite Lodge complex, has about 10 beers on tap. Weather permitting, take your drink out onto the small back patio. [$] *Average main: $24* ✉ *Yosemite Lodge, Northside Dr. about ¾ mile west of the visitor center, Yosemite Village* ☎ *209/372–1403* 🌐 *www.yosemitepark.com* 🕒 *No lunch.*

$ FAST FOOD

🍴 **Tuolumne Meadows Grill.** Serving continuously throughout the day until 5 or 6 pm, this fast-food eatery cooks up basic breakfast, lunch, and snacks. It's possible that ice cream tastes better at this altitude. Stop in for a quick meal before exploring the meadows. [$] *Average main: $8* ✉ *Tioga Rd. (Rte. 120), 1½ mile east of Tuolumne Meadows Visitor Center* ☎ *209/372–8426* 🕒 *Closed Oct.–Memorial Day. No dinner.*

$$ AMERICAN

🍴 **Tuolumne Meadows Lodge.** At the back of a small building that contains the lodge's front desk and small gift shop, this restaurant serves a menu of hearty American fare at breakfast and dinner. The decor is woodsy, with dark-wood walls, red-and-white-checkered tablecloths, and a handful of communal tables, which give it the feeling of an old-fashioned summer camp. The menu is small, often featuring a few meat and seafood dishes and one pasta or other special, including a vegetarian choice. If you have any dietary restrictions, let the front desk know in advance and the cooks will not let you down. Order box lunches from here for before hikes. [$] *Average main: $20* ✉ *Tioga Rd. (Rte. 120)* ☎ *209/372–8413* 🌐 *www.yosemitepark.com* ✍ *Reservations essential* 🕒 *Closed late Sept.–mid-June. No lunch.*

$$$ AMERICAN 🍴 **Wawona Hotel Dining Room.** Watch deer graze on the meadow while you dine in the romantic, candlelit dining room of the whitewashed Wawona Hotel, which dates from the late 1800s. The American-style cuisine favors fresh ingredients and flavors; trout and flatiron steaks are menu staples. There's also a brunch on some Sunday holidays, like Mother's Day and Easter, and a barbecue on the lawn Saturday evening in summer. [$] *Average main: $28* ✉ *8308 Wawona Rd., Wawona* ☎ *209/375–1425* 🕒 *Closed most of Dec., Jan., Feb., and Mar.*

PICNIC AREAS

Considering how large the park is and how many visitors come here—some 4 million people every year, most of them just for the day—it is somewhat surprising that Yosemite has so few formal picnic areas, though in many places you can find a smooth rock to sit on and enjoy breathtaking views along with your lunch. The convenience stores all sell picnic supplies, and prepackaged sandwiches and salads are widely available. Those options can come in especially handy during the middle of the day, when you might not want to spend precious daylight hours in such a spectacular setting sitting in a restaurant for a formal meal.

WHERE TO STAY

Hotel reviews have been shortened. For full information, visit Fodors.com.

$$$$ HOTEL Fodor's Choice ★ 🏨 **Ahwahnee Hotel.** A National Historic Landmark, the hotel is constructed of sugar-pine logs and features Native American design motifs; public spaces are enlivened with art deco flourishes, oriental rugs, and elaborate iron- and woodwork. **Pros:** best lodge in Yosemite; helpful concierge. **Cons:** expensive rates; some reports that service has slipped in recent years. [$] *Rooms from: $471* ✉ *Ahwahnee Rd., about ¾ miles east of Yosemite Valley Visitor Center, Yosemite Village* ☎ *801/559–4884* 🌐 *www.yosemitepark.com* 🛏 *95 lodge rooms, 6 suites, 24 cottage rooms* 🍽 *No meals.*

$$ HOTEL 🏨 **Curry Village.** Opened in 1899 as a place for budget-conscious travelers, Curry Village has plain accommodations: standard motel rooms, simple cabins with either private or shared baths, and tent cabins with shared baths. **Pros:** close to many activities; family-friendly atmosphere. **Cons:** not that economical after a recent price surge; can be crowded; sometimes a bit noisy. [$] *Rooms from: $124* ✉ *South side of Southside Dr.* ☎ *801/559–4884* 🌐 *www.yosemitepark.com* 🛏 *18 rooms, 485 cabins* 🍽 *No meals.*

Best Campgrounds in Yosemite

If you are going to concentrate solely on valley sites and activities, you should endeavor to stay in one of the "Pines" campgrounds, which are clustered near Curry Village and within an easy stroll from that busy complex's many facilities. For a more primitive and quiet experience, and to be near many backcountry hikes, try one of the Tioga Road campgrounds.

National Park Service Reservations Office. Reservations are required at many of Yosemite's campgrounds, especially in summer. You can book a site up to five months in advance, starting on the 15th of the month. Unless otherwise noted, book your site through the central National Park Service Reservations Office. If you don't have reservations when you arrive, many sites, especially those outside Yosemite Valley, are available on a first-come, first-served basis. ☎ 877/444–6777 ⊕ www.recreation. gov ☉ Daily 10–10.

Bridalveil Creek. This campground sits among lodgepole pines at 7,200 feet, above the valley on Glacier Point Road. From here, you can easily drive to Glacier Point's magnificent valley views. ⊠ From Rte. 41 in Wawona, go north to Glacier Point Rd. and turn right; entrance to campground is 25 miles ahead on right side.

Camp 4. Formerly known as Sunnyside Walk-In, and extremely popular with rock climbers who don't mind that a total of six are assigned to each campsite, no matter how many are in your group, this is the only valley campground available on a first-come, first-served basis. ⊠ Base of Yosemite Falls Trail, just west of Yosemite Lodge on Northside Dr., Yosemite Village.

Housekeeping Camp. Composed of three concrete walls and covered with two layers of canvas, each unit has an open-ended fourth side that can be closed off with a heavy white canvas curtain. You can rent "bedpacks," consisting of blankets, sheets, and other comforts. ⊠ Southside Dr., ½ mile west of Curry Village.

Porcupine Flat. Sixteen miles west of Tuolumne Meadows, this campground sits at 8,100 feet. If you want to be in the high country, this is a good bet. ⊠ Rte. 120, 16 miles west of Tuolumne Meadows.

Tuolumne Meadows. In a wooded area at 8,600 feet, just south of its namesake meadow, this is one of the most spectacular and sought-after campgrounds in Yosemite. ⊠ Rte. 120, 46 miles east of Big Oak Flat entrance station.

Upper Pines. This is one of the valley's largest campgrounds and the closest one to the trailheads. Expect large crowds in the summer—and little privacy. ⊠ At east end of valley, near Curry Village.

Wawona. Near the Mariposa Grove, just downstream from a popular fishing spot, this year-round campground has larger, less densely packed sites than campgrounds in the valley. ⊠ Rte. 41, 1 mile north of Wawona.

White Wolf. Set in the beautiful high country at 8,000 feet, this is a prime spot for hikers from early July to mid-September. ⊠ Tioga Rd., 15 miles east of Big Oak Flat entrance.

$$$
HOTEL

Wawona Hotel. This 1879 National Historic Landmark at Yosemite's southern end is an old-fashioned New England–style estate, with whitewashed buildings, wraparound verandas, and pleasant, no-frills rooms decorated with period pieces. **Pros:** lovely building; peaceful atmosphere. **Cons:** few modern amenities, such as phones and TVs; an hour's drive from Yosemite Valley. $ *Rooms from: $159* ⊠ *8308 Wawona Rd., Wawona* ☎ *801/559–4884* ⊕ *www.yosemitepark.com* ↝ *104 rooms, 50 with bath* ⊗ *Closed Dec.–Mar., except mid-Dec.–Jan. 2* ⦿ *Breakfast.*

LODGING TIP

Reserve your room or cabin in Yosemite as far in advance as possible. You can make a reservation up to a year before your arrival (within minutes after the reservation office makes a date available, the Ahwahnee, Yosemite Lodge, and Wawona Hotel often sell out their weekends, holiday periods, and all days between May and September).

$$
HOTEL

White Wolf Lodge. Set in a subalpine meadow, the rustic accommodations at White Wolf Lodge make it an excellent base camp for hiking the backcountry. **Pros:** quiet location; near some of Yosemite's most beautiful, less crowded hikes; good restaurant. **Cons:** far from the valley. $ *Rooms from: $124* ⊠ *Off Tioga Rd. (Rte. 120), 25 miles west of Tuolumne Meadows and 15 miles east of Crane Flat* ☎ *801/559–4884* ↝ *24 tent cabins, 4 cabins* ⊗ *Closed mid-Sept.–mid-June* ⦿ *No meals.*

$$$$
HOTEL

Yosemite Lodge at the Falls. This 1915 lodge near Yosemite Falls more closely resembles a 1960s resort with its numerous two-story structures tucked beneath the trees, and it doesn't help that the brown buildings are surrounded by large parking lots. **Pros:** centrally located; dependably clean rooms; lots of tours leave from out front. **Cons:** can feel impersonal; appearance is a little dated; prices recently skyrocketed. $ *Rooms from: $250* ⊠ *9006 Yosemite Lodge Dr., Yosemite Village* ☎ *801/559–4884* ⊕ *www.yosemitepark.com/yosemite-lodge.aspx* ↝ *245 rooms* ⦿ *No meals.*

SEQUOIA AND KINGS CANYON NATIONAL PARKS

WELCOME TO SEQUOIA AND KINGS CANYON NATIONAL PARKS

TOP REASONS TO GO

★ **Gentle giants:** You'll feel small—in a good way—walking among some of the world's largest living things in Sequoia's Giant Forest and Kings Canyon's Grant Grove.

★ **Because it's there:** You can't even glimpse it from the main part of Sequoia, but the sight of majestic Mt. Whitney is worth the trek to the eastern face of the High Sierra.

★ **Underground exploration:** Far older even than the giant sequoias, the gleaming limestone formations in Crystal Cave will draw you along dark, marble passages.

★ **A grander-than-Grand Canyon:** Drive the twisting Kings Canyon Scenic Byway down into the jagged, granite Kings River Canyon, deeper in parts than the Grand Canyon.

★ **Regal solitude:** To spend a day or two hiking in a subalpine world of your own, pick one of the 11 trailheads at Mineral King.

1 **Giant Forest–Lodgepole Village.** The most heavily visited area of Sequoia lies at the base of the "thumb" portion of Kings Canyon National Park and contains major sights such as Giant Forest, General Sherman Tree, Crystal Cave, and Moro Rock.

2 **Grant Grove Village–Redwood Canyon.** The "thumb" of Kings Canyon National Park is its busiest section, where Grant Grove, General Grant Tree, Panoramic Point, and Big Stump are the main attractions.

3 **Cedar Grove.** The drive through the high-country portion of Kings Canyon National Park to Cedar Grove Village, on the canyon floor, reveals magnificent granite formations of varied hues. Rock meets river in breathtaking fashion a few miles beyond Cedar Grove in Zumwalt Meadow.

4 **Mineral King.** In the southeast section of Sequoia, the highest road-accessible part of the park is a good place to hike, camp, and soak up the unspoiled grandeur of the Sierra Nevada.

5 **Mount Whitney.** The highest peak in the Lower 48 stands on the eastern edge of Sequoia; to get there from Giant Forest you must either backpack eight days through the mountains or drive nearly 400 miles around the park to its other side.

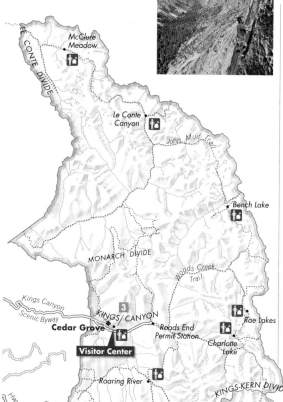

CALIFORNIA

GETTING ORIENTED

The two parks comprise 865,964 acres (1,353 square miles), mostly on the western flank of the Sierra. A map of the adjacent parks looks vaguely like a mitten, with the palm of Sequoia National Park south of the north-pointing, skinny thumb and long fingers of Kings Canyon National Park. Between the western thumb and eastern fingers, north of Sequoia, lies part of Sequoia National Forest, which includes Giant Sequoia National Monument.

McClure Meadow

Le Conte Canyon

John Muir Trail

Bench Lake

MONARCH DIVIDE

Woods Creek Trail

Kings Canyon Scenic Byway

KINGS CANYON

Cedar Grove

Visitor Center

Roads End Permit Station

Rae Lakes

Charlotte Lake

Roaring River

KINGS-KERN DIVIDE

Stony Creek Village

Table Mountain 13,630 ft

Tyndall Creek

Whitney Portal

Wuksachi Village

Lodgepole Village

Visitor Center

Crystal Cave

Mount Whitney 14,491 ft

Giant Forest Museum

General Sherman Tree

Bearpaw Meadow

Crabtree

John Muir Trail

Moro Rock

Buckeye Flat

Mount Kaweah 13,802 ft

Potwisha

Visitor Center

Mount Guyot 12,300 ft

Rock Creek

Ash Mountain Entrance

Little Five Lakes

Lookout Point Entrance

Mineral King

Cold Springs

KERN CANYON

Hockett Meadows

South Fork

Kern Canyon

Sheep Mountain 10,050 ft

0 ___ 5 mi
0 ___ 5 km

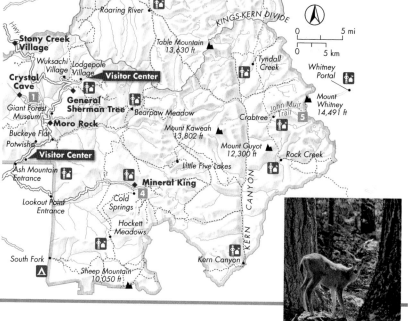

Updated by
Steve Pastorino

Although *Sequoiadendron giganteum* is the formal name for the redwoods that grow here, everyone outside the classroom calls them sequoias, big trees, or Sierra redwoods. Their monstrously thick trunks and branches, remarkably shallow root systems, and neck-craning heights are almost impossible to believe, as is the fact they can live for more than 2,500 years. Many of these towering marvels are in the Giant Forest stretch of Generals Highway, which connects Sequoia and Kings Canyon national parks.

Next to or a few miles off the 43-mile Generals Highway are most of Sequoia National Park's main attractions and Grant Grove Village, the orientation hub for Kings Canyon National Park. The two parks share a boundary that runs from the Central Valley in the west, where the Sierra Nevada foothills begin, to the range's dramatic eastern ridges. Kings Canyon has two portions: the smaller is shaped like a bent finger and encompasses Grant Grove Village and Redwood Mountain Grove (the two parks' largest concentration of sequoias), and the larger is home to stunning Kings River Canyon, whose vast, unspoiled peaks and valleys are a backpacker's dream. Sequoia is in one piece and includes Mt. Whitney, the highest point in the Lower 48 states (although it is impossible to see from the western part of the park and is a chore to ascend from either side).

SEQUOIA AND KINGS CANYON PLANNER

WHEN TO GO

The best times to visit are late spring and early fall, when temperatures are moderate and crowds thin. Summertime can draw hordes of tourists to see the giant sequoias, and the few, narrow roads mean congestion at peak holiday times. If you must visit in summer, go during the week. By contrast, in wintertime you may feel as though you have the parks all to yourself. But because of heavy snows, sections of the main park roads can be closed without warning, and low-hanging clouds can move in and obscure mountains and valleys for days. From mid-November to late April, check road and weather conditions before venturing out.

GETTING HERE AND AROUND
CAR TRAVEL

Sequoia is 36 miles east of Visalia on Route 198; Grant Grove Village in Kings Canyon is 56 miles east of Fresno on Route 180. There is no automobile entrance on the eastern side of the Sierra. Routes 180 and 198 are connected by Generals Highway, a paved two-lane road that sometimes sees delays at peak times due to ongoing improvements. The road is extremely narrow and steep from Route 198 to Giant Forest, so keep an eye on your engine temperature gauge, as the incline and congestion can cause vehicles to overheat; to avoid overheated brakes, use low gears on downgrades.

If you are traveling in an RV or with a trailer, study the restrictions on these vehicles. Do not travel beyond Potwisha Campground on Route 198 with an RV longer than 22 feet; take straighter, easier Route 180 instead. Maximum vehicle length on Generals Highway is 40 feet, or 50 feet combined length for vehicles with trailers.

From May through September, the Sequoia Shuttle offers free transportation within the park along four routes in and around the Giant Forest and Lodgepole areas. Buses run every 15 minutes.

Generals Highway between Lodgepole and Grant Grove is sometimes closed by snow. The Mineral King Road from Route 198 into southern Sequoia National Park is closed 2 miles below Atwell Mill either on November 1 or after the first heavy snow. The Buckeye Flat–Middle Fork Trailhead Road is closed from mid-October to mid-April, when the Buckeye Flat Campground closes. The lower Crystal Cave Road is closed when the cave closes in November. Its upper 2 miles, as well as the Panoramic Point and Moro Rock–Crescent Meadow roads, close with the first heavy snow. Because of the danger of rockfall, the portion of Kings Canyon Scenic Byway east of Grant Grove closes in winter. For current road and weather conditions, call ☎ *559/565–3341.*

■ **TIP→** Snowstorms are common from late October through April. Unless you have a four-wheel-drive vehicle with snow tires, you should carry chains and know how to install them.

PARK ESSENTIALS
PARK FEES AND PERMITS

The admission fee is $20 per vehicle and $10 for those who enter by bus, on foot, bicycle, motorcycle, or horse; it is valid for seven days in both parks. U.S. residents over the age of 62 pay $10 for a lifetime pass, and permanently disabled U.S. residents are admitted free.

If you plan to camp in the backcountry, you need a permit, which costs $15 for hikers or $30 for stock users (e.g., horseback riders). One permit covers the group. Availability of permits depends upon trailhead quotas. Reservations are accepted by mail or fax for a $15 processing fee, beginning March 1, and must be made at least 14 days in advance

(☎ 559/565–3766). Without a reservation, you may still get a permit on a first-come, first-served basis starting at 1 pm the day before you plan to hike. For more information on backcountry camping or travel with pack animals (horses, mules, burros, or llamas), contact the Wilderness Permit Office (☎ 530/565–3761).

PARK HOURS
The parks are open 24/7 year-round.

PRICES

WHAT IT COSTS			
	$	**$$**	**$$$**	**$$$$**
Restaurants	under $12	$12–$20	$21–$30	over $30
Hotels	under $100	$100–$150	$151–$200	over $200

Restaurant prices are the average cost of a main course at dinner or, if dinner is not served, at lunch. Hotel prices are the lowest cost of a standard double room in high season, excluding taxes and service charges.

VISITOR INFORMATION
NATIONAL PARK SERVICE
Sequoia and Kings Canyon National Parks ✉ *47050 Generals Hwy.(Rte. 198), Three Rivers* ☎ *559/565–3341* ⊕ *www.nps.gov/seki.*

SEQUOIA VISITOR CENTERS
Foothills Visitor Center. Exhibits here focus on the foothills and resource issues facing the parks. You can pick up books, maps, and a list of ranger-led walks, and get wilderness permits. ✉ *47050 Generals Hwy., Rte. 198, 1 mile north of Ash Mountain entrance, Sequoia National Park* ☎ *559/565–4212* ⊙ *Daily 8–4:30.*

Lodgepole Visitor Center. Along with exhibits on the area's history, geology, and wildlife, the center screens an outstanding 22-minute film about bears. You can buy books, maps, and tickets to cave tours and the Wolverton barbecue here. ✉ *Generals Hwy. (Rte. 198), 21 miles north of Ash Mountain entrance, Sequoia National Park* ☎ *559/565–4436* ⊙ *Late May–early Sept., daily 7–7; Apr.–late May and early Sept.–Dec., days and hrs vary* ⌒ *Shuttle: Giant Forest or Wuksachi-Lodgepole-Dorst.*

KINGS CANYON VISITOR CENTERS
Cedar Grove Visitor Center. Off the main road and behind the Sentinel Campground, this small ranger station has books and maps, plus information about hikes and other activities. ✉ *Kings Canyon Scenic Byway, 30 miles east of Rte. 180/198 junction, Kings Canyon National Park* ☎ *559/565–3793* ⊙ *Late May–early Sept., Tues.–Sun. 9–5.*

Kings Canyon Park Visitor Center. The center's 15-minute film and various exhibits provide an overview of the park's canyon, sequoias, and human history. Books, maps, and weather advice are dispensed here, as are (if available) free wilderness permits. ✉ *Grant Grove Village, Generals Hwy. (Rte. 198), 3 miles northeast of Rte. 180, Big Stump entrance, Kings Canyon National Park* ☎ *559/565–4307* ⊙ *Daily 9–4:30; may vary seasonally.*

SEQUOIA NATIONAL PARK

EXPLORING

SCENIC DRIVES

Fodor'sChoice ★ **Generals Highway.** One of California's most scenic drives, this 43-mile road is the main asphalt artery between Sequoia and Kings Canyon national parks. Some portions are also signed as Route 180, others as Route 198. Named after the landmark Grant and Sherman trees that leave so many visitors awestruck, Generals Highway runs from Sequoia's Foothills Visitor Center north to Kings Canyon's Grant Grove Village. Along the way, it passes the turnoff to Crystal Cave, the Giant Forest Museum, Lodgepole Village, and other popular attractions. The lower portion, from Hospital Rock to the Giant Forest, is especially steep and winding. If your vehicle is 22 feet or longer, avoid that stretch by entering the parks via Route 180 (from Fresno) rather than Route 198 (from Visalia or Three Rivers). ■TIP→ Take your time on this road—there's a lot to see, and wildlife can scamper across at any time.

SCENIC STOPS

Sequoia National Park is all about the trees, and to understand the scale of these giants you must walk among them. But there is much more to the park than the trees. Try to access one of the vista points that provide a panoramic view over the forested mountains. Generals Highway (on Routes 198 and 180) will be your route to most of the park's sights. A few short spur roads lead from the highway to some sights, and Mineral King Road branches off Route 198 to enter the park at Lookout Point, winding east from there to the park's southernmost section.

Crescent Meadow. A sea of ferns signals your arrival at what John Muir called the "gem of the Sierra." Walk around for an hour or two and you might decide that the Scotland-born naturalist was exaggerating a wee bit, but the verdant meadow is quite pleasant and you just might see a bear. ■TIP→ Wildflowers bloom here throughout the summer. ⊠ *End of Moro Rock–Crescent Meadow Rd., 2.6 miles east off Generals Hwy.* ↷ *Shuttle: Moro Rock–Crescent Meadow.*

Fodor'sChoice ★ **Crystal Cave.** One of more than 200 caves in Sequoia and Kings Canyon, Crystal Cave is composed largely of marble, the result of limestone being hardened under heat and pressure. It contains several eye-popping formations. There used to be more, but some were damaged or obliterated by early-20th-century dynamite blasting. You can only see the cave on a tour. The Daily Tour ($15), a great overview, takes about 50 minutes. To immerse yourself in the cave experience—at times you'll be crawling on your belly—book the exhilarating Wild Cave Tour ($130). ■TIP→ Purchase Daily Tour tickets at either the Foothills or Lodgepole visitor center; they're not sold at the cave itself. ⊠ *Crystal Cave Rd., off Generals Hwy.* ☎ *559/565–3759* ⊕ *www.sequoiahistory.org* ⊠ *$15* ☉ *Mid-May–Nov., daily 10–4.*

Fodor'sChoice ★ **General Sherman Tree.** The 274.9-foot-tall General Sherman is one of the world's tallest and oldest sequoias, and it ranks No. 1 in volume, adding the equivalent of a 60-foot-tall tree every year to its approximately

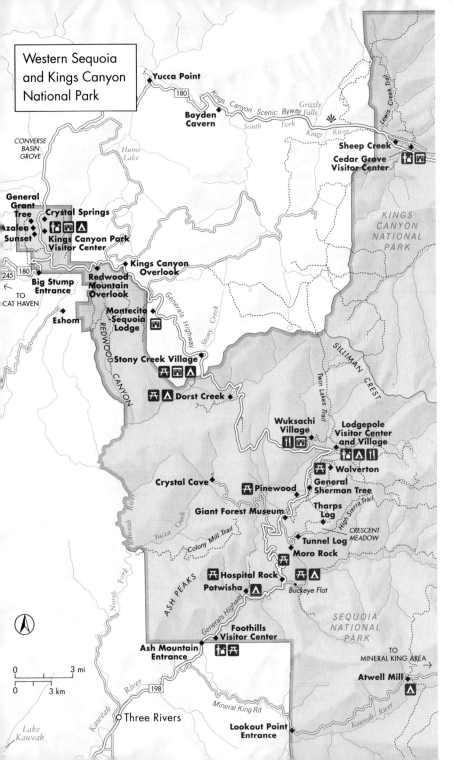

Western Sequoia and Kings Canyon National Park

Yucca Point

180

Kings Canyon Scenic Byway

Boyden Cavern

South Fork

Grizzly Falls

Kings River

Sheep Creek

Cedar Grove Visitor Center

CONVERSE BASIN GROVE

Hume Lake

KINGS CANYON NATIONAL PARK

Lewis Creek Trail

General Grant Tree

Crystal Springs

Azalea

Sunset

Kings Canyon Park Visitor Center

245

180

Big Stump Entrance

TO CAT HAVEN

Kings Canyon Overlook

Redwood Mountain Overlook

Eshom

Montecito Sequoia Lodge

Generals Highway

Stony Creek

Stony Creek Village

REDWOOD CANYON

Dorst Creek

SILLIMAN CREST

Twin Lakes Trail

Wuksachi Village

Lodgepole Visitor Center and Village

Wolverton

Crystal Cave

Pinewood

Kaweah River

Yucca Creek

Colony Mill Trail

Giant Forest Museum

General Sherman Tree

Tharps Log

High Sierra Trail

CRESCENT MEADOW

Tunnel Log

Moro Rock

ASH PEAKS

Hospital Rock

Potwisha

Buckeye Flat

North Fork

Generals Highway

Foothills Visitor Center

SEQUOIA NATIONAL PARK

TO MINERAL KING AREA

Ash Mountain Entrance

0   3 mi

0   3 km

Atwell Mill

River

198

Three Rivers

Mineral King Rd

Kaweah River

Lookout Point Entrance

Lake Kaweah

52,500 cubic feet of mass. The tree doesn't grow taller, though—it's dead at the top. A short, wheelchair-accessible trail leads to the tree from Generals Highway, but the main trail (½ mile) winds down from a parking lot off Wolverton Road. ▪TIP➜ The walk back up the main trail is steep, but benches along the way provide rest for the short of breath. ⊠ *Main trail Wolverton Rd. off Generals Hwy. (Rte. 198)* ☞ *Shuttle: Giant Forest or Wolverton–Sherman Tree.*

12

Mineral King Area. A subalpine valley of fir, pine, and sequoia trees, Mineral King sits at 7,500 feet at the end of a steep, winding road. This is the highest point to which you can drive in the park. It is open only from Memorial Day through late October. ⊠ *Mineral King Rd., 25 miles east of Generals Hwy. (Rte. 198)* ⊘ *June–late Oct., daily.*

Fodor's Choice
★

Moro Rock. Sequoia National Park's best non-tree attraction offers panoramic views to those fit and determined enough to mount its 350 or so steps. In a case where the journey rivals the destination, Moro's stone stairway is so impressive in its twisty inventiveness that it's on the National Register of Historic Places. The rock's 6,725-foot summit overlooks the Middle Fork Canyon, sculpted by the Kaweah River and approaching the depth of Arizona's Grand Canyon, although smoggy, hazy air often compromises the view. ⊠ *Moro Rock–Crescent Meadow Rd., 2 miles east off Generals Hwy. (Rte. 198) to parking area* ☞ *Shuttle: Moro Rock–Crescent Meadow.*

Tunnel Log. This 275-foot tree fell in 1937, and soon a 17-foot-wide, 8-foot-high hole was cut through it for vehicular passage (not to mention the irresistible photograph) that continues today. Large vehicles take the nearby bypass. ⊠ *Moro Rock–Crescent Meadow Rd., 2 miles east of Generals Hwy. (Rte. 198)* ☞ *Shuttle: Moro Rock–Crescent Meadow.*

EDUCATIONAL OFFERINGS
PROGRAMS AND SEMINARS

Evening Programs. The Sequoia Natural History Association presents film and slide shows, hikes, and evening lectures during the summer and winter. From May through October the popular Wonders of the Night Sky programs celebrate the often stunning views of the heavens experienced at both parks. ☏ *559/565–3341* ⊕ *www.sequoiahistory. org/snhacalendar.asp* ⊘ *Locations and times vary.*

Free Nature Programs. Almost any summer day, half-hour to 1½-hour ranger talks and walks explore subjects such as the life of the sequoia, the geology of the park, and the habits of bears. Giant Forest, Lodgepole Visitor Center, Wuksachi Village, and Dorst Creek Campground are frequent starting points. Look for less frequent tours in the winter from Grant Grove. Check bulletin boards throughout the park for the week's offerings.

Seminars. Expert naturalists lead seminars on a range of topics, including birds, wildflowers, geology, botany, photography, park history, backpacking, and pathfinding. Reservations are recommended. Information about times and prices is available at the visitor centers or through the Sequoia Natural History Association. ☏ *559/565–3759* ⊕ *www. sequoiahistory.org.*

TOURS

Fodor'sChoice ★ **Sequoia Field Institute.** The Sequoia Natural History Association's highly regarded educational division conducts single-day and multi-day "EdVenture" tours that include backpacking hikes, natural-history walks, and kayaking excursions. ⊠ *47050 Generals Hwy., Unit 10, Three Rivers* ☎ *559/565–4251* ⊕ *www.sequoiahistory.org.*

Sequoia Sightseeing Tours. This operator's friendly, knowledgeable guides conduct interpretive sightseeing tours in a 10-passenger van. Reservations are essential. The company also offers private tours of Kings Canyon. ⊠ *Three Rivers* ☎ *559/561–4189* ⊕ *www.sequoiatours.com* ▧ *From $69 tour of Sequoia; from $129 tour of Kings Canyon.*

SPORTS AND THE OUTDOORS

The best way to see Sequoia is to take a hike. Unless you do so, you'll miss out on the up-close grandeur of mist wafting between deeply scored, red-orange tree trunks bigger than you've ever seen. If it's winter, put on some snowshoes or cross-country skis and plunge into the snow-swaddled woodland. There are not too many other outdoor options: no off-road driving is allowed in the parks, and no special provisions have been made for bicycles. Boating, rafting, and snowmobiling are also prohibited.

BIRD-WATCHING

More than 200 species of birds inhabit Sequoia and Kings Canyon national parks. Not seen in most parts of the United States, the white-headed woodpecker and the pileated woodpecker are common in most mid-elevation areas here. There are also many hawks and owls, including the renowned spotted owl. Species are diverse in both parks due to the changes in elevation, and range from warblers, kingbirds, thrushes, and sparrows in the foothills to goshawks, blue grouse, red-breasted nuthatches, and brown creepers at the highest elevations. Ranger-led bird-watching tours are held on a sporadic basis. Call the park's main information number to find out more about these tours. The Sequoia Natural History Association (☎ *559/565–3759* ⊕ *www.sequoiahistory. org*) also has information about bird-watching in the southern Sierra.

CROSS-COUNTRY SKIING

Wuksachi Lodge Rentals. Rent cross-country skis and snowshoes here. Depending on snowfall amounts, instruction may also be available. Reservations are recommended. Marked trails cut through Giant Forest, about 5 miles south of the lodge. ⊠ *Off Generals Hwy. (Rte. 198), 2 miles north of Lodgepole* ☎ *559/565–4070* ☉ *Nov.–May (unless no snow), daily 9–4* ↝ *Shuttle: Wuksachi-Lodgepole-Dorst.*

HIKING

The best way to see the park is to hike it. Carry a hiking map and plenty of water. Visitor center gift shops sell maps and trail books and pamphlets. Check with rangers for current trail conditions, and be aware of rapidly changing weather. As a rule of thumb, plan on covering about a mile per hour.

EASY

Fodor's Choice ★ **Congress Trail.** This 2-mile trail, arguably the best hike in the parks in terms of natural beauty, is a paved loop that begins near General Sherman Tree. You'll get close-up views of more big trees here than on any other Sequoia hike. Watch for the clusters known as the House and Senate. The President Tree, also on the trail, supplanted the General Grant Tree in 2012 as the world's second largest in volume (behind the General Sherman). ■ TIP → An offshoot of the Congress Trail leads to Crescent Meadow, where in summer you can catch a free shuttle back to the Sherman parking lot. *Easy.* ⊠ *Trail begins off Generals Hwy. (Rte. 198), 2 miles north of Giant Forest* ⌗ *Shuttle: Giant Forest.*

Crescent Meadow Trails. A 1-mile trail loops around lush Crescent Meadow to Tharp's Log, a cabin built from a fire-hollowed sequoia. From there you can embark on a 60-mile trek to Mt. Whitney, if you're prepared and have the time. ■ TIP → Brilliant wildflowers bloom here in midsummer. *Easy.* ⊠ *Trail begins at the end of Moro Rock–Crescent Meadow Rd., 2.6 miles east off Generals Hwy. (Rte. 198)* ⌗ *Shuttle: Moro Rock–Crescent Meadow.*

MODERATE

Tokopah Falls Trail. This trail with a 500-foot elevation gain follows the Marble Fork of the Kaweah River for 1.75 miles one way and dead-ends below the impressive granite cliffs and cascading waterfall of Tokopah Canyon. The trail passes through a mixed-conifer forest. It takes 2½ to 4 hours to make the round-trip journey. *Moderate.* ⊠ *Trail begins off Generals Hwy. (Rte. 198), ¼ mile north of Lodgepole Campground* ⌗ *Shuttle: Lodgepole-Wuksachi-Dorst.*

DIFFICULT

Mineral King Trails. Many trails to the high country begin at Mineral King. Two popular day hikes are Eagle Lake (6.8 miles round-trip) and Timber Gap (4.4 miles round-trip). ■ TIP → At the Mineral King Ranger Station (559/565–3768) you can pick up maps and check about conditions from late May to late September. *Difficult.* ⊠ *Trailheads at end of Mineral King Rd., 25 miles east of Generals Hwy. (Rte. 198).*

HORSEBACK RIDING

TOURS AND OUTFITTERS

Grant Grove Stables. Grant Grove Stables (⇨ *Horseback Riding in Kings Canyon National Park*) isn't too far from parts of Sequoia National Park, and is perfect for short rides from June to September. Reservations are recommended. ⊕ *www.visitsequoia.com/grant-grove-stables. aspx* ⊒ *From $40 per person.*

Horse Corral Pack Station. One- and two-hour trips through Sequoia are available for beginning and advanced riders. ⊠ *Big Meadow Rd., 12 miles east of Generals Hwy. (Rte. 198) between Sequoia and Kings Canyon national parks* ☏ *559/565–3404* ⊕ *www.highsierrapackers.org* ⊒ *From $45* ☾ *May–mid.-Sept.*

KINGS CANYON NATIONAL PARK

EXPLORING

SCENIC DRIVES

Fodor's Choice ★ **Kings Canyon Scenic Byway.** The 30-mile stretch of Route 180 between Grant Grove Village and Zumwalt Meadow delivers eye-popping scenery—granite cliffs, a roaring river, waterfalls, and Kings River Canyon itself—much of which you can experience at vista points or on easy walks. The canyon comes into view about 10 miles east of the village at **Junction View.** Five miles beyond, at **Yucca Point,** the canyon is thousands of feet deeper than the more famous Grand Canyon. **Canyon View,** a special spot 1 mile east of the Cedar Grove Village turnoff, showcases evidence of the area's glacial history. Here, perhaps more than anywhere else, you'll understand why John Muir compared Kings Canyon vistas with those in Yosemite. ■ TIP➜ Driving the byway takes about an hour each way without stops. ⊠ *Rte. 180 north and east of Grant Grove village.*

HISTORIC SITES

Fallen Monarch. This toppled sequoia's hollow base was used in the second half of the 19th century as a home for settlers, a saloon, and even to stable U.S. Cavalry horses. As you walk through it (assuming entry is permitted, which is not always possible), notice how little the wood has decayed, and imagine yourself tucked safely inside, sheltered from a storm or protected from the searing heat. ⊠ *Grant Grove Trail, 1 mile north of Kings Canyon Park Visitor Center.*

SCENIC STOPS

General Grant Tree. President Coolidge proclaimed this to be the "nation's Christmas tree," and 30 years later President Eisenhower designated it as a living shrine to all Americans who have died in wars. Bigger at its base than the General Sherman Tree, it tapers more quickly. It's estimated to be the world's third-largest sequoia by volume. ■ TIP➜ A spur trail winds behind the tree, where scars from a long-ago fire remain visible. ⊠ *Trailhead 1 mile north of Grant Grove Visitor Center.*

Redwood Mountain Sequoia Grove. One of the world's largest sequoia groves, Redwood contains within its 2,078 acres nearly 2,200 sequoias whose diameters exceed 10 feet. You can view the grove from afar at an overlook or hike 6 to 10 miles down into the richest regions, which include two of the world's 25 heaviest trees. ⊠ *Drive 6 miles south of Grant Grove on Generals Hwy. (Rte. 198), then turn right at Quail Flat; follow it 2 miles to the Redwood Canyon trailhead.*

SPORTS AND THE OUTDOORS

The siren song of beauty, challenge, and relative solitude (by national parks standards) draws hard-core outdoors enthusiasts to the Kings River Canyon and the backcountry of the park's eastern section. Backpacking, rock-climbing, and extreme-kayaking opportunities abound, but the park also has day hikes for all ability levels. Winter brings

12

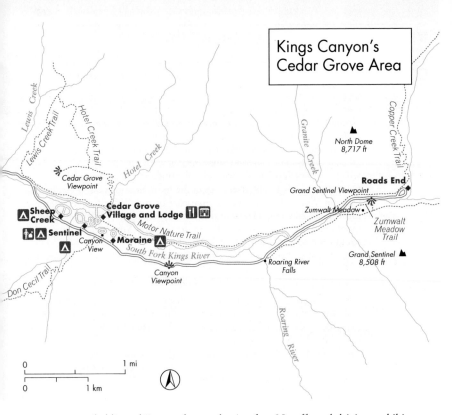

Kings Canyon's
Cedar Grove Area

Lewis Creek

Lewis Creek Trail

Hotel Creek Trail

Hotel Creek Trail

Hotel Creek

Granite Creek

Copper Creek Trail

North Dome
8,717 ft

Roads End

Grand Sentinel Viewpoint

Cedar Grove
Viewpoint

Zumwalt Meadow

Zumwalt
Meadow
Trail

Sheep
Creek

Cedar Grove
Village and Lodge

Sentinel

Motor Nature Trail

Canyon
View

Moraine

South Fork Kings River

Grand Sentinel
8,508 ft

Don Cecil Trail

Canyon
Viewpoint

Roaring River
Falls

Canyon
Viewpoint

Roaring River

0   1 mi

0   1 km

sledding, skiing, and snowshoeing fun. No off-road driving or biking
is allowed in the park, and snowmobiling is also prohibited.

CROSS-COUNTRY SKIING

Roads to Grant Grove are accessible even during heavy snowfall, making the trails here a good choice over Sequoia's Giant Forest when harsh
weather hits.

HIKING

You can enjoy many of Kings Canyon's sights from your car, but the
giant gorge of the Kings River Canyon and the sweeping vistas of some
of the highest mountains in the United States are best seen on foot.
Carry a hiking map—available at any visitor center—and plenty of
water. Check with rangers for current trail conditions, and be aware of
rapidly changing weather. Except for one trail to Mt. Whitney, permits
are not required for day hikes.

Roads End Permit Station. You can obtain wilderness permits, maps, and
information about the backcountry at this station, where bear canisters, a must for campers, can be rented or purchased. When the station is closed, complete a self-service permit form. ⊠ *Eastern end of
Kings Canyon Scenic Byway, 6 miles east of Cedar Grove Visitor Center*
⊙ *Mid-May–Sept., daily 7–4.*

CLOSE UP

Plants and Wildlife in Sequoia and Kings Canyon

12

The parks can be divided into three distinct zones. In the west (1,500–4,500 feet) are the rolling, lower elevation foothills, covered with shrubby chaparral vegetation or golden grasslands dotted with oaks. Chamise, red-barked manzanita, and the occasional yucca plant grow here. Fields of white popcorn flower cover the hillsides in spring, and the yellow fiddleneck flourishes. In summer, intense heat and absence of rain cause the hills to turn golden brown. Wildlife includes the California ground squirrel, noisy blue-and-gray scrub jay, black bears, coyotes, skunks, and gray foxes.

At middle elevation (5,000–9,000 feet), where the giant sequoia belt resides, rock formations mix with meadows and huge stands of evergreens—red and white fir, incense cedar, and

ponderosa pines, to name a few. Wildflowers like yellow blazing star and red Indian paintbrush bloom in spring and summer. Mule deer, golden-mantled ground squirrels, Steller's jays, mule deer, and black bears (most active in fall) inhabit the area, as does the chickaree.

The high alpine section of the parks is extremely rugged, with a string of rocky peaks reaching above 13,000 feet to Mt. Whitney's 14,494 feet. Fierce weather and scarcity of soil make vegetation and wildlife sparse. Foxtail and whitebark pines have gnarled and twisted trunks, the result of high wind, heavy snowfall, and freezing temperatures. In summer you can see yellow-bellied marmots, pikas, weasels, mountain chickadees, and Clark's nutcrackers.

EASY

Fodor's Choice ★ **Zumwalt Meadow Trail.** Rangers say this is the best (and most popular) day hike in the Cedar Grove area. Just 1.5 miles long, it offers three visual treats: the South Fork of the Kings River, the lush meadow, and the high granite walls above, including those of Grand Sentinel and North Dome. *Easy.* ⊠ *Trailhead 4½ miles east of Cedar Grove Village turnoff from Kings Canyon Scenic Byway.*

MODERATE

Big Baldy. This hike climbs 600 feet and 2 miles up to the 8,209-feet summit of Big Baldy. Your reward is the view of Redwood Canyon. Round-trip the hike is 4 miles. *Moderate.* ⊠ *Trailhead 8 miles south of Grant Grove on Generals Hwy. (Rte. 198).*

Redwood Canyon Trails. Two main trails lead into Redwood Canyon Grove, the world's largest sequoia grove. The 6.5-mile **Hart Tree and Fallen Goliath Loop** passes by a 19th-century logging site, pristine Hart Meadow, and the hollowed-out Tunnel Tree before accessing a side trail to the grove's largest sequoia, the 277.9-foot-tall Hart Tree. The 6.4-mile **Sugar Bowl Loop** provides views of Redwood Mountain and Big Baldy before winding down into its namesake, a thick grove of mature and young sequoias. *Moderate.* ⊠ *Trail begins off Quail Flat ⊕ Drive 5 miles south of Grant Grove on Generals Hwy. (Rte. 198), turn right at Quail Flat and proceed 1½ miles to trailhead.*

Mt. Whitney

At 14,494 feet, Mt. Whitney is the highest point in the contiguous United States and the crown jewel of Sequoia National Park's wild eastern side. The peak looms high above the tiny, high-mountain desert community of Lone Pine, where numerous Hollywood Westerns have been filmed. The high mountain ranges, arid landscape, and scrubby brush of the eastern Sierra are beautiful in their vastness and austerity.

Despite the mountain's scale, you can't see it from the more traveled west side of the park because it is hidden behind the Great Western Divide. The only way to access Mt. Whitney from the main part of the park is to circumnavigate the Sierra Nevada via a 10-hour, nearly 400-mile drive outside the park. No road ascends the peak; the best vantage point from which to catch a glimpse of the mountain is at the end of Whitney Portal Road. The 13 miles of winding road lead from U.S. 395 at Lone Pine to the trailhead for the hiking route to the top of the mountain. Whitney Portal Road is closed in winter.

DIFFICULT

Hotel Creek Trail. For gorgeous canyon views, take this trail from Cedar Grove up a series of switchbacks until it splits. Follow the route left through chaparral to the forested ridge and rocky outcrop known as Cedar Grove Overlook, where you can see the Kings River Canyon stretching below. This strenuous 5-mile round-trip hike gains 1,200 feet and takes three to four hours to complete. *Difficult.* ⊠ *Trailhead at Cedar Grove Pack Station, 1 mile east of Cedar Grove Village.*

HORSEBACK RIDING

One-day destinations by horseback out of Cedar Grove include Mist Falls and Upper Bubb's Creek. In the backcountry, many equestrians head for Volcanic Lakes or Granite Basin, ascending trails that reach elevations of 10,000 feet. Costs per person range from $35 for a one-hour guided ride to around $250 per day for fully guided trips for which the packers do all the cooking and camp chores.

TOURS AND OUTFITTERS

Cedar Grove Pack Station. Take a day ride or plan a multiday adventure along the Kings River Canyon with Cedar Grove Pack Station. Popular routes include the Rae Lakes Loop and Monarch Divide. ⊠ *Kings Canyon Scenic Byway, 1 mile east of Cedar Grove Village* ☎ *559/565–3464* ⊕ *www.nps.gov/seki/planyourvisit/horseride.htm* ☜ *From $40 per hour or $100 per day* ☉ *Late May–early Sept.*

Grant Grove Stables. A one- or two-hour trip through Grant Grove leaving from the stables provides a taste of horseback riding in Kings Canyon. ⊠ *Rte. 180, ½ mile north of Grant Grove Visitor Center* ☎ *559/335–9292 mid-June–Sept.* ⊕ *www.nps.gov/seki/planyourvisit/ horseride.htm* ☜ *From $45* ☉ *June–Labor Day, daily 8–6.*

Hiking in the Sierra Mountains is a thrilling experience, putting you amid some of the world's highest trees.

SLEDDING AND SNOWSHOEING

In winter Kings Canyon has a few great places to play in the snow. Sleds, inner tubes, and platters are allowed at both the Azalea Campground area on Grant Tree Road, ¼ mile north of Grant Grove Visitor Center, and at the Big Stump picnic area, 2 miles north of the lower Route 180 entrance to the park.

Snowshoeing is good around Grant Grove, where you can take naturalist-guided snowshoe walks on Saturdays and holidays from mid-December through mid-March as conditions permit. For a small donation, you can rent snowshoes at the Grant Grove Visitor Center for the guided walks. Grant Grove Market rents sleds and snowshoes.

WHERE TO EAT

SEQUOIA

$ CAFÉ 🍴 **Lodgepole Market and Snack Bar.** The choices here run the gamut from simple to very simple, with the three counters only a few strides apart in a central eating complex. For hot food, venture into the snack bar. The deli sells prepackaged salads, sandwiches, and wraps along with ice cream scooped from tubs. You'll find other prepackaged foods in the market. [$] *Average main: $6* ✉ *Next to Lodgepole Visitor Center* ☎ *559/565–3301* ⏲ *Closed late Sept.–mid-Apr.*

$$$ MODERN AMERICAN 🍴 **The Peaks.** Huge windows run the length of the Wuksachi Lodge's high-ceilinged dining room, and a large fireplace on the far wall warms both body and soul. The diverse dinner menu—by far the best at both

parks—reflects a commitment to locally sourced and sustainable products. The menu might include venison, pan-seared mountain trout, and vegetarian options like pho and chili. The wine selection is serviceable but lacks imagination. Breakfast and lunch are also served. $ *Average main: $28* ⊠ *Wuksachi Village* 🕾 *559/565–4070* ⊕ *www.visitsequoia. com/the-peaks-restaurant.aspx* ⌂ *Reservations essential.*

$$$ ✕ **Wolverton Barbeque.** Weather permitting, diners congregate nightly on a
BARBECUE   wooden porch that looks directly out onto a small but strikingly verdant meadow. In addition to the predictable meats such as ribs and chicken, the all-you-can-eat buffet has sides that include baked beans, corn on the cob, and potato salad. Following the meal, listen to a ranger talk and then clear your throat for a campfire sing-along. Purchase tickets at Lodgepole Market, Wuksachi Lodge, or Wolverton Recreation Area's office. $ *Average main: $25* ⊠ *Wolverton Rd., 1½ mile northeast off Generals Hwy. (Rte. 198)* 🕾 *559/565–4070* ☉ *No lunch. Closed early Sept.–mid-June.*

KINGS CANYON

$$ ✕ **Cedar Grove Snack Bar.** The menu here is surprisingly extensive, with
AMERICAN   dinner entrées such as pasta, pork chops, trout, and steak. For breakfast, try the biscuits and gravy, French toast, pancakes, or cold cereal. Burgers (including vegetarian patties) and hot dogs dominate the lunch choices. Outside, a patio dining area overlooks the Kings River. $ *Average main: $14* ⊠ *Cedar Grove Village* 🕾 *559/565–0100* ☉ *Closed Oct.–May.*

$$ ✕ **Grant Grove Restaurant.** In a no-frills, open room, this restaurant offers
AMERICAN   utterly standard American fare such as pancakes for breakfast or hot sandwiches and chicken for later meals. Take-out service is available year-round, and during the summer there's also a pizza parlor. $ *Average main: $16* ⊠ *Grant Grove Village* 🕾 *559/335–5500.*

WHERE TO STAY

SEQUOIA

$$$$ 🏨 **Wuksachi Lodge.** The striking cedar-and-stone main building is a fine
HOTEL   example of how a structure can blend effectively with lovely mountain
Fodor's Choice   scenery. **Pros:** best place to stay in the parks; lots of wildlife. **Cons:**
★   rooms can be small; main lodge is a few-minutes' walk from guest rooms. $ *Rooms from: $229* ⊠ *64740 Wuksachi Way, Wuksachi Village* 🕾 *559/565–4070, 888/252–5757* ⊕ *www.visitsequoia.com/ lodging.aspx* ⇱ *102 rooms* ⦿| *No meals.*

KINGS CANYON

$$$$ 🏨 **John Muir Lodge.** This modern, timber-sided lodge occupies a wooded
HOTEL   area in the hills above Grant Grove Village. **Pros:** open year-round; common room stays warm; lodge is far enough from the main road to be quiet. **Cons:** check-in is down in the village. $ *Rooms from: $205* ⊠ *Kings Canyon Scenic Byway, ¼ mile north of Grant Grove Village, 86728 Highway 180* 🕾 *559/335–5500* ⊕ *www.visitsequoia.com/John-Muir-Lodge.aspx* ⇱ *36 rooms* ⦿| *No meals.*

SACRAMENTO AND THE GOLD COUNTRY

WELCOME TO SACRAMENTO AND THE GOLD COUNTRY

TOP REASONS TO GO

★ **Gold Rush:** Marshall Gold Discovery State Park and Hangtown's Gold Bug & Mine conjure up California's mid-19th-century boom.

★ **State Capital:** Easygoing Sacramento offers sights like the Capitol and historic Old Sacramento along with a sophisticated dining scene.

★ **Bon appétit:** Sacramento is home to the California state fair in July and several ethnic food festivals. Nevada City and environs are known for summer mountain-music festivals and Victorian and Cornish winter-holiday celebrations.

★ **Wine Tasting:** With bucolic scenery and friendly tasting rooms, the Gold Country's Shenandoah Valley has become an acclaimed wine-making region, specializing in Zinfandel.

★ **Sequoias and Caverns:** Calaveras Big Trees State Park is filled with giant sequoias, and Moaning Cavern's main chamber is big enough to hold the Statue of Liberty.

1 Sacramento and Nearby. The gateway to the Gold Country, the seat of state government, and an agricultural hub, Sacramento plays many important contemporary roles. About 2.5 million people live in the metropolitan area, which offers up more sunshine and lower prices than coastal California.

2 The Gold Country— South. South of its junction with U.S. 50, Highway 49 traces in asphalt the famed Mother Lode. The peppy former gold-rush towns strung along the road have for the most part been restored and made presentable to visitors with an interest in one of the most frenzied episodes of American history.

3 The Gold Country— North. Highway 49 north of Placerville links the towns of Coloma, Auburn, Grass Valley, and Nevada City. Most are gentrified versions of once-rowdy mining camps, vestiges of which remain in roadside museums, old mining structures, and restored homes now serving as inns.

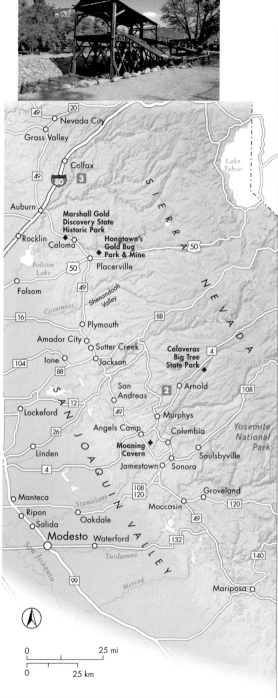

GETTING ORIENTED

The Gold Country is a largely laid-back destination popular with those seeking a reasonably priced escape from Southern California and the Bay Area. Sacramento, Davis, and Woodland are in an enormous valley just west of the Sierra Nevada range. Foothill communities Nevada City, Placerville, and Sutter Creek were products of the gold rush, and remain popular stopovers with travelers en route to Lake Tahoe.

13

Updated by
Steve Pastorino

The Gold Country is one of California's less expensive destinations, a region of the Sierra Nevada foothills that's filled with natural and cultural pleasures. Visitors come to Nevada City, Auburn, Coloma, Sutter Creek, and Columbia not only to relive the past but also to explore art galleries, shop for antiques, and stay at friendly, atmospheric inns. Spring brings wildflowers, and in fall the hills are colored by bright red berries and changing leaves. Because it offers plenty of outdoor diversions, the Gold Country is a great place to take kids.

Old Sacramento's museums provide a good introduction to the region's considerable history, but the Gold Country's heart lies along Highway 49, which winds the approximately 300-mile north–south length of the historic mining area. The highway—often a twisting, hilly two-lane road—begs for a convertible with the top down.

A new era dawned for California when James Marshall turned up a gold nugget in the tailrace of a sawmill he was constructing along the American River. On January 24, 1848, Mexico and the United States were still wrestling for ownership of what would become the Golden State. Marshall's discovery helped compel the United States to tighten its grip on the region, and prospectors from all over the world soon came to seek their fortunes in the Mother Lode.

As gold fever seized the nation, California's population of 15,000 swelled to 265,000 within three years. The mostly young, male adventurers who arrived in search of gold—the forty-niners—became part of a culture that discarded many of the button-down conventions of the eastern states. It was also a violent time. Yankee prospectors chased Mexican miners off their claims, and California's leaders initiated a plan to exterminate the local Native American population. Bounties were paid and private militias were hired to wipe out the Native Americans or sell them into slavery. California was to be dominated by the Anglo.

The gold-rush boom lasted scarcely 20 years, but it changed California forever, producing 546 mining towns, of which fewer than 250 remain. The hills of the Gold Country were alive, not only with prospecting and mining but also with business, the arts, gambling, and a fair share of crime. Opera houses went up alongside brothels, and the California State Capitol, in Sacramento, was built partly with the gold dug out of the hills.

The mild climate and rich soil in and around Sacramento Valley are responsible for the region's current riches: fresh and bountiful food and high-quality wines. Gold Country restaurants and wineries continue to earn national acclaim, and they're without the high prices of the Bay Area and Sonoma and Napa wine regions. There's a growing local craft beer scene, too.

13

PLANNING

WHEN TO GO

The Gold Country is most pleasant in spring, when the wildflowers are in bloom, and in fall. Summers can be hot: temperatures of 100°F are fairly common. Sacramento winters tend to be cool, with occasionally foggy or rainy days; many Sacramentans drive to the foothills (or the coast) for a dose of winter sunshine. Throughout the year Gold Country towns stage community and ethnic celebrations. In December many towns are decked out for Christmas.

GETTING HERE AND AROUND

AIR TRAVEL

Sacramento International Airport (SMF) is served by Aeromexico, Alaska/Horizon, American, Delta, Hawaiian, JetBlue, Southwest, United, and Volaris. A private taxi from the airport to Downtown Sacramento costs about $40; the Super Shuttle fare starts at $13. Public buses (⇨ *Bus and Light-Rail Travel*) are also an option.

Contacts Sacramento International Airport ⊠ *6900 Airport Blvd., 12 miles northwest of downtown off I-5, Sacramento* ☎ *916/929–5411* ⊕ *www. sacramento.aero/smf.* **Super Shuttle** ☎ *800/258–3826* ⊕ *www.supershuttle. com.*

BUS AND LIGHT-RAIL TRAVEL

Greyhound serves Sacramento from San Francisco and Los Angeles. Sacramento Regional Transit serves the capital area with buses and light-rail vehicles. Yolobus public buses Nos. 42A and 42B connect SMF airport and Downtown Sacramento, West Sacramento, Davis, and Woodland.

Contacts Greyhound ⊠ *420 Richards Blvd.* ☎ *800/231–2222* ⊕ *www. greyhound.com.* **Sacramento Regional Transit** ☎ *916/321–2877* ⊕ *www.sacrt. com.* **Yolobus** ☎ *530/666–2877, 916/371–2877* ⊕ *www.yolobus.com.*

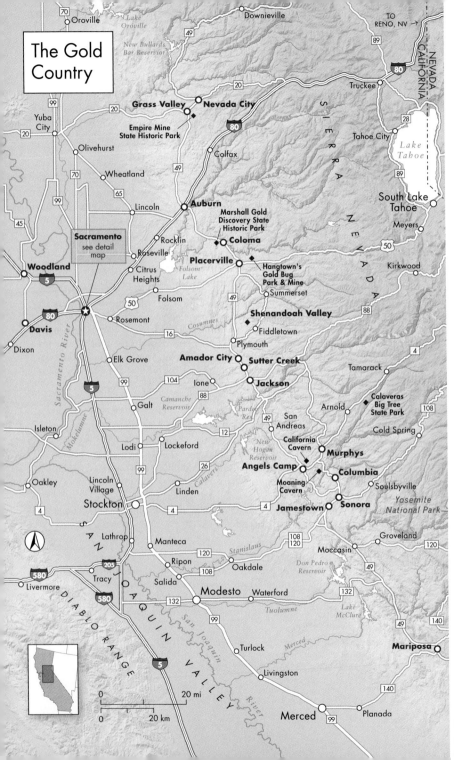

CAR TRAVEL

Interstate 5 (north–south) and Interstate 80 (east–west) are the two main routes into and out of Sacramento. From Sacramento, three highways fan out toward the east, all intersecting with historic Highway 49: Interstate 80 heads northeast 34 miles to Auburn; U.S. 50 goes east 40 miles to Placerville; and Highway 16 angles southeast 45 miles to Plymouth. Highway 49 is an excellent two-lane road that winds and climbs through the foothills and valleys, linking the principal Gold Country towns. Traveling by car is the only practical way to explore the Gold Country.

TRAIN TRAVEL

One of the most authentic ways to relive the Old West is traveling via train. On the Amtrak *California Zephyr*, you can ride the same route traveled by prospectors in the late 1800s. Docents from the Sacramento Railroad Museum ride the route from Sacramento to Reno daily, and are available to answer questions. The route into the Sierra Nevada is memorable, especially if you book a sleeper car. Amtrak trains serve Sacramento and Davis from San Jose, Oakland, and Emeryville (Amtrak buses transport passengers from San Francisco's Ferry Building to Emeryville). Amtrak also runs trains and connecting motor coaches from the Central Valley.

Contacts Amtrak ⊠ *401 I St.* ☎ *800/872–7245* ⊕ *www.amtrak.com.*

RESTAURANTS

American, Italian, and Mexican are common Gold Country fare, but chefs also prepare ambitious European, French, and contemporary regional cuisine that mixes California ingredients with international preparations. Grass Valley's meat- and vegetable-stuffed *pasties*, introduced by 19th-century gold miners from Cornwall, are one of the region's more unusual treats.

HOTELS

Sacramento has plenty of full-service hotels, budget motels, and small inns. Larger towns along Highway 49—among them Auburn, Grass Valley, and Jackson—have chain motels and inns. Many Gold Country bed-and-breakfasts occupy former mansions, miners' cabins, and other historic buildings. *Hotel reviews have been shortened. For full information, visit Fodors.com.*

Contacts Amador Council of Tourism ⊠ *115 Valley View Way, Sutter Creek* ☎ *209/267–9249, 877/868–7262* ⊕ *www.touramador.com.* **California Association of Bed & Breakfast Inns** ☎ *800/373–9251* ⊕ *www.cabbi.com/region/ sierra-foothills.* **Gold Country Inns of Tuolumne County** ⊕ *www.goldbnbs.com.*

VISITOR INFORMATION

Contacts Amador County Chamber of Commerce & Visitors Bureau ⊠ *115 Main St., Jackson* ☎ *209/223–0350* ⊕ *www.amadorcountychamber.com.* **El Dorado County Visitors Authority** ⊠ *542 Main St., Placerville* ☎ *530/621– 5885, 800/457–6279* ⊕ *visit-eldorado.com.* **Grass Valley/Nevada County Chamber of Commerce** ⊠ *128 E. Main St., Grass Valley* ☎ *530/273–4667* ⊕ *www.grassvalleychamber.com.* **Yosemite/Mariposa County Tourism Bureau** ⊠ *5158 Hwy. 140, Mariposa* ☎ *209/742–4567* ⊕ *www.yosemiteexperience.com.*

Tuolumne County Visitors Bureau ✉ *542 W. Stockton Rd., Sonora* ☎ *209/533–4420, 800/446–1333* ⊕ *www.yosemitegoldcountry.com.*

WHAT IT COSTS			
$	$$	$$$	$$$$
Restaurants	under $16	$16–$22	$23–$30	over $30
Hotels	under $120	$120–$175	$176–$250	over $250

Restaurant prices are the average cost of a main course at dinner or, if dinner is not served, at lunch, excluding sales tax. Hotel prices are the lowest cost of a standard double room in high season, excluding taxes.

SACRAMENTO AND NEARBY

California's capital is an ethnically diverse city, with sizable Mexican, Hmong, and Ukrainian populations, among many others.

SACRAMENTO

87 miles northeast of San Francisco; 384 miles north of Los Angeles.

All around the Golden State's seat of government you'll experience echoes of the gold-rush days, most notably in Old Sacramento, whose wooden sidewalks and horse-drawn carriages on cobblestone streets lend the waterfront district a 19th-century feel. The California State Railroad Museum and other venues hold artifacts of state and national significance, and historic buildings house shops and restaurants. River cruises and train rides are fun family diversions for an hour or two.

Due east of Old Sacramento is Downtown, where landmarks include the Capitol building and the surrounding Capitol Park. The convention center is also here. The area is a little uneven economically, but some of the boarded-up storefronts have begun to enjoy some revitalization in recent years.

Farther east, starting at about 15th Street, lies the city's most interesting neighborhood, Midtown, a mix of genteel Victorian edifices, ultramodern lofts, and innovative restaurants and cozy wine bars. The neighborhood springs to life on the second Saturday evening of the month, when art galleries hold open houses and the sidewalks are packed. A few intersections are jumping most evenings when the weather's good; they include the corner of 20th and L streets in what's known as Lavender Heights, the center of the city's gay and lesbian community.

GETTING HERE AND AROUND

Most people drive to Sacramento and get around by car. Yellow Cab is a reliable company.

BUS TRAVEL   Sacramento Regional Transit buses and light-rail vehicles serve the area. The No. 30 DASH shuttle bus links Old Sacramento, Midtown, and Sutter's Fort.

CAR TRAVEL   Assuming that traffic is not a factor (though it often is), Sacramento is a 90-minute drive from San Francisco and a seven-hour drive from Los

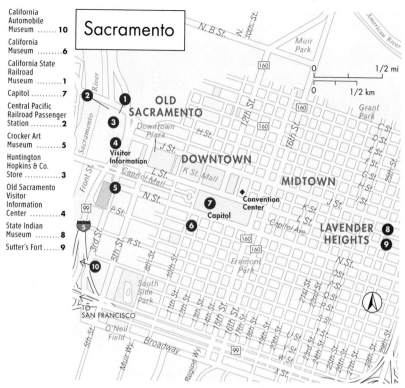

Angeles. Parking garages serve Old Sacramento and other tourist spots; on-street parking in Downtown can be difficult to find.

ESSENTIALS

Transportation Contacts Sacramento Regional Transit ☏ *916/321–2877* ⊕ *www.sacrt.com.* **Yellow Cab Co. of Sacramento** ☏ *916/444–2222* ⊕ *www. yellowcabsacramento.com.*

Visitor Information Old Sacramento Visitor Information Center ✉ *1002 2nd St.* ☏ *916/442–7644* ⊕ *www.oldsacramento.com* ⊙ *Daily 10–5.*

Sacramento Convention and Visitors Bureau ✉ *1608 I St.* ☏ *916/808–7777* ⊕ *www.visitsacramento.com.*

EXPLORING

TOP ATTRACTIONS

American River Bicycle Trail. The Jedediah Smith Memorial Trail, as it's formally called, runs for 32 miles from Old Sacramento to Beals Point in Folsom. Walk or ride a bit of it and you'll see why local cyclists and pedestrians adore its scenic lanes, if not always each other: confrontations do occur between humorless speeders and meandering gawkers. Enjoy great views of the American River and the bluffs overlooking it. ■TIP→ **Bring lunch or a snack. Pretty parks and picnic areas dot the trail.** ⊕ *www.americanriverbiketrail.com.*

The California State Railroad Museum is North America's most popular railroad museum.

California Automobile Museum. More than 150 vintage automobiles—including Model Ts, Hudsons, Studebakers, Pontiacs, and other bygone makes and models—are on display at this museum that pays tribute to automotive history and car culture. Check out a replica of Henry Ford's 1896 Quadracycle and a 1920s roadside café and garage exhibit. The docents are ready to explain everything you see. The museum is near Downtown and Old Sacramento, with ample free parking. ⊠ *2200 Front St., Downtown* ☎ *916/442–6802* ⊕ *www.calautomuseum.org* 🔤 *$8* ⏱ *Daily 10–6.*

FAMILY **California State Railroad Museum.** Near what was the terminus of the transcontinental and Sacramento Valley railroads, this 100,000-square-foot museum is a re-creation of the original train station and round-house. There are 21 locomotives and railroad cars on display along with dozens of other exhibits. You can walk through a post-office car and peer into cubbyholes and canvas mailbags, enter a sleeping car that simulates the swaying on the roadbed and the flashing lights of a passing town at night, or glimpse inside the first-class dining car. The room containing the gold "Last Spike," one of two cast in 1869 to commemorate the completion of the transcontinental railroad, is quietly compelling. Kids have lots of fun at this museum, especially in the play area upstairs. ■ **TIP→ You can visit an original roundhouse, not just a replica, at Railtown 1897 in Jamestown, near Sonora.** ⊠ *125 I St., at 2nd St., Old Sacramento* ☎ *916/323–9280* ⊕ *www.csrmf.org* 🔤 *$10* ⏱ *Daily 10–5.*

Capitol. The lacy plasterwork of the Capitol's 120-foot-high rotunda has the complexity and colors of a Fabergé egg. Underneath the gilded dome are marble floors, glittering chandeliers, monumental staircases, reproductions of century-old state offices, and legislative chambers decorated in the style of the 1890s (the Capitol was built in 1869). Guides conduct tours of the building and the 40-acre Capitol Park, which contains a rose garden, a fragrant display of camellias (Sacramento's city flower), and the California Vietnam Veterans Memorial. ■TIP➜ Wander the Capitol's botanical grounds to glimpse the diverse collection of trees, shrubs, and flowers, including some 1,200 trees from around the world. The original Deodar Cedars on the west side date back to 1872. ☒ *Capitol Mall and 10th St., Downtown* ☏ *916/324-0333* ⊕ *www.statecapitol museum.com* ☒ *Free* ☺ *Daily 9-5; tours hourly 9-4.*

Fodor's Choice
★
Crocker Art Museum. Established in 1885, this esteemed art museum contains one of the finest collections of Californian art in the nation—two highlights include *Sunday Morning in the Mines* (1872), a large canvas by Charles Christian Nahl depicting the original mining industry, and the magnificent *Great Canyon of the Sierra, Yosemite* (1871), by Thomas Hill. The Crocker has exceptional holdings of master drawings as well as an impressive collection of international ceramics and works from Europe, Asia, and Africa. A huge contemporary wing was added in 2010 and regularly hosts outstanding traveling exhibitions. On view in 2015 are works by Toulouse-Lautrec, William S. Rice, David Ligare, and Armin Hansen. ☒ *216 O St., at 3rd St., Downtown* ☏ *916/808-7000* ⊕ *www.crockerartmuseum.org* ☒ *$10* ☺ *Tues., Wed., and Fri.-Sun. 10-5, Thurs. 10-9.*

WORTH NOTING

FAMILY **California Museum.** Some of the exhibits at this celebration of all things California are high-tech and interactive, but there are also scores of archival drawers that you can pull out to see the real artifacts of history and culture—from the California State Constitution to surfing magazines. Board a 1949 cross-country bus to view a video on immigration, visit a Chinese herb shop maintained by a holographic proprietor, or find familiar names inducted into the annually expanded California Hall of Fame. The museum's café is open on weekdays until 2:30 pm. ☒ *1020 O St., at 11th St., Downtown* ☏ *916/653-7524* ⊕ *www. californiamuseum.org* ☒ *$9* ☺ *Tues.-Sat. 10-5, some Sun. noon-5.*

FAMILY **Central Pacific Railroad Passenger Station.** At this reconstructed 1876 depot there's rolling stock to admire, a typical waiting room, and a small restaurant. Part of the year a train departs from the freight depot, south of the passenger station, making a 40-minute out-and-back trip between the Sacramento River and, less interestingly, Interstate 5. ☒ *930 Front St., at J St., Old Sacramento* ☏ *916/445-6645* ⊕ *www.csrmf.org* ☒ *Train rides $10* ☺ *Train rides Apr.-Sept., weekends 11-4; Oct.-Mar., call for hrs.*

Huntington, Hopkins & Co. Store. Picks, shovels, gold pans, and other paraphernalia used by gold-rush miners are on display at this re-creation of a 19th-century hardware store. Though it's named for two of the Big Four railroad barons, their store was far more elaborate. ☒ *113 I St., at Front St., Old Sacramento* ☏ *916/323-9280* ☒ *Free* ☺ *Mon.-Thurs. 11-4.*

State Indian Museum. Among the interesting displays at this museum near Sutter's Fort is one about Ishi, the last Yahi Indian to emerge from the mountains, in 1911. Ishi provided anthropologists with insight into his people's traditions and culture. Arts-and-crafts exhibits, a demonstration village, and an evocative 10-minute video also explore the lives and history of California's native peoples. ✉ *2618 K St., at 27th St.* ☎ *916/324–0971* 🌐 *www.parks.ca.gov* 🎟 *$3* 🕒 *Daily 10–5.*

FAMILY **Sutter's Fort.** German-born Swiss immigrant John Augustus Sutter founded Sacramento's earliest Euro-American settlement in 1839. Audio speakers give information at each stop along a self-guided tour that includes a blacksmith's shop, bakery, prison, living quarters, and livestock areas. Costumed docents sometimes reenact fort life, demonstrating crafts, food preparation, and firearms maintenance. ✉ *2701 L St., at 27th St., Midtown* ☎ *916/445–4422* 🌐 *www.parks.ca.gov* 🎟 *$5 most days, $7 on interpretive program days* 🕒 *Daily 10–5.*

WHERE TO EAT

$$$ ITALIAN Fodor's Choice ★ 🍴 **Biba.** Owner Biba Caggiano is a nationally recognized authority on Italian cuisine, having written numerous cookbooks, several of which are sold here in her inviting restaurant. The Capitol crowd flocks here for exceptional renditions of lasagna with Bolognese sauce, classic Milanese-style veal osso buco with saffron-risotto cakes, and pan-roasted halibut topped with a light caper-lemon-butter sauce. For dessert, try delicious *zuccotto Florentino* (a layer of rum-soaked cake with chocolate ganache crowned with a mountain of whipped cream, and bites of hazelnuts, almonds and chocolate). A pianist adds to the upscale ambience nightly. [$] *Average main: $28* ✉ *2801 Capitol Ave., at 28th St., Midtown* ☎ *916/455–2422* 🌐 *www.biba-restaurant.com* ✍ *Reservations essential* 🕒 *Closed Sun. No lunch Mon. or Sat.*

$$ AMERICAN 🍴 **Cafeteria 15L.** An easygoing comfort-food haven, 15L makes a great first impression on newbies and a lasting one on its many repeat local customers. Generous portions of sides such as macaroni and cheese and tater tots just might be the biggest hits, but entrées like pork sliders and grilled-cheese sandwiches are also popular. The food here consistently receives high marks, as does the attentive service. On Friday and Saturday nights the place turns into a hopping club with DJs spinning dance music. [$] *Average main: $18* ✉ *1116 15th St., at L St., Downtown* ☎ *916/492–1960* 🌐 *www.cafeteria15l.com* 🕒 *No lunch weekends.*

$ MEXICAN 🍴 **Ernesto's Mexican Food.** Customers often have to wait for a table on Friday and Saturday evenings at this traditional Mexican restaurant that's a reliably good bet for shrimp Veracruz, pork carnitas, *chile colorado* (steak in ancho and pasilla chili sauce), and Mexico City–style street-food tacos. The margaritas are strong and affordable. Sister restaurant **Zocalo** (*1801 Capitol Ave.,* ☎ *916/441–0303*) has an indoor-outdoor dining space and is a popular launching spot for nights out on the town. [$] *Average main: $13* ✉ *1901 16th St., at S St., Midtown* ☎ *916/441–5850* 🌐 *www.ernestosmexicanfood.com.*

$$$$ MODERN AMERICAN 🍴 **Ella.** With fresh white calla lilies on the tables, ivory linen curtains, and distressed-wood shutters installed across the ceiling, this swank restaurant and bar near the Capitol building is artfully designed and

thoroughly modern—a nice fit for the stellar California-French farm-to-table cuisine served within. The menu changes seasonally, but typical are the steak tartare with garlic popovers and a farm egg, seared local sturgeon with caul fat, grilled endive, and romanesco sauce, and wood-fried pork chop with root vegetables. The impeccable waitstaff works with ninja-like precision, paying close attention to every detail. $ *Average main: $34* ✉ *1131 K St., Downtown* ☎ *916/443–3772* ⊕ *www.ella diningroomandbar.com* ⊘ *Closed Sun.*

$$$$
AMERICAN
Fodor's Choice
★

✕ **The Firehouse.** Long celebrated by locals and foodies as one of the city's top restaurants, this historic eatery has a full bar, breezy courtyard seating, and creative American cooking, such as char-grilled spring rack of lamb served with roasted French fingerling potatoes and baby artichoke and fava bean succotash. Visitors who can afford to treat themselves to a fine and leisurely meal can do no better in Old Sacramento—although they might also opt for the less-pricey **Ten 22.** Located a block away and under the same ownership as the Firehouse, it serves pizza and other fancified comfort food. $ *Average main: $41* ✉ *1112 2nd St., at L St., Old Sacramento* ☎ *916/442–4772* ⊕ *www.firehouseoldsac.com* ⊘ *No lunch weekends.*

$$
MODERN
AMERICAN

✕ **Hook & Ladder Manufacturing Company.** Youthful and hip, with found-art decorative elements and exposed vents, this historic former fire station is a favorite stop for creative cocktails, craft beers, and creative gastropub fare. Lighter dishes include pizza with gooey burrata cheese and fresh tomatoes, house-made sausages with assorted chutneys and mustards, and seared-ahi bahn mi sliders. There's more complex fare, too, such as bacon-wrapped pork tenderloin with gnocchi and smoked tomato, and roasted-pumpkin risotto with mascarpone. A refined drink list includes rotating local wine and beers on tap. $ *Average main: $18* ✉ *1630 S. St., Midtown* ☎ *916/442–4885* ⊕ *www.hookandladder 916.com.*

$$
AMERICAN
Fodor's Choice
★

✕ **Magpie Cafe.** This hip Midtown eatery with a casual vibe takes its food quite seriously: nearly all the produce is sourced locally, and menus are printed each day, reflecting availability from local farms. The array of small-batch farmstead cheeses, all from California, is mouthwatering (especially the Point Reyes Blue, drizzled with honey). Recent offerings have included roasted chicken for two with a chervil-ginger green sauce, and—at lunch—a smoked-trout and Meyer lemon sandwich with dill, capers, and cream cheese. Be sure to choose a couple of the perfectly braised or roasted side vegetable dishes, perhaps asparagus with green-garlic oil, or pan-seared creamy polenta with sage. If you make it here for brunch, consider the savory bread pudding with bacon, chipotle-cheddar, and chives. The pub next door can get loud after 9, so arrive before if aiming for a relaxed dinner. $ *Average main: $22* ✉ *1409 R St., No. 102, Midtown* ☎ *916/452–7594* ⊕ *www.magpiecafe.com* ⌣ *Reservations not accepted* ⊘ *No dinner Sun.*

$$
AMERICAN

✕ **Rio City Café.** Contemporary and seasonal Mediterranean and Californian cuisine, and huge floor-to-ceiling windows and an outdoor deck overlooking the river are the attractions of this popular restaurant that's designed to resemble a vintage steamship warehouse. Consider dining here for lunch or brunch, when you can enjoy the beautiful water

13

views. The food is unfussy and consistently good—burgers with rosemary fries, Baja-style fish tacos with pineapple-papaya salsa, Dungeness crab and shrimp Louie salad. The big draw here, however, is the ambience. [$] *Average main: $18* ✉ *1110 Front St., at L St., Old Sacramento* ☎ *916/442–8226* 🌐 *www.riocitycafe.com.*

$$$ EUROPEAN Fodor's Choice ★ 🍴 **The Waterboy.** Rural French cooking with locally sourced, high-quality (often organic) ingredients is the hallmark of this upscale but refreshingly unfussy Midtown restaurant that's as appealing for a casual meal with friends as it is for a drawn-out romantic dinner for two. The artisan cheese and antipasto plates are appealing starters for sharing, as is a standout chicken-liver crostini with fennel, frisée, apple, and caramelized shallots. Among the mains, try the braised Niman Ranch pork cheeks with green garlic jus, or pan-seared dayboat scallops with a celery root–sunchoke–bacon hash and a Meyer lemon–brown butter sauce. [$] *Average main: $28* ✉ *2000 Capitol Ave., at 20th St., Midtown* ☎ *916/498–9891* 🌐 *www.waterboyrestaurant.com* ⏲ *No lunch weekends.*

WHERE TO STAY

$$$ B&B/INN 🏨 **Amber House Bed & Breakfast Inn.** About a mile from the Capitol, this B&B has rooms in a 1905 Craftsman-style home and an 1895 Dutch colonial–revival home. **Pros:** Midtown location; attentive service. **Cons:** freeway access isn't easy. [$] *Rooms from: $199* ✉ *1315 22nd St., Midtown* ☎ *916/444–8085, 800/755–6526* 🌐 *www.amberhouse.com* 🛏 *10 rooms* 🍽 *Breakfast.*

$$ HOTEL Fodor's Choice ★ 🏨 **Citizen Hotel.** This boutique hotel built within the historic 1926 Cal Western Life building is dapper and refined, with marble stairs, stripped wallpaper, and plush velvet chairs, lending the place a Roaring '20s charm. **Pros:** hip, sophisticated decor; smooth and solicitous service; terrific restaurant and bar. **Cons:** rooms near elevator can be noisy; rates vary widely depending on conventions, legislature, season. [$] *Rooms from: $159* ✉ *926 J St., Downtown* ☎ *916/447–2700* 🌐 *www.jdvhotels.com* 🛏 *183 rooms, 15 suites* 🍽 *No meals.*

$$ HOTEL 🏨 **Delta King.** For the opportunity to sleep in one of Sacramento's most unusual and historic relics, book a stay in this riverboat that's been gloriously restored. **Pros:** exudes old-world charm; steps from historic Old Town shopping and dining. **Cons:** slanted floors can feel a bit jarring; rooms are a bit cramped. [$] *Rooms from: $167* ✉ *1000 Front St., Old Sacramento* ☎ *916/444–5464, 800/825–5464* 🌐 *www.deltaking.com* 🛏 *44 rooms* 🍽 *Breakfast.*

$$$ HOTEL 🏨 **Hyatt Regency Sacramento.** With a marble-and-glass lobby and luxurious rooms, this hotel across from the Capitol and adjacent to the convention center is arguably Sacramento's finest. **Pros:** beautiful Capitol Park is across the street; some rooms have small balconies. **Cons:** nearby streets can feel a little dodgy at night; somewhat impersonal. [$] *Rooms from: $179* ✉ *1209 L St., Downtown* ☎ *916/443–1234, 800/633–7313* 🌐 *www.sacramento.hyatt.com* 🛏 *485 rooms, 18 suites* 🍽 *No meals.*

NIGHTLIFE AND PERFORMING ARTS

NIGHTLIFE

Blue Cue. A billiard lounge known for its selection of single-malt scotches, the Blue Cue is upstairs from the popular Mexican restaurant Centro. Wednesday night's trivia contest is a spirited event. ✉ *1004 28th St., at J St., Midtown* ☎ *916/441–6810* ⊕ *www.bluecue.com.*

Dive Bar. Live "mermaids" and "mermen" swim in a massive tank above the bar at this lively downtown nightspot known for its extensive list of craft cocktails and local beers. ✉ *1016 K St., Downtown* ☎ *916/737–5999* ⊕ *divebarsacramento.com.*

Fox and Goose. This casual pub with live music serves fish-and-chips, Cornish pasties, and other traditional items—plus vegetarian/vegan fare—on weekdays until 9:30. ✉ *1001 R St., at 10th St., Downtown* ☎ *916/443–8825* ⊕ *www.foxandgoose.com.*

Harlow's. This sceney restaurant draws a youngish crowd to its art-deco bar-nightclub for live music after 9 pm. ✉ *2708 J St., at 27th St., Midtown* ☎ *916/441–4693* ⊕ *www.harlows.com.*

Streets of London Pub. A favorite among Anglophiles, Streets is open until 2 am nightly. Darts and TV soccer, anyone? ✉ *1804 J St., at 18th St., Midtown* ☎ *916/498–1388* ⊕ *www.streetsoflondon.net.*

PERFORMING ARTS

California Musical Theatre. This group presents Broadway shows at the Sacramento Community Center Theater and the summer Music Circus offerings (think *Oklahoma, Annie*) at the theater-in-the-round Wells Fargo Pavilion. ✉ *1419 H St., at 14th St., Downtown* ☎ *916/557–1999* ⊕ *www.calmt.com.*

Crest Theatre. It's worth peeking inside the Crest even if you don't catch a show there, just to see the swirling and flamboyant art deco design in the foyer. It's a beloved venue for classic and art-house films, along with concerts and other cultural events. ✉ *1013 K St., at 10th St., Downtown* ☎ *916/476–3356* ⊕ *www.crestsacramento.com.*

SHOPPING

Greater Sacramento is filled with familiar shops. To try something new, wander through Midtown, especially J, K, and L streets between 16th and 26th streets.

Westfield Galleria at Roseville. The Sacramento region's largest shopping complex is a sprawling, heavily trafficked collection of chain stores and restaurants. It's always jumping. ✉ *1151 Galleria Blvd., north of Sacramento off I–80 Exit 105A, Roseville* ⊕ *www.westfield.com/galleria atroseville.*

WOODLAND

20 miles northwest of Sacramento.

In its heyday, Woodland was among California's wealthiest cities. Established by gold seekers and entrepreneurs, it later became an agricultural gold mine. The legacy of the old land barons lives on in the restored Victorian and Craftsman architecture downtown; the best examples are south of Main Street on College, Elm, 1st, and 2nd streets. The town's top attraction is the splendid Heidrick Ag History Center.

GETTING HERE AND AROUND

Yolobus (🌐 *www.yolobus.com*) serves downtown Woodland from Sacramento, but it's far more practical to drive here via Interstate 5.

ESSENTIALS

Visitor Information Woodland Chamber of Commerce ✉ *307 1st St., at Dead Cat Alley* ☎ *530/662–7327* 🌐 *www.woodlandchamber.org.*

EXPLORING

FAMILY **Heidrick Ag History Center Tractor & Truck Museum.** This gigantic space provides a marvelous overview of the entire history of motorized agricultural vehicles. Souped-up and shiny, the antique threshers, harvesters, combines, tractors, and proto-tractors on display here look ready to service the farms of their eras all over again. And there's more. A separate wing surveys the evolution of the truck, with an emphasis on ones used for farm work. ✉ *1962 Hays La., off County Rd. 102* ☎ *530/666–9700* 🌐 *www.aghistory.org* 🎫 *$10* 🕒 *Mid-Mar.–early Nov., Wed.–Sun. 10–5; early Nov.–mid-Mar., Wed.–Sun. 10–4.*

Woodland Opera House. This 1896 structure hosted minstrel shows, John Philip Sousa's marching band, and early vaudeville acts before closing for six decades (a sad saga that involved a penny-pinching Hershey's chocolate heir). Now restored, it hosts plays, musicals, and concerts. If the box office is open, ask for a backstage tour or a peek at the auditorium. ✉ *340 2nd St.* ☎ *530/666–9617* 🌐 *www.woodlandoperahouse.org* 🕒 *Tours Tues. 2–4 or by appointment.*

Yolo County Historical Museum. This 10-room classical-revival home of settler William Byas Gibson was purchased by volunteers and restored to what you see today. You can see collections of furnishings and artifacts from the 1850s to 1930s. Old trees and an impressive lawn cover the 2½-acre site. ✉ *512 Gibson Rd., at College St.* ☎ *530/666–1045* 🌐 *www.gibsonhouse.org* 🕒 *Tues.–Fri. 10–3.*

WHERE TO EAT

$$ AMERICAN 🍴 **Mojo's Kitchen428.** Woodland's dining scene turned a shade greener when Mojo's opened with restored furnishings reportedly rescued from other businesses. The steaks, lamb shanks, and turkey potpies all have their adherents, but if you're not into meat you'll find salmon and other seafood on the menu, along with vegetarian and even a few vegan items. There's a popular brunch on weekends. A friendly, stylish place, Mojo's rewards customers for also adopting green practices: ride a bike here, and you'll receive 10% off your bill. [$] *Average main: $21* ✉ *428 1st St., off Main St.* ☎ *530/661–0428* 🌐 *www.mojoskitchen428.com.*

DAVIS

10 miles west of Sacramento.

Davis began as a rich agricultural area and remains one, but it doesn't feel like a cow town. It's home to the University of California at Davis, whose 35,000-plus students hang at downtown cafés, galleries, and bookstores (most of the action takes place between 1st and 4th and C and G streets), lending the city a decidedly college-town feel.

GETTING HERE AND AROUND

Most people arrive here by car via Interstate 80. In a pinch, you can get here via Yolobus (⊕ *www.yolobus.com*) from Sacramento. Downtown is walkable. Touring by bicycle is also a popular option—Davis is very flat.

ESSENTIALS

Visitor Information Davis Chamber of Commerce ⊠ *640 3rd St.* ☎ *530/756– 5160* ⊕ *www.davischamber.com.*

EXPLORING

University of California, Davis. A top research university, UC Davis educates many of the Wine Country's vintners and grape growers. Campus tours depart from Buehler Alumni and Visitors Center. On a tour or not, worthy stops include the **Arboretum** (*arboretum.ucdavis.edu*)—this is a major agricultural school, and it shows—and the **Mondavi Center for the Performing Arts** (*www.mondaviarts.org*), a striking modern glass structure that presents top-tier artists. ⊠ *Visitor Center, Alumni La.* ☎ *530/752–8111* ⊕ *visit.ucdavis.edu* ⊗ *Visitor Center weekdays 8–5, Sat. 9–3.*

Artery. The work of Northern California craftspeople is displayed at the Artery, an artists' cooperative that includes decorative and functional ceramics, glass, wood, jewelry, fiber arts, painting, sculpture, drawing, and photography. ⊠ *207 G St.* ☎ *530/758–8330* ⊕ *www.theartery.net* ⊗ *Mon.–Thurs. and Sat. 10–6, Fri. 10–9, Sun. noon–5.*

WHERE TO EAT AND STAY

$ ✕ **Bistro 33.** This striking venue, in and outside what long ago was Davis

AMERICAN   City Hall, does brisk business well into the evenings. Wood-fired pizza and a small but diverse selection of entrées draw big crowds for lunch and dinner in a renovated building that has a large, attractively arranged courtyard. Brunch is served on Sunday. Ⓢ *Average main: $15* ⊠ *226 F St.* ☎ *530/756–4556* ⊕ *davis.bistro33.com.*

$$ 🛏 **Aggie Inn.** This simple hotel, less than a block from the campus, is

HOTEL   named for the University of California at Davis Aggies, the school's team name. **Pros:** clean; windows open; good location; not a chain. **Cons:** so-so breakfasts; bare-bones decor. Ⓢ *Rooms from: $135* ⊠ *245 1st St.* ☎ *530/756–0352* ⊕ *www.aggieinn.com* ⇗ *25 rooms, 9 suites* ⏐⊘⏐ *Breakfast.*

$$ 🛏 **Hallmark Inn.** Two buildings with clean, modern rooms make up this

HOTEL   inn, which is five blocks from the University of California campus and is next door to a restaurant. **Pros:** within walking distance of campus and downtown; safe neighborhood; updated rooms. **Cons:** limited ventilation; rooms can feel small. Ⓢ *Rooms from: $155* ⊠ *110 F St.* ☎ *800/753–0035* ⊕ *www.hallmarkinn.com* ⇗ *120 rooms* ⏐⊘⏐ *No meals.*

13

THE GOLD COUNTRY—SOUTH

This hilly region has an old-timey vibe. It's rich with antiques shops, quaint coffee shops, and delightfully appointed Victorian B&Bs.

PLACERVILLE

44 miles east of Sacramento.

It's hard to imagine now, but in 1849 about 4,000 miners staked out every gully and hillside in Placerville, turning the town into a rip-roaring camp of log cabins, tents, and clapboard houses. The area was then known as Hangtown, a graphic allusion to the nature of frontier justice. It took on the name Placerville in 1854 and became an important supply center for the miners. (*Placer* is defined roughly as valuable minerals found in riverbeds or lakes.) Mark Hopkins, Philip Armour, and John Studebaker were among the industrialists who got their starts here. Today Placerville ranks among the hippest towns in the region, its Main Street abuzz with indie shops, coffeehouses, and wine bars, many of them inside rehabbed historic buildings.

GETTING HERE AND AROUND

You'll need a car to get to and around Placerville; it's a 45-minute drive from Sacramento via U.S. 50.

EXPLORING

FAMILY   **Apple Hill.** During the fall harvest season (September through December), the members of the Apple Hill Growers Association open their orchards and vineyards for apple and berry picking, picnicking, and wine and cider tasting. Start your tour at High Hill Ranch, where there are fishing ponds for kids (they'll clean and pack the fish for you). Nibble on apple doughnuts or buy jewelry from local crafters. Stop at Larsen Apple Barn, a legacy farm. Family-favored Kid's Inc. serves apple pie and empanadas, and you can sample Cabernet and Bordeaux-style blends at Grace Patriot Wines, and fresh-pressed juices at Barsotti. Stop at Wofford Acres Vineyard just to see a dramatic view of the American River canyon below. ⚠ Traffic on weekends is often backed up, so take the Camino exit or go during the week to avoid the crowds (although kid-centric events are on weekends). ⊠ *About 5 miles east of Hwy. 49; take Camino exit from U.S. 50* ☎ *530/644–7692* ⊕ *www.applehill.com.*

FAMILY   **Hangtown's Gold Bug Park & Mine.** Take a self-guided tour of this fully lighted mine shaft owned by the City of Placerville. The worthwhile audio tour (included) makes clear what you're seeing. ■TIP➜ A shaded stream runs through the park, and there are picnic facilities. ⊠ *2635 Goldbug La., off Bedford Ave., 1 mile off U.S. 50* ☎ *530/642–5207* ⊕ *www.goldbugpark.org* ⌦ *Park free; mine tour $6* ☉ *Apr.–Oct., daily 10–4; Nov.–Mar., weekends noon–4.*

WHERE TO EAT AND STAY

$ ✕ **The Cozmic Cafe.** Crowds come for healthful wraps, burritos, sandwiches, salads, and the like, plus breakfast (served anytime), smoothies, and espresso drinks. Portions are big, prices are low, and the ambience is distinctive. The eatery is in the 1859 Pearson's Soda Works

VEGETARIAN

Building and extends back into the side of a mountain, into what used to be a mineshaft. The live music here is among the best in the foothills, and an upstairs pub beckons with local wines and microbrews. $ *Average main: $9* ⊠ *594 Main St.* ☎ *530/642–8481* ⊕ *www.ourcoz. com* ☺ *Closed Mon.*

$$$$
B&B/INN
Fodor's Choice
★

Eden Vale Inn. Handcrafted by the owners, this lavish but rustic B&B occupies a converted turn-of-the-20th-century hay barn, the centerpiece of which is a 27-foot slate fireplace that rises to a sloping roof of timber beams. **Pros:** rooms are exceptionally plush; the patio and grounds are stunning; plenty of places outside for kids to run. **Cons:** fairly expensive for the area; book summer weekends well in advance. $ *Rooms from: $298* ⊠ *1780 Springvale Rd.* ☎ *530/621-0901* ⊕ *www.edenvaleinn.com* ↻ *5 rooms, 2 suites* ⏉*Breakfast.*

$$
B&B/INN

Seasons Bed & Breakfast. One of Placerville's oldest homes has been transformed into a lovely and relaxing oasis. **Pros:** quiet setting; short walk to downtown; attentive hosts; great breakfasts. **Cons:** B&B environment not for everyone. $ *Rooms from: $135* ⊠ *2934 Bedford Ave.* ☎ *530/626–4420* ⊕ *www.theseasons.net* ↻ *2 rooms, 1 suite, 1 cottage* ⏉*Breakfast.*

SHENANDOAH VALLEY

20 miles south of Placerville.

The most concentrated Gold Country wine-touring area lies in the hills of the Shenandoah Valley, east of Plymouth. Robust Zinfandel is the primary grape grown here, but vineyards here produce plenty of other varietals, from Rhône blends to Italian Barberas and Sangioveses. Most wineries are open for tastings at least on weekend afternoons, and some of the top ones are open daily; several have shaded picnic areas. ■TIP→ This region is gaining steam as a less-congested alternative to the Napa Valley.

GETTING HERE AND AROUND

Reach the Shenandoah Valley by turning east on Fiddletown Road in Plymouth, between Placerville and Sutter Creek, and then north on Plymouth-Shenandoah Road. You will need a car to explore the valley and its vineyards.

EXPLORING

Shenandoah Vineyards. A plummy Barbera and an almost chocolaty Zinfandel top this winery's repertoire, but for a contrast you can also try a startlingly crisp Sauvignon Blanc. The Tempranillo is also good. An adjacent gallery sells contemporary art, pottery, photographs, and souvenirs. ■TIP→ Shenandoah is affiliated with the nearby Sobon Estate Winery, which has an engaging on-site museum about the area. ⊠ *12300 Steiner Rd.* ☎ *209/245–4455* ⊕ *www.sobonwine.com* ▧ *Tasting $5* ☺ *Daily 10–5.*

Sobon Estate. You can sip fruity, robust Zinfandels—old vine and new—and learn about winemaking and Shenandoah Valley pioneer life at the museum here. This winery was established in 1856 and has been run since 1989 by the owners of Shenandoah Vineyards (whose wines you can also taste). ■TIP→ To sample the best of the Zins, pay the modest fee for the reserve tasting. ⊠ *14430 Shenandoah Rd.* ☎ *209/245–4455* ⊕ *www.sobonwine.com* ⊠ *Tasting $5* ⊙ *Daily 10–5.*

Terre Rouge and Easton Wines. The winery of Bill and Jane Easton has two labels with two different wine-making styles: Terre Rouge focuses on Rhône-style wines, while Easton covers old-vine Zinfandel and Barbera. The winery has had good results with inky, soft Syrahs and Enigma, a Rhône-style white blend of Marsanne, Viognier, and Roussane. ■TIP→ You can picnic on the shaded patio here and there's a pétanque court nearby. ⊠ *10801 Dickson Rd.* ☎ *209/245–4277* ⊕ *www.terrerougewines.com* ⊠ *Tasting $5* ⊙ *Nov.–Aug., Thurs.–Mon. 11–4; Sept.–Oct., daily 11–4.*

Vino Noceto. This winery is an example of the benefits of focusing mostly on one varietal—in this case Sangiovese—and doing it well. Owners Suzy and Jim Gullett produce their Sangioveses in several different styles, from light and fruity to rich and heavy. They also produce small lots of wines from other varietals. ⊠ *11011 Shenandoah Rd., at Dickson Rd.* ☎ *209/245–6556* ⊕ *www.noceto.com* ⊠ *Tasting free* ⊙ *Weekdays 11–4, weekends 11–5.*

WHERE TO EAT AND STAY

$$$$
MODERN
AMERICAN
Fodor'sChoice
★

✕ **Taste.** A serendipitous find on the dusty streets of tiny Plymouth, Taste serves eclectic modern dishes made from fresh local fare. Phyllo-wrapped mushroom "cigars" or pan-seared scallops served with golden-beet risotto, kumquat, mint, fennel, and orange butter. Toss in tahini-grilled cauliflower with red-wine braised carrots and turnip greens, and even the vegetarians leave happy. ■TIP→ Gold Country winemaking can be hit or miss, but with several sommeliers on staff, this is a terrific place to find out which producers are worth seeking out. There's also a great beer list. $ *Average main: $33* ⊠ *9402 Main St.* ☎ *209/245–3463* ⊕ *www.restauranttaste.com* ⊙ *Closed Tues. and Wed. No lunch weekdays.*

$$
B&B/INN

⌂ **Amador Harvest Inn.** This B&B adjacent to the Deaver Vineyards tasting room occupies a bucolic lakeside spot in the Shenandoah Valley. **Pros:** rustic charm; reasonable rates; hearty breakfasts. **Cons:** spare decor; a bit old-fashioned. $ *Rooms from: $165* ⊠ *12455 Steiner Rd.* ☎ *209/245–5512, 800/217–2304* ⊕ *www.amadorharvestinn.com* ⇄ *4 rooms* ⦿*Breakfast.*

AMADOR CITY

6 miles south of Plymouth.

The history of tiny Amador City mirrors the boom-bust-boom cycle of many Gold Country towns. With an output of $42 million in gold, its Keystone Mine was one of the most productive in the Mother Lode. After all the gold was extracted, the miners cleared out, and the area

Continued on page 498

EUREKA! CALIFORNIA'S GOLD RUSH

When James W. Marshall burst into John Sutter's Mill on January 24, 1848, carrying flecks of gold in his hat, the millwright unleashed the glittering California gold rush with these immortal words:

"Boys, I believe I've found a gold mine!"

Before it was over, drowsy San Francisco had become the boomtown of the Golden West, Columbia's mines alone yielded $87,000,000, and California's Mother Lode—a vein of gold-bearing quartz that stretched 150 miles across the Sierra Nevada foothills—had been nearly tapped dry. Even though the gold rush soon became the gold bust, today you can still strike it rich by visiting the historic sites where it all happened.

Journey down the Gold Country Highway—a serpentine, nearly 300-mile-long two-lane route appropriately numbered 49—to find pure vacation treasure: fascinating mother lode towns, rip-roaring mining camps, and historic strike sites. In fact, in Placerville—as the former Hangtown, this spot saw so much new money and crime that outlaws were hanged in pairs—you can still pan the streams. And after you've seen the sights, the prospects remain just as golden: the entire region is a trove of gorgeous wineries, fun eateries, and Victorian-era hotels.

ALL THAT GLITTERED: '49ER FEVER

From imagination springs adventure, and perhaps no event in the 19th century provoked more wild adventures than the California gold rush of 1848 to 1855.

James Marshall

1856 U.S. quarter

John Sutter

GOLD IN THEM THAR HILLS California's golden lava was discovered purely by accident. Upon finding his cattle ranch had gone to ruin while he was away fighting in the Mexican-American War, New Jersey native James W. Marshall decided to build a sawmill, with John Sutter, outside the town of Coloma, 40 miles upstream of Sutter's Fort on the American River. To better power the mill, he had a wider siphon created to divert the river water and, one morning, spotted golden flakes in the trench. Rich fur magnate Sutter tried to keep the mother strike quiet, but his own staff soon decamped to pan the streams, and the secret was out. The gold rush's impact was so profound that, practically overnight, it catapulted San Francisco into one of the nation's—and the world's—wealthiest cities.

BROTHER, CAN YOU SPARE AN INGOT? After Marshall, 37 at the time, saw his fledgling mill abandoned by workers who went to pan the streams, he left Coloma for almost a decade. During the 1860s he made some money as a vintner there—a dicey profession for a reported alcoholic. Eventually Marshall's wine business dried up, and he returned to prospecting in the 1870s. But without success. For six years starting in 1872, the state Legislature gave him a small pension as an acknowledgment of his gold rush importance, but for the last years of his life he was practically penniless. He died on Aug. 10, 1885, at age 74.

THE GOLD CRUSH Before the gold rush ended, in 1855, it is estimated that it drew 300,000 people—Americans, Europeans, and Chinese—to the Sierra Nevada foothills to seek their fortune. Sadly, accidents, disease, and skirmishes with Native Americans took their toll on both the prospectors and the environment. In addition, the gold lust of '49er fever left more than a thousand murders in its wake (not counting the infamous "suspended" sentences meted out at Hangtown).

BOOM TO BUST

Jan. 24, 1848: James W. Marshall spies specks of bright rock in the streambed at his sawmill's site; Sutter certifies they are gold.

May, 1848: California's coastal communities empty out as prospectors flock to the hills to join the "forty-eighters."

Aug. 19, 1848: The *New York Herald* is the first East Coast newspaper to report a gold rush in California.

Oct. 13, 1849: California's state constitution is approved in Monterey. The state's new motto becomes "Eureka!"

1855: The California gold rush effectively ends, as digging for the precious mineral becomes increasingly difficult, and large corporations monopolize mining operations.

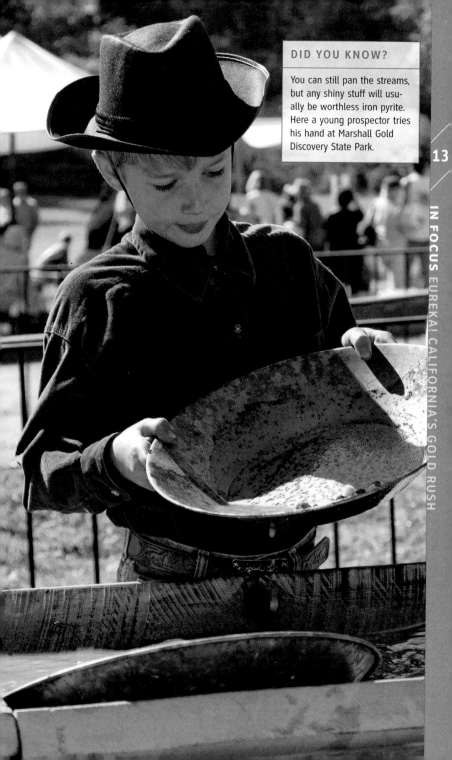

DID YOU KNOW?

You can still pan the streams, but any shiny stuff will usually be worthless iron pyrite. Here a young prospector tries his hand at Marshall Gold Discovery State Park.

GOING FOR THE GOLD

Marshall Gold Discovery State Park

If you want to go prospecting for the best sightseeing treasures in Gold Country, just follow this map.

Coloma

Empire Mine State Historic Park, Grass Valley: During the century that it was operating, Empire Mine produced some 5.6 million ounces of gold. More than 350 miles of tunnels were dug, most under water. Operations ceased in 1956, but today visitors to the 800-acre park can go on guided tours of the mines and enjoy great hiking trails and picnic spots.

Marshall Gold Discovery State Historic Park, Coloma: Here's where it all began—a can't-miss gold rush site. See the stone cairn that marks the spot of James Marshall's discovery, the huge statue of him that rests on his grave site, and visit—together with crowds of schoolchildren—the updated museum, and more.

Hangtown's Gold Bug Park & Mine, Placerville: Put on a hardhat and step into the 19th century at Gold Bug, located a few miles south of Marshall's jackpot site. Take a self-guided audio tour of a mine that opened in 1888, or a special tour of a mine opened in the 1850s, and do some panning for gems outside the gift shop. "Fool's gold" (used for billiard tables and chalkboards) was mostly found here before digging stopped in 1942.

Man pans for gold during gold rush.

Empire Mine State Historic Park   Gold sifting pan   Columbia State Historic Park

Angels Camp Museum: Gold-rush relics are on display here: photos, rocks, petrified wood, blacksmith and mining equipment, even a horse-drawn hearse. The carriage house out back holds 3 carriages and impressive mineral specimens.

Kennedy Gold Mine, Jackson: At 5,912 feet below ground, this is one of the world's deepest mines. Its head frame is one of the most dominant man-made sights along Highway 49's 295 miles. In operation from 1880 until World War II, the mine produced tens of millions of dollars of gold. One-hour tours, offered weekends and holidays from March through October, include a look inside the stately Mine Office.

Columbia State Historic Park. Just north of Sonora, this is the best extant example of a gold rush-era town as it appeared in the mid-19th century. During its "golden" years, Columbia yielded more than $85 million in gold. Since World War II, the

town has been restored. Fandango halls, Wells Fargo stage coaches, and a costumed staff bring a working 1850's mining town to life again.

Mariposa Museum and History Center, Mariposa: Find all sorts of mining equipment, including a five-stamp ore mill, at this modest museum in the gold rush region's southernmost area. Also here is the fascinating California State Mining and Mineral Museum, home to a famous 13-pound golden nugget.

Gold dollars

A PROSPECTING PRIMER

Grab any non-Teflon-coated pan with sloping sides and head up to "them thar hills." Find a stream—preferably one containing black sand—you can stoop beside, and then:

■ Scoop out sediment to fill your pan.

■ Add water, then gently shake the pan sideways, back and forth. This allows any gold to settle at the bottom.

■ Pick out and toss away any larger rocks.

■ Keep adding water, keep shaking the pan, and slowly pour the loosened waste gravel over the rim of the pan, making sure not to upend the pan while doing so.

■ If you're left with gold, yell "Eureka!" then put it in a glass container. Your findings may not make you rich, but will entitle you to bragging rights for as long as you keep the gold handy to show friends.

■ TIP→ If you'd rather not pan on your own, plenty of attractions and museums in the Gold Country will let you try your hand at prospecting. See listings in this chapter for more details on these historic sites.

Columbia State Historic Park

suffered. Amador City now derives its wealth from tourists, who come to browse through its antiques and specialty shops, most of them on or just off Highway 49.

GETTING HERE AND AROUND

Park where you can along Old Highway 49 (a bypass diverts Highway 49 traffic around Sutter Creek and Amador City), and walk around.

WHERE TO STAY

$$ B&B/INN 🏨 **Imperial Hotel.** The whimsically decorated mock-Victorian rooms at this 1879 hotel give a modern twist to the excesses of the era. **Pros:** comfortable; good restaurant and bar; tiny-town charm. **Cons:** no nightlife. [$] *Rooms from: $135* ✉ *14202 Old Hwy. 49* ☎ *209/267–9172* 🌐 *www.imperialamador.com* 🛏 *6 rooms, 3 suites* 🍴 *Breakfast.*

SUTTER CREEK

2 miles south of Amador City.

Sutter Creek is a charming conglomeration of balconied buildings, Victorian homes, and neo–New England structures. The stores on Main Street (formerly part of Highway 49, which was rerouted) are worth visiting for works by the many local artists and craftspeople.

GETTING HERE AND AROUND

Arrive here by car on Highway 49. There's no public transit, but downtown is walkable. The visitor center organizes walking tours.

ESSENTIALS

Information **Sutter Creek Visitor Center** ✉ *71A Main St.* ☎ *209/267–1344* 🌐 *www.suttercreek.org.*

EXPLORING

Monteverde Store Museum. This store, opened 1896, is a relic from the past: its final owner walked out more than four decades ago and never returned. These days you can peruse what he left behind, including typical wares from a century ago, an elaborate antique scale, and a chair-encircled potbellied stove. ✉ *3 Randolph St.* ☎ *209/267–0493* 🕒 *Weekends, if volunteers available, hrs vary.*

WHERE TO STAY

$$ B&B/INN 🏨 **Eureka Street Inn.** The lead- and stained-glass windows and the original redwood paneling, wainscoting, and beams—and, oh yes, those gas-log fireplaces in most rooms—lend the Eureka Street Inn a cozy feel. **Pros:** quiet location; lovely porch; engaging owners. **Cons:** only four rooms. [$] *Rooms from: $145* ✉ *55 Eureka St.* ☎ *209/267–5500, 800/399–2389* 🌐 *www.eurekastreetinn.com* 🛏 *4 rooms* 🍴 *Breakfast.*

$$$ B&B/INN 🏨 **The Foxes Inn of Sutter Creek.** The rooms in this 1857 white-clapboard house are handsome, with high ceilings, antique beds, and armoires; five have gas fireplaces. **Pros:** lovely inside and out; friendly owners. **Cons:** pricey. [$] *Rooms from: $200* ✉ *77 Main St.* ☎ *209/267–5882, 800/987–3344* 🌐 *www.foxesinn.com* 🛏 *5 rooms, 2 suites* 🍴 *Breakfast.*

$$ B&B/INN 🏨 **Grey Gables Inn.** Charming yet modern, this inn brings a touch of the English countryside to the Gold Country; the rooms, named after British poets, have gas-log fireplaces. **Pros:** English feel; tasteful interiors.

Cons: hovers over main road; not much to do in town after dark. [$] *Rooms from: $168* ✉ *161 Hanford St.* ☎ *209/267–1039, 800/473–9422* 🌐 *www.greygables.com* 🛏 *8 rooms* 🍴 *Breakfast.*

$$ HOTEL **Days Inn Sutter Creek.** If you're on a budget, this hotel is a good choice; the rooms have coffeemakers, and most have queen-size beds. **Pros:** affordable; convenient; clean. **Cons:** can feel a bit impersonal. [$] *Rooms from: $124* ✉ *271 Hanford St.* ☎ *209/267–9177* 🌐 *www.daysinn.com/suttercreek* 🛏 *52 rooms* 🍴 *Breakfast.*

JACKSON

8 miles south of Sutter Creek.

Jackson wasn't the Gold Country's rowdiest town, but the party lasted longer here than most anywhere else: "girls' dormitories" (aka brothels) and nickel slot machines flourished until the mid-1950s. Jackson also had the world's deepest and richest gold mines, the Kennedy and the Argonaut, which together produced $70 million in gold. Most of the miners who worked the lode were of Serbian or Italian origin, and they gave the town a European character that persists to this day. Jackson has pioneer cemeteries whose headstones tell the stories of local Serbian and Italian families. The city's official website (🌐 *ci.jackson.ca.us; click on "Visitor Center"*) has great cemetery and walking-tour maps; there are some interesting shops downtown.

GETTING HERE AND AROUND

Arrive by car on Highway 49. You can walk to downtown sights but otherwise will need a car.

EXPLORING

Kennedy Gold Mine. On weekends, docents offer guided surface tours of one the most prolific mines of the Gold Rush era. Exhibits inside the remaining buildings illustrate how the mine used "skips" to lower miners and materials into the mile-long shaft, and to carry ore and tailings to the surface. The tour, including a short film, takes 60 to 90 minutes. ✉ *½ mile east of Hwy. 49, Kennedy Mine Rd., at Argonaut Ln.* ☎ *209/223–9542* 🌐 *www.kennedygoldmine.com* 🎟 *Free; guided tours $10* 🕒 *Mar.–Oct., weekends 10–3.*

Fodor's Choice ★ **Preston Castle.** History buffs and ghost hunters regularly make the trip to this fantastically creepy building that was built to house troubled youth in 1894. Having fallen into a state of disrepair, the building is slowly undergoing a full renovation. Tours are available by appointment and on certain Thursdays and Saturdays throughout the year (it's best to call ahead to confirm schedule). Ask about evening and overnight tours when tales of paranormal activity are truly spooky. The dramatic Romanesque Revival structure has appeared on TV's *Ghost Hunters,* and during tours of this 156-room building you'll learn all sorts of spine-tingling tales, including one about a student murdering a housekeeper and then rolling her up in a carpet. ✉ *909 Palm Dr., 12 miles west of Jackson via Hwys. 88 and 104, Ione* ☎ *209/256–3623* 🌐 *www.prestoncastle.com* 🎟 *$10* 🕒 *Apr.–Sept., Sat. 10–1; hrs vary for evening and overnight tours.*

St. Sava Serbian Orthodox Church. The terraced cemetery on the grounds of the handsome church is an impressive sight. ✉ *724 N. Main St.* 🌐 *www.saintsavajackson.org.*

WHERE TO EAT AND STAY

$ AMERICAN 🍴 **Mel and Faye's Diner.** A local hangout famous for its "Moo Burger"—so big it still makes cow sounds, presumably—the diner is run by its namesakes' son, who has added slightly more sophisticated fare for breakfast, lunch, and dinner. [$] *Average main: $10* ✉ *31 Main St.* ☎ *209/223–0853* 🌐 *www.melandfayesjackson.com* 🕒 *Closed Tues.*

$ HOTEL 🏨 **Hotel Leger.** Home to a still convivial old saloon that was one of the rowdiest miners' haunts back in the day, this atmospheric 1851 inn, which is about 8 miles south of Jackson, is inhabited today by friendly ghosts. **Pros:** friendly and accommodating proprietors; rich in history; reasonably priced. **Con:** bathrooms are private but some are located across the hall; thin walls and creaky floorboards. [$] *Rooms from: $115* ✉ *8304 Main St., Mokelumme Hill* ☎ *209/286–1401* 🌐 *www.hotelleger.com* 🛏 *7 rooms, 7 suites* 🍽 *No meals.*

ANGELS CAMP

20 miles south of Jackson.

Angels Camp is famous chiefly for its May jumping-frog contest, based on Mark Twain's short story "The Celebrated Jumping Frog of Calaveras County." The writer reputedly heard the story of the jumping frog from Ross Coon, proprietor of Angels Hotel, which has been in operation since 1856. It's a favorite destination these days among outdoor adventurers, who love exploring the subterranean caverns and fishing for salmon, trout, and bass in the area's crystal clear rivers and lakes.

GETTING HERE AND AROUND

Angels Camp is at the intersection of Highway 49 and Highway 4. You'll need a car to get here and around.

EXPLORING

Angels Camp Museum. Gold-rush relics are on display here: photos, rocks, petrified wood, blacksmith and mining equipment, even a horse-drawn hearse. The carriage house out back holds 31 carriages and impressive mineral specimens. ✉ *753 S. Main St.* ☎ *209/736–2963* 🌐 *www.angelscampmuseumfoundation.org* 🎟 *$5* 🕒 *Mar.–Nov., Thurs.–Mon. 10–4; Dec.–Feb., weekends 10–4.*

FAMILY **California Cavern.** A ½-mile subterranean trail winds through large chambers and past underground streams and lakes. There aren't many steps to climb, but it's a strenuous walk with some narrow passageways and steep spots. The caverns, at a constant 55°F, contain crystalline formations not found elsewhere, and the 80-minute guided tour explains local history and geology. ✉ *9565 Cave City Rd., 9 miles east of San Andreas on Mountain Ranch Rd., then about 3 miles on Cave City Rd., Mountain Ranch* ☎ *209/736–2708* 🌐 *www.caverntours.com* 🎟 *$14.95* 🕒 *Apr.–Oct., daily 10–5; Nov.–Feb. weekends 10–4; hrs can vary, call to confirm.*

FAMILY   **Moaning Cavern.** There's no better way to see what life was like under-
Fodor's Choice   ground for prospectors than to descend into the belly of the land. This
★   fascinating tour let's you wander down a chasm into the wonder of
an ancient limestone cave. Take the 235-step spiral staircase built in
1922 into this vast cavern. More intrepid explorers can rappel into
the chamber—ropes and instruction are provided. Otherwise, the only
way inside is via the 45-minute tour, during which you'll see giant
(and still growing) stalactites and stalagmites and an archaeological
site that holds some of the oldest human remains yet found in America.
Outside there are three zip lines, starting at $44 per person. ⊠ *5350
Moaning Cave Rd., off Parrots Ferry Rd., about 2 miles south of Vallecito, Vallecito* 🕾 *209/736–2708* ⊕ *www.caverntours.com* 🖃 *$14.95*
⊗ *Apr.–Oct., daily 9–6; Nov.–Mar., weekdays 10–4, weekends 9–5; hrs
can vary, call to confirm.*

MURPHYS

10 miles northeast of Angels Camp.

Murphys is the Gold Country's most compact, most orderly town, with
enough shops and restaurants to keep families busy for at least a half-
day, and more than 20 tasting rooms within walking distance. A well-
preserved town of white-picket fences, Victorian houses, and interesting
shops, it exhibits an upscale vibe. Horatio Alger and Ulysses S. Grant
came through here, staying at what's now called the Murphys Historic
Hotel & Lodge when they, along with many other 19th-century tourists, came to investigate the giant sequoia groves in nearby Calaveras
Big Trees State Park.

GETTING HERE AND AROUND
Murphys is 10 miles northeast of Highway 49 on Highway 4. You'll
need to drive here. Parking can be difficult on summer weekends.

EXPLORING
Calaveras Big Trees State Park. The park protects hundreds of the largest and rarest living things on the planet—magnificent giant sequoia
redwood trees. Some are 3,000 years old, 90 feet around at the base,
and 250 feet tall. There are campgrounds and picnic areas; swimming,
wading, fishing, and sunbathing on the Stanislaus River are popular in
summer. Enjoy the "three senses" trail, designated for the blind, with
interpretive signs in braille that guide visitors to touch the bark and
encourage children to slow down and enjoy the forest in a more sensory
way. ⊠ *Off Hwy. 4, 15 miles northeast of Murphys, 4 miles northeast
of Arnold, Angels Camp* 🕾 *209/795–2334* ⊕ *www.parks.ca.gov* 🖃 *$10
per vehicle* ⊗ *Park: daily sunrise–sunset. Visitor center: daily 10–4.*

Ironstone Vineyards. Tours here take in spectacular gardens and underground tunnels cooled by a waterfall, and include the automated performance of a restored silent-movie-era pipe organ. On display near the
tasting room is a 44-pound specimen of crystalline gold. The winery,
known for Merlot, Cabernet Sauvignon, and Cabernet Franc, hosts
concerts and other events. Its deli has picnic items. ■**TIP➔ Ironstone is
worth a visit even if you don't drink wine.** ⊠ *1894 6 Mile Rd.* ⊹ *From*

Jones St. in town, head south on Scott St. ☎ *209/728–1251* 🌐 *www.ironstonevineyards.com* 🎫 *Tastings $5* 🕒 *Daily 10–5; open until 6 in summer.*

WHERE TO EAT AND STAY

$$ AMERICAN 🍴 **Grounds.** Light entrées, grilled vegetables, chicken, seafood, and steak are the specialties at this bustling bistro and coffee shop with a good wine list. Sandwiches, salads, and homemade soups are served for lunch. The crowd is friendly and the service attentive. [$] *Average main: $20* ✉ *402 Main St.* ☎ *209/728–8663* 🌐 *www.groundsrestaurant.com.*

$$$ B&B/INN 🏨 **Dunbar House 1880.** The oversize rooms in this elaborate Italianate-style home have brass beds, down comforters, gas-burning stoves, and claw-foot tubs. **Pros:** great breakfasts; lovely gardens; wonderful town. **Cons:** pricey. [$] *Rooms from: $207* ✉ *271 Jones St.* ☎ *209/728–2897, 800/692–6006* 🌐 *www.dunbarhouse.com* 🛏 *3 rooms, 2 suites* 🍽 *Breakfast.*

$ HOTEL 🏨 **Murphys Historic Hotel & Lodge.** This 1855 stone hotel, whose register has seen the signatures of Mark Twain and the bandit Black Bart, figured in a Bret Harte short story. **Pros:** historical ambience; great bar; downtown location. **Cons:** dated; creaky. [$] *Rooms from: $119* ✉ *457 Main St.* ☎ *209/728–3444, 800/532–7684* 🌐 *www.murphyshotel.com* 🛏 *29 rooms, 21 with bath* 🍽 *No meals.*

COLUMBIA

14 miles south of Angels Camp.

Columbia is the gateway for Columbia State Historic Park, one of the Gold Country's most visited sites. The historic Fallon House Theater is a great place for families to participate in living history activities like candle dipping and soap making on weekends. There are several inviting spots for a picnic in the area.

GETTING HERE AND AROUND

The only way to get here is by car, via either Highway 4 (the northern route) or Highway 49 (the southern) from Angels Camp.

EXPLORING

FAMILY Fodor's Choice ★ **Columbia State Historic Park.** Columbia comes as close to a gold-rush town in its heyday as any site in the Gold Country. Usually you can ride a stagecoach, pan for gold, and watch a blacksmith working at an anvil. Street musicians perform in summer. Restored or reconstructed buildings include a Wells Fargo Express office, a Masonic temple, an old-fashioned candy store, saloons, a firehouse, churches, a school, and a newspaper office. At times, all are staffed to simulate a working 1850s town. The park also includes the must-stop, **Historic Fallon House Theater,** where Broadway-quality shows are performed Wednesday through Sunday—Mark Twain once performed in this gorgeous Victorian structure. The town's two 19th-century historic lodgings, the Fallon Hotel ($) and City Hotel ($–$$) perch you in the past; to reserve a hotel or cottage go to 🌐 *www.reserveamerica.com.* ✉ *11255 Jackson St.* ☎ *209/588–9128* 🌐 *www.parks.ca.gov/columbia* 🎫 *Free* 🕒 *Daily 9–5.*

SONORA

4 miles south of Columbia.

Miners from Mexico founded Sonora and made it the biggest town in the Mother Lode. Following a period of racial and ethnic strife, the Mexican settlers moved on, and Yankees built the commercial city visible today. Sonora's historic downtown section sits atop the Big Bonanza Mine, one of the richest in the state. Another mine, on the site of nearby Sonora High School, yielded 990 pounds of gold in a single week in 1879. Reminders of the gold rush are everywhere in Sonora, in prim Victorian houses, typical Sierra-stone storefronts, and awning-shaded sidewalks. Reality intrudes beyond the town's historic heart, with strip malls, shopping centers, and modern motels.

GETTING HERE AND AROUND

Arrive in Sonora by car via Highway 49 (if coming from Columbia, drive south on Parrots Ferry Road). Parking can be difficult on the busy main drag, Washington Street (Highway 49).

EXPLORING

Tuolumne County Museum and History Center. The small museum occupies a historic gold rush–era building that served as a jail until 1960. Vintage firearms and paraphernalia, gold specimens, and MiWuk baskets are among the many artifacts on display. ✉ *158 W. Bradford St.* ☎ *209/532–1317* 🌐 *www.tchistory.org* 🎟 *Free* 🕒 *Weekdays 10–4, Sat. 10–3:30.*

WHERE TO EAT AND STAY

$ AMERICAN 🍴 **Diamondback Grill and Wine Bar.** The bright decor and refined atmosphere suggest more ambitious fare, but burgers are what this place is about. Locals crowd the tables, especially after 6 pm, for the ground-meat patties, beer-battered onion rings, veggie burgers, and fine wines. [$] *Average main: $11* ✉ *93 S. Washington St.* ☎ *209/532–6661* 🌐 *www.thediamondbackgrill.com* 🕒 *Closed Sun.*

$$ B&B/INN 🏨 **Barretta Gardens Bed and Breakfast Inn.** This inn is perfect for a romantic getaway, with elegant Victorian rooms varying in size, all furnished with period pieces. **Pros:** lovely grounds; yummy breakfasts; romantic. **Cons:** only seven rooms. [$] *Rooms from: $159* ✉ *700 S. Barretta St.* ☎ *209/532–6039, 800/206–3333* 🌐 *www.barrettagardens.com* 🛏 *7 rooms* 🍽 *Breakfast.*

JAMESTOWN

4 miles south of Sonora.

Compact Jamestown supplies a touristy view of gold rush–era life. Shops in brightly colored buildings along Main Street sell antiques and gift items. You can try your hand at panning for gold here or explore a bit of railroad history.

GETTING HERE AND AROUND

Jamestown lies at the intersection of north–south Highway 49 and east–west Highway 108. You'll need a car to tour here.

EXPLORING

FAMILY **Gold Prospecting Adventures.** You'll get a real feel (sort of) for the life of a prospector on the three-hour gold-panning excursions led by this outfit's congenial tour guides. You might even strike gold at the Jimtown Mine. Reservations recommended. ✉ *18170 Main St.* ☎ *209/984–4653, 800/596–0009* 🌐 *www.goldprospecting.com* ☞ *Call for hrs and fees.*

Fodor's Choice ★ **Railtown 1897.** A must for rail enthusiasts and families with kids, this is one of the most intact early roundhouses (maintenance facilities) in North America. You can hop aboard a steam train for a 40-minute journey—bring along the family dog if you'd like. The docents entertain guests with tales about the history of locomotion. Listen to the original rotor and pulleys in the engine house and take in the smell of axle grease. Walk through a genteel passenger car with dusty-green velvet seats and ornate metalwork, where Grace Kelly and Gary Cooper filmed a scene in the epic Western *High Noon.* You can also climb onto a historic train to see where the fireman once shoveled coal into the tender. ✉ *18115 5th Ave.* ☎ *209/984–3953* 🌐 *www.railtown1897.org* 🎟 *Roundhouse tour $5; train ride $15* ⏲ *Apr.–Oct., daily 9:30–4:30; Nov.–Mar., daily 10–3; train ride, weekends Apr.–Oct. (additional holiday rides are offered some weekends in late Nov. and Dec.).*

WHERE TO STAY

$$$ RESORT FAMILY 🏨 **Black Oak Casino Resort.** About 12 miles east of Jamestown off Highway 108, this flashy, contemporary property appeals heavily to casino gamers, but it's also just a nice place to stay with well-outfitted rooms (comfy bedding, down pillows, and alarm clocks with MP3 players) and a central Gold Country location. **Pros:** clean and spacious rooms; plenty of diversions on hand for both kids and adults. **Cons:** must go through smoky casino to reach bowling alley and restaurants; there's nothing quaint or historic about this place. [$] *Rooms from: $189* ✉ *19400 Tuolumne Rd. N, Tuolumne* ☎ *209/928–9300* 🌐 *www.blackoakcasino.com* 🛏 *148 rooms* 🍴 *No meals.*

$$ B&B/INN 🏨 **McCaffrey House Bed and Breakfast Inn.** Remoteness is one of McCaffrey's appeals—it's about 20 miles east of Jamestown on Highway 108 in the mountain community of Twain Harte. **Pros:** large rooms; wonderful nearby hiking; romantically remote. **Cons:** too remote for some. [$] *Rooms from: $169* ✉ *23251 Hwy. 108, Twain Harte* ☎ *209/586–0757, 888/586–0757* 🌐 *www.mccaffreyhouse.com* 🛏 *8 rooms* 🍴 *Breakfast.*

$$ HOTEL 🏨 **National Hotel.** The National has been in business since 1859, and its furnishings—brass beds, regal comforters, and lace curtains—are authentic but not overly embellished. **Pros:** historic feel; great brunches. **Cons:** not much happens in town after dark. [$] *Rooms from: $140* ✉ *18183 Main St.* ☎ *209/984–3446, 800/894–3446 in California* 🌐 *www.national-hotel.com* 🛏 *9 rooms* 🍴 *Breakfast.*

MARIPOSA

50 miles south of Jamestown.

Mariposa marks the southern end of the Mother Lode. Much of the land in this area was part of a 44,000-acre land grant Colonel John C.

Fremont acquired from Mexico before gold was discovered and California became a state. Many people stop here on the way to Yosemite National Park, about an hour's drive east on Highway 140.

GETTING HERE AND AROUND

If driving, take Highway 49 or Highway 140. YARTS (🌐 *www.yarts.com*), the regional transit system, can get you to Mariposa from the Central Valley town of Merced (where you can also transfer from Amtrak) or from Yosemite Valley. Otherwise, you'll need a car to get here and around.

EXPLORING

FAMILY **California State Mining and Mineral Museum.** A California State Park since 1999, the museum has displays on gold-rush history including a replica hard-rock mine shaft to walk through, a miniature stamp mill, and a 13-pound chunk of crystallized gold. In 2012 thieves stole almost $2 million in gold and jewels; suspects were soon arrested, but only some of the items were recovered. ✉ *5005 Fairground Rd., off Hwy. 49* ☎ *209/742–7625* 🌐 *www.parks.ca.gov* 🎟 *$4* 🕒 *May–Sept., Thurs.–Sun. 10–5; Oct.–Apr., Thurs.–Sun. 10–4.*

Mariposa Museum and History Center. You'll leave this small museum feeling like you just found your own gold nugget. Detailed exhibits, both indoors and out, tell the history of Mariposa County. Visit a replica of a typical miner's cabin; see a working stamp mill; tour the blacksmith shop. Artifacts, photographs, and maps, along with the knowledgeable staff, will capture your imagination and transport you back to 1849. ✉ *5119 Jessie St.* ☎ *209/966–2924* 🌐 *www.mariposamuseum.com* 🎟 *$5* 🕒 *Daily 10–4.*

WHERE TO EAT AND STAY

$$ AMERICAN 🍴 **Savoury's.** The pasta and fresh bread at Savoury's receive especially enthusiastic praise from locals; vegetarians and vegans will find lots of options. Everything about this place exudes competence and class. Kids might find it stuffy, though. [$] *Average main: $22* ✉ *5034 Hwy. 140* ☎ *209/966–7677* 🌐 *www.savouryrestaurant.com* 🕒 *Closed Wed. No lunch.*

$$ HOTEL 🏨 **Mariposa Lodge.** Thoroughly modern and tastefully landscaped, the Mariposa is a solid option for those who want to stay within 30 miles of Yosemite National Park without spending a fortune. **Pros:** convenient; relatively inexpensive; clean. **Cons:** chainlike feel. [$] *Rooms from: $129* ✉ *5052 Hwy. 140* ☎ *209/966–3607, 800/966–8819* 🌐 *www.mariposalodge.com* 🛏 *45 rooms* 🍽 *No meals.*

THE GOLD COUNTRY—NORTH

Gold has had a significant presence along this northern stretch of Highway 49, whose highlights include the bucolic Empire State Historic Park and Coloma, where the discovery of a few nuggets triggered the gold rush.

COLOMA

8 miles northwest of Placerville.

The California gold rush started in Coloma. "My eye was caught with the glimpse of something shining in the bottom of the ditch," James Marshall recalled. Marshall himself never found any more "color," as gold came to be called.

GETTING HERE AND AROUND
A car is the only practical way to get to Coloma, via Highway 49. Once parked, you can walk to all the worthwhile sights.

EXPLORING
FAMILY **Marshall Gold Discovery State Historic Park.** Most of Coloma lies within the historic park. Though crowded with tourists in summer, Coloma hardly resembles the mob scene it was in 1849, when 2,000 prospectors staked out claims along the streambed. The town's population grew to 4,000, supporting seven hotels, three banks, and many stores and businesses. But when reserves of the precious metal dwindled, prospectors left as quickly as they had come. A working reproduction of an 1840s mill lies near the spot where James Marshall first saw gold. A trail leads to a modest sign (considering the impact) marking his discovery. ■TIP➜ Take a stroll up the surrounding hills for sublime views. ⊠ *310 Back St., off Hwy. 49* ☎ *530/622–3470* ⊕ *www.parks. ca.gov* ⌦ *$8 per vehicle* ⊙ *Park daily 8–sunset. Museum Mar.–Nov., 10–5; Nov.–Mar., 10–4.*

AUBURN

18 miles northwest of Coloma; 34 miles northeast of Sacramento.

Auburn is the Gold Country town most accessible to travelers on Interstate 80. An important transportation center during the gold rush, downtown Auburn has a small Old Town district with narrow climbing streets, cobblestone lanes, wooden sidewalks, and many original buildings. ■TIP➜ Fresh produce, flowers, baked goods, and gifts are for sale at the farmers' market, held on Saturday morning year-round.

GETTING HERE AND AROUND
Amtrak serves Auburn, though most visitors arrive by car on Highway 49 or Interstate 80. Once downtown, you can tour on foot.

EXPLORING
Bernhard Museum Complex. Party like it's 1889 at this space whose main structure opened in 1851 as the Traveler's Rest Hotel and for 100 years was the residence of the Bernhard family. The congenial docents, dressed in Victorian garb, describe the family's history and 19th-century life in Auburn. ⊠ *291 Auburn–Folsom Rd.* ☎ *530/889–6500* ⊕ *www. placer.ca.gov* ⌦ *Free* ⊙ *Tues.–Sun. 11–4.*

FAMILY **Gold Country Museum.** You'll get a feel for life in the mines at this museum whose highlights include a re-created mine tunnel, a gold-panning stream, and a reproduction saloon. ⊠ *601 Lincoln Way* ☎ *530/889– 6500* ⌦ *Museum free, $3 to pan for gold* ⊙ *Tues.–Sun. 11–4.*

13

Placer County Courthouse. Auburn's standout structure is the Placer County Courthouse. The classic gold-dome building houses the Placer County Museum, which documents the area's history—Native American, railroad, agricultural, and mining—from the early 1700s to 1900. ⊠ *101 Maple St.* ☎ *530/889–6500* ⚏ *Free* ⊘ *Daily 10–4.*

WHERE TO EAT AND STAY

$$$ ✕ **Carpe Vino.** Chef Eric Alexander is known for his hearty and imaginative French-inspired dishes—sophisticated fare presented in a nonchalant, almost effortless way, as if ingredients rolled right from the farm basket onto your plate. Consider purple and yellow beets in olive oil with fans of sliced fennel stalks and creamy panna cotta, roasted bone marrow, duck-fat fries, and brothy mussels steamed with lemon and chilies. This gem is tucked into an old downtown saloon and mine with a handsome old bar. Note the extensive and varied wine list. $ *Average main: $28* ⊠ *1568 Lincoln Way* ☎ *530/823–0320* ⊕ *www.carpevino auburn.com* ⊘ *Closed Mon.*

MODERN
AMERICAN
Fodor'sChoice
★

$$ 🛏 **Holiday Inn Auburn Hotel.** Above the freeway across from Old Town, this hotel has a welcoming lobby and chain-standard but nice rooms. **Pros:** full-service restaurant on premises; convenient; clean; books available on loan. **Cons:** noise in rooms near parking lot. $ *Rooms from: $162* ⊠ *120 Grass Valley Hwy.* ☎ *530/887–8787, 800/814–8787* ⊕ *www.auburnhi.com* ⇗ *89 rooms, 7 suites* ⦿ *No meals.*

HOTEL

GRASS VALLEY

24 miles north of Auburn.

More than half of California's total gold production was extracted from mines around Grass Valley, including the Empire Mine, which, along with the North Star Mining Museum, is among the Gold Country's most fascinating attractions.

GETTING HERE AND AROUND

You'll need a car to get here. Take Highway 20 east from Interstate 5 or west from Interstate 80. Highway 49 is the north–south route into town. Gold Country Stage vehicles (☎ *530/477–0103* ⊘ *Weekdays 7–6*) serve some attractions. Expect to wait, though.

EXPLORING

FAMILY **Empire Mine State Historic Park.** Relive the days of gold, grit, and glory, when this mine was one of the biggest and most prosperous hard-rock gold mines in North America. Visit Bourn Cottage with its exquisite woodwork, lovely fountains, and stunning gardens. On a tour, you can walk into a mineshaft and peer into its dark, deep recesses—you can almost imagine what it felt like to work this vast operation. An estimated 5.8 million ounces of gold were extracted from the mine's 367 miles of underground passages during its lifetime. Dressed-up docents portraying colorful characters who shaped Northern California's history share stories about the period. The grounds have picnic tables and gentle trails—perfect for a family outing. ⊠ *10791 E. Empire St.* ☎ *530/273–8522* ⊕ *www.empiremine.org* ⚏ *$7* ⊘ *Daily 10–5.*

Almost 6 million ounces of gold were extracted from the Empire Mine.

Holbrooke Hotel. The recently refurnished landmark hotel ($$), built in 1851, hosted entertainer Lola Montez and writer Mark Twain as well as Ulysses S. Grant and other U.S. presidents. The restaurant-saloon ($$) is one of the oldest operating west of the Mississippi. ✉ *212 W. Main St.* ☎ *530/273–1353, 800/933–7077* 🌐 *www.holbrooke.com.*

FAMILY **North Star Mining Museum.** Housed in a former powerhouse, the museum displays the 32-foot-high Pelton Water Wheel, said to be the largest ever built. It was used to power mining operations and was a forerunner of the modern turbines that generate hydroelectricity. Hands-on displays are geared to children. You can picnic nearby. ✉ *10933 Allison Ranch Rd.* ☎ *530/273–4255* 🌐 *www.nevadacountyhistory.org* 🎟 *By donation* 🕒 *May–Oct., Wed.–Sat. 11–5, Sun. 12–4.*

WHERE TO EAT

$ BRITISH 🍴 **Cousin Jack Pasties.** Meat- and vegetable-stuffed pasties are a taste of the region's history, having come across the Atlantic with Cornish miners and their families in the mid-19th century. The flaky crusts practically melt in your mouth. A simple food stand, Jack's is nonetheless a local landmark. [$] *Average main: $8* ✉ *100 S. Auburn St.* ☎ *530/272–9230* 💳 *No credit cards* 🕒 *Mon.–Sat. 11–5, Sun. 11–4:15.*

NEVADA CITY

4 miles north of Grass Valley.

Nevada City, once known as the Queen City of the Northern Mines, is the most appealing of the northern Mother Lode towns. The iron-shutter brick buildings that line the narrow downtown streets contain antiques shops, galleries, boutiques, B&Bs, restaurants, and a winery. Horse-drawn carriage tours add to the romance, as do gas street lamps. At one point in the 1850s, Nevada City had a population of nearly 10,000—enough to support much cultural activity. Today, about 3,000 people live here.

GETTING HERE AND AROUND

You'll need a car to get here. Take Highway 20 east from Interstate 5 or west from Interstate 80. Highway 49 is the north–south route into town. Gold Country Stage vehicles (☎ *530/477–0103* ⏲ *Weekdays 7–6*) serve some attractions.

ESSENTIALS

Visitor Information **Nevada City Chamber of Commerce** ✉ *132 Main St.* ☎ *530/265–2692* 🌐 *www.nevadacitychamber.com.*

EXPLORING

Firehouse No. 1. With its gingerbread-trim bell tower, Firehouse No. 1 is one of the Gold Country's most distinctive buildings. A museum, it houses gold-rush artifacts and the altar from a Chinese joss house (temple). ✉ *214 Main St.* ☎ *530/265–5468* 🌐 *www.nevadacountyhistory.org* 🎟 *Donation suggested* ⏲ *May–Oct., Tues.–Sun. 1–4.*

Nevada City Winery. Watch wine being created while you sip at this winery whose tasting room overlooks the production area. Syrah and Zinfandel are among the strengths here. ✉ *Miners Foundry Garage, 321 Spring St., at Bridge St.* ☎ *530/265–9463, 800/203–9463* 🌐 *www.ncwinery.com* 🎟 *Tasting and tour free* ⏲ *Sun.–Thurs. noon–5, Fri. and Sat. noon–6; tour on Sat. at 1:30.*

WHERE TO EAT AND STAY

$$$ ECLECTIC 🍴 **Friar Tuck's.** Popular Friar Tuck's specializes in creative, interactive fondues and has an extensive menu of seafood, steaks, and pasta dishes, too. The sparkling interior has a late-19th century ambience—it's one of Nevada City's best indoor spaces. [$] *Average main: $25* ✉ *111 N. Pine St.* ☎ *530/265–9093* 🌐 *friartucks.com* ⏲ *No lunch.*

$ AMERICAN 🍴 **South Pine Cafe.** Locals flock here, especially for brunch. Lobster and beef are on the menu, but the real attention-grabbers are vegetarian entrées and side dishes, such as breakfast potatoes and apple-ginger muffins. There's a branch in Grass Valley at 102 North Richardson Street. [$] *Average main: $11* ✉ *110 S. Pine St.* ☎ *530/265–0260* 🌐 *www.southpinecafe.com* ⏲ *No dinner.*

LAKE TAHOE

With Reno, Nevada

WELCOME TO LAKE TAHOE

TOP REASONS TO GO

★ **The lake:** Blue, deep, and alpine pure, Lake Tahoe is far and away the main reason to visit this High Sierra paradise.

★ **Skiing:** Daring black-diamond runs or baby-bunny bumps—whether you're an expert, a beginner, or somewhere in between, the numerous Tahoe-area ski parks abound with slopes to suit your skills.

★ **The great outdoors:** A ring of national forests and recreation areas linked by miles of trails makes Tahoe excellent for nature lovers.

★ **Dinner with a view:** You can picnic lakeside at state parks or dine in restaurants perched along the shore.

★ **A date with lady luck:** Whether you want to roll dice, play the slots, or hope the blackjack dealer goes bust before you do, you'll find round-the-clock gambling at the casinos on the Nevada side of the lake and in Reno.

1 **California Side.** With the exception of Stateline, Nevada—which, aside from its casino-hotel towers, seems almost indistinguishable from South Lake Tahoe, California—the California side is more developed than the Nevada side. Here you can find both commercial enterprises—restaurants, motels, lodges, ski resorts, residential subdivisions—and public-access facilities, such as historic sites, parks, campgrounds, marinas, and beaches.

2 **Nevada Side.** You don't need a highway sign to know when you've crossed from California into Nevada: the flashing lights and elaborate marquees of casinos announce legal gambling in garish hues. But you'll find more here than tables and slot machines. Reno, the Biggest Little City in the World, has a vibrant arts scene and a serene downtown RiverWalk. And when you really need to get away from the chip-toting crowds, you can hike through pristine wilderness at Lake Tahoe–Nevada State Park, or hit the slopes near Incline Village.

GETTING ORIENTED

In the northern section of the Sierra Nevada mountain range, the Lake Tahoe area covers portions of four national forests, several state parks, and rugged wilderness areas with names like Desolation and Granite Chief. Lake Tahoe, the star attraction, straddles California and Nevada and is one of the world's largest, clearest, and deepest alpine lakes. The region's proximity to the Bay Area and Sacramento to the west and Reno to the east draws thrill seekers during ski season and again in summer when water sports, camping, and hiking are the dominant activities.

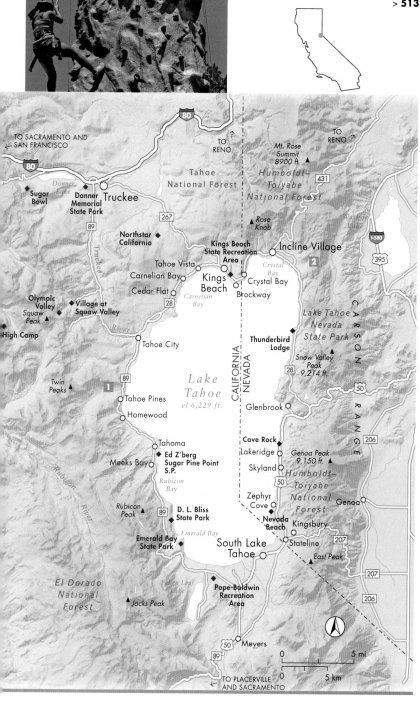

TO SACRAMENTO AND
← SAN FRANCISCO

80

TO
RENO

TO
RENO

Mt. Rose
Summit
8900 ft.

431

Sugar
Bowl

Donner
Lake

Donner
Memorial
State Park

Truckee

Tahoe
National Forest

Humboldt–
Toiyabe
National Forest

Washington
Lake

I-580

Rose
Knob

267

Northstar
California

Kings Beach
State Recreation
Area

Incline Village

2

395

Tahoe Vista

Crystal
Bay

89

Truckee

Carnelian Bay

Cedar Flat

28

Kings
Beach

Crystal Bay

Brockway

Olympic
Valley

Squaw
Peak

Village at
Squaw Valley

Carnelian
Bay

River

Lake Tahoe
Nevada
State Park

C
A
R
S
O
N

R
A
N
G
E

High Camp

Tahoe City

Thunderbird
Lodge

Snow Valley
Peak
9,214 ft.

28

50

Twin
Peaks

89

1

Lake
Tahoe
el 6,229 ft.

CALIFORNIA
NEVADA

Glenbrook

206

Tahoe Pines

Homewood

Cave Rock

Lakeridge

Genoa Peak
9,150 ft.

Rubicon
River

Tahoma

Ed Z'berg
Sugar Pine Point
S.P.

Skyland

50

Humboldt–
Toiyabe
National
Forest

Meeks Bay

Rubicon
Bay

Zephyr
Cove

Genoa

Rubicon
Peak

89

D. L. Bliss
State Park

Nevada
Beach

Kingsbury

Emerald Bay
State Park

Emerald Bay

South Lake
Tahoe

Stateline

207

El Dorado
National
Forest

Fallen Leaf
Lake

Jacks Peak

Pope-Baldwin
Recreation
Area

East Peak

207

206

50

Meyers

89

0   5 mi
0   5 km

TO PLACERVILLE
AND SACRAMENTO

Updated
by Christine
Vovakes

Whether you swim, fish, sail, or simply rest on its shores, you'll be wowed by the overwhelming beauty of Lake Tahoe, the largest alpine lake in North America. Famous for its cobalt-blue water and surrounding snowcapped peaks, Lake Tahoe straddles the state line between California and Nevada. The border gives this popular Sierra Nevada resort region a split personality. About half its visitors are intent on low-key sightseeing, hiking, camping, and boating. The rest head directly to the Nevada side, where bargain dining, big-name entertainment, and the lure of a jackpot draw them into the glittering casinos.

To explore the lake area and get a feel for its many differing communities, drive the 72-mile road that follows the shore through wooded flatlands and past beaches, climbing to vistas on the rugged southwest side of the lake and passing through busy commercial developments and casinos on its northeastern and southeastern edges. Another option is to actually go out *on* the 22-mile-long, 12-mile-wide lake on a sightseeing cruise or kayaking trip.

The lake, the communities around it, the state parks, national forests, and protected tracts of wilderness are the region's main draws, but other nearby destinations are gaining in popularity. Truckee, with an Old West feel and innovative restaurants, entices visitors looking for a relaxed pace and easy access to Tahoe's north shore and Olympic Valley ski parks. And today Reno, once known only for its casinos, attracts tourists with its buzzing arts scene, revitalized downtown riverfront, and campus events at the University of Nevada.

PLANNING

WHEN TO GO

A sapphire-blue lake shimmering deep in the center of an ice-white wonderland—that's Tahoe in winter. But those blankets of snow mean lots of storms that often close roads and force chain requirements on the interstate. In summer the roads are open, but the lake and lodgings are clogged with visitors seeking respite from valley heat. If you don't ski, the best times to visit are early fall—September and October—and late spring. The crowds thin, prices dip, and you can count on Tahoe being beautiful.

Most Lake Tahoe accommodations, restaurants, and even a handful of parks are open year-round, but many visitor centers, mansions, state parks, and beaches are closed from October through May. During those months, winter-sports enthusiasts swamp Tahoe's downhill resorts and cross-country centers, North America's largest concentration of skiing facilities. In summer it's cooler here than in the scorched Sierra Nevada foothills, the clean mountain air is bracingly crisp, and the surface temperature of Lake Tahoe is an invigorating 65°F to 70°F (compared with 40°F to 50°F in winter). This is also the time, however, when it may seem as if every tourist at the lake—100,000 on peak weekends—is in a car on the main road circling the shoreline (especially on Highway 89, just south of Tahoe City; on Highway 28, east of Tahoe City; and on U.S. 50 in South Lake Tahoe). Christmas week and July 4th are the busiest times, and prices go through the roof; plan accordingly.

GETTING HERE AND AROUND

AIR TRAVEL

The nearest airport to Lake Tahoe is Reno–Tahoe International Airport (RNO), in Reno, 50 miles northeast of the closest point on the lake. Airlines serving RNO include Alaska, Allegiant Air, American, Delta, Jet Blue, Southwest, United, U.S. Airways, and Volaris. Except for Allegiant Air, these airlines plus Aeromexico and Hawaiian serve Sacramento International Airport (SMF), 112 miles from South Lake Tahoe. North Lake Tahoe Express runs buses ($49 each way) between RNO and towns on the lake's western and northern shores, plus Incline Village, Truckee, Squaw Valley, and Northstar. South Tahoe Express runs buses ($29.75 one-way, $53 round-trip) between Reno–Tahoe Airport and resort hotels in the South Lake Tahoe area.

Airport Contacts Reno–Tahoe International Airport ⊠ *2001 E. Plumb La., off U.S. 395/I–580, at Reno-Tahoe International Airport Exit, Reno, Nevada* ☎ *775/328–6400* ⊕ *www.renoairport.com.* **Sacramento International Airport** ⊠ *6900 Airport Blvd., 12 miles northwest of downtown off I-5, Sacramento* ☎ *916/929–5411* ⊕ *www.sacramento.aero/smf.*

Transfer Contacts North Lake Tahoe Express ☎ *866/216–5222* ⊕ *www. northlaketahoeexpress.com.* **South Tahoe Express** ☎ *775/325–8944, 866/898– 2463* ⊕ *www.southtahoeexpress.com.*

BUS TRAVEL

Greyhound stops in San Francisco, Sacramento, Truckee, and Reno. BlueGO ($2 per ride) provides year-round local service in South Lake Tahoe. On the north shore, Tahoe Area Regional Transit (TART; $1.75) operates buses between Tahoma and Incline Village and runs shuttles to Truckee. RTC RIDE buses ($2) serve the Reno area. All local rides require exact change.

In winter, BlueGO provides free ski shuttle service from South Lake Tahoe hotels and resorts to various Heavenly Mountain ski lodge locations. Most of the major ski resorts offer shuttle service to nearby lodging.

Bus Contacts Greyhound ☎ 800/231–2222 ⊕ www.greyhound.com. **BlueGO** ☎ 530/541–7149 ⊕ www.tahoetransportation.org/transit/south-shore-services. **RTC RIDE** ☎ 775/348–7433 ⊕ www.rtcwashoe.com. **Tahoe Area Regional Transit (TART)** ☎ 530/550–1212, 800/736–6365 ⊕ www.placer.ca.gov/departments/works/transit/tart.

CAR TRAVEL

Lake Tahoe is 198 miles northeast of San Francisco, a drive of less than four hours in good weather and light traffic—if possible avoid heavy weekend traffic, particularly leaving the San Francisco area for Tahoe on Friday afternoon and returning on Sunday afternoon. The major route is Interstate 80, which cuts through the Sierra Nevada about 14 miles north of the lake. From there Highway 89 and Highway 267 reach the west and north shores, respectively.

U.S. 50 is the more direct route to the south shore, a two-hour drive from Sacramento. From Reno you can get to the north shore by heading south on U.S. 395/Interstate 580 for 10 miles, then west on Highway 431 for 25 miles. For the south shore, head south on U.S. 395/Interstate 580 through Carson City, and then turn west on U.S. 50 (56 miles total).

The scenic 72-mile highway around the lake is marked Highway 89 on the southwest and west shores, Highway 28 on the north and northeast shores, and U.S. 50 on the east and southeast. Sections of Highway 89 sometimes close during snowy periods, usually at Emerald Bay because of avalanche danger, which makes it impossible to complete the circular drive around the lake. Interstate 80, U.S. 50, and U.S. 395/Interstate 580 are all-weather highways, but there may be delays while snow is cleared during major storms.

Interstate 80 is a four-lane freeway; much of U.S. 50 is only two lanes with no center divider. Carry tire chains from October through May, or rent a four-wheel-drive vehicle. Most rental agencies do not allow tire chains to be used on their vehicles; ask when you book.

Contacts California Highway Patrol ☎ 530/577–1001 South Lake Tahoe ⊕ www.chp.ca.gov. **Caltrans Current Highway Conditions** ☎ 800/427–7623 ⊕ www.dot.ca.gov. **Nevada Department of Transportation Road Information** ☎ 877/687–6237 ⊕ nvroads.com. **Nevada Highway Patrol** ☎ 775/687–5300 ⊕ nhp.nv.gov.

TRAIN TRAVEL

Amtrak's cross-country rail service makes stops in Truckee and Reno. Amtrak also operates several buses daily between Reno and Sacramento to connect with coastal train routes.

Train Contact Amtrak ☎ *800/872–7245* ⊕ *www.amtrak.com.*

RESTAURANTS

On weekends and in high season, expect a long wait at the more popular restaurants. And expect to pay resort prices almost everywhere. During the "shoulder seasons" (from April to May and September to November), some places may close temporarily or limit their hours, so call ahead. Also, check local papers for deals and discounts during this time, especially two-for-one coupons. Many casinos use their restaurants to attract gamblers. Marquees often tout "$8.99 prime rib dinners" or "$2.99 breakfast specials." Some of these meals are downright lousy and they are usually available only in the coffee shops and buffets, but at those prices, it's hard to complain. The finer restaurants in casinos deliver pricier food, as well as reasonable service and a bit of atmosphere. Unless otherwise noted, even the most expensive area restaurants welcome customers in casual clothes.

HOTELS

Quiet inns on the water, suburban-style strip motels, casino hotels, slope-side ski lodges, and house and condo rentals throughout the area constitute the lodging choices at Tahoe. The crowds come in summer and during ski season; reserve as far in advance as possible, especially for holiday periods when prices skyrocket. Spring and fall give you a little more leeway and lower—sometimes significantly lower, especially at casino hotels—rates. Check hotel websites for the best deals.

Head to South Lake Tahoe for the most activities and the widest range of lodging options. Heavenly Village in the heart of town has an ice rink, cinema, shops, fine-dining restaurants, and simple cafés, plus a gondola that will whisk you up to the ski park. Walk two blocks south from downtown, and you can hit the casinos.

Tahoe City, on the west shore, has a small-town atmosphere and is accessible to several nearby ski resorts. A few miles northwest of the lake, Squaw Valley USA has its own self-contained upscale village, an aerial tram to the slopes, and numerous outdoor activities once the snow melts.

Looking for a taste of Old Tahoe? The north shore with its woodsy backdrop is your best bet, with Carnelian Bay and Tahoe Vista on the California side. And across the Nevada border are casino resorts where Hollywood's glamour-stars once romped. *Hotel reviews have been shortened. For full information, visit Fodors.com.*

WHAT IT COSTS			
$	$$	$$$	$$$$
Restaurants	under $16	$16–$22	$23–$30	over $30
Hotels	under $120	$120–$175	$176–$250	over $250

Restaurant prices are the average cost of a main course at dinner or, if dinner is not served, at lunch. Hotel prices are the lowest cost of a standard double room in high season.

OUTDOORS AND BACKCOUNTRY TIPS

If you're planning to spend any time outdoors around Lake Tahoe, whether hiking, climbing, skiing, or camping, be aware that weather conditions can change quickly in the Sierra. To avoid hypothermia, always bring a pocket-size, fold-up rain poncho (available in all sporting-goods stores) to keep you dry. Wear long pants and a hat. Carry plenty of water. Because you'll likely be walking on granite, wear sturdy, closed-toe hiking boots, with soles that grip rock. If you're going into the backcountry, bring a signaling device (such as a mirror), emergency whistle, compass, map, energy bars, and water purifier. When heading out alone, tell someone where you're going and when you expect to return.

If you plan to ski, be aware of resort elevations. In the event of a winter storm, determine the snow level before you choose the resort you'll ski. Often the level can be as high as 7,000 feet, which means rain at some resorts' base areas but snow at others.

BackCountry, in Truckee, operates an excellent website with current information about how and where to (and where not to) ski, mountain bike, and hike in the backcountry around Tahoe. The store also stocks everything from crampons to transceivers. For storm information, check the National Weather Service's website; for ski conditions, visit ⊕ *onthesnow.com*. For reservations at campgrounds in California state parks, contact Reserve America. If you plan to camp in the backcountry of the national forests, you'll need to purchase a wilderness permit, which you can pick up at the forest service office or at a ranger station at any forest entrance. If you plan to ski the backcountry, check the U.S. Forest Service's recorded information for conditions.

Contacts and Information BackCountry ✉ *11400 Donner Pass Rd., at Meadow Way, Truckee* ☎ *530/582–0909 Truckee* ⊕ *www.thebackcountry. net.* **National Weather Service** ⊕ *www.wrh.noaa.gov/rev.* **OntheSnow. com** ⊕ *www.onthesnow.com/california/skireport.html.* **Reserve America** ☎ *800/444–7275* ⊕ *www.reserveamerica.com.* **U.S. Forest Service** ✉ *Office, 35 College Dr., South Lake Tahoe* ☎ *530/543–2600 general backcountry information, 530/587–3558 backcountry information recording after office hours* ⊕ *www.fs.usda.gov/ltbmu.*

SKIING AND SNOWBOARDING

The mountains around Lake Tahoe are bombarded by blizzards throughout most winters and sometimes in fall and spring; 10- to 12-foot bases are common. Indeed, the Sierras often have the deepest snowpack on the continent, but because of the relatively mild temperatures over the Pacific, falling snow can be very heavy and wet—it's nicknamed "Sierra Cement" for a reason. The upside is that you can sometimes ski and board as late as May (snowboarding is permitted at all Tahoe ski areas). The major resorts get extremely crowded on weekends. If you're going to ski on a Saturday, arrive early and quit early. Avoid moving with the masses: eat at 11 am or 1:30 pm, not noon. Also consider visiting the ski areas with few high-speed lifts or limited lodging and real estate at their bases: Alpine Meadows, Sugar Bowl, Homewood, Mt. Rose, Sierra-at-Tahoe, Diamond Peak, and Kirkwood. And to find out the true ski conditions, talk to waiters and bartenders—most of them are ski bums.

The Lake Tahoe area is also a great destination for Nordic skiers. "Skinny" (i.e., cross-country) skiing at the resorts can be costly, but you get the benefits of machine grooming and trail preparation. If it's bargain Nordic you're after, take advantage of thousands of acres of public forest and parkland trails.

TOURS

Lake Tahoe Balloons. Take a hot-air balloon flight over the lake from mid-May through mid-October with this experienced company. The excursion begins shortly after sunrise and takes four hours total, including a traditional champagne toast at journey's end. ⊠ *Tahoe Keys Marina, at end of Venice Dr. East, South Lake Tahoe* ☎ *530/544–1221, 800/872–9294* ⊕ *www.laketahoeballoons.com* 🖃 *From $295.*

MS Dixie II. The 520-passenger *MS Dixie II*, a stern-wheeler, sails year-round from Zephyr Cove to Emerald Bay on sightseeing and dinner cruises. ⊠ *Zephyr Cove Marina, 760 U.S. Hwy. 50, near Church St., Zephyr Cove, Nevada* ☎ *775/589–4906, 800/238–2463* ⊕ *www.zephyr cove.com/cruises* 🖃 *From $51.*

Sierra Cloud. From May to September, the *Sierra Cloud*, a 41-passenger catamaran, departs from the Hyatt Regency beach at Incline Village and cruises the north and east shore areas. ⊠ *Hyatt Regency Lake Tahoe, 111 Country Club Dr., Incline Village* ☎ *775/831–4386* ⊕ *www. awsincline.com* 🖃 *From $65.*

Tahoe Boat Cruises. From April to October, this company offers various boating experiences. The *Woodwind II*, a 50-passenger catamaran, sails from Zephyr Cove on regular and champagne cruises. The company's *Safari Rose*, an 80-foot-long wooden motor yacht, departs from Tahoe Keys Marina for half-day cruises around the lake. From late May to mid-October, their classic wooden boat, the *Tahoe*, takes passengers on an east shore cruise with a walking tour of Thunderbird Lodge historic site. ⊠ *Zephyr Cove Resort, 760 U.S. Hwy. 50, near Church St., Zephyr Cove* ☎ *775/588–1881, 888/867–6394* ⊕ *www.tahoecruises. com* 🖃 *From $34.*

Tahoe Queen. The 312-passenger *Tahoe Queen*, a partially glass-bottomed paddle wheeler, departs from South Lake Tahoe daily for 2½-hour sightseeing cruises year-round by reservation and 3-hour dinner-dance cruises daily from late spring to early fall (weekly the rest of the year). Fares range from $51 to $83. ⊠ *Ski Run Marina, 900 Ski Run*

Blvd., off U.S. 50, South Lake Tahoe ☎ *530/543–6191, 800/238–2463* ⊕ *www.zephyrcove.com/cruises* 🎫 *From $51.*

VISITOR INFORMATION

Contacts Lake Tahoe Visitors Authority ✉ *169 U.S. Hwy. 50, Stateline, Nevada* ☎ *775/588–5900, 800/288–2463* ⊕ *tahoesouth.com.* **U.S. Forest Service** ☎ *530/587–3558 backcountry recording* ⊕ *www.fs.usda.gov/tahoe.*

THE CALIFORNIA SIDE

The most hotels, restaurants, ski resorts, and state parks are on the California side of the lake, but you'll also encounter the most congestion and developed areas.

SOUTH LAKE TAHOE

60 miles south of Reno, 198 miles northeast of San Francisco.

The city of South Lake Tahoe's raison d'être is tourism: the casinos of adjacent Stateline, Nevada; the ski slopes at Heavenly Mountain; the beaches, docks, bike trails, and campgrounds all around the south shore; and the backcountry of Eldorado National Forest and Desolation Wilderness. The main road into town, however, shows less attractive features: older motels, strip malls, and low-rise prefab-looking buildings that line both sides of U.S. 50. Though there are plenty of places to stay, we haven't recommended many because they're not top choices. The small city's saving grace is its convenient location and bevy of services, as well as its gorgeous lake views.

GETTING HERE AND AROUND

The main route into and through South Lake Tahoe is U.S. 50; signs say "Lake Tahoe Boulevard" in town. Arrive by car or, if coming from Reno Airport, take the South Tahoe Express bus. BlueGO operates daily bus service in the south shore area year-round, plus a ski shuttle from the large hotels to Heavenly Ski Resort in the winter.

ESSENTIALS

Visitor Information Lake Tahoe Visitors Authority ✉ *Visitor Center, 169 U.S. Hwy. 50, at Kingsbury Grade, Stateline, Nevada* ☎ *775/588–5900, 800/288–2463* ⊕ *tahoesouth.com* ✉ *Visitor Center, 3066 Lake Tahoe Blvd., at San Francisco Ave.* ☎ *530/541–5255* ⊕ *tahoesouth.com.*

EXPLORING

FAMILY

Fodor'sChoice

★

Heavenly Gondola. Whether you ski or not, you'll appreciate the impressive view of Lake Tahoe from the Heavenly Gondola. Its eight-passenger cars travel from the middle of town 2.4 miles up the mountain in 15 minutes. When the weather's fine, you can take one of three hikes around the mountaintop and then have lunch at Tamarack Lodge. Heavenly also offers day care for children. ✉ *4080 Lake Tahoe Blvd.* ☎ *775/586–7000, 800/432–8365* ⊕ *www.skiheavenly.com* 🎫 *$48* ☉ *Summer daily 10–5; winter weekdays 9–4, weekends 8:30–4.*

Heavenly Village. The centerpiece of South Lake Tahoe's efforts to reinvent itself and provide a focal point for tourism, this complex at the base of the gondola has restaurants, some good shopping, a cinema, an arcade for kids, the Heavenly Village Outdoor Ice Rink in winter, and miniature golf in summer. ✉ *1001 Heavenly Village Way, at U.S. 50* 🌐 *www.theshopsatheavenly.com.*

WHERE TO EAT

$ ECLECTIC 🍴 **Blue Angel Café.** A favorite of locals, who fill the dozen or so wooden tables, this cozy spot with Wi-Fi serves basic sandwiches and salads along with internationally inspired dishes like chipotle shrimp tacos and Thai curry. On cold days warm up with wine or an espresso in front of the fireplace. [$] *Average main: $14* ✉ *1132 Ski Run Blvd., at Larch Ave.* ☎ *530/544–6544* 🌐 *www.blueangelcafe.com.*

$ MEXICAN 🍴 **The Cantina.** A casual Tahoe favorite, the Cantina serves traditional Mexican dishes—huge burritos, enchiladas, and rellenos—as well as stylized Southwestern fare such as smoked-chicken polenta with grilled vegetables, and crab cakes in jalapeño cream sauce. The bartenders make great margaritas and serve 30 different kinds of beer. [$] *Average main: $14* ✉ *765 Emerald Bay Rd., Hwy. 89, at 10th St.* ☎ *530/544–1233* 🌐 *www.cantinatahoe.com* ✍ *Reservations not accepted.*

$$$$ ECLECTIC Fodor's Choice ★ 🍴 **Evan's American Gourmet Cafe.** Its excellent service, world-class food, and superb wine list make this the top choice for high-end dining in South Lake. Inside a converted cabin, the restaurant serves creative American cuisine that includes catch-of-the-day seafood offerings and meat dishes such as rack of lamb marinated with rosemary and garlic and served with raspberry demi-glace. Some diners find the table spacing a tad close. Evan's is intimate, to be sure, but the food always pleases. [$] *Average main: $33* ✉ *536 Emerald Bay Rd., Hwy. 89, at 15th St.* ☎ *530/542–1990* 🌐 *evanstahoe.com* 🕒 *No lunch.*

$$ ECLECTIC 🍴 **Freshies.** When you've had your fill of junk food, come here for delicious, healthful meals prepared with an "earth-friendly" attitude and commitment. Specialties include seafood and vegetarian dishes, but good grilled meats are always available, such as teriyaki beef stir fry, and spare ribs with Hawaiian barbecue sauce. Freshies is in a mini-mall, and can be loud and crowded—try to snag a spot on the upstairs lake-view deck. [$] *Average main: $16* ✉ *Lakeview Plaza, 3330 Lake Tahoe Blvd., at Fremont Ave.* ☎ *530/542–3630* 🌐 *www.freshiestahoe.com* ✍ *Reservations not accepted* 🕒 *Closed Nov. until weekend after Thanksgiving.*

$$$ SEAFOOD 🍴 **Fresh Ketch.** Fish is the specialty at this dockside restaurant, where you can look out at the yachts in the Tahoe Keys marina. The upstairs dining room serves full dinners (no lunch) that feature fresh seafood and meats. The menu downstairs in the lively fireside seafood bar, beginning with lunch, is lighter and more eclectic, with reasonably priced hot and cold appetizers, salads, and sandwiches served through dinner. Have a hankering for something sweet? Stop by for dessert only and enjoy the view. There's live entertainment on Thursday, Friday, and Saturday nights year-round. [$] *Average main: $24* ✉ *2435 Venice Dr., off Tahoe Keys Blvd.* ☎ *530/541–5683* 🌐 *www.thefreshketch.com* 🕒 *Daily in summer; winter hrs vary.*

$$$$ ASIAN 🍴 **Kalani's.** Fresh-off-the-plane seafood gets delivered from the Honolulu fish market to Heavenly Village's sexiest (and priciest) restaurant. The

sleek, white-tablecloth dining room is decked out with carved bamboo, a burnt-orange color palette, and a modern-glass sculpture, all of which complement contemporary Pacific Rim specialties such as melt-off-the-bone baby-back pork ribs with sesame-garlic soy sauce. Sushi selections with inventive rolls and sashimi combos, plus less expensive vegetarian dishes, add depth to the menu. [$] *Average main: $34* ✉ *1001 Heavenly Village Way, #26, at U.S. 50* ☎ *530/544–6100* 🌐 *www.kalanis.com* 🕒 *No lunch weekdays in winter.*

$ THAI 🍴 **Orchid's Thai.** If you're hungry for Thai, stop here for good food at reasonable prices served in an attractive dining room. Tucked into a tiny mall, the restaurant isn't fantastic, but it's reliably good, and when every place in town is booked, this is a great backup. Carryout is available. [$] *Average main: $13* ✉ *2180 Lake Tahoe Blvd., at 3rd St.* ☎ *530/544–5541* 🌐 *www.orchidstahoe.com.*

$ AMERICAN 🍴 **Red Hut Café.** A vintage-1959 Tahoe diner, all chrome and red plastic, the Red Hut is a tiny place with a wildly popular breakfast menu: huge omelets; banana, pecan, and coconut waffles; and other tasty vittles. A second South Lake branch has a soda fountain and is the only one that serves dinner. There's a third location in Stateline. [$] *Average main: $10* ✉ *2723 Lake Tahoe Blvd., near Blue Lake Ave.* ☎ *530/541–9024* 🌐 *www.redhutcafe.com* ✍ *Reservations not accepted* 🕒 *No dinner* [$] *Average main: $10* ✉ *3660 Lake Tahoe Blvd., at Ski Run Blvd.* ☎ *530/544–1595* 🌐 *www.redhutcafe.com* [$] *Average main: $10* ✉ *229 Kingsbury Grade, off U.S. 50, Stateline, Nevada* ☎ *775/588–7488* 🌐 *www.redhutcafe.com* 🕒 *No dinner.*

$$ ITALIAN 🍴 **Scusa! Italian Ristorante.** This longtime favorite turns out big plates of veal scallopine, chicken piccata, and garlicky linguine with clams—straightforward Italian-American food (and lots of it), served in an intimate dining room warmed by a crackling fire on many nights. There's an outdoor patio that's open in warm weather. [$] *Average main: $21* ✉ *2543 Lake Tahoe Blvd., at Sierra Blvd.* ☎ *530/542–0100* 🌐 *www.scusalaketahoe.com* 🕒 *No lunch.*

WHERE TO STAY

$$$ B&B/INN Fodor's Choice ★ 🏨 **Black Bear Inn Bed and Breakfast.** The rooms and cabins at South Lake Tahoe's most luxurious inn feature 19th-century American antiques, fine art, and fireplaces; cabins also have kitchenettes. **Pros:** intimate; serene, woodsy grounds; within walking distance of good restaurants. **Cons:** not appropriate for children under 16; pricey. [$] *Rooms from: $225* ✉ *1202 Ski Run Blvd.* ☎ *530/544–4451, 877/232–7466* 🌐 *www.tahoeblackbear.com* 🛏 *5 rooms, 4 cabins* 🍽 *Breakfast.*

$$ HOTEL 🏨 **Forest Suites Resort.** The location of this resort is excellent—5½ acres bordering a forest, right behind the Heavenly Village, a half block from the casinos, and adjacent to a supermarket, cinema, and shops. **Pros:** as close to the city center as pricier hotels; good bet for families. **Cons:** an older facility. [$] *Rooms from: $159* ✉ *1 Lake Pkwy.* ☎ *530/541–6655, 800/822–5950* 🌐 *www.forestsuites.com* 🛏 *17 rooms, 102 suites* 🍽 *Breakfast.*

$$$ HOTEL 🏨 **Inn by the Lake.** Across the road from a beach, this "inn" is essentially a high-end motel, with spacious, spotless rooms and suites. **Pros:** great

Continued on page 530

TAHOE A LAKE FOR ALL SEASONS

by Christine Vovakes

Best known for its excellent skiing, Lake Tahoe is a year-round resort and outdoor sports destination. All kinds of activities are available, from snowboarding some of the best runs in North America and gliding silently along the lakeshore on cross-country skis in winter, to mountain biking through lush forests and puttering around the alpine lake in a classic yacht in summer. Whatever you do—and whenever you visit—the sapphire lake is at the center of it all, pulling you out of your posh resort or rustic cabin rental like a giant blue magnet. There are many ways to enjoy and experience Lake Tahoe, but here are some of our favorites.

(top) Heavenly Mountain Resort, (bottom) Sand Harbor Beach.

WINTER WONDERLAND

Home to a host of world-famous Sierra resorts, Tahoe is a premier ski destination. Add sledding, ice skating, cross-country skiing, and jingly sleigh rides under the stars to the mix, and you begin to get a glimpse of Tahoe's cold-weather potential.

DOWNHILL SKIING AND SNOWBOARDING

Even if you've never made it off the bunny hill before, you should definitely hit the slopes here at least once. The Lake Tahoe region has the deepest snowpack in North America, and you can ski from Thanksgiving until it melts—which is sometimes July.

One of the top-rated resorts in the country, Olympic Valley's **Squaw Valley USA** hosted the 1960 Winter Olympics that put Tahoe on the map. A great classic resort is **Sugar Bowl,** where you can revel in a bit of Disney nostalgia while you swoop down the slopes. Walt helped start the resort, which opened in 1939 and had Tahoe's first chair lift.

Even if you're not hitting the slopes at South Lake Tahoe's **Heavenly Mountain,** be sure to take a ride on their **Heavenly Gondola** so you can take in awe-inspiring views of the frozen circle of white ice that rings the brilliant lake.

(top) Skiing in Lake Tahoe,. (above left) Cross-country skiing, (above right) Snow boarding at Heavenly Mountain.

SKI RESORT	LOCATION	TRAILS	ACRES	BEGIN.	INTER.	ADV./ EXP.
CALIFORNIA						
Alpine Meadows	Tahoe City	100	2,400	25%	40%	35%
Heavenly Mountain	South Lake Tahoe	97	4,800	20%	45%	35%
Homewood Mountain	Homewood	64	2,010	15%	40%	45%
Kirkwood	Kirkwood	87	2,300	12%	20%	68%
Northstar California	Truckee	97	3,170	13%	60%	27%
Sierra-at-Tahoe	South Lake Tahoe	46	2,000	25%	50%	25%
Squaw Valley USA	Olympic Valley	170	3,600	25%	45%	30%
Sugar Bowl	Truckee	102	1,650	17%	45%	38%
NEVADA						
Diamond Peak	Incline Village	30	655	18%	46%	36%
Mt. Rose Ski Tahoe	Incline Village	61	1,200	20%	30%	50%

CROSS-COUNTRY SKIING

Downhill skiing may get all the glory here, but Lake Tahoe is also a premier cross-country (or Nordic) skiing destination. "Skinny" skiers basically have two options: pony up the cash to ski the groomed trails at a resort, or hit the more rugged (but cheaper—or free) public forest and parkland trails.

Beautiful **Royal Gorge** is the country's largest cross-country ski resort. Other resorts with good skinny skiing include **Kirkwood, Squaw Valley USA, Tahoe Donner,** and **Northstar California.** Private operators **Spooner Lake Cross Country** and **Hope Valley Outdoors** will also have you shushing through pristine powder in no time.

For bargain Nordic on public trails, head to **Sugar Pine Point State Park.** Other good low-cost cross-country skiing locations include **Donner Memorial State Park, Lake Tahoe—Nevada State Park,** and **Tahoe Meadows** near Incline Village.

CAUTION⚠ Cross-country skiing is relaxing and provides a great cardiovascular workout—but it's also quite strenuous. If it's your first time out or you're not in great shape, start out slow.

SLEDDING AND TUBING

Kirkwood, Squaw Valley USA, Boreal, Soda Springs, and many other Tahoe resorts have areas where you can barrel down hills on inflatable tubes. Some good non-resort sledding spots are **Tahoe National Forest** and **Tahoe Meadows,** near Incline Village.

ICE SKATING

Want to work on your triple lutz? You can skate seasonally at **Heavenly Village Outdoor Ice Rink,** or year-round at the **South Tahoe Ice Arena.** Other great gliding spots include **Squaw Valley USA's Olympic Ice Pavilion.**

WARMING UP

To defrost your ski-stiff limbs, take a dip in a resort's heated pool, de-stress in a hotel spa...or enjoy a brandy by the fire at a cozy restaurant. Our favorite places to warm up and imbibe include Graham's of Squaw Valley and Soule Domain, near Crystal Bay.

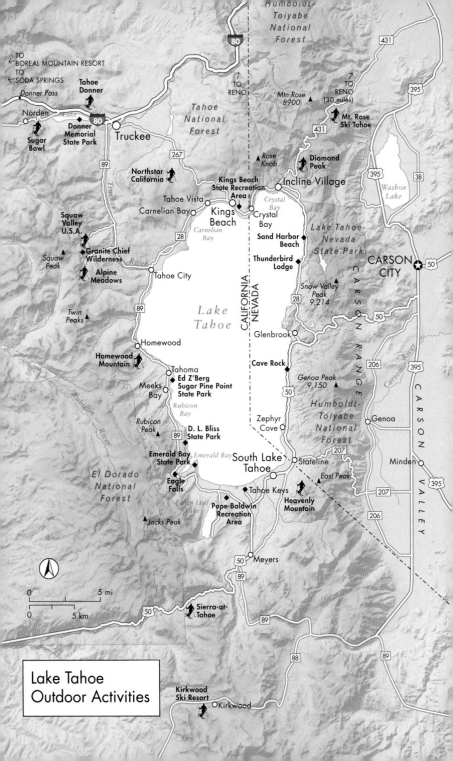

Lake Tahoe
Outdoor Activities

FROSTY CATCH

Too cold to fish? Nonsense. South Lake's Tahoe Sport Fishing runs charters year-round with crews that will clean and package your catch.

IN THE WARM CALIFORNIA SUN

Summer in Tahoe means diving into pure alpine waters, hiking a mountain trail with stunning lake views, or kayaking on glorious Emerald Bay. From tennis to golf to fishing, you can fill every waking moment with outdoor activity—or just stretch out on a sunny lakeside beach with a good book and a cool drink.

HIKING

The lake is surrounded by protected parkland, offering countless opportunities to take jaunts through the woods or rambles along lakeside trails.

One of the most unique hiking experiences in Tahoe is at Heavenly Mountain Resorts, where the **Heavenly Gondola** runs up to three nice trails. When you're done enjoying sky-high views of the lake, grab lunch at the nearby Tamarack Lodge.

Another out-of-the-ordinary option is a romantic moonlit trek. **Camp Richardson** has lots of trails and a long curve of lake to catch the moonlight.

In **Eldorado National Forest and Desolation Wilderness,** you can hike a small portion of the famous Pacific Crest Trail and branch off to discover beautiful backcountry lakes. Nearby **Eagle Falls** has stunning views of Emerald Bay.

One of Tahoe's best hikes is a 4½-mi trail at **D.L. Bliss State Park;** it has lovely views of the lake and leads to bizarre **Vikingsholm** (*see box on next page*).

Other great places to hike in Lake Tahoe include **Sugar Pines Point State Park, Olympic Valley's Granite Chief Wilderness, Squaw Valley USA's High Camp, Donner Memorial State Park,** and **Lake Tahoe—Nevada State Park.**

You can pick up hiking maps at the **U.S. Forest Service** office at the **Lake Tahoe Visitor Center.**

HIT THE BEACH

Lake Tahoe has some gorgeous lakeside sunbathing terrain; get to perennial favorite **Kings Beach State Recreation Area** early to snag a choice spot. Or, if you never want to be far from the water, reserve one of the prime beachside spots at **D.L. Bliss State Park Campground.**

(left) Fannette Island in Emerald Bay. (right) A young man leaps off a cliff into Lake Tahoe.

MOUNTAIN BIKING AND CYCLING

You don't need to be preparing for the Tour de France to join the biking fun. While there are myriad rugged mountain biking trails to choose from, the region is also blessed with many flat trails.

Truly intrepid cyclists take the lift up **Northstar California** and hit the resort's 100 mi of trails. Another good option is **Sugar Pine Point State Park,** where you can hop on a 10-mi trail to Tahoe City.

Tahoe Sports in South Lake Tahoe is a good place for bike rentals and tips for planning your trip. **Cyclepaths Mountain Bike Adventures** in Truckee leads guided mountain biking tours, and **Flume Trail Bikes** on the Nevada side of the lake, near Glenbrook, rents bikes and operates a bike shuttle to popular trails.

LAKE TOURS AND KAYAKING

One of the best ways to experience the lake is by getting out on the water.

The *Tahoe Queen* is a huge glass-bottomed paddle-wheel boat that offers sightseeing cruises and dinner-dance cruises. The *Sierra Cloud, MS Dixie II,* and

Woodwind II also ply the lake, offering a variety of memorable cruises.

Another enjoyable option is taking a throwback wooden cruiser from Tahoe Keys Marina in South Lake Tahoe to tour **Thunderbird Lodge,** the meticulously crafted stone mansion built in 1936 by socialite George Whittell.

For a more personal experience, rent a kayak and glide across **Emerald Bay. Kayak Tahoe** in South Lake Tahoe will have you paddling in no time.

VIKINGS?

As you kayak around Tahoe, you'll see many natural wonders…and a few manmade ones as well. One of the most impressive and strangest is **Vikingsholm,** a grand 1929 estate that looks like an ancient Viking castle. You can see it from **Emerald Bay** (which, appropriately, resembles a fjord), or hike to it via a steep one-mile trail.

(left top) Biking along the shore. (left bottom) Kayaking. (right) Steamboat cruise.

value; stellar service; short drive from Heavenly Mountain. **Cons:** on busy Lake Tahoe Boulevard. ⓢ *Rooms from: $180* ✉ *3300 Lake Tahoe Blvd., at Fremont Ave.* ☎ *530/542–0330, 800/877–1466* ⊕ *www.innby thelake.com* ↻ *90 rooms, 10 suites* ⑩ *No meals.*

$$$ ⛺ **Marriott's Grand Residence and Timber Lodge.** You can't beat the loca-
RESORT   tion of these two gigantic, modern condominium complexes right at the base of Heavenly Gondola, smack in the center of town. **Pros:** central location; great for families; near excellent restaurants. **Cons:** can be jam-packed on weekends. ⓢ *Rooms from: $195* ✉ *1001 Heavenly Village Way* ☎ *530/542–8400 Marriott's Grand Residence; 800/845–5279, 530/542–6600 Marriott's Timber Lodge* ⊕ *www.marriott.com* ↻ *431 condos* ⑩ *No meals.*

$$ ⛺ **Sorensen's Resort.** Escape civilization by staying in a log cabin at this
RESORT   woodsy 165-acre resort within the Eldorado National Forest, 20 minutes south of town. **Pros:** gorgeous, rustic setting. **Cons:** nearest nightlife is 20 miles away. ⓢ *Rooms from: $135* ✉ *14255 Hwy. 88, Hope Valley* ☎ *530/694–2203, 800/423–9949* ⊕ *www.sorensensresort.com* ↻ *2 rooms with shared bath, 29 cabins, 5 houses* ⑩ *No meals.*

$$ ⛺ **Tahoe Seasons Resort.** At this all-suites time-share hotel, a mere 150-
HOTEL   yard walk from the Heavenly Mountain Resort ski area, every room has a two-person sunken hot tub. **Pros:** steps from ski resort; less touristy location. **Cons:** no casinos or outside restaurants within walking distance. ⓢ *Rooms from: $170* ✉ *3901 Saddle Rd.* ☎ *530/541–6700 front desk, 800/540–4874 reservations* ⊕ *www.tahoeseasons.net* ↻ *183 suites* ⑩ *No meals.*

NIGHTLIFE

Most of the area's nightlife is concentrated in the casinos over the border in Stateline. To avoid slot machines and blinking lights, try the California-side nightspots in and near Heavenly Village. The Marriott Timber Lodge bars are always dependable.

BARS

Mc P's Taphouse & Grill. You can hear live bands—rock, jazz, blues, alternative—on most nights at Mc P's while you sample a few of their 40 beers on draft. Lunch and dinner are served daily. ✉ *4125 Lake Tahoe Blvd., Ste A, near Friday Ave.* ☎ *530/542–4435* ⊕ *www. mcpstaphousetahoe.com.*

SPORTS AND THE OUTDOORS

FISHING

Tahoe Sport Fishing. One of the area's largest and oldest fishing-charter services offers morning and afternoon trips. Outings include all necessary gear and bait, and the crew cleans and packages your catch. ✉ *900 Ski Run Blvd., off U.S. 50* ☎ *530/541–5448, 800/696–7797 in CA* ⊕ *www.tahoesportfishing.com* ✉ *From $110.*

GOLF

Lake Tahoe Golf Course. Set in a meadow with mountain views, this public championship course was designed by William Bell. The Upper Truckee River comes into play on several holes. The twilight rate ($39) starts at 4 pm. ✉ *2500 Emerald Bay Rd, Hwy. 89/U.S. 50* ☎ *530/577–0788*

⊕ *www.laketahoegc.com* ✉ *$67 for weekdays, $87 for weekends; $20 for golf cart* ⚑ *18 holes, 6741 yards, par 71.*

HIKING

The south shore is a great jumping-off point for day treks into nearby Eldorado National Forest and Desolation Wilderness.

Desolation Wilderness. Trails within the 63,960-acre wilderness lead to gorgeous backcountry lakes and mountain peaks. It's called Desolation Wilderness for a reason, so bring a topographic map and compass, and carry water and food. You need a permit for overnight camping (877/444–6777). In summer you can access this area by boarding a boat taxi ($12 one-way) at **Echo Chalet** (*9900 Echo Lakes Rd., off U.S. 50, 530/659–7207, www.echochalet.com*) and crossing Echo Lake. The Pacific Crest Trail also traverses Desolation Wilderness. ⊠ *El Dorado National Forest Information Center* ☎ *530/644–2349* ⊕ *www.fs.usda. gov/eldorado.*

Pacific Crest Trail. Hike a couple of miles on this famous mountain trail that stretches from Mexico to Canada. ⊠ *Echo Summit, about 12 miles southwest of South Lake Tahoe off U.S. 50* ☎ *916/285–1846, 888/728–7245* ⊕ *www.pcta.org.*

ICE-SKATING

FAMILY **Heavenly Village Outdoor Ice Rink.** If you're here in winter, practice your jumps and turns at this rink between the gondola and the cinema. ⊠ *1001 Heavenly Village Way* ☎ *530/542–4230* ⊕ *www.theshopsatheavenly. com* ✉ *$20, includes skate rental* ⊙ *Nov.–Mar., daily 10–8, weather permitting.*

South Tahoe Ice Arena. For year-round fun, head to this city-operated, NHL regulation–size indoor rink where you can rent equipment and sign up for lessons. In the evening the lights are turned low and a disco ball lights up the ice. ⊠ *1176 Rufus Allen Blvd.* ☎ *530/544–7465* ⊕ *tahoearena.com* ✉ *$15, includes skate rental* ⊙ *Daily, hrs vary.*

KAYAKING

Kayak Tahoe. Sign up for lessons and excursions (to the south shore, Emerald Bay, and Sand Harbor), offered from May through September. You can also rent a kayak and paddle solo on the lake. ⊠ *Timber Cove Marina, 3411 Lake Tahoe Blvd., at Balbijou Rd.* ☎ *530/544–2011* ⊕ *www.kayaktahoe.com* ✉ *From $40.*

MOUNTAIN BIKING

Tahoe Sports Ltd. You can rent road and mountain bikes and get tips on where to ride from the friendly staff at this full-service sports store. ⊠ *Tahoe Crescent V Shopping Center, 4008 Lake Tahoe Blvd.* ☎ *530/542–4000* ⊕ *www.tahoesportsltd.com.*

SKIING

If you don't want to pay the high cost of rental equipment at the resorts, you'll find reasonable prices and expert advice at Tahoe Sports Ltd. (⇨ *Mountain Biking, above*).

Fodor's Choice **Heavenly Mountain Resort.** Straddling two states, vast Heavenly Mountain Resort—composed of nine peaks, two valleys, and four base-lodge areas, along with the largest snowmaking system in the western United

14

States—has terrain for every skier. Beginners can choose wide, well-groomed trails, accessed from the California Lodge or the gondola from downtown South Lake Tahoe; kids have short and gentle runs in the Enchanted Forest area all to themselves. The Sky Express high-speed quad chair whisks intermediate and advanced skiers to the summit for wide cruisers or steep tree-skiing. Mott and Killebrew canyons draw experts to the Nevada side for steep chutes and thick-timber slopes. For snowboarders and tricksters, there are five different terrain parks.

The ski school is big and offers everything from learn-to-ski packages to canyon-adventure tours. Call about ski and boarding camps. Skiing lessons are available for children ages four and up; there's day care for infants older than six weeks. ⊠ *Ski Run Blvd., off U.S. 50* ☎ *775/586–7000, 800/432–8365* ⊕ *www.skiheavenly.com* ☞ *97 trails on 4,800 acres, rated 20% beginner, 45% intermediate, 35% expert. Longest run 5½ miles, base 6,540 feet, summit 10,067 feet. Lifts: 30, including 1 aerial tram, 1 gondola, 2 high-speed 6-passenger lifts, and 8 high-speed quads.*

Hope Valley Outdoors. Operating from a yurt at Pickett's Junction, Hope Valley provides lessons and equipment rentals to prepare you for cross-country skiing and snowshoeing. The outfit has 60 miles of trails through Humboldt–Toiyabe National Forest, 10 of which are groomed. ⊠ *Hwy. 88, at Hwy. 89, Hope Valley* ☎ *530/721–2015* ⊕ *www.hopevalleycrosscountry.com.*

Kirkwood Ski Resort. Thirty-six miles south of Lake Tahoe, Kirkwood is the hard-core skiers' and boarders' favorite south-shore mountain, known for its craggy gulp-and-go chutes, sweeping cornices, steep-aspect glade skiing, and high base elevation. But there's also fantastic terrain for newbies and intermediates down wide-open bowls, through wooded gullies, and along rolling tree-lined trails. Tricksters can show off in two terrain parks on jumps, wall rides, rails, and a half-pipe, all visible from the base area. The mountain normally gets hammered with more than 600 inches of snow annually, and often has the most in all of North America. If you're into out-of-bounds skiing, check out Expedition Kirkwood, a backcountry-skills program that teaches basic safety awareness. Kirkwood is also the only Tahoe resort to offer Cat-skiing. If you're into cross-country, the resort has 80 km (50 miles) of superb groomed-track skiing, with skating lanes, instruction, and rentals. Nonskiers can snowshoe, snow-skate, and go dogsledding or snow-tubing. The children's ski school has programs for ages 3 to 12. ⊠ *1501 Kirkwood Meadows Dr., off Hwy. 88, 14 miles west of Hwy. 89, Kirkwood* ☎ *800/967–7500 information, 209/258–7248 cross-country, 209/258–7293 lodging information, 209/258–7332 snow phone* ⊕ *www.kirkwood.com* ☞ *87 trails on 2,300 acres, rated 12% beginner, 20% intermediate, 38% advanced, 30% expert. Longest run 2½ miles, base 7,800 feet, summit 9,800 feet. Lifts: 15, including 2 high-speed quads.*

Sierra-at-Tahoe. Often overlooked by skiers and boarders rushing to Heavenly or Kirkwood, Sierra-at-Tahoe has meticulously groomed intermediate slopes, some of the best tree-skiing in California, and gated backcountry access. Extremely popular with snowboarders, Sierra also has six terrain parks, including a super-pipe with 17-foot walls. For nonskiers there's a snow-tubing hill. Sierra has a low-key atmosphere that's great for families. Kids and beginners take the slow routes in the Mellow Yellow Zone. ⊠ *1111 Sierra-at-Tahoe Rd., 12 miles from South Lake Tahoe off U.S. 50, past Echo Summit, Twin Bridges* ☎ *530/659–7453 information, 530/659–7475 snow phone* ⊕ *www.sierraattahoe. com* ⌒ *46 trails on 2,000 acres, rated 25% beginner, 50% intermediate, 25% advanced. Longest run 2½ miles, base 6,640 feet, summit 8,852 feet. Lifts: 14, including 3 high-speed quads.*

POPE-BALDWIN RECREATION AREA

5 miles west of South Lake Tahoe.

To the west of downtown South Lake Tahoe, U.S. 50 and Highway 89 come together, forming an intersection nicknamed "the Y." If you head northwest on Highway 89, also called Emerald Bay Road, and follow the lakefront, commercial development gives way to national forests and state parks. One of these is Pope-Baldwin Recreation Area.

GETTING HERE AND AROUND

The entrance to the Pope-Baldwin Recreation Area is on the east side of Emerald Bay Road. The area is closed to vehicles in winter, but you can cross-country ski here.

EXPLORING

Tallac Historic Site. At this site you can stroll or picnic lakeside, and then explore three historic estates. The **Pope House** is the magnificently restored 1894 mansion of George S. Pope, who made his money in shipping and lumber and played host to the business and cultural elite of 1920s America. The **Baldwin Museum** is in the estate that once belonged to entrepreneur "Lucky" Baldwin; today it houses a collection of family memorabilia and Washoe Indian artifacts. The **Valhalla** (⊕ *valhallatahoe.com*), with a spectacular floor-to-ceiling stone fireplace, belonged to Walter Heller. Its Grand Hall and a lakeside boathouse, refurbished as a theater, host summertime concerts, plays, and cultural activities. Docents conduct tours of the Pope House in summer; call for tour times. In winter you can cross-country ski around the site. ⊠ *Hwy. 89* ☎ *530/541–5227 late May–Oct., 530/543–2600 year-round* ⊕ *tahoeheritage.org* ▨ *Free, Pope House tour $8* ⊗ *Grounds daily sunrise–sunset. Pope House and Baldwin Museum late May–late Sept., call for hrs.*

FAMILY **Taylor Creek Visitor Center.** At this center operated by the U.S. Forest Service you can visit the site of a Washoe Indian settlement; walk self-guided trails through meadow, marsh, and forest; and inspect the Stream Profile Chamber, an underground display with windows right into Taylor Creek. In fall you may see spawning kokanee salmon digging their nests. In summer Forest Service naturalists organize discovery walks and evening programs. ⊠ *Hwy. 89, 3 miles north of junction with U.S. 50* ☎ *530/543–2674 late May–Oct., 530/543–2600 year-round* ⊕ *www.fs.usda.gov/recarea/ltbmu/recarea/?recid=11785* ▨ *Free* ⊗ *Late May–late Sept., 8:30–4:30; call for Oct. hrs.*

Fjord-like Emerald Bay is possibly the most scenic part of Lake Tahoe.

EMERALD BAY STATE PARK

4 miles west of Pope-Baldwin Recreation Area.

You can hike, bike, swim, camp, scuba dive, kayak, or tour a lookalike Viking castle at this state park. Or you can simply enjoy the most popular tourist stop on Lake Tahoe's circular drive: the high cliff overlooking Emerald Bay, famed for its jewel-like shape and color.

GETTING HERE AND AROUND

The entrance to Emerald Bay State Park is on the east side of a narrow, twisting section of Highway 89. Caution is the keyword for both drivers and pedestrians. The park is closed to vehicles in winter.

EXPLORING

Fodor'sChoice
★
Emerald Bay. A massive glacier millions of years ago carved this 3-mile-long and 1-mile-wide fjordlike inlet. Famed for its jewel-like shape and colors, the bay surrounds Fannette, Tahoe's only island. Highway 89 curves high above the lake through Emerald Bay State Park; from the Emerald Bay lookout, the centerpiece of the park, you can survey the whole scene. This is one of the don't-miss views of Lake Tahoe. The light is best in mid- to late morning, when the bay's colors really pop. ✉ *Hwy. 89, 20 miles south of Tahoe City* ☎ *530/525–7232* ⊕ *www. parks.ca.gov* ✉ *$10 parking fee.*

Vikingsholm. This 38-room estate was completed in 1929. The original owner, Lora Knight, had this precise copy of a 1,200-year-old Viking castle built out of materials native to the area. She furnished it with Scandinavian antiques and hired artisans to build period reproductions. The sod roof sprouts wildflowers each spring. There are picnic tables nearby and a gray-sand beach for strolling. A steep 1-mile-long trail from the Emerald Bay lookout leads down to Vikingsholm, and the hike back up is hard (especially if you're not yet acclimated to the elevation), although there are benches and stone culverts to rest on. At the 150-foot peak of Fannette Island are the ruins of a stone structure known as the Tea House, built in 1928 so that Knight's guests could have a place to enjoy afternoon refreshments after a motorboat ride. The island is off-limits from February through mid-June to protect nesting Canada geese. The rest of the year it's open for day use. ⊠ *Hwy. 89* ☎ *530/541–6498 summer, 530/525–7232 year-round* ⊕ *www. vikingsholm.com* 🖭 *Day-use parking fee $10; mansion tour $10* ☉ *Late May–Sept., daily 10:30–4.*

SPORTS AND THE OUTDOORS

HIKING

Eagle Falls. To reach these falls, leave your car in the parking lot of the Eagle Falls picnic area (near Vikingsholm; arrive early for a good spot), and walk up the short but fairly steep canyon nearby. You'll have a brilliant panorama of Emerald Bay from this spot near the boundary of Desolation Wilderness. For a strenuous full-day hike, continue 5 miles, past Eagle Lake, to Upper and Middle Velma Lakes. Pick up trail maps at Taylor Creek Visitor Center in summer, or year-round at the main U.S. Forest Service Office in South Lake Tahoe, at 35 College Drive. ⊠ *Hwy. 89, South Lake Tahoe.*

D.L. BLISS STATE PARK

3 miles north of Emerald Bay State Park, 17 miles south of Tahoe City.

This park shares six miles of shoreline with adjacent Emerald Bay State Park, and has two white-sand beaches. Hike the Rubicon Trail for stunning views of the lake.

GETTING HERE AND AROUND

The entrance to D.L. Bliss State Park is on the east side of Highway 89 just north of Emerald Bay. No vehicles are allowed in when the park is closed for the season.

EXPLORING

D.L. Bliss State Park. This park takes its name from Duane LeRoy Bliss, a 19th-century lumber magnate. At one time Bliss owned nearly 75% of Tahoe's lakefront, along with local steamboats, railroads, and banks. The park shares 6 miles of shoreline with Emerald Bay State Park; combined the two parks cover 1,830 acres, 744 of which the Bliss family donated to the state. At the north end of Bliss is Rubicon Point, which overlooks one of the lake's deepest spots. Short trails lead to an old lighthouse and Balancing Rock, which weighs 250,000 pounds and balances on a fist of granite. The 4.5-mile Rubicon Trail—one of Tahoe's premier hikes—leads to Vikingsholm and provides stunning lake views. Two white-sand beaches front some of Tahoe's warmest water. ⊠ *Hwy. 89* ☎ *530/525–3345, 800/777–0369* ⊕ *www.parks.ca.gov* 🖭 *$10 per vehicle, day use* ☉ *Late May–Sept., daily sunrise–sunset.*

ED Z'BERG SUGAR PINE POINT STATE PARK

8 miles north of D. L. Bliss State Park, 10 miles south of Tahoe City.

Visitors love to hike, swim, and fish here in the summer, but this park is also popular in winter, when a small campground remains open. Eleven miles of cross-country ski and snowshoe trails allow beginners and experienced enthusiasts alike to whoosh through pine forests and glide past the lake.

GETTING HERE AND AROUND

The entrance to Sugar Pine Point is on the east side of Highway 89, about a mile south of Tahoma. A bike trail links Tahoe City to the park.

EXPLORING

Hellman-Ehrman Mansion. The main attraction at Sugar Pine Point State Park is Ehrman Mansion, a 1903 stone-and-shingle summer home furnished in period style. In its day it was the height of modernity, with electric lights and complete indoor plumbing. Also in the park are a trapper's log cabin from the mid-19th century, a nature preserve with wildlife exhibits, a lighthouse, the start of the 10-mile biking trail to Tahoe City, and an extensive system of hiking and cross-country skiing trails. If you're feeling less ambitious, you can relax on the sun-dappled lawn behind the mansion and gaze out at the lake. ⊠ *Hwy. 89* 🕾 *530/525–7982 mansion in season, 530/525–7232 year-round* ⊕ *www.parks.ca.gov* 🎫 *$10 per vehicle, day use; mansion tour $10* 🕙 *Mansion late May–Aug., daily 10–3; call for Sept. hrs.*

Ed Z'Berg Sugar Pine Point State Park. Named for a state lawmaker who sponsored key conservation legislation, Lake Tahoe's largest state park has 2,000 acres of dense forests and nearly 2 miles of shore frontage. A popular spot during snow season, Sugar Pine provides 11 miles of cross-country trails and winter camping on a first-come, first-served basis. Rangers lead full-moon snowshoe tours from January to March. ⊠ *Hwy. 89, 1 mile south of Tahoma* 🕾 *530/525–7982, 530/525–7232 year-round* ⊕ *www.parks.ca.gov* 🎫 *$10 per vehicle, day use.*

TAHOMA

1 mile north of Ed Z'berg Sugar Pine Point State Park, 23 miles south of Truckee.

With its rustic waterfront vacation cottages, Tahoma exemplifies life on the lake in its quiet early days before bright-lights casinos and huge crowds proliferated. In 1960 Tahoma was host of the Olympic Nordic-skiing competitions. Today there's little to do here except stroll by the lake and listen to the wind in the trees, making it a favorite home base for mellow families and nature buffs.

GETTING HERE AND AROUND

Approach Tahoma by car on Highway 89, called West Lake Boulevard in this section. From the northern and western communities, take a TART bus to Tahoma. A bike trail links Tahoe City to Tahoma.

WHERE TO STAY

$$ **Tahoma Meadows B&B Cottages.** It's hard to beat this serene prop-
B&B/INN   erty for atmosphere and woodsy charm; it's a great retreat for families
and couples. **Pros:** lovely setting; good choice for families; close to
Homewood ski resort. **Cons:** far from the casinos. $ *Rooms from:
$169 ⊠ 6821 W. Lake Blvd. ☎ 530/525–1553, 866/525–1553 ⊕ www.
tahomameadows.com ⤳ 16 cabins* ⎜○⎜ *Breakfast.*

SPORTS AND THE OUTDOORS

SKIING

Homewood Mountain Resort. Schuss down these slopes for fantastic
views—the mountain rises across the road from the Tahoe shoreline.
This small, usually uncrowded resort is the favorite area of locals on a
snowy day, because you can find lots of untracked powder. It's also the
most protected and least windy Tahoe ski area during a storm; when
every other resort's lifts are on wind hold, you can almost always count
on Homewood's to be open. There's only one high-speed chairlift, but
there are rarely any lines, and the ticket prices are some of the cheapest
around—kids 5 to 12 ski for $24, and those four and under are free.
The resort may look small as you drive by, but most of it isn't visible
from the road. ⊠ *5145 W. Lake Blvd., Hwy. 89, 6 miles south of Tahoe
City, Homewood* ☎ *530/525–2992 information, 530/525–2900 snow
phone* ⊕ *www.skihomewood.com* ⤳ *64 trails on 2,010 acres, rated
15% beginner, 40% intermediate, and 45% advanced. Longest run 2
miles, base 6,230 feet, summit 7,880 feet. Lifts: 4 chairlifts, 4 surface
lifts.*

14

TAHOE CITY

9 miles north of Tahoma, 14 miles south of Truckee.

Tahoe City is the only lakeside town with a charming downtown area
good for strolling and window-shopping. Stores and restaurants are
all within walking distance of the Outlet Gates, where water is spilled
into the Truckee River to control the surface level of the lake. You can
spot giant trout in the river from Fanny Bridge, so-called for the views
of the backsides of sightseers leaning over the railing.

GETTING HERE AND AROUND

Tahoe City is at the junction of Highway 28, also called North Lake
Boulevard, and Highway 89 where it turns northwest toward Squaw
Valley and Truckee. TART buses serve the communities along the north
and west shores, and connect them to Truckee.

ESSENTIALS

Visitor Information Tahoe Visitor Information Center ☎ *530/581–6900,
888/434–1262* ⊕ *www.gotahoenorth.com.*

EXPLORING

Gatekeeper's Museum. This museum preserves a little-known part of the
region's history. Between 1910 and 1968 the gatekeeper who lived on
this site was responsible for monitoring the level of the lake, using a
hand-turned winch system (still used today) to keep the water at the
correct level. Also on this site, the fantastic Marion Steinbach Indian

Basket Museum displays 800 baskets from 85 tribes. ✉ *130 W. Lake Blvd.* ☎ *530/583–1762* 🌐 *www.northtahoemuseums.org* 🎟 *$5* 🕒 *Late June–Sept., daily 10–5.*

Watson Cabin Living Museum. In the middle of Tahoe City sits a 1909 log cabin built by Robert M. Watson and his son. Now a museum, it's filled with century-old furnishings and many reproductions. Docents are available to answer questions and will lead tours if you call ahead. ✉ *560 N. Lake Blvd.* ☎ *530/583–8717, 530/583–1762* 🌐 *www.northtahoemuseums.org* 🎟 *$2* 🕒 *Late May–early Sept., Thurs.–Mon. 10–5.*

WHERE TO EAT

$$$ AMERICAN 🍴 **Christy Hill.** Huge windows give diners here some of the best lake views in Tahoe. The menu features solid Euro–Cal preparations of fresh seafood, filet of beef, and vegetarian dishes, as well as small plate offerings. The extensive wine list and exceptionally good desserts earn accolades, as do the gracious service and casual vibe. If the weather is balmy, have dinner on the deck. In any season, this is a romantic choice for lake gazing and wine sipping. [$] *Average main: $27* ✉ *115 Grove St., at N. Lake Blvd.* ☎ *530/583–8551* 🌐 *www.christyhill.com* 🕒 *No lunch.*

$ AMERICAN 🍴 **Fire Sign Café.** Watch the road carefully or you'll miss this great little diner two miles south of Tahoe City on Highway 89. There's often a wait for breakfast and lunch, but it's worth it. The pastries are made from scratch, the salmon is smoked in-house, the salsa is hand cut, and there's real maple syrup for the many types of pancakes and waffles. Leave room for dessert; a fruit cobbler is almost always on the menu. [$] *Average main: $10* ✉ *1785 W. Lake Blvd., at Fountain Ave.* ☎ *530/583–0871* 🌐 *www.firesigncafe.com* ✍ *Reservations not accepted* 🕒 *No dinner.*

$ AMERICAN 🍴 **Syd's Bagelry & Espresso.** For breakfast bagels and pastries and lunchtime salads and sandwiches, locals head to Syd's, which brews good coffee and provides free Wi-Fi, too. Want the skinny on Tahoe City? Talk to Dean, the affable owner. [$] *Average main: $8* ✉ *550 N. Lake Tahoe Blvd., at Grove St.* ☎ *530/584–2384* 🕒 *No dinner.*

$$$ ECLECTIC Fodor's Choice ★ 🍴 **Wolfdale's.** Consistent, inspired cuisine makes Wolfdale's one of the top restaurants on the lake. Seafood is the specialty on the changing menu; the imaginative entrées merge Asian and European cooking and lean toward the light and healthful, rather than the heavy and overdone. Everything from teriyaki glaze to smoked fish is made in-house. Request a window table, and book early enough to see the lake view from the elegantly simple dining room. [$] *Average main: $30* ✉ *640 N. Lake Blvd., near Grove St.* ☎ *530/583–5700* 🌐 *www.wolfdales.com* 🕒 *Closed Tues. No lunch.*

WHERE TO STAY

$$ B&B/INN 🏨 **Cottage Inn.** Avoid the crowds by staying in one of these charming circa-1938 log cottages under the towering pines on the lake's west shore. **Pros:** romantic, woodsy setting; each room has a fireplace; full breakfast. **Cons:** no kids under 12. [$] *Rooms from: $160* ✉ *1690 W. Lake Blvd.* ☎ *530/581–4073, 800/581–4073* 🌐 *www.thecottageinn.com* 🛏 *22 rooms* 🍽 *Breakfast.*

$$$$
HOTEL
Fodor'sChoice
★

Sunnyside Steakhouse and Lodge. The views are superb and the hospitality gracious at this lakeside lodge three miles south of Tahoe City. **Pros:** complimentary continental breakfast and afternoon tea; most rooms have balconies overlooking the lake. **Cons:** can be pricey for families. $ *Rooms from: $265 ⊠ 1850 W. Lake Blvd. ☎ 530/583–7200, 800/822–2754 ⊕ www.sunnysideresort.com ⇆ 18 rooms, 5 suites ⓘ Breakfast.*

SPORTS AND THE OUTDOORS

GOLF

Tahoe City Golf Course. This 9-hole course, which opened in 1917, gives golfers views of Lake Tahoe. Rent a cart for $10. ■TIP➜ **All greens break toward the lake.** ⊠ *251 N. Lake Blvd. ☎ 530/583–1516 ⊕ www. playtcgc.com ⓐ $30 for 9 holes; $50 for 18 ⚑ 18 holes, 5261 yards, par 66.*

RAFTING

FAMILY **Truckee River Rafting.** In summer you can take a self-guided raft trip down a gentle 5-mile stretch of the Truckee River. This outfitter will shuttle you back to Tahoe City at the end of your two- to three-hour trip. On a warm day, this makes a great family outing. ⊠ *175 River Rd., near W. Lake Blvd. ☎ 530/583–1111 ⊕ www.truckeeriverrafting. com ⓐ From $28.*

SKIING

Fodor'sChoice
★

Alpine Meadows Ski Area. With 450 inches of snow annually, Alpine has some of Tahoe's most reliable conditions. It's usually one of the first areas to open in November and one of the last to close in May or June. Alpine isn't the place for show-offs; instead, you'll find down-to-earth alpine fetishists. The two peaks here are well suited to intermediate skiers, with a number of runs for experts only. Snowboarders and hot-dog skiers will find a terrain park with a super-pipe, rails, and tabletops, as well as a boarder-cross course. Alpine is a great place to learn to ski and has a ski school that coaches those with physical and mental disabilities. On Saturday, because of the limited parking, there's more acreage per person than at other resorts. Lift tickets are good at neighboring Squaw Valley; a free shuttle runs all day between the two ski parks. ⊠ *2600 Alpine Meadows Rd., off Hwy. 89, 6 miles northwest of Tahoe City and 13 miles south of Truckee ☎ 530/583–4232, 800/403–0206, 800/403–0206 snow phone ⊕ www.squawalpine.com ☞ 100 trails on 2,400 acres, rated 25% beginner, 40% intermediate, 35% advanced. Longest run 2½ miles, base 6,835 feet, summit 8,637 feet. Lifts: 13, including 1 high-speed 6-passenger lift and 2 high-speed quads.*

Tahoe Dave's Skis and Boards. You can rent skis, boards, and snowshoes at this shop, which has the area's best selection of downhill rental equipment. ⊠ *590 N. Lake Blvd. ☎ 530/583–6415 ⊕ www.tahoedaves.com.*

14

Squaw Valley USA has runs for skiers of all ability levels, from beginner to expert trails.

OLYMPIC VALLEY

7 miles north of Tahoe City to Squaw Valley Road; 8½ miles south of Truckee.

Olympic Valley got its name in 1960, when Squaw Valley USA, the ski resort here, hosted the Winter Olympics. Snow sports remain the primary activity, but once summer comes, you can hike into the adjacent Granite Chief Wilderness, explore wildflower-studded alpine meadows, or lie by a swimming pool in one of the Sierra's prettiest valleys.

GETTING HERE AND AROUND

Squaw Valley Road, the only way into Olympic Valley, branches west off Highway 89 about 8 miles south of Truckee. TART connects the Squaw Valley ski area with the communities along the north and west shores, and Truckee, with year-round public transportation. Squaw Valley Ski Resort provides a free shuttle to many stops in those same areas.

EXPLORING

High Camp. You can ride the Squaw Valley Aerial Tram to this activity hub, which at 8,200 feet commands superb views of Lake Tahoe and the surrounding mountains. In summer, go for a sunset hike, sit by the pool, or have a cocktail and watch the sunset. In winter you can ski, ice-skate, snow-tube, or go for a full-moon hike. There's also a restaurant, a lounge, and a small Olympic museum. Pick up trail maps at the tram building. ⊠ *Aerial Tram Bldg., Squaw Valley* ☎ *800/403–0206* ⊕ *www.squawalpine.com/events-things-do/aerial-tram-rides* ✉ *Aerial Tram, $39* ☾ *Daily; call for hrs.*

FAMILY **Village at Squaw Valley.** The centerpiece of Olympic Valley is a pedestrian mall at the base of several four-story ersatz Bavarian stone-and-timber buildings, where you'll find restaurants, high-end condo rentals, boutiques, and cafés. ✉ *1750 Village East Rd.* ☎ *530/584–1000, 800/403–0206 information, 800/731–8021 condo reservations* 🌐 *www.squawalpine.com/explore/about/squaw-valley-village-map.*

WHERE TO EAT

$$ PIZZA FAMILY 🍴 **Fireside Pizza Company.** Adults might opt for the signature pear and Gorgonzola pizza at this modern Italian restaurant, but most kids clamor for the house favorite: an Italian-sausage-and-pepperoni combo with a bubbly blend of four cheeses. Salads and pasta dishes round out the menu at this family-friendly spot. [$] *Average main: $16* ✉ *The Village at Squaw Valley, 1985 Squaw Valley Rd., #25* ☎ *530/584–6150* 🌐 *www.firesidepizza.com.*

$$$ ECLECTIC 🍴 **Graham's of Squaw Valley.** Sit by a floor-to-ceiling river-rock hearth under a knotty-pine peaked ceiling in the intimate dining room in the Christy Inn Lodge. The southern European–inspired menu changes often, but expect hearty entrées such as grilled beef tenderloin with wild mushroom sauce, along with lighter-fare small plates like quail with fig demi-glace or tasty crab salad. You can also stop in at the fireside bar for appetizers and wine from Graham's highly regarded wine list. [$] *Average main: $30* ✉ *1650 Squaw Valley Rd.* ☎ *530/581–0454* ⏲ *Closed Mon. and Tues. No lunch.*

$$ JAPANESE 🍴 **Mamasake.** The hip sushi spot at Squaw serves stylized presentations. On some evenings you can sit at the bar and watch extreme ski movies, many of them filmed right outside the window. From 3 to 5 enjoy the afternoon special: a spicy-tuna or salmon hand roll and a can of Bud for six bucks. [$] *Average main: $16* ✉ *1850 Village South Rd. #52, off Squaw Valley Rd.* ☎ *530/584–0110* 🌐 *mamasake.com.*

$$$$ AMERICAN Fodor's Choice ★ 🍴 **PlumpJack Café.** The best restaurant in the entire Tahoe Basin is the epitome of discreet chic for serious foodies. The menu changes seasonally, but look for filet mignon "Oscar" with Dungeness crab, braised short ribs with kimchi-Asian pear slaw, and inventive vegetarian dishes. Rather than complicated, heavy sauces, the chef uses simple reductions to complement a dish. The result: clean, dynamic flavors. The wine list is exceptional for its variety and reasonable prices. A less expensive but equally adventurous menu, including lunch, is served at the bar. [$] *Average main: $35* ✉ *1920 Squaw Valley Rd.* ☎ *530/583–1578, 800/323–7666* 🌐 *www.plumpjacksquawvalleyinn.com* ✍ *Reservations essential.*

WHERE TO STAY

$$$$ HOTEL Fodor's Choice ★ 🏨 **PlumpJack Squaw Valley Inn.** Stylish and luxurious, this two-story, cedar-sided inn has a snappy, sophisticated look and laid-back sensibility, perfect for the Bay Area cognoscenti who flock here on weekends. **Pros:** small; intimate; lots of attention to details. **Cons:** not the best choice for families with small children. [$] *Rooms from: $275* ✉ *1920 Squaw Valley Rd.* ☎ *530/583–1576, 800/323–7666* 🌐 *www.plumpjacksquawvalleyinn.com* 🛏 *56 rooms, 8 suites* 🍽 *Breakfast.*

$$$$ RESORT 🏨 **Resort at Squaw Creek.** This multi-facility Squaw Valley resort offers a plethora of year-round activities. **Pros:** every conceivable amenity;

private chairlift to Squaw Valley USA for ski-in, ski-out. **Cons:** large and pricey. Ⓢ *Rooms from: $259* ✉ *400 Squaw Creek Rd.* ☎ *530/583–6300, 800/327–3353* ⊕ *www.squawcreek.com* ↳ *205 rooms, 200 suites* ❑ *No meals.*

$$$　❑ **The Village at Squaw Valley USA.** Right at the base of the slopes, at the
HOTEL　center point of Olympic Valley, the Village's condominiums (from studio to three bedrooms) come complete with gas fireplaces, daily maid service, and heated slate-tile bathroom and kitchen floors. **Pros:** family-friendly; near Village restaurants and shops. **Cons:** claustrophobia-inducing crowds on weekends. Ⓢ *Rooms from: $199* ✉ *1750 Village East Rd.* ☎ *530/584–1000, 888/259–1428* ⊕ *www.squawalpine.com/ lodging* ↳ *198 suites* ❑ *No meals.*

SPORTS AND THE OUTDOORS

GOLF

Resort at Squaw Creek Golf Course. For beautiful views of Squaw Valley's surrounding peaks, play this narrow, challenging championship course designed by Robert Trent Jones Jr. Rates start at $99 with mid-range twilight fees beginning at noon for $79; the lowest rate, $59, starts at 3 pm. All fees include a golf cart plus valet parking. ✉ *400 Squaw Creek Rd.* ☎ *530/583–6300, 530/581–6637 pro shop* ⊕ *www.squawcreek. com* ▤ *$99* ⛳ *18 holes, 6931 yards, par 71.*

ICE-SKATING

FAMILY　**Olympic Ice Pavilion.** Ice-skate here from late November to early March. A ride up the mountain in the Aerial Tram costs $39, plus $12 for skate rental and one hour of skate time. End your outing in the hot tub ($10). In summer the pavilion converts into a roller-skating rink. Year-round, you get fabulous views of the lake and the Sierra Nevada. ✉ *1960 Squaw Valley Rd., High Camp, Squaw Valley* ☎ *800/403–0206* ⊕ *www.squawalpine.com/events-things-do/ice-skating.*

MINIATURE GOLF

FAMILY　**Squaw Valley Adventure Center.** Next to the Olympic Village Lodge, on the far side of the creek, this seasonal activities center has an 18-hole miniature golf course, a ropes course, and sometimes a bungee trampoline, a blast for kids. ✉ *1960 Squaw Valley Rd.* ☎ *530/581–7563* ⊕ *www.squawadventure.com.*

ROCK CLIMBING

Headwall Climbing Wall. Before you rappel down a granite monolith, hone your skills at this challenging wall at the base of the Aerial Tram. ✉ *Squaw Valley Adventure Center, 1960 Squaw Valley Rd.* ☎ *530/581– 7563* ⊕ *www.squawadventure.com.*

SKIING

Resort at Squaw Creek. Cross-country skiers enjoy looping through the valley's giant alpine meadow. The resort rents ski equipment and provides trail maps. ✉ *400 Squaw Creek Rd.* ☎ *530/583–6300, 530/581– 6637 pro shop* ⊕ *www.squawcreek.com.*

Fodor's Choice　**Squaw Valley USA.** Known for some of the toughest skiing in the Tahoe
★　area, this park was the centerpiece of the 1960 Winter Olympics. Today it's the definitive North Tahoe ski resort and among the top-three mega-resorts in California (the other two are Heavenly and Mammoth).

Although Squaw has changed significantly since the Olympics, the skiing is still world-class and extends across vast bowls stretched between six peaks. Experts often head directly to the untamed terrain of the infamous KT-22 face, which has bumps, cliffs, and gulp-and-go chutes, or to the nearly vertical Palisades, where many famous extreme-skiing films have been shot. Fret not, beginners and intermediates: you have plenty of wide-open, groomed trails at High Camp (which sits at the *top* of the mountain) and around the more challenging Snow King Peak. Snowboarders and show-off skiers can tear up the five fantastic terrain parks, which include a giant super-pipe. Ski passes are good at neighboring Alpine Meadows; free shuttles run all day between the two ski parks. ⊠ *1960 Squaw Valley Rd., off Hwy. 89, 7 miles northwest of Tahoe City* ☏ *800/731–8021 lodging reservations, 530/452–4355 snow phone, 800/403–0206 information* ⊕ *www.squawalpine.com* ⚲ *170 trails on 3,600 acres, rated 25% beginner, 45% intermediate, 30% advanced. Longest run 3.2 miles, base 6,200 feet, summit 9,050 feet. Lifts: 29, including a gondola-style funitel, a tram, 7 high-speed chairs, and 15 fixed-grip chairs and 5 surface lifts.*

Tahoe Dave's Skis and Boards. If you don't want to pay resort prices, you can rent and tune downhill skis and snowboards at this shop. ⊠ *3039 Hwy. 89, at Squaw Valley Rd.* ☏ *530/583–5665* ⊕ *www.tahoedaves. com.*

TRUCKEE

13 miles northwest of Kings Beach, 14 miles north of Tahoe City.

Formerly a decrepit railroad town in the mountains, Truckee is now the trendy first stop for many Tahoe visitors. The town was officially established around 1863, and by 1868 it had gone from a stagecoach station to a major stopover for trains bound for the Pacific via the new transcontinental railroad. Every day, freight trains and Amtrak's California Zephyr still idle briefly at the depot in the middle of town. Step inside the depot for a walking-tour map of historic Truckee.

Across from the station, where Old West facades line the main drag, you'll find galleries, gift shops, boutiques, old-fashioned diners, and several remarkably good restaurants. Look for outlet stores, strip malls, and discount skiwear shops along Donner Pass Road, north of the freeway. Because of its location off Interstate 80, Truckee is a favorite stopover for people traveling from the San Francisco Bay Area to the north shore of Lake Tahoe, Reno, and points east.

GETTING HERE AND AROUND

Truckee is off Interstate 80 between highways 89 and 267. Greyhound and Amtrak stop here, Enterprise and Hertz provide car rentals, and TART buses serve Truckee and north shore communities.

ESSENTIALS

Visitor Information Truckee Donner Chamber of Commerce and the California Welcome Center ⊠ *Amtrak depot, 10065 Donner Pass Rd., near Spring St.* ☏ *530/587–8808 chamber of commerce, 866/443–2027 welcome center* ⊕ *www.truckee.com.*

EXPLORING

Donner Memorial State Park and Emigrant Trail Museum. The park and museum commemorate the Donner Party, westward-bound pioneers—about 90; historians debate the exact number—who became trapped in the Sierra in the winter of 1846–47 in snow 22 feet deep. Barely more than half the pioneers survived, some by resorting to cannibalism. In the park, you can picnic, hike, camp, and go boating, fishing, and waterskiing in summer; winter brings cross-country skiing and snowshoeing on groomed trails. A new visitor's center and museum contains exhibits about the Donner Party's plight, regional Native Americans, and railroad and transportation development through Donner Pass and the Sierra. ✉ *12593 Donner Pass Rd., off I–80, 2 miles west of Truckee* ☎ *530/582–7892 museum, 800/444–7275 camping reservations* 🌐 *www.parks.ca.gov* 🎟 *$8 parking, day use* 🕒 *Museum daily 10–5.*

OFF THE BEATEN PATH

Tahoe National Forest. Draped along the Sierra Nevada Crest north of Lake Tahoe, the national forest offers abundant outdoor recreation: hiking, picnicking, and camping in summer, and snowshoeing, skiing, and sledding over some of the deepest snowpack in the West in winter. ✉ *Truckee ranger station, 10811 Stockrest Springs Rd.* ☎ *530/587–3558 Truckee ranger station, 530/265–4531 forest headquarters* 🌐 *www.fs.usda.gov/tahoe.*

WHERE TO EAT

$$$ ECLECTIC Fodor's Choice ★

🍴 **Cottonwood Restaurant & Bar.** Perched above town on the site of North America's first chairlift, this restaurant is an institution. The bar is decked out with old wooden skis, sleds, skates, and photos of Truckee's early days. The ambitious menu includes such dishes as grilled steak, baby-back short ribs with Cajun spices, and butternut-squash enchiladas with Ancho chile mole—plus fresh-baked breads and desserts. But people come here mainly for the atmosphere and hilltop views. [$] *Average main: $25* ✉ *10142 Rue Hilltop Rd., off Brockway Rd., ¼ mile south of downtown* ☎ *530/587–5711* 🌐 *www.cottonwoodrestaurant.com* 🕒 *No lunch.*

$$ AMERICAN

🍴 **FiftyFifty Brewing Company.** In this Truckee brewpub warm red tones and comfy booths, plus a pint of the Donner Party porter, will take the nip out of a cold day on the slopes. The menu includes salads, burgers, and the house specialty, a pulled-pork sandwich, plus barbecued ribs and pan-seared salmon. Their inventive pizzas are popular anytime. There's a full bar along with the brews, and lots of après-ski action. [$] *Average main: $21* ✉ *11197 Brockway Rd.* ☎ *530/587–2337* 🌐 *www.fiftyfiftybrewing.com.*

$$$ ECLECTIC

🍴 **Moody's Bistro, Bar & Beats.** Head here for contemporary-Cal cuisine in a sexy dining room with pumpkin-color walls, burgundy velvet banquettes, and art-deco fixtures. The earthy, sure-handed cooking features organically grown ingredients: look for ahi poke, snazzy pizzas bubbling-hot from a brick oven, braised lamb shanks, pan-roasted wild game, fresh seafood, and organic beef. Lunch fare is lighter. In summer dine alfresco surrounded by flowers. From Thursday through Saturday there's music in the borderline-raucous bar that gets packed with

Truckee's bon vivants. $ *Average main: $25* ✉ *10007 Bridge St., at Donner Pass Rd.* ☎ *530/587–8688* ⊕ *www.moodysbistro.com.*

$$$ ✕ **Truckee Tavern & Grill.** The wood-fired grill in this downtown Truckee
AMERICAN   restaurant turns out steaks, chicken, and chops along with buffalo tri-
tip and other house specialties. Non-carnivores enjoy pasta and fish
entrées. The full bar features inventive cocktails plus, in tribute to
Truckee's bootlegging past during prohibition, artisanal small-batch
gin and whiskey. $ *Average main: $26* ✉ *10118 Donner Pass Rd., near
Spring St.* ☎ *530/587–3766* ⊕ *www.truckeetavern.com* ⊘ *No lunch.*

WHERE TO STAY

$$$ ⌂ **Cedar House Sport Hotel.** The clean, spare lines of the Cedar House's
HOTEL   wooden exterior evoke a modern European feel, while energy-saving
heating, cooling, and lighting systems emphasize the owners' commitment to sustainability. **Pros:** environmentally friendly; comfortable;
hip. **Cons:** some bathrooms on the small side. $ *Rooms from: $190*
✉ *10918 Brockway Rd.* ☎ *530/582–5655, 866/582–5655* ⊕ *www.cedar
housesporthotel.com* ⤳ *40 rooms* ⦿| *Breakfast.*

$$$ ⌂ **Northstar California Resort.** The area's most complete destination resort
RESORT   entices families with its sports activities and concentration of restau-
rants, shops, and accommodations. **Pros:** array of lodging types; on-
site shuttle; several dining options in Northstar Village. **Cons:** family
accommodations are very pricey. $ *Rooms from: $249* ✉ *100 North-
star Dr., off Hwy. 267, 6 miles southeast of Truckee* ☎ *530/562–1010,
800/466–6784* ⊕ *www.northstarcalifornia.com* ⤳ *250 units* ⦿| *No
meals.*

$$$$ ⌂ **Ritz-Carlton Highlands Court, Lake Tahoe.** Nestled mid-mountain on the
RESORT   Northstar ski resort, the plush accommodations of the Ritz-Carlton
Fodor'sChoice   have floor-to-ceiling windows for maximum views, along with fire-
★   places, cozy robes, and down comforters. **Pros:** superb service; gorgeous
setting. **Cons:** prices as breathtaking as the views; must go off-site for
golf and tennis. $ *Rooms from: $469* ✉ *13031 Ritz-Carlton High-
lands Court* ☎ *530/562–3000, 800/241–3333* ⊕ *www.ritzcarlton.com/
laketahoe* ⤳ *153 rooms, 17 suites* ⦿| *No meals.*

$$ ⌂ **River Street Inn.** On the banks of the Truckee River, this 1885 wood-
B&B/INN   and-stone inn has uncluttered, comfortable rooms that are simply deco-
rated, with attractive, country-style wooden furniture and extras like
flat-screen TVs. **Pros:** tidy rooms; good value. **Cons:** parking is a half-
block from inn. $ *Rooms from: $145* ✉ *10009 E. River St.* ☎ *530/550–
9290, 530/550–9222 restaurant* ⊕ *www.riverstreetinntruckee.com*
⤳ *11 rooms* ⦿| *Breakfast.*

SPORTS AND THE OUTDOORS
GOLF

Coyote Moon Golf Course. With towering pine trees lining the fairways
and no houses to spoil the view, this course is as beautiful as it is
challenging. Fees include a shared cart; the green fee drops at 1 pm
and dips again at 3. ✉ *10685 Northwoods Blvd., off Donner Pass Rd.*
☎ *530/587–0886* ⊕ *www.coyotemoongolf.com* ⌦ *$160* ⛳ *18 holes,
7177 yards, par 72* ⊘ *Closed late fall–late spring.*

14

Northstar. The front nine holes here are open-links style, while the challenging back nine move through tight, tree-lined fairways. Fees include a shared cart. Twilight rates begin at 2 pm. You can play nine holes for $50; special teen rates encourage family outings. The restaurant serves breakfast and lunch only. ⊠ *168 Basque Dr., off Northstar Dr., west off Hwy. 267* ☏ *530/562–3290 pro-shop* ⊕ *www.northstarcalifornia.com/info/summer/golf.asp* ⌾ *$85* ⚑ *18 holes, 6781 yards, par 72.*

Old Greenwood. Beautiful mountain and forest views add to the pleasure of a round played at north Lake Tahoe's only Jack Nicklaus Signature Golf Course. The regular fees are high, but there's a $75 twilight rate beginning at 4 pm. ⊠ *12915 Fairway Dr., off Overland Trail Rd., off I–80, Exit 190* ☏ *530/550–7010* ⊕ *www.golfintahoe.com/old_greenwood* ⌾ *$200* ⚑ *18 holes, 7518 yards, par 72.*

MOUNTAIN BIKING

Cyclepaths Mountain Bike Adventures. This combination full-service bike shop and bike-adventure outfitter offers instruction in mountain biking, guided tours, tips for self-guided bike touring, bike repairs, and books and maps on the area. ⊠ *10095 W. River St., by Bridge St.* ☏ *530/582–1890* ⊕ *www.cyclepaths.net.*

Northstar California. In summer you can rent a bike and ride the lifts ($50, ages 13 and up) to the mountain-biking park for 100 miles of challenging terrain. The season extends from mid-June through September with varying hours. ⊠ *Northstar Dr., off Hwy. 267* ☏ *530/562–1010* ⊕ *www.northstarcalifornia.com/bike-and-hike/mtn-biking-rentals.aspx.*

SKIING

Several smaller resorts around Truckee offer access to the Sierra's slopes for less than half the price of the big resorts. Though you'll sacrifice vertical rise, acreage, and high-speed lifts, you can ski or ride and still have money left over for room and board. These are great places for first-timers and families with kids learning to ski.

Boreal Mountain Resort. These slopes have 380 skiable acres and 500 vertical feet of terrain visible from the freeway. Lift-served snow-tubing and night skiing go until 9. ⊠ *19749 Boreal Ridge Rd., at I–80, Boreal/Castle Peak exit, Soda Springs* ☏ *530/426–3666* ⊕ *www.rideboreal.com.*

Donner Ski Ranch. This ski park has 505 acres and 750 vertical feet. A popular area with kids in this small, family-friendly park is the Tubing Hill. Riders whisk down the slope in a huge inflated inner tube and then go back to the top on a moving carpet. ⊠ *19320 Donner Pass Rd., Norden* ☏ *530/426–3635* ⊕ *www.donnerskiranch.com.*

Fodor's Choice ★   **Northstar California.** With two tree-lined, northeast-facing, wind-protected bowls, this park is the ideal place in a storm, and just may be the best all-around family ski resort at Tahoe. Hotshot experts unfairly call the mountain "Flatstar," but the meticulous grooming and long cruisers make it an intermediate skier's paradise. Boarders are especially welcome, with awesome terrain parks, including a 420-foot-long superpipe, a half-pipe, rails and boxes, and lots of kickers. Experts can ski the steeps and bumps off Lookout Mountain, where there's rarely a line for the high-speed quad. Northstar's cross-country center has 35 km

(22 miles) of groomed trails, including double-set tracks and skating lanes. The school has programs for skiers ages three and up, and day care is available for tots two and older. The mountain gets packed on busy weekends, but when there's room on the slopes, Northstar is loads of fun. ⊠ *5001 Northstar Dr.* ☎ *530/562–1010 information, 800/466–6784 lodging, 530/562–1330 snow phone* ⊕ *www.northstarcalifornia. com* ☞ *97 trails on 3,170 acres, rated 13% beginner, 60% intermediate, 27% advanced. Longest run 1.4 miles, base 6,330 feet, summit 8,610 feet. Lifts: 20, including 2 gondolas and 7 high-speed quads.*

Royal Gorge. If you love to cross-country, don't miss Royal Gorge, which serves up 200 km (124 miles) of track for all abilities, 75 trails on a whopping 6,000 acres, a ski school, and eight warming huts. Two trailside cafés and a lodge round out the facilities. Because the complex sits right on the Sierra Crest, the views are drop-dead gorgeous. ⊠ *9411 Pahatsi Dr., off I–80, Soda Springs/Norden exit, Soda Springs* ☎ *530/426–3871, 800/500–3871* ⊕ *www.royalgorge.com.*

14

Soda Springs. Along with 200 acres and 500 vertical feet, this ski park also has lift-served snow-tubing. ⊠ *10244 Soda Springs Rd., I–80 Soda Springs exit, Soda Springs* ☎ *530/426–3901* ⊕ *www.ski sodasprings.com.*

Fodor's Choice
★

Sugar Bowl Ski Resort. Opened in 1939 by Walt Disney, this is the oldest—and one of the best—resorts at Tahoe. Atop Donner Summit, it receives an incredible 500 inches of snowfall annually. Four peaks are connected by 1,650 acres of skiable terrain, with everything from gentle groomed corduroy to wide-open bowls to vertical rocky chutes and outstanding tree skiing. Snowboarders can hit two terrain parks with numerous boxes, rails, and jumps. Because it's more compact than some of the area's megaresorts, there's a gentility here that distinguishes Sugar Bowl from its competitors, making this a great place for families and a low-pressure, low-key place to learn to ski. It's not huge, but there's some very challenging terrain (experts: head to the Palisades). There's limited lodging at the base area. ⊠ *629 Sugar Bowl Rd., off Donner Pass Rd., 3 miles east of I–80 Soda Springs/Norden exit, 10 miles west of Truckee, Norden* ☎ *530/426–9000 information and lodging reservations, 530/426–1111 snow phone, 866/843–2695 lodging referral* ⊕ *www.sugarbowl.com* ☞ *102 trails on 1,650 acres, rated 17% beginner, 45% intermediate, 38% advanced. Longest run 3 miles, base 6,883 feet, summit 8,383 feet. Lifts: 13, including 5 high-speed quads.*

Tahoe Dave's. You can save money by renting skis and boards at this shop, which has the area's best selection and also repairs and tunes equipment. ⊠ *10200 Donner Pass Rd., near Spring St.* ☎ *530/582–0900* ⊕ *www.tahoedaves.com.*

Tahoe Donner. Just north of Truckee, this park covers 120 acres and 600 vertical feet; the cross-country center includes 51 trails on 100 km (62 miles) of groomed tracks on 4,800 acres, with night skiing on Wednesday in January and February. ⊠ *11603 Snowpeak Way* ☎ *530/587–9444* ⊕ *www.tahoedonner.com.*

CARNELIAN BAY TO KINGS BEACH

5–10 miles northeast of Tahoe City.

The small lakeside commercial districts of Carnelian Bay and Tahoe Vista service the thousand or so locals who live in the area year-round and the thousands more who have summer residences or launch their boats here. Kings Beach, the last town heading east on Highway 28 before the Nevada border, is to Crystal Bay what South Lake Tahoe is to Stateline: a bustling town full of basic motels and rental condos, restaurants, and shops, used by the hordes of hopefuls who pass through on their way to the casinos.

GETTING HERE AND AROUND

To reach Kings Beach and Carnelian Bay from the California side, take Highway 89 north to Highway 28 north and then east. From the Nevada side, follow Highway 28 north and then west. TART provides public transportation in this area.

BEACHES

FAMILY **Kings Beach State Recreation Area.** The north shore's 28-acre Kings Beach State Recreation Area, one of the largest such areas on the lake, is open year-round. The 700-foot-long sandy beach gets crowded in summer with people swimming, sunbathing, Jet Skiing, riding in paddleboats, spiking volleyballs, and tossing Frisbees. If you're going to spend the day, come early enough to snag a table in the picnic area; there's also a good playground. **Amenities**: food and drink; parking (fee); toilets; water sports. **Best For**: sunrise; sunset; swimming; windsurfing. ✉ *8318 N. Lake Blvd., Hwy. 28, Kings Beach* ☎ *530/546–7248* 🌐 *www.parks.ca.gov* 🎟 *$10 parking fee.*

WHERE TO EAT AND STAY

$$$ ECLECTIC 🍴 **Gar Woods Grill and Pier.** The view's the thing at this lakeside stalwart, where you can watch the sun shimmer on the water through the dining room's plate-glass windows or from the heated outdoor deck. Grilled steak and fish are menu mainstays, but be sure to try specialties like crab chiles rellenos and chipotle chicken salad. At all hours in season, the bar gets packed with boaters who pull up to the restaurant's private pier. [$] *Average main: $29* ✉ *5000 N. Lake Blvd., Hwy. 28, Carnelian Bay* ☎ *530/546–3366* 🌐 *www.garwoods.com.*

$$$ AMERICAN 🍴 **Spindleshanks American Bistro and Wine Bar.** Relocated to the Old Brockway Golf Course, this local favorite serves mostly classic American cooking—ribs, steaks, and seafood updated with adventurous sauces—as well as house-made ravioli. Savor a drink from the full bar or choose a wine from the extensive list while you enjoy views of Lake Tahoe or the historic green where Bing Crosby hosted his first golf tournament in 1934. When the weather's balmy, dine on the patio. [$] *Average main: $23* ✉ *400 Brassie Ave., at Hwy. 267 & N. Lake Tahoe Blvd., Kings Beach* ☎ *530/546–2191* 🌐 *www.spindleshankstahoe.com.*

$ HOTEL FAMILY 🏨 **Ferrari's Crown Resort.** Great for families with kids, the family-owned and -operated Ferrari's has straightforward motel rooms in a resort setting. **Pros:** family-friendly; lakeside location. **Cons:** older facility. [$] *Rooms from: $105* ✉ *8200 N. Lake Blvd., Kings Beach* ☎ *530/546–3388, 800/645–2260* 🌐 *www.tahoecrown.com* 🛏 *72 rooms* 🍽 *Breakfast.*

THE NEVADA SIDE

The difference on the Nevada side of the lake is, of course, gambling, with all its repercussions.

CRYSTAL BAY

1 mile east of Kings Beach, 30 miles north of South Lake Tahoe.

Right at the Nevada border, Crystal Bay features a cluster of casinos, a few spunky ones with personality and some smaller ones that locals tend to favor. There's not much lodging; the largest property, the Cal-Neva Resort, Spa and Casino that Frank Sinatra owned, is, as of this writing, undergoing a multimillion-dollar remodel. Look for it to reopen with great hoopla in 2016. For now, one of Tahoe's best restaurants, Soule Domain, is reason enough for a stop in Crystal Bay.

14

GETTING HERE AND AROUND

From the California side, reach Crystal Bay via Highway 89 or 267 to Highway 28. TART serves the communities along the north and west shores.

WHERE TO EAT

$$$ ECLECTIC 🍴 **Soule Domain.** Rough-hewn wood beams, a vaulted wood ceiling, and, in winter, a roaring fireplace lend high romance to this cozy 1927 pine-log cabin next to the Tahoe Biltmore. Chef-owner Charlie Soule's specialties include curried almond chicken, fresh sea scallops poached in champagne with a kiwi and mango cream sauce, and a vegan sauté with ginger, jalapeños, and tofu. If you're looking for a place with a sterling menu where you can hold hands by candlelight, this is it. [$] *Average main: $27* ✉ *9983 Cove St., ½ block up Stateline Rd. off Hwy. 28, Kings Beach* ☎ *530/546–7529* 🌐 *www.souledomain.com* 🕒 *No lunch.*

NIGHTLIFE

CASINOS

Crystal Bay Club. Known for its classic steak and lobster dinner, the restaurant in this casino has a distinctive open-truss ceiling. With entertainment in two venues, and accommodations in its historic 10-room Border House ($$$) next to the club, this refurbished casino tempts tourists to linger on Tahoe's north shore. ✉ *14 Hwy. 28, near Stateline Rd.* ☎ *775/833–6333* 🌐 *www.crystalbaycasino.com.*

Tahoe Biltmore. A daily happy hour keeps this old favorite hopping, along with dinner specials in Bilty's Brew & Q restaurant, and inexpensive breakfasts in their café. Expect simple accommodations ($-$$) in the casino's hotel. The circular Tahoe Biltmore sign is a 1962 "Googie-style" architectural riff off the Seattle Space Needle, which debuted the same year. ✉ *5 Hwy. 28, at Stateline Rd.* ☎ *800/245–8667, 775/831–0660* 🌐 *www.tahoebiltmore.com.*

INCLINE VILLAGE

3 miles east of Crystal Bay.

Incline Village dates to the early 1960s, when an Oklahoma developer bought 10,000 acres north of Lake Tahoe. His idea was to sketch out a plan for a town without a central commercial district, hoping to prevent congestion and to preserve the area's natural beauty. One-acre lakeshore lots originally fetched $12,000 to $15,000; today you couldn't buy the same land for less than several million.

GETTING HERE AND AROUND

From the California side, reach Incline Village via Highway 89 or 267 to Highway 28. From South Lake Tahoe, take U.S. 50 north to Highway 28 north. TART serves the communities along Lake Tahoe's north and west shores from Incline Village to Tahoma.

ESSENTIALS

Visitor Information Lake Tahoe Incline Village/Crystal Bay Visitors Bureau ⊠ *969 Tahoe Blvd.* ☎ *775/832–1606, 800/468–2463* ⊕ *www.gotahoenorth.com.*

EXPLORING

Lakeshore Drive. Take this beautiful drive to see some of the most expensive real estate in Nevada. The route is discreetly marked: to find it, start at the Hyatt hotel and drive westward along the lake.

Fodor's Choice ★

Thunderbird Lodge. George Whittell, a San Francisco socialite who once owned 40,000 acres of property along the lake, built this lodge in 1936. You can tour the mansion and the grounds by reservation only, and though it's pricey to do so, you'll be rewarded with a rare glimpse of a time when only the very wealthy had homes at Tahoe. The lodge is accessible via a bus from the Incline Village Visitors Bureau, a catamaran from the Hyatt in Incline Village ($120), or a 1950 wooden cruiser from Tahoe Keys Marina in South Lake Tahoe, which includes continental breakfast and lunch ($139). ⊠ *5000 Nevada 28* ☎ *775/832–8752 lodge info, 800/468–2463 tour reservations, 775/588–1881, 888/867–6394 Tahoe Keys boat, 775/831–4386 Hyatt Incline catamaran* ⊕ *www.thunderbirdtahoe.org/tours* ⊡ *$39 bus tour, $120 and $139 for boat tours* ☉ *May–Oct., Tues.–Sat., call for tour times.*

BEACHES

Lake Tahoe–Nevada State Park and Sand Harbor Beach. Protecting much of the lake's eastern shore from development, this park comprises several sections that stretch from Incline Village to Zephyr Cove. Beaches and trails provide access to a wilder side of the lake, whether you're into cross-country skiing, hiking, or just relaxing at a picnic. With a gently sloping beach for lounging, crystal-clear water for swimming and snorkeling, and a picnic area shaded by cedars and pines, **Sand Harbor Beach** is so popular that it sometimes fills to capacity by 11 am on summer weekends. Boaters have two launch ramps. A handicap-accessible nature trail has interpretive signs and beautiful lake views. Pets are not allowed. **Amenities:** food and drink; parking (fee)); toilets; water sports. **Best For:** snorkeling; sunset; swimming; walking. ⊠ *Sand Harbor Beach, Hwy. 28, 3 miles south of Incline Village* ☎ *775/831–0494*

🎟 Parking $12 mid-Apr.–mid-Oct., $7 rest of the year 🌐 parks.nv.gov/parks/sand-harbor.

WHERE TO EAT AND STAY

$$$ ECLECTIC 🍴 **Fredrick's Fusion Bistro.** Copper-top tables lend a chic look to the dining room at this intimate bistro. The menu consists of a mélange of European and Asian dishes, most of them prepared with organic produce and free-range meats. Try the braised short ribs, roasted duck with caramel-pecan glaze, or the deliciously fresh sushi rolls. **■ TIP→ On cold nights ask for a table by the fire.** [$] *Average main: $24 ✉ 907 Tahoe Blvd., at Village Blvd. ☎ 775/832–3007 🌐 fredricksbistro.com ⏲ Closed Sun. and Mon. No lunch.*

$$$ FRENCH Fodor's Choice ★ 🍴 **Le Bistro.** Incline Village's hidden gem serves expertly prepared French-country cuisine in a relaxed, romantic dining room. The chef-owner makes everything himself, using organically grown ingredients. Expect such dishes as pâté de campagne, escargots, herb-crusted roast lamb, and fresh fish. Try the five-course prix-fixe menu ($55), which can be paired with award-winning wines. Service is gracious and attentive. **■ TIP→ This restaurant is hard to find, so ask for directions when you book.** [$] *Average main: $30 ✉ 120 Country Club Dr., #29, off Lakeshore Blvd. ☎ 775/831–0800 🌐 www.lebistrorestaurant.net ⏲ Closed Sun. and Mon. No lunch.*

$ SOUTHERN 🍴 **T's Mesquite Rotisserie.** There's nothing fancy about T's (it looks like a small snack bar), but the mesquite-grilled chicken and tri-tip steaks are delicious and inexpensive—a rare combination in pricey Incline Village. It's mainly a take-out spot; seating is limited. [$] *Average main: $9 ✉ 901 Tahoe Blvd., at Village Blvd. ☎ 775/831–2832 💳 No credit cards.*

$$$$ RESORT 🏨 **Hyatt Regency Lake Tahoe.** A full-service destination resort on 26 acres of prime lakefront property, the Hyatt has a range of luxurious accommodations, from tower-hotel rooms to lakeside cottages. **Pros:** incredible views; low-key casino. **Cons:** pricey (especially for families). [$] *Rooms from: $379 ✉ 111 Country Club Dr. ☎ 775/832–1234, 888/899–5019 🌐 www.laketahoe.hyatt.com 🛏 386 rooms, 36 suites 🍽 No meals.*

SPORTS AND THE OUTDOORS

GOLF

Incline Championship. Robert Trent Jones Sr. designed this challenging course of tightly cut, tree-lined fairways laced with water hazards that demand accuracy as well as distance skills. Green fee includes a cart, except the 4:30 pm Super Twilight rate of $3 per hole (cart $25). *✉ 955 Fairway Blvd., at Northwood Blvd., north off Hwy. 28 ☎ 866/925–4653 reservations, 775/832–1146 pro shop 🌐 www.yourtahoeplace.com/golf-incline 🎟 $179 ⛳ 18 holes, 7106 yards, par 72.*

Incline Mountain. Robert Trent Jones Jr. designed this executive (shorter) course that requires accuracy more than distance skills. The green fee includes a cart. *✉ 690 Wilson Way, at Golfer's Pass, south off Hwy. 431 ☎ 866/925–4653 reservations, 775/832–1150 pro shop 🌐 www.yourtahoeplace.com/golf-incline 🎟 $70 ⛳ 18 holes, 3527 yards, par 58.*

Get to Sand Harbor Beach in Lake Tahoe–Nevada State Park early; the park sometimes fills to capacity before lunchtime in summer.

MOUNTAIN BIKING

Flume Trail Bikes. You can rent bikes and get helpful tips from this company, which also operates a bike shuttle to popular trailheads. Ask about the secluded backcountry rental cabins for overnight rides. ⊠ *1115 Tunnel Creek Rd., at Ponderosa Ranch Rd., off Hwy. 28* ☎ *775/298–2501* ⊕ *www.flumetrailtahoe.com.*

SKIING

Diamond Peak. A fun family mood prevails at Diamond Peak, which has affordable rates and many special programs. Snowmaking covers 75% of the mountain, and runs are groomed nightly. The ride up the 1-mile Crystal Express rewards you with fantastic views. Diamond Peak is less crowded than Tahoe's larger ski parks and provides free shuttles to nearby lodgings. A great place for beginners and intermediates, it's appropriately priced for families. Though there are some steep-aspect black-diamond runs, advanced skiers may find the acreage too limited. For snowboarders there's a small terrain park. ⊠ *1210 Ski Way, off Country Club Dr.* ☎ *775/832–1177* ⊕ *www.diamondpeak.com* ↳ *30 trails on 655 acres, rated 18% beginner, 46% intermediate, 36% advanced. Longest run 2½ miles, base 6,700 feet, summit 8,540 feet. Lifts: 7, including 1 high-speed quad and a surface lift.*

Mt. Rose Ski Tahoe. At this park, ski some of Tahoe's highest slopes and take in bird's-eye views of Reno, the lake, and Carson Valley. Though more compact than the bigger Tahoe resorts, Mt. Rose has the area's highest base elevation and consequently the driest snow. The mountain has a wide variety of terrain. The most challenging is the Chutes, 200 acres of gulp-and-go advanced-to-expert vertical. Intermediates can choose steep groomers or mellow, wide-open boulevards. Beginners have their own corner of the mountain, with gentle, wide slopes. Boarders and tricksters have three terrain parks to choose from, on opposite sides of the mountain, allowing them to follow the sun as it tracks across the resort. The mountain gets hit hard in storms; check conditions before heading up during inclement weather or on a windy day. ✉ *22222 Mt. Rose Hwy., Hwy. 431, 11 miles north of Incline Village, Reno* ☎ *775/849–0704, 800/754–7673* 🌐 *www.skirose.com* ☞ *61 trails on 1,200 acres, rated 20% beginner, 30% intermediate, 40% advanced, 10% expert. Longest run 2½ miles, base 8,260 feet, summit 9,700 feet. Lifts: 8, including 2 high-speed 6-passenger lifts.*

TAHOE TESSIE

Local lore claims this huge sea monster slithers around Lake Tahoe. Skeptics laugh, but true believers keep their eyes peeled for surprise sightings.

Tahoe Meadows Snowplay Area. This is the most popular area near the north shore for noncommercial cross-country skiing, sledding, tubing, snowshoeing, and snowmobiling. ✉ *Off Hwy. 431, between Incline Village and Mt. Rose.*

ZEPHYR COVE

22 miles south of Incline Village.

The largest settlement between Incline Village and the Stateline area is Zephyr Cove, a tiny resort. It has a beach, marina, campground, picnic area, coffee shop in a log lodge, rustic cabins, and nearby riding stables.

GETTING HERE AND AROUND

From the north shore communities, reach Zephyr Cove by following Highway 28 along the eastern side of the lake. From South Lake Tahoe, take U.S. 50 north and then west. Public transportation isn't available in Zephyr Cove.

EXPLORING

Cave Rock. Near Zephyr Cove, this 75 feet of solid stone at the southern end of Lake Tahoe–Nevada State Park is the throat of an extinct volcano. Tahoe Tessie, the lake's version of the Loch Ness monster, is reputed to live in a cavern below the impressive outcropping. Cave Rock towers over a parking lot, a lakefront picnic ground, and a boat launch. The views are some of the best on the lake; this is a good spot to stop and take a picture. However, this area is a sacred burial site for the Washoe Indians, and climbing up to the cave, or through it, is prohibited. ✉ *U.S. 50, 4 miles north of Zephyr Cove* ☎ *775/831–0494* 🌐 *www.parks.nv.gov/parks/cave-lake-state-park/cave%20rock* 🎟 *$10 day use fee.*

WHERE TO STAY

$$$ RENTAL FAMILY 🏨 **Zephyr Cove Resort.** Beneath towering pines at the lake's edge stand 28 cozy, modern vacation cabins with peaked knotty-pine ceilings. **Pros:** family-friendly. **Cons:** lodge rooms are basic; can be noisy. [$] *Rooms from: $200* ✉ *760 U.S. 50, 4 miles north of Stateline* ☎ *775/589–4906,*

800/238–2463 🌐 *www.zephyrcove.com* 🛏 *28 cabins; 4 lodge rooms* 🍴 *No meals.*

STATELINE

5 miles south of Zephyr Cove.

Stateline is the archetypal Nevada border town. Its four high-rise casinos are as vertical and contained as the commercial district of South Lake Tahoe, on the California side, is horizontal and sprawling. And Stateline is as relentlessly indoors-oriented as the rest of the lake is focused on the outdoors. This strip is where you'll find the most concentrated action at Lake Tahoe: restaurants (including typical casino buffets), showrooms with famous headliners and razzle-dazzle revues, tower-hotel rooms and suites, and 24-hour casinos.

GETTING HERE AND AROUND

From South Lake Tahoe take U.S. 50 north across the Nevada border to reach Stateline and its casinos. If coming from Reno's airport, take U.S. 395/Interstate 580 south to Carson City, and then head west on U.S. 50 to the lake and head south. Or take the South Tahoe Express bus. BlueGO operates daily bus service in the south shore area year-round, plus a ski shuttle from the large hotels to Heavenly in the winter.

BEACHES

Nevada Beach. Although less than a mile long, this is the widest beach on the lake and especially good for swimming (many Tahoe beaches are rocky). You can boat and fish here, and there are picnic tables, barbecue grills, and a campground beneath the pines. This is the best place to watch the July 4th or Labor Day fireworks, but most of the summer the subdued atmosphere attracts families and those seeking a less-touristy spot. **Amenities:** parking (fee), water sports, toilets. **Best For:** sunrise, swimming, walking. ✉ *Elk Point Rd., off U.S. 50, 3 miles north of Stateline* ☎ *530/543–2600, 877/444–6777 camping reservations* 🕒 *Open daily late May–Oct.* 🎫 *Parking $8* ☞ *No pets.*

WHERE TO EAT AND STAY

$$$ FRENCH

🍴 **Mirabelle at Lake Tahoe.** Don't be put off by this restaurant's nondescript exterior. Inside there's an airy dining room with creamy yellow walls and white tablecloths. Enticing scents drift from the kitchen, where all menu offerings are housemade. Specialties include sautéed veal sweetbreads, garlicky escargots, and rack of lamb with sauce ravigote. There's always a fresh fish entrée, plus a $45 prix-fixe three-course menu. [$] *Average main: $28* ✉ *290 Kingsbury Grade, off U.S. 50* ☎ *775/586–1007* 🌐 *www.mirabelleatlaketahoe.com* 🕒 *Closed Mon. No lunch Oct.–May.*

$ HOTEL

🏨 **Harrah's Tahoe Hotel/Casino.** The hotel's major selling point is that every room has two full bathrooms, a boon if you're traveling with family. **Pros:** central location; great midweek values. **Cons:** can get noisy. [$] *Rooms from: $109* ✉ *15 U.S. 50, at Stateline Ave.* ☎ *775/588–6611, 800/427–7247* 🌐 *www.caesars.com/harrahs-tahoe* 🛏 *470 rooms, 62 suites* 🍴 *No meals.*

$ HOTEL 🏨 **Harveys Resort Hotel/Casino.** This resort began as a cabin in 1944, and now it's Tahoe's largest casino-hotel; premium rooms have custom furnishings, oversize marble baths, minibars, and good lake views. **Pros:** hip entertainment; just a few blocks north of the Heavenly Gondola. **Cons:** can get loud at night. [$] *Rooms from: $89* ✉ *18 U.S. 50, at Stateline Ave.* ☎ *775/588–2411, 800/648–3361* 🌐 *www.caesars.com/harveys-tahoe* 🛏 *742 rooms, 36 suites* 🍴 *No meals.*

NIGHTLIFE

Each of the major casinos has its own showroom, featuring everything from comedy to magic acts to sexy floor shows to Broadway musicals.

DANCE CLUBS

Peek. You can dance the night away with top-notch DJs, and often hear live performances, at this club that emulates a Vegas vibe. ✉ *Harrah's Lake Tahoe, 15 U.S. 50* ☎ *775/588–6611 information, 775/586–6705 Peek reservations* 🌐 *www.caesars.com/peek.*

LIVE MUSIC

Harveys Outdoor Summer Concert Series. Harveys Lake Tahoe books outdoor concerts on weekends in summer with headliners such as the Dave Matthews Band and country music star Kenny Chesney. ✉ *18 U.S. 50* ☎ *775/588–2411* 🌐 *www.caesars.com/harveys-tahoe/shows.html.*

South Shore Room. Classic acts like the Jefferson Starship, singer-songwriter Leon Russell, and legendary reggae band The Wailers play Harrah's big showroom, along with tribute shows for groups such as the Rolling Stones and Bruce Springsteen and the E Street Band. ✉ *Harrah's Lake Tahoe, 15 U.S. 50* ☎ *775/586–6244 tickets, 775/588–6611* 🌐 *www.caesars.com/harrahs-tahoe/shows.html.*

SPORTS AND THE OUTDOORS

GOLF

Edgewood Tahoe. Golfers of all skill levels enjoy this scenic lakeside course that has four sets of tees, offering a variety of course lengths. The green fee includes an optional cart. ✉ *100 Lake Pkwy., at U.S. 50* ☎ *775/588–3566, 866/761–4653* 🌐 *www.edgewood-tahoe.com* 🎫 *$220 for weekdays, $240 for weekends* ⛳ *18 holes, 7543 yards, par 72.*

RENO

32 miles east of Truckee, 38 miles northeast of Incline Village.

Established in 1859 as a trading station at a bridge over the Truckee River, Reno grew along with the silver mines of nearby Virginia City and the transcontinental railroad that chugged through town. Train officials named it in 1868, but gambling—legalized in 1931—put Reno on the map. This is still a gambling town, with most of the casinos crowded into five square blocks downtown, but a thriving university scene and outdoor activities also attract tourists.

Parts of downtown are sketchy, but things are changing. Several defunct casinos are being converted into condominiums, and the riverfront is being reconceived. Reno now touts family-friendly activities like kayaking on the Truckee, museums, and a downtown climbing wall. New shops and excellent restaurants have sprung up outside the hotels. With over 300 days of sunshine annually, temperatures year-round in this high-mountain-desert climate are warmer than at Tahoe, though rarely as hot as in Sacramento and the Central Valley, making strolling around town a pleasure.

> ### RENO'S RIVERWALK
>
> Stroll along the Truckee River and check out the art galleries, cinema, specialty shops, theater, and restaurants that line this lively refurbished section of town near Reno's casino district.

GETTING HERE AND AROUND

Interstate 80 bisects Reno east–west, U.S. 395 north–south (south of town the road is signed U.S. 395/Interstate 580). Greyhound and Amtrak stop here, and several airlines fly into Reno-Tahoe International Airport. RTC Ride provides bus service in the greater Reno area.

ESSENTIALS

Bus Contact RTC Ride ✉ *Transit Center, E. 4th and Lake Sts.* ☎ *775/348–7433* ⊕ *www.rtcwashoe.com.*

Visitor Information Reno-Sparks Convention and Visitors Authority ✉ *4001 S. Virginia St.* ☎ *775/827–7650, 800/367–7366* ⊕ *www.visitrenotahoe. com.*

EXPLORING

TOP ATTRACTIONS

FAMILY   **National Automobile Museum.** Antique and classic automobiles, including an Elvis Presley Cadillac, a Mercury coupe driven by James Dean in the movie *Rebel Without a Cause,* and the experimental and still futuristic-looking 1938 Phantom Corsair, are all on display at this museum. ✉ *10 S. Lake St., at Mill St.* ☎ *775/333–9300* ⊕ *www.automuseum.org* 🎟 *$10* ☉ *Mon.–Sat. 9:30–5:30, Sun. 10–4.*

Nevada Museum of Art. A dramatic four-level structure designed by Will Bruder houses this splendid museum's collection, which focuses on themes such as the Sierra Nevada/Great Basin and altered-landscape photography. The building's exterior torqued walls are sided with a black zinc-based material that has been fabricated to resemble textures found in the Black Rock Desert. Inside the building, a staircase installed within the central atrium is lit by skylights and suspended by a single beam attached to the atrium ceiling; visitors can climb 55 feet to the fourth floor rooftop landing. ✉ *160 W. Liberty St., and Hill St.* ☎ *775/329–3333* ⊕ *www.nevadaart.org* 🎟 *$10* ☉ *Wed. and Fri.–Sun. 10–6, Thurs. 10–8.*

Fodor's Choice ★   **Riverwalk District.** The makeover of Reno's waterfront has transformed this formerly dilapidated area into the toast of the town. The Riverwalk itself is a half-mile promenade on the north side of the Truckee River, which flows around lovely Wingfield Park, where outdoor festivals and other events take place. On the third Saturday of each month, local merchants host a **Wine Walk** between 2 and 5. For $20 you receive a wine glass and can sample fine wines at participating shops, bars, restaurants, and galleries. In July, look for stellar outdoor art, opera, dance, and kids' performances as part of the monthlong **Artown festival** (🌐 *renoisartown.com*), presented mostly in Wingfield Park. Also at Wingfield is the **Truckee River Whitewater Park.** With activities for all skill levels, it's become a major attraction for water-sports enthusiasts. ✉ *Riverwalk, north side of Truckee River between Lake and Ralston Sts.* 🌐 *renoriver.org.*

WORTH NOTING

FAMILY **Fleischmann Planetarium.** Digital star shows provide the glittering lights inside this facility. The shows aim to make learning about astronomy entertaining for kids and adults. ✉ *University of Nevada, 1664 N. Virginia St., near E. 15th St.* ☎ *775/784–4811 recorded information, 775/784–4812 office* 🌐 *www.planetarium.unr.nevada.edu* 🎫 *Exhibits free, films and star shows $7* 🕒 *Mon.–Thurs. noon–7, Fri. noon–9, Sat. 10–9, Sun. 10–7.*

WHERE TO EAT

$ THAI 🍴 **Bangkok Cuisine.** To eat well but not break the bank, come to this busy Thai restaurant and sample the delicious soups, salads, stir-fries, and curries. [$] *Average main: $12* ✉ *55 Mt. Rose St., at S. Virginia St.* ☎ *775/322–0299* 🌐 *thaifoodreno.com* 🕒 *No lunch Sun.*

$$$ FRENCH Fodor's Choice ★ 🍴 **Beaujolais Bistro.** Across from the Truckee River, this Reno favorite serves earthy, country-style French food with zero pretension. Expect classics like escargots, steak frites with red wine sauce, cassoulet, and crisp sweetbreads with Madeira, along with fish and vegetarian selections. Wood floors, large windows, and brick walls with a fireplace create a welcoming and intimate atmosphere. Diners who want a more casual experience can dine at the long bar. Less expensive small plates as well as an inventive cocktail menu are also offered. [$] *Average main: $29* ✉ *753 Riverside Dr., near Winter St.* ☎ *775/323–2227* 🌐 *www.beaujolaisbistro.com* 🕒 *No lunch. Closed Mon.*

$$ CAFÉ 🍴 **Chocolate Bar.** Part café, part cocktail bar, this hip little spot close to the river makes truffles, chocolate fondue, fabulous fruity cocktails, hot chocolate, gourmet small plates, and entrées, all served at a long wooden bar or at several tables and leather banquettes. Chocolate Bar is open late each night for those craving dessert, a chocolate cocktail, or a simple, unadorned cognac. [$] *Average main: $16* ✉ *95 N. Sierra St., at W. 1st St.* ☎ *775/337–1122* 🌐 *thechocbar.com.*

$$$ AMERICAN Fodor's Choice ★ 🍴 **4th St. Bistro.** For deliciously simple, smart cooking, head to this charming little bistro on the edge of town. The chef-owner uses organic produce and meats in her soulful preparation of dishes like grilled cobia wrapped in Serrano ham or Moroccan spiced organic chicken breast with braised rainbow chard and couscous. Ochre-color sponge-painted walls, tablecloths from Provence, and a roaring fireplace in winter warm the dining room. In summer months there's delightful deck dining. [$] *Average main: $30* ✉ *3065 W. 4th St.* ☎ *775/323–3200* 🌐 *www.4thstbistro.com* 🕒 *Closed Sun. and Mon. No lunch.*

14

WHERE TO STAY

$ HOTEL 🏨 **Eldorado Hotel Casino.** In the middle of glittering downtown, this resort's huge tower has rooms overlooking either the mountains or the lights of the city. **Pros:** fun; good food; amusingly kitschy decor. **Cons:** noisy. [$] *Rooms from: $60* ✉ *345 N. Virginia St.* ☎ *775/786–5700, 800/879–8879* 🌐 *www.eldoradoreno.com* 🛏 *679 rooms, 137 suites* 🍴 *No meals.*

$ HOTEL 🏨 **Harrah's Reno.** Of the big-name casino hotels in downtown Reno, double-towered Harrah's is still the best, with no surprises. **Pros:** sets the standard for downtown Reno; great online midweek rates. **Cons:** huge property. [$] *Rooms from: $70* ✉ *219 N. Center St., at E. 2nd St.* ☎ *775/786–3232, 800/427–7247* 🌐 *www.harrahsreno.com* 🛏 *876 rooms, 52 suites* 🍴 *No meals.*

$ HOTEL 🏨 **Peppermill Reno.** A few miles removed from downtown's flashy main drag, this property sets a new standard for luxury in Reno; its 600 baroque suites in the Tuscan Tower have plush king-size beds, marble bathrooms, and European soaking tubs. **Pros:** luxurious rooms; casino decor; good coffee shop. **Cons:** deluge of neon may be off-putting to some. [$] *Rooms from: $90* ✉ *2707 S. Virginia St., at Peppermill La.* ☎ *775/826–2121, 866/821–9996* 🌐 *www.peppermillreno.com* 🛏 *915 rooms, 720 suites* 🍴 *No meals.*

NIGHTLIFE

CASINOS

FAMILY **Circus Circus.** Families with kids head to this casino, where a midway above the floor has clowns, games, fun-house mirrors, and circus acts. ✉ *500 N. Sierra St., at W. 5th St.* ☎ *775/329–0711, 800/648–5010* 🌐 *www.circusreno.com.*

Eldorado. Action packed, with lots of slots and popular bar-top video poker, this casino also has good coffee-shop and food-court fare. Don't miss the Fountain of Fortune with its massive Florentine-inspired sculptures. ✉ *345 N. Virginia St., at W. 4th St.* ☎ *775/786–5700, 800/879–8879* 🌐 *www.eldoradoreno.com.*

Harrah's Reno. Occupying two city blocks, this landmark property has a sprawling casino and an outdoor promenade. ✉ *219 N. Center St., at E. 2nd St.* ☎ *775/786–3232, 800/427–7247* 🌐 *www.harrahsreno.com.*

Peppermill. A few miles from downtown, this casino is known for its excellent restaurants and neon-bright gambling areas. The Fireside cocktail lounge is a blast. ✉ *2707 S. Virginia St., at Peppermill La.* ☎ *775/826–2121, 866/821–9996* 🌐 *www.peppermillreno.com.*

Silver Legacy. A 120-foot-tall mining rig and video poker games draw gamblers to this razzle-dazzle casino. ✉ *407 N. Virginia St., at W. 4th St.* ☎ *775/329–4777, 800/687–8733* 🌐 *www.silverlegacyreno.com.*

THE FAR NORTH

With Lake Shasta, Mt. Shasta, and
Lassen Volcanic National Park

WELCOME TO THE FAR NORTH

TOP REASONS TO GO

★ **Mother Nature's wonders:** California's Far North has more rivers, streams, lakes, forests, and mountains than you'll ever have time to explore.

★ **Rock and roll:** With two volcanoes to entice you—Lassen and Shasta— you can learn firsthand what happens when a mountain blows its top.

★ **Fantastic fishing:** Whether you like casting from a riverbank or letting your line bob beside a boat, you'll find fabulous fishing in all the northern counties.

★ **Cool hops:** On a hot day there's nothing quite as inviting as a visit to Chico's world-famous Sierra Nevada Brewery. Take the tour, and then savor a chilled glass on tap at the adjacent brewpub.

★ **Shasta:** Wonderful in all its forms: lake, dam, river, mountain, forest, and town.

1 From Chico to Mt Shasta. The Far North is bisected, south to north, by Interstate 5, which passes through several historic towns and state parks, as well as miles of mountainous terrain. Halfway to the Oregon border is Lake Shasta, a favorite recreation destination, and farther north stands the spectacular snowy peak of Mt. Shasta.

2 The Backcountry. East of Interstate 5, the Far North's main corridor, dozens of scenic two-lane roads crisscross the wilderness, leading to dramatic mountain peaks and fascinating natural wonders. Small towns settled in the second half of the 19th century seem frozen in time, except that they are well equipped with tourist amenities.

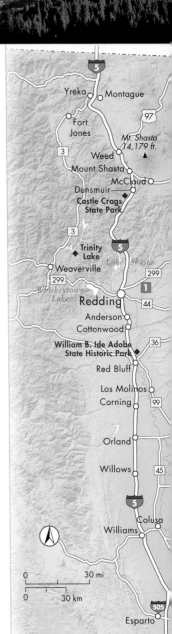

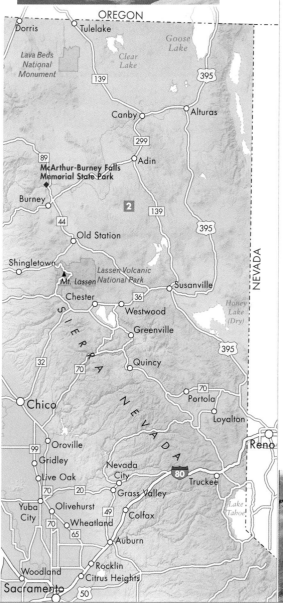

GETTING ORIENTED

The Far North is a vast area that stretches from the upper reaches of the Sacramento Valley north to the Oregon border and east to Nevada. The region includes all or part of eight counties with sparsely populated rural farming and mountain communities, as well as thriving small cities in the valley. Much of the landscape was shaped by two volcanoes—Mt. Shasta and Mt. Lassen—that draw amateur geologists, weekend hikers, and avid mountain climbers to their rugged terrain. An intricate network of high-mountain watersheds feeds lakes large and small, plus streams and rivers that course through several forests.

15

Updated by Christine Vovakes

The Far North's soaring mountain peaks, trail-filled national forests, alpine lakes, and wild rivers teeming with trout make it the perfect destination for outdoor enthusiasts, including hikers, cyclists, kayakers, and bird-watchers. You won't find many hot nightspots or cultural enclaves in this region, but you will find crowd-free national and state parks, crystal-clear mountain streams, superlative hiking and fishing, plus small towns worth exploring. And the spectacular land-scapes of Lassen Volcanic National Park and Mt. Shasta are sure to impress.

The wondrous landscape of California's northeastern corner, relatively unmarred by development, congestion, and traffic, is the product of volcanic activity. At the southern end of the Cascade Range, Lassen Volcanic National Park is the best place to witness the Far North's fascinating geology. Beyond the sulfur vents and bubbling mud pots, the park owes much of its beauty to 10,457-foot Mt. Lassen and 50 wilderness lakes.

The most enduring image of the region, though, is Mt. Shasta, whose 14,179-foot snowcapped peak beckons outdoor adventurers of all kinds. There are many versions of Shasta to enjoy—the mountain, the lake, the river, the town, the dam, and the forest—all named after the Native Americans known as the Shatasla, or Sastise, who once inhab-ited the region.

PLANNING

WHEN TO GO
Heat scorches the valley in summer. Temperatures above 110°F are common, but the mountains provide cool respite. Fall throughout the Far North is beautiful, rivaled only by spring, when wildflowers and

almond orchards bloom and mountain creeks fed by the snowmelt splash through the forests. Winter is usually temperate in the valley, but cold and snowy in high country. A few favorite tourist attractions are closed in winter.

GETTING HERE AND AROUND

AIR TRAVEL

For the cheapest fares, fly into Sacramento and then rent a car—you'll need one anyway—and drive north. Redding, which is served by United Express, has a small airport. There's no shuttle service, but you can take a taxi for about $32 to downtown Redding.

Air Contacts Redding Municipal Airport ✉ *6751 Woodrum Circle, off Airport Rd., Redding* ☎ *530/224–4320* ⊕ *www.ci.redding.ca.us/transeng/airports/rma. htm.*

Ground Transportation Taxi Service, Chico ☎ *530/893–4444, 530/898–1776.* **Taxi Service, Redding** ☎ *530/246–0577, 530/222–1234.*

BUS TRAVEL

Greyhound buses stop in Chico, Red Bluff, Redding, and Weed. Various transit authorities provide local bus transportation *(see individual town listings for details)*, though few tourists avail themselves of it.

Bus Contact Greyhound ☎ *800/231–2222* ⊕ *www.greyhound.com.*

CAR TRAVEL

Interstate 5 runs up the center of California through Red Bluff and Redding. Chico is east of Interstate 5 on Highway 32. Lassen Volcanic National Park can be reached by Highway 36 from Red Bluff or (except in winter) Highway 44 from Redding. Highway 299 connects Weaverville, Redding, and Alturas. U.S. 395 leads from Susanville to Alturas. Highway 89 will take you from Mt. Shasta to Quincy. Highway 36 links Chester and Susanville. Check weather reports and carry detailed maps, warm clothing, and tire chains whenever you head into mountainous terrain in winter.

Road Conditions Caltrans Current Highway Conditions ☎ *800/427–7623* ⊕ *www.dot.ca.gov.*

TRAIN TRAVEL

Amtrak serves Chico, Redding, and Dunsmuir.

Train Contacts Amtrak ☎ *800/872–7245* ⊕ *www.amtrak.com.*

RESTAURANTS

Redding, the urban center of the Far North, and college-town Chico have the greatest selection of restaurants. Cafés and simple eateries are the rule in the smaller towns, though trendy, innovative restaurants have been popping up. Dress is always informal.

HOTELS

Aside from the large chain hotels and motels in Redding and Chico, most accommodations in the Far North blend rustic appeal, simplicity, and coziness. Rooms in Redding, Chico, and Red Bluff are usually booked solid only during popular local events. Wilderness resorts close in fall and reopen after the snow season ends in May. For summer

15

holiday weekends in towns such as Mt. Shasta, Dunsmuir, and Chester, and at camping sites within state or national parks, make lodging reservations well in advance. *Hotel reviews have been shortened. For full information, visit Fodors.com.*

B&B Info California Association of Boutique & Breakfast Inns ☎ 800/373-9251 ⊕ www.cabbi.com/region/Mount-Shasta.

WHAT IT COSTS			
$	$$	$$$	$$$$
Restaurants	under $16	$16–$22	$23–$30	over $30
Hotels	under $120	$120–$175	$176–$250	over $250

Restaurant prices are the average cost of a main course at dinner or, if dinner is not served, at lunch. Hotel prices are the lowest cost of a standard double room in high season.

VISITOR INFORMATION
Contacts Lassen County Chamber of Commerce ✉ 75 N. Weatherlow St., Susanville ☎ 530/257-4323 ⊕ lassencountychamber.com. **Shasta Cascade Wonderland Association** ✉ 1699 Hwy. 273, Anderson ☎ 530/365-7500, 800/474-2782 ⊕ www.shastacascade.com. **Trinity County Chamber of Commerce** ✉ 509 Main St., Weaverville ☎ 530/623-6101 ⊕ www.trinitycounty. com. **Visit Siskiyou** ☎ 800/926-4865 Mt. Shasta Chamber of Commerce ⊕ visit siskiyou.org.

FROM CHICO TO MT. SHASTA

From the blooming almond orchards of the fertile Sacramento River valley through the forested mountains and to the dominating peak of a dormant volcano, this section of the Far North entices tourists in all seasons.

CHICO

180 miles from San Francisco, east on I–80, north on I–505 to I–5, and east on Hwy. 32; 86 miles north of Sacramento on Hwy. 99.

Chico (Spanish for "small") lies in the Sacramento Valley and offers a welcome break from the monotony of Interstate 5. The Chico campus of California State University, the scores of local artisans, and the area's agriculture (primarily almond orchards) all influence the culture here. Chico's true claim to fame, however, is the popular Sierra Nevada Brewery, which keeps beer drinkers across the country happy with its distinctive brews.

GETTING HERE AND AROUND
Both Highway 99, coming north from Sacramento or south off Interstate 5 at Red Bluff, and Highway 32, going east off Interstate 5 at Orland, intersect Chico. Amtrak and Greyhound stop here, and United Express flies into the Chico airport. Butte Regional Transit's B-Line

buses serve Chico and nearby towns. Anchored by a robust university scene, the downtown neighborhoods are great for walking.

ESSENTIALS

Bus Contact B-Line ☎ *530/342–0221, 800/822–8145* ⊕ *www.blinetransit.com.*

Visitor Information Chico Chamber of Commerce ⊠ *441 Main St., Ste. 150, near E. 5th St.* ☎ *530/891–5556, 800/852–8570* ⊕ *www.chicochamber.com.*

TOURS

Sacramento River Eco Tours. Chico wildlife biologist Henry Lomeli guides boat tours down the Sacramento River to explore the diverse fish, fowl, and plant life that thrives in and around one of California's major waterways. ⊠ *Ord Bend County Park boat launch, Ord Ferry Rd. and Sacramento River, 14 miles southwest of Chico* ☎ *530/864–8594* ⊕ *www.sacramentoriverecotours.com* 🖃 *From $85.*

EXPLORING

Bidwell Mansion State Historic Park. Built between 1865 and 1868 by General John Bidwell, the founder of Chico, this mansion was designed by Henry W. Cleaveland, a San Francisco architect. Bidwell and his wife welcomed many distinguished guests to their distinctive pink Italianate home, including President Rutherford B. Hayes, naturalist John Muir, suffragist Susan B. Anthony, and General William T. Sherman. A one-hour tour takes you through most of the mansion's 26 rooms. Credit cards are not accepted. ⊠ *525 The Esplanade, at Memorial Way* ☎ *530/895–6144* ⊕ *www.parks.ca.gov* 🖃 *$6* ⊗ *Sat.–Mon. 11–5; last tour at 4.*

Bidwell Park. The sprawling 3,670-acre Bidwell Park is a community green space straddling Big Chico Creek, where scenes from *Gone With the Wind* and the 1938 version of *Robin Hood* (starring Errol Flynn) were filmed. The region's recreational hub, it includes a golf course, swimming areas, and biking, hiking, horseback riding, and in-line skating trails. One of the largest city-run parks in the country, Bidwell starts as a slender strip downtown and expands eastward 11 miles toward the Sierra foothills. Chico Creek Nature Center serves as the official information site for Bidwell Park. ⊠ *1968 E. 8th St., off Hwy. 99* ☎ *530/896–7800 Chico Public Works Dept., 530/891–4671 Chico Creek Nature Center* ⊕ *www.ccnaturecenter.org.*

Fodor's Choice ★ **Sierra Nevada Brewing Company.** This pioneer of the microbrewery movement still has a hands-on approach to beer making. Tour the brew house and see how the beer is produced—from the sorting of hops through fermentation and bottling, and concluding with a complimentary tasting. You can also visit the gift shop and enjoy a hearty lunch or dinner in the brewpub. ■TIP→ **Tours fill up fast; call or sign up online before you visit.** ⊠ *1075 E. 20th St., at Sierra Nevada St.* ☎ *530/345–2739 brewpub, 530/899–4776 tours* ⊕ *www.sierranevada.com* 🖃 *Free* ⊗ *Tours daily, call for times.*

WHERE TO EAT AND STAY

$$$ **STEAKHOUSE** ✕ **5th Street Steakhouse.** Hand-cut steak is the star in this refurbished early 1900s building, the place to come when you're craving red meat and a huge baked potato. Exposed redbrick walls warm the dining rooms, and a long mahogany bar catches the overflow crowds that jam the place on weekends. Lunch is served on Fridays only. No reservations for parties smaller than six persons are accepted on Fridays and Saturdays. [$] *Average main: $30* ✉ *345 W. 5th St., at Normal Ave.* ☎ *530/891–6328* 🌐 *www.5thstreetsteakhouse.com* 🕒 *No lunch Thurs.–Sat.*

$ AMERICAN 🍴 **Madison Bear Garden.** This downtown favorite two blocks south of the Chico State campus is a great spot for checking out the vibrant college scene while enjoying a burger and a brew. [$] *Average main: $8* ✉ *316 W. 2nd St., at Salem St.* ☎ *530/891–1639* 🌐 *www.madisonbeargarden.com.*

$$$ MEDITERRANEAN 🍴 **Red Tavern.** With its burgundy carpet, white linen tablecloths, and mellow lighting, this is one of Chico's coziest restaurants. The Mediterranean-influenced menu, inspired by fresh local produce, changes seasonally. There's a great California wine list, and a full bar. **TIP→ Try their popular Sunday brunch.** [$] *Average main: $24* ✉ *1250 The Esplanade, at E. 3rd Ave.* ☎ *530/894–3463* 🌐 *www.redtavern.com* 🕒 *Closed Mon. No lunch Tues.–Sat.*

$$ HOTEL 🏨 **Hotel Diamond.** Crystal chandeliers and gleaming wood floors and banisters elegantly welcome guests into the foyer of this restored gem in downtown Chico near the university. **Pros:** refined; great location; breakfast voucher included in room rate. **Cons:** street scene can be noisy on weekends. [$] *Rooms from: $140* ✉ *220 W. 4th St., near Broadway* ☎ *530/893–3100, 866/993–3100* 🌐 *www.hoteldiamondchico.com* 🛏 *39 rooms, 4 suites* 🍽 *Breakfast.*

RED BLUFF

41 miles north of Chico on Hwy 99.

Historic Red Bluff is a gateway to Lassen Volcanic National Park. Established in the mid-19th century as a shipping center on the Sacramento River, and named for the color of its soil, the town is filled with dozens of restored Victorians. It's a great home base for outdoor adventures in the area.

GETTING HERE AND AROUND

Access Red Bluff via exits off Interstate 5, or by driving north on Highway 99. Highway 36 is a long, twisting road that begins near the Pacific Coast and goes to Red Bluff, then east to the towns near Lassen Volcanic National Park. Greyhound buses stop here and also provide connecting service to Amtrak. TRAX (Tehama Rural Area Express) serves Red Bluff and neighboring towns.

ESSENTIALS

Bus Information TRAX ☎ *530/385–2877* 🌐 *www.taketrax.com.*

Visitor Information Red Bluff–Tehama County Chamber of Commerce ✉ *100 Main St., at Rio St.* ☎ *530/527–6220* 🌐 *www.redbluffchamber.com.*

EXPLORING

William B. Ide Adobe State Historic Park. Named for the first and only president of the short-lived California Republic of 1846, William B. Ide Adobe State Historic Park is on an oak-lined bank of the Sacramento River. The Bear Flag Party proclaimed California a sovereign nation, separate from Mexican rule, and the republic existed for 22 days before it was taken over by the United States. The republic's flag has survived, with minor refinements, as California's state flag. At press time, the park's main attraction, an adobe home built in the 1850s and outfitted with period furnishings, was being refurbished after a giant oak tree fell on it during a storm. ✉ *21659 Adobe Rd., at Park Pl., ½ mile east of I–5* ☎ *530/529–8599* 🌐 *www.parks.ca.gov/?page_id=458* 🎫 *$6 per vehicle* 🕒 *Park and picnic facilities, and historic sites Fri.–Sun. 10–4.*

RED BLUFF ROUND-UP

Check out old-time rodeo at its best during the Red Bluff Round-Up. Held the third weekend of April, this annual event attracts some of the best cowboys in the country. For more information, visit 🌐 *redbluffroundup.com.*

WHERE TO EAT AND STAY

$$ STEAKHOUSE 🍴 **Green Barn Steakhouse.** You're likely to find cowboys sporting Stetsons and spurs feasting on sizzling porterhouse, baby back ribs, and prime rib at Red Bluff's premier steak house. For lighter fare, try the fish or pasta entrées. Don't miss the bread pudding with rum sauce. The lounge is usually hopping, especially when there's an event at the nearby rodeo grounds. [$] *Average main: $20* ✉ *5 Chestnut Ave., at Antelope Blvd.* ☎ *530/527–3161* ✍ *Reservations not accepted* 🕒 *Closed Sun. no lunch Sat.*

$ HOTEL 🏨 **Sportsman Lodge.** On-site owners keep this small motel neat and inviting, with practical amenities like refrigerators, microwaves, cable TV, and free Wi-Fi. **Pros:** spacious rooms; helpful owners; pet-friendly. **Cons:** an older facility. [$] *Rooms from: $68* ✉ *768 Antelope Blvd., near Trinity Ave.* ☎ *530/527–2888* 🌐 *www.sportsmanlodgemotel.com* 🛏 *19 rooms* 🍽 *No meals.*

REDDING

32 miles north of Red Bluff on I–5.

As the largest city in the Far North, Redding is an ideal headquarters for exploring the surrounding countryside.

GETTING HERE AND AROUND

Reach Redding from exits off Interstate 5 or via Highway 299, which originates near coastal Eureka and crosses Weaverville and Redding before heading northeast to Burney and Alturas. Highway 44 stretches from Susanville past Lassen Park's north entrance before ending in Redding. United Express serves the Redding airport. Amtrak and Greyhound make stops here.

ESSENTIALS

Bus Information Redding Area Bus Authority ☎ *530/241–2877* 🌐 *www.rabaride.com.*

Visitor Information Redding Convention and Visitors Bureau ✉ *2334 Washington Ave., Ste. B* ☎ *530/225–4100, 800/874–7562* 🌐 *www.visitredding.com.*

Anglers fish under Santiago Calatrava's striking Sundial Bridge next to Turtle Bay Exploration Park.

EXPLORING

FAMILY Fodor's Choice ★ **Turtle Bay Exploration Park.** This park features walking trails, an arboretum and botanical gardens, and lots of interactive exhibits for kids, including a gold-panning area and the seasonal butterfly exhibit. The main draw is the stunning **Sundial Bridge,** which links the Sacramento River Trail and the park's arboretum and gardens. Access to the bridge and arboretum is free, but there's a fee for the museum. ✉ *844 Sundial Bridge Dr., off Hwy. 44* ☎ *530/243–8850, 800/887–8532* 🌐 *www.turtlebay.org* 🎟 *Museum $16* ⏲ *May–early Sept., Mon.–Sat. 9–5, Sun. 10–5; early Sept.–Apr., Wed.–Sat. 9–4, Sun. 10–4.*

WHERE TO EAT AND STAY

$$$ STEAKHOUSE 🍴 **Jack's Grill.** Famous for its 16-ounce steaks, this popular bar and steak house also serves shrimp and chicken. A town favorite, the place is usually jam-packed and noisy. The bar serves great martinis. [$] *Average main: $27* ✉ *1743 California St., near Sacramento St.* ☎ *530/241–9705* 🌐 *www.jacksgrillredding.com* ⏲ *Closed Sun. No lunch.*

$ AMERICAN 🍴 **Klassique Kafe.** Two sisters run this small, bustling restaurant that caters to locals looking for simple but hearty breakfast and lunch fare. The hot luncheon specials served daily might include butter beans and ham with corn bread, or chicken and dumplings. [$] *Average main: $10* ✉ *2427 Athens Ave., at Locust St.* ☎ *530/244–4939* 🌐 *www.klassiquekafe.com* ⏲ *Closed weekends. No dinner.*

$$$ ITALIAN 🍴 **Nello's Place.** Fine Italian dining and romantic ambience go hand-in-hand at Nello's Place, one of Redding's best restaurants. You'll find a varied selection of veal, chicken, beef, and pasta dishes mixed with lighter fish and vegetarian fare. For special presentations, order a

Caesar salad prepared tableside for two, and bananas flambé for dessert. There's a full bar in addition to an extensive wine list. $ *Average main: $25 ⊠ 3055 Bechelli La., near Hartnell Ave.* ☎ *530/223–1636* ⊕ *www.nellosrestaurant.net* ⊘ *No lunch. Closed Mon.*

$ 🛌 **The Red Lion.** Close to Redding's convention center and regional recreation sites, this hotel is a top choice for both business and vacation travelers. **Pros:** family-friendly; close to a major shopping and dining area. **Cons:** on a noisy street. $ *Rooms from: $119 ⊠ 1830 Hilltop Dr., Hwy. 44/299 exit off I–5* ☎ *530/221–8700, 800/733–5466* ⊕ *www. redlion.com* ⌇ *192 rooms, 2 suites* ⏉ *No meals.*

HOTEL

SPORTS AND THE OUTDOORS
FISHING
Fly Shop. This store sells fishing licenses and has information about guides, conditions, and fishing trips. ⊠ *4140 Churn Creek Rd., at Denton Way* ☎ *530/222–3555, 800/669–3474* ⊕ *www.flyshop.com.*

WEAVERVILLE

46 miles west of Redding on Hwy. 299.

A man known only as Weaver struck gold here in 1849, and the fledgling community that developed at the base of the Trinity Alps was named after him. With its impressive downtown historic district, today Weaverville is a popular headquarters for family vacations and biking, hiking, fishing, and gold-panning excursions.

GETTING HERE AND AROUND
Highway 299 becomes Main Street down the center of Weaverville. Take the highway either east from the Pacific Coast or west from Redding. Highway 36 from Red Bluff to Highway 3 heading north leads to Weaverville. Trinity Transit provides minimal local bus service plus a line that links Weaverville to Interstate 5 at Redding.

ESSENTIALS
Visitor Information Trinity County Visitors Bureau ⊠ *509 Main St.* ☎ *530/623–6101* ⊕ *www.visittrinity.com.*

EXPLORING
Trinity County Courthouse. Built in 1856 as a store, office building, and hotel, Trinity County Courthouse was converted to county use in 1865. The Apollo Saloon, in the basement, became the county jail. It's the oldest courthouse still in use in California. ⊠ *Court and Main Sts.*

Trinity County Hal Goodyear Historical Park. For a vivid sense of Weaverville's past, visit the Trinity County Hal Goodyear Historical Park, especially its **Jake Jackson Memorial Museum.** A blacksmith shop and a stamp mill (where ore is crushed) from the 1890s are still in use during certain community events. Also here are the original jail cells of the Trinity County Courthouse. ⊠ *780 Main St., at Bartlett La.* ☎ *530/623–5211* ⊕ *www.trinitymuseum.org* ⊘ *Jan.–Mar., Wed. and Sat. noon–4; Apr. and Oct., daily 11–4; May–Sept., daily 10–5; Nov. and Dec., Wed.–Sat. 11–4.*

15

Fodor's Choice ★ **Weaverville Joss House.** Weaverville's main attraction is the Joss House, a Taoist temple built in 1874 and called Won Lim Miao ("the temple of the forest beneath the clouds") by Chinese miners. The oldest continuously used Chinese temple in California, it attracts worshippers from around the world. With its golden altar, antique weaponry, and carved wooden canopies, the Joss House is a piece of California history that can best be appreciated on a guided 30-minute tour. The original temple building and many of its furnishings—some of which came from China—were lost to fire in 1873, but members of the local Chinese community soon rebuilt it. ✉ *630 Main St., at Oregon St.* ☎ *530/623–5284* 🌐 *www.parks.ca.gov* 🎟 *Museum free; guided tour $4* 🕒 *Thurs.–Sun. 10–5; last tour at 4.*

WHERE TO EAT AND STAY

$$ STEAKHOUSE 🍴 **Beckett's Trail's End Steakhouse.** The chef-owner of this small restaurant serves big steaks along with chicken and fish entrées. The blackened shrimp tacos with a spicy corn and bean salsa are superb, as are the fresh wild salmon and the black 'n blue Cajun burger. Jeans and kick-back attire are perfectly suited to this super casual eatery. [$] *Average main: $18* ✉ *1324 Nugget La., at Main St.* ☎ *530/623–2900* 🕒 *Closed Sun. no lunch Thurs.*

$ MEXICAN 🍴 **La Casita.** A traditional selection of Mexican food is on the menu here, including quesadillas (try the version with roasted chili peppers), tostadas, enchiladas, tacos, and tamales. Many dishes are available without meat. Open from late morning through dinner, this casual spot is great for a mid-afternoon snack. [$] *Average main: $9* ✉ *570 Main St.* ☎ *530/623–5797* 🕒 *Closed Sun.*

$ HOTEL 🏨 **Red Hill Motel.** This 1940s-era property is popular with anglers, who appreciate the outdoor fish-cleaning area on the premises. **Pros:** close to popular bass fishing sites; inexpensive. **Cons:** older facility; some rooms need sprucing up. [$] *Rooms from: $53* ✉ *50 Red Hill Rd., off Main St./Hwy. 299* ☎ *530/623–4331* 🛏 *4 rooms, 6 cabins, 2 duplexes* 🍽 *No meals.*

$$ HOTEL 🏨 **Weaverville Hotel.** Originally built during the gold rush, this beautifully restored hotel is filled with antiques and period furniture. **Pros:** gracious on-site owners; in heart of town's historic district. **Cons:** no pets allowed. [$] *Rooms from: $140* ✉ *481 Main St., near Court St.* ☎ *530/623–2222, 800/750–8853* 🌐 *www.weavervillehotel.com* 🛏 *7 rooms* 🍽 *No meals.*

SPORTS AND THE OUTDOORS

Fly Stretch. Below the Lewiston Dam, east of Weaverville on Highway 299, is the Fly Stretch of the Trinity River, an excellent fly-fishing area.

Pine Cove Boat Ramp. This ramp on Lewiston Lake provides fishing access for those with disabilities—decks here are built over prime trout-fishing waters.

Weaverville Ranger Station. Check here for maps and information about local fishing and hiking trails in the Trinity Alps Wilderness. ✉ *360 Main St.* ☎ *530/623–2121.*

LAKE SHASTA AREA

12 miles north of Redding on I–5.

When you think of the Lake Shasta Area, picture water, wilderness, dazzling stalagmites—and a fabulous man-made project in the midst of it all.

GETTING HERE AND AROUND

Interstate 5 north of Redding is the main link to the entire Lake Shasta area. Get to the dam by passing through the tiny city of Shasta Lake. There is no local bus service.

ESSENTIALS

Shasta Cascade Wonderland Association. Stop in the association's visitor center in the Anderson outlet mall off I–5 between Red Bluff and Redding, or check the website for special events taking place during your visit to California's northernmost counties. A weekly fishing report informs anglers about stream closures and which spots are yielding the best catches. ⊠ *1699 Hwy. 273, Anderson* ☎ *530/365–7500, 800/474–2782* ⊕ *www.shastacascade.com.*

EXPLORING

Lake Shasta. Numerous types of fish inhabit the lake, including rainbow trout, salmon, bass, brown trout, and the humble catfish. The lake region also has the largest nesting population of bald eagles in California. You can rent fishing boats, ski boats, sailboats, canoes, paddleboats, Jet Skis, and windsurfing boards at one of the many marinas and resorts along the 370-mile shoreline. ⊠ *Shasta Lake* ⊕ *www.shastacascade.com.*

Fodor'sChoice
★ **Lake Shasta Caverns.** Stalagmites, stalactites, flowstone deposits, and crystals entice visitors to the Lake Shasta Caverns. To see this impressive spectacle, you must take the two-hour tour, which includes a catamaran ride across the McCloud arm of Lake Shasta and a bus ride up North Grey Rocks Mountain to the cavern entrance. The caverns are 58°F year-round, making them a cool retreat on a hot summer day. The most awe-inspiring of the limestone rock formations is the glistening Cathedral Room, which appears to be gilded. A gift shop is open from 8 to 4:30. ⊠ *20359 Shasta Caverns Rd., Exit 695 off I–5, 17 miles north of Redding, Lakehead* ☎ *530/238–2341, 800/795–2283* ⊕ *www.lakeshastacaverns.com* 🖭 *$24* ☉ *June–Aug., tours on the half hr, daily 9–4; Apr., May, and Sept., tours on the hr, daily 9–3; Oct.–Mar., tours at 10, noon, and 2.*

Shasta Dam. This is the second-largest concrete dam in the United States (only Grand Coulee in Washington is bigger). The visitor center has computerized photographic tours of the dam construction, video presentations, fact sheets, and historical displays. Hour-long guided tours inside the dam and its powerhouse leave from the center. ⊠ *16349 Shasta Dam Blvd., off Lake Blvd., Shasta Lake* ☎ *530/275–4463* ⊕ *www.usbr.gov* 🖭 *Free* ☉ *Visitor center daily 8–5; call for tour times.*

SPORTS AND THE OUTDOORS

FISHING

The Fishen Hole. A couple of miles from the lake, this bait-and-tackle shop sells fishing licenses and provides information about conditions. ✉ *3844 Shasta Dam Blvd., at Red Bluff Ave., Shasta Lake* ☎ *530/275–4123.*

HOUSEBOATING

Houseboats here come in all sizes except small. As a rule, rentals are outfitted with cooking utensils, dishes, and most of the equipment you'll need—you supply the food and the linens. When you rent a houseboat, you receive a short course in how to maneuver your launch before you set out. You can fish, swim, sunbathe on the flat roof, or sit on the deck and watch the world go by. The shoreline of Lake Shasta is beautifully ragged, with countless inlets; it's not hard to find privacy. Expect to spend a minimum of $350 a day for a craft that sleeps six. A three-day, two-night minimum is customary. Prices are often lower during the off-season (September through May). Bridge Bay Resort rents houseboats, fishing boats, ski boats, and patio boats. Shasta Cascade offers general information.

Bridge Bay Resort. This resort offers modest lakeside lodging, a restaurant, boat and Jet Ski rentals, and a full-service marina. If you want to sleep on the lake rather than beside it, rent one of the houseboats that come in sizes large enough to accommodate up to a dozen people. ✉ *10300 Bridge Bay Rd., Redding* ☎ *800/752–9669, 530/275–3021* ⊕ *www.bridgebayhouseboats.com.*

DUNSMUIR

10 miles south of Mt. Shasta on I–5.

Surrounded by towering forests and boasting world-class fly-fishing in the Upper Sacramento River, tiny Dunsmuir was named for a 19th-century Scottish coal baron who offered to build a fountain if the town was renamed in his honor. Another major attraction is the Railroad Park Resort, where you can spend the night in restored cabooses.

GETTING HERE AND AROUND

Reach Dunsmuir via exits off Interstate 5 at the north and south ends of town. When snow hasn't closed the route, you can take Highway 89 from the Lassen Park area toward Burney then northeast to Interstate 5 at Mt. Shasta. From there it's a 10-mile drive south to Dunsmuir. Amtrak stops here; Greyhound stops in Weed, 20 miles north. On weekdays, STAGE buses serve Dunsmuir.

ESSENTIALS

Bus Information STAGE ☎ *530/842–8295* ⊕ *www.co.siskiyou.ca.us/content/transportation-division-stage.*

Visitor Information Dunsmuir Chamber of Commerce ✉ *5915 Dunsmuir Ave., Ste. 100* ☎ *530/235–2177* ⊕ *dunsmuir.com.*

EXPLORING

Fodor's Choice ★ **Castle Crags State Park.** Named for its 6,000-foot glacier-polished crags, which were formed by volcanic activity centuries ago, this park offers fishing in Castle Creek, hiking in the backcountry, and a view of Mt. Shasta. The crags draw climbers and hikers from around the world. The 4,350-acre park has 28 miles of hiking trails, including a 2¾-mile access trail to **Castle Crags Wilderness,** part of the **Shasta-Trinity National Forest.** There are excellent trails at lower altitudes. Camping is allowed in winter on a first-come, first-served basis. ✉ *6 miles south of Dunsmuir, Castella/Castle Crags exit off I–5, 20022 Castle Creek Rd., Castella* ☎ *530/235–2684* 🌐 *www.parks.ca.gov* 🎟 *$8 per vehicle, day use.*

FINE FISHING

The upper Sacramento River near Dunsmuir is consistently rated one of the best fishing spots in the country. Check with the chamber of commerce for local fishing guides.

WHERE TO EAT AND STAY

$$ MEDITERRANEAN 🍴 **Café Maddalena.** The chef here gained experience working in top San Francisco restaurants before moving north to prepare adventurous Mediterranean fare with a French influence. Selections change seasonally but always feature a vegetarian dish, along with fish, beef, and chicken entrées. Wines from Spain, Italy, and France complement the meals. Ask about the daily prix-fixe menu. [$] *Average main: $21* ✉ *5801 Sacramento Ave.* ☎ *530/235–2725* 🌐 *www.cafemaddalena.com* ⏲ *Closed Mon.–Wed. and Jan.–mid-Feb. No lunch.*

$$ HOTEL FAMILY 🏨 **Railroad Park Resort.** The antique cabooses here were collected over more than three decades and have been converted into cozy motel rooms in honor of Dunsmuir's railroad legacy. **Pros:** gorgeous setting; kitschy fun. **Cons:** cabooses can feel cramped. [$] *Rooms from: $125* ✉ *100 Railroad Park Rd.* ☎ *530/235–4440* 🌐 *www.rrpark.com* 🛏 *23 cabooses, 4 cabins* 🍽 *No meals.*

MT. SHASTA

34 miles north of Lake Shasta on I–5.

While a snow-covered dormant volcano is the area's dazzling draw, the town of Mt. Shasta charms visitors with its small shops, friendly residents, and beautiful scenery in all seasons.

GETTING HERE AND AROUND

Three exits off Interstate 5 lead to the town of Mt. Shasta. When snow hasn't closed the route, you can take Highway 89 from the Lassen Park area toward Burney then northeast to Mt. Shasta. The ski park is off Highway 89. Greyhound stops at Weed, 10 miles north; Amtrak stops at Dunsmuir, 10 miles south. There's no local bus system.

ESSENTIALS

Visitor Information Mt. Shasta Chamber of Commerce and Visitors Bureau ✉ *300 Pine St., at W. Lake St., Mt. Shasta* ☎ *530/926–4865, 800/926–4865* 🌐 *www.mtshastachamber.com.*

15

EXPLORING

Fodor's Choice ★ **Mt. Shasta.** The crown jewel of the 2.5-million-acre Shasta-Trinity National Forest, Mt. Shasta, a 14,179-foot-high dormant volcano, is a mecca for day hikers. It's especially enticing in spring, when fragrant Shasta lilies and other flowers adorn the rocky slopes. A paved road, the Everitt Memorial Highway, reaches only as far as the timberline; the final 6,000 feet are a tough climb of rubble, ice, and snow (the summit is perpetually ice-packed). Only a hardy few are qualified to make the trek to the top. **TIP→ Always check weather predictions; sudden storms have trapped climbers with snow and freezing temperatures.**

The town of Mt. Shasta has real character and some fine restaurants. Lovers of the outdoors and backcountry skiers abound, and they are more than willing to offer advice on the most beautiful spots in the region, which include out-of-the-way swimming holes, dozens of high mountain lakes, and a challenging 18-hole golf course with 360 degrees of spectacular views. 🌐 *www.mtshastachamber.com.*

WHERE TO EAT AND STAY

$$ ECLECTIC 🍴 **Lilys.** This restaurant in a white-clapboard home, framed by a picket fence and arched trellis, offers an eclectic menu. Try bourbon-glazed French toast for breakfast. Lunch and dinner selections vary seasonally, but often include roasted beet salad with poached pear, walnuts, and blue cheese; steak and beef dishes; and marinated pork chops with cannellini beans. Daily fish entrées might include herb-stuffed fresh trout or seared mahi. For innovative vegetarian fare, try the walnut garbanzo veggie burger. Brunch is served on the weekend. [$] *Average main: $20* ✉ *1013 S. Mt. Shasta Blvd., at Holly St., Mt. Shasta* ☎ *530/926–3372* 🌐 *www.lilysrestaurant.com.*

$ CAFÉ 🍴 **Seven Suns Coffee and Cafe.** A favorite gathering spot for locals, this small coffee shop serves specialty wraps for breakfast and lunch, plus soup and salad selections. Pastries, made daily, include muffins, cookies, and blackberry scones in season. If the weather's nice, grab a seat on the patio. [$] *Average main: $9* ✉ *1011 S. Mt. Shasta Blvd., at Holly St., Mt. Shasta* ☎ *530/926–9701* 🌐 *www.mtshastacoffee.com.*

$$ HOTEL 🏨 **Best Western Tree House Motor Inn.** The clean, standard rooms at this motel less than a mile from downtown Mt. Shasta are decorated with natural-wood furnishings. **Pros:** close to ski park; indoor pool; lobby's roaring fireplace is a big plus on winter days. **Cons:** not all lodging buildings have elevators. [$] *Rooms from: $170* ✉ *111 Morgan Way, Mt. Shasta* ☎ *530/926–3101, 800/545–7164* 🌐 *www.bestwesterncalifornia.com/hotels/best-western-plus-tree-house* 🛏 *91 rooms, 7 suites* 🍽 *Breakfast.*

$$ RENTAL 🏨 **Mount Shasta Resort.** Private chalets are nestled among tall pine trees along the shore of Lake Siskiyou, all with gas-log fireplaces and full kitchens. **Pros:** incredible views; romantic woodsy setting; some pet-friendly rooms for extra fee. **Cons:** kids may get bored. [$] *Rooms from: $170* ✉ *1000 Siskiyou Lake Blvd., Mt. Shasta* ☎ *530/926–3030, 800/958–3363* 🌐 *www.mountshastaresort.com* 🛏 *65 units* 🍽 *No meals.*

SPORTS AND THE OUTDOORS

HIKING

Mt. Shasta Forest Service Ranger Station. Check in here for current trail conditions and avalanche reports. ⊠ *204 W. Alma St., at Pine St., Mt. Shasta* ☎ *530/926–4511, 530/926–9613 avalanche conditions.*

MOUNTAIN CLIMBING

Fifth Season Mountaineering Shop. This shop rents bicycles and skiing and climbing equipment, and operates a recorded 24-hour climber-skier report. ⊠ *300 N. Mt. Shasta Blvd.* ☎ *530/926–3606, 530/926–5555 ski phone* ⊕ *www.thefifthseason.com.*

Shasta Mountain Guides. These guides lead hiking, climbing, and ski-touring groups to the summit of Mt. Shasta. ⊠ *Mt. Shasta* ☎ *530/926–3117* ⊕ *shastaguides.com.*

SKIING

FAMILY **Mt. Shasta Board & Ski Park.** On the southeast flank of Mt. Shasta, this ski park has three triple-chairlifts and two surface lifts on 425 skiable acres. Three-quarters of the trails are for beginning or intermediate skiers. The area's vertical drop is 1,435 feet, with a top elevation of 6,890 feet. The longest of the 32 trails is 1.75 miles. A package for beginners, available through the ski school, includes a lift ticket, ski rental, and a lesson. The school also runs ski and snowboard programs for children. There's night skiing for those who want to see the moon rise as they schuss. The base lodge has a simple café, a ski shop, and a ski-snowboard rental shop. ⊠ *Hwy. 89 exit east from I–5, south of Mt. Shasta, Mt. Shasta* ☎ *530/926–8610, 800/754–7427* ⊕ *www.skipark. com* ☉ *Winter ski season schedule: Sun.–Wed. 9–4, Thurs.–Sat. 9–9.*

Mt. Shasta Nordic Center. This center, run by a nonprofit, maintains 15 miles of groomed cross-country ski trails. ⊠ *Ski Park Hwy., off Hwy. 89 (take I–5's McCloud exit), Mt. Shasta* ☎ *530/926–2142* ⊕ *mtshasta nordic.org.*

THE BACKCOUNTRY

The Far North's primitive, rugged backcountry is arguably full of more natural wonders than any other region in California.

MCARTHUR–BURNEY FALLS MEMORIAL STATE PARK

Hwy. 89, 52 miles southeast of Mt. Shasta and 41 miles north of Lassen Volcanic National Park.

One of the most spectacular sights in the Far North is Burney Falls, where countless ribbon-like streams pour from moss-covered crevices. You have to travel forested back roads to reach this gem, but the park's beauty is well worth the trek.

GETTING HERE AND AROUND

To see some stunning falls, head east off Interstate 5 on Highway 89 at Mt. Shasta. The drive is 52 miles. From Interstate 5 in Redding, head east 55 miles on Highway 299 to connect with Highway 89; follow signs 6 miles to the park. From Alturas, head west on Highway 299 for about 86 miles and hook up with Highway 89.

EXPLORING

FAMILY

Fodor'sChoice

★

McArthur–Burney Falls Memorial State Park. Just inside the park's southern boundary, Burney Creek wells up from the ground and divides into two falls that cascade over a 129-foot cliff into a pool below. Countless ribbonlike streams pour from hidden moss-covered crevices; resident bald eagles are frequently seen soaring overhead. You can walk a self-guided nature trail that descends to the foot of the falls, which Theodore Roosevelt—according to legend—called "the eighth wonder of the world." On warm days, swim at Lake Britton; lounge on the beach; rent motorboats, paddleboats, and canoes; or relax at one of the campsites or picnic areas. The camp store is open from mid-April to mid-October. ⊠ *24898 Hwy. 89, 6 miles north of Hwy. 299, Burney* ☎ *530/335–2777* ⊕ *www.parks.ca.gov* ⊠ *$8 per vehicle, day use.*

ALTURAS

86 miles northeast of McArthur–Burney Falls Memorial State Park on Hwy. 299.

Alturas is the county seat and largest town in Modoc County. The Dorris family arrived in the area in 1874, built Dorris Bridge over the Pit River, and later opened a small wayside stop for travelers. As in the past, travelers today come to see eagles and other wildlife, the Modoc National Forest, and active geothermal areas.

GETTING HERE AND AROUND

To get to Alturas from Susanville, take Main Street/Highway 36 south for about 4 miles; turn left at U.S. 395 and stay on that highway for 99 miles. From Redding, take the Lake Blvd./299E exit off Interstate 5, head east and stay on Highway 299 for 140 miles. Sage Stage buses serve Alturas from Redding and Susanville.

ESSENTIALS

Bus Information Modoc County Sage Stage ☎ *530/233-6410* ⊕ *www. sagestage.com.*

Visitor Information Alturas Chamber of Commerce ⊠ *600 S. Main St.* ☎ *530/233-4434* ⊕ *www.alturaschamber.org.*

EXPLORING

Modoc National Forest. Encompassing 1.6 million acres in the northeast corner of California, Modoc National Forest protects 300 species of wildlife, including Rocky Mountain elk, wild horses, mule deer, and pronghorn antelope. In spring and fall, watch for migratory waterfowl as they make their way along the Pacific Flyway above the forest. The numerous campsites within the forest are all available on a "first come, first served" basis. ⊠ *Park Headquarters, 225 W. 8th St.* ☎ *530/233-5811* ⊕ *www.fs.usda.gov/modoc.*

Modoc National Wildlife Refuge. The 7,021-acre Modoc National Wildlife Refuge was established in 1961 to protect migratory waterfowl. You might see Canada geese, sandhill cranes, mallards, teal, wigeon, pintail,

white pelicans, cormorants, and snowy egrets. The refuge is open for hiking, bird-watching, and photography, but one area is set aside for hunters. Regulations vary according to season. ✉ *5364 County Rd. 115, U.S. 395, 1½ miles south of Alturas, left on Rd. 56, then right on Rd. 115* ☎ *530/233–3572* 🌐 *www.fws.gov/refuge/modoc* 🎟 *Free* 🕒 *Daily dawn–dusk.*

WHERE TO EAT

$$ SPANISH 🍴 **Brass Rail.** Prix-fixe dinners at this authentic Basque restaurant include wine, homemade bread, soup, salad, side dishes, coffee, and ice cream. Steak, lamb chops, fried chicken, shrimp, and scallops are among the best entrée selections. A lounge with a full bar adjoins the dining area. [$] *Average main: $22* ✉ *395 Lakeview Hwy.* ☎ *530/233–2906* 🕒 *Closed Mon.*

SUSANVILLE

104 miles south of Alturas via U.S. 395; 65 miles east of Lassen Volcanic National Park via Highway 36.

Susanville, established as a trading post in 1854, tells the tale of its rich history through murals painted on buildings in the historic uptown area. You can take a self-guided tour around the original buildings and stop for a bite at one of the restaurants now housed within them. If you'd rather work up a sweat, you can hit the Bizz Johnson Trail and Eagle Lake recreation areas just outside town.

GETTING HERE AND AROUND

U.S. 395 connects Susanville and Alturas, about a 100-mile trip. From Red Bluff, take Interstate 5's Highway 36E/Fairgrounds exit and drive east for about 3 miles; turn left at Highway 36E and continue through the mountains for 103 miles. Lassen Rural Bus serves Susanville Monday through Saturday, and surrounding areas on weekdays only.

ESSENTIALS

Bus Information Lassen Rural Bus ☎ *530/252–7433* 🌐 *www.lassentransportation.com/a/Lassen-Rural-Bus-LRB.php.*

Visitor Information Lassen County Chamber of Commerce ✉ *75 N. Weatherlow St., off Main St.* ☎ *530/257–4323* 🌐 *lassencountychamber.com.*

EXPLORING

Bizz Johnson Trail. This trail follows a defunct line of the Southern Pacific Railroad for 25 miles. Known to locals as the Bizz, the trail is open for hikers, walkers, mountain bikers, horseback riders, and cross-country skiers. It skirts the Susan River through a scenic landscape of canyons, bridges, and forests abundant with wildlife. ✉ *Trailhead, old railroad depot, 601 Richmond Rd., near N. Railroad Ave.* ☎ *530/257–0456* 🌐 *www.blm.gov/ca/st/en/fo/eaglelake/bizztrail.html* 🎟 *Free.*

Eagle Lake. Anglers travel great distances to fish the waters of this large lake where the trout is prized for its size and fighting ability. Surrounded by high desert to the north and alpine forests to the south, Eagle Lake is also popular for picnicking, hiking, boating, waterskiing and windsurfing, and bird-watching—ospreys, pelicans, and many other waterfowl visit the lake. On land you might see mule deer, small mammals, and even pronghorn antelope—and be sure to watch for bald-eagle nesting sites. ⊠ *16 miles north of Susanville, Eagle Lake Rd. off Hwy. 139* ☎ *530/257–0456 for Eagle Lake Recreation Area, 530/825–3454 for Eagle Lake Marina* ⊕ *www.blm.gov/ca/st/en/fo/eaglelake.html.*

WHERE TO EAT AND STAY

$ ✕ **Mazatlan Grill.** The sauces are prepared on-site in this friendly, family-
MEXICAN run restaurant and lounge, with a full bar, which serves lunch and dinner daily. The dining room is simple and tidy, with comfortable upholstered booths. The extensive menu offers authentic, inexpensive Mexican fare ranging from fajitas and enchiladas to a vegetarian burrito. $ *Average main: $10* ⊠ *1535 Main St., at Park St.* ☎ *530/257–1800.*

$ ⌂ **High Country Inn.** Rooms are spacious in this colonial-style motel on
HOTEL the eastern edge of town. **Pros:** great mountain views; seasonal heated pool. **Cons:** lots of traffic in the area. $ *Rooms from: $93* ⊠ *3015 Riverside Dr., at Main St.* ☎ *530/257–3450, 866/454–4566* ⊕ *www.high-country-inn.com* ⇗ *66 rooms* ¶⊙¶ *Breakfast.*

LASSEN VOLCANIC NATIONAL PARK

45 miles east of Redding on Hwy. 44; 48 miles east of Red Bluff on Hwy. 36.

Fissures and fumaroles burble and belch as reminders of Lassen Peak's dramatic eruption a century ago. Four different types of volcanoes form part of this park's fascinating geothermal landscape.

GETTING HERE AND AROUND

Whether coming from the west or the east, reach the park's southern entrance via Highway 36E, and turn onto Highway 89 for a short drive to the park. The northwest entrance is reached via Highway 44 from Redding and Susanville. No buses serve the area.

EXPLORING

Fodor's Choice **Lassen Scenic Byway.** This 185-mile scenic drive begins in Chester and
★ loops through the forests, volcanic peaks, geothermal springs, and lava fields of Lassen National Forest and Lassen Volcanic National Park, providing an all-day excursion into dramatic wilderness. From Chester, take Route 36 west to Route 89 north through the park, then Route 44 east to Route 36 west back to Chester. Parts of the road are inaccessible in winter. ☎ *800/427–7623 CA Highway info service, 530/595–4480 Lassen Park visitor center* ⊕ *www.nps.gov/lavo.*

Fodor's Choice **Lassen Volcanic National Park.** A dormant plug dome, Lassen Peak is
★ the focus of Lassen Volcanic National Park's 165.6 square miles of distinctive landscape. The peak began erupting in May 1914, sending pumice, rock, and snow thundering down the mountain and gas and hot ash billowing into the atmosphere. Lassen's most spectacular outburst occurred in 1915 when it blew a cloud of ash some 7 miles into the stratosphere. The resulting mudflow destroyed vegetation for miles in some directions; the evidence is still visible today, especially in the Devastated Area. The volcano finally came to rest in 1921. Today fumaroles, mud pots, lakes, and bubbling hot springs create a fascinating but

15

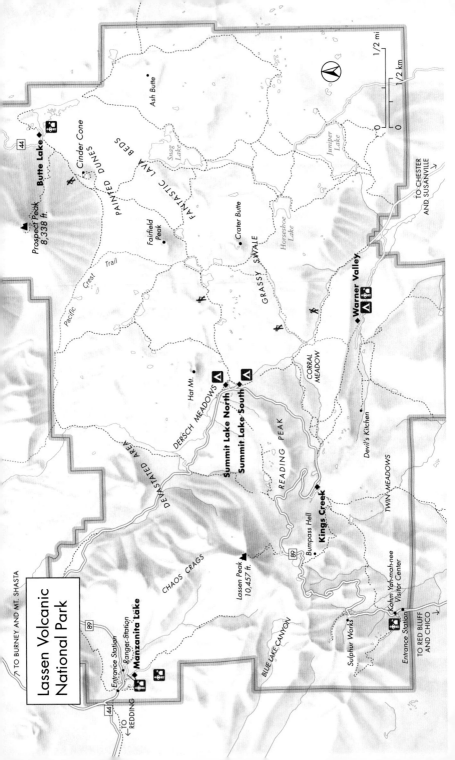

Lassen Volcanic National Park

TO BURNEY AND MT. SHASTA

TO REDDING

Entrance Station

Ranger Station

Manzanita Lake

CHAOS CRAGS

BLUE LAKE CANYON

Lassen Peak
10,457 ft.

Sulphur Works

DEVASTATED AREA

DERSCH MEADOWS

Hat Mt.

Summit Lake North

Summit Lake South

READING PEAK

Bumpass Hell

Kings Creek

Kohm Yah-mah-nee Visitor Center

Entrance Station

TO RED BLUFF AND CHICO

Devil's Kitchen

TWIN MEADOWS

CORRAL MEADOW

Prospect Peak
8,338 ft.

Cinder Cone

Butte Lake

Ash Butte

PAINTED DUNES

FANTASTIC LAVA BEDS

Snag Lake

Fairfield Peak

Crater Butte

GRASSY SWALE

Horseshoe Lake

Juniper Lake

TO CHESTER AND SUSANVILLE

Warner Valley

Pacific Crest Trail

1/2 mi

1/2 km

0

0

dangerous landscape that can be viewed throughout the park, especially via a hiked descent into Bumpass Hell. Because of its significance as a volcanic landscape, Lassen became a national park in 1916. Several volcanoes—the largest of which is now Lassen Peak—have been active in the area for roughly 600,000 years. The four types of volcanoes found in the world are represented in the park, including shield (Prospect Peak), plug dome (Lassen Peak), cinder cone (Cinder Cone), and composite (Brokeoff Volcano). Lassen Park Road (the continuation of Highway 89 within the park) and 150 miles of hiking trails provide access to many of these volcanic wonders. ■ TIP→ **Caution is key here: heed signs that warn visitors to stay on the trails and railed boardwalks to avoid falling into boiling water or through dangerous thin-crusted areas of the park.** Although the park is closed to cars in winter, it's usually open to intrepid cross-country skiers and snowshoers. The Kohm Yah-mah-nee Visitor Center is open year-round with closures on Monday and Tuesday from November 1 to March 31. ✉ *Mineral* 🌐 *www.nps.gov/lavo* 🎟 *$20 per car, $10 per person if not in a car.*

FAMILY **Sulphur Works Thermal Area.** Proof of Lassen Peak's volatility becomes evident shortly after you enter the park at the southwest entrance. Sidewalks skirt boiling springs and sulphur-emitting steam vents. This area is usually the last site to close because of snow. ✉ *Lassen Park Rd., 1 mile from the southwest entrance ranger station* 🌐 *www.nps.gov/lavo.*

WHERE TO STAY

$$$$ B&B/INN 🏨 **Drakesbad Guest Ranch.** With propane furnaces and kerosene lamps, everything about this century-old property harks back to a simpler time. **Pros:** a true back-to-nature experience; great for family adventures. **Cons:** accessible only via a partially paved road leading out of Chester. [$] *Rooms from: $348* ✉ *End of Warner Valley Rd., Chester* ☎ *866/999–0914* 🌐 *www.drakesbad.com* 🛏 *19 rooms* 🕒 *Closed mid-Oct.–early June* 🍴 *All meals.*

SPORTS AND THE OUTDOORS

HIKING

Fodor's Choice ★ **Bumpass Hell Trail.** Boiling springs, steam vents, and mud pots highlight this 3-mile round-trip hike. Expect the loop to take about two hours. During the first mile of the hike there's a gradual climb of 500 feet before a steep 300-foot descent to the basin. You'll encounter rocky patches, so wear hiking boots. ⚠ **Stay on trails and boardwalks near the thermal areas, as what appears to be firm ground may be only a thin crust over scalding mud.** *Moderate.* ✉ *Trailhead at end of paved parking area off Lassen Park Rd., 6 miles from the southwest entrance ranger station* 🌐 *www.nps.gov/lavo.*

Fodor's Choice ★ **Lassen Peak Hike.** This trail winds 2½ miles to the mountaintop. It's a tough climb—2,000 feet uphill on a steady, steep grade—but the reward is a spectacular view. At the peak you can see into the rim and view the entire park (and much of California's far north). Bring sunscreen, water, and a jacket, since it's often windy and much cooler at the summit. ■ TIP→ **After a multiyear restoration project, the trail is open again.** ✉ *Trailhead past a paved parking area off Lassen Park Rd., 7* *miles north of the southwest entrance ranger station* ☎ *530/595–4480* 🌐 *www.nps.gov/lavo.*

CHESTER

36 miles west of Susanville on Hwy 36.

The population of this small town on Lake Almanor swells from 2,500 to nearly 5,000 in summer as tourists come to visit. Chester serves as a gateway to Lassen Volcanic National Park.

GETTING HERE AND AROUND

Chester is on Highway 36E. When snow doesn't close Highway 89, the main road through Lassen Park, visitors can take Highway 44 from Redding to Highway 89 through the park and to Highway 36E and onto Chester and Lake Almanor. Plumas County Transit connects Chester to the Quincy area.

ESSENTIALS

Bus Information Plumas County Transit ☎ *530/283–2538* 🌐 *www.plumastransit.com.*

Visitor Information Lake Almanor Area Chamber of Commerce and Visitors Bureau ✉ *328 #6 Main St., near Reynolds Rd.* ☎ *530/258–2426* 🌐 *www.lakealmanorarea.com.*

EXPLORING

Lake Almanor. This lake's 52 miles of forested shoreline are popular with campers, swimmers, water-skiers, and anglers. At an elevation of 4,500 feet, the lake warms to above 70°F for about eight weeks in summer. ✉ *Off Hwys. 89 and 36* ☎ *530/258–2426* 🌐 *www.lakealmanorarea.com.*

WHERE TO EAT AND STAY

$ AMERICAN 🍴 **Kopper Kettle Cafe.** Locals return again and again to this tidy restaurant that serves home-cooked lunches and dinners. Head here for breakfast whenever you've got a hankering for scrambled eggs or biscuits and gravy. [$] *Average main: $15* ✉ *243 Main St., at Myrtle St.* ☎ *530/258–2698.*

$$ HOTEL 🏨 **Best Western Rose Quartz Inn.** Down the road from Lake Almanor and close to Lassen Volcanic National Park, this small-town inn balances traditional decor and up-to-the-minute amenities like Wi-Fi. **Pros:** near national park; within easy walking distance of town's restaurants. **Cons:** standard rooms on the pricey side. [$] *Rooms from: $140* ✉ *306 Main St.* ☎ *530/258–2002, 888/571–4885* 🌐 *www.rosequartzinn.com* 🛏 *51 rooms* 🍽 *Breakfast.*

$$ B&B/INN Fodor's Choice ★ 🏨 **Bidwell House.** Some guest rooms at this 1901 ranch house have wood-burning stoves, claw-foot tubs, and antique furnishings; a separate cottage with a kitchen sleeps six. **Pros:** unique decor in each room; beautiful wooded setting; near Lake Almanor. **Cons:** not ideal for kids. [$] *Rooms from: $135* ✉ *1 Main St.* ☎ *530/258–3338* 🌐 *www.bidwellhouse.com* 🛏 *14 rooms, 2 with shared bath* 🍽 *Breakfast.*

Lassen Volcanic National Park's King Creek Falls Hike, which takes you through forests and meadows dotted with wildflowers, is a good hike for nature photographers.

QUINCY

67 miles southwest of Susanville via Hwys. 36 and 89.

A center for mining and logging in the 1850s, Quincy is nestled against the western slope of the Sierra Nevada. The county seat and largest community in Plumas County, the town is rich in historic buildings that have been the focus of preservation and restoration efforts. The four-story courthouse on Main Street, one of several stops on a self-guided tour, was built in 1921 with marble posts and staircases. The arts are thriving in Quincy, too: catch a play or a bluegrass performance at the Town Hall Theatre.

GETTING HERE AND AROUND

Quincy is on Highway 70 and is accessible from all directions via mountain roads. Highway 70 goes through the Feather River Canyon to Highway 149, then Highway 99 to Chico and Red Bluff, a 198-mile trip. From Quincy, Highway 70 connects to Highway 89 and then to Highway 36E toward Susanville in the east, or westward toward Chester and Lassen Park. Plumas County Transit serves Chester and Quincy. Lassen Rural Bus connects Quincy and Susanville.

ESSENTIALS

Bus Information Lassen Rural Bus ☎ *530/252–7433* ⊕ *www. lassentransportation.com/a/Lassen-Rural-Bus-LRB.php.* **Plumas County Transit** ☎ *530/283–2538* ⊕ *www.plumastransit.com.*

Visitor Information Quincy Chamber of Commerce ✉ *336 Main St., inside Plumas Bank* ☎ *530/283–0188* ⊕ *www.quincychamber.com.*

EXPLORING

Bucks Lake Recreation Area. The main recreational attraction in central Plumas County is 17 miles southwest of Quincy at elevation 5,200 feet. During warm months the lake's 17-mile shoreline, two marinas, and eight campgrounds attract anglers and water-sports enthusiasts. Trails through the tall pines beckon hikers and horseback riders. In winter much of the area remains open for snowmobiling and cross-country skiing. ⊠ *Bucks Lake Rd.* ☎ *530/283–0188* ⊕ *www.plumascounty.org/communities/buckslake.htm.*

Plumas County Museum. The cultural, home arts, and industrial history displays at the Plumas County Museum contain artifacts dating to the 1850s. Highlights include collections of Maidu Indian basketry, pioneer weapons, and rooms depicting life in the early logging and mining days of Plumas County. Out in the Exhibit Yard are a working blacksmith shop, a restored goldminer's cabin, and a railroad exhibit. ⊠ *500 Jackson St., at Coburn St.* ☎ *530/283–6320* ⊕ *www.plumasmuseum.org* ⊡ *$2* ☾ *Tues.–Sat. 10–4.*

Plumas National Forest. Plumas County is known for its wide-open spaces, and the 1.2-million-acre Plumas National Forest, with its high alpine lakes and crystal clear woodland streams, is a beautiful example. Hundreds of campsites are maintained in the forest, and picnic areas and hiking trails abound. You can enter the forest along highways 70 and 89. ⊠ *U.S. Forest Service, 159 Lawrence St., near W. Main St.* ☎ *530/283–2050* ⊕ *www.fs.usda.gov/plumas* ☾ *Office weekdays 8–4:30.*

WHERE TO EAT AND STAY

$$
AMERICAN
✕ **Sweet Lorraine's.** Hearty fare served in this casual, bustling restaurant in Quincy's historic downtown area includes meaty dishes like St. Louis–style ribs as well as vegetarian options and lighter fare; there's also a good selection of wines. If the weather is mild, dine alfresco on the patio. Counter seating is fast and friendly. Ⓢ *Average main: $18* ⊠ *384 Main St., at Harbison Ave.* ☎ *530/283–5300* ☾ *Closed Sun. and Mon.*

$
RENTAL
Fodor'sChoice
★
🛏 **Ada's Place.** This place is actually four uniquely beautiful cottages, secluded on a quiet street one block from the county courthouse and downtown Quincy. **Pros:** on-site owners' meticulous upkeep. **Cons:** no pets allowed. Ⓢ *Rooms from: $110* ⊠ *562 Jackson St., near Court St.* ☎ *530/283–1954, 877/234–2327* ⊕ *www.adasplace.com* ⇱ *4 cottages* ⦿ *No meals.*

TRAVEL SMART NORTHERN CALIFORNIA

GETTING HERE AND AROUND

Wherever you plan to go in California, getting there will likely involve driving, even if you fly. Major airports are usually far from main attractions. In San Francisco, expect a 30-minute-plus trip between any Bay Area airport and Downtown. California's major airport hubs are LAX in Los Angeles and SFO in San Francisco, but you can find satellite airports around most major cities. When booking flights, it pays to check these options for more convenient times and a better location in relation to your hotel.

FROM SAN FRANCISCO TO:	BY AIR	BY CAR
San Jose		1 hr
Monterey	45 mins	2 hrs
Los Angeles	1 hr 30 mins	5 hrs 40 mins
Portland, OR	1 hr 50 mins	10 hrs
Mendocino		3 hrs
Yosemite NP/ Fresno	1 hr	4 hrs
Lake Tahoe/ Reno	1 hr	3 hrs 30 mins

▮ AIR TRAVEL

Flying time to California is about 5½ hours from New York and 4 hours from Chicago. Travel from London to either Los Angeles or San Francisco is 11 hours and from Sydney approximately 15. Flying between San Francisco and Los Angeles takes about 90 minutes.

AIRPORTS

Northern California's gateways are San Francisco International Airport (SFO), Oakland International Airport (OAK), Sacramento International Airport (SMF), and San Jose International Airport (SJC).

Airport Information Oakland International Airport ☏ 510/563-3300 ⊕ www.oaklandairport.com. **Sacramento**

International Airport ☏ 916/929-5411 ⊕ www.sacramento.aero/smf. **San Francisco International Airport** ☏ 650/821-8211, 800/435-9736 ⊕ www.flysfo.com. **San Jose International Airport** ☏ 408/392-3600 ⊕ www.flysanjose.com.

FLIGHTS

With hubs in San Francisco and Los Angeles, United has the greatest number of flights into and within California. But most national and many international airlines fly to the state. Southwest Airlines and United Airlines connect smaller cities within California, often from satellite airports near major cities.

Airline Contacts Air Canada ☏ 888/247-2262 ⊕ www.aircanada.com **Alaska Airlines/ Horizon Air** ☏ 800/252-7522 ⊕ www.alaskaair.com. **American Airlines** ☏ 800/433-7300 ⊕ www.aa.com. **British Airways** ☏ 800/247-9297 ⊕ www.britishairways.com. **Cathay Pacific** ☏ 800/233-2742 ⊕ www.cathaypacific.com. **Delta Airlines** ☏ 800/221-1212 for U.S. reservations, 800/241-4141 for international reservations ⊕ www.delta.com. **Frontier Airlines** ☏ 800/432-1359 ⊕ www.flyfrontier.com. **Japan Airlines** ☏ 800/525-3663 ⊕ www.jal.com. **JetBlue** ☏ 800/538-2583 ⊕ www.jetblue.com. **Qantas** ☏ 800/227-4500 ⊕ www.qantas.com.au. **Southwest Airlines** ☏ 800/435-9792 ⊕ www.southwest.com. **Spirit Airlines** ☏ 801/401-2200 ⊕ www.spirit.com. **United Airlines** ☏ 800/864-8331 for U.S. reservations, 800/538-2929 for international reservations ⊕ www.united.com. **US Airways** ☏ 800/428-4322 for U.S. and Canada reservations, 800/622-1015 for international reservations ⊕ www.usairways.com.

▮ BOAT TRAVEL

CRUISES

A number of major cruise lines offer trips that begin or end in California. Most voyages sail north along the Pacific coast to Alaska or south to Mexico. Northern California's cruise port is San Francisco.

Cruise Lines Carnival Cruise Line ☎ 305/599–2600, 888/227–6482 ⊕ www. carnival.com. **Celebrity Cruises** ☎ 800/647–2251, 800/437–3111 ⊕ www.celebritycruises. com. **Crystal Cruises** ☎ 310/785–9300, 888/722–0021 ⊕ www.crystalcruises.com. **Disney Cruise Line** ☎ 800/951–3532 ⊕ www. disneycruise.disney.go.com. **Holland America Line** ☎ 206/281–3535, 877/932–4259 ⊕ www. hollandamerica.com. **Norwegian Cruise Line** ☎ 305/436–4000, 866/234–7350 ⊕ www. ncl.com. **Princess Cruises** ☎ 661/753–0000, 800/774–6237 ⊕ www.princess.com. **Regent Seven Seas Cruises** ☎ 954/776–6123, 844/473–4368 ⊕ www.rssc.com. **Royal Caribbean International** ☎ 305/539–6000, 866/562–7625 ⊕ www.royalcaribbean. com. **Silversea Cruises** ☎ 954/522–4477, 877/276–6816 ⊕ www.silversea.com.

▮ BUS TRAVEL

Greyhound is the major bus carrier in California. Regional bus service is available in metropolitan areas.

Bus Information Greyhound ☎ 800/231–2222 ⊕ www.greyhound.com.

▮ CAR TRAVEL

There are two basic north–south routes in California: Interstate 5 runs inland most of the way from the Oregon border to the Mexican border; and U.S. Highway 101 hugs the coast for part of the route from Oregon to Mexico. A slower but much more scenic option is to take California State Route 1, also referred to as Highway 1 and the Pacific Coast Highway, which winds along much of the California coast and provides an occasionally hair-raising, but breathtaking, ride.

From north to south, the state's east–west interstates are Interstate 80, Interstate 15, Interstate 10, and Interstate 8. Much of California is mountainous, and you may encounter winding roads, frequently cliff-side, and steep mountain grades. In

winter, roads crossing the Sierra from east to west may close at any time due to weather. Also in winter, Interstate 5 north of Los Angeles closes during snowstorms.

FROM SAN FRANCISCO TO:	ROUTE	DISTANCE
San Jose	U.S. 101	50 miles
Monterey	U.S. 101 to Hwy. 156 to Hwy. 1	120 miles
Los Angeles	U.S. 101 to Hwy. 156 to I-5	382 miles
Portland, OR	I-80 to I-505 to I-5	635 miles
Mendocino	Hwy. 1	174 miles
Yosemite NP	I-80 to I-580 to I-205 to Hwy. 120 east	184 miles
Lake Tahoe/ Reno	I-80	220 miles

GASOLINE

Gasoline prices in California vary widely, depending on location, oil company, and whether you buy it at a full-service or self-serve pump. It's less expensive to buy fuel in the southern part of the state than in the north. If you're planning to travel near Nevada, you can sometimes save a bit by purchasing gas over the border. Gas stations are plentiful throughout the state. Most stay open late (24 hours along major highways and in big cities), except in rural areas, where Sunday hours are limited and where you may drive long stretches without a chance to refuel.

ROAD CONDITIONS

Rainy weather can make driving along the coast or in the mountains treacherous. Some of the smaller routes over mountain ranges and in the deserts are prone to flash flooding. When the rains are severe, coastal Highway 1 can quickly become a slippery nightmare, buffeted by strong winds and obstructed by falling debris from the cliffs above. When the weather is particularly bad, Highway 1 may be closed due to mud and rock slides.

Many smaller roads over the Sierra Nevada are closed in winter, and if it's snowing, tire chains may be required on routes that are open. From October through April, if it's raining along the coast, it's usually snowing at higher elevations. Consider renting a four-wheel-drive vehicle, or purchase chains before you get to the mountains. (Chains or cables generally cost $40 to $70, depending on tire size; cables are easier to attach than chains, but chains are more durable.) If you delay and purchase them in the vicinity of the chain-control area, the cost may double. Be aware that most rental-car companies prohibit chain installation on their vehicles. If you choose to risk it and do not tighten them properly, they may snap—your insurance likely will not cover any resulting damage.

In Northern California uniformed chain installers on Interstate 80 and U.S. Highway 50 will apply chains at the checkpoint for about $40 and take them off for less than that. Chain installers are independent business people, not highway employees, and set their own fees. They are not allowed to sell or rent chains. On smaller roads, you're on your own.

Always carry extra clothing, blankets, water, and food when driving to the mountains in the winter, and keep your gas tank full to prevent the fuel line from freezing.

Road Conditions Caltrans Current Highway Conditions ☎ 800/427–7623 ⊕ www.dot. ca.gov.

Weather Conditions National Weather Service ☎ 707/443–6484 northernmost California, 831/656–1725 San Francisco Bay area and central California, 775/673–8100 Reno, Lake Tahoe, and northern Sierra, 805/988–6610 Los Angeles area, 858/675–8700 San Diego area, 916/979–3051 Sacramento area ⊕ www.weather.gov.

ROADSIDE EMERGENCIES

Dial 911 to report accidents and to reach the police, the California Highway Patrol (CHP), or the fire department. On some rural highways and on most interstates, look for emergency phones on the side of the road.

RULES OF THE ROAD

All passengers must wear seat belts at all times. It is illegal to leave a child six years of age or younger unattended in a motor vehicle. A child must be secured in a federally approved child passenger restraint system and ride in the back seat until at least eight years of age or until the child is at least 4 feet 9 inches tall. Children who are eight but don't meet the height requirement must ride in a booster seat or a car seat. Unless indicated, right turns are allowed at red lights after you've come to a full stop. Left turns between two one-way streets are allowed at red lights after you've come to a full stop.

Drivers with a blood-alcohol level higher than 0.08 who are stopped by police are subject to arrest, and those under 21 convicted of driving with a level of 0.01 or more can have their driving privileges revoked for a year. California's drunk-driving laws are extremely tough—violators may have their licenses immediately suspended, pay hefty fines, and spend the night in jail.

The speed limit on many interstate highways is 70 mph; unlimited-access roads are usually 55 mph. In cities, freeway speed limits are between 55 mph and 65 mph. Many city routes have commuter lanes during rush hour.

You must turn on your headlights whenever weather conditions require the use of windshield wipers.

Those 18 and older must use a hands-free device for their mobile phones while driving; those under 18 may not use mobile phones or wireless devices while driving. Texting on a wireless device is illegal for all drivers. Smoking in a vehicle where a minor is present is an infraction. For more information, refer to the Department of Motor Vehicles driver's handbook at ⊕ *www.dmv.ca.gov.*

CAR RENTAL

When you reserve a car, ask about cancellation penalties, taxes, drop-off charges (if you're planning to pick up the car in one city and leave it in another), and surcharges (for being under or over a certain age, for additional drivers, or for driving across state or country borders or beyond a specific distance from your point of rental). All these things can add substantially to your costs. Request car seats and extras such as GPS when you book.

Rates are sometimes—but not always—better if you book in advance or reserve through a rental agency's website. There are other reasons to book ahead, though: for popular destinations, during busy times of the year, or to ensure that you get certain types of cars (vans, SUVs, exotic sports cars).

■TIP→ Make sure that a confirmed reservation guarantees you a car. Agencies sometimes overbook, particularly for busy weekends and holiday periods.

A car is essential in most parts of California. In compact San Francisco it's better to use public transportation to avoid parking headaches.

Rates statewide for the least expensive vehicle begin as low as $30 a day, usually on weekends, and less than $200 a week (though they increase rapidly from here, especially in some of the larger metropolitan areas). This does not include additional fees and the tax on car rentals, which is 9% in San Francisco. Be sure to shop around—you can get a decent deal by shopping the major car-rental companies' websites. Compare prices by city before you book, and ask about "drop charges" if you plan to return the vehicle in a city other than the one where you rented it. If you pick up at an airport, there may also be a facility charge of as much as $12 per rental, plus higher tax rates; ask when you book.

In California you must have a valid driver's license and be 21 to rent a car; rates may be higher if you're under 25. Some agencies will not rent to those under 25; check when you book. Non-U.S. residents must have a license with text in the Roman alphabet that is valid for the entire rental period. Though it need not be entirely written in English, it must have English letters that clearly identify it as a driver's license. In addition, most companies also require an international license; check in advance.

If you dream of driving down the coast with the top down, or you want to explore the desert landscape not visible from the road, consider renting a specialty vehicle. Agencies that specialize in convertibles and sport-utility vehicles will often arrange airport delivery in larger cities. Unlike most of the major agencies, the following companies guarantee the car class that you book.

Specialty Car Agencies Enterprise Exotic Car Rentals ☎ *800/400–8412, 866/458–9227 locations in San Francisco, Los Angeles, and other Southern California locations* ⊕ *exotic-cars.enterprise.com.* **Beverly Hills Rent a Car** ☎ *800/479–5996 San Francisco and several locations in Los Angeles, 310/274–6969* ⊕ *www.bhrentacar.com.*

Major Rental Agencies Alamo ☎ *800/462–5266* ⊕ *www.alamo.com.* **Avis** ☎ *800/331–1212* ⊕ *www.avis.com.* **Budget** ☎ *800/527–0700* ⊕ *www.budget.com.* **Hertz** ☎ *800/654–3131* ⊕ *www.hertz.com.* **National Car Rental** ☎ *877/222–9058* ⊕ *www.nationalcar.com.*

▌ TRAIN TRAVEL

Amtrak's *Coast Starlight* begins in Los Angeles and hugs the Pacific Coast to San Luis Obispo before it turns inland for the rest of its journey to Portland and Seattle.

In the northern part of the state, the *California Zephyr* travels from Chicago to Emeryville (San Francisco) via Denver.

Information Amtrak ☎ *800/872-7245* ⊕ *www.amtrak.com.*

ESSENTIALS

▮ ACCOMMODATIONS

The lodgings we review are the top choices in each price category. ⇨ *For an expanded review of each property, please see ⊕ www.fodors.com.* We don't specify whether the facilities cost extra; when pricing accommodations, ask what's included and what costs extra. ⇨ *For price information, see the planner in each chapter.*

Most hotels require you to give your credit-card details before they will confirm your reservation. If you don't feel comfortable emailing this information, ask if you can fax it or call and give details over the phone. However you book, get confirmation in writing and have a copy of it handy when you check in.

Be sure you understand the hotel's cancellation policy. Some places allow you to cancel without any kind of penalty—even if you prepaid to secure a discounted rate—if you cancel at least 24 hours in advance. Others require you to cancel a week in advance or penalize you the cost of one night. Small inns and B&Bs are most likely to require you to cancel far in advance. Most hotels allow children under a certain age to stay in their parents' room at no extra charge, but others charge for them as extra adults; find out the cutoff age for discounts.

Many B&Bs are entirely no-smoking, and hotels and motels are decreasing their inventory of smoking rooms; if you require one, ask when you book if any are available.

BED-AND-BREAKFASTS
California has more than 1,000 bed-and-breakfasts. You'll find everything from simple homestays to lavish luxury lodgings, many in historic hotels and homes. The California Association of Boutique and Breakfast Inns has about 300 member properties that you can locate and book through its website.

Reservation Services Bed & Breakfast.com ☎ 512/322–2710, 800/462–2632 ⊕ www.bedandbreakfast.com. Bed & Breakfast Inns Online ☎ 800/215–7365 ⊕ www.bbonline.com. BnB Finder.com ☎ 212/480–0414, 888/547–8226 ⊕ www.bnbfinder.com. California Association of Boutique and Breakfast Inns ☎ 800/373–9251 ⊕ www.cabbi.com.

▮ COMMUNICATIONS

INTERNET
Internet access is widely available in urban areas, but it's usually more difficult to get online in the state's rural communities. Most hotels offer some kind of connection—usually broadband or Wi-Fi. Many hotels charge a daily fee (about $10) for Internet access. Cybercafés are located throughout California.

▮ EATING OUT

California has led the pack in bringing natural and organic foods to the forefront of American dining. Though rooted in European cuisine, California cooking sometimes has strong Asian and Latin influences. Wherever you go, you're likely to find that dishes are made with fresh produce and other local ingredients.

The restaurants we list are the cream of the crop in each price category. ⇨ *For price information, see the planner in each chapter.*

CUTTING COSTS
▮TIP➜ If you're on a budget, take advantage of the "small plates" craze sweeping California by ordering several appetizer-size portions and having a glass of wine at the bar, rather than having a full meal. Also, the better grocery and specialty-food stores have grab-and-go sections, with prepared foods on a par with restaurant cooking, perfect for picnicking (remember, it infrequently rains between May and October). At resort areas in the

off-season you can often find two-for-one dinner specials at upper-end restaurants; check coupon apps or local papers or with visitor bureaus.

RESERVATIONS AND DRESS

Regardless of where you are, it's a good idea to make a reservation if you can. We only mention reservations specifically when they are essential (there's no other way you'll ever get a table) or when they are not accepted. For popular restaurants, book as far ahead as you can (often 30 days), and reconfirm as soon as you arrive. (Large parties should always call ahead to check the reservations policy.) We mention dress only when men are required to wear a jacket or a jacket and tie.

Online reservation services make it easy to book a table before you even leave home. OpenTable covers many California cities.

Contacts OpenTable ⊕ *www.opentable.com.*

WINES, BEER, AND SPIRITS

Throughout the state, most famously in the Napa and Sonoma valleys, you can visit wineries, many of which have tasting rooms and offer tours. Microbreweries are an emerging trend in the state's cities and in some rural areas in Northern California. The legal drinking age is 21.

▌ HEALTH

Smoking is illegal in all California bars and restaurants, including on outdoor dining patios in some cities. If you have an existing medical condition that may require emergency treatment, be aware that many rural and mountain communities have only daytime clinics, not hospitals with 24-hour emergency rooms.

Outdoor sports are a huge draw in California's moderate climate, but caution, especially in unfamiliar areas, is key. Drownings occur each year because beach lovers don't heed warnings about high surfs with their deadly rogue waves. Do not fly within 24 hours of scuba diving.

▌ HOURS OF OPERATION

Banks in California are typically open weekdays from 9 to 6 and Saturday morning; most are closed on Sunday and most holidays. Smaller shops usually operate from 10 to 6, with larger stores remaining open until 8 or later. Hours vary for museums, historical sites, and state parks, and many are closed one or more days a week, or for extended periods during off-season months. It's a good idea to check before you visit a tourist site.

▌ MONEY

San Francisco tends to be an expensive city to visit, and rates at coastal and wine country resorts are almost as high. A day's admission to a major theme park can run as much as $99 per person, though you may be able to get discounts by purchasing tickets in advance online. Hotel rates average $150 to $250 a night (though you can find cheaper places), and dinners at even moderately priced restaurants often cost $20 to $40 per person. Costs in the Gold Country and the Far North are considerably less—many fine Gold Country bed-and-breakfasts charge around $100 a night, and some motels in the Far North charge $70 to $90.

CREDIT CARDS

It's a good idea to inform your credit-card company before you travel. Otherwise, unusual activity might prompt the company to put a hold on your card—not a good thing halfway through your trip.

Record all your credit-card numbers—as well as the phone numbers to call if your cards are lost or stolen—in a safe place, so you're prepared should something go wrong. Both MasterCard and Visa give general numbers you can call (collect if you're abroad) if your card is lost or not working.

Reporting Lost Cards American Express
☏ 800/528–4800 in U.S., 715/343–7977 collect from abroad ⊕ www.americanexpress.com. **Discover** ☏ 800/347–2683 in U.S., 801/902–3100 collect from abroad ⊕ www.discover.com. **Diners Club** ☏ 800/234–6377 in U.S., 514/877–1577 collect from abroad ⊕ www.dinersclub.com. **MasterCard** ☏ 800/627–8372 in U.S., 636/722–7111 collect from abroad ⊕ www.mastercard.com. **Visa** ☏ 800/847–2911 in U.S., 303/967–1096 collect from abroad ⊕ www.visa.com.

▌ SAFETY

California is a safe place to visit, as long as you take the usual precautions. In large cities ask the concierge or desk clerk to point out areas on your map that you should avoid. Lock valuables in a hotel safe when you're not using them. (Some hotels have in-room safes large enough to hold a laptop computer.) Keep an eye on your handbag when you're out in public. Security is high (but mostly invisible) at theme parks and resorts.

▌ TAXES

Sales tax in the state of California is 7.5%, but local taxes vary and may be as much as an additional 2%. Sales tax applies to all purchases except for food bought in a grocery store; food consumed in a restaurant is taxed, but take-out food is not. Hotel taxes vary widely by region, from about 8% to 15.5%.

▌ TIME

California is in the Pacific time zone. Pacific daylight time (PDT) is in effect from mid-March through early November; the rest of the year the clock is set to Pacific standard time (PST).

▌ TIPPING

Most service workers in California are fairly well paid compared to those in the rest of the country, and extravagant tipping is not the rule here. Exceptions include wealthy enclaves such as San Francisco in Northern California, as well as the most expensive resort areas.

TIPPING GUIDELINES FOR CALIFORNIA	
Bartender	$1 per drink, or 10%–15% of tab per round of drinks
Bellhop	$1–$2 per bag, depending on the level of the hotel
Hotel Concierge	$5–$10, if he/she performs a service for you
Hotel Doorman	$1–$2 if he/she helps you get a cab
Valet Parking Attendant	$3–$5 when you get your car
Hotel Maid	$2–$5 per day; more in high-end hotels
Waiter	15%–20% (20%–25% is standard in upscale restaurants); nothing additional if a service charge is added to the bill
Skycap at Airport	$1–$2 per bag
Hotel Room-Service Waiter	15%–20% per delivery, even if a service charge was added since that fee goes to the hotel, not the waiter
Taxi Driver	15%–20%, but round up the fare to the next dollar amount
Tour Guide	15% of the cost of the tour, more depending on quality

▌ TOURS

Guided tours are a good option when you don't want to do it all yourself. You travel along with a group (sometimes large, sometimes small), stay in prebooked hotels, eat with your fellow travelers (the cost of meals is sometimes included in the price of your tour, sometimes not), and follow a schedule.

But not all guided tours are an if-it's-Tuesday-this-must-be-Yosemite experience. A knowledgeable guide can take you places that you might never discover on your own, and you may be pushed to see more than you would have otherwise. Tours aren't for everyone, but they can be just the thing for trips to places where making travel arrangements is difficult or time-consuming.

Whenever you book a guided tour, find out what's included and what isn't. A "land-only" tour includes all your travel (by bus, in most cases) in the destination, but not necessarily your flights to and from or even within it. Also, in most cases prices in tour brochures don't include fees and taxes. And remember that you'll be expected to tip your guide (in cash) at the end of the tour.

SPECIAL-INTEREST TOURS

BIKING

Biking is a popular way to see the California countryside, and commercial tours are available throughout the state. Most three- to five-day trips are all-inclusive—you'll stay in delightful country inns, dine at good regional restaurants, and follow experienced guides. When booking, ask about level of difficulty, as nearly every trip will involve some hill work. Tours fill up early, so book well in advance.

■TIP→ Most airlines accommodate bikes as luggage, provided they're dismantled and boxed.

The Northern California Wine Country, with its flat valley roads, is one of the most popular destinations.

Napa and Sonoma Valley Bike Tours. Single-day bike tours through beautiful Napa and Sonoma wine country offer a casual pace and frequent winery stops. ⊠ 6500 Washington St., Yountville ☎ 707/251–8687 Napa tours, 707/996–2453 Sonoma tours ⊕ www.napavalleybiketours.com ⊠ From $99.

Bicycle Adventures. Based in Washington state, this outfitter plans all the meal, lodging, and travel details of multiday bike trips through some of California's most engaging scenery, including the redwoods, wine country, the North Coast, Big Sur, and rugged Death Valley. ⊠ 29700 S.E. High Point Way, Issaquah, Washington ☎ 800/443–6060, 425/250–5540 ⊕ www.bicycleadventures.com.

▮ VISITOR INFORMATION

The California Travel and Tourism Commission's website takes you to each region of California, with digital visitor guides in multiple languages, driving tours, maps, welcome center locations, information on local tours, links to bed-and-breakfasts, and a complete booking center. It also links you—via the Destinations menu—to the websites of city and regional tourism offices and attractions. ⇨ For the numbers and websites of regional and city visitor bureaus and chambers of commerce, see the Planning section in each chapter.

Contacts California Travel and Tourism Commission ⊠ Sacramento ☎ 916/444–4429 CA Tourism Commission office, 800/862–2543 brochures and information ⊕ www.visit california.com.

INDEX

PHOTO CREDITS

Front cover: Natta Ang / Shutterstock [Description: Coastline along Highway 1, Big Sur, California]. 1, Yuen Kwan, Fodors.com member. 2, Gordon Swanson/Shutterstock. 5, Heavenly Mountain Resort. Chapter 1: Experience California: 8-9, Jay Anderson, Fodors.com member. 12, Clinton Steeds/Flickr. 13, comfortablynirm, Fodors.com member. 14 (left), Lorcel / Shutterstock. 14 (top right), Corbis. 14 (bottom right), Warren H. White. 15 (top left), Alan A. Tobey/iStockphoto. 15 (bottom left), Gary C. Tognoni / Shutterstock. 15 (right), Aaron Kohr/iStockphoto. 16, Warren H. White. 17, Thomas Kranzel/Venture Media. 18, vathomp, Fodors.com member. Chapter 2: Northern California's Best Road Trips: 19, sd_Foodie, Fodors.com member. 21, Paul Giamou/iStockphoto. 22 (top), Janine Bolliger/ iStockphoto. 22 (bottom), Lise Gagne/iStockphoto. 23, iStockphoto. 24 (top), Evan Meyer/ iStockphoto. 24 (center), Kyle Maass iStockphoto. 24 (bottom left), iStockphoto. 24 (bottom right), Lise Gagne iStockphoto. 25, Tom Baker/Shutterstock. 26 (left), SuperStock/age fotostock. 26 (top right), CURAphotography/Shutterstock. 26 (bottom right), Michael Almond/iStockphoto. 27 (top), iStockphoto. 27 (bottom), Lise Gagne/iStockphoto. 28 (top), Ross Stapleton-Gray/iStockphoto. 28 (center), Jay Spooner/iStockphoto. 28 (bottom),nTebNad/Shutterstock. 29 (top), Jay Spooner/iStockphoto. 29 (bottom), Lise Gagne/iStockphoto. Chapter 3: The Central Coast: 41, Shippee | Dreamstime.com. 42, Stephen Walls/iStockphoto. 43, Robert Holmes. 44, David M. Schrader/Shutterstock. 58, S. Greg Panosian/iStockphoto. 59, Ruben G. Mendoza. 60 (top), Richard Wong/www.rwongphoto.com/Alamy. 60 (bottom), Ruben G. Mendoza. 61 (top left), Witold Skrypczak/Alamy. 61 (top right), S. Greg Panosian/ iStockphoto. 61 (bottom), Janet Fullwood. 62 (top left), GIPhotoStock Z/Alamy. 62 (top right), Craig Lovell/Eagle Visions Photography/Alamy. 62 (bottom) and 63 (top), S. Greg Panosian/iStockphoto. 63 (bottom), Eugene Zelenko/wikipedia.org. 68, David M. Schrader/Shutterstock. 74, Doreen Miller, Fodors.com member. 86, Aimee M Lee / Shutterstock. 104-105, Valhalla Design & Conquer, Fodors. com member. Chapter 4: The Monterey Bay Area: 109, mellifluous, Fodors.com member. 111 (top), vittorio sciosia/age fotostock. 111 (bottom). Jeff Greenberg/age fotostock. 112, Brent Reeves/Shutterstock. 120, Robert Holmes. 127, Holger Mette/iStockphoto. 134, laurel stewart/iStockphoto. Chapter 5: San Francisco: 155, Prisma Bildagentur AG / Alamy. 156, Brett Shoaf/Artistic Visuals Photography. 158, Robert Schlie / Shutterstock. 164, San Francisco Travel Association/Scott Chernis. 170 (top), Arnold Genthe. 170 (bottom), Library of Congress Prints and Photographs Division. 171 (left), Sandor Balatoni/SFCVB. 171 (right), Detroit Publishing Company Collection, Photography Collection, Miriam and Ira D. Wallach Division of Art, Prints and Photographs, The New York Public Library, Astor, Lenox and Tilden Foundation. 172, Brett Shoaf/Artistic Visuals Photography. 181, travelstock44/Alamy. 183, Brett Shoaf/Artistic Visuals Photography. 184, San Francisco Municipal Railway Historical Archives. 189, Andresr | Dreamstime.com. 200, Robert Holmes. 207, aprillilacs, Fodors. com member. 213, Rafael Ramirez Lee/iStockphoto. 218, San Francisco Travel Association/Scott Chernis. 219 (top), T photography / Shutterstock. 219 (bottom), Walleyelj | Dreamstime.com. 240, Rough Guides/Alamy. 251, Robert Holmes. Chapter 6: The Bay Area: 255 and 257 (top), Robert Holmes. 257 (bottom), Jyeshern Cheng/iStockphoto. 258, Brett Shoaf/Artistic Visuals Photography. 266, California Travel and Tourism Commission / Bongo. 270, Nancy Hoyt Belcher / Alamy. 288, Robert Holmes. 299, Robert Holmes. 303, Mark Rasmussen/iStockphoto. 309, S. Greg Panosian/iStockphoto. Chapter 7: Napa and Sonoma: 311, Andrew Zarivny / Shutterstock. 312, iStockphoto. 313, Robert Holmes. 314, Warren H. White. 320, Robert Holmes. 321 (top), kevin miller/iStockphoto. 321 (bottom), Far Niente+Dolce+Nickel & Nickel. 322 (top and bottom) Robert Holmes. 323 (top) Domaine Carneros. 323 (bottom), star5112/Flickr. 324 (top left), Rubicon Estate. 324 (top right and bottom) and 325 (top and bottom), Robert Holmes. 326 (top), Philippe Roy/Alamy. 326 (center), Agence Images/Alamy. 326 (bottom), Cephas Picture Library/Alamy. 327 (top), Napa Valley Conference Bureau. 327 (second and third from top), Wild Horse Winery (Forrest L. Doud). 327 (fourth from top), Napa Valley Conference Bureau. 327 (fifth from top), Panther Creek Cellars (Ron Kaplan). 327 (sixth from top), Clos du Val (Marvin Collins). 327 (seventh from top), Panther Creek Cellars (Ron Kaplan). 327 (bottom), Warren H. White. 328, courtesy of the di Rosa Collection. 330, Robert Holmes. 340, Far Niente+Dolce+Nickel & Nickel. 343, Terry Joanis/Frog's Leap. 353, Castello di Amorosa. 363, 364, and 370-371, Robert Holmes. Chapter 8: The North Coast: 381, Thomas Barrat/Shutterstock. 382 (all), Robert Holmes. 383 (top), Russ Bishop/age fotostock. 383 (bottom), Robert Holmes. 384, Janet Fullwood. 387, 395, and 399, Robert Holmes. Chapter 9: Redwood National Park: 407, iStockphoto. 408 (top), Michael Schweppe/wikipedia.org. 408 (center), Agnieszka Szymczak/iStockphoto. 408 (bottom), Natalia Bratslavsky/Shutterstock. 410, WellyWelly/Shutterstock. Chapter 10: The Southern Sierra: 415, Randall Pugh, Fodors.com member. 416, Craig Cozart/iStockphoto. 417 (top), David T Gomez/iStockphoto. 417 (bottom left and bottom right), Robert Holmes. 418, christinea78, Fodors.com member. 424, moonjazz/Flickr. 432, Douglas Atmore/iStockphoto. Chapter 11: Yosemite National Park: 435, Sarah

NOTES

ABOUT OUR WRITERS

Native Californian **Cheryl Crabtree**—who updated the Central Coast, Monterey Bay Area, and Southern Sierra chapters—has worked as a freelance writer since 1987. She has contributed to *Fodor's California* since 2003. Cheryl is editor of *Montecito Magazine*. Her articles have appeared in many regional and national publications, including US Airways in-flight magazine and *Santa Barbara Seasons,* and annual visitor magazines in Santa Barbara, Ventura, and Pismo Beach. She also authors California Central Coast Web content and travel apps for mobile devices, and co-authors *The California Directory of Fine Wineries books,* Central Coast and Napa/Sonoma/Mendocino editions.

Longtime Fodor's writer, editor, and contributor to our San Francisco chapter, **Denise M. Leto** roams the city out of sheer love for SF, peeking down overgrown alleyways and exploring tucked-away corners from the Tenderloin to the Richmond, often with her three homeschooled kids in tow.

Daniel Mangin returned to California, where he's maintained a home for three decades, after two stints at the Fodor's editorial offices in New York City, the second one as the editorial director of Fodors.com and the Compass American Guides. With several-dozen wineries less than a half-hour's drive from home, he often finds himself transported as if by magic to a tasting room bar, communing with a sophisticated Cabernet or savoring the finish of a smooth Pinot Noir. For this edition, Daniel, the writer of *Fodor's Travel Napa & Sonoma,* updated the Napa and Sonoma chapter.

Steve Pastorino has visited nearly a dozen national parks on behalf of Fodor's and has favorite spots in all of them. In the summer, the long-time sports marketer and his family of five are often found at baseball diamonds. He updated the Yosemite National Park, Sequoia and Kings Canyon National Parks, and Sacramento and the Gold Country chapters.

A veteran traveler, **Claire Deeks van der Lee** feels lucky to call San Diego home. Claire loves roadtripping around her adopted state of California, so it was a perfect fit for her to work on the Experience and Northern California's Best Road Trips chapters of this book. Claire has traveled to more than 40 countries, and has contributed to *Everywhere* magazine and several Fodor's guides.

Freelance writer **Christine Vovakes**—who updated the North Coast, Lake Tahoe, Far North, the Redwoods, and Travel Smart chapters—has contributed to *Fodor's California* since 2004, and also has written for *Fodor's Complete Guide to the National Parks of the West, Fodor's Pacific Northwest,* and *Fodor's Essential USA.* Her travel articles and photographs have appeared in many publications, including *The Washington Post, The Christian Science Monitor, The Sacramento Bee,* and the *San Francisco Chronicle.*

Updating our San Francisco chapter was a team of writers from Fodor's San Francisco: **Michele Bigley, Christine Ciarmello, Denise M. Leto, Fiona Parrott,** and **Jerry James Stone.**